American Sentencing—What Happens and Why?

Associate Editors
Philip J. Cook
Francis T. Cullen
Anthony N. Doob
Jeffrey A. Fagan
Daniel S. Nagin

*American Sentencing—
What Happens and Why?*

Edited by Michael Tonry

VOLUME 48

The University of Chicago Press, Chicago and London

The University of Chicago Press, Chicago 60637
The University of Chicago Press, Ltd., London

© 2019 by The University of Chicago
All rights reserved.
Printed in the United States of America

ISSN: 0192-3234

ISBN-13: 978-0-226-64491-2 (cloth)
ISBN-13: 978-0-226-64507-0 (paper)
ISBN-13: 978-0-226-64510-0 (e-book)

LCN: 80-642217

Library of Congress Cataloging-in-Publication Data:

Names: Tonry, Michael H., editor.
Title: American sentencing : what happens and why? / edited by Michael Tonry.
Description: Chicago : The University of Chicago Press, 2019. | Series: Crime and justice: a review of research ; volume 48 |
Identifiers: LCCN 2019009745 (print) | LCCN 2019012446 (ebook) | ISBN 9780226645100 (E-book) | ISBN 9780226644912 (cloth) | ISBN 9780226645070 (pbk.)
Subjects: LCSH: Sentences (Criminal procedure)—United States. | Punishment—United States. | Law reform—United States.
Classification: LCC KF9225 (ebook) | LCC KF9225 .A44 2019 (print) | DDC 345.73/0772—dc23
LC record available at https://lccn.loc.gov/2019009745

COPYING BEYOND FAIR USE. The code on the first page of an essay in this volume indicates the copyright owner's consent that copies of the essay may be made beyond those permitted by Sections 107 or 108 of the U.S. Copyright Law provided that copies are made only for personal or internal use or for the personal or internal use of specific clients and provided that the copier pay the stated per-copy fee through the Copyright Clearance Center, 222 Rosewood Drive, Danvers, Massachusetts 01923. To request permission for other kinds of copying, such as copying for general distribution, for advertising or promotional purposes, for creating new collective works, or for sale, kindly write to the Permissions Department, The University of Chicago Press, 1427 East 60th Street, Chicago, Illinois 60637. If no code appears on the first page of an essay, permission to reprint may be obtained only from the author.

The paper used in this publication meets the minimum requirements of American National Standard for Information Sciences—Permanence of Paper for Printed Library Materials, ANSI Z39.48-1984. ♾

Contents

Preface   vii
Michael Tonry

Fifty Years of American Sentencing Reform: Nine Lessons   1
Michael Tonry

The Wild West of Sentencing Reform: Lessons from California   35
Robert Weisberg

Forty Years of American Sentencing Guidelines: What Have We Learned?   79
Richard S. Frase

Federal Sentencing after *Booker*   137
Paul J. Hofer

The Evolution of Sentencing Guidelines in Minnesota and England and Wales   187
Julian V. Roberts

Model Penal Code: Sentencing—Workable Limits on Mass Punishment   255
Kevin R. Reitz and Cecelia M. Klingele

Trials and Tribulations: The Trial Tax and the Process of Punishment   313
Brian D. Johnson

Have Racial and Ethnic Disparities in Sentencing Declined?   365
Ryan D. King and Michael T. Light

Predictions of Dangerousness in Sentencing: Déjà Vu All Over Again   439
Michael Tonry

Criminal Courts as Inhabited Institutions: Making Sense of Difference and Similarity in Sentencing   483
Jeffery T. Ulmer

Index   523

Preface

American sentencing policies and practices have been being "reformed" for nearly 50 years. In 1975, every state and the federal government operated an indeterminate sentencing system. Judges had unreviewable discretion to sentence convicted offenders to prison, jail, or probation. Parole boards decided when prisoners got out. In theory, and to some extent in practice, rehabilitation and reintegration of offenders were the system's primary aims.

That was then, before support for indeterminate sentencing dissolved, remarkably quickly, in the mid-1970s. Sentencing reform was in the air. There was wide agreement about the problems. Judges' and parole boards' decisions, critics contended, were too often idiosyncratic and racially biased; unjust and unwarranted disparities were ubiquitous; treatment programs were seldom effective; and the system was fundamentally unfair. Support for radical change was bipartisan. Civil liberties, civil rights, and prisoners' rights groups, and political liberals generally, focused on finding solutions for disparities, unfairness, and racial bias. Police and prosecutors' organizations, and political conservatives generally, focused on preventing unwarranted leniency and increasing emphasis on crime prevention through deterrence and incapacitation.

The result was a law reform explosion. Since 1975, American jurisdictions have established statutory sentencing standards; enacted mandatory minimum sentence, truth in sentencing, and life without parole laws; created parole and sentencing guidelines systems; and abolished parole release.

The new policies and institutions made fundamental changes to traditional ways of doing business. They coincided with enormous expansion of government and foundation support for criminal justice research and correspondingly large increases in the numbers of university departments and scholarly specialists in criminology. No one knows how many research projects, evaluations, and PhD theses on sentencing and corrections have been completed in the past 50 years. Tens of thousands is a realistic estimate.

Given the scale and diversity of the changes, and the proliferation of efforts to assess their effects, we should know a great deal about what works, what doesn't, and in each case why. We know less than we should, but we know a lot, as the essays in this volume explain.

We followed the standard *Crime and Justice* developmental process. Essays were commissioned from well-known, widely respected senior scholars. Two, on important subjects, sentencing of women and prosecutors' sentencing roles, did not work out because of health problems that afflicted the writers or members of their families. The remaining writers and as many more other scholarly specialists attended a May 2018 conference in Minneapolis to discuss and illuminate initial drafts. The essays, rewritten after the meeting, were distributed to paid referees for critical reactions and suggestions for improvement. The essays in this volume are the result.

Su Smallen coordinated and managed the Minneapolis event. The attendees, besides the writers, were Mark Bergstrom (Pennsylvania Sentencing Commission), Douglas Berman (Ohio State University), Robert Crutchfield (University of Washington), Anthony Doob (University of Toronto), Rhys Hester (Clemson University), Marc Mauer (The Sentencing Project), Kelly Mitchell (University of Minnesota; president, National Association of Sentencing Commissions), Ojmarrh Mitchell (University of South Florida), and Rossella Selmini (University of Minnesota).

Many of the attendees served later on as anonymous referees of particular essays. The other referees for one or more essays were Nora Demleitner (Washington and Lee University), Malcolm Feeley (University of California, Berkeley), Arie Freiberg (Monash University), Hadar Aviram (University of California, Hastings), Marc Miller (University of Arizona), Noah Painter-Davis (University of New Mexico), Cassia Spohn (Arizona State University), and Ronald Wright (Wake Forest University).

The writers endured a long, arduous process with remarkable patience and good will. Meeting participants did their reading ahead of time and offered useful advice and challenging criticism. Referees prepared reports substantially more detailed and reflective than is common; writers took the reports seriously. Su Smallen provided indispensable help on stage and behind the curtains. I am enormously grateful to them all. Readers will decide for themselves whether the effort was worthwhile.

Michael Tonry
Bagnaia, Isola d'Elba, December 2018

Michael Tonry

Fifty Years of American Sentencing Reform: Nine Lessons

Major turbulence in American sentencing policy began 50 years ago, more or less. At the latest, it began in 1975, when Maine abolished parole release and became the first determinate sentencing state since the early 1930s. Earlier dates are also plausible. Don M. Gottfredson and Leslie T. Wilkins began foundational work on parole guidelines in the mid-1960s. Their efforts led successively to the US Parole Board's path-breaking release guidelines, the first voluntary sentencing guidelines in Vermont and Colorado, and presumptive guidelines in Minnesota and elsewhere. Another possibility is 1969, when, in *Discretionary Justice*, Kenneth Culp Davis, America's leading administrative law scholar, disparaged the lack of basic fairness in the criminal justice system. Or 1971, when the American Friends Service Committee's *Struggle for Justice* decried racial injustice and sentencing disparities and blamed indeterminate sentencing. Or 1973, when Judge Marvin Frankel's *Criminal Sentences: Law without Order* condemned judicial "lawlessness" and proposed creation of an administrative agency to set standards for sentencing. National newspapers and public affairs journals seldom review scholarly books on specialized subjects. These they did.

Sentencing reform was in the air. There was wide agreement about the problems. Judges had unreviewable authority to set sentences and parole boards to release prisoners. Among the results, critics contended, were idiosyncratic and racially biased decisions, unjust and unwarranted disparities, and procedural unfairness. Support for change was bipartisan. Civil liberties, civil rights, and prisoners' rights groups, and political liberals generally, focused on disparities, unfairness, and racial bias. Police and prosecutors' organizations, and political conservatives generally, focused on unwarranted leniency, inconsistency, and insufficient emphasis on crime prevention.[1]

The result was a law reform explosion that rivaled the nineteenth-century inventions of the reformatory, the prison, parole, probation, and the juvenile court. Together they constituted the indeterminate sentencing systems that critics disdained. Since 1975, American jurisdictions have established statutory sentencing standards; enacted mandatory minimum sentence, truth in sentencing, and life without parole laws; created parole and sentencing guidelines systems; and abolished parole release. Together those initiatives constitute determinate sentencing.

Big differences distinguish indeterminate from determinate sentencing. The former extended broad authority to officials so they could make individualized decisions in every case; the latter narrowed or eliminated officials' discretion. Supporters of indeterminate sentencing viewed offenders as malleable and their crimes as products of adverse social and environmental conditions. Many supporters of determinate sentencing viewed human nature as fixed and crimes as products of immorality, greed, and lack of self-discipline. Indeterminate sentencing rested on the idea that most offenders should and can be rehabilitated, and the incorrigible few incapacitated. Determinate sentencing rests on the idea that the primary purpose of sentencing is to assure that offenders receive the punishments they deserve.

The new policies and institutions involved fundamental changes in traditional ways of doing business. They coincided with enormous expansion of government and foundation support for criminal justice research and correspondingly large increases in the numbers of university departments and scholarly specialists in criminology. No one knows how many research projects, evaluations, and PhD theses on sentencing and corrections have been completed in the past 50 years. Tens of thousands is a realistic estimate.

---

[1] Rothman (1971, 1980) provided the classic historical accounts of the origins, operations, and chronic problems of indeterminate sentencing. Besides the seminal works mentioned in the text, a number of influential liberal (e.g., Morris 1974; Dershowitz 1976; von Hirsch 1976) and conservative (e.g., Fleming 1974; van den Haag 1975; Wilson 1975) books offered overlapping critiques of indeterminate sentencing but proposed substantially different solutions. The richest accounts of the left/right, due process/crime control coalitions favoring the shift to determinate sentencing describe early changes in California (Messenger and Johnson 1978; Parnas and Salerno 1978) and Pennsylvania and Minnesota (Martin 1984).

Given the scale and diversity of the changes, and the proliferation of efforts to assess their effects, we should know a great deal about what works, what doesn't, and in each case why. We know less than we should, but we know a lot. Nine lessons, summarized in table 1, stand out.

TABLE 1
Sentencing Reform, Nine Lessons

1. Sentencing Guidelines	Presumptive sentencing guidelines developed by sentencing commissions are the most effective means to improve consistency, reduce disparity, and control corrections spending.
2. Mandatory Sentences	Mandatory sentencing laws should be repealed, and no new ones enacted; they produce countless injustices, encourage cynical circumventions, and seldom achieve demonstrable reductions in crime.
3. Federal Sentencing	Federal sentencing guidelines have been remarkably unsuccessful; they should be rebuilt from the ground up.
4. Racial Disparities	Black and Hispanic defendants are more likely than whites and Asians to be sentenced to imprisonment, and for longer; presumptive sentencing guidelines reduced racial disparities initially and over time, but most states do not have presumptive guidelines.
5. Predicting Dangerousness	Use of predictions of dangerousness to determine who is imprisoned and for how long is unjust; predictive accuracy has improved little in 50 years, and current methods too often lengthen prison terms of people who would not have committed violent crimes.
6. Case Processing	Efforts to standardize sentences and eliminate disparities in a state or the federal system cannot succeed; distinctive practices and norms, diverse local cultures, and practical and political needs of officials and agencies assure major local differences in sentencing practice.
7. Punishments	Many community correctional programs can reduce reoffending, improve offenders' and their families' lives, and compared with imprisonment reduce public expenditure; imprisonment increases reoffending, damages prisoners and their families, and wastes enormous amounts of money.
8. Parole Release	Except in the handful of states that have effective systems of presumptive sentencing guidelines, parole release is an essential component of a just and cost-effective sentencing system in the United States.
9. Luck and Leadership	Some sentencing systems and policies are demonstrably superior to others. Whether they are successful often depends, alas, on auspicious circumstances and the involvement of unusually effective leaders.

1. SENTENCING GUIDELINES.—*Presumptive sentencing guidelines developed by sentencing commissions are the most effective means to improve consistency, reduce disparity, and control corrections spending.*

Judge Frankel proposed the establishment of specialized administrative agencies, now usually called sentencing commissions, to develop, promulgate, monitor, and, as needed, revise presumptively applicable guidelines for sentencing. He reasoned that legislatures lack the specialized knowledge, staff continuity, and attention spans needed to do those things well and are too vulnerable to day-to-day political and media influence. He expected appellate courts to review contested sentences and gradually to develop a "common law of sentencing" to deal with difficult kinds of cases.

What Judge Frankel proposed worked. Commissions in Kansas, Minnesota, North Carolina, Oregon, and Washington created presumptive guidelines systems that established sentencing standards for typical cases, made the process fairer and more consistent, reduced disparities, including by race and gender, and managed prison population sizes and correctional spending. They accomplished these things in somewhat different ways and more and less successfully, but showed that presumptive guidelines can remedy many of the problems of indeterminate sentencing. Richard Frase (2019, p. X), summing up the most exhaustive and authoritative survey of guidelines experience ever published, observes, "The preguidelines regime of unstructured, highly discretionary sentencing is unacceptable. Guidelines offer the only proven sentencing reform model."

Frankel's was but one of six contending sentencing reform proposals in the 1970s.[2] None of the five others proved effective. Most were abandoned. The first was creation, under judicial leadership, of voluntary guidelines based on research documenting prior sentencing patterns. The logic was that judges would want to observe local conventions once they knew what they were. The second, an alternative to voluntary guide-

---

[2] Blumstein et al. (1983) and Tonry (1996, 2016) through their respective dates summarize the major changes in American sentencing laws and policies and their effects. On sentencing guidelines generally, see Frase (2013, 2019). On the 1970s experience with judge-led voluntary guidelines, see Gottfredson, Wilkins, and Hoffman (1978), Kress (1980), Rich et al. (1982), and Carrow et al. (1985). On sentencing information systems, see Doob (1990) and Miller (2004). On sentencing councils, see Zeisel and Diamond (1975). On sentence appeals without guidelines, see Zeisel and Diamond (1977). Shane-Dubow, Brown, and Olsen (1985) and Austin et al. (1994) provide broader overviews of sentencing policy changes, including adoption of mandatory sentence laws, through their respective dates.

lines, was to establish computerized "sentencing information systems" that judges could consult to learn how they and their colleagues had previously dealt with particular kinds of cases. They were quickly abandoned everywhere they were tried. The third, adopted in Arizona, California, Colorado, Illinois, Indiana, and North Carolina, was to amend criminal codes to specify recommended sentences for typical cases. No other state enacted a "statutory determinate sentencing law" after 1979, and Colorado and North Carolina repealed theirs. The fourth, without guidelines, was to create sentence appeal systems, sometimes involving appellate courts and other times involving "sentencing councils" composed of trial judges. The fifth was for sentencing commissions rather than judges to develop voluntary sentencing guidelines systems.

Except for Judge Frankel's presumptive sentencing guidelines, none of those efforts demonstrably improved consistency, reduced racial and other disparities, or effectively controlled correctional resource planning and spending. The early voluntary guidelines and sentencing information systems failed because, as Anthony Doob observed after evaluating information systems, "Judges do not, as a rule, care to know what sentences other judges are handing down in comparable cases" (1989, p. 6). The early appeal systems failed because of "lawlessness." In the absence of standards indicating what sentence should ordinarily be imposed, there was no basis for deciding whether a particular one was appropriate or not. Some sentences were overturned, but on the ad hoc bases that they were too severe or inappropriate under the circumstances. Those rationales are not generalizable and provided little guidance for subsequent cases.

Evaluations of the early voluntary guidelines systems in Colorado, Vermont, Maryland, and Florida uniformly concluded that they had no discernible effects on sentencing disparities. Nonetheless, most of the 16 current state systems are voluntary (now usually called "advisory"). No subsequent research has shown that the newer voluntary systems have reduced disparities compared with sentencing patterns before their adoption. Proponents argue that they improve consistency for two reasons: newly appointed judges without prior sentencing experience are socialized into the idea that the guidelines express local conventions, and over time the guidelines become points of reference around which "going rates" take shape and charging and plea bargaining take place (Ulmer 2019).

Every American state should establish a sentencing commission and direct it to develop presumptive guidelines, as the recently approved *Model Penal Code—Sentencing* proposes (Reitz and Klingele 2019). Auguries are not promising, however, at least in the short term. The newest of the presumptive guidelines systems, in Kansas and North Carolina, took effect in 1993 and 1994. Practitioners generally oppose major law reforms for fear of the unknown, judges oppose presumptive guidelines for fear they will lose discretion, and prosecutors oppose them for fear they will lose plea bargaining leverage. Frase (2019, p. X), on the rationale that half a loaf is better than none, observes, "But even if we can eventually agree on what an ideal guidelines system should look like, some jurisdictions will be unable or unwilling to adopt all of its features. In some, an incomplete system may be 'as good as it gets.' Such guidelines may be better than if there were no guidelines at all."

2. MANDATORY SENTENCES.—*Mandatory sentencing laws should be repealed, and no new ones enacted; they produce countless injustices, encourage cynical circumventions, and seldom achieve demonstrable reductions in crime.*

Mandatory sentencing laws are a fundamentally bad idea.[3] From eighteenth-century England, when pickpockets worked the crowds at hangings of pickpockets and juries refused to convict people of offenses subject to severe punishments, to twenty-first-century America, the evidence has been clear. Mandatory minimum sentences have few, if any, discernible deterrent effects and, because of their rigidity, result in unjustly harsh punishments in many cases and willful circumvention by prosecutors, judges, and juries in others. In our time, when plea bargaining is ubiquitous, mandatories are routinely used to coerce guilty pleas, sometimes from innocent people (Johnson 2019).

In the 1950s, the American Bar Foundation undertook the most extensive research ever conducted on day-to-day operations of American crim-

---

[3] The classic summaries of the historical evidence are Michael and Wechsler (1940) and Hay (1975). The most comprehensive studies of day-to-day use of mandatories were carried out in the 1950s for the American Bar Foundation and published in the 1960s (Newman 1966; Dawson 1969). I have several times summarized the 1950s–90s case studies (e.g., Tonry 2016) and other countries' limited experience (Tonry 2009, 2012). The authoritative surveys of research on deterrent effects are National Academy of Sciences reports (Blumstein, Cohen, and Nagin 1978; Travis, Western, and Redburn 2014). Comprehensive recent surveys of the evidence include Chalfin and McCrary (2017) and Tonry (2018*b*).

inal courts. They learned that prosecutors applied mandatories selectively and that judges and juries refused to convict when penalties seemed too severe. Frank Remington, who directed the project, observed in 1969, "Legislative prescription of a high mandatory sentence for certain offenders is likely to result in a reduction in charges at the prosecution stage, or if this is not done, by a refusal of the judge to convict at the adjudication stage. The issue . . . thus is not solely whether certain offenders should be dealt with severely, but also how the criminal justice system will accommodate to the legislative charge" (1969, p. xvii). A large number of sophisticated case processing studies in the 1970s, 1980s, and 1990s reached the same conclusion.

The evidence on deterrent effects is equally damning. Countless authoritative surveys, in many countries, have concluded that mandatories' deterrent effects are modest at best. National Academy of Sciences reports in 1978 and 2014 serve as contemporary bookends. The 1978 Panel on Research on Deterrent and Incapacitative Effects concluded, "In summary . . . we cannot assert that the evidence warrants an affirmative conclusion regarding deterrence" (Blumstein, Cohen, and Nagin 1978, p. 7). The 2014 Committee on the Causes and Consequences of High Rates of Incarceration similarly observed that "knowledge about mandatory minimum sentences has changed remarkably little in the past 30 years. Their ostensible primary rationale is deterrence. The overwhelming weight of the evidence, however, shows that they have few if any deterrent effects. . . . Existing knowledge is too fragmentary [and] estimated effects are so small or contingent on particular circumstances as to have no practical relevance for policy making" (Travis, Western, and Redburn 2014, p. 83).

Contemporary research thus confirms long-standing cautions against enactment of mandatory sentencing laws. Their use to coerce guilty pleas is new and distinctive to our times. Even innocent defendants are sorely tempted to plead guilty and accept probation or a short prison term rather than risk a mandatory 10- or 20-year sentence. The late Harvard Law School professor William Stuntz observed that "outside the plea bargaining process" prosecutors' threats to file charges subject to mandatories "would be deemed extortionate" (2011, p. 260). Federal Court of Appeals Judge Gerald Lynch similarly observed that prosecutors' power to threaten mandatories has enabled them to displace judges from their traditional role: It is "the prosecutor who decides what sentence the defendant should be given in exchange for his plea" (2003, p. 1404). American sentencing has become more severe in recent decades; prosecutors bear much of the responsibility (Johnson 2019).

This is a uniquely American problem. Nothing similar occurs in any other developed country. It has two causes. One is that American prosecutors are elected or appointed by elected politicians; elsewhere they are nonpartisan career civil servants. The second is that, under US constitutional law, prosecutors' day-to-day decisions are almost never subject to judicial review. American prosecutors have the same interests and motives, however, as other elected politicians to curry favor with the electorate and the media. In recent "tough-on-crime" decades, prosecutors have favored severe punishments.

This is not how things are supposed to work. Until mandatory sentencing laws proliferated, prosecutors filed charges and presented evidence, judges with or without juries decided whether the evidence justified a conviction, and judges imposed sentences. This division of labor made sense and remains the norm in other Western countries.

American prosecutors are adversaries. Their aims are to achieve convictions and, often, severe punishments. Mandatory sentencing laws increased their power to do both. Offers to dismiss charges subject to mandatories are often too good to refuse; that is why many fewer cases go to trial than in earlier times. In tried cases resulting in convictions, judges have no legally legitimate way to do anything but impose at least the mandated punishment.

Prosecutors in other countries are expected, like judges, to focus equally on conviction of the guilty and exoneration of those whose guilt cannot be proven. American prosecutors are seldom so evenhanded. Their adversary role and foreseeable identification with victims make personal animus toward many defendants likely and psychologically understandable. Personal political interests, especially in controversial or notorious cases, exacerbate those tendencies. Those are reasons why judges, not prosecutors, should set sentences. Good judges should be above the battle—unemotional, impartial, and motivated to do justice. That may sometimes be difficult, but good judges try. Because of the coercive power of mandatories, the avenging prosecutor often displaces the neutral judge.

Every authoritative law reform organization that has examined American sentencing in the last 50 years has proposed elimination of mandatory minimum sentence laws. These included, in earlier times, the 1967 President's Commission on Law Enforcement and Administration of Justice, the 1971 National Commission on Reform of Federal Laws, the 1973 National Advisory Commission on Criminal Justice Standards and Goals, the 1979 Model Sentencing and Corrections Act proposed by the Uniform Law Commissioners, and the American Bar Association's 1994 Sentencing Standards. The American Law Institute's *Model Penal Code—Sentencing* offered the same recommendation in 2017 (Reitz and Klingele 2019).

3. FEDERAL SENTENCING.—*Federal sentencing guidelines have been remarkably unsuccessful; they should be rebuilt from the ground up.*

The federal guidelines were the most controversial and disliked sentencing reform initiative in American history. Within 2 years of their taking effect, more than 200 federal district judges invalidated the guidelines and declared all or part of the Sentencing Reform Act of 1984 unconstitutional. In *Mistretta v. United States*, 488 U.S. 361 (1989), however, the US Supreme Court rejected the lower courts' holdings. Little changed until the Court in *U.S. v. Booker*, 543 U.S. 220 (2005), reversed course, declaring major parts of the 1984 act unconstitutional after all and converting the guidelines from "mandatory," as the federal sentencing commission called them, to "advisory."

The federal guidelines' failure is ironic; prospects for success could not have been better. Senate Bill 2699, introduced by Senator Edward Kennedy in 1975, was the first legislative proposal for a sentencing commission anywhere. The bill, developed by Yale Law School faculty in collaboration with Judge Frankel, quickly obtained bipartisan support; the Senate approved it several times. When the 1984 act took effect, the future looked rosy. The commission had a staff of 70 (state commissions had five to 10), a correspondingly large budget, and the good fortune that Kay A. Knapp, director of the successful Minnesota commission, signed on as executive director.

After that, it was all downhill. The initial commission was poorly led and faction-ridden. Knapp was forced out within months. The commission made no effort to learn from the experiences of existing commissions in Minnesota, Pennsylvania, and Washington. Most importantly, although Frankel viewed administrative agencies' partial insulation from political influence as a key element—and benefit—of his proposal, the commission and key commissioners openly pursued personal and partisan political ends. The "tough-on-crime" politics of the 1980s displaced the original goals of reduced disparities and greater fairness.

Detailed discussions of how and why the guidelines proved so unsuccessful and unpopular are available elsewhere.[4] They were too severe, too complex, and too detailed. Most sitting federal judges hated them. The guidelines nearly eliminated the use of probation as a federal sanction. Half of federal offenders received probation before the guidelines took effect; 7 percent did in 2017. The commission's unprecedented "relevant conduct" policy required sentencing judges to take account of alleged crimes that were not prosecuted or that resulted in acquittals.

Federal judges in recent years have imposed sentences that fall within applicable guideline ranges about half of the time. Paul Hofer (2019), in the most exhaustive analysis to date of federal sentencing data, concludes that sentencing disparities, including racial disparities, are probably greater now than before the guidelines took effect. The existence of numerous mandatory sentencing laws in the federal system is part of the explanation, but the US Sentencing Commission deserves most of the blame.

The federal guidelines are not salvageable. Fundamental problems result from decisions made when they were initially developed. The US Sentencing Commission's guidelines are much too detailed. They divide offense severity into 43 categories; most states use eight to 12. They attempt to micromanage judges' decisions concerning the pertinence of offenders' personal characteristics and backgrounds; state guidelines simply identify aggravating and mitigating characteristics judges may take into account, among others, when they believe it appropriate. They authorize probationary sentences for only 5–7 percent of federal offenders; states authorize use of probation for any offender not subject to a mandatory minimum sentence law. Finally, they direct judges to increase sentences on the basis of "relevant conduct" whether or not it was proven at trial or admitted, including conduct occurring in crimes of which the offender was acquitted. No state guidelines contain a comparable provision.

Those provisions are straitjackets. Just, fair, and accountable sentencing will remain an impossible dream in federal courts until they are repu-

---

[4] Stith and Cabranes (1998) and Tonry (1996, 2016) provide the fullest historical accounts including detailed discussions of the federal guidelines' major provisions, their rationales, and the controversies they generated. US Supreme Court Justice Stephen Breyer (1988, 1999) provided spirited apologia.

diated. If and when that happens, state experience can guide a new commission in creating a new system of federal guidelines.

4. RACIAL DISPARITIES.—*Black and Hispanic defendants are more likely than whites and Asians to be sentenced to imprisonment, and for longer; presumptive sentencing guidelines reduced racial disparities initially and over time, but most states do not have presumptive guidelines.*

Racial and ethnic disparities in sentencing and imprisonment continue to be an American dilemma.[5] They have been common throughout American history. Racial disparities among prison inmates in the twentieth century increased slowly through the 1970s and then rose rapidly through the early 1990s. At the peak, the imprisonment rate for black Americans was eight times higher than the white rate. In our time, black and Hispanic offenders, compared with whites, are more likely to receive prison sentences, and for longer. In jurisdictions with sentencing guidelines, minority defendants receive mitigated sentences less often than whites and are more likely than whites to receive sentences at the top of the applicable guideline range. Minority offenders are less likely to be sentenced to community punishments than whites or to receive early release from prison.

The explanations are complex and simple. The first simple one is that judges react differently to minority offenders. In earlier times, racial bias and stereotyping were major reasons. In our time, implicit racial biases and no doubt some invidious bias remain part of the problem. The second simple explanation is that deeply disadvantaged backgrounds more often characterize minority offenders than whites. Many judges believe disadvantaged offenders are especially likely to reoffend and thus should be punished more severely.

The complex reasons involve the nature of American sentencing laws. Legislatures enacted laws that mandated especially severe sentences for crimes of which disproportionately large numbers of minority offenders are convicted. The mandatory minimum sentence, three-strikes, dangerous offender, truth in sentencing, and life without parole laws enacted in the 1980s and 1990s targeted violent and drug crimes. Relatively more

---

[5] Classic early sources include Du Bois (1899), Sellin (1935), and Myrdal (1944). Tonry (1995, 2011) and Travis, Western, and Redburn (2014, chap. 2) provide comprehensive overviews of knowledge concerning racial disparities in imprisonment since 1970. The best surveys of research on sentencing disparities through their respective dates are Mitchell (2005), Baumer (2013), Spohn (2015), and King and Light (2019).

minority than white people commit violent crimes—though the difference is declining. Making punishments more severe for violent crimes necessarily affected more minority than white offenders. Some might argue that concern about victims of violence justifies harsher punishments. Others disagree, noting the effects on minority offenders of discrimination, police practices, and structural disadvantage.

There is no equivalent debate to be had about drug crimes. Minority citizens neither use illicit drugs nor engage in trafficking more than whites. They are, however, much more likely to be arrested, prosecuted, and convicted. The reasons are that police drug enforcement targets inner-city neighborhoods, that minority citizens are vastly—eight to 10 times—more likely than whites to be stopped on the street, and that prosecutors less often divert minority arrestees from prosecution. Racial profiling is a big part of the story.

Critics of American drug policy note that governmental responses to the crack and heroin outbreaks of the 1970s, 1980s, and 1990s emphasized arrests and harsh punishments that disproportionately ensnared minority citizens. Responses to the recent methamphetamine and heroin epidemics, mostly involving white users and sellers, emphasize treatment, education, and other public health and social welfare solutions. Go figure.

The disparate effects of seemingly neutral laws on members of racial and ethnic groups are a major cause of racial disparities in imprisonment. The classic example, which filled federal prisons with black prisoners, was the 100-to-1 law that punished low-level sellers of 5 grams of crack, mostly black, as severely as major sellers, mostly white, of 500 grams of powder cocaine. It is now an 18-to-1 law and continues to punish blacks more severely than whites. Similar laws survive in many American states. Few mandatory sentencing laws for violent and drug crimes have been repealed or substantially narrowed. As long as they survive, racial disparities will remain endemic.

Disparities have slightly declined. The black/white difference in imprisonment rates in recent years has been about 4:1 (higher for males). This resulted partly from major declines in prosecutions for drug crimes. The news about racial and ethnic disparities in sentencing is good and bad. The good part is that they have declined in jurisdictions with strong guidelines systems (King and Light 2019). The bad part is that only a few jurisdictions have strong guidelines. Elsewhere business continues as usual.

There are some easy partial solutions to the racial disparities problems. One is to repeal all mandatory minimum sentence and similar laws. They are the principal drivers of mass incarceration and of racial disparities in imprisonment. The second is to create enforceable mechanisms to prohibit racial profiling. The third is to double and redouble efforts to educate police, prosecutors, judges, and other officials about explicit and implicit bias. It is humanly understandable, even if regrettable, that officials react with greater empathy toward people whose lives they understand, but it is fundamentally unjust. The fourth is to undertake racial impact studies throughout the criminal justice system to learn whether laws, policies, and practices do disproportionate damage to members of particular groups and to reconsider the justifiability of those that do (Reitz and Klingele 2019).

5. PREDICTING DANGEROUSNESS.—*Use of predictions of dangerousness to determine who is imprisoned and for how long is unjust; predictive accuracy has improved little in 50 years, and current methods too often lengthen prison terms of people who would not have committed violent crimes.*

Use of predictions of dangerousness has proliferated throughout the criminal justice system from bail to prison release.[6] They have no morally justifiable role to play in sentencing (Tonry 2019). They do have appropriate correctional uses in classifying offenders for admission to treatment programs. Three sets of problems bedevil use of predictions in sentencing.

First, they are seldom very accurate. Violence is rare, even among known offenders. Predicting rare events is inherently difficult. As a result, violence predictions are more often inaccurate than accurate. Norval Morris (1974) and John Monahan (1981) in influential early syntheses concluded that predictions of future violence were wrong two-thirds of the time. "'Dangerousness,'" Morris wrote, "must be rejected for [sentencing], since it presupposes a capacity to predict future criminal behavior quite beyond our present technical ability" (1974, p. 62). Locking up

---

[6] Particularly insightful analyses of ethical and technical issues by proponents of use of predictions include Monahan and Skeem (2016), Monahan (2017), Berk et al. (2018), and Berk (2019). The leading meta-analyses of research on the accuracy and reliability of violence prediction instruments are Campbell, French, and Gendreau (2009), Yang, Wong, and Coid (2010), and Fazel et al. (2012); they offer remarkably similar conclusions.

three people predicted to be violent when only one will be is, he said, deeply unjust.

The technology of violence prediction is vastly more sophisticated than it was four decades ago. One might expect that violence predictions today would be vastly more accurate. They aren't.

The most influential meta-analysis on violence prediction analyzed research on the nine most commonly used instruments. It concluded that positive violence predictions are correct, on average, 42 percent of the time (Fazel et al. 2012; Fazel 2019). Morris, recall, was troubled that only one-third of positive predictions (two of six) were correct. Forty-two percent accuracy, put differently, is two of five. The false positives are disproportionately black and other minority offenders (Angwin et al. 2016). As in Morris's time, substantially more than half of people predicted to be violent in our time will not be.

Two leading meta-analyses explicitly conclude that positive predictions of violence are too inaccurate to be used in sentencing:

> Because of their moderate level of predictive efficacy, they should not be used as the sole or primary means for clinical or criminal justice decision making that is contingent on a high level of predictive accuracy, such as preventive detention. (Yang, Wong, and Coid 2010, p. 761)

> These tools are not sufficient on their own for the purposes of risk assessment. . . . The current level of evidence is not sufficiently strong for definitive decisions on sentencing, parole, and release or discharge to be made solely using these tools. (Fazel et al. 2012, pp. 5, 6)

The second problem concerns variables used in prediction instruments. Most use characteristics such as youth and gender that are per se unjust. Like eye color or height, they are matters over which individuals have no control and for which they are not morally responsible. Gender in most settings is simply not an acceptable basis for distinguishing between people. Nor is youth. Common practice in all Western countries, consistently with findings of recent neurological and developmental research, calls for treating young offenders more sympathetically than adults, and less severely.

All prediction instruments incorporate socioeconomic variables such as marital status, employment record, education, and residential stability that are not the state's business. These are quintessentially personal choices;

people in free societies are entitled to make those decisions for themselves and not to suffer because of the choices they make. On all of these socioeconomic factors, minority offenders fare less well than whites. Their use causes and aggravates invidious disparities.

The third problem is that all prediction instruments incorporate criminal history variables that are inflated for black and other minority offenders by racially biased and disparate practices and racial profiling (Starr 2014). Group differences in some criminal history variables—including age at first arrest, custody status, and numbers of prior arrests, convictions, and punishments—result in substantial part from racial profiling and police targeting of poor and minority neighborhoods and individuals. Young black and Hispanic people are arrested at younger ages than whites, and more often. Schools expel more minority than white students for conduct problems and refer more to the police. Police drug enforcement targets substances sold by minority drug dealers and places where they sell them. All of these practices exaggerate the criminal records of minority individuals compared with other people.

Use of predictions of dangerousness in sentencing thus cannot be justified either empirically or morally. To many people, however, it is intuitively plausible. It expresses sympathy toward hypothetical future victims and disdain for people believed—usually incorrectly—to be likely to be violent. What to do?

The best answer is to abandon use of violence predictions in sentencing. Prevention of crime is an important public policy goal, but so are justice, fairness, and equal treatment. Each derives from fundamental ideas about human dignity. Each should limit the exercise of state power over individual lives. Predictive sentencing, by contrast, sacrifices the lives of individuals in order to protect hypothetical victims.

Law and order politics and prevailing emotionalism may make elimination of preventive sentencing unachievable. A less morally justifiable but more saleable option is to establish limits on increments of additional punishment that can be imposed, for example, sentences to confinement not more than 20 or 30 percent longer than would otherwise be ordered.

Monahan (2017) and the *Model Penal Code—Sentencing* propose use of predictions as a basis only for mitigation of sentences and never for aggravation. BUT—a big but—Monahan's proposal can work only if there are strong meaningful limits on sentencing severity, from which the mitigated sentence offers a reduction. This might be achievable in the handful of jurisdictions with presumptive sentencing guidelines systems. Otherwise, and elsewhere, nothing would stop judges and prosecutors from using predictions to reduce sentences for low-risk offenders and increase them for high-risk offenders.

6. CASE PROCESSING.—*Efforts to standardize sentences and eliminate disparities in a state or the federal system cannot succeed; distinctive practices and norms, diverse local cultures, and practical and political needs of officials and agencies assure major local differences in sentencing practice.*

It is impossible to micromanage sentencing decisions successfully throughout a state or the federal system. Sentencing will be fairer, more just, and more rational when legislators and other political officials acknowledge this. Those who were judges, prosecutors, or defense lawyers earlier in their careers know it even if for political reasons they act as if they do not. Only uninformed and naive people believe, and disingenuous people claim to believe, that any criminal law will be consistently and mechanically applied. Exceptions are inevitable and sometimes are the norm. The inexorable implication is that sentencing laws should provide frameworks for decision making and presumptions about decisions, but never more than that.

There are three reasons. The first is that almost all judges, prosecutors, defense lawyers, and correctional officials take their jobs seriously. Circumstances of criminal offenses and characteristics of offenders, offenses, and victims vary enormously. Decent practitioners know this and want to make, or be involved in making, decisions that are sensible and just under the particular circumstances, even if applicable laws direct them to make decisions that are neither sensible nor just. This is why three centuries of experience and a half century of social science research show that mandatory sentence laws are never applied consistently. Sometimes prescribed punishments that everyone involved believes to be palpably unjust are imposed; often they are not.

The second is that criminal court processes are local. State and federal legislatures enact criminal laws, but local officials apply them. They live and work in particular places that have distinctive histories, norms, traditions, and political, religious, and legal cultures. That is why big cities, small towns, suburbs, and rural areas differ in the severity of the punishments their courts impose generally and in particular kinds of cases. That is why punishments are and long have been far more severe in southeastern than in northeastern states. Stereotyped examples involve comparisons of sentences for theft of lobster traps in Maine or cattle in Nebraska with sentences for those crimes elsewhere. Those examples, though, can trivialize a general phenomenon.

Officials in culturally and religiously conservative communities are likely to regard drug, sexual, and violent crimes differently than officials in big cities. Officials in rural courts, who know the people whose cases they process and where caseloads are small, tend to operate differently than officials in anonymous urban settings. Judges, prosecutors, and other officials usually reflect prevailing attitudes and beliefs; people new to a community quickly become socialized into the local culture. Prosecutors often say their overriding goal is to reflect local values in their office's work. What, therefore, local practitioners believe to be just and sensible outcomes in individual cases varies from place to place.

The third is that sentencing is a process and not simply a product of judicial idiosyncrasies. Prosecutors control charging and most dismissals. Judges control case processing. Judges, prosecutors, and defense counsel interact regularly and develop well-understood conventions and "going rates" that inform plea bargaining and predict sentences. All of them work within institutions that have limited resources, policy priorities, and standard ways of doing business. People who regularly ignore established conventions and others' institutional interests do not usually get along. It is business as usual for most cases. Notorious crimes are different, but they are a minuscule fraction of any court's caseload.

There is nothing new about any of this. It explains the history and research findings concerning mandatory sentencing. Social scientists studying courts document it.[7] An early political science literature on "local legal culture" demonstrated the interplays of local norms, going rates, institutional interests, and personal idiosyncrasies. A criminology literature on "focal concerns" emphasized practitioners' needs, and wishes, to reconcile public safety, offenders' moral responsibility, and practical institutional interests. A sociology literature on "inhabited institutions" takes those analyses further to explore interactions among institutions, of individuals within institutions, and resulting interplays.

---

[7] The classic works on local legal culture are Blumberg (1967), Eisenstein and Jacob (1977), and Eisenstein, Flemming, and Nardulli (1988). Steffensmeier, Ulmer, and Kramer (1998) and Kramer and Ulmer (2009) are foundational to the focal concerns literature. Kramer and Ulmer (2009) integrate the theories and literatures on focal concerns and local legal cultures. Ulmer (2019) canvasses the inhabited institutions literature that attempts to explain how and why local differences matter.

The bottom line: Courts are local, the people who work in them are local (or soon socialized into local norms), nearly all victims are local, and most offenders are local. Laws in books are statewide or national. Laws in action are local. When law in books conflicts with law in action, small wonder that local norms usually come out on top.

That does not mean that policy changes cannot shape sentencing outcomes. Passage or repeal of a mandatory sentence law will alter sentencing patterns, though not consistently. Increases and decreases in sentences specified in presumptive sentencing guidelines, or in other guidelines that have become part of the local legal culture, will affect sentencing outcomes. All else being equal, most practitioners want to comply with applicable laws and rules. Plea bargaining takes place in the shadow of the law or guidelines. The more, however, that laws or guidelines call on practitioners to behave in ways they believe to be unjust or unnecessary, the less likely they will pay attention.

7. PUNISHMENTS.—*Many community correctional programs can reduce reoffending, improve offenders' and their families' lives, and compared with imprisonment reduce public expenditure; imprisonment increases reoffending, damages prisoners and their families, and wastes enormous amounts of money.*

The case for greater use of community punishments is a no-brainer.[8] Compared with confinement in a jail or prison, they cost less, are less likely to lead to future offending, and are more humane. They do less collateral damage to the lives and futures of offenders and their loved ones. They can be scaled to the seriousness of crimes for which they are imposed. Well-managed, well-targeted, and adequately funded programs achieve lower reoffending rates. Other Western countries use community punishments much more, and imprisonment much less, than do American jurisdictions.

---

[8] Cullen, Lero Jonson, and Mears (2017) and Tonry (2018*a*) provide up-to-date surveys of knowledge concerning community punishments and their effects. Morris and Tonry (1990) and MacKenzie (2006) tell the story through their respective dates. Travis, Western, and Redburn (2014) contains authoritative summaries of knowledge concerning the effects of imprisonment on prisoners, their families, their communities, and public safety. Nagin, Cullen, and Lero Jonson (2009) and Cullen, Lero Jonson, and Nagin (2011) demonstrate that, all else being equal, imprisonment makes future offending by released prisoners more, not less, likely.

There are many effective community punishment programs. These include victim-offender mediation; diversion from prosecution conditioned on payment of fines, making restitution, or participating in treatment programs; fines for nontrivial crimes; suspended prison sentences; community service; and diverse forms of supervision and community-based treatment.

Unconditional discharges following conviction and unsupervised probation are important options. In neither instance do convicted offenders escape punishment. Anyone convicted of crime has endured fear and anxiety. All experience demeaning assembly line case processing. Many spend time overnight in jail awaiting a preliminary hearing. Many remain in jail until their cases are resolved. As the title of a classic 1979 book by Malcolm Feeley declared, for many *The Process Is the Punishment*.

Unconditional discharges and unsupervised or nominally supervised probation should be the defaults. Otherwise, probation agencies will waste scarce resources supervising low-risk offenders. Researchers have repeatedly shown, and most corrections officials believe, that resources are best devoted to working with higher-risk offenders. Reducing their likelihood of reoffending is more cost-effective and pays greater crime prevention dividends.

For offenders for whom supervision makes sense, well-managed, well-targeted, and adequately funded community programs can reduce reoffending. Many hundreds of evaluations show that participants in community punishments, at worst, do no worse than comparable people sentenced to confinement do. That last finding means that, except for the small percentage of unusually dangerous people, the vast sums spent on imprisonment are—from a crime-prevention perspective—wasted.

A steadily accumulating literature confirms the observation two centuries ago by John Howard, the first prominent English prison reformer, that prisons are "schools for crime." All else being equal, people sentenced to imprisonment are more, not less, likely to reoffend. There is nothing surprising about this. Imprisonment immerses people in inmate subcultures and exposes them to the deviant values of chronic offenders. Many prisons are brutal and brutalizing places to which prisoners must accommodate for self-protection. Almost all prisons are resource-poor and unable to provide adequate drug, mental health, and other treatment, vocational training, and education programs that can help prisoners lead law-abiding lives later on.

Imprisonment worsens prisoners' physical and mental health and shortens their life expectancies. The resulting stigma and collateral legal consequences foreclose opportunities and access to resources that make their later lives more difficult, their employment prospects worse, and their lifetime earnings less. Imprisonment damages and often impoverishes prisoners' families and children.

Nothing I have written here is new, controversial, or likely to surprise knowledgeable professionals or other well-informed people. Most of it has been known for decades, some for centuries.

8. PAROLE RELEASE.—*Except in the handful of states that have effective systems of presumptive sentencing guidelines, parole release is an essential component of a just and cost-effective sentencing system in the United States.*

Parole release has been the missing component of American sentencing reform since the late 1970s.[9] Its absence has been a huge loss. Well-designed and managed parole systems provide important capacities. They can establish and implement rational, evidenced-based release policies. They can even out disparities in the lengths of prison sentences judges impose. They can attempt to address prison overcrowding and control corrections costs by adjusting release standards. They can tailor supervision and conditions to individual parolees' needs. Not least, they give prisoners hope of an early release and motivation to achieve it.

The usefulness of parole release has been ignored for 40 years. In 20 states and the federal system, it was abolished. A few states later re-established it. In states that retained parole release, parole boards stopped performing their traditional roles.

In retrospect, parole's problem is that important developments occurred during a transition period. Parole release guidelines were a harbinger of the sentencing reform movement, a response to concerns about inconsistency, lack of official accountability, and racial and other dispar-

---

[9] The literature on parole release is scanty except for recidivism studies (e.g., Petersilia and Rosenfeld 2008). Few researchers or policy analysts have been interested since it fell out of favor. Petersilia (1999) is the most comprehensive survey of parole policy issues. Gottfredson, Wilkins, and Hoffman (1978) document early parole reforms and the development of evidence-based release guidelines. Arthur D. Little, Inc. (1981) reports the results of an evaluation of the first, largely successful, parole guidelines systems.

ities that undermined indeterminate sentencing. That is why I described their development in the introduction as one plausible beginning of modern sentencing reform efforts. To many critics, however, parole release was the paradigm institution of indeterminate sentencing. Ironically, evaluations showed that the best early parole guidelines systems successfully reduced disparities and improved accountability. That evidence made no difference. Oregon, Minnesota, and the federal system abandoned successful parole guidelines systems in the 1980s.

After the mid-1980s, parole boards became highly risk averse; most still are. Few, if any, tried to control prison populations. The percentages of prisoners released fell sharply. Average times served before release increased. The numbers held until their sentences expired ballooned. The numbers returned to prison for breach of conditions skyrocketed.

Elected officials deserve most of the blame. Especially during the tough-on-crime period from 1980 to 2000, but also more recently, governors made it clear they did not want to be associated with "parole leniency." In one of the best-known incidents, liberal Democratic Massachusetts governor Deval Patrick demanded that the entire parole board resign after a notorious crime by a parolee; releases under the new board, headed by a conservative former prosecutor, plummeted. Notorious crimes by parolees are inevitable, however, even in the best system. Auto accidents and bathtub slips are also inevitable, but no one suggests we should stop using cars or bathing. In earlier times in US history, governors and parole boards expressed deep sorrow about crimes by parolees. Life went on.

Parole boards can do a number of things better than any alternative. Modern prediction instruments, for example, include "dynamic" factors, things that treatment programs can change and that make future success on and after parole more likely. Judges cannot know about those future changes when they impose sentences.

Parole boards can use release guidelines to even out disparities, especially gross ones, in sentences judges impose. In almost all states, no other mechanism exists to do that. Except for a handful of states with presumptive sentencing guidelines, meaningful systems of appellate sentence review are nonexistent. Even in that handful of states, successful appeals are rare. Part of the reason is that prosecutors often require defendants to waive any appeal rights as a condition of a plea bargain.

Parole boards cannot prevent prison overcrowding in periods like the 1980s and 1990s, when imprisonment rates doubled and redoubled, but they can ameliorate the increases. In stable periods, their ability to advance release dates can make the difference between operating within a system's capacity and exceeding it. This was a standard function of parole release in earlier times. Even earlier, governors commonly used their pardon powers to control the size of the prison population.

No plausible arguments have been made against parole release. No other institution can release people because they have changed in important ways or can even out sentencing disparities. Demagogic arguments against parole release center on "leniency," but demagoguery is morally irrelevant. Romantic arguments are made that judges, not bureaucrats, should determine sentences, but that ignores three realities. Judges seldom know much about defendants; they rarely receive comprehensive presentence investigation reports. They know less about individuals than parole authorities can. In any case, prosecutors through their charging and bargaining decisions, not judges, control most sentences for moderately serious and serious crimes. And, as a practical matter, unjust decisions by judges are usually irremediable.

It is possible that parole release authority is unnecessary in states that have presumptive sentencing guidelines. That could be true, but only if meaningful opportunities exist to appeal sentences. Given that prosecutors have the same powers in those states as everywhere else and that successful appeals are rare, meaningful appeal opportunities are unlikely.[10] A solution is for parole boards and sentencing commissions to promulgate identical guidelines. If judges impose sentences from within the applicable guideline ranges, parole boards would seldom have reason to release prisoners early. If judges impose sentences longer than the applicable range indicates, parole boards would normally set a release date within the range.

A critic might fairly say that I have described aspirations for parole release rather than accomplishments (e.g., Frase 2019). Parole boards have long been demoralized, underfunded, and risk averse. Parole board members are too often political appointees, serving at the governor's pleasure,

---

[10] The *Model Penal Code—Sentencing* offers a number of proposals to reinvigorate sentence appeals, including authorizing appellate judges to overturn disproportionately severe sentences (including those resulting from mandatory sentence laws) and to take a "second look" at the need for continued confinement of prisoners who have served 15 or more years (Reitz and Klingele 2019). The code has not, however, been enacted anywhere and does not address the problem that prosecutors often insist that defendants waive appeal rights as a condition of plea bargains.

and often lack appropriate professional expertise. Those things were not true in the best parole systems in the 1970s and need not be true in the future. Blueprints are available to guide development and reinvigoration of parole boards so that they can operate systems for implementing rational evidence-based release policies, reducing disparities in sentences judges impose, and ameliorating prison overcrowding (Rhine, Petersilia, and Reitz 2017).

9. LUCK AND LEADERSHIP.—*Some sentencing systems and policies are demonstrably superior to others. Whether they are successful often depends, alas, on auspicious circumstances and the involvement of unusually effective leaders.*

On a cosmic report card, the sentencing reform movement of the last half century deserves a low or failing grade. The initial aims were to reduce disparities, make processes fairer, and in Judge Frankel's terms bring the rule of law to sentencing. Credible evidence of reduction in disparities exists only for a few initiatives and a few states. During the tough-on-crime period, the 1980s and 1990s, the aims of mandatory minimum and similar laws were ostensibly to reduce crime and increase "uniformity." They had few, if any, crime reduction effects and increased disparities. Proliferation of mandatory minimums and resulting increases in prosecutorial power have made processes less fair, sentences less consistent, and efforts to improve fairness, consistency, and accountability less successful.

In most places, the rule of law is no more evident today in sentencing than it was 50 years ago. The core elements are established and knowable rules, fair procedures, impartial decision makers, and opportunities for review of initial decisions. Of these, only the requirement of an impartial decision maker is generally satisfied. Less than a third of states have sentencing guidelines. Most cases everywhere are resolved by plea bargaining, a process few would describe as fair, transparent, or accountable. Appeals of sentence are meaningfully available only in four or five jurisdictions, and they are not common there. Even that picture is a bit rosy. Many guidelines systems have had few or no general effects on sentencing in general or on disparities.

Table 2 summarizes major changes in state sentencing systems since 1970; the federal government enacted all of them. Three patterns stand out. Legislatures enacted many more mandatory minimum sentence and

TABLE 2
Major State Sentencing Reforms

Initiative	Total	Pre-1970	1970–79	1980–89	1990–99	2000–2009	Post-2009
Mandatory minimums[a]	50	Unknown	49	Many	Many	Some	A few
Three-strikes[b]	27	None	None	None	24	3	
Truth in sentencing[c]	29	1	None	2	26		
Life without parole	49	7	12	11	16	4	
Sentencing commission[d]	16	None	2	9	10 [−4]	1 [−1]	[−1]
Presumptive guidelines	5	None	None	4	3	[−2]	
Any state guidelines[d]	19	None	None	10	10 [−1]	2 [−1]	[−1]

SOURCE.—Three-strikes: Chen (2008); truth in sentencing: Sabol et al. (2002); sentencing commissions and sentencing guidelines: Frase (2019, table 1); life without parole: Ogletree and Sarat (2012); mandatory minimums: Shane-Dubow, Brown, and Olsen (1985); Tonry (2016, table 2.2).

[a] After 1979, innumerable mandatory sentence laws were enacted and amended, making decadal counts nearly impossible. The 1970–79 laws mostly required 1- or 2-year sentence enhancements, often for use of a gun in the underlying crime.

[b] Earlier habitual offender laws, mostly enacted in the 1920s and 1930s, targeted chronic property offenders; people sentenced to imprisonment were usually eligible for parole release.

[c] Jurisdictions qualifying for prison construction funds under the federal Violent Crime Control and Law Enforcement Act of 1994.

[d] Totals refer to status in 2018 and include District of Columbia. Annual accounts show adoptions and in brackets repeals. Totals are adoptions less repeals.

similar laws than sentencing guidelines laws, mostly in the 1980s and 1990s. Except in Michigan in 2003 for most drug offenses, no significant mandatory minimum sentence laws have been repealed. By contrast, a quarter of all sentencing commissions went out of business, two of the seven presumptive guidelines systems were converted to voluntary systems, and three of the 22 guidelines jurisdictions terminated their use.

Table 2 understates the fragility of sentencing commissions. A number created in the 1980s failed to develop guidelines, and several, most famously in New York, were unable to persuade legislatures to approve their proposals (von Hirsch, Knapp, and Tonry 1987; Griset 1991).

Table 2 explains the failing or near-failing grade on the cosmic report card. However, some sentencing policy initiatives have worked reasonably well and a few jurisdictions in recent decades, most famously California, have pulled back from the worst excesses of the tough-on-crime period. Four lessons can be drawn.

First, some policy initiatives can make sentencing fairer, more predictable, and more consistent. The presumptive sentencing guidelines systems in Minnesota, North Carolina, Oregon, and Washington reduced sentencing disparities, including racial disparities, achieved compliance with changed policies, established meaningful systems of appellate sentence review, and improved corrections systems' planning and budgeting. Those things probably also happened in Kansas, but there is less evidence. North Carolina's guidelines reduced prison population growth more successfully there than occurred in any other state. Some of the voluntary guidelines systems, notably in Delaware, Pennsylvania, and Virginia, are widely said to have achieved legitimacy in judges' eyes and to have improved consistency in those states (though sophisticated evaluations have not demonstrated this). Those three states have institutionalized competent commissions that regularly revise their guidelines, maintain extensive data systems, and provide impact projections concerning proposed legislation. So, some successes.

Second, it is vastly harder to achieve the political support needed to enact sentencing commission legislation and to develop, promulgate, and oversee implementation of successful guidelines than it is to enact mandatory sentence and similar laws. That is not surprising. Proponents of those laws tend to have little compassion or concern for offenders, not to think or much care about implementation issues, and to have personal, political, and ideological objectives in mind. Enactment of the proposed laws achieves those objectives. The supporting rhetoric often insists that the goal is to prevent victim suffering; who could possibly be against that?

That so few mandatory sentence laws have been repealed is also not surprising. Their human costs are borne by offenders. State and local agencies pay any operations costs. There is no easy way to show that a particular law is ineffective, especially to politicians who distrust research findings and know intuitively that deterrence and incapacitation work.

Vocal opposition comes from civil liberties and ex-prisoners groups, defense lawyers, and sometimes judges, but they carry less weight than police and prosecutors, victims' organizations, and conservative activists.

Sentencing and parole commissions, by contrast, are continuing targets. Individual judges, prosecutors' organizations, and victims' groups usually oppose their creation and favor their expiration. They require state funding, and opponents can propose to save money by closing them down. Unlike a mandatory sentence law, a guidelines commission can be palpably ineffective. The leadership may be politically ineffective, important constituencies may disapprove policy choices, and the guidelines may fail to achieve legitimacy in practitioners' eyes.

Third, despite all that, some guidelines systems have succeeded and survived. Some other major reform initiatives, notably California's "Realignment" to date, have succeeded. There are few policy histories of successful sentencing initiatives.[11] All stress the commitment of politically savvy leaders and unusually able senior staff. In Oregon, longtime Republican Attorney General Hardy Myers supported the enabling legislation for the commission and guidelines and ran continuous political interference. In Washington, Republican District Attorney Norm Maleng of King County (Seattle) was the godfather; his former deputy David Boerner (later the commission's longtime chair) and executive director Roxanne Lieb made the trains run on time. Judge, then Justice, then Chief Justice Douglas Amdahl provided the political weight in Minnesota and commission executive directors Dale Parent and Kay Knapp produced a first-rate product. Judge Thomas Ross as commission chair did the heavy lifting in North Carolina. And so on.

Unusually effective individuals were also behind the successful parole guidelines systems. The federal prototype resulted in part from a decade's work by Don M. Gottfredson and Leslie T. Wilkins, formerly head of corrections research in the UK Home Office, and in part from the support of Maurice Sigler, chair of the Federal Parole Board. The key person in developing Oregon's successful parole guidelines was Parole Board chair Ira Blalock. In Minnesota, it was the parole board's chief executive, Dale Parent. Parole guidelines, however, were easier. All of these people worked at a time when indeterminate sentencing was taken

---

[11] Martin (1984), Parent (1988), and Frase (2005) tell the Minnesota story; the Washington story, Boerner and Lieb (2001); North Carolina, Wright (2002); Pennsylvania, Martin (1984) and Kramer and Ullmer (2009).

for granted. Parole abolition was on no one's agenda, judges and prosecutors had no reason to oppose parole reforms, criminal justice policy was not highly politicized, and reducing disparities and improving efficiency were uncontroversial ambitions.

The most dramatic sentencing reform story of our time is California's work in progress Realignment. The story Robert Weisberg (2019) tells includes many important players—prison reform litigators who kept at it for two decades, determined activist groups who launched successful referenda, three federal district court judges who stayed the course—but centers on Governor Jerry Brown. During two terms as governor, Brown repeatedly spent political capital, successfully managed the legislature, and stimulated referenda that made the difference. Realignment is not perfect and may in the end fail, but for now California sentencing is in better shape than it has been for 40 years. You will have to read the story to learn the details.

Fourth, prevailing ways of thinking change. As recently as the 1960s, few people challenged indeterminate sentencing. Emphasizing rehabilitation of offenders made sense to almost everyone. The American Law Institute's *Model Penal Code* (1962) and three high-profile national commissions in 1967, 1971, and 1973 endorsed it wholeheartedly.[12] That is a major reason why parole commissions had easier law reform jobs than sentencing commissions. The latter came into being after indeterminate sentencing imploded but also when tough-on-crime politics was in full swing: rehabilitation and sympathetic concern for offenders were out; deterrence, incapacitation, and do the crime, do the time were in. That Hardy Myers, Norm Maleng, Doug Amdahl, and Tom Ross superintended substantial guidelines successes during that period is in retrospect remarkable. They marched their commissions into the prevailing winds and somehow overcame the political obstacles on which most sentencing commissions foundered.

The tough-on-crime period is not completely past, but its influence is waning. Liberal and conservative movements, the ACLU and Right on Crime, and totemic liberal and conservative activists, George Soros and the Koch brothers, find law reform common cause. Legislatures mostly stopped enacting new mandatory sentence laws two decades ago. Some

---

[12] President's Commission on Law Enforcement and Administration of Justice (1967), National Commission on Reform of Federal Criminal Laws (1971), and National Advisory Commission on Criminal Justice Standards and Goals (1973).

legislatures have whittled away at them though not yet repealed them. That shift in the zeitgeist may partly explain California's successes. Changes may be possible in many states that were not able to make them one or two decades ago. If so, lessons have been learned about what does and does not work that may be helpful if fairness, consistency, and accountability reappear on sentencing reform agendas.

REFERENCES

American Bar Association. 1994. *ABA Standards for Criminal Justice: Sentencing*. 3rd ed. Washington, DC: American Bar Association.
American Friends Service Committee. 1971. *Struggle for Justice: A Report on Crime and Punishment in America*. New York: Hill & Wang.
American Law Institute. 1962. *Model Penal Code—Proposed Official Draft*. Philadelphia: American Law Institute.
———. 2017. *Model Penal Code—Sentencing*. Proposed Final Draft. Philadelphia: American Law Institute.
Angwin, Julia, Jeff Larson, Surya Mattu, and Lauren Kirchner. 2016. "Machine Bias: There's Software Used across the Country to Predict Future Criminals. And It's Biased Against Blacks." ProPublica, May 23. https://www.propublica.org/article/machine-bias-risk-assessments-in-criminal-sentencing.
Arthur D. Little, Inc. 1981. *An Evaluation of Parole Guidelines in Four Jurisdictions*. Washington, DC: National Institute of Corrections.
Austin, James, Charles Jones, John Kramer, and Phil Renninger. 1994. *National Assessment of Structured Sentencing*. Washington, DC: US Department of Justice, Bureau of Justice Assistance.
Baumer, Eric P. 2013. "Reassessing and Redirecting Research on Race and Sentencing." *Justice Quarterly* 30(2):231–61.
Berk, Richard. 2019. *Machine Learning Risk Assessments in Criminal Justice Settings*. New York: Springer.
Berk, Richard, Hoda Heidari, Shahin Jabbari, Michael Kearns, and Aaron Roth. 2018. "Fairness in Criminal Justice Risk Assessments: The State of the Art." *Sociological Methods and Research*. DOI:10.1177/0049124118782533.
Blumberg, Abraham S. 1967. *Criminal Justice*. New York: Quadrangle.
Blumstein, Alfred, Jacqueline Cohen, Susan E. Martin, and Michael Tonry, eds. 1983. *Research on Sentencing: The Search for Reform*. 2 vols. Washington, DC: National Academy Press.
Blumstein, Alfred, Jacqueline Cohen, and Daniel Nagin, eds. 1978. *Deterrence and Incapacitation: Estimating the Effects of Criminal Sanctions on Crime Rates*. Washington, DC: National Academy of Sciences.

Boerner, David, and Roxanne Lieb. 2001. "Sentencing Reform in the Other Washington." In *Crime and Justice: A Review of Research*, vol. 28, edited by Michael Tonry. Chicago: University of Chicago Press.

Breyer, Stephen. 1988. "The Federal Sentencing Guidelines and the Key Compromises upon Which They Rest." *Hofstra Law Review* 17:1–50.

———. 1999. "Federal Sentencing Guidelines Revisited." *Federal Sentencing Reporter* 11:180–86.

Campbell, Mary Ann, Sheila French, and Paul Gendreau. 2009. "The Prediction of Violence in Adult Offenders: A Meta-Analytic Comparison of Instruments." *Criminal Justice and Behavior* 36:567–90.

Carrow, Deborah M., Judith Feins, Beverly N. W. Lee, and Lois Olinger. 1985. *Guidelines without Force: An Evaluation of the Multi-jurisdictional Sentencing Guidelines Field Test*. Report to the National Institute of Justice. Cambridge, MA: Abt Associates.

Chalfin, Aaron, and Justin McCrary. 2017. "Criminal Deterrence: A Review of the Literature." *Journal of Economic Literature* 55(1):5–48.

Chen, Elsa Y. 2008. "Impacts of 'Three Strikes and You're Out' on Crime Trends in California and Throughout the United States." *Journal of Contemporary Criminal Justice* 24:345–70.

Cullen, Francis T., Cheryl Lero Jonson, and Daniel P. Mears. 2017. "Reinventing Community Corrections." In *Reinventing American Criminal Justice*, edited by Michael Tonry and Daniel S. Nagin. Vol. 46 of *Crime and Justice: A Review of Research*, edited by Michael Tonry. Chicago: University of Chicago Press.

Cullen, Francis T., Cheryl Lero Jonson, and Daniel S. Nagin. 2011. "Prisons Do Not Reduce Recidivism." *Prison Journal* 91(3):48–65.

Davis, Kenneth Culp. 1969. *Discretionary Justice: A Preliminary Inquiry*. Baton Rouge: Louisiana State University Press.

Dawson, Robert O. 1969. *Sentencing*. Boston: Little, Brown.

Dershowitz, Alan. 1976. *Fair and Certain Punishment*. New York: Twentieth Century Fund.

Doob, Anthony N. 1989. "Sentencing Aids Final Report." Unpublished manuscript. Toronto: University of Toronto, Institute of Criminology.

———. 1990. "Computerized Sentencing Information for Judges: An Overview of Progress Reports on the Sentencing Aids Project." Unpublished report. Toronto: University of Toronto, Institute of Criminology.

Du Bois. W. E. B. 1899. *The Philadelphia Negro: A Social Study*. Philadelphia: University of Pennsylvania.

Eisenstein, James, Roy Flemming, and Peter Nardulli. 1988. *The Contours of Justice: Communities and Their Courts*. Boston: Little, Brown.

Eisenstein, James, and Herbert Jacob. 1977. *Felony Justice: An Organizational Analysis of Criminal Courts*. Boston: Little, Brown.

Fazel, Seena. 2019. "The Scientific Validity of Current Approaches to Violence and Criminal Risk Assessment." In *Predictive Sentencing: Normative and Empirical Perspectives*, edited by Jan W. de Keijser, Julian V. Roberts, and Jesper Ryberg. Oxford: Hart.

Fazel, Seena, Jay P. Singh, Helen Doll, and Martin Grann. 2012. "Use of Risk Assessment Instruments to Predict Violence and Antisocial Behavior in 73 Samples Involving 24,827 People: Systematic Review and Meta-Analysis." *BMJ* 345: e4692. DOI:10.1136/bmj.e4692.

Feeley, Malcolm J. 1979. *The Process Is the Punishment: Handling Cases in a Lower Criminal Court*. New York: Russell Sage Foundation.

Fleming, MacKlin. 1974. *The Price of Perfect Justice: The Adverse Consequences of Current Legal Doctrine on the American Courtroom*. New York: Basic Books.

Frankel, Marvin. 1973. *Criminal Sentences: Law Without Order*. New York: Hill & Wang.

Frase, Richard S. 2005. "Sentencing Guidelines in Minnesota, 1978–2003." In *Crime and Justice: A Review of Research*, vol. 32, edited by Michael Tonry. Chicago: University of Chicago Press.

———. 2013. *Just Sentencing: Principles and Procedures for a Workable System*. New York: Oxford University Press.

———. 2019. "Forty Years of American Sentencing Guidelines: What Have We Learned?" In *American Sentencing*, edited by Michael Tonry. Vol. 48 of *Crime and Justice: A Review of Research*, edited by Michael Tonry. Chicago: University of Chicago Press.

Gottfredson, Don M., Leslie T. Wilkins, and Peter B. Hoffman. 1978. *Guidelines for Parole and Sentencing*. Lanham, MD: Lexington.

Griset, Pamela. 1991. *Determinate Sentencing: The Promise and the Reality of Retributive Justice*. Albany: State University of New York Press.

Hay, Douglas. 1975. "Property, Authority, and the Criminal Law." In *Albion's Fatal Tree: Crime and Society in Eighteenth Century England*, edited by Douglas Hay, Peter Linebaugh, E. P. Thompson, and Cal Winslow. New York: Pantheon.

Hofer, Paul J. 2019. "Federal Sentencing after *Booker*." In *American Sentencing*, edited by Michael Tonry. Vol. 48 of *Crime and Justice: A Review of Research*, edited by Michael Tonry. Chicago: University of Chicago Press.

Johnson, Brian D. 2019. "Trials and Tribulations: The Trial Tax and the Process of Punishment." In *American Sentencing*, edited by Michael Tonry. Vol. 48 of *Crime and Justice: A Review of Research*, edited by Michael Tonry. Chicago: University of Chicago Press.

King, Ryan D., and Michael T. Light. 2019. "Have Racial and Ethnic Disparities in Sentencing Declined?" In *American Sentencing*, edited by Michael Tonry. Vol. 48 of *Crime and Justice: A Review of Research*, edited by Michael Tonry. Chicago: University of Chicago Press.

Kramer, John H., and Jeffery T. Ulmer. 2009. *Sentencing Guidelines: Lessons from Pennsylvania*. Boulder, CO: Rienner.

Kress, Jack M. 1980. *Prescription for Justice: The Theory and Practice of Sentencing Guidelines*. Cambridge, MA: Ballinger.

Lynch, Gerard E. 2003. "Screening versus Plea Bargaining: Exactly What Are We Trading Off?" *Stanford Law Review* 55:1399–1408.

MacKenzie, Doris Layton. 2006. *What Works in Corrections: Reducing the Criminal Activities of Offenders and Delinquents*. Cambridge: Cambridge University Press.

Martin, Susan. 1984. "Interests and Politics in Sentencing Reform: The Development of Sentencing Guidelines in Pennsylvania and Minnesota." *Villanova Law Review* 29:21–113.

Messenger, Sheldon L., and Phillip E. Johnson. 1978. "California's Determinate Sentencing Statute: History and Issues." In *Determinate Sentencing: Reform or Regression*, edited by the National Institute of Justice. Washington, DC: US Government Printing Office.

Michael, Jerome, and Herbert Wechsler. 1940. *Criminal Law and Its Administration*. Chicago: Foundation.

Miller, Marc L. 2004. "Sentencing 'Reform' through Sentencing Information Systems." In *The Future of Imprisonment*, edited by Michael Tonry. New York: Oxford University Press.

Mitchell, Ojmarrh. 2005. "A Meta-Analysis of Race and Sentencing Research: Explaining the Inconsistencies." *Journal of Quantitative Criminology* 21(4):439–66.

Monahan, John. 1981. *The Clinical Prediction of Violent Behavior*. Washington, DC: National Institute of Mental Health.

———. 2017. "Risk Assessment in Sentencing." In *Reforming Criminal Justice: Punishment, Incarceration, and Release*, edited by Erik Luna, Barry C. Feld, and Michael Tonry. Phoenix: Arizona State University Press (for Academy for Justice).

Monahan, John, and Jennifer L. Skeem. 2016. "Risk Assessment in Criminal Sentencing." *Annual Review of Clinical Psychology* 12:489–513.

Morris, Norval. 1974. *The Future of Imprisonment*. Chicago: University of Chicago Press.

Morris, Norval, and Michael Tonry. 1990. *Between Prison and Probation: Intermediate Punishments in a Rational Sentencing System*. New York: Oxford University Press.

Myrdal, Gunnar. 1944. *An American Dilemma: The Negro Problem and Modern Democracy*. New York: Harper & Bros.

Nagin, Daniel S., Francis Cullen, and Cheryl Lero Jonson. 2009. "Imprisonment and Reoffending." In *Crime and Justice: A Review of Research*, vol. 38, edited by Michael Tonry. Chicago: University of Chicago Press.

National Advisory Commission on Criminal Justice Standards and Goals. 1973. *A National Strategy to Reduce Crime*. Washington, DC: US Government Printing Office.

National Commission on Reform of Federal Criminal Laws. 1971. *Report: Proposed Federal Code*. Washington, DC: US Government Printing Office.

Newman, Donald. 1966. *Conviction*. Boston: Little, Brown.

Ogletree, Charles J., Jr., and Austin Sarat, eds. 2012. *Life Without Parole: America's New Death Penalty?* New York: New York University Press.

Parent, Dale G. 1988. *Structuring Criminal Sentences: The Evolution of Minnesota's Sentencing Guidelines*. New York: LEXIS.

Parnas, Raymond I., and Michael B. Salerno. 1978. "The Influence Behind, Substance, and Impact of the New Determinate Sentencing Law in California." *University of California at Davis Law Review* 11:29–41.

Petersilia, Joan. 1999. "Parole and Prisoner Reentry in the United States." In *Prisons*, edited by Michael Tonry and Joan Petersilia. Vol. 26 of *Crime and Jus-*

tice: A Review of Research*, edited by Michael Tonry. Chicago: University of Chicago Press.

Petersilia, Joan, and Richard Rosenfeld, eds. 2008. *Parole, Desistance from Crime, and Community Integration*. Washington, DC: National Academies Press.

President's Commission on Law Enforcement and Administration of Justice. 1967. *The Challenge of Crime in a Free Society*. Washington, DC: US Government Printing Office.

Reitz, Kevin R., and Cecelia M. Klingele. 2019. "Model Penal Code: Sentencing—Workable Limits on Mass Punishment." In *American Sentencing*, edited by Michael Tonry. Vol. 48 of *Crime and Justice: A Review of Research*, edited by Michael Tonry. Chicago: University of Chicago Press.

Remington, Frank. 1969. "Introduction." In *Sentencing*, edited by Robert Dawson. Boston: Little, Brown.

Rhine, Edward E., Joan Petersilia, and Kevin R. Reitz. 2017. "The Future of Parole Release." In *Reinventing American Criminal Justice*, edited by Michael Tonry and Daniel S. Nagin. Vol. 46 of *Crime and Justice: A Review of Research*, edited by Michael Tonry. Chicago: University of Chicago Press.

Rich, William D., L. Paul Sutton, Todd D. Clear, and Michael J. Saks. 1982. *Sentencing by Mathematics: An Evaluation of the Early Attempts to Develop Sentencing Guidelines*. Williamsburg, VA: National Center for State Courts.

Rothman, David. 1971. *The Discovery of the Asylum: Social Order and Disorder in the New Republic*. Boston: Little, Brown.

———. 1980. *Conscience and Convenience: The Asylum and Its Alternatives in Progressive America*. Boston: Little, Brown.

Sabol, William J., Katherine Rosich, Kamala Mallik Kane, David Kirk, and Glenn Dubin. 2002. *Influences of Truth-in-Sentencing Reforms on Changes in States' Sentencing Practices and Prison Populations*. Washington, DC: Urban Institute.

Sellin, Thorsten. 1935. "Race Prejudice in the Administration of Justice." *American Journal of Sociology* 41:212–17.

Shane-DuBow, Sandra, Alice P. Brown, and Erik Olsen. 1985. *Sentencing Reform in the United States: History, Content, and Effect*. Washington, DC: US Government Printing Office.

Spohn, Cassia. 2015. "Race, Crime, and Punishment in the Twentieth and Twenty-First Centuries." In *Crime and Justice: A Review of Research*, vol. 44, edited by Michael Tonry. Chicago: University of Chicago Press.

Starr, Sonja. 2014. "Evidence-Based Sentencing and the Scientific Rationalization of Discrimination." *Stanford Law Review* 66:803–72.

Steffensmeier, Darrell, Jeffery Ulmer, and John Kramer. 1998. "The Interaction of Race, Gender, and Age in Criminal Sentencing: The Punishment Cost of Being Young, Black, and Male." *Criminology* 36:763–98.

Stith, Kate, and José Cabranes. 1998. *Fear of Judging: Sentencing Guidelines in the Federal Courts*. Chicago: University of Chicago Press.

Stuntz, William J. 2011. *The Collapse of American Criminal Justice*. Cambridge, MA: Harvard University Press.

Tonry, Michael. 1995. *Malign Neglect: Race, Crime, and Punishment in America*. New York: Oxford University Press.

———. 1996. *Sentencing Matters*. New York: Oxford University Press.
———. 2009. "The Mostly Unintended Effects of Mandatory Penalties: Two Centuries of Consistent Findings." In *Crime and Justice: A Review of Research*, vol. 38, edited by Michael Tonry. Chicago: University of Chicago Press.
———. 2011. *Punishing Race: An American Dilemma Continues*. New York: Oxford University Press.
———. 2012. "Prosecutors and Politics in Comparative Perspective." In *Prosecutors and Politics in Comparative Perspective*, edited by Michael Tonry. Vol. 41 of *Crime and Justice: A Review of Research*. Chicago: University of Chicago Press.
———. 2016. *Sentencing Fragments*. New York: Oxford University Press.
———. 2018*a*. "Community Punishments." In *Reforming Criminal Justice: Punishment, Incarceration, and Release*, edited by Erik Luna, Barry C. Feld, and Michael Tonry. Phoenix: Arizona State University Press (for Academy for Justice).
———. 2018*b*. "An Honest Politician's Guide to Deterrence: Certainty, Severity, Celerity, and Parsimony." In *Deterrence, Choice, and Crime: Contemporary Perspectives*, edited by Daniel S. Nagin, Cheryl Lero Jonson, and Francis T. Cullen. New York: Routledge.
———. 2019. "Predictions of Dangerousness in Sentencing: Déjà Vu All Over Again." In *American Sentencing*, edited by Michael Tonry. Vol. 48 of *Crime and Justice: A Review of Research*, edited by Michael Tonry. Chicago: University of Chicago Press.
Travis, Jeremy, Bruce Western, and Steve Redburn, eds. 2014. *The Growth of Incarceration in the United States: Exploring Causes and Consequences*. Washington, DC: National Academies Press.
Ulmer, Jeffery T. 2019. "Criminal Courts as Inhabited Institutions: Making Sense of Difference and Similarity in Sentencing." In *American Sentencing*, edited by Michael Tonry. Vol. 48 of *Crime and Justice: A Review of Research*, edited by Michael Tonry. Chicago: University of Chicago Press.
van den Haag, Ernst. 1975. *Punishing Criminals: Concerning a Very Old and Painful Question*. New York: Basic Books.
von Hirsch, Andrew. 1976. *Doing Justice*. New York: Hill & Wang.
von Hirsch, Andrew, Kay A. Knapp, and Michael Tonry. 1987. *The Sentencing Commission and Its Guidelines*. Boston: Northeastern University Press.
Weisberg, Robert. 2019. "The Wild West of Sentencing Reform: Lessons from California." In *American Sentencing*, edited by Michael Tonry. Vol. 48 of *Crime and Justice: A Review of Research*, edited by Michael Tonry. Chicago: University of Chicago Press.
Wilson, James Q. 1975. *Thinking about Crime*. New York: Basic Books.
Wright, Ronald. 2002. "Counting the Cost of Sentencing in North Carolina, 1980–2000." In *Crime and Justice: A Review of Research*, vol. 29, edited by Michael Tonry. Chicago: University of Chicago Press.
Yang, Min, Stephen C. Wong, and Jeremy Coid. 2010. "The Efficacy of Violence Prediction: A Meta-Analytic Comparison of Nine Risk Assessment Tools." *Psychology Bulletin* 136:740–67.

Zeisel, Hans, and Shari Seldman Diamond. 1975. "Sentencing Councils: A Study of Sentence Disparity and Its Reduction." *University of Chicago Law Review* 43:109–49.

———. 1977. "Search for Sentencing Equity: Sentence Review in Massachusetts and Connecticut." *American Bar Foundation Research Journal* 2(4):881,883–940.

Robert Weisberg

The Wild West of Sentencing Reform: Lessons from California

ABSTRACT

As the United States became notorious for mass incarceration, California received outsized attention. Not so much for the sheer volume of California imprisonment but because of its chaotic operation. Populist political mood swings led to Eighth Amendment violations that caused a federal court to declare the whole system unconstitutional, a decision ultimately upheld by the US Supreme Court in *Brown v. Plata*, 563 U.S. 493 (2011). The state responded with innovations commonly referred to as realignment, which include a dramatic devolution of incarcerative power from state to county, among other major changes. Disaster has been avoided, thanks to clever low-level and low-visibility workings of legal and political mechanisms to control populist democracy. But the DNA of California's mode of governing cautions that nothing remains stable without foundational reform.

What makes the recent history of sentencing in California a worthy source of lessons of wider significance? A few basic reasons stand out. First, for three decades after the late 1970s, as the national incarceration rate became an international anomaly and embarrassment, California experienced a quintupling of its incarceration rate from 1978 to 2007, matching or slightly exceeding the national increase. The excess of its prison population over its rated capacity was so great as to warrant federal court intervention. Second, in the last decade, as the overall American prison population stabilized and

Electronically published February 8, 2019
  Robert Weisberg is the Edwin E. Huddleson Jr. Professor of Law at Stanford Law School and faculty codirector, Stanford Criminal Justice Center.

© 2019 by The University of Chicago. All rights reserved.
0192-3234/2019/0048-0006$10.00

somewhat decreased, California's more than 20 percent reduction in its prison plus jail population has been sharper than the overall national reduction. Given California's inmate population in absolute numbers, its decrease is a significant share of the national total. Thus, California has reflected and even epitomized national trends. But third, and most important, the means by which these California numbers changed involves a complex interaction of vectors implicating all branches and levels of government and all the criminal justice agencies that have any power, explicit or implicit, to influence the size and nature of the incarceration population. In a state notorious for wild swings between harshness and leniency, California has served as a legal and political laboratory in which we can observe the relative powers and the catalytic reactions among these authorities.

The history is recounted in detail later in this essay, but here is the gist. For most of the twentieth century, California had a robust form of indeterminate sentencing, with great discretion in judges and considerable power lodged in highly professionalized parole officials (Petersilia 2008; Barker 2009). In 1976 it reversed things with the Uniform Determinate Sentencing Law, which structured trial judges' sentencing discretion and abolished parole release for most felons. Further, through both legislation and the state's famously active popular initiative process, the penal code gained an array of sentencing enhancements for many felonies (the famous three-strikes law is but one example). As California's incarceration rate rose, especially for state prisons, moral and political denunciations of mass incarceration that were heard all over the nation became especially loud here.

But key to the changes in California were legal efforts to use federal Section 1983 civil rights class action lawsuits claiming that inadequate mental health treatment (*Coleman v. Wilson*) and inadequate overall medical care for state prisoners (*Plata v. Davis*)[1] constituted cruel and unusual punishment in violation of the Eighth Amendment of the US Constitution. Ultimately the illegal conditions in both cases were traced to overcrowding, and the lawsuits were consolidated into a direct attack on overcrowding per se. The mega *Plata* case proceeded under the authority and constraints of the Prison Reform Litigation Act of 1995, a law designed to limit the power of the federal courts to order prison population reductions.

---

[1] Because of the numerous pleadings and published and unpublished orders in these two cases, unless otherwise indicated the best source for them is the comprehensive listing in the Civil Rights Litigation Clearinghouse of the University of Michigan Law School under the plaintiffs' names (https://www.clearinghouse.net/).

Plata proceeded, and its injunction was upheld by the Supreme Court in *Brown v. Plata*, 563 U.S. 493 (2011). The three-judge district court ultimately ordered a huge population reduction, and the case entered a back-and-forth phase in which the state argued for different numbers and more time (Schlanger 2013). But in 2011, a new governor realized that California had to take drastic action, and the legislature acquiesced in the 2011 "realignment law," perhaps the most dramatic state-to-county devolution of responsibility for prisoners in American history. The law did not call for release of any current prison inmates, but it mandated that going forward large numbers of offenders convicted of a variety of less serious felonies would be incarcerated in county jails, rather than in state prisons. In addition, large numbers of felons who earlier would have been placed on state parole after release, and then returned to prison for violating a parole condition, would be supervised by county probation officers and would be incarcerated in jail for violations, and for shortened terms (Petersilia 2014*a*).

Unsurprisingly, the state prison population and crowding experienced quick and large reductions,[2] winning some credit from the three-judge federal district court handling *Plata*, but not quite enough to terminate the injunction. And while in theory realignment might simply have shifted population and crowding burdens to county jails, certain provisions of the law and practices of local officials stabilized the jail populations enough that the state's overall incarceration rate dropped (Lofstrom and Raphael 2013*a*).

The immediate motivation of realignment may have been to obey federal law, but it was also a response to powerful anti-incarceration campaigns. Those campaigns, if anything, stepped up their efforts through the ballot box. In 2012, Proposition 36 mitigated the harshness of the three-strikes law.[3] In 2014, Proposition 47 reduced large numbers of low-level felonies to misdemeanors. And in 2016, Proposition 57 created new parole opportunities for large numbers of long-term felons.

The bottom line is that California is in a nervous state of equilibrium. It has impressively reduced prison crowding and the chaos in its parole

---

[2] In the first year, new admissions to the prisons dropped 65 percent and readmissions of parolees revoked for technical violations dropped 87 percent. The first year also saw a 10 percent drop in prison population, which was about half that year's total national reduction (which as an average dropped about 1.7 percent; Petersilia 2014*a*).

[3] For all the California propositions discussed in this essay, details can be found at https://ballotpedia.org/California.

system. Its crime rate is respectable by national standards (Lofstrom and Raphael 2013*b*). The medical and psychiatric treatment of its state prisoners has notably improved, and it has committed significant amounts of new funding to local jurisdictions to enhance rehabilitation and reentry (Petersilia 2014*b*).

These events show that when a criminal justice system gets roiled by strong and opposing vectors without a well-designed way to mediate them, the "physics" of government may somehow produce a decent equilibrium—but often at great cost (Petersilia 2008). The cost is literal because remedying the Eighth Amendment violations has meant a large rise in the prison budget even as the prison population has declined. Further, while much of the devolution via realignment has potential to alleviate recidivism and achieve cost internalization, it has also created large agency costs by lodging remarkable new power in county officials to set the correctional rules. For example, county sheriffs now serve as de facto prison wardens, and both sheriffs and county probation officers now serve as de facto parole officials (Bird et al. 2016). Their new power and their broad discretion to allocate state-reimbursed funds by their own criteria have led to widely disparate and unpredictable correctional policies around the state. Sky-is-falling warnings that the reforms would cause a big rise in crime were clearly wrong (Lofstrom and Raphael 2013*c*), but there are signs of small spikes here and there, leading to complaints that too many unsupervised dangerous people are on the streets.

Now, declaring a change in a criminal justice (or sentencing and correctional) system to be a teachable moment may imply any number of assumptions or predicates to justify the exercise. Perhaps we first need to choose among contestable criteria that define a system as good or bad (by virtue of crime control, treatment of prisoners, cost efficiency, etc.). Then, the first step for a specific lesson may be that the system is a good or bad one—in an "absolute" sense (i.e., in comparison with other jurisdictions), or, in terms of historical change within the jurisdiction, an improvement or a worsening according to the chosen criteria. But while these steps involve approval or disapproval,[4] assigning credit or blame may wrongly assume that changes were actually chosen. The condition of a criminal justice sys-

---

[4] We can also be normatively indifferent about those changes within a jurisdiction and only concern ourselves with significant degrees of change in any system feature as interesting for their own sake.

tem results from some combination of relatively freely chosen human decisions, unavoidable exogenous forces, stubborn structural forces, and economic, political, and legal constraints. Drawing sharp distinctions among these poses both conceptual and empirical challenges. Whether our criteria for judging a system are deontological or utilitarian, we can assume, or discover, a fair degree of human and institutional agency and thereby generate recommendations for policy makers. Or we can adopt a positive political science posture, or a kind of sociobiology of institutions, taking a diagnostic approach to draw causal inferences while being skeptical or agnostic about human or institutional agency.

There is a middle ground in which deep governmental structures either enable or block changes in a system; even if we can identify policy choices that led to these structures, they may lie far too deep for the type of change we think of as "policy reform." The result would be to treat these as essentially exogenous, and, even if they produce a bad system, the lesson may have the tone of either neutral diagnosis or tragic wisdom. A source for this idea comes from Barker (2009), who traced the paths of sentencing and correctional reform in California, Washington, and New York. All can plausibly be described as "progressive states." None has had the egregiously high imprisonment rates of many southern states that continue to reflect the legacy of slavery. But these states sharply differ in their traditional modes of governing, or what might be called "political culture." Washington is a populist state in a certain sense, a highly participatory democracy in which individuals and small groups engage in the institutions of governing at every level. The result is a highly deliberative popular democracy that enables rational discussion of policy choices. By contrast, in California's popular democracy most people avoid the hard work of institutional governance and are not closely allied to parties. Rather, they participate with visceral expressions of passion and let officials work out the details. New York is "less democratic" (in any populist sense) than both the others. Its officials act as policy managers and rely heavily on managerial expertise, although with an implicit delegation from voters. By contrast, California voters favor their raw instincts and condemn experts as elitists or virtual dictators. Barker's cautious conclusion is that Washington and New York have done far better in the era of mass incarceration.

Blending or alternating among these possible approaches, in this essay I offer analytic observations, tentative causal inferences, cautionary tales, and occasional critiques. I assay some modest normative criteria for a good sentencing and corrections system. I judge California, in its current state, as mediocre to fair by these criteria. I show how this current condition reflects a remarkable set of responses to a threatened crisis that just barely saved California from having a catastrophic and scandalous system. I diagnose the effects of California's popular democracy, and in some cases I credit numerous actors who finessed, avoided, or manipulated its siren songs. But, echoing Barker, I worry that Californian democracy poses serious obstacles to any durable reform. The mood swings of recent decades are so deep in the neural networks of public life in California that it may take a revolution in the form of government to create a punishment system that is fair, efficient, and stable.

Section I of this essay narrates the history of California sentencing law from the state's early deep investment and century-long practice of indeterminate sentencing to its dramatic reversal toward a determinate model in the 1970s. Section II recounts how the confluence of new determinate sentencing laws and California's volatile populist crime politics led to a dysfunctional system that a federal court declared unconstitutional. This confluence marked California as a state in penal crisis and subjected the whole apparatus of state government to the equity powers of a federal court. Section III analyzes how California responded with its realignment law and other measures. It describes the aftermath of these laws as a complex decentralized sentencing system that promises pragmatic flexibility but shows signs of institutional instability traceable to the conflictual means by which the changes came about. Section IV briefly assays the range of criteria by which we can evaluate the quality or success of a sentencing and corrections system or the nature and degree of change. I argue that California should blame itself for allowing the crisis to develop, but I acknowledge that its officials deserve modest credit for political creativity in finding a way out, although at high costs financially and in institutional fragility. Section V draws lessons, most diagnostic, on how the nature of public life in California destined its sentencing and correction systems to fall into disarray. Working around and outside arenas of popular democracy, clever officials and others used old-fashioned and flexible tools to avoid catastrophe. The nature of things in California warns that fundamental changes in governing are needed.

I. The Rise and Fall of Indeterminacy

Now to retell the story in some detail. It recapitulates and epitomizes the American shift from indeterminacy to determinacy.

A. The Early Legacy of Indeterminacy

The complex and often self-contradictory nature of California's sentencing law and practice has a deep provenance. At the start of its history as a state, California, generally adopting the common law of England for its definition of crimes, cobbled together a penal code without declaration of a philosophy of punishment and legislated very severe sentences (Dansky 2008). Although, in theory, trial judges were left with some discretion, these sentences would have been described as "determinate" in modern parlance, because the law provided no mechanism for release based on evidence of rehabilitation. In an eerily prescient pattern, the places of incarceration (originally the county jails and then the first state prison at San Quentin) quickly became overcrowded. For that reason, but because of the perceived excessive lengths of sentences, officials sought means of mitigation. The law did not provide for parole release. Governors could and did use their pardon power but were constitutionally unable to create a quasi-parole system through commutation of sentences. Reformers pushed for a more flexible system accommodating rehabilitation, but the tough-on-crime wrath of voters deterred major changes for decades.

Things changed around the turn of the twentieth century, beginning with the formal introduction of parole in 1893 (applicable to murderers in 1901) and probation in 1903 (Dansky 2008). This was still, in effect, a determinate system, although with an administrative pressure-release valve through fairly generous use of parole.[5] After looking at expressly indeterminate sentencing systems in other states, the legislature in 1917 enacted the Indeterminate Sentencing Act. Judges were to hand down indeterminate terms, with the formerly rigid sentencing laws providing statutory minimums and maximums. Broad discretion was granted to the Board of Prison Directors to choose release dates.[6] Rehabilitation and reform were not mentioned in the legislative history, so it is unclear whether those principles or financial and overcrowding concerns better explain the change. For two decades after World War II, the state remained strongly committed to the

---

[5] On this specific point and in general in this essay, I do not address treatment of juvenile offenders, who until 1941 were generally held in either jails or prisons or reform schools. But a fair generalization is that however convoluted California's approach to adult imprisonment, it has been very successful in reducing unwarranted and criminogenic incarceration of youths (Hayes and Tafoya 2014).

[6] The legislature also augmented the probation system with a 50 percent state subsidy to counties.

indeterminacy model, with a heavy government investment in rehabilitation efforts (Petersilia 2008; Barker 2009).

B. The Pivot to Determinacy

Everything that has happened in recent decades is a response to the 1976 Uniform Determinate Sentencing Law (DSL) that replaced indeterminate sentencing and was signed by the then-young governor Jerry Brown.[7] The turn against indeterminacy probably reflects the motives that led to the national move toward determinacy in the 1970s and to the creation of the United States Sentencing Guidelines and similar bodies in other states. The guiding view was that a more formulaic scheme would be fairer, less discriminatory, and less capricious, although some proponents of the DSL also thought it would lead to shorter sentences (Tonry 2015).

The DSL was in effect a whole new penal code, generally built around sentencing triads within which the judge could choose, for example, 4, 5, or 6 years for a particular crime;[8] in extreme cases the judge could go above the top of the triad (Ricciardulli 2006). By itself the DSL was fairly straightforward and typical for its time as a response to the perceived ills of the indeterminate regime. However, there emerged another dimension of the new determinacy, the result of aggressive politicking about crime by legislators and, even more important, the power of direct voters' democracy, which soon distorted the DSL. This was the proliferation of sentencing "enhancements," mostly enacted from 1975 to 1995, a period of great public anxiety about crime (Lewis, Pfingst, and Thomas 2002; Begovich et al. 2014). As always in California, the initiative process joined regular legislation as a mechanism of passionate social reaction, although often it worked in partnership with the legislature.

The term "enhancement" first appeared in the penal code in 1977 with a firearm sentence enhancement (Lizotte and Zatz 1986). Other enhancements proliferated and now range from possession of a gun during a

---

[7] It is somewhat more precise to use the vocabulary suggested by Chanenson (2005); he distinguished controls on the initial sentence (structured/unstructured sentencing) from controls on the ultimate time served (determinate/indeterminate). In those terms, the DSL was structured and determinate.

[8] There is a presumption that the middle term should be imposed, but a judge's choice of the lower or upper is essentially unreviewable. Traditional indeterminate sentencing continued for the most egregious crimes, especially noncapital murder (Ricciardulli 2006).

crime[9] to interfering with a police horse (Sigal 2007). In 1988, the legislature enacted the Street Terrorism Enforcement and Prevention (STEP) Act to "eradicate" criminal gang activity (Yoshino 2008). It originally added gang enhancements of 1, 2, or 3 years; in 1994, the legislature amended the statute to set a 16-month minimum. California gang law now includes a mélange of overlapping, almost double-jeopardy-threatening statutes that outdo federal Racketeer Influenced and Corrupt Organizations (RICO) law in the art of prosecuting guilt by association. In 1997, the legislature enacted the "10-20-Life" gun enhancement, which adds 10-year enhancements for use of a gun during a felony, 20 years for firing a gun, or 25 years to life for killing or seriously injuring another person with a gun. In 2000 came Proposition 21, which increased prison terms for gang-related crime and provided that serious or violent crimes receive mandatory 5- and 10-year enhancements (Bigelow, Couzens, and Prickett 2013).

California law currently provides for at least 153 enhancements, spread across the Penal Code, Health and Safety Code, Insurance Code, and Vehicle Code. While some enhancements are tied to specific base crimes, the numerous general enhancements apply to broad categories of offenses, such as all violent crimes or all felonies, using such criteria as the defendant's criminal record or motivation or mechanical measures of the weight of drugs.[10]

Some of the tougher sentencing laws of this era are not enhancements in the determinate sense but augmentations to habitual offender laws that expose more offenders to life sentences. In 1982 came Proposition 8, the "Victims' Bill of Rights," which helped make a meme by its title. It is a collection of both tough-on-crime and victim-focused procedural rules. It was the first initiative to augment sentences for offenders with prior convictions that were prison-sentenced crimes (Barker 2009; Begovich et al. 2014).

Then in 1994 came Proposition 184, the "three-strikes" initiative, overhauling California's recidivist enhancements. It required that offenders receive 25-to-life sentences after their third "strike," which originally

---

[9] Ironically, some of the impetus for severe gun enhancements came from progun groups deflecting gun control campaigns by arguing that the only sensible gun control laws were those aimed at "bad guys with guns."

[10] The drug enhancements to some extent reflect the nationwide pattern of mandatory minimum drug laws associated with the war on drugs. Overall, the California enhancements were enacted for two decades after the wave of "Rockefeller" drug laws in the early 1970s.

included even nonserious, nonviolent felonies and crimes that could "wobble" between misdemeanor and felony status.[11] More recently, there have been new laws deploying the popular title meme "Victims' Bill of Rights" or the names of young female victims, such as the 2008 Marsy's Law (California Victims' Bill of Rights Act of 2008). That initiative expanded victims' procedural rights and penalized a rejected request for parole release by a lifer with a multiyear delay in his right to try again.

II. The Road to Crisis

The enactment of the DSL was a dramatic change, but it was fairly typical of a national shift in that direction. The vigorous program to enact sentencing enhancements, however, signaled California's extreme (though not unique) investment in populist tough-on-crime politics. It would be a daunting statistical project to determine how much the enhancements (or particular pairings of base sentences and enhancements) contributed to increased imprisonment, whether because of the enhanced sentences or because they were used to coerce guilty pleas to nonenhanced sentences. But they surely made some contribution and may reflect tougher prosecutorial and judicial actions that led to the *Plata* case.

A. Crime and the Political "Culture" of the Golden State

Ultimately, the decisive legal fact of the modern California story was prison overcrowding. That is surprising because California was profligate in its prison building in the late twentieth century. Although its crime rate rose dramatically after the late 1970s, it stayed close to the national average (Petersilia 2008). But the rising crime rate was in the public eye, and it fueled a number of tough-on-crime measures that were enacted through voter initiatives. And however expensive these measures were in requiring more prison beds, prison construction was financed by lease bonds that delayed payment for decades and were outside of annual budgets and the public eye (Anderson 2008). This unusual, if not unique, feature of California government[12] allowed anticrime populism to increase impris-

---

[11] As noted below, in 2012 California voters passed Proposition 36, which revised the law to require the third strike to be a serious or violent felony.

[12] Many states have on their books, and often deploy, a variety of popular referenda mechanisms, but few have used them to increase criminal penalties, and few have used them to reduce penalties or prison populations (Potyondy 2018).

onment more than equivalent tough-on-crime innovations did elsewhere, while its financing was buried in the esoterica of the bond market. We see then that the story of California's prison crisis—and of its current reforms—lies to a great extent in the hydraulics of government operations and diffusions of authority.

Some relevant political history has been well documented (Lynch 2001; Petersilia 2008; Barker 2009; Greenhut 2017). California has been a remarkably volatile—indeed labile—state in terms of its politics of crime. However liberal it sometimes seems to be, it has a long history of populist law-and-order campaigns, especially through the initiative.[13]

Republican governors Ronald Reagan (1967–75), George Deukmejian (1983–91), and Pete Wilson (1991–99) certainly encouraged the spirit behind such measures. Even the young Jerry Brown, governor between Republicans from 1975–83, readily signed on to the determinate sentencing movement of the 1970s. As a good government figure, he represented the liberal side of the paradoxical convergence underlying determinate sentencing—he subscribed to the idea that discretionary sentencing lodged too much freedom in judges and parole boards and led to capricious and biased outcomes, at a time when conservatives viewed it as overly lenient. But Brown was also a political pragmatist, sensitive to the huge defeat of his very liberal father Governor Pat Brown by Reagan in 1966. Governor Gray Davis (1999–2003), an otherwise conventional Democrat who wanted to secure his right flank on crime issues and who became in effect a wholly owned subsidiary of the prison guards' union, pushed the state in this direction as well.

B. Manifestation of Crisis

It is arbitrary to pick a point at which a complex crisis materializes or becomes fully manifest, but a decade ago works well for California. In 2007, the Little Hoover Commission (2007), an unusual entity that serves as a venerable official oversight conscience of the state's government but

---

[13] Mona Lynch brilliantly traces these forces to strange new populist phenomena in midcentury California. Middle-class people finding themselves in anomic, soulless suburbs denounced the progressive state welfare reforms that, they believed, both raised their taxes and coddled immoral poor people. The state built more prisons in a rise of retributive fervor. Those same middle-class people found themselves living in gated communities. Poor people found themselves in urban housing projects that were themselves highly regulated "gated communities." And, of course, the prisons were the reductio ad absurdum of the gated community (Lynch 2001).

has limited formal power, sounded the theme of crisis and elaborated its features. Here are the key features (somewhat further elaborated).

As fast as California built prisons, the number of prisoners increased faster, the imprisonment rate rising over 500 percent between 1980 and 2007.

Despite the lobbying of the California Correctional Peace Officers Association (CCPOA)—popularly known as the prison guards' union—the staff to inmate ratio fell, leading to serious security problems.

As was demonstrably true but also, significantly, became better conveyed to the public and the courts, prisoner health, both physical and mental, was in jeopardy, with scandals including horrifying numbers of preventable emphysema deaths and dismal failures to deliver the most basic medicines.

Prison costs doubled as a proportion of the state budget between 1980 and 2006.

Responding to the financing problem was especially difficult in California. California depends more than most states on a state income tax, which in turn is contingent on an often thriving but unpredictable economy (especially via Silicon Valley). Thus, revenue was erratic and hard to project; the exotica of lease financing for prisons and the compartmentalization of certain funds under weird California laws made money less fungible and adaptable; and especially under Governor Davis, the CCPOA was able to lock the state into onerous salary and benefits packages for prison guards (Petersilia 2008). In addition, in the liberal and progressive spirit of the Golden State, California was committed to such megaexpensive projects as a generous health care system and the nation's best public university and college system, and to vast water control projects required by the vagaries of the delta system. Worse yet, in the early 2000s the state created a pension benefit scheme for state employees that it could not afford, creating a huge unfunded mandate. In those senses, the Golden State was beginning to see the bill become due for its California dream of progressive social, educational, and economic programs for an ever-rising population (Barker 2009).

Yet in this heterogeneous state there has always been a dialectical counterforce of antigovernment ideology that manifested itself in the famous or infamous Proposition 13 in 1978, which permanently froze the property tax liability of vast numbers of Californians. Proposition 13 was a right-wing populist measure enacted while the liberal Jerry Brown was governor, and the political sentiments that motivated it aligned with those that motivated many of the tough-on-crime and prison-building measures. However right-wing, the antitax ideology behind Proposition 13 in theory could conceivably have led politicians to rethink the costs of a harsh sentencing system. But many in recent decades believed (or said they believed) that tough-on-crime laws were why the crime rate was dropping—even though states such as New York were achieving equal or better crime reductions without such expensive investments in punishment. So Proposition 13 exacerbated the financial stresses the criminal justice changes caused, especially by shifting the costs of education from local governments to the state. Proposition 13 was thus both a factor in and a symptom of the volatility story of California sentencing and corrections (Barker 2009).

Pressures for change also came from within the criminal justice system. California's unusual parole system was broken. California law required great numbers of released midlevel prisoners to serve mandatory parole terms for up to 3 years with violations sending the offender back to state prison (Petersilia 2006). Reabsorption of revoked parolees only slightly increased the imprisonment rate (terms were usually short), but it meant that the prisons experienced the chaotic inflows and outflows common in county jails.[14] This made it even more difficult for prisons to provide decent health care.

Further, because of California's vast size and the diversity of its local jurisdictions, it exhibited an extreme version of a common phenomenon in political economy—negative externalities (Ball 2012). The number of offenders sent to state prison was largely a function of the preferences of county prosecutors and county-based judges (and local police), and these preferences varied widely between counties. But the costs of state imprisonment were borne by the state. The proportion of felons individual counties sent to state prison bore little relation to crime rates; it was mostly a matter of political choice. The discrepancies among big and small counties and rural and urban counties were enormous.

Let us review the basic responses to the crisis: The state had resisted any structural reform of the penal code and governors resisted calls for establishment of a state sentencing commission (Little Hoover Commission 2007; Weisberg 2009). Although many blamed this on the CCPOA, the union probably lost power when Gray Davis was recalled and replaced by a self-funded Arnold Schwarzenegger. The major force against reform was probably the California District Attorneys Association, which

---

[14] It is a linguistic wonder that the entry and sorting area of each prison is called the "reception center."

resisted any penal code reform because the incoherent maze of statutes and enhancements was a great prosecutorial tool for inducing guilty pleas (Teji 2011).

C. The Constitutional Coup

Schlanger (2006) has documented the long history of class action injunction cases involving prisons and jails, many affecting California jails. The litigation campaign launched by public interest lawyers against the state prison system in the 1990s was hardly novel, but it eventually led to novel consequences. For all the "mass imprisonment" rhetoric that suggests that the sheer scale of imprisonment had become the paradigm evil of American criminal justice, the modern California story involves prison conditions. In 1991 a class action was brought under Section 1983 condemning the prison system's mistreatment or nontreatment of mentally ill prisoners. The *Coleman* case (first titled *Coleman v. Wilson* and still ongoing as *Coleman v. Brown*, 912 F. Supp. 1282 [E.D.CA. 1195]) led to a 1995 order. Judge Lawrence Karlton found an Eighth Amendment violation and appointed a special master to help oversee improvements in the system. Then in 2001, some of the *Coleman* lawyers joined others in a parallel suit in the Northern District of California making similar claims about overall health care. In that case (first titled *Plata v. Davis* and then *Plata v. Brown*), the plaintiffs' lawyers cited frightening evidence of disease and death due to gross medical neglect and called for vast expenditures to overhaul the health care system.[15]

As the health care litigation proceeded, the state was a begrudging but sometimes passive-aggressive defendant. In 2002, it almost conceded the inadequacy of the prison health care system and began a regular back-and-forth about the scope of the remedy. The original *Plata* case went a step further when, instead of appointing a special master, Judge Thelton Henderson created a court receivership. The result has been a large de facto state agency that continues to run the medical care system in the prisons. The receiver was effectively empowered to write vast checks on the government's account, whether the state agreed or not. Thus, once the court identified a minimal level of health care needed to avoid cruel and unusual punishment, the Eighth Amendment served as its own deontological force, not subject to cost-benefit analysis (Schlanger 2013).

---

[15] Unless otherwise indicated, the sources for the numerous stages in this original *Plata* case or the later three-judge case can be found at the Civil Rights Litigation Clearinghouse, University of Michigan Law School.

Recognizing that the plaintiffs and judges were homing in on overcrowding as the underlying problem, the state adopted interim measures to stave off constitutional disaster. In 2006, Governor Schwarzenegger declared a state of emergency to trigger his power to ship prisoners out of state (Cal. Proclamation No. 4278, Oct. 4, 2006). In 2009, the legislature enacted the California Community Corrections Performance Incentives Act of 2009, which incentivized counties to reduce the number of revoked probationers sent to prison by sharing the state's savings with the counties and also subsidized evidence-based risk assessment. In the first year, the prison return rate for probationers declined by 23 percent (Pew Center 2012).

Also in 2009, the legislature addressed the problem of revolving-door parole revocations by enacting a law placing large numbers of paroled felons on a regime of "nonrevocable parole." This meant that a large share of the felons on 1- to 3-year terms were not supervised; the sole legal consequence was that these parolees were subject to suspicionless police searches. But these measures did little to quell the prison controversy. The emergency order of 2006 may even have energized the litigants to take their boldest step: invoking the Prison Litigation Reform Act (PLRA) process by alleging that the unconstitutional conditions in both predicate cases were traceable to crowding (Schlanger 2013).

The PLRA was enacted to discourage federal district court judges from imposing population caps (Schlanger 2013). No longer could a single judge do so. Only a specially appointed three-judge court had that authority, and any population reduction order could be directly appealed to the US Supreme Court. The PLRA also gave generous statutory rights of intervention to all manner of stakeholders (even legislators). It placed high burdens on plaintiffs to prove that crowding was the true cause of unconstitutional conditions, required that remedies be narrowly tailored (among other things, to respect public safety concerns), and established a presumption that any order be terminated within 2 years. By law, the petition to assemble the three-judge court went to the chief judge of the Ninth Circuit, Mary Schroeder, who granted it, and she appointed both district court judges Karlton and Henderson and added the extremely liberal circuit court judge Stephen Reinhardt.

The three-judge court saw some hope for settlement. In 2007, in an intriguing reach across the federal-state line, it appointed two settlement referees—one a former state court of appeal justice and the other a current one who had earlier been a deputy attorney general who litigated prison cases for the state (Schlanger 2013). The referees met with a range of the intervenor-stakeholders, but settlement talks broke down. So the case went to trial, leading to an order that the system get the overall prison population down to 137.5 percent of rated capacity in 2 years, by 2013, with interim 6-month benchmark targeted percentages. Given the number of inmates at that time, this meant that the number would have to decline to about 100,000, a number last seen in 1993. Notably, at least initially the three-judge court did not dictate how the state should get to that number. In the course of the numerous follow-up orders it nodded in approval concerning such possibilities as increasing the rate at which prisoners accrue good-time credits.

The US Supreme Court, in a bitterly divided decision, upheld the reduction order (*Brown v. Plata*, 563 U.S. 493 [2011]). The case continues in the three-judge court, with the court alternately granting and refusing extensions of time to a begrudging state, while sounding increasingly more exasperated in focusing on reforms it wants to see.[16] The three-judge order in *Plata* is one of the most dramatic court-ordered inmate population cap cases in history, and the first that has gotten past the objections of defendants under the PLRA (Schlanger 2013).

III. Responses to the Crisis

In 2011, newly elected Governor Brown inherited *Plata*. Like his predecessor, he fought the court fairly vigorously, but within a week of taking office he set out to create the great legislative solution to the case—the 2011 realignment law (officially entitled "the 2011 Realignment Legislation Addressing Public Safety").[17] The complex political and legislative compromise that led to its quick passage probably resulted from the more formal negotiations within the *Plata* case.

A. The Design of Realignment

The realignment law was an exercise in "state-local federalism." In promoting it, Brown emphasized to the public that it did not mean the release of current prison inmates. Rather, going forward, large numbers of offenders convicted of certain felonies that were designated as less egre-

---

[16] The Supreme Court decision and these later developments are discussed below.

[17] This is the original realignment statute (2011 Cal. Stat. Ch. 15, § 1 at 7). It has frequently been amended, especially to deal with financing.

gious,[18] and whose sentences would normally require commitment to state prison, would be sent to county jails, regardless of the length of their sentences. Equally importantly, most offenders who were eligible for parole (mostly nonlifers) would fall under a new regime called Post Release Community Supervision (PRCS). County probation officers would supervise them. If deemed in violation they would be sent to county jails, not state prisons, and for much shorter penalty terms than under the old parole regime (Schlanger 2013). The state would transfer a large share of the state prison budget to the counties as reimbursement and sweeten the pot by leaving allocation of the funds among local law enforcement and other agencies almost entirely to the discretion of county governments.

A secondary goal of realignment, or hoped for by-product, was that prisoner reentry would happen more effectively if the last place of incarceration was the jail, usually closer to the inmate's home and family (Petersilia 2014b). Thus, counties were free to deploy the reimbursement funds generously toward reentry programs. It is probably true that inmates just leaving county jails have more access to services from local agencies and nonprofits. Policy makers acting on such a belief, however, risk being mesmerized by the elusive phrase "in the community," when the definition and the very existence of this phenomenon called "the community" are in doubt (Weisberg 2003; Cullen and Petersilia 2015).

B. *The Initiative Process Goes Soft on Crime*

Then came popular initiatives fueled by nonprofits and advocacy groups and passed by large voter majorities. In 2012, Proposition 36, which changed the three-strikes law, passed by 64 to 35 percent—impressive but not quite as large as the vote supporting the original law. This initiative drastically reduced the scope of crimes that count as third strikes[19] and allowed for retroactivity by providing postconviction review for resentencing. It thus reduced the number of current and future life prison-

---

[18] The long list of felonies that qualify for jail in incarceration—known as "triple-nons" (nonserious, nonviolent, nonsexual)—defies any intuitive understanding as to how some of them differ from felonies that can still send offenders to prison.

[19] Here, too, distinctions are not intuitive. A felony inflicting great bodily injury can still be a third strike, but not if the "GBI" is caused indirectly; assault with a deadly weapon can still be a third strike, but not an assault done by means likely to cause great bodily injury (Bigelow and Couzens 2017).

ers in the prisons.[20] In 2014, Proposition 47, a major penal code reform, passed by a 60–40 vote and reduced the level of many crimes, especially drug and theft crimes, from felonies to misdemeanors, at least when the defendant did not have significant prior convictions (Camacho 2016). A good example is that shoplifting of expensive items that formerly could have been punished as grand theft or commercial burglary was reduced to petty theft.

In 2016, Proposition 57, virtually written by Governor Brown, was approved by voters. It extended the possibility of discretionary parole release from only life prisoners to include large numbers of prisoners sentenced under recidivist and other enhancement laws. Proposition 57 is complex (and includes changes in juvenile corrections), but the gist is that thousands of "nonviolent"[21] felons became eligible for parole consideration when their base term expired, regardless of any term extension based on an enhancement. Prisoners can also shorten their terms through more generous credits for rehabilitation, good behavior, and education under regulations the Department of Corrections and Rehabilitation was ordered to develop (CDCR 2018c). Proposition 57 was Brown's "workaround" to control the effects of California's enhancements. It is too soon to know how it will operate, but it was an act of political savvy for Brown to exploit the power of the ballot instead of asking the legislature to do this and then to have a state agency generate early release rules so labyrinthine as to defy legislative override.

Notice that two of these changes were politically initiated populist measures. One was enacted by the legislature as a result of pressure from the governor that amounted almost to an edict. The other, though a ballot proposition, was essentially the work of the governor (and partly financed by his own surplus campaign funds; Ashton 2016). Aside from acquiescing in Brown's pressure to enact realignment, the legislature proved itself as feckless as usual. The sense of crisis, widely reported in the media as a national embarrassment because of the *Plata* litigation, led a majority of voters to support the initiative.

---

[20] A year after enactment, Proposition 36 had led to resentencing and release of about 1,500 inmates, with minimal short-term recidivism (Three Strikes Project 2014).

[21] Yet again, we see a distinction between egregious and less egregious felonies—here the test is whether the felony is defined as violent under Cal. Pen. Code § 667.5. It defies easy explanation in conceptual terms.

C. Short-Term Results

Overall, these recent changes have surely relieved some of the population pressure on the state prisons, although with a lag time as we await parole releases. However, one large element of the prison system, that of lifers, was unaffected by all these legal changes; lifers remain subject to old-fashioned parole with great discretion in the parole board and the governor and will not see any earlier release by virtue of the good-time credit extensions of Proposition 57. Yet the practical difficulty of winning release makes lifer sentences pretty determinate (Mukamal, Segall, and Weisberg 2011). Complicating things further, California's parole system has actually become even more oddly heterogeneous since realignment was implemented. Many felons convicted of serious crimes remain under the rigid prerealignment parole system; most lifers remain under the prior scheme. Further, realignment essentially made the county sheriff a new de facto sentencing authority. In their role as jailers, the sheriffs have to manage a larger, and more dangerous, population of inmates diverted from prison and have accrued implicit power to release inmates to address the second-order crowding problems in the jails (often with GPS bracelets). No statute or regulation sets criteria for this new power of sheriffs, so this is the most indeterminate of all features of California sentencing (Bird et al. 2016).

IV. Report Card

How is California performing? Earlier I suggested that drawing lessons may require asserting or stipulating criteria for approval or disapproval. In terms of sentencing law, we can easily (if not very helpfully) say that the sentencing laws should reconcile the often competing demands of utilitarian and retributive goals, be clear and coherent enough to be comprehensible to the public, and at least mitigate the tendency of American criminal justice to produce arbitrary outcomes and racial disparities. The incarceration system should be safe, humane, and cost efficient, and it should ensure public safety in the short run by incapacitating enough prisoners and in the long run by reducing recidivism. And if indeed the United States merits criticism for "mass incarceration," the system should not be too capacious and offer prospects for some degree of shrinkage.

We can split the difference between success and failure by noting that California has come close to having a constitutionally permissible prison system. The state has managed some interesting changes in the severity and determinacy of sentences, fostered and funded local programs that may be useful models of assisting offender reentry, and done these things without any significant uptick in crime. But we need to dig a bit deeper.

A. What Goes on the Report Card?

The criteria for diagnosing good and bad conditions and decisions are and always will be contested, especially if we try to advance beyond the obvious and vague ones mentioned above. As Johnson (2019) deftly argues, the bizarre variety of American sentencing schemes makes it difficult even to make cross-jurisdictional comparisons. The further step of comparative evaluation seems almost quixotic. Even the common notion that we have moved toward determinacy in recent decades is too simplistic, with many states retaining or moving back to various forms of indeterminacy. Nevertheless, I suggest here a few possible implications of the California story, looking both at current conditions, absolutely or relative to peer states, at where California was before, and how it got to where it now is.

In an earlier article I offered impressionistic speculations about several possible criteria (Weisberg 2009). One is the relative incarceration rate (on the theory that all states have overincarcerated, so the lower the rate the better). A second is the relative rate of recent decarceration (because the direction of change is a proxy for the current system's health). A third is crowding, the ratio of prisoners to prison space (reflecting treatment quality and risk of Eighth Amendment litigation). A fourth is the ratio of imprisonment rates to crime rates, or the ratio of imprisonment rates to new commitments (on the theory that this would show the efficacy of prison as a general deterrent and as an instrument of specific deterrence, incapacitation, or rehabilitation). A fifth is the ratio of new court commitments to parole violations. Also of special salience is how disproportionate the prison population is to the demographics of the jurisdiction, and how that disproportion compares with those of other states.

Another possible measure is the ratio of prison to jail inmates, but this could be meaningful in opposite ways. Lower might be better if we assume that this ratio correlates with sentence lengths (if we think shorter is better), or more plausibly if we believe local incarceration is more likely to aid reentry. But a higher prison/jail ratio might be better if it results from less use of jails for pretrial detention, thus reflecting more enlightened bail policies. We can also look to racial disparities. And we can look to budgets, comparing correctional expenditures to any number of other measures.

The silver lining to Johnson's bad news about our capacity for comparative evaluation is that we cannot do it very systematically, and so we are liberated to proceed roughly and even impressionistically. It is easiest to compare California to the nation, but occasionally direct comparisons to individual states are helpful. Texas is one good point of comparison.

B. *California Gets a B Minus*

California looks somewhere between fair and good on some of the reckonings sketched. The state imprisonment rate (not counting jails), 330 per 100,000 population, is now well below the national average of 450 (Bureau of Justice Statistics 2018*b*). The pattern of incarceration has a couple of anomalies. One is the relatively high percentage of lifers, roughly 20 percent in 2017 (CDCR 2018*a*); perhaps not coincidentally the lifer population is the least affected by recent changes in state law.

Another is the degree and nature of its reliance on jails. In the United States overall there are about half as many jail inmates as prison inmates. The California ratio is slightly higher (Bureau of Justice Statistics 2018*a*). California has an unusually high percentage of pretrial detainees, another group not directly affected by recent legal changes.[22] A high percentage of jail inmates were convicted of felonies and serving sentences longer than a year, often several years, and that is a direct result of realignment (of course, a lot of factors get tangled here). California is again unremarkable, by national standards, concerning racial disparities between the general population and prison inmates (Bureau of Justice Statistics 2018*a*, 2018*b*).

That California's prison rate looks good by national standards could be viewed as misleading, given that realignment shifted so many potential state prisoners to the jails. Total incarceration would be a more meaningful measure. This particular shift happened quickly and in large magnitude because of realignment, but it is always true that the ratio of prison inmates to convicted jail inmates is a function of the overall workings and gradations of that state's penal code. Yet another measure would mitigate this criticism. Although in theory realignment changed only the place, not the length, of felony prison sentences, convicted felons in "county jail prison" generally can get out sooner than they would from prison. So a measure of total years of sentences being served would show California

---

[22] Pretrial Release or Detention: Pretrial Services, 2018 Cal. Stat. Ch. 244 (2018). https://leginfo.legislature.ca.gov/faces/billTextClient.xhtml?bill_id=201720180SB10.

to be respectable. If we subtract the pretrial jail inmates from the incarceration total, the total convicted incarcerated population in California is unremarkable.

In any event, realignment created new pressures for county jails, at a time when some were subject to court-ordered population caps imposed well before the new state crisis (Lawrence 2014). After an extended period of decline, jail populations increased under realignment (Board of State and Community Corrections 2002–16). The monthly average daily jail population had declined by 15 percent from a high of 84,275 inmates in September 2007, before realignment took effect, but increased by 14 percent in the following 3 years. This is way over the rated capacity set by a new state agency, the California Board of State and Community Corrections.

In response, counties released large numbers of inmates (14,000 in 1 month alone). Relief arrived from Proposition 47 in November 2014, and the average daily population dropped by almost 10,000 between October 2014 and January 2015. The jail population has remained relatively flat since. Releases clearly due to crowding have dropped significantly, but roughly half the jails are still rated as overcrowded.[23]

And as for public safety, the numbers suggest that recidivism rates of inmates released from the jails have not declined, as the most optimistic of proponents of "community corrections" hoped, but rates have not increased either (Lofstrom and Martin 2015). The state continues to provide assistance: more than $2.5 billion for county jail construction (Lofstrom and Raphael 2013*a*).

California has been cited, along with New York and New Jersey, as showing that punishment system reforms can at least be correlated with exceptional decreases in crime rates over the past two decades (The Sentencing Project 2018). California's crime rate is slightly higher than the national average, but it started that period well above the national average. Its current violent and property crime rates are 445 and 2,550 per 100,000, respectively, compared with 386 and 2,450 for the nation as a whole.

Dire predictions that realignment would lead to higher crime have not been borne out. Violent crime has not changed much at all, especially relative to national averages; only a spike in car theft rates stands out as a rise (Lofstrom and Raphael 2013*b*, 2013*c*). Given the somewhat organized

---

[23] Release figures include both nonsentenced and sentenced inmates.

nature of car theft rings, and their allied chop shops, even that spike is hard to attribute to an increase in the number of generally bad people on the streets.

Another dimension that is indirectly related to crime rates is comparison of prison admissions to releases. In the United States overall, the ratio of new admissions to releases is about 2:3, whereas in California it is close to 1:1 (CDCR 2018*b*). That could mean that California is underimprisoning, but given California's reduced use of state prisons, it may simply be imprisoning more parsimoniously. In any case, the ratio would look different if we took jails into account.

C. At What Cost the Outcome?

California has reduced incarceration with no notable increase in crime. Some might praise the changes as noble, progressive reform achievements. The state faced its crisis. It met the federal court's injunctive demands. It enacted realignment, shifting much incarceration from state prisons to county jails. Its citizens approved Propositions 36, 47, and 57. Some might say that California, because of the size of its population, deserves the majority of the statistical credit for reversal of national trends in the imprisonment rate.[24]

Some would say, however, that the primary impetus for change, the federal court order, makes these reforms something less than noble, and that these much-publicized measures deserve attention mainly as flawed if marginally positive efforts to mitigate the disaster that the state itself recklessly created. A California-Texas comparison is instructive.

Texas and California have roughly equal crime rates. Both have experienced a significant drop in imprisonment rates over the last decade. The long-time ratio of California's rate to Texas's (about 2:3) has remained steady. California's ratio of jail population to prison population is much higher than in Texas, so their total incarceration rates are not that far apart (Bureau of Justice Statistics 2018*a*).[25]

Texas has won publicity as an all-happy story, free of legal Sturm und Drang. For Texas the term "crisis" tends to refer only to a financial problem that spurred reform (Texas Public Policy Foundation 2017). California

---

[24] From 2007 to 2015 the national imprisonment rate dropped from 470 per 100,000 to just over 400. If we take California out of the picture the drop would have been from 465 to 427 (Bureau of Justice Statistics 2018*b*).

[25] Texas's ratio of admissions to releases is close to the national number of 2:3, so in that sense it could justify its higher imprisonment rate in terms of its efficacy.

is seen by many, rightly, as having been a political and legal mess that blinded itself to crisis until the *Plata* injunctive hammer came down, responding in ways that bring the negative connotation of "reactive" to its last-minute scrambling (Petersilia 2014*a*).

One explanation for the difference is expectations. California is increasingly the epitome of liberalism and progressivism, while Texas epitomizes the red state and has long been derided for its crudely harsh and racist criminal justice system. Low expectations may explain why the Texas news is seen as straightforwardly good while California is seen, at best, as melodramatically averting disasters.

But the most striking point of comparison with Texas is in cost. Adjusting for size of prison population, California spends three times as much as Texas (Mai and Subramanian 2017). Explanations include anomalously high prison guard salaries in California (and anomalously low ones in Texas) and great recent expenditures resulting from federal court control. But the Texas cost comparison, while stark, reminds us that California is near the top nationally in cost per prisoner (and correctional share of the state budget), and that costs keep rising dramatically while its incarceration rate goes down (Graves 2018). By that reckoning, we could lower California's report card grade considerably: even if it is doing reasonably well by most measures, the correctional system is eating up too much of the state's wealth.

How much credit California deserves for its reforms, or for decarceration, requires us to consider how much sympathy or scorn it merits for its incarceration problems. To appreciate the distinct things that California did to address "mass incarceration," we need to understand the California-specific version of the phenomenon. For decades, California's per capita imprisonment rate had been rising to unprecedented levels, but by the 1990s it was not a distinct outlier. California was as bad as the rest of the nation in rate and trajectory but not far from average.

That upward trajectory resulted from factors that were fairly typical. They included increases in the length of sentences; increasing rigidity and severity of new sentencing laws; the American rise in crime rates from the 1970s through the early 1990s; a sharp increase in the tendency of prosecutors to ask for prison sentences (Zimring 1994; Pfaff 2017); and more broadly, if amorphously, the national political demagoguery on crime, most evident in the war on drugs.

The key point is that these wild swings (and increasing costs) implicate more than the nature of public life in California as explanations for the complexity of its sentencing and correctional history. They signal a set of "structural" factors that undermine confidence in the durability of any solution to the contemporary crisis—and any confidence that the state's "grade" will stay at least up in the B-minus range.

The three-judge court itself is a wonderfully revealing source for this concern. Over the many years of litigation and negotiation, the state argued many times that the injunction should be modified or even terminated. Again and again the court, with reactions that varied among skepticism, caution, disbelief, and exasperation, showed just this lack of confidence. Many of these moments can demonstrate this, but the best example occurred on April 11, 2013.

At stake was the state's obligation to meet the cap of 137.5 percent of the stated capacity of its prisons. The state, proclaiming the success of realignment, alternately requested further extensions of time and a declaration that the health and mental health care systems had improved sufficiently to make a population cap moot. It acknowledged that there was more work to do in improving the medical care systems but insisted that remaining problems were no longer due to overcrowding. In one other framing of the issues, the state argued that changed conditions since the original order had undermined the necessity of the 137.5 percent figure.

The court ferociously rejected all these arguments and declared that realignment had not accomplished enough. It virtually accused the state of bad faith in its evidentiary claims about the state of the system and mocked its arguments that practical obstacles beyond its control should excuse its missing the targets. One long-standing issue had been so-called waivers of state law. Under the PLRA, a three-judge court can order a state to waive state law rules if clearly necessary to carry out a required remedy. The *Plata* court deployed this power. Earlier it did this one at a time and usually following negotiations. This time it bluntly required waiver of a number of barriers—including restrictions on physician licensing, budgetary allocations, and zoning laws governing placement of nonprison places of incarceration. The court rejected the state's claim that it had not yet been able to identify reliable risk-assessment instruments it needed to identify which prisoners could be safely released. "That was not a factual assessment based on current circumstances. Rather, it was a determination of what population level *would be required in the future* to allow defendants to be able to produce constitutional care. As the Supreme Court recognized, there are 'no scientific tools available to determine the precise population reduction necessary to remedy a constitutional violation of this sort'" (Three-Judge Court, Opinion and Order Denying Defendants' Motion to Vacate or Modify Population Reduction Order, April 11, 2013, Civil Rights Litigation Clearinghouse, University of Michigan Law School). Thus, it would weaken the power of an equity court to allow such a "changed conditions" argument to undermine a predictive judgment when time has passed. The judges declared that opening opportunities for reconsideration of the prediction instrument would invite endless relitigation. A truly decisive "changed circumstance" would have to affect the constitutional foundation of the equity order—such as a change in Eighth Amendment doctrine announced by the Supreme Court. They told the state to consider reducing the lifer population and to expand good-time credits. They urged the state to change its penal code to mitigate the enhancements and to create a sentencing commission.

The *Plata* case itself is now in a strange state of inaction. The court has issued few orders in recent years. The state publishes required monthly status reports that genially proclaim that the prisons meet the ordered cap (but not by much), and that projections for future years are promising (CDCR 2018*d*). But the court holds on to its power and may worry that some of the steps taken are unstable. Proposition 57, for example, allows the governor to use below-the-radar administrative rulemaking to grant greater good-time credits to increase releases. But the countervector, as usual, is California's big-money interest group version of direct democracy: the California District Attorneys' Association. Private donors are pushing for virtual repeal of Proposition 57.

So, overall, this very mixed picture does not mark California as an outlier. Its recent and longer history show that it is somewhere between doing somewhat well and treading water. Other states have achieved this status in fairly undramatic ways; California has been the national drama queen. So the lessons concern the causes and costs of volatility and the means and costs of finding equilibrium. One might say that California has taken one for the national team. It has played out every good and bad thing that can be done in the complex hydraulics of criminal justice and corrections and so may provide a reference manual for other states.

V. Some Lessons

The lessons laid out here are more impressionistic and speculative than sharply diagnostic or prescriptive. They overlap in subject and data.

A. Honestly Acknowledging Necessity Is a Predicate to Addressing It Sensibly

We now know this: a polity finds a way of getting things done, with various fingers pressing various buttons, when it realizes that necessity demands it. But a sense of crisis by itself does not create acknowledgment of necessity. So where does necessity come from, and what mechanisms respond to it and how?

Consider again Texas, where the adage that necessity is the mother of invention became a popular meme (Texas Public Policy Foundation 2017). Its prison population followed the national trajectory, growing to more than 150,000 inmates by the early 2000s (proportionately substantially more than California). Texas initially responded like California, by building more and more prisons, reflecting judges' and prosecutors' lack of faith in alternatives to incarceration. In 2007, however, an entity called the Legislative Budget Board (LBB) scared the state straight by projecting a need to double prison capacity in just 5 years, and then political enthusiasm for spending more money on prisons waned. The LBB is essentially a joint legislative committee, with a well-endowed research staff. It operates in some ways like a sentencing commission. Here is its general self-description (Legislative Budget Board 2017): "The Legislative Budget Board (LBB) is a permanent joint committee of the Texas Legislature that develops budget and policy recommendations for legislative appropriations, completes fiscal analyses for proposed legislation, and conducts evaluations and reviews to improve the efficiency and performance of state and local operations." One of its typical reports on criminal justice begins this way:

Correctional Population Projections: Overview
- Correctional population projections are produced to serve as a basis for biennial funding determinations.
- Projections are based on current laws, policies, and practices. Subsequent shifts in these factors will be incorporated into future LBB projections.
- The LBB simulation model incorporates these factors into the population projections and tracks an individual's movement into, through, and out of the criminal justice system.

Guided by the LBB, the legislature effected a huge shift toward alternatives and passed a $241 million "justice reinvestment" package that proved far more efficient than prison building. Changes were made in rehabilitative resources at the front and back ends, and the harmony of public safety and cost control became the new vocabulary. Among many markers of success: far more offenders and inmates were directed to probation and parole, revocation rates declined, and crime rates dropped in line with national rates. The whole reform panoply was adopted: more good-time credits, county performance incentive funding, good-time credit power allocated to both judges and jailers, and sealing of offender records to enhance their employability. Similar stories can be told in blue states such as Maryland, and red ones such as Georgia and Louisiana (DeBor, Bauer, and Schrantz 2018).

Now back to California's recognition of and response to its crisis. We could see it as a kind of cultural epiphany, but it had no clear financial manifestation in the legislature. Nor was there any formally empowered research entity putting cost-benefit projections in the face of the legislature. Instead, the governor drafted a bill and confronted the legislature with an emergency and the admonition that the federal court could no longer be resisted. So California was cowardly and evasive and then impulsive and reactive, while Texas was relatively systematic. Nevertheless, somewhat more optimistically, California's experience suggests that sometimes the hydraulics of American government push a jurisdiction toward some degree of cost-benefit rationality.

B. There Is an Art to Constructive Crisis Provocation

Perceived forces of necessity often depend on unusually forceful agents, individual or institutional. With respect to the California federal court intervention, there were several:

- A man named Donald Spector and his small nonprofit called the Prison Law Office. The innocuous-looking, owlish Mr. Spector deployed the resources of his small but brilliant staff to precipitate the class action lawsuits that enabled the court to be the irresistible force. Notably, the Prison Law Office has been litigating about crowding and maltreatment in numerous county jail systems as well as the state system. And also notably, its success is partly due to the unusually ample supply of public interest–oriented young lawyers in Northern California, employed not only by nonprofits but also by very aggressive for-profit firms that specialize in civil rights litigation (Schlanger 2013).

- It is a mistake, an act of gross underestimation, to view Judge Thelton Henderson solely as an idealistic civil rights icon. He is a ferociously tough and stubborn hander-down of orders, not at all afraid of confrontation with resistant state officials, and a cold pragmatist when he needs to be. In the original *Plata* litigation, the first court-appointed receiver was an especially aggressive public health official who seemed indifferent to state fiscal realities as he called for supercomprehensive, state-of-the-art medical systems. Judge Henderson fired him, with the reminder to all that his judicial mandate was to induce the creation of a constitutionally permissible health care system, not a world-class one (Rothfeld 2008).

C. *However Contingent on the Vagaries of Majoritarian Politics, the Appointment of Federal Judges with the Power to Take Countermajoritarian Measures Is Crucial to Reform*

One result of the convergence of the Prison Law Office and Judge Henderson (and the other two judges on the three-judge court) was the production of an encyclopedic documentation of evidence—raw data and expert inference, on matters legal and medical—that was proof against attack by appellate courts committed to deference to trial courts on matters of fact. This point in turn leads us to another singular individual but also to the nature of appellate court review.

Consider the Supreme Court case in *Brown v. Plata*, 563 U.S. 493 (2011), which confirmed the three-judge court's injunction. It was a bitterly divided 5–4 decision, and had it not been for the adventitious historical presence of Anthony Kennedy, it might have gone the other way. Kennedy was not the swing vote on the Supreme Court because, or entirely because, he was typically a moderate on controversial issues. Rather, he was a paradoxical extremist, going far right on some matters (the commerce clause in the Obamacare case) and left on such matters as capital punishment, gay rights, and prison conditions.

Kennedy took the occasion of *Plata* to deliver a passionate, indeed florid, denunciation of mass incarceration. His vote to uphold the injunction caused Justice Scalia to denounce the three-judge court hyperbolically for what he called the worst act of equity jurisprudence since the origin of the chancellor, and Justice Alito to fulminate that we had better lock up our children's bedrooms immediately. But it is a mistake to say that the Supreme Court ordered the decarceration of California's prisons. Rather, it upheld a lower court order in large part because it could defer to the trial record (Weisberg 2013). Kennedy read into its opinion passages from the damning expert reports on which the lower court judges had relied. He even had estoppel available: "The Corrections Independent Review Panel, a body appointed by the Governor and composed of correctional consultants and representatives from state agencies, concluded that California's prisons are 'severely overcrowded, imperiling the safety of both correctional employees and inmates.' In 2006, then-Governor Schwarzenegger declared a state of emergency in the prisons, as 'immediate action is necessary to prevent death and harm caused by California's severe prison overcrowding'" (563 U.S. at 502–3). Hence, even Kennedy's role traces back to the legal situation down in the trial court trenches. Presumably, random assignment (admittedly in two very liberal federal districts) gave the *Plata* and *Coleman* cases to Judges Henderson and Karlton. It was a political fact that the chief judge of the Ninth Circuit decided to appoint those two judges and the even more liberal Judge Reinhardt to the three-judge court. It was the diligent work of the Prison Law Office to turn the Prison Litigation Reform Act, designed to limit the power of the courts to order decarceration, into a mechanism of aggressive decarceration.[26]

In theory the plaintiffs could have brought these Eighth Amendment claims in state court, which shares authority for Section 1983 lawsuits and is not subject to the limits of the Prison Litigation Reform Act. But, as in many states, California's own courts have played only a minor role in prison reform efforts. To the extent that litigation has been a driver of decarceration, the American tradition of civil rights plaintiffs investing their trust in the expected independence of the federal courts abides. The state courts are mostly left to monitor individual sentencing decisions under whatever power they have under the state penal code. In California, the state supreme court, widely respected for its sophistication and, in some areas, great legal innovation, has not played a major role.

---

[26] As a side note to the mundane administrative side of the case—the deference to the trial court—Schlanger (2013) observes that his background as a government person in Sacramento predisposed Kennedy to a kind of ad hoc, problem-solving, reformist approach to big issues.

D. Hope for the Accident of the Right Leader at the Right Time

When Jerry Brown was elected in 2010, he was perhaps the most experienced public official in the country. Son of a two-term governor, he had already served as secretary of state, governor, mayor of Oakland, and attorney general. He knew which buttons to press. He knew how to move the legislature on realignment. He knew how to break bread with powerful groups such as the nurses' and teachers' unions while avoiding any obligation to the prison guards' union. He knew when he needed the initiative process and how to use his own campaign funds to promote it. Finally, when prison reform required more state revenue, he had the credibility and savvy to win popular approval of new tobacco and gasoline taxes in a state known for virulent antitax popular revolts.

One need not subscribe to a "great person theory of history" to appreciate that an individual acting at the right time and place can make a difference. Brown had a history on this issue. As a boy-wonder governor starting in 1975, he committed himself to the Determinate Sentencing law. But as a contemplative Jesuit-trained intellectual, he had the capacity for self-scrutiny that ultimately enabled him to think through the troubled legacy of the 1970s. After again becoming governor in 2011, Brown made clear that he suffered from buyer's remorse. Elected in 2010 by a huge margin against a plausible Republican candidate who spent $150 million of her own money in the race, and at a time when he enjoyed a Democratic supermajority in the legislature, he entered office in as unassailable a political position as can be imagined in a large American state. With unshakable motivation he moved the lumbering state machinery toward his goal, with some twists.

Many believe that Brown, and his predecessor Schwarzenegger, cleverly allowed the federal court to play "bad cop" in order to lean on the state's politicians without looking like a reckless reformer. This is probably not quite right. Both governors fought reasonably hard as defendants in the litigation, at least to negotiate for more time and more flexibility in meeting the decarceration orders. But Brown appreciated the force of necessity better than others, and, to abuse this cliché, he saw that it was the mother of invention when he promoted the realignment concept. Moreover, the new, older Governor Brown had become a fiscal pragmatist who wanted to leave the state with a rainy-day surplus. Thus, he drew on his political capital to pass new taxes; by doing so he was able to mitigate the financial distress caused by the necessary correctional reforms.

E. The Particular Structures of a Government Can Be Both Obstacles and Toolkits

Each state has its own structure of authority. The particular allocation of authority can delay or thwart reform but can also be deployed to serve reform if the party doing the deploying is experienced and adept. California's distinct structural features are notable (Zasloff 2004). The governor has unusual dominance over the legislature because he initiates the annual budget process and can remove budget lines. However, the governor has full control over state agencies only for budget purposes. A fair amount of policy-making authority lies in the so-called cabinet officials—the attorney general, comptroller, treasurer, and others who are popularly elected separately from the governor. But also, the California attorney general has relatively little power over criminal justice. Almost all the powers of prison regulation lie within the Department of Corrections and Rehabilitation, which sits under the governor (except for legislative confirmation of its secretary). But most notably, all elected and appointed officials must yield to the powers of the populace. The process for ballot propositions can moot or override any executive or legislative action. Some ballot propositions involve constitutional amendments, which means that only a new one, not mere legislation, can change an old one.

Brown was able to maximize his powers within these structures. We can trace his efforts through these various permutations of power allocation. Thus, for many years the legislature partnered with the populace (or well-resourced lobbies) to create the highly incarcerative system that created the crisis. When the legislature proved mostly useless in addressing the crisis, Propositions 36 and 47 did the major work; in parallel Brown coerced the legislature into enacting realignment. Then, reading the reform mood in the state, Brown offered Proposition 57, bypassing the legislature to correct the effects of the legislative tradition of enhancements. Proposition 57 proved to be a kind of double bypass. Passed by the voters, it authorized the governor to instruct his own Department of Corrections and Rehabilitation to create the highly complex regulations that would implement the mandate to enable earlier parole consideration for the vast numbers of lower-level felons who were not affected by realignment because they were already in state prison.

Finally, a word about the most important character in the story—the three-judge court, as a dramatic example of managerial justice under modern civil rights and jurisdictional statutes but also as an adherent of venerable principles of equity. In its response to the state's efforts and evasions, in its resilience in titrating its doses, and in its sanctions and permissions, the court was mindful that it is a three-person chancellor of equity. Operating within a centuries-old tradition of jurisprudence, equity judges can act when the "law" side proves insufficient.

F. Authority Is Vertically Fungible, but with Agency Costs (and Benefits)

As realignment devolved authority to the counties, vast numbers of potential state prisoners were sent to county jails, and a vast share of parole authority was given to county probation authorities. Counties were given broad discretion to handle new prisoners in their own ways, with diverse probation policies, localized judicial attitudes toward split sentencing and revocation, and de jure and de facto authority lodged in county sheriffs to open and close the spigots on the jail population. This has been an extreme exercise in "state-county federalism" in terms of allowing experimentation with correctional policy. But it has also been an expensive bargain. The state gave up its power to set uniform policies, and counties have widely varied in their positions on a spectrum of surveillance-and-control to treatment-and-rehabilitation.

If by determinate sentencing we mean that the judge's sentence cannot be reduced later by a discretionary parole board (though perhaps by a good-behavior formula), California achieved Brown's goal of bringing back some degree of indeterminacy (King 2015). The most obvious example is Proposition 57, but realignment fits here as well. County officials, including probation officers, sheriffs, and judges making bail and revocation decisions, now have power to identify jail inmates as plausible candidates for early release or for alternative forms of incapacitation. If by determinacy we mean sentencing rules or guidelines that limit front-end discretion, then the "split-sentencing" alternative afforded trial judges under realignment moves California in the indeterminacy direction. Perhaps the key point is that California moved in this direction in subtle incremental steps, without requiring or provoking foundational debates about a paradigm shift. That is the mirror opposite of what happened in the 1970s.

But recall that one potential effect of this devolution is cost internalization. California offers a possible example or test case of realigning cost and correctional/sentencing power so that counties must internalize the consequences of their prosecutors' decisions. Measuring this is difficult, but this reconfiguration may have succeeded to the extent that jail populations are not increasing to offset prison downsizing, and parole and probation populations have also declined. Some argue that the changes have put more criminals on the street, but there is little evidence of a crime uptick except the anomalous case of auto theft. To the extent that police feel overwhelmed by low-level street criminals, that may be more the result of budget cuts following the 2008 financial crisis than of correctional reforms.

But assuming realignment spurred cost internalization, what form has that taken? The first-round answer is, many different forms. Lin and Petersilia (2014) analyzed the allocation plans that realignment required each county to produce, and they show a complex matrix of possibilities. After sorting pre- and postrealignment policies according to key types of allocation (i.e., police, sheriff, jails, courts, prosecutors, rehabilitation programs, probation personnel), they roughly distinguished realignment county allocations into two models: "control" counties (that emphasized law enforcement, surveillance, and harsh sentencing) and "treatment" counties (that emphasized rehabilitation programs and mental health services). They coded the counties for various factors involving demographics, economic metrics, crime rates, and political voting patterns, as well as long-standing budget allocations to various organs of local government, sentencing patterns, and expressions of public trust or distrust in law enforcement.

Various of these factors cluster at two ends of the spectrum to help explain why some counties were on the control side or on the treatment side and remain there after realignment. The overall theme is that allocations turn on perceptions of local law enforcement needs, tilted by political orientation. Some highly nuanced factors emerged. For example, treatment counties exhibit high degrees of faith in law enforcement, which tends to liberate officials to emphasize social needs. Where sheriffs enjoy high public confidence, counties tend to follow the key secondary goal of realignment, which was to improve local reentry services. Control counties exhibit high rates of serious crimes and perceptions of underenforcement of drug-crime laws, paired with high rates of harsh prison sentences for those prosecuted for drug crimes.

Many counties continued their earlier patterns after receiving realignment money. Others moved one way or the other on the control-treatment continuum as they anticipated new jail population pressures or new large numbers of released offenders. Depending on the county, they were seen as mainly posing challenges for police or needs for mental health and drug programs. In some counties in which money had been short for prosecutors or probation, the response was to spend much of the money on these agencies. In others, the money went more toward social services.

Longer term, we do not know how these diverse county allocations of money would look were we to perform the presumably impossible task of evaluating each county system under the report card criteria discussed above. There has been no great legal scandal about any county nor any notorious new mistreatment scandal about any prison, and the crime rates are reasonable, but this devolution story is still clearly a cautionary tale. In effect, indeterminacy in the technical sense also means indeterminacy in the more common sense. There will be less truth in sentencing when the truth is so complicated and the data for any scrutiny into the truth are so hard to identify. When a state has devolved authority as California has done, the predictability of sentence lengths becomes much more uncertain for large numbers of prisoners. Authority to release them has become more diffuse, more discretionary, and less visible.

Finally, many observers speculated on how realignment might affect lawyering. Some predicted that prosecutors would up the ante in their charges to ensure prison sentences (Keel, Landin, and Warp 2012). Some predicted that defense lawyers, realizing their clients faced less severe sentences, would resist plea offers, force more trials, and thus burden the courts (Owens 2014). From another angle, some predicted that state parole agents would be swamped by the loss of funding that went to probation while being left with the most dangerous parolees to supervise (Vilkin and Williams 2014). The data to measure such phenomena are far too scattered and spaced to draw any clear inferences, but so far none of the more dramatic predictions seems to have been proved out.

G. Beware the Risk of Narrowness or Simplicity in Tying Means to Ends

Efforts to reduce incarceration may be too narrowly focused if they ignore contributors to the imprisonment rate. Although prison crowding has lessened, and jails appear to be managing secondary crowding, California has failed to reckon with continued population pressures on both. A high fraction of the prison population are lifers, who present a dilemma. Utilitarian cost-benefit analyses would call for release of large numbers: once they reach a certain age, most lifers pose almost no risk of recidivism, especially for violent crimes, while their imprisonment becomes much more expensive because of medical care costs. However, they are lifers because they committed the most heinous of the noncapital crimes. The public spirit of moral desert probably makes wholesale releases politically impossible.

The problem for jails is bail. Many jail inmates in every state are pretrial detainees, and for reasons not fully understood that proportion is anomalously high in California. Sheriffs must triage space use between detainees and convicted misdemeanants and felons, and in relation to public perceptions about danger and public safety. It is far from obvious that the detainees should be the first to be released.

None of the decarceration measures has addressed bail, at least directly. County-level authorities have traditionally set bail schedules, and prosecutors and judges tend to go high on bail demands. The forces that led to realignment and the other measures did not target this issue. Moreover, the commercial bail industry, ideologically allied with the California District Attorneys Association, has been a powerful opponent of bail reform. Proposed legislation may change this, but the issue is a latecomer to decarceration efforts.

Bail reform is happening around the nation. Because of its unusually high percentage of pretrial detainees, California has been a laboratory for proposed solutions. Civil rights groups have attacked money bail as discriminatory, and in a remarkable recent case, *In re Humphrey*, 19 Cal. App. 5th 1006 (2018), a court of appeal held it unconstitutional to condition release on ability to pay. There was pressure for legislative change and suddenly we have a newly enacted statute that, in uncoordinated parallel with *Humphrey*, essentially abolishes all cash bail in California (Pretrial Release or Detention: Pretrial Services, 2018 Cal. Stat. Ch. 244 [2018]).

Some civil rights groups opposed this new law because in their view it leaves too much discretion in judges even though it replaced harsh money formulas. Others believe that the problem is not cash bail but commercial cash bail, and that state-run cash security systems would be fair and efficient. How this plays out will, of course, be a function of many different legal and political forces interacting. The various actors so far are not talking to each other very thoughtfully; bail reform may prove to be the negative story for reformist pragmatics.

VI. Direct and Indirect Democracy

The most temptingly plausible lesson from California concerns the disadvantages of direct popular democracy in relation to punishment. A mildly positive story can be told of California's adventures with ballot initiatives: they fueled the volatility of the politics of punishment and helped create the crisis, but other forces of government ultimately intervened to manage the crisis, and smart leaders learned how to circumvent the legislature[27] and bring some rationality to the system. That positive version of the story feels like a rationalization. The simpler negative version remains more plausible. Direct democracy has been too costly for California criminal justice. Barker's comparison of California with Washington and New York is deeply instructive.

The most publicized counterstories come from the South, and not just Texas. Typical is a report lauding Tennessee, Arkansas, Mississippi, Kentucky, and South Carolina for a wide range of sensible reforms (Justice Policy Institute 2011). Of course, these states benefit from the low expectations of national reform leaders about the South, and the Nixon-can-go-to-China phenomenon that makes conservative politicians less afraid of appearing soft on crime. In any event, in statistical terms, very high imprisonment rates in the South leave ample room for impressive percentage reductions.

These southern achievements have largely come from the legislatures. Referenda have played little role in criminal justice in the nation in recent years—except in California. The databases of popular ballot votes in recent years reveal hardly any large structural ones dealing with criminal justice (Schwartzapfel 2016; Potyondy 2018). Oregon's Measure 94, in 2000, repealed mandatory minimum sentences enacted by ballot measure in 1994 for very serious crimes. Oregon's 2010 Measure 73 increased mandatory minimum sentences (up to 25 years) for certain repeat sex offenders and repeat intoxicated drivers. On the decarceration side, Oklahoma voters in 2016 passed State Question 780, reducing certain property and drug offenses to misdemeanors, and companion State Question 781, creating the County Community Safety Investment Fund. The fund distributes costs saved through these penal code reductions to counties to fund mental health and substance abuse treatment programs. In Arizona, Proposition 302 in 2002 restored the possibility of probation for certain drug-related crimes where for years a prison sentence had been mandatory. Altogether this represents only a tiny slice of major structural changes in American sentencing in recent decades.

However, the political passions exploited (or deployed) through ballot propositions find outlets elsewhere in other mechanisms of government.

---

[27] A key feature of California law is that "legislation" enacted by the voters after a voter-created initiative cannot be repealed except by the voters (Cal. Const. art. II, sec. 10 (c)).

Here is a cautionary tale from the Midwest. O'Hear (2017) observes that California experienced a 24 percent drop in imprisonment from 2005–15, but Midwestern states, with the exception of Michigan (14 percent drop), experienced increases, ranging up to 16 percent. The irony, O'Hear notes, is that these states worked hard to bring data-driven research to their sentencing systems. Some had sentencing commissions, and many drew on the resources of the national "Justice Reinvestment" initiative.

Thus, the absence of ballot populism is hardly a panacea for reform. Responsibility remains where it best belongs, in the legislature and commissions, but the legislature also can become the voice through which raw populism speaks. To the extent that lobbies such as prosecutors' associations or prison guards' unions play a role, they can play it more directly with legislators.

Nevertheless, the safest inference remains: however salutatory the hydraulic tropism toward equilibrium, we need stable structures of government, including bureaucracies, to discipline the politics of punishment. California may appear stable, but the fault lines are always here. Slight upticks in crime, especially property crime, get media coverage as police and others blame realignment and Proposition 47. Alas, there is already talk of a ballot proposition to repeal Proposition 47. Had officially authorized experts, inside or outside the legislature, "costed out" the likely effects of Proposition 47 and other measures, overreactions might have been avoided or weakened. Finances may also threaten the current stability. Realignment mainly aimed at satisfying the federal court and secondarily at easing reentry. Protecting the state budget was tertiary at best. Proposition 47, however, was sold in part as a money saver. Now viewed as part of a larger decarceration effort, it is criticized for failing to deliver a sufficiently large decarceration dividend. A new governor less skillful at coordinating progressive reform and frugality than Brown may see volatility return.

In recent years, many states have achieved admirable reforms by delegating some degree of planning to sentencing commissions (Weisberg 2007). If California had overcome its stubborn aversion to a sentencing commission, it might have avoided the crisis or smoothed the path toward overcoming it. Law-and-order leaders in California have always feared that a sentencing commission would accrue power to control sentencing without democratic review. California instead ceded vast amounts of sentencing power to such "de facto commissions" as the federal district court and the 58 counties (Weisberg 2011). One might say that the county sheriffs became the ultimate cost-benefit analysts. If the overall lesson is that punishment is a government program subject to cost-benefit analysis, not a theological imperative, the California story shows that someone will wind up doing the calculations.

REFERENCES

Anderson, Alex. 2008. "Hiding Out in Prison Bonds." *Forbes*, October 22.
Ashton, Adam. 2016. "Gov. Jerry Brown Contemplates Second Chances in Backing Prison-Reform Measure." *Sacramento Bee*, October 12.
Ball, W. David. 2012. "Tough on Crime (on the State's Dime): How Violent Crime Does Not Drive California Counties' Incarceration Rates—and Why It Should." *Georgia State University Law Review* 28(4):987–1084.
Barker, Vanessa. 2009. *The Politics of Imprisonment*. New York: Oxford University Press.
Begovich, Michael, William R. Bennett, Matthew C. Braner, Nancy Brewer, Robyn L. Chew, Ronald J. Freitas, Steven I. Katz, Michael Ogul, Philip Pennypacker, Kenneth L. Shapero, and Catherine Stephenson. 2014. *California Criminal Sentencing Enhancements*. Oakland: California Continuing Education of the Bar.
Bigelow, Tricia A., and J. Richard Couzens. 2017. *The Amendment of the Three Strikes Law*. http://www.courts.ca.gov/documents/Three-Strikes-Amendment-Couzens-Bigelow.pdf.
Bigelow, Tricia A., J. Richard Couzens, and Greg L. Prickett. 2013. *Sentencing California Crimes*. Encino, CA: Thomson Reuters/Rutter Group.
Bird, Mia, Ryken Grattet, Viet Nguyen, and Sonya Tafoya. 2016. *California's County Jails in the Era of Reform*. San Francisco: Public Policy Institute of California.
Board of State and Community Corrections. 2002–16. *Jail Profile Survey—Quarter Survey Results Reports*. Sacramento, CA: Board of State and Community Corrections. http://www.bscc.ca.gov/s_fsojailprofilesurvey.php.
Bureau of Justice Statistics. 2018*a*. *Jail Inmates in 2016*. Washington, DC: Office of Justice Programs.
———. 2018*b*. *Prisoners in 2016*. Washington, DC: Office of Justice Programs.
Camacho, Albert, Jr. 2016. "Everything You Wanted to Know about Prop 47 but Were Afraid to Ask." *Criminal Law Journal* 16(1):1–4.
CDCR (California Department of Corrections and Rehabilitation). 2018*a*. *Budget and Policy Post: The 2017–18 Budget*. Sacramento, CA: Legislative Analyst's Office. https://lao.ca.gov/Publications/Report/3595.
———. 2018*b*. *Offender Data Points: Offender Demographics for the 24-Month Period, Ending December 2017*. Sacramento, CA: Office of Research, Division of Internal Oversight and Research, CDCR. https://sites.cdcr.ca.gov/research/wp-content/uploads/sites/9/2018/07/Offender-Data-Points-as-of-December-31-2017-1.pdf.

———. 2018c. *Proposition 57, the Public Safety and Rehabilitation Act of 2016*. Sacramento, CA: CDCR.

———. 2018d. *Three Judge Panel Updates*. Sacramento, CA: CDCR. https://www.cdcr.ca.gov/News/3-judge-panel.html.

Chanenson, Steven L. 2005. "The Next Era of Sentencing Reform." *Emory Law Journal* 54:377–460.

Cullen, Francis T., and Joan Petersilia. 2015. "Liberal but Not Stupid: Meeting the Promise of Downsizing Prisons." *Stanford Journal of Criminal Law and Policy* 2:1–43.

Dansky, Kara. 2008. "Understanding California Sentencing." *University of San Francisco Law Review* 43(1):45–86.

DeBor, Stephen, Marc Bauer, and Dennis Schrantz. 2018. *Decarceration Strategies: How 5 States Achieved Substantial Prison Population Reductions*. Washington, DC: The Sentencing Project.

Graves, Scott. 2018. *Despite the Recent Decline in Incarceration, Corrections Spending in the Governor's Proposed 2018–19 Budget Remains High*. Sacramento: California Budget and Policy Center. https://calbudgetcenter.org/resources/despite-the-recent-decline-in-incarceration-corrections-spending-in-the-governors-proposed-2018-19-budget-remains-high/.

Greenhut, Steven. 2017. "How California Softened Its 'Tough on Crime' Approach." *R Street Policy Study* 102:1–8.

Hayes, Joseph, and Sonya Tafoya. 2014. *Juvenile Justice in California*. San Francisco: Public Policy Institute of California.

Johnson, Brian. 2019. "Trials and Tribulations: The Trial Tax and the Process of Punishment." In *American Sentencing*, edited by Michael Tonry. Vol. 48 of *Crime and Justice: A Review of Research*, edited by Michael Tonry. Chicago: University of Chicago Press.

Justice Policy Institute. 2011. *Due South: Looking to the South for Criminal Justice Innovations*. Washington, DC: Justice Policy Institute. http://www.justicepolicy.org/research/2472.

Keel, Corinne, Marisa Landin, and Lindsey Warp. 2012. *Early Impacts of California's Criminal Justice Realignment on District Attorneys' Strategies and Use of Discretion*. Stanford, CA: Criminal Justice Center.

King, Ryan. 2015. "Balancing the Goals of Determinate and Indeterminate Sentencing Systems." *Federal Sentencing Reporter* 28(2):85–87.

Lawrence, Sarah. 2014. *Court-Ordered Population Caps in California County Jails*. Stanford, CA: Criminal Justice Center.

Legislative Budget Board, State of Texas. 2017. "Overview of Criminal Justice Correctional Population Projections, Recidivism Rates, and Costs per Day." House Committee on Corrections Hearing. Austin: State of Texas. http://www.lbb.state.tx.us/Documents/Publications/Presentation/3754_HCC_OVERVIEW FEB2017.pdf.

Lewis, Kathleen M., Paul J. Pfingst, and Gregory Thomas. 2002. "'The Genie Is Out of the Jar': The Development of Criminal Justice Policy in California." *McGeorge Law Review* 33:717–47.

Lin, Jeffrey, and Joan Petersilia. 2014. *Follow the Money: How California Counties Are Spending Their Public Safety Realignment Funds*. Stanford, CA: Criminal Justice Center.

Little Hoover Commission, State of California. 2007. "Solving California's Corrections Crisis: Time Is Running Out." Report no. 185, January 27. https://lhc.ca.gov/sites/lhc.ca.gov/files/Reports/185/Report185.pdf.

Lizotte, Alan, and Marjorie S. Zatz. 1986. "The Use and Abuse of Sentence Enhancement for Firearm Offenses in California." *Law and Contemporary Problems* 49(1):199–221.

Lofstrom, Magnus, and Brandon Martin. 2015. *Public Safety Realignment: Impacts So Far*. San Francisco: Public Policy Institute of California.

Lofstrom, Magnus, and Steven Raphael. 2013*a*. *Impact of Realignment on County Jail Populations*. San Francisco: Public Policy Institute of California.

———. 2013*b*. *Public Safety Realignment and Crime Rates in California*. San Francisco: Public Policy Institute of California.

———. 2013*c*. *Realignment and Crime Trends in California*. San Francisco: Public Policy Institute of California.

Lynch, Mona. 2001. "From the Punitive City to the Gated Community: Security and Segregation across the Social and Penal Landscape." *University of Miami Law Review* 56:89–112.

Mai, Chris, and Ram Subramanian. 2017. *The Price of Prisons: Examining State Spending Trends, 2010–2015*. New York: Vera Institute of Justice.

Mukamal, Debbie A., Jordon D. Segall, and Robert Weisberg. 2011. *A Life in Limbo: An Examination of Parole Release for Prisoners Serving Life Sentences with the Possibility of Parole in California*. Stanford, CA: Criminal Justice Center.

O'Hear, Michael M. 2017. "Mass Incarceration in the Heartland: Midwestern States Struggle to Tame Historically High Prison Populations." *Federal Sentencing Reporter* 30(2):91–93.

Owens, Matthew. 2014. *Bargaining in the Wake of Realignment*. Stanford, CA: Criminal Justice Center.

Petersilia, Joan. 2006. *Understanding California Corrections*. A Policy Research Program Report. San Francisco: California Policy Research Center.

———. 2008. "California's Correctional Paradox of Excess and Deprivation." In *Crime and Justice: A Review of Research*, vol. 37, edited by Michael Tonry. Chicago: University of Chicago Press.

———. 2014*a*. "California's Prison Downsizing and Its Impact on Local Criminal Justice Systems." *Harvard Law and Policy Review* 8:327–58.

———. 2014*b*. "Voices from the Field: How California Stakeholders View Public Safety Realignment." Working paper. Stanford, CA: Criminal Justice Center.

Pew Center on the States. 2012. *The Impact of California's Probation Performance Incentive Funding Program*. Washington, DC: Pew Center on the States.

Pfaff, John F. 2017. *Locked In: The True Causes of Mass Incarceration and How to Achieve Real Reform*. New York: Basic.

Potyondy, Patrick. 2018. Statewide Ballot Measures Database. Denver: National Conference of State Legislatures. http://www.ncsl.org/research/elections-and-campaigns/ballot-measures-database.aspx.

Ricciardulli, Alex. 2006. "Clearing Up Sentencing Confusion: Everything You Ever Wanted to Know about the Determinate Sentencing Law but Were Afraid to Ask." *California Bar Journal* (September). http://archive.calbar.ca.gov/archive/Archive.aspx?articleId=81193&categoryId=81182&month=9&year=2006.

Rothfeld, Michael. 2008. "State Prison Health Czar Is Fired." *Los Angeles Times*, January 24.

Schlanger, Margo. 2006. "Civil Rights Injunctions over Time: A Case Study of Jail and Prison Court Orders." *New York University Law Review* 81:550–630.

———. 2013. "*Plata v. Brown* and Realignment: Jails, Prisons, Courts, and Politics." *Harvard Civil Rights–Civil Liberties Review* 48:165–215.

Schwartzapfel, Beth. 2016. "The States Where Voters Decided to Give Criminal Justice Reform a Try." *Marshall Project*, November 9.

The Sentencing Project. 2018. *State of Sentencing 2017: Developments in Policy and Practice*. Washington, DC: The Sentencing Project.

Sigal, J. Franklin. 2007. "Out of Step: When the California Street Terrorism Enforcement Act Stumbles into Penal Code Limits." *Golden Gate University Law Review* 38(1):1–32.

Teji, Selena. 2011. *Ignoring the Evidence: The Role of the California District Attorneys Association in California's Prison Crisis*. San Francisco: California Center on Juvenile and Criminal Justice.

Texas Public Policy Foundation. 2017. "Ten Years of Criminal Justice Reform in Texas." *Veritas*. http://rightoncrime.com/2017/08/ten-years-of-criminal-justice-reform-in-texas/.

Three Strikes Project. 2014. *Proposition 36 Progress Report*. Stanford, CA: Stanford Law School.

Tonry, Michael. 2015. "Federal Sentencing 'Reform' since 1984: The Awful as Enemy of the Good." In *Crime and Justice: A Review of Research*, vol. 44, edited by Michael Tonry. Chicago: University of Chicago Press.

Vilkin, Camden, and Jennifer Williams. 2014. *Post-realignment Parole: Loud Bark, Soft Bite*. Stanford, CA: Criminal Justice Center.

Weisberg, Robert. 2003. "Restorative Justice and the Danger of Community." *Utah Law Review* 2003:343–74.

———. 2007. "How Sentencing Commissions Turned Out to Be a Good Idea." *Berkeley Journal of Criminal Law* 12:179–230.

———. 2009. "Tragedy, Skepticism, Empirics, and the *MPCS*." *Florida Law Review* 61:797–826.

———. 2011. "California's De Facto Sentencing Commissions." *Stanford Law Review Online* 64:1–7.

———. 2013. "Kennedy and the Prisons—Moral Exhortation and Technical Fastidiousness." *McGeorge Law Review* 44:247–68.

Yoshino, Erin R. 2008. "California's Criminal Gang Enhancements: Lessons from Interviews with Practitioners." *Review of Law and Social Justice* 18:117–52.

Zasloff, Jonathan. 2004. "Taking Politics Seriously: A Theory of California's Separation of Powers." *UCLA Law Review* 51:1079–1150.

Zimring, Franklin E. 1994. "The Growth of Imprisonment in California." *British Journal of Criminology* 34:83–96.

Richard S. Frase

Forty Years of American Sentencing Guidelines: What Have We Learned?

ABSTRACT

Since 1980, 22 state and federal jurisdictions have adopted sentencing guidelines. Nineteen still have them. No two systems are alike. Experience suggests that any well-designed system requires five core features: a permanent, balanced, independent, and adequately funded sentencing commission; typical-case presumptive sentences and departure criteria; a hybrid sentencing theory that recognizes both retributive and crime control purposes; balance between the competing benefits of rules and discretion; and sentence recommendations informed by resource and demographic impact assessments. Balance is needed in terms of commission composition, between conflicting sentencing purposes, between rules and discretion, and between the influence of the commission, the legislature, and case-level actors. Guidelines proponents disagree about a number of important issues. Some relate to which crimes and sentencing issues should be regulated. Others concern the design details that determine how the system actually works. It is clear, however, that preguidelines regimes of unstructured, highly discretionary sentencing are unacceptable and that commission-drafted guidelines, endorsed by the American Bar Association and the American

Electronically published February 7, 2019
Richard S. Frase is Benjamin N. Berger Professor of Criminal Law at the University of Minnesota. He is grateful to the Robina Foundation for funding much of the research supporting this essay and to Michael Tonry and two anonymous reviewers for their very helpful comments and suggestions. He would also like to thank his colleagues at the Robina Institute of Criminal Law and Criminal Justice for their contributions to this essay and to our joint efforts to document and improve sentencing guidelines systems: Rhys Hester, Kelly Lyn Mitchell, Julian Roberts, and our numerous student research assistants over the years. Our projects have also greatly benefited from the advice of many present and former guidelines commission members and staff, whom we gratefully acknowledge.

© 2019 by The University of Chicago. All rights reserved.
0192-3234/2019/0048-0001$10.00

Law Institute, are the only successful sentencing reform model. In four decades, no competing model of comparable detail and scope has been seriously proposed.

Forty years ago, the Minnesota and Pennsylvania legislatures each created a commission tasked with proposing statewide sentencing guidelines.[1] In 1980, Minnesota became the first state to implement such a system. Pennsylvania's guidelines took effect 2 years later. Since then, 18 other states, the District of Columbia, and the federal courts have implemented commission-drafted guidelines,[2] although some guidelines, their parent commissions, or both were subsequently abolished.[3] In 2017 the American Law Institute gave final approval to the Model Penal Code–Sentencing (MPCS) rules, which strongly endorsed legally binding guidelines developed and monitored by a permanent commission. The American Bar Association's Sentencing Standards (ABA 1994) likewise strongly endorsed this approach. In the last four decades, no competing sentencing reform model of comparable detail and scope has been seriously proposed, let alone implemented.

But there is no single, or even clear, "consensus" model of sentencing guidelines and guidelines commissions. The Minnesota and Pennsylvania prototypes are quite different from each other in important respects.

---

[1] The idea of commission-drafted sentencing guidelines was first proposed in the early 1970s by federal judge Marvin Frankel (1973). The first commissions were established in Minnesota and Pennsylvania in 1978.

[2] Those 18 states are Alabama, Arkansas, Delaware, Florida, Kansas, Louisiana, Maryland, Massachusetts, Michigan, Missouri, North Carolina, Ohio, Oregon, Tennessee, Utah, Virginia, Washington, and Wisconsin. In total (including Minnesota, Pennsylvania, Washington, DC, and the federal courts), 22 American state and federal jurisdictions have, or once had, some form of commission-drafted, jurisdiction-wide guidelines. For further details on how "guidelines" system is defined in this essay, see the text at nn. 4 and 5.

[3] Sentencing guidelines commissions were abolished, or left as nonguidelines commissions, in five states: the guidelines or successor laws are still in effect in Florida and Tennessee despite abolition of the sentencing commission; in Louisiana and Missouri guidelines were repealed but nonguidelines commissions remain; Wisconsin abolished both its guidelines and its commission. Massachusetts has a sentencing commission and proposed guidelines that the legislature has not approved but that many judges take into consideration. And, in addition to Louisiana and Missouri, there are sentencing or broader criminal justice commissions without a charge to develop guidelines in Alaska, Connecticut, Illinois, New Mexico, and New York. Finally, Nevada currently has a commission to consider writing guidelines (the Nevada Legislative Counsel Bureau: https://www.leg.state.nv.us/App/InterimCommittee/REL/Interim2017/Committee/1391/Meetings). For further information on the guidelines systems that are still operating, as well as on states with nonguidelines commissions, visit the University of Minnesota's Sentencing Guidelines Resource Center, Robina Institute of Criminal Law and Criminal Justice (Robina Institute 2018).

The state and federal guidelines and commissions that were created later are even more diverse in their goals, scope of coverage, and major structural features. In light of the new impetus given to guidelines reforms by completion of the MPCS project, and growing opposition to the excesses of mass incarceration, now seems like a good time to review the history and future of guidelines reforms. What have we learned about what works and what does not? What structural and other policy choices enjoy widespread support, and which continue to be vigorously debated? What are the most important issues requiring additional research to inform these policy debates? What is the likely future of this and competing sentencing structures?

Here are my main findings and conclusions:

- The diversity of guidelines structures and rules suggests a high degree of contingency in what American jurisdictions want in a sentencing system, or at least in what they can successfully implement and sustain.
- From a normative perspective, some guidelines structures are much more likely to produce good sentencing policy and practice. Five essential features characterize a well-designed sentencing system: first, a permanent, balanced, independent, and adequately funded sentencing commission; second, specified typical-case presumptive sentences and departure criteria; third, hybrid sentencing theory that recognizes both retributive and crime control purposes; fourth, balance between the competing benefits of rules and discretion: rules promote uniformity and predictability; discretion promotes efficiency, flexibility, and case-specific justice; and fifth, recommended sentences that are informed by resource and demographic impact assessments. In many jurisdictions it will not be possible to implement all of these features (although a few state systems have), but the more of them a system has, the better.
- A recurring theme is the need to maintain workable and reasonable balances, not only in terms of commission makeup, and between conflicting sentencing purposes and between rules and discretion, but also between the powers and influence of the sentencing commission relative to the legislature and to judges, attorneys, and correctional authorities.
- Guidelines reformers have disagreed about a number of important policy issues. Some relate to coverage—which crimes and sentencing

issues should be regulated. Other issues relate to design—the necessary details that determine how the system actually works. There are good arguments on both sides of each of these contested issues. On some, one approach seems clearly preferable; on others, more research is needed.
- The preguidelines regime of unstructured, highly discretionary sentencing is unacceptable. Guidelines offer the only proven sentencing reform model.

The remainder of this essay is organized as follows. Section I surveys the wide variety of guidelines systems that currently exist in American jurisdictions, showing their similarities and differences with respect to major structural features and operation, identifying features recommended by the MPCS, and examining available data on the effects of guidelines on sentencing practices, inmate populations, and achievement of important reform and policy goals. Section II examines the most important policy issues raised by guidelines sentencing and seeks to identify issues on which there is, or should be, broad agreement and issues that are more contestable. Section III identifies priority issues for research, including development of better cross-jurisdictional measures and efforts to promote better understanding about how best to achieve widely shared sentencing reform goals. Section IV considers the future of guidelines sentencing.

I. Where, When, and What Kinds of Guidelines?

Several types of "structured" sentencing systems seek to reduce sentencing discretion and disparities (US Department of Justice 1996, 1998), and not all true guidelines are referred to as "guidelines."[4] For purposes of this essay a "sentencing guidelines" system is one with three features. First, judges are given a set of recommended sentences or sentence ranges for most types of crime or at least most felonies. Second, the guidelines are deemed to be appropriate in typical cases of that type (i.e., cases that do not present aggravating or mitigating factors that might permit departure from the recommendation). Third, they were developed by a legislatively created sentencing commission (regardless of whether the rules are embodied in

---

[4] For previous surveys of American guidelines systems, as of 2004 and 2012, see Frase (2005; 2013, chap. 3). See also Tonry (1988; 1996, esp. chaps. 2 and 3).

statutes, and even if the commission ceased to exist at some point after the guidelines went into effect).

This definition excludes legislatively drafted presumptive sentences set out in statutes like those that California and several other states adopted in the mid- to late 1970s.[5] Florida is a borderline case; its commission-drafted guidelines were replaced in 1998 with statutory presumptive minimum sentences (Griset 1999). I include it as a guidelines state because its current punishment code carries over elements of the former commission-drafted guidelines system. Massachusetts is another borderline case; it is included because, even though initial and revised commission-drafted guidelines have not received legislative approval (Robina Institute 2018), judges appear generally to follow the commission's recommended sentences. In effect, the commission's proposals are functioning like advisory guidelines (Massachusetts Sentencing Commission 2014, pp. 44–45). Finally, I include Ohio as a guidelines system since its entirely statutory recommended sentence system was developed by a sentencing commission, even though it lacks a feature found in all other systems that meet the definition: Ohio has nothing that could be called a criminal history score or scoring system (Griffin and Katz 2002; Robina Institute 2018).

A. Where and When

The 22 state and federal jurisdictions that have or once had sentencing guidelines under my definition are shown in table 1, listed in order of the initial effective dates of their commission-drafted guidelines, and also showing the years when the guidelines commission was in operation.[6]

---

[5] For further discussion of legislatively drafted presumptive sentence reforms, see Tonry (1988) and Frase (2013). Some researchers have classified Alaska as a "guidelines" system (National Center for State Courts 2008). I exclude Alaska because its statutory presumptive sentences were not developed by a commission (although they were later studied and endorsed by a short-lived sentencing commission); they were drafted by the legislature and supplemented with appellate case law that added additional presumptive sentences (Carnes 1993).

[6] Some of these states previously had guidelines drafted by courts or other agencies. Utah implemented statewide felony guidelines, written by judicial and correctional authorities, in 1979 (Oldroyd 1994), but in 1998 these were replaced with commission-drafted guidelines. Florida, Maryland, Michigan, and Virginia likewise had judicial guidelines that preceded their commission-drafted guidelines. Maryland considers its current guidelines system to have begun with the judicial guidelines that were implemented statewide, with legislative approval, in 1983. Florida had commission-drafted guidelines from 1983 to 1998, which were replaced with a statute that carried over some of the guidelines rules. Judicial guidelines in Michigan and Virginia were replaced by completely different commission-drafted guidelines. For further details on each of these systems, see Robina Institute (2018).

TABLE 1
Sentencing Guidelines Systems, Guidelines Commissions, and Model Codes and Standards Recommending Guidelines.

Agency or Jurisdiction	Guidelines Commissions: Years in Operation	(Commission's) Guidelines Initial Effective Dates
ABA Sentencing Standards, 2nd ed.		Approved: Aug. 1979
Minnesota	1978–	May 1980–
Pennsylvania	1978–	July 1982–
Maryland	1996–	July 1983–
Florida	1982–97	1983–98, 1998–
Washington	1981–	July 1984–
Wisconsin	1984–95, 2001–7	1985–95, 2003–7
Delaware	1984–	Oct. 1987–
Federal	1984–	Nov. 1987–
Oregon	1985–	Nov. 1989–
Tennessee	1986–95	Nov. 1989–
Louisiana	1987–95	1992–95
ABA Sentencing Standards, 3rd ed.		Approved: Feb. 1993
Kansas	1989–	July 1993–
Arkansas	1993–	Jan. 1994–
North Carolina	1990–	Oct. 1994–
Virginia	1994–	Jan. 1995–
Massachusetts	1994–	April 1996–
Ohio	1990–	July 1996–
Missouri	1993–2012	1997–2012
Michigan	1994–2002, 2015–	Jan. 1999–
Washington, DC	1998–	June 2004–
Alabama	2006–	Oct. 2006–
ALI Revised Model Penal Code		Sections approved: 2007, 2011, 2014, 2016, and 2017

SOURCE.—Robina Institute (2018).

These systems vary considerably; moreover, several have made significant changes over time. Some have expanded the scope of their guidelines. Delaware in 1990 eliminated parole release discretion; its guidelines now determine prison duration and prison commitment. Alabama in 2013 made some of its guidelines rules—those that apply to nonviolent crimes—legally binding rather than purely advisory. Other jurisdictions have gone in the opposite direction. Florida replaced the tops of its guidelines ranges with the almost-always-higher applicable statutory maximums. Ohio and Tennessee in 2006 made their legally binding guidelines mostly advisory, to avoid the increased constitutional requirements, under *Blakely v. Washington* (542 U.S. 296 [2004]), for proof of aggravating facts permitting upward departure from guidelines "typical-case" sentence recommendations. For the same reason, the US Supreme Court made the federal guidelines advisory, in *U.S. v. Booker* (543 U.S. 220 [2005]). Louisiana, Missouri, and Wisconsin completely abolished their guidelines; Wisconsin did it twice. Subtracting those three states leaves 19 state and federal jurisdictions that currently have a guidelines system meeting my definition.

Table 1 also shows when the American Bar Association (ABA) and the American Law Institute (ALI) adopted their recommendations in favor of commission-drafted guidelines. The second edition of the ABA's (1979) sentencing standards provided the rough outlines of a system of guidelines drafted by an agency independent of the legislature and located in the judicial branch. The third edition (ABA 1994) provided greater detail on the duties and organization of such an agency (and also provided alternative standards for an agency located within the legislature to perform that function). Further details, and a strong endorsement of the independent agency concept, are contained in the ALI's revised MPCS provisions; these were approved in five stages, beginning in 2007 and ending in 2017 with approval of the proposed final draft containing all of the revised code sentencing provisions (ALI 2017).

B. *Varieties of Guidelines*

State and federal guidelines systems display considerable structural variation on each of the dimensions discussed below. Except where otherwise noted, the sources for these summaries are jurisdiction-specific profiles and multijurisdiction overviews available from the University of Minnesota's Sentencing Guidelines Resource Center (Robina Institute 2018) or my compilation and interpretation of materials posted on the center's website.

1. *The Guidelines Commission.* These bodies vary in size, composition, duties, and policy-making powers relative to the legislature. The commissions currently in operation have between seven and 31 members, with an average of about 17 (Watts 2016). The membership always includes judges and usually includes defense and prosecution representatives. The federal commission is unusual in its small size (seven voting members) and composition: there is prosecution but not de-

fense representation. Other frequent membership categories include correctional officials, legislators, police officers, victim representatives, and other "public" members. A few commissions reserve a spot for an academic or other sentencing or correctional expert. In about a quarter of the systems, members are appointed solely by the executive (governor or president); the rest include judicial, legislative, or other appointing authorities. In addition to drafting, monitoring, and revising the guidelines, most commissions collect and analyze data on sentences imposed and use those data to project future prison populations (Frase 1995; Watts 2017). About half of the systems allow the commission's initial or amended guidelines to go into effect subject only to initial or later legislative override. The remainder require affirmative legislative enactment before any proposal or modified version can go into effect or require such approval within a limited period after the initial effective date (Mitchell 2017).

2. *Reform and Punishment Goals.* All guidelines seek to reduce sentencing discretion and its resulting disparities, but only a few systems explicitly define an underlying normative framework—disparity relative to what criteria? In particular, what punishment purposes and factors render two offenders "similarly situated" so that "disparity" exists if they receive different penalties?

Minnesota adopted a theory of "modified just deserts." Sentences are determined by a mix of retributive and crime control purposes. Both kinds of purposes determine typical-case recommendations on prison duration and whether the prison term will be immediately executed or suspended (the "disposition" decision).[7] Durational departures are governed solely by retributive values, while dispositional departures are based on crime control considerations (Frase 2013). Washington went further, giving greater emphasis to desert (Boerner and Lieb 2001, pp. 84–85).

Most guidelines systems pursue, and seek disparity reduction relative to, all traditional sentencing purposes. Sometimes they state that sentences should be uniform and proportionate relative to offense severity

---

[7] As noted below, Minnesota and a number of other guidelines systems deem an offender's desert to be enhanced in proportion to not only the seriousness of the conviction offense(s) but also the offender's prior conviction record. These systems thus allow the latter factor to increase the recommended prison duration (sometimes very substantially); prior record will also often make the difference between recommended prison and recommended probation.

and prior record, without specifying how each of those dimensions, and the particular scales employed, relates to punishment goals.[8] Minnesota and several other systems expressly endorse the principle of sentencing "parsimony": a penalty should be no more severe than is necessary to achieve its purposes adequately (see, e.g., MSGC 2018, sec. 1.A.5).

Another closely related question is whether the guidelines seek to encourage judges more consistently to apply existing sentencing norms ("descriptive" or "historical" guidelines) or whether the guidelines are intended to change some of those norms ("prescriptive" guidelines). Even systems of the first type, however, may recognize goals such as reduced racial disparity or the implementation of legislative mandates (such as the numerous congressional directives in the 1984 Sentencing Reform Act).[9] Even prescriptive guidelines such as those in Minnesota (which, like many guidelines reforms, sought to send more violent offenders to prison and fewer property offenders) are often heavily based on prior practice (sometimes pursuant to legislative directive).[10]

Many guidelines reforms have recognized the goals of managing prison and other correctional resources and avoiding prison overcrowding. Minnesota pioneered this approach, taking advantage of the greater uniformity and predictability of sentencing under guidelines, and a sentencing commission's capacity to collect and analyze detailed data on sentencing practices. The Minnesota legislature directed the new commission to "take into substantial consideration . . . existing correctional resources, including but not limited to the capacities of local and state correctional facilities."[11] The commission took this directive seriously and developed a prison bed

---

[8] See, e.g., Or. Admin. R. 213-002-001(d): "the appropriate punishment for a felony conviction should depend on the seriousness of the crime of conviction when compared to all other crimes and the offender's criminal history."

[9] See, e.g., 28 U.S.C. § 994(m) (2018): "The Commission shall insure that the guidelines reflect the fact that, in many cases, current sentences do not accurately reflect the seriousness of the offense." See also USSC (2016, sec. 5H1.10): race, sex, national origin, creed, religion, and socioeconomic status are "not relevant in the determination of a sentence."

[10] See, e.g., Minn. Laws 1978, c. 723, art. 1, § 9: commission "shall take into substantial consideration current sentencing and release practices."

[11] Minn. Laws 1978, c. 723, art. 1, § 9. However, in 1989 this provision was given reduced weight; the current version of the commission's mandate states that "in establishing and modifying the Sentencing Guidelines, the primary consideration of the commission shall be public safety. The commission shall also consider current sentencing and release practices; correctional resources, including but not limited to the capacities of local and state correctional facilities; and the long-term negative impact of the crime on the community" (Minn. Stat. § 244.09, subdiv. 5 [MSGC 2018]).

impact model, which it used to ensure that predicted prison populations would stay within 95 percent of existing and expected (already-funded) prison capacity (Parent 1988). In contrast, the next-oldest guidelines system, Pennsylvania's, did not recognize correctional resource management as a reform goal; its guidelines were expected to increase the prison population (Tonry 1996, p. 50). But almost all subsequent guidelines reforms have recognized the value of guidelines as a means of controlling prison growth and avoiding overcrowding (Watts 2017); that has sometimes been the primary goal in adopting guidelines (Frase 1995). The federal guidelines remain a notable exception, probably for two reasons: first, in contrast to most states, the federal budget need not be balanced, and deficit spending is the norm; second, even dramatically increased prison costs constitute a tiny fraction of the massive federal budget.

Although a number of guidelines systems (e.g., Alabama, Arkansas, Kansas, Minnesota) have recognized the goal of reducing racial and ethnic disparities in sentencing, a few systems have gone further to ensure that this goal is given serious consideration when guidelines and other sentencing rules are written or revised (Porter 2014). These jurisdictions have adapted their prison bed impact projection model so that it shows the predicted effects of proposed new or revised sentencing rules on racial and ethnic disparities among prison inmate populations. If a rule is found to increase disparity, its policy goals are scrutinized further and the rule might then be rejected or modified.

3. *Sentencing Decisions Covered by the Guidelines.* Some of the most basic differences among American guidelines systems relate to their scope. Most apply only to felony-level offenses; others also cover some or all misdemeanors. The federal guidelines cover the most serious (class A) misdemeanors, and in six states all non–petty misdemeanors are covered (Delaware, Maryland, Massachusetts, North Carolina, Pennsylvania, and Utah). I discuss other major differences in coverage below (whether judges retain their traditional unfettered discretion to choose between consecutive and concurrent sentencing of multiple conviction offenses; whether the guidelines regulate conditions of probation or other non-prison sanctions; and whether, because of abolition of parole release discretion, the guidelines govern both the imposition of active prison sentences and the duration of prison terms).

4. *Grids and Other Formats.* Most American guidelines systems employ one or more two-dimensional grids to summarize and present guidelines recommendations, with offense severity represented on the

vertical axis (grid rows) and prior record on the horizontal axis (grid columns).[12] The federal system and several states have a single grid. Nine jurisdictions have multiple grids (usually a "main" or "standard" grid, with separate ones for sex, drug, or other offenses). Alabama, Florida, and Virginia use worksheets rather than grids. Delaware and Ohio use neither grids nor worksheets. The Delaware guidelines provide typical-case sentence ranges for each felony and misdemeanor crime class and type (violent, nonviolent), with specified mitigations and aggravations (e.g., for acceptance of responsibility and prior convictions). Ohio statutes contain general standards to help judges decide between prison and probation and select a prison duration.

Among systems using grids, the formats vary considerably:[13]

- number of offense severity levels: most have about 10, but Tennessee has only five and the federal grid has 43;
- number of criminal history categories: most have five to seven, but Kansas, Oregon, and Washington have nine or 10;
- widths of grid cells: on some grids the cell ranges are very wide and overlap substantially, but on other grids the ranges are narrow and hardly overlap at all;
- use of a "disposition" line or other demarcation separating grid cells with recommended executed prison sentences from cells recommending probation: most grids have this kind of disposition zone structure, but some have "border boxes" or entire grid zones in which judges may, without departure, select from two or more disposition options such as prison, more intensive probation, or less intensive probation; and
- display of separate aggravated or mitigated prison duration ranges: most grids do not have such separate ranges.

Another basic difference between grids relates to the meaning of the prison-duration numbers on the grid (almost always shown in months). In most systems these numbers, and any higher or lower numbers chosen

---

[12] Utah is the sole exception: on its grids, criminal history categories define the grid rows, and offense severity defines grid columns. For further details, see Watts (2018*a*).

[13] There are also purely visual differences in the order of offense severity levels and criminal history categories. On most grids the highest-severity offenses are on the top row of the grid and the highest criminal history category is the far-right column.

by judges in case of departure, are the maximum prison terms offenders will serve in prison, subject to reduction by good conduct credits, discretionary parole release if that was retained, or both. In Michigan, North Carolina, and Pennsylvania the numbers on the grid, or terms chosen by judges, represent minimum terms of imprisonment, which assume that offenders will receive all available good-conduct credits or be paroled at the earliest allowable time. In these systems, the maximum prison term is then determined by other rules or by a formula (e.g., in North Carolina the maximum term for less serious felonies is 120 percent of the minimum term).

The numbers shown on guidelines grids also vary in how recommended terms of imprisonment relate to statutory maximum and minimum prison terms. In most systems the longest recommended prison term for offenders in the highest criminal history category is lower than the statutory maximum for most or all of the applicable offenses;[14] longer prison terms may be imposed by means of an upward durational departure. In a few state systems, the tops of the ranges in each grid cell replace previous statutory maximums. In North Carolina the maximum for each grid cell is the number shown as the top of the "aggravated range." In Kansas upward durational departures cannot exceed twice the top of the range for that cell. State systems sometimes take statutory minimum terms into account when setting guidelines sentences, but more often the guidelines were determined independently (and are overridden if a longer statutory minimum applies). In contrast, the federal commission took a consistently more punitive approach: recommended guidelines sentences are always equal to or greater than any applicable or related mandatory minimum (Tonry 1996, pp. 96–98; Hofer 2019).

5. *Uncharged and Unconvicted Offenses.* In all state guidelines systems, the recommended sentence and almost all recognized grounds for departure are based on the offense or offenses of which the offender was convicted (along with his or her criminal history). The federal guidelines are unique in permitting crimes that did not result in conviction (because they were dismissed, acquitted, or never charged) to enhance recommended sentences and justify upward departures.[15]

---

[14] However, in some systems (e.g., District of Columbia, Florida, and Tennessee) the tops of the ranges for highest-history offenders are equal to the statutory maximum.

[15] See USSC (2016, sec. 1B1.3): definition of "relevant conduct" that may be considered when calculating the recommended guidelines sentence, or when departing from that sen-

6. *Criminal History.* Some of the most important differences among guidelines systems concern prior convictions and other aspects of an offender's criminal history.[16] Most systems have a separate criminal history score that forms one axis of the guidelines grid or grids (almost always the horizontal axis defining grid columns); in nongrid systems, prior record factors add points on one or more worksheets that determine the form and severity of the recommended sentence. Some grid-based systems use a categorical rather than a points-based system. For example, Kansas places offenders with three or more prior violent felonies in the highest criminal history category (A); those with a single prior violent felony go in a midlevel category (D); category E is for offenders with three nonviolent prior felonies and no violent felonies; offenders with only misdemeanors or no prior convictions are placed in the lowest category (I).

Criminal history scores and worksheet point systems vary in the kinds of prior convictions and other components that are counted, how they are weighted, and how strongly they affect recommended sentences. These differences do not seem to be explained by differing views about punishment purposes. A few systems explicitly justify such enhancements on the basis of the assumed higher culpability or higher recidivism risk of repeat offenders. Most seem simply to have assumed that prior record is an "obviously" relevant sentencing factor (Roberts 2015*b*), basing criminal history scoring and weighting on rough, "back-of-the-envelope" calculations (Tonry 2010, p. 93) or on prior record factors that judges in the jurisdiction traditionally considered (see, e.g., Parent 1988). The culpability-based (retributive, just deserts) rationale is highly contested by punishment theorists (Roberts and von Hirsch 2010; Frase and Roberts, forthcoming, chap. 1). And although there are abundant data showing that, in general, an offender's risk of recidivism is correlated with the extent of his or her prior record, the strength of that relationship depends on many factors. Very few guidelines systems have attempted to validate the risk-predictive

---

tence. Although most state guidelines allow upward departures to be based on aggravating facts of the conviction offense(s) that were not proven or admitted by the defendant, such facts only occasionally (e.g., weapon use, victim injury) increase the ordinary-case recommended sentence. State systems rarely permit aggravating facts based on nonconviction offenses to serve as grounds for departure and almost never allow them to increase the recommended sentence.

[16] For a survey of 18 state and federal guidelines systems that use some form of overall criminal history score or point system, see Frase et al. (2015). For further discussion of the rationales for criminal history enhancements, their intended and unintended effects, and the most important needed reforms, see Hester et al. (2018) and Frase and Roberts (forthcoming).

accuracy of their criminal history scores and score components (Frase and Roberts, forthcoming, chap. 2).

All guidelines systems count prior adult felony convictions, and almost all include at least some prior misdemeanor convictions and juvenile court adjudications (Frase et al. 2015). The latter are often further limited in various ways (e.g., by counting only juvenile offenses committed after age 14 or that are felony-level or counting only qualifying adjudications if the current [adult] offense was committed prior to age 25). Prior adult misdemeanors usually exclude traffic offenses and may be limited only to designated crimes or the highest misdemeanor class. About two-thirds of the systems include "custody status" (the offender was on probation, parole, or certain other forms of criminal justice supervision, or was in jail or prison, when he or she committed the offense being sentenced).[17]

Almost all point-based systems use some sort of weighting formula that counts prior felonies more heavily than misdemeanors and juvenile adjudications (Hester et al. 2018). Many point systems further limit the weight of misdemeanor and juvenile priors by means of caps on the maximum number of points each can contribute to the total score (Mitchell 2015*a*, 2015*b*). Almost all systems weight prior felonies according to their seriousness (the federal system weights according to prior sentences imposed); the weights used are quite varied (Hester 2015). On average, a single prior felony moves the offender about one-third of the way across the sentencing grid. In some systems a single serious felony can move the offender two-thirds or even three-quarters of the way across. However, about half of the systems limit eligibility for the highest criminal history categories to offenders with one or several prior violent or high-severity felonies. In these systems, nonviolent or low-severity felonies, no matter how many, can move the offender only about halfway across the grid.

Many systems stop counting very old priors at some point; most such "look-back" limits are stricter (shorter) for prior misdemeanors and juvenile adjudications. Some systems employ unconditional look-back limits based solely on the passage of time, while other systems use "gap" rules requiring that the offender have remained crime-free for a specified pe-

---

[17] Several other states include custody status not as a criminal history score component, but as a recognized aggravating factor that courts may consider (Roberts 2015*a*). A few systems also count whether the offender has ever violated the terms of community release or has ever had release revoked (see, e.g., Maryland State Commission on Criminal Sentencing Policy 2018, p. 30).

riod.[18] However, more than half of systems count all or at least the most serious prior felonies for the remainder of the offender's life, despite evidence showing that very old convictions, and advancing age, are associated with lower recidivism risk (Frase and Roberts, forthcoming, chap. 3). Even when a prior conviction is subject to a look-back limit, the period is typically 10 or 15 years, and the "clock" usually does not begin to run until a date long after the prior conviction was entered (e.g., when the offender is discharged from probation, released from prison, or discharged from postprison supervision). Thus, a 15-year limit can easily count convictions 20 or 25 years old.

A high criminal history score, category, or point total can have a dramatic effect on the form and severity of an offender's recommended sentence. As to form, on most guidelines grids offenders convicted of medium- or low-severity offenses are recommended for community-based sanctions if they have little or no prior record; a more substantial record pushes them across the grid into cells that recommend an executed prison sentence. Since a high proportion of offenders are convicted at lower offense severity levels and often have substantial prior records, many prison commitments result from criminal history, not offense severity (in Washington, e.g., over one-third of convicted offenders have recommended prison sentences for this reason; Frase, Roberts, and Hester, forthcoming *c*).

Criminal history also dramatically increases the length of recommended custody sentences. On average, across American guidelines systems, the recommended custody sentence in the highest criminal history category is six times longer than in the lowest, and in some guidelines states the highest-history/lowest-history ratio is over 10. These substantial enhancements greatly increase the size and expense of prison populations (Frase, Roberts, and Hester, forthcoming *b*). They also have other undesirable consequences. They make sentences less proportional to the conviction offense. They distort prison use priorities by sending many nonviolent offenders to prison (since those offenders tend to have higher criminal history scores). They increase the number of aging, low-risk but high-cost prison inmates (since, especially with lax or no look-back limits, older offenders tend to have higher history scores). They increase racial disproportionality (since black and Native American offenders usually have

---

[18] Recent-gap rules require that there have been no convictions in the period immediately before the current offense, whereas any-gap rules give offenders credit for earlier crime-free periods. For further discussion of look-back rules, see Frase and Roberts (forthcoming, chap. 9).

higher history scores). All of these effects may increase over time as a result of rising criminal history scores.[19]

7. *Other Offense- or Offender-Based Guidelines Criteria.* Many systems enhance penalties for certain crimes because of similarity between the current and prior offenses, but no system applies such a "patterning" rule across the board (Roberts 2015c). Perhaps surprisingly, no system takes into account whether the offender's past and current crimes show a trend toward increasing or decreasing severity. Perhaps most surprising of all, very few systems factor in the offender's current age or other known risk and protective factors. The two systems that make the most use of such risk factors consider them only as an adjustment after the recommended sentence has been determined on the basis of current offense severity and prior record (Virginia Criminal Sentencing Commission 2018) or as a screening tool to identify offenders in need of additional offender-specific risk and needs assessment (Pennsylvania Commission on Sentencing 2018).[20]

8. *Multiple Current Offenses.* Sentencing theorists and policy makers have traditionally focused on individual offenders being sentenced for a single crime, but many offenders are sentenced for multiple crimes. Such crimes can be multiple counts in a single case or convictions entered in two or more cases sentenced at about the same time. Similar issues can arise when the offender about to be sentenced is already serving a sentence for a prior crime (Frase 2018a; see, generally, Ryberg, Roberts, and de Keijser [2018]). Traditionally, this problem was dealt with by giving judges total discretion to sentence multiple crimes fully concurrently, fully consecutively, or partially consecutively. About two-thirds of guidelines systems take this approach (Frase 2015a, table 10.2). The remaining systems make concurrent sentencing presumptive for many if not most cases; however, these systems also recognize "concurrent-plus" options, including the following (Frase 2018a, pp. 205–7):

- multiple crimes involving similar, "addable" harm amounts (dollar losses to victims; quantity of drugs or other contraband) are deemed to be "one big crime";

---

[19] See, e.g., MSGC (2017, table 10), reporting substantial declines in the proportion of offenders with zero history and substantial increases for the highest scores.

[20] Some state systems, by either case law or guidelines provisions, allow courts to depart downward from a recommended prison sentence on the basis of a finding of the offender's particular amenability to probation or unamenability to prison or to depart upward on the basis of the offender's unamenability to probation (Frase and Roberts, forthcoming, chap. 3).

- multiple closely related crimes are treated as aggravating factors for the most serious of the crimes;
- multiple counts are included when computing the criminal history score applied to some or all current offenses; or
- additional counts increase recommended sentence severity according to other formulas (e.g., under the federal guidelines, multiple counts can cause offense severity to be increased by up to five levels).

9. *Suspended Sentences and Other Ways of Structuring Nonprison Sanctions.* Most American guidelines systems impose probation and other community-based felony sentences as conditions of a suspended prison sentence (Frase 2018*b*). Some require the court to first pronounce a prison sentence and then suspend its execution. In others, community-based sentences can be imposed only when the court suspends imposition of sentence (in effect, deferring completion of the sentencing process). In a third group, a community sentence can be a condition of either a suspended-execution prison sentence (SEPS) or an order suspending imposition of sentence (SIS). A few states (e.g., Oregon and Washington) often impose community sanctions as stand-alone penalties rather than as conditions of either kind of suspended sentence.[21]

Each approach employs a different set of procedures to sanction violations of the conditions of release.[22] Under the SEPS option, the suspended prison term may be executed as a sanction for violation, with minimal hearing and fact-finding safeguards. If a sentencing court invokes the SIS option and later wishes to use imprisonment to sanction violations of release conditions, it must hold a standard sentencing hearing, with all of the procedural requirements and sentencing alternatives that would apply if a hearing had been held when the community sanction was imposed. When probation or other nonprison penalties are imposed as stand-alone penalties, not as conditions of a SEPS or SIS suspended sentence, prison is usually not available as a sanction for violation of release conditions. Violations are sanctioned by short jail terms,

---

[21] Although Washington purported to abolish suspended sentences as part of its guidelines reform, formal SEPS or de facto SIS were retained for certain groups of offenders (Frase 2013, chap. 3).

[22] For further discussion of the advantages and disadvantages of the probation-structure approaches described in the text, see Frase (2018*b*).

home detention, increased release conditions, or other community-based alternatives.[23]

Regardless of the form in which community-based sanctions are imposed, however, judges in all guidelines systems retain broad or even total discretion when deciding whether to revoke release and in choosing among available sanctions for violations of release conditions.

10. *Conditions of Nonprison Sentences.* Most guidelines rules focus on prison commitment and prison duration and provide little or no guidance or structure concerning conditions of community-based sentences. Systems that attempt to regulate such sentences usually do so in one of two ways:[24] by defining two or more broad levels of sanction intensity that may be imposed for different groups of offenders or by providing a maximum or a permitted range of local jail custody, with rules translating nonjail community penalties into jail days. North Carolina and Pennsylvania use the first of these approaches: in grid cells in which prison is not the sole recommended sentence, judges may choose from one or more sanction types: intensive community sanctions, less restrictive sanctions, or in some grid cells, either.[25] Oregon and Washington use the second approach. Each nonprison cell on the Oregon grid contains two numbers: the maximum number of jail days allowed without departure and the maximum number of sanction units (including any jail days imposed, as well as units contributed by other community sanctions that the judge has imposed). The Washington grid provides a custody range in every cell, but some ranges call for durations (a year or less) that would be served in a local jail. In addition, "alternative conversion" formulas permit some or all of the required jail time to be converted into work release, part-time custody, home detention, community service, a fine, or a combination.

11. *Departures.* Some states (e.g., Pennsylvania, Utah, Virginia) have no stated standard that judges must meet before departing from recom-

---

[23] Five guidelines systems strongly discourage the use of prison as a sanction for probation violations. Oregon and Washington often impose stand-alone probation orders, with designated jail sanctions for violations and no option of revoking a suspended sentence. North Carolina, Utah, and the federal system retain the revocation option but discourage its use; probation is combined with a suspended sentence, which could be revoked, but courts are encouraged (and for some violations are required) to use shorter custodial backup sanctions.

[24] For further discussion, see Frase (2013, chap. 3) and Robina Institute (2018; North Carolina, Oregon, Pennsylvania, and Washington "profiles").

[25] In some of these cells, judges also have the option of imposing a prison sentence.

mended guidelines sentences. When a standard is stated, it sometimes requires only that the case be "atypical" (Arkansas Sentencing Commission 2018, p. 1) or that there are "aggravating" or "mitigating" circumstances (Mass. Gen. Laws ch. 211E, § 3(a)(2) [2018]). However, a number of states adhere to a stricter standard, requiring the presence of "substantial and compelling" circumstances (e.g., Delaware, Minnesota, and Washington; Robina Institute 2018).

The departure standard under the federal guidelines requires that the case involve aggravating or mitigating circumstances "of a kind, or to a degree, not adequately taken into consideration by the sentencing commission in formulating the guidelines" (USSC 2016, § 5K2.0). Given the extremely detailed nature of the federal guidelines, this standard strongly discouraged departures in the pre-*Booker* period when the guidelines were legally binding. The pre-*Booker* guidelines were also very strict with respect to mitigation based on offender cooperation. Offenders who show "acceptance of responsibility" (almost always in the form of a guilty plea) may receive at most a three-level reduction in their offense severity level, on a grid that contains 43 levels (§ 3E). Offenders who provide "substantial assistance" to law enforcement can receive sentence mitigation only upon a motion by the government (§ 5K1). In all of these ways, the federal guidelines (especially pre-*Booker*) strike a balance too heavily weighted toward commission or prosecution power, at the expense of judges and defense attorneys.

The varying departure standards reflect differing views about how much discretion trial judges should have and about which sentencing purposes should be considered or given priority.

Most systems provide lists of allowed grounds for departure and sometimes lists of forbidden criteria (especially race, gender, and family or socioeconomic status). The allowed grounds tend to focus on factors that make the conviction offense more or less serious than a typical case, which implies a preference for retributive punishment goals. But in a number of states, the lists include offender factors such as amenability to supervision or treatment that are more relevant to risk-based, crime prevention goals.[26] And even in states that give strong emphasis to

---

[26] In North Carolina, listed mitigating factors include defendant supports his or her family; defendant has a support system in the community; defendant has a positive employment history or is gainfully employed; and defendant "has a good treatment prognosis and a workable treatment plan is available" (N.C. Gen. Stat. § 15A-1340.16(e) [2013]). In

retributive goals, both in general and in lists of departure factors, courts have sometimes recognized nonretributive, offender-based departure grounds such as "particular amenability to probation."[27]

Only a few systems expressly give courts power to depart based on atypical aspects of the offender's prior record.[28] This is surprising, given the universal endorsement of departures based on atypical aspects of the conviction offense (and the fact that offense and prior record are the two primary determinants of recommended sentences). Finally, some guidelines systems have special rules that expand departure powers (e.g., by providing that certain deviations are not deemed departures) or that limit departure powers (e.g., by providing that upward durational departures, except in very unusual cases, cannot exceed twice the recommended prison term for a typical case).

Utah, the listed aggravating circumstances include "previous willful inability to comply in less restrictive setting ... willful failure to attend or to participate in appropriate educational, vocational, or treatment programs ... willful failure to obtain and/or maintain verifiable lawful employment ... [and] regular association with individuals engaged in criminal or unlawful behavior"; listed mitigating circumstances include that the offender "has demonstrated compliance with all pretrial conditions ... is engaged in community based supervision and/or treatment services consistent with a validated risk and needs assessment ... his current living environment is stable and supportive of offense specific interventions which do not enable continued criminal or unlawful conduct ... is engaged in positive, supportive, pro-social relationships ... is engaged in positive, supportive, pro-social community activities ... [and] has implemented positive educational or employment plans" (Utah Sentencing Commission 2017, p. 31). See also Ohio Rev. Stat. § 2929.12 (D): list of factors "indicating that the offender is likely to commit future crimes" includes the following: that the offender "has not responded favorably" to prior juvenile court adjudications or adult court sanctions and that the offenders has shown "a pattern of drug or alcohol abuse that is related to the offense" and refuses to acknowledge the pattern, or refuses to accept treatment for it.

[27] The Minnesota case law allowing "amenability" and "unamenability" departures is summarized in Frase (2005). Such departures have also been recognized by courts in Kansas (Frase 2013, chap. 3).

[28] The federal guidelines' "inadequacy of criminal history" provision permits departure up or down if the offender's criminal history score "substantially" understates or overstates "the seriousness of the defendant's criminal history or the likelihood that the defendant will commit other crimes" (USSC 2016, secs. 4A1.3(a)(1) and 4A1.3(b)(1)). Three states authorize adjustments in one direction only. Washington permits upward departure if the omission of certain prior crimes from the offender's criminal history score yields a recommended sentence that is "clearly too lenient" (Wash. Rev. Code §§ 9.94A.535(2)(b)–(d) 2013). A similar Pennsylvania provision, Adequacy of the Prior Record Score, permits the sentencing court to consider prior convictions and juvenile adjudications or dispositions that were not counted in the calculation of the score (204 Pa. Code § 303.5(d)). Minnesota permits downward departure where the offender's prior convictions were all entered in a single court appearance (medium-low current offense severity) or in one or two court appearances (low offense severity; MSGC 2018, sec. 2.D.3.a(4)).

12. *Degree to Which the Guidelines Are Legally Binding and Available Enforcement Methods.* It is sometimes said that guidelines are either "mandatory" or "advisory" (see, e.g., *U.S. v. Booker* [543 U.S. at 233]), but these terms are misleading. Very few guidelines rules are "mandatory" in the way in which a mandatory minimum sentence statute is (judges can depart from guidelines), nor are there two homogeneous types of guidelines. The degree of binding force is best seen as a continuum, not a simple mandatory-advisory dichotomy. It is better to ask about the degree to which a given system's typical-case recommendations and departure standards are formally or in practice legally binding on judges. Relevant factors include the extent to which they are enforced by active appellate review, procedural requirements to state reasons for departure, and other factors tending to encourage compliance.

Legally binding systems with active appellate review, generating a large body of appellate case law, are found in Kansas, Minnesota, Oregon, and Washington. The guidelines recommendations in these states, however, are only presumptive, not mandatory; trial courts retain considerable discretion as to both the type and the severity of sanctions. Appellate review does not appear to have unduly limited trial court discretion.[29]

At the other end of the continuum are systems in which the guidelines recommendations and departure standards are purely advisory (at least as a formal matter), allowing judges to ignore the recommendations and impose any sentence up to the statutory maximum for that offense (and at or above the statutory minimum, if any). Examples of jurisdictions following this model include Arkansas, Delaware, the District of Columbia, Maryland, Massachusetts, Utah, and Virginia. The guidelines in these systems are described as "voluntary" or "advisory," and departures are not subject to appeal.

Numerous variations lie between these polar extremes (for further details, see Frase [2015*b*]). Some purely advisory systems have features that encourage judges to follow the guidelines. These include informal peer or political pressure generated by publication of judge-specific departure rates or by location in a small, geographically concentrated jurisdiction where judges are well known to each other (Ulmer 2019). Conversely, some legally binding guidelines leave judges with very broad or even

---

[29] Reitz (1997, pp. 1458–71) compares appellate review of sentences in the Minnesota, Pennsylvania, and federal guidelines systems.

complete discretion in certain respects, thus functioning, in those contexts, more like an advisory system.

13. *Prison Release and Postprison Supervision.* Eleven guidelines jurisdictions (Delaware, District of Columbia, Florida, Kansas, Minnesota, North Carolina, Ohio, Oregon, Virginia, US federal courts, and Washington) have abolished parole release discretion for all or most offenders (Robina Institute 2018). Inmates serve the entire executed prison term subject only to reduction for good conduct (which usually includes completion of in-prison programming and compliance with disciplinary rules). Eight guidelines states (Alabama, Arkansas, Maryland, Massachusetts, Michigan, Pennsylvania, Tennessee, and Utah) retain discretionary parole release for most offenders serving felony sentences. Five of those states (all but Arkansas, Massachusetts, and Tennessee) use or are in the process of developing parole release guidelines (Watts 2018*b*).

In parole abolition systems, good-time reductions vary from as little as 15 percent (e.g., the federal system and the District of Columbia) to as much as 50 percent for some offenders (e.g., Washington); in many states it is 33 percent. In these systems, most offenders spend some time under postrelease, parole-like supervision. Some abolition states (e.g., Minnesota) retain the traditional parole-based rule that both the period of supervision and the possible prison term if release is revoked are equal to the remaining unserved prison sentence (i.e., the amount of good-conduct credit). In the federal system and several states (e.g., Washington, Oregon, and Kansas) periods of postprison supervision and allowable custody terms in case of revocation are independent of the prison sentence and usually depend on the seriousness of the offense. In North Carolina, postprison supervision periods are quite short, in comparison to traditional parole terms: either 9 or 12 months, depending on the offense severity level (Robina Institute 2018).

As with probation, few guidelines rules limit the conditions of postprison supervision. Almost no rules regulate decisions to revoke release or impose other sanctions for violations of release conditions.

C. *Summary: Major Similarities and Differences*

The preceding summary reveals a number of similarities and differences in guidelines systems. Some features (e.g., identifying management of prison resources as a goal) are found in almost all. However, state systems differ from each other in important ways (e.g., in the extent to which prison bed or other resource-impact assessments are used to shape guidelines rules, not just to warn of overcrowding after the rules are written without regard to resource impact). The differences between the federal system and most state systems are even greater (e.g., enhancement of recommended sentence severity based on unconvicted offenses).

D. Major Features of State Guidelines Reforms Embodied in Model Rules and Standards

Several model codes and standards have endorsed the concept of sentencing guidelines drafted and monitored by an independent sentencing commission. The MPCS is the most detailed proposal (ALI 2017; Robina Institute 2018). The MPCS includes features found in well-developed state guidelines systems and some added features not found in any current system. Those modeled on state systems suggest a degree of consensus on some sentencing policy issues, at least among practitioners and scholars most interested in sentencing policy. The added features are worthy of serious consideration, debate, and further research.

1. *MPCS Features Found in Well-Developed State Guidelines Systems.* The sentencing commission proposed by MPCS is a permanent, broadly representative body charged with drafting and monitoring guidelines, conducting research, and maintaining data on sentencing. Impact assessments are required when drafting or modifying guidelines rules and to periodically assess operations of existing rules; these assessments include fiscal impacts and effects on racial and ethnic disproportionality in prison populations. The MPCS expressly adopts a hybrid, limiting retributive sentencing theory. The offender's deserved punishment sets upper and lower limits on penalty severity, within which crime control purposes are pursued "when reasonably feasible." A general principle of parsimony directs that the sentence be "no more severe than necessary to achieve the applicable purposes [of punishment]" (ALI 2017, sec. 1.02(2)(a)).

The proposed guidelines cover all crimes, including misdemeanors. Limits are placed on criminal history enhancements and consecutive sentencing of multiple current offenses. The use at sentencing of validated risk assessment instruments is encouraged. Probation, fines, and other nonprison sanctions can be imposed as stand-alone penalties, without being a condition of a suspended execution or suspended imposition sentence. Recommended sentences are legally binding, not purely advisory. Departure sentences are subject to a moderate degree of appellate review;

nondeparture sentences are subject to discretionary review. Parole release discretion is abolished, but inmates may reduce their prison terms by up to 15 percent for good conduct and another 15 percent for program participation. Most released inmates are subject to a period of postprison supervision; the period of supervision and the permissible revocation sanction for violation of release conditions do not depend on the remaining unserved prison term.

2. *MPCS Features Not Found in Existing Guidelines Systems.* Suggested guidelines rules or principles for legislation to authorize such rules are provided for a number of matters not regulated by any existing system: adult court sentencing of crimes committed when the offender was a juvenile; forfeitures, restitution, and other onerous economic sanctions; pretrial diversion (deferred prosecution or deferred adjudication); and collateral consequences of conviction. Appellate courts are authorized to reverse disproportionately severe sentences, even if the sentence does not exceed constitutional proportionality limits. Mandatory minimum sentences are strongly discouraged, and where they still apply, trial courts may depart below the minimum in exceptional cases. There are multiple "second-look" sentencing provisions, permitting release from prison or reduction of the term (including mandatory terms) based on age or infirmity, other changed circumstances, or overcrowding of prison, jail, or supervision populations. The commission is directed to conduct an omnibus review of how the guidelines are working; the suggested frequency is every 10 years.

E. Effects of Guidelines Reforms

How well have guidelines achieved their goals? In particular, have sentencing disparities—the original impetus for structured sentencing reforms—been reduced? And since almost all guidelines systems originally or eventually identified correctional resource management as a reform goal, have those systems had slower rates of growth in prison populations, with fewer problems of prison overcrowding?

1. *Disparity Reduction.* Answering this question is very difficult, for a variety of reasons. First, one would need to compare sentencing before and after implementation of the guidelines (while attempting to control for other changes in the system), but preguidelines data are usually not available. In the few cases in which they are, researchers have generally

concluded that disparities were reduced, at least in state guidelines systems (see, e.g., Miethe and Moore 1985; Tonry 1996). Second, most evaluations of pre- versus postguidelines sentencing have measured disparity by examining compliance and departure rates relative to the guidelines definitions of factors (primarily guidelines offense severity ranking and prior record score) that are deemed to render two offenders "similarly situated." That baseline, however, biases the comparison in favor of finding "success" in disparity reduction; preguidelines sentencing might very well have been just as consistent relative to the accepted, highly offender-based criteria of that time (Doob 1995; Tonry 1996). Third, almost all pre- and postguidelines comparisons are based on the offense of conviction, even though it might be expected—and in many systems has been clearly documented—that prosecution charging and plea bargaining practices changed under the guidelines (Frase 1993; Tonry 1996). Where "real offense" data are available, they tend to show a lesser degree of "improvement" in disparity reduction (again, measured relative to guidelines criteria) than appears when pre- and postguidelines disparity are examined relative to conviction offenses (Frase 1993).

Finally, measures of disparity and disparity reduction based on rates of compliance with the guidelines are very difficult to compare across jurisdictions, because of substantial variations in what crimes are covered by the guidelines and, even more importantly, what qualifies as a "departure" (Tonry 1996). Guidelines grids and worksheets vary substantially in how wide a range is provided, for each grid cell or other offense/offender group, within which judges may sentence without departing. Moreover, some guidelines use border boxes and other special rules that either give judges multiple dispositional options (prison, intensive probation, regular probation) or define certain deviations from guidelines recommendation as nondepartures. For example, Washington has a "first-offender waiver" provision and several other options for mitigation without formally departing; if those mitigations were treated as departures, departure rates would be higher. A further problem with cross-jurisdictional comparisons results from the very different approaches jurisdictions have taken when designing their guidelines. A system in which the guidelines seek to model prior sentencing and parole-release practices (descriptive or historical guidelines) would be expected to have higher compliance rates than a system in which the guidelines seek to change prior practice (prescriptive guidelines).

Subject to the major caveats just stated, here are some illustrative recent data on compliance rates (showing the year the cases were sentenced in brackets):[30]

- District of Columbia [2017] (District of Columbia Sentencing Commission 2018, pp. 40–52): 97.2 percent of sentenced felony counts were "compliant" (including 2.4 percent that were plea-agreed sentences, some of which would otherwise have been departures, 0.7 percent that were deemed compliant because sentenced concurrently with another count receiving an equal or longer sentence, and 1.5 percent that were deemed "compliant departures" because the court stated listed aggravating or mitigating factors).
- Federal courts [fiscal year (FY) 2017] (USSC 2018, table N): 49.1 percent of sentences were "within" the guidelines; that is, they were neither departures under guidelines rules nor "variances" permitted by the *Booker* decision rendering the guidelines "advisory." However, some of the not-within sentences are required by statutory mandatory minimums that are higher than the top of the guidelines range (Hofer 2019); and more than one-sixth of the not-within sentences were entered under a special mitigation rule applicable to "early disposition" programs that are designed to expedite guilty pleas in nonserious immigration cases.
- Kansas [FY 2017] (Kansas Sentencing Commission 2018, p. 65): 79.1 percent of cases had no departure as to either prison disposition or prison duration, including 14.1 percent that were sentenced within a "border box" permitting either prison or a nonprison sentence.
- Minnesota [2016] (MSGC 2017, p. 23): 74 percent of cases had no departure as to either prison disposition or prison duration.
- Pennsylvania [2016] (Pennsylvania Commission on Sentencing 2017, p. 41): 89 percent of cases were deemed to be in "conformity" with the guidelines and not "departures," including 6 percent sentenced in the "aggravated" sentencing range and 8 percent sentenced in the "mitigated" range; excluding the latter two groups, 75 percent of cases were sentenced within the "standard" sentencing ranges shown on the

---

[30] For an earlier review of compliance rates in several guidelines systems, see Tonry (1996, pp. 33–39).

guidelines grids (all of these figures include misdemeanor crimes, which have higher compliance rates than felonies [Tonry 1996]).[31]
- Virginia [FY 2017] (Virginia Criminal Sentencing Commission 2017, p. 12): 81.2 percent of sentences were in compliance with the guidelines as to both prison disposition and duration (including, as compliant, variances based on the commission's validated risk assessment tools or statutory diversion options, sentences within 5 percent of the recommended duration, and sentences to time served in pretrial detention where the guidelines call for probation).
- Washington [FY 2017] (Washington State Caseload Forecast Council 2018, p. 33): 94.8 percent of sentences were within the standard range or were outside that range but not defined as "departures" (81 percent were within the standard range).

Note that adjusted compliance rates (excluding cases that would be counted as departures in other systems) are not consistently higher in the three jurisdictions with legally binding guidelines and frequent appellate review (Kansas, Minnesota, and Washington) than they are in the four systems with advisory or only loosely binding guidelines (District of Columbia, federal, Pennsylvania, and Virginia). The highest and lowest adjusted compliance rates are found in advisory guidelines systems. The District of Columbia, with the highest compliance rates, has descriptive guidelines (based on prior practice), very wide grid cell ranges, and a relatively small and geographically concentrated judiciary. The lowest compliance rate is in the federal system, whose guidelines have probably been more unpopular with judges than guidelines in any other jurisdiction.

2. *Prison Population Growth.* All US jurisdictions experienced substantial increases in prison populations and incarceration rates from the early 1970s until at least the mid-2000s. Several studies have found that states with sentencing guidelines, especially those that also abolished

---

[31] Although the Pennsylvania guidelines apply to most nontraffic misdemeanors, misdemeanors of the first and second class carry maximum penalties of more than 1 year, which would be considered a felony penalty in most other states. However, third-degree misdemeanors (maximum penalty: 1 year) are comparable to misdemeanors in other states; these crimes (ranked at the lowest severity level, Offense Gravity Score = 1) constituted 29 percent of cases sentenced under the guidelines in 2016, and they had a "conformity" rate of 97 percent (Pennsylvania Commission on Sentencing 2017, p. 83). Excluding these cases, the overall conformity rate falls from 89 percent to 86 percent (data on the use of the aggravated and mitigated sentencing ranges are not reported by offense severity level).

parole release discretion, had slower rates of growth (Reitz 2011, pp. 154–55). Reitz reports that from the year in which each state abolished parole discretion, through 2009, all nine states with parole-abolition guidelines had slower-than-average rates of prison growth than the average for all states during the same periods (p. 153);[32] if the federal system is included, all 10 parole-abolition guidelines systems had slower-than-average growth.[33]

Of course, this was not a controlled experiment. Jurisdictions were not randomly assigned to the parole-abolition-guidelines "treatment" group. Other features of many of those guidelines systems—including the same good-government concerns that led to adoption of parole-abolition guidelines—may have contributed to slower prison growth (Zimring 2005, pp. 336–37).

Another potential problem with the 10-out-of-10 finding reported above is that it is based on comparison of absolute increases in the number of prisoners per capita (per 100,000 population). On this basis prison growth in Minnesota, for example, is much less than all-states growth; from 1980 to 2009 Minnesota's per capita rate rose by 141 (from 49 to 190), while the all-states rate grew by 314 (from 129 to 443; Carson 2018). But prison growth can also be measured in relative or percentage terms (see, e.g., Zimring 2010; Pew Charitable Trusts 2018). In other contexts, especially when comparing jurisdictions, growth over time is usually expressed in percentage terms. We usually say that the murder rate in city X increased by 10 percent, while the rate increased by 5 percent in city Y. We do not say that the rate increased by two murders per 100,000 residents in city X and three murders per 100,000 residents in city Y.

Comparing prison growth in percentage terms can yield quite different results. Minnesota's prison rate increased by 288 percent: its 2009 rate was 3.88 times its 1980 rate. That percentage increase was a bit higher than the 243 percent growth in all states during these years.

For some purposes it makes sense to measure prison growth in per capita units, or even in absolute numbers of inmates. Such measures em-

---

[32] The nine state guidelines systems are Delaware, Florida, Kansas, Minnesota, North Carolina, Ohio, Oregon, Virginia, and Washington.

[33] For annual federal and state prison rates from 1978 through 2016, see Carson (2018). Another parole-abolition guidelines jurisdiction, the District of Columbia, is excluded from the analysis here since most of its custody-sentenced offenders are housed by the federal Bureau of Prisons, which provides no separate breakdown of DC and non-DC inmates.

phasize the fiscal and human costs of escalating prison populations and show which jurisdictions are making the largest contributions to nationwide prison growth (Reitz 2018). But if we want to understand changes in prison populations and the factors that make those populations grow faster or slower in different jurisdictions, we need to examine growth in percentage terms. Equal percentage growth provides a better baseline for comparison: whatever caused Minnesota to have a very low incarceration rate at the outset would likely also cause Minnesota to increase its rate less than states that started at much higher levels. If, as happened, the national rate increased by 300 units from 150 to 450 per 100,000, we would not expect Minnesota's rate to increase from 50 to 350 (a 600 percent increase). If it did, we would immediately want to know: What changed in Minnesota?

Most of the parole-abolition guidelines systems come out the same under the absolute and percentage change measures, but two systems besides Minnesota come out differently: Kansas and the federal system. Both had slower-than-average prison growth when measured by the increased number of per capita units but higher-than-average growth when measured in percentage terms (Carson 2018). Thus, in percentage terms, seven of the 10 parole-abolition guidelines systems had below-average rates of prison growth.[34]

Here is some further detail on the three parole abolition systems with above-average growth. Kansas was only slightly higher than the national average following implementation of that state's guidelines in 1993. Its rate had risen 37 percent by 2009, compared with the all-states rise of 34 percent (Carson 2018).

Minnesota's higher-than-average increase from 1980 to 2009 (288 percent compared with 243 percent for all states) appears largely to be

---

[34] This record was better than in the six states that abolished parole without adopting guidelines: Arizona, California, Indiana, Illinois, Maine, and Wisconsin (Reitz 2011, pp. 51–52). (As shown in table 1, Wisconsin had advisory guidelines for less than half of the period 1999–2009 after parole discretion was abolished.) Of these six states, only Maine experienced below-average percentage growth in its prison rate; three (Illinois, Arizona, and Wisconsin) had average or slightly above-average growth; the other two (California and Indiana) had much greater-than-average growth (Carson 2018). The eight states that adopted sentencing guidelines but retained parole release discretion provide another point of comparison: half of these states had above-average rates of prison growth after implementing guidelines (Alabama, Arkansas, Pennsylvania, and Tennessee); Utah had average growth; Maryland, Massachusetts, and Michigan had below-average growth (Carson 2018).

explained by higher-than-average increases in felony caseloads.[35] And there were several additional reasons to expect above-average growth in Minnesota after 1980. First, rates tend to grow faster in states with the lowest rates than in high-rate states (Zimring and Hawkins 1991, p. 221; Reitz 2018). There are plausible reasons for this. Low-rate states probably have more marginal offenders who can be shifted from probation to prison (in high-rate states, those offenders are mostly already in prison). Low-rate states are also likely to have more room in their budgets to increase prison costs. Another explanation is more speculative but seems plausible (and testable). In an era of rising sentence severity, low-rate states may feel pressure to "catch up," if only to allay the public's fear that "all the bad guys will come here to commit their crimes."

Second, Minnesota is a relatively prosperous state and could have afforded even greater increases in its prison populations than those that occurred. Third, to the extent that racial hostility and lack of empathy with offenders and their families produce harsher punishments, Minnesota sentencing might be expected to become more severe. The proportions of blacks among the state's residents and among convicted offenders increased substantially after 1980.[36]

In contrast, the federal system's 281 percent prison growth rate (from 16 inmates per 100,000 US residents in 1987 to 61 in 2009) was far greater than the all-states growth rate (107 percent) in those years, even though the annual number of sentenced cases grew only modestly faster in federal than in state courts.[37] One plausible explanation is that the federal system lacks the budget constraints that limit state prison growth. Perhaps for this reason the federal commission has never used prison impact assessments to restrain the severity of recommended sentences. The commission appar-

---

[35] See Frase (2016, sec. III.B.4): from 1988 through 2006, annual felony convictions increased by 117 percent in Minnesota and by an estimated 70 percent for all states. From 1981 to 1988, Minnesota's moderate prison growth was exactly equal to its caseload increase, but in later years prison growth exceeded caseload increases. From 2001 to 2015 Minnesota's prison population, including inmates held in local jails with sentences of over 1 year, increased by 63 percent while the sentenced felony caseload increased by 55 percent (Frase and Mitchell 2017).

[36] Minnesota's black population more than quadrupled from 1980 to 2005 (Frase 2009), and from 1981 to 2009 the percentage of blacks among sentenced felons rose from 11 percent to 28 percent (MSGC 2017, table 7).

[37] See Carson (2018; prison rates) and Hindelang Criminal Justice Research Center (2018, table 5.23.2010): Criminal Defendants Sentenced in US District Courts, by Type and Length of Sentence, 1945–2010. Sentenced federal offenders increased by 86 percent from 1988 to 2006; as noted previously, the all-states sentenced felony caseload increased by 70 percent during this period.

ently did not view dramatic growth in prison populations, or serious prison overcrowding, as problems it should address.

There are potential selection bias problems in these comparisons. Is it plausible to suppose that the adoption of parole abolition guidelines by itself causes slower prison growth? I believe the answer is yes. Discretionary parole release is subject to politically motivated slowdowns or even temporary cessation.[38] Moreover, the availability of parole encourages judges to impose unreasonably severe prison terms in reliance on the unreliable and often illusory possibility of early release. The variable nature of parole release policy also makes it much more difficult for legislators to predict and take political responsibility for the prison bed and fiscal impacts of severe sentencing laws.

Parole abolition makes these predictions more accurate, especially when combined with guidelines that increase the uniformity of sentences. Average or below-average prison growth is even more likely in a system in which sentencing guidelines are created by an independent commission that takes seriously the goals of avoiding prison overcrowding and setting priorities for prison use and that incorporates prison bed impact projections into its guidelines development process. Projections can be quite accurate and credible, making clear the fiscal and bed impacts of severe sentences and the trade-offs that are often necessary: unless taxes are raised or funds are taken away from nonprison budgets, more severity for crime X requires less severity for crime Y.

3. *Prison Overcrowding.* Guidelines are sometimes adopted as a tool to avoid uncontrolled prison population growth, overcrowding, and all of the dangers associated with overcrowding. These include reduced security for inmates and staff, insufficient prison space and resources for treatment programs, and court intervention. Overcrowding is thus another important outcome measure. It is not necessarily redundant with measures of prison growth. A low-growth jurisdiction can develop serious overcrowding problems if its prisons are already full and the legislature declines to fund new construction. A high-growth jurisdiction can avoid overcrowding by timely expansion of its prison capacity or contracting with private prisons or other states. Guidelines commissions can manage prison growth and avoid overcrowding. They can use their sentencing data to update projected population numbers. These predictions can

---

[38] For several examples, see Reitz (2011, n. 84).

be used to scale back proposals for severe penalty increases, reduce penalties for some offenses to free up beds for others, and warn the legislature of the need to fund new construction.

However, it is difficult to tell whether guidelines have helped avoid or reduce prison overcrowding. The federal government collects and reports data on state and federal prison populations relative to prison capacities, but these data are based on a single, year-end count that may not be representative of other days throughout the year. Moreover, there is reason to doubt whether these data are comparable across jurisdictions. Definitions of "capacity" vary; some prison systems have raised capacity simply by adding bunks to existing cells (Zimring 1992). Nor is there any reason to believe that all state and federal prison authorities have made equally heavy use of this strategy so that estimates of overcrowding are understated to approximately equal degree across jurisdictions. Finally, available data include only prison custody populations and do not take into account the extent to which jurisdictions have reduced prison overcrowding by placing inmates in overcrowded local jails.

Subject to these caveats, here is what the overcrowding data showed at year-end 2007, 2008, and 2009 (Bureau of Justice Statistics 2008, 2009, 2010). These were the years when, depending on the jurisdiction, prison rates stopped rising (Carson 2018). These data are reported in two ways: inmates as a percentage of the highest measure of capacity reported for that jurisdiction and inmates as a percentage of the lowest reported capacity measure.[39] In table 2, "overcrowding" is defined as exceeding 105 percent of the lowest reported capacity measure. The 105 percent cutoff is used to disregard minor, possibly temporary, overcrowding; use of the lowest-capacity measure recognizes that prison officials may have reasons to overstate true capacity.

Table 2 shows the overcrowding rates for these three years, broken down by sentencing system type (Alabama is treated as a nonguidelines state because its guidelines became effective only for crimes committed on or after October 1, 2006).

These data suggest that guidelines jurisdictions have been more successful in avoiding prison overcrowding than nonguidelines systems.

---

[39] For example, in 2008, New York reported that its "design" capacity was 57,403, its "rated" capacity was 59,830, and its "operational" capacity was 60,978, so the first of these represents the "lowest reported capacity measure." Connecticut did not report capacity information in any of these years; Maine, Illinois, and Nevada did not report in 2007, and Oregon did not report in 2009.

TABLE 2
Prison Overcrowding in States With and Without Guidelines and Discretionary Parole

	Percent of Systems That Were Overcrowded in			
System Type (No. of Systems in 2008)	2007	2008	2009	3-Year Means
Guidelines with parole abolition (10)	60	50	44	51
Guidelines with parole retention (7)	29	14	29	24
All guidelines systems (17)	47	35	38	40
No guidelines, parole abolition (6)	n.a.*	67	50	58
No guidelines, parole retention (27)	58	44	52	51
All nonguidelines systems (33)	57	48	52	52
All reporting jurisdictions (50)	53	44	47	48

SOURCE.—Bureau of Justice Statistics (2008, 2009, 2010).

* Two of the six states in this category did not report capacity data.

Within each group, however, parole retention systems were more successful. The difference between parole abolition and retention was particularly strong for states with guidelines; perhaps guidelines states that retained parole did so precisely because they wanted to (and did) use parole release as a means of combating overcrowding. These findings suggest the need for parole abolition guidelines systems to include some sort of emergency release mechanism to relieve prison overcrowding, as the MPCS recommends (§ 305.8).

4. *Other Guidelines Impacts.* Little is known about differences among and between guidelines and nonguidelines jurisdictions concerning two subjects that suffuse writing about American sentencing: racial disparities in imprisonment and whether overall punishment severity becomes more proportionate to crime seriousness.

a. Racial Disparity. Sentencing guidelines reforms seek to reduce sentencing disparities among comparable offenders, particularly disparities related to race and ethnicity (King and Light 2019). Evaluations conducted by commissions and outside researchers have generally found that this goal was achieved: racial disparities were reduced (Tonry 1996). However, these studies have mostly viewed offense severity and offender prior record as control variables when defining groups of "similarly situated" offenders; and in some guidelines systems it is possible that the guidelines have changed these control variables in ways that actually increase racial disparities. The reasons are that guidelines reforms often seek to increase penalties for violent crimes, criminal history scores may increase under guidelines, and some nonwhite offender groups are more likely to be convicted of violent crimes or have more extensive prior records.

There do not appear to have been any national-level studies comparing racial disparity in states with and without guidelines, controlling for relevant confounding variables. Overall, there is no indication that guidelines states have higher rates of disparity. As of 2014, the most recent year for which national data are available, the 17 states that currently have some form of sentencing guidelines were widely distributed across the racial disparity rankings, with about equal numbers in the top (higher disparity) and bottom halves of the rankings.[40]

b. Offense Proportionality. A number of sentencing guidelines reforms are meant to give increased weight to retributive punishment goals and thus to increase the proportionality of sentence severity relative to offense severity, thereby "making the punishment fit the crime." However, as noted above, some guidelines systems give great weight to the offender's prior record of convictions in making dispositional and durational decisions. There is an inherent trade-off: giving more weight to prior record means giving less weight to offense severity. Thus, in some guidelines jurisdictions, the adoption of guidelines may have reduced offense proportionality.

No studies have sought to examine whether prior record receives greater weight as a sentencing factor following implementation of guidelines. There is limited evidence that guidelines cause criminal history scores to increase over time (Frase and Mitchell 2017; MSGC 2017). Such increases may occur because prosecutors file and retain a larger number of separate charges in order to increase the severity of current and future recommended sentences (MSGC 1984). It is possible that criminal history records have become more extensive even in systems without guidelines because of improved data systems, the criminogenic effects of mass incarceration, or both.

II. Major Sentencing Policy Issues

Section I summarized current knowledge about the nature, operation, and effects of guidelines systems. This section addresses questions for

---

[40] Nellis (2016, table C) reports ratios of black to white per capita prison rates, by state.

the future. What are the policy implications of experiences with guidelines sentencing in America? What are the essential features of a workable and worthwhile system? What additional features seem highly desirable, even if not essential? Can we reach consensus on what's good and what's not? What are the major arguments pro and con concerning issues lacking consensus? What additional research is needed to address these issues?

A. Essential Features

Here are features I believe are essential to well-designed guidelines systems and for which I believe there is widespread support. These features are present in most guideline systems and model codes or standards, or the arguments for them are in my view overwhelming. However, I do not mean to suggest that a system lacking one or more of these features should be rejected if proposed or abolished if it already exists. The success of sentencing reform is highly dependent on context (Zimring and Hawkins 1991, pp. 156–62, 201–4).

1. *A Permanent, Balanced, Independent, and Adequately Funded Sentencing Commission.* Every jurisdiction needs the kind of sentencing commission found in the best state systems and recommended by the ABA Standards and the MPCS. In theory, the same work could be done by a legislative committee or subcommittee. California and a half dozen other states tried that approach in the 1970s; but several of those abandoned it, and no state has adopted it since 1979. As Zimring (1976) long ago warned, legislatures are poorly equipped to develop well-considered rules to cover case-level sentencing and assess the effects of policies after they are implemented. Criminal codes are mostly too crude to use as a template. Legislators are subject to strong law-and-order political pressures. Legislative committees are unlikely to develop and maintain the necessary statistical databases and substantive policy expertise.

A sentencing commission can develop such data and expertise and is at least partly insulated from direct electoral pressures. To do its job well, a commission must be adequately funded, free of legislative or executive branch interference, balanced politically, and representative of the most important actors and perspectives within and outside the criminal justice system. The commission must also be permanent. Some states abolished their commissions after guidelines went into effect, but that is shortsighted and unwise. Guidelines need monitoring and updating on a regular basis or they will not achieve their purposes (and will eventually be ignored by judges and others). Given the huge costs and impacts of criminal punishment, creating and retaining a well-funded sentencing commission is money well spent.

2. *Presumptive Typical-Case Sentences with Specified Departure Criteria.* Judges must be given at least two kinds of guidance. First, there must be a common starting point for each kind of case, consisting of the sentence or sentence range deemed appropriate in that jurisdiction. Second, there must be standards and illustrative (but not exclusive) lists of permitted and forbidden factors to consider when deciding whether and by how much to depart from the applicable starting point. All guidelines systems have the first and most the second. These features are essential not only to guidelines but to any system governed by the rule of law. Judges need at least this much guidance when exercising their awesome powers over the liberty, property, and future life chances of offenders (and their potential victims).

3. *Hybrid Sentencing Theory.* Presumptive sentences and departure standards and factors must accommodate both retributive and crime control sentencing purposes. No guidelines system—indeed, no modern sentencing system of any type—has ever adopted a purely retributive or a purely crime control–focused punishment model, nor should they. Retributive values and the pursuit of crime control goals are both essential features of any workable and worthwhile sentencing system.

Fundamental fairness to offenders demands that they never be punished more severely than they deserve, even if greater severity would provide cost-effective crime control benefits. The importance of avoiding undeservedly severe punishment is something about which all proponents of retributive values agree, even when they strongly disagree about other aspects of deserved punishment. "Positive" desert theories assert that society has the right and the duty to impose exactly the deserved punishment, or at least a punishment falling within a very narrow range of severity (Moore 1997). Negative (or "limiting") retributive theories posit a range of deserved punishment. Some negative retributive accounts emphasize the imprecision of desert assessments and envision a range of "not undeserved" punishment (see, e.g., Morris and Tonry 1990; ALI 2003). Other negative accounts (e.g., Armstrong 1969; Frase 2013) view desert assessments as reasonably precise, at least as to relative degrees of blameworthiness. These writers propose an asymmetric theory under which it is more important to avoid punishment in excess of desert than punishment less than desert.[41]

Crime prevention is an essential government function, and governments must spend their limited funds efficiently. A purely retributive model would often require significant public expenditures, and significantly burden offenders and their families, with limited crime control benefits. Benefits may be outweighed by their costs and burdens or could be achieved more effectively or efficiently with nonpunitive measures. Hybrid guidelines models should specify that, within outer bounds set by retributive principles, custodial sanctions and conditions of community release should be no more onerous than is necessary to achieve their crime control purposes (the parsimony principle).

4. *Balance between Uniformity and Flexibility.* Guidelines must strike and preserve a workable balance between rule and discretion. Rules tend to make decisions more consistent and predictable. Discretion promotes flexibility and efficiency, allowing atypical case facts to be considered in order to do justice and avoid unnecessary burdens and expense. Mandatory minimum sentences statutes are rules that seek to impose excessive uniformity (in practice, they are only as uniform as prosecutors want them to be). Traditional indeterminate sentencing, with unfettered judicial and parole discretion, allows excessive flexibility.

Many guidelines systems are more or less "advisory," with little or no appellate review even of departure sentences. I believe (and so did the drafters of the MPCS) that advisory guidelines allow too much case-level flexibility. Legally binding guidelines with moderate appellate review provide a better balance between rule and discretion (Reitz 1997). Appel-

---

[41] Under the asymmetric conception of negative desert limits, undeservedly severe punishment is a serious abuse of government power, whereas failure to give offenders their full just deserts raises different issues (fairness to other equally culpable offenders who were punished more severely, fairness to victims and their families). For further discussion, see Frase (2013). Asymmetric desert limits may be appropriate even under a positive retributive account (Frase 2018*a*). Desert assessments can err in both directions—too much or too little. In assessing these inherent risks of error, a positive retributivist could decide that imposing punishment in excess of desert is normatively "worse" than imposing a less than fully deserved punishment. Such asymmetry is also a feature of utilitarian/consequentialist punishment models that incorporate the concept of parsimony—no greater severity than necessary to achieve crime control and other practical goals; in these models there is no corresponding directive to avoid penalties that are less severe than necessary. Asymmetry is a central feature of modern criminal justice systems: the requirement of proof beyond reasonable doubt and other procedural rules reflect deliberate choices to err on the side of too few criminal convictions rather than too many.

late review of sentences serves to clarify and enforce guidelines rules and to aid in development of sentencing policy as common-law courts have traditionally done, taking into account factual variations and patterns that a sentencing commission cannot foresee and regulate in advance.

A workable balance is also necessary in the degree to which guidelines rules are prescriptive (changing prior sentencing norms) or descriptive (encouraging judges to follow existing norms more consistently). Of course, when existing sentencing practices are demonstrably unfair or wasteful, an effort must be made to change them. But existing practice will often embody practical wisdom or, at least, strongly held views shared by judges and other practitioners. If guidelines rules are too prescriptive, they invite widespread evasion. When penalties seem too severe, judges are more likely to depart downward, and prosecutors are more likely to grant charging leniency. When guidelines recommendations seem too lenient, prosecutors can file and retain additional counts.

All of these processes occurred in Minnesota, where the guidelines commission took a relatively prescriptive approach (Frase 1993). The commission sought to increase use of imprisonment for people convicted of high-severity crimes who had low criminal histories. This goal was substantially undercut by charging leniency combined with high rates of downward departure. The commission sought to decrease imprisonment rates for people convicted of low-severity crimes who had sizable criminal histories. This was increasingly undermined by rising criminal history scores (due, at least in part, to prosecution decisions) that pushed many low-severity offenders across the guidelines grid to the recommended prison zone (MSGC 1984).[42]

5. *Resource and Demographic Impact Assessments.* Guidelines permit more accurate projections of the size and composition of future custody and supervision populations. This allows a jurisdiction to set priorities in the use of limited correctional resources and to avoid overcrowding by expanding capacity, adjusting recommended sentences for some crimes, or both. Such projections, especially when factored into drafting and revision processes, can help a system control the growth of its prison population and avoid serious overcrowding problems.

Similar projections are used in some guidelines states (e.g., Minnesota, Oregon) to predict the effects of current or proposed penalties on racial

---

[42] For an earlier summary of effects of prescriptive changes in several guidelines systems, see Tonry (1996, pp. 49–54).

and ethnic disparities. When a penalty is projected to cause or increase prison disparity, the commission and the legislature can examine it more closely to make sure it has a strong policy rationale and is narrowly tailored to minimize its disparate impact. There is room for debate as to how policy makers should respond to predicted new or increased racial disparate impacts.

B. Contested Guidelines Policy Issues—How Should They Be Resolved?

Substantial policy disagreements are raised by many aspects of guidelines sentencing. Here are some of the major disagreements and my thoughts about the underlying policy issues. Some relate to coverage—which crimes and sentencing issues should be regulated? Others relate to design details that determine how the system works.

1. *Coverage.* Guidelines systems vary considerably in terms of whether, and to what extent, they regulate each of the following sentencing matters.

a. Sentencing of Misdemeanor Offenses. Limiting guidelines to felonies, as a majority of guidelines systems do, makes sense in terms of reform priorities. The more severe penalties given in felony cases impose greater costs and create greater potentials for disparity. However, failure to regulate misdemeanor sentencing creates problems because of frequent overlap between penalties for more serious misdemeanors and less serious felonies. Using costly or scarce community-based sentences for misdemeanants means that fewer of those resources are available for felons. There are also issues of fairness, proportionality, and crime control when some misdemeanants are punished more severely than some felons; that is sure to occur if misdemeanor sentencing is unregulated. These problems will be worse if guidelines do not regulate conditions of nonprison felony sentences.

b. Sentencing of Multiple Current Offenses. One of the curious things about guidelines is their inconsistent treatment of repeat offenders. Guidelines closely regulate the ways in which judges take into account convictions entered before the date of the current sentencing, but sentencing of multiple current convictions is not regulated at all in the majority of systems. Judges retain unfettered discretion to sentence these multiple convictions concurrently, consecutively, or with a mix of concurrent and consecutive sentences.[43] One reason is the complexity of the subject. Multiple offenses may be closely related in time and place,

---

[43] For a variety of perspectives on sentencing of multiple current offenses, see Ryberg, Roberts, and de Keijser (2018).

loosely related, unrelated, similar, or dissimilar. They vary in their underlying circumstances and motivations (single or multiple objectives), similarity to prior offenses, and degree of police inducement (e.g., selling or buying drugs). Similar concurrent/consecutive choices arise when offenses are sentenced at the same time but in different courts or when the offender is serving a previously imposed sentence. Given this complexity, guidelines should provide only broad presumptive rules subject to departure (Frase 2018*a*). Most sentences for multiple offenses should be presumptively concurrent, with a few types being presumptively consecutive. Jurisdictions should also make use of "concurrent-plus" sentencing options that take account of additional convictions but recommend sentences shorter than under full consecutive sentencing. Each of these solutions has been implemented in a number of guidelines states.

c. Conditions of Nonprison Sentences. Most guidelines regulate only decisions about who goes to prison and for how long. This choice reflects in part the desire to give reform priority to the penalties imposing the highest costs and with the greatest potential for serious disparities. But nonprison sentences can also be onerous, especially when jail terms up to 1 year are combined with fines, other probation conditions, or both. The absence of detailed guidelines for community-based felony sentences reflects the complexity and case-specific nature of these decisions and a desire to retain some local control over sentences, particularly when they are paid for locally and must accommodate widely varying local resources.

Of course, state funding could be provided to expand and maintain adequate community-based sentencing options. Such funding should be provided, along with a charge-back formula, in order to eliminate the "correctional free lunch" problem (Zimring and Hawkins 1991, pp. 211–15). Local judges and prosecutors in almost all states are free to commit state prison resources, without fiscal or political accountability, by imposing prison terms on offenders who ought to be sanctioned in the community. At a minimum, guidelines should do as Oregon and Washington have done: place presumptive upper limits on the severity of nonprison sanctions (maximum jail days and "sanction unit" equivalents) for cases not ordinarily warranting state imprisonment.

d. Decisions to Revoke Probation and Postprison Release. Guidelines systems impose few limits on decisions to revoke conditional release, even when a substantial prison term may result. Revocations impose substantial public and private costs and in some states account for a high percentage of all prison admissions. Unregulated revocation decisions are also another source of sentencing disparity. Decisions to revoke release can be difficult to regulate if they are primarily offender-based and focus on whether the offender is too high-risk to remain at liberty or not amenable to supervision. But to the extent that revocation is intended to sanction and deter violations of release conditions, it involves the kind of "punishment" decision that can and should be regulated, at least as to sanction severity. Jurisdictions wishing to limit revocations can also do so by eliminating unnecessary release conditions and lengthy periods of supervision (thereby reducing alleged violations) and by providing guidance, or presumptive rules, specifying kinds of release violations that justify revocation. Revocations to prison and their impacts on prison populations can be further limited by rules that limit the duration of prison or jail sanctions used to sanction violations.

e. Discretionary Parole Release. Some US guidelines systems have abolished discretionary parole release. A substantial minority have not. The MPCS recommends abolition; that in my view is the right choice. Unregulated parole release discretion is, prima facie, an affront to transparency and the rule of law; prison duration is a sentencing decision that should be made by a judge, in a public courtroom, with the full due process protections of sentencing proceedings. Proponents of retaining parole discretion have a heavy burden of proof. I do not believe they can satisfy it.

There is no reason to believe that parole boards can accurately and consistently assess whether individuals have been rehabilitated or for other reasons are less likely to reoffend. Prisoners know how to "act reformed," and behavior in a prison environment is sometimes a poor predictor of behavior in the community. Of course, parole guidelines can make these decisions more consistent. They can also take into account dynamic high- or low-risk factors that cannot be known at the time of sentencing. One of the most reliable factors of this type is whether the offender completed assigned prison programming. But it is not necessary to retain parole discretion in order to take this into account; good-conduct credits can and should include credit for program completion. Parole discretion is likewise not needed to take advantage of two other important recidivism predictors: pre-prison offending and age at release; both can be known or estimated at the time of sentencing.

Some have argued that parole discretion is a necessary safety valve to relieve prison crowding or that parole abolition may cause prison populations to swell when it becomes public knowledge how long offenders actually spend in prison (Zimring 1976). It appears, however, that abolition is actually associated with slower prison growth—but only when combined with adoption of sentencing guidelines. On the other hand, available data suggest that, with or without guidelines, prison overcrowding is more often found in systems that have abolished parole release discretion than in states that retained it.

One solution to overcrowding is to adopt "control release" procedures as recommended by the MPCS (§ 305.8) The code provides that when prison population exceeds operational capacity (which the code defines) for 30 days, the director of the department of corrections may declare "an overcrowding state of emergency" and advance inmate release dates by specified amounts, award additional good-time credits, or advance individuals' release dates on the basis of reliable risk-assessment measures.[44]

Here are some other essential features of any system, with or without guidelines, that chooses to abolish parole release discretion:

- Offenders should receive substantial sentence reductions for good conduct and program participation. Any particular figure is arbitrary, but higher credits are needed in systems with relatively long prison terms. The credit should exceed the 15 percent granted in the federal system and should generally fall within the 30–35 percent range adopted by most guidelines states and the MPCS (§ 305.1).
- There should be other grounds for exceptional early release. A "second-look" procedure, as recommended by the MPCS (§ 305.6), would permit courts to reconsider and reduce very long sentences that no longer seem appropriate (and that in our time are rarely commuted). Other procedures should permit release for advanced age, serious illness or infirmity, exigent family circumstances, or other compelling reasons (§ 305.7).
- Periods of postprison supervision and sanctions for violations of release conditions should be independent of the remaining unserved prison term at the time of release. This is the approach in several guidelines systems and is endorsed by the MPCS (§ 6.09[5]). Supervision periods and sanctions should be as short as possible and be selected in light of research on recidivism rates after varying periods of time on release. In systems retaining parole, and in some parole abolition systems, the supervision period, and the maximum sanction for

---

[44] The cited Model Penal Code provision also recommends procedures to deal with jail, probation, and postprison supervision populations that exceed operational capacity.

release violations, are each set equal to the remaining prison term. This provides both too much and too little control. Offenders who "max out" their original sentence before release (many of whom are high-risk) have little or no period on supervision and little or no threatened revocation sanction. Those released earliest (many are low-risk) have the longest supervision term and the most time in prison if they are revoked.

f. Other Important Decisions That Are Rarely Regulated but May Need to Be. Important decisions that affect sentencing occur before sentencing occurs. These decisions, which no guidelines system has adequately addressed, can fundamentally undercut guidelines rules and undermine guidelines goals.

Prosecutorial Charging and Bargaining: Prosecutors "sentence" large numbers of offenders every day. They effectively impose the most lenient possible sentence when they decline to file provable charges. They impose probation-like obligations as conditions of pretrial diversion. They use their charging powers to expand or contract the judge's sentencing options when they decide whether to invoke a mandatory penalty or to select a conviction offense to trigger a recommended guidelines sentence they prefer. They decide whether to allow concurrent sentencing and shape the offender's criminal record when they dismiss or retain provable counts. Washington is the only guidelines state that has attempted to deal with prosecutorial discretion, and it did so only to a very limited extent (Boerner and Lieb 2001). No guidelines jurisdiction has addressed pretrial diversion and deferred adjudication. The MPCS does (§§ 6.02A and 6.02B).

Failures to regulate prosecutorial discretion result from practical and political difficulties. Even so, the nature and scope of the problem need recognition. In any given case, the prosecution charging decision may be too severe or too lenient. Unreasonable severity is not a serious problem in well-designed guidelines systems that set reasonable penalty levels, avoid mandatory minimums, and retain substantial judicial discretion to depart downward from typical-case guidelines. In systems lacking these safeguards, prosecutorial discretion is more likely to undermine the guidelines' goals. Thus one solution to excessive prosecutorial severity is to create well-designed sentencing rules.

Excessive prosecutorial leniency is unlikely to pose a systemic problem in any American jurisdiction. Nor is there any practical way to prevent the occasional grant of excessive leniency. US prosecutors define their roles in "adversary" terms (Pizzi 1999) and face electoral pressure not to appear "soft on crime." In most cases they are motivated to seek as severe a sentence as the evidence will support.[45] Unless victims are given broad rights of private prosecution, there is no practical way for courts to identify, let alone control, excessive leniency.

Pretrial Release and Detention Decisions: Offenders in pretrial detention receive a "custody sentence" in all but name. Their detention makes it more likely they will be convicted and receive a formal custody sentence. If released pending trial, conditions are often indistinguishable from probation conditions. No guidelines system has addressed these problems, in part because their solution would almost certainly require guideline rules governing nonprison sentences (now largely absent from existing systems). There is no reason in principle why guidelines could not set presumptive limits for pretrial detention and regulate conditions of pretrial release. Rules could provide that offenders normally may not be held in pretrial detention longer than the recommended maximum jail or prison sentence under applicable sentencing guidelines and that conditions of release in the aggregate may not be more onerous than could be imposed following conviction. However, without stricter standards on prosecutorial charging decisions, such limits might encourage (further) overcharging.

2. *Design and Details.* Numerous details need to be considered when designing a guidelines system about which little consensus has emerged favoring one approach over another. Here is a short, high-priority list.

a. Use of a Grid, Multiple Grids, or No Grid. Sentencing grids convey a lot of information in a simple form but tend to limit sentencing considerations to two dimensions. Multiple grids allow different formulas for different kinds of crimes but make inconsistency in degrees of severity or other treatment more likely. Worksheets allow more factors to be considered and permit criminal history to be given different definitions and weights for different offenses (Hester et al., forthcoming). However, worksheet calcula-

---

[45] Even when American prosecutors are appointed, as in the federal system, they do not seem predisposed to grant undue leniency (I base this conclusion on 35 years of supervising students in my law school's federal prosecution and defense clinics). For that reason, the much-criticized "relevant conduct" enhancements under the federal guidelines (USSC 2016, sec. 1B1.3), designed to counteract prosecutorial leniency, appear to be addressing a nonexistent problem.

tions tend to be more complex, and their greater detail and seeming completeness may unduly discourage departures.

Another set of issues concerns relations between the range of recommended sentences and statutory minimums and maximums. Some guidelines systems use mandatory minimum penalties as a base and build up, while others set guidelines sentences independently, subject to override by a mandatory. The latter approach gives less weight to mandatories and thus is preferable because mandatory penalties fail to provide a reasonable balance between rule and discretion. Some guidelines systems use statutory maximums to set the tops of the recommended ranges for offenders with the highest criminal history. That seems unwise; it occupies all of the statutory range, making sentence enhancements based on aggravated offense factors impossible. It also overpunishes high-history offenders whose crimes lack such factors.

b. Criminal History Scoring and Impact on Recommended Sentences. Existing guidelines rules on criminal history vary greatly. Differences include their stated rationales; the choice and weighting of score components; look-back limits (decay and gap rules); limits on eligibility for the highest score categories; validation of scores and score components as proxies for recidivism risk; magnitude of enhancements; and overall effects of enhancements on prison costs, prison-use priorities, racial disparities, and sentence proportionality relative to the conviction offense. Criminal history enhancements need closer scrutiny and curtailment in all of these areas (Frase 2013; Frase et al. 2015; Frase and Roberts, forthcoming). Rationales need to be clearly stated. If one rationale is that prior record is a proxy for recidivism risk, the predictive accuracy and efficiency of the score and its components must be validated. Problematic score components need especially close attention: juvenile record, misdemeanor convictions, custody status points, heavy weighting of higher-severity prior felonies, and formulaic enhancement based on prior and current offense similarity. Look-back periods need to be shorter (or added where they are currently missing), with more credit given for crime-free gap periods. Eligibility for inclusion in the highest history score categories should require one or more violent or very serious prior crimes. Finally, all of the potential adverse effects of each system's criminal history enhancements (prison costs, racial disparities, etc.) need to be measured and kept as low as possible.

c. Use of Validated Risk Assessment Tools at Sentencing. Very few guidelines systems use such tools, and those that do seem to use them only after the recommended sentence has been decided, based solely or primarily on offense severity and prior record. This may reflect the continued influence on guidelines policy makers of just deserts sentencing theory or an assumption that such assessments should be based only on prior convictions that have been reliably determined by a court. However, most criminal history scores are not well designed to serve as proxies for recidivism risk. They typically include prior record factors of unknown or doubtful risk and ignore nonprior record factors that are known to be strongly associated with lower or higher risk.

The use of nonrecord factors must, however, overcome important normative concerns. Strong objections are made to such factors as marriage or other family circumstances, past and current employment, drug and alcohol use, current or end-of-sentence offender age, and gender. These factors are contested because they do not (or often do not) reflect culpable offender choices, and many have a disparate negative impact on nonwhite offenders (Starr 2015; Tonry 2019). The strength of normative objections to contested nonhistory factors may depend on how they are used (Frase 2014). For example, it may be appropriate to mitigate penalties for middle-aged and older offenders even if we conclude that fairness prohibits enhancing penalties for offenders in their late teens and early 20s (who cannot help being in high-risk age groups).

Another important variable concerns the kinds of future offending sought to be prevented. Many risk assessment instruments were validated using broad outcome measures such as arrest or conviction for any crime within X years. Granted, it is much more difficult to predict serious violent crimes, since they are relatively rare events. But if and when risk assessment tools are developed that predict such crimes with relatively few false positives, it can be argued that fairness to potential victims justifies using them (Frase 2011). That may be true even if they rely on socioeconomic or legal lifestyle choices, as long as sentence severity does not exceed the offender's deserved punishment for the current offense or offenses.

   d. What to Do about Racial Disparate Impacts.   Many sentencing rules have an adverse disparate impact on nonwhite offenders. These result from not only racial differences in the type and seriousness of conviction offenses (which may or may not reflect racial differences in behavior) but also racial differences in prior record. Black and Native American offenders tend to have higher criminal history scores than whites, especially non-Hispanic whites (Frase 2009, 2013; Frase, Roberts, and Hester, forthcoming *a*). Some guidelines systems have taken advantage of improved data and increased sentence predictability to examine past and predicted future impacts of guidelines rules on racial disparity. Demographic impact assessments allow a commission to identify and measure foreseeable disparate impacts; they should be an essential feature of a guidelines system.

But how should the results of these assessments be used? Some (Mauer 2007; Tonry 2011) argue that any sentencing rule with a demonstrated or predicted disparate impact should be presumed invalid, with the burden being on proponents to provide data and convincing arguments to justify the rule. But we need much more debate on what justifications could overcome such a presumption. In short, when are demonstrated racial disparate impacts unacceptable? The easiest cases are those in which the rule lacks any convincing justification. Only a few rules meet this standard; the crack/powder distinction is a clear example. Strong objections can also be raised when the goals supposedly achieved could be equally well served by a more narrowly tailored rule with less disparate impact. An example is overbroad "school-zone" drug laws that, given residential patterns, are much more likely to apply to nonwhite offenders (such laws are often unnecessarily broad, e.g., enhancing penalties for crimes committed in the middle of the night; Mauer and Cole 2011).

A substantial argument can be made against penalty enhancements that reflect racial profiling or other systematic bias (e.g., black offenders have more drug priors than whites because of law enforcement targeting, not racial differences in drug offending). Many enhancements with disparate racial impact could also be attacked because the harms they cause (including worsening of disadvantage and exacerbating entrenched social inequalities) outweigh the value of retributive or crime control punishment (Frase 2009, 2013). Ruth and Reitz (2003, pp. 103, 116) argued that a penalty with disparate impact should be allowed only if it helps prevent serious crimes.

III. Priority Issues for Research

Much is unknown about the effects of variations in guidelines systems on outcomes and inmate populations. Examples include the composition and permanence of the commission, use of grids versus worksheets, each system's location on the mandatory-to-advisory continuum, and retention or abolition of parole release discretion.

Some research topics are primarily methodological; solving these puzzles will open up greater potential for comparative research across diverse guidelines systems:

- measures of "disparity" and disparity reduction that are comparable across jurisdictions;
- measurement of prison, probation, and postprison supervision population growth (e.g., per capita or percentage change), and how to relate those measures to variations in systems' structure, design, or operation;
- measures of prison overcrowding and of the extent to which supervision populations exceed operational capacity that are comparable across jurisdictions.

Other priority research topics concern whether some kinds of guidelines are better able to achieve widely shared sentencing reform goals:

- How do different kinds of guidelines relate to variations in sentencing disparities, growth in prison and jail populations, correctional overcrowding, and levels of racial disproportionality?
- Do prior records receive more weight at sentencing in jurisdictions with guidelines than in those without guidelines? Do criminal history scores rise more under guidelines than under nonguidelines systems, and if so, why?
- How well do criminal history scores, score components, and nonrecord risk factors predict recidivism, especially for violent or other serious crime? This research has been done only for the federal system, Minnesota, Pennsylvania, and Virginia.
- How well have less commonly employed guidelines provisions worked in practice? Examples include coverage of misdemeanors, structuring of sentences for multiple current convictions, limits on severity of nonprison sentences, and limits on custodial sanctions for violations of probation and postprison release conditions.
- Are some kinds of guidelines more or less susceptible to being undermined by unregulated prosecutor charging and plea bargaining decisions?
- Should pretrial detention, pretrial release conditions, pretrial diversion, and deferred adjudication be regulated, and if so, how?
- What do judges, prosecutors, defense counsel, offenders, probation officers, and other correctional officers think about various guidelines

rules, and how do their opinions support or undermine guidelines reforms?[46]
- What is the public's opinion about guidelines rules, and how well do such attitudes reflect the content of the rules?[47] To what extent does public opinion support or undermine guidelines reforms?
- Why have guidelines been adopted, or survived, in some states but not in others?

IV. Conclusion

Although American guidelines systems share many common features, each is unique in some ways. This diversity is not surprising, given the distinctive histories and politics of each jurisdiction. In the end, sentencing reform is highly contingent as to both place and time (Zimring and Hawkins 1991). Nevertheless, it is useful to identify and seek to expand areas of consensus about what a well-designed sentencing guidelines system should look like. I have proposed a short list of essential features of such a system and have discussed policy arguments, practical considerations, and research that may help to resolve other, more contested issues. A number of guidelines states have adopted most of the essential features I identify and satisfactorily resolved many contested issues. Overall, and recognizing that any "best of" list is inherently imprecise and subjective, I believe that the guidelines systems in five states qualify, each in its own way, as models: Kansas, Minnesota, North Carolina, Oregon, and Washington (for further details, see Frase [2013, chap. 3]).

But even if we can eventually agree on what an ideal guidelines system should look like, some jurisdictions will be unable or unwilling to adopt all of its features. In some, an incomplete system may be "as good as it gets." Such guidelines may be better than if there were no guidelines at all. This characterization fits the post-*Booker* advisory federal guidelines, but also the guidelines of some states. Pennsylvania, for example, retained parole release discretion, has minimal appellate review or interpretive case law, and has experienced much faster prison population growth than the

---

[46] The federal sentencing commission has conducted a series of surveys of judges' views about the operation of the guidelines (USSC 2003, 2010, 2015).

[47] For a survey of public attitudes about punishment of four federal crimes (drug trafficking, bank robbery, immigration offenses, and fraud), with comparisons to the corresponding federal guidelines sentencing range, see USSC (1997).

average state (Carson 2018). However, Pennsylvania's guidelines usefully structure nonprison sanctions and provide guidance on the choice of punishment purposes. Pennsylvania's commission has an active research program and has conducted cutting-edge work on risk assessment scales and use of criminal history as a predictor of recidivism.

Saying that an incomplete guidelines system is better than none poses the question, what alternative sentencing structures are possible? No other sentencing reform of comparable scope has been implemented in even a single US state or federal jurisdiction in the past four decades. The only competing model is the statutory presumptive sentence approach that California and several other states adopted beginning in 1976, but 1979 was the last year such a system was adopted. In theory it would be possible to design a sentencing system based on restorative justice principles, but no such effort has been made in any American jurisdiction. Nor, to my knowledge, has any other comprehensive sentencing reform model been proposed or widely discussed.[48] By contrast, 22 jurisdictions adopted guidelines, and 19 still use them.

There are two basic choices, each with two alternative versions: sentencing guidelines and traditional unfettered judicial sentencing, each with or without parole release discretion. Discretionary sentencing and parole, however, are no more defensible today than they were when they began to fall from favor in the 1970s (ALI 2003; Frase 2013). That is why both the ABA (1994) and the ALI (2017) favored parole-abolition sentencing guidelines. Parole-abolition guidelines strike a better balance between rule and discretion than discretionary sentencing and releasing and permit more rational, fiscally responsible, and transparent decisions to be made about who should go to prison and for how long. They have proved to be workable and sustainable in a variety of states, in some cases for decades.

---

[48] The Justice Reinvestment (JRI) programs sponsored in recent years by the Council on State Governments (2018) could perhaps be seen as promoting systemwide reforms comparable in scope to sentencing guidelines. But JRI programs focus on efficient achievement of crime control goals and do not give much attention to widely felt concerns about sentencing proportionality and disparity. It is also unclear what the long-term effects of JRI programs will be, especially where those programs have not created or strengthened state and local institutions involved in criminal justice operations and tasked with long-term planning (including, and especially, sentencing commissions).

Unstructured, highly discretionary punishment should be unacceptable in any state claiming to be governed by the rule of law. There is no better reform alternative than the parole-abolition guidelines model.

REFERENCES

ABA (American Bar Association). 1979. *Standards Relating to the Administration of Criminal Justice*. 2nd ed.: *Sentencing Alternatives and Procedures*. Washington, DC: American Bar Association.
———. 1994. *ABA Standards for Criminal Justice: Sentencing*. 3rd ed. Washington, DC: American Bar Association.
ALI (American Law Institute). 2003. *Model Penal Code: Sentencing, Report*. Philadelphia: American Law Institute.
———. 2017. *Model Penal Code: Sentencing, Proposed Final Draft*. Philadelphia: American Law Institute.
Arkansas Sentencing Commission. 2018. *Sentencing Standards Grid Offense Seriousness Rankings and Related Material*. https://www.arsentencing.com/.
Armstrong, K. G. 1969. "The Retributivist Hits Back." In *The Philosophy of Punishment: A Collection of Papers*, edited by H. B. Acton. London: Macmillan.
Boerner, David, and Roxanne Lieb. 2001. "Sentencing Reform in the Other Washington." In *Crime and Justice: A Review of Research*, vol. 28, edited by Michael Tonry. Chicago: University of Chicago Press.
Bureau of Justice Statistics. 2008. *Prisoners in 2007*. Washington, DC: US Department of Justice.
———. 2009. *Prisoners in 2008*. Washington, DC: US Department of Justice.
———. 2010. *Prisoners in 2009*. Washington, DC: US Department of Justice.
Carnes, Teresa. 1993. "Sentencing Reform in Alaska." *Federal Sentencing Reporter* 6:134–37.
Carson, E. Ann. 2018. "Imprisonment Rate of Sentenced Prisoners under the Jurisdiction of State or Federal Correctional Authorities." https://www.bjs.gov/index.cfm?ty=nps.
Council on State Governments. 2018. *Justice Reinvestment*. Washington, DC: CSG Justice Center. https://csgjusticecenter.org/jr.
DC Sentencing Commission. 2018. *2017 Annual Report*. Washington, DC: DC Sentencing and Criminal Code Revision Commission. https://scdc.dc.gov/node/1328161.
Doob, Anthony. 1995. "The United States Sentencing Commission Guidelines: If You Don't Know Where You Are Going, You Might Not Get There." In *The Politics of Sentencing Reform*, edited by Chris Clarkson and Rod Morgan. New York: Oxford University Press.
Frankel, Marvin. 1973. *Criminal Sentences: Law without Order*. New York: Hill & Wang.

Frase, Richard S. 1993. "Implementing Commission-Based Sentencing Guidelines: The Lessons of the First Ten Years in Minnesota." *Cornell Journal of Law and Public Policy* 2:279–337.

———. 1995. "Lessons of State Guideline Reforms." *Federal Sentencing Reporter* 8:39–41.

———. 2005. "State Sentencing Guidelines: Diversity, Consensus, and Unresolved Policy Issues." *Columbia Law Review* 105:1190–1232.

———. 2009. "What Explains Persistent Racial Disproportionality in Minnesota's Prison and Jail Populations?" In *Crime and Justice: A Review of Research*, vol. 38, edited by Michael Tonry. Chicago: University of Chicago Press.

———. 2011. "Can Above-Desert Penalties Be Justified by Competing Deontological Theories?" In *Retributivism Has a Past: Has It a Future?* edited by Michael Tonry. New York: Oxford University Press.

———. 2013. *Just Sentencing: Principles and Procedures for a Workable System*. New York: Oxford University Press.

———. 2014. "Recurring Policy Issues of Guidelines (and *Non*-Guidelines) Sentencing: Risk Assessments, Criminal History Enhancements, and the Enforcement of Release Conditions." *Federal Sentencing Reporter* 26:145–57.

———. 2015a. "The Treatment of Multiple Current Offenses." In *Criminal History Enhancements Sourcebook*, edited by Richard S. Frase, Julian V. Roberts, Rhys Hester, and Kelly Lyn Mitchell. Minneapolis: Robina Institute of Criminal Law and Criminal Justice.

———. 2015b. "Varying Binding Effects of Guidelines—the Mandatory-to-Advisory Continuum." Minneapolis: Sentencing Guidelines Resource Center, Robina Institute of Criminal Law and Criminal Justice. https://sentencing.umn.edu/content/varying-binding-effects-guidelines-mandatory-advisory-continuum.

———. 2016. "Sentencing Policies and Practices in Minnesota." In *Oxford Handbooks Online*. Oxford: Oxford University Press. http://www.oxfordhandbooks.com/view/10.1093/oxfordhb/9780199935383.001.0001/oxfordhb-9780199935383-e-148?print=pdf.

———. 2018a. "Principles and Procedures for Sentencing of Multiple Current Offenses." In *Sentencing Multiple Crimes*, edited by Jesper Ryberg, Julian V. Roberts, and Jan W. de Keijser. New York: Oxford University Press.

———. 2018b. "Suspended Sentences and Free-Standing Probation Orders in US Guidelines Systems: A Survey and Assessment." *Law and Contemporary Problems* 82(1).

Frase, Richard S., and Kelly Lyn Mitchell. 2017. "Why Are Minnesota's Prison Populations Continuing to Rise in an Era of Decarceration?" *Federal Sentencing Reporter* 30:114–24.

Frase, Richard S., and Julian V. Roberts, eds. Forthcoming. *Paying for the Past: Exploring the Intended and Unintended Consequences of Prior Record Sentencing Enhancements*. New York: Oxford University Press.

Frase, Richard S., Julian V. Roberts, and Rhys Hester. Forthcoming a. "Disparate Impact on Minority Offenders." In *Paying for the Past: Exploring the*

Intended and Unintended Consequences of Prior Record Sentencing Enhancements, edited by Richard S. Frase and Julian V. Roberts. New York: Oxford University Press.

———. Forthcoming *b*. "Impact of Criminal History Enhancements on Prison Bed Needs and Costs." In *Paying for the Past: Exploring the Intended and Unintended Consequences of Prior Record Sentencing Enhancements*, edited by Richard S. Frase and Julian V. Roberts. New York: Oxford University Press.

———. Forthcoming *c*. "Magnitude of Criminal History Impacts on Sentence Severity." In *Paying for the Past: Exploring the Intended and Unintended Consequences of Prior Record Sentencing Enhancements*, edited by Richard S. Frase and Julian V. Roberts. New York: Oxford University Press.

Frase, Richard S., Julian V. Roberts, Rhys Hester, and Kelly Lyn Mitchell. 2015. *Criminal History Enhancements Sourcebook*. Minneapolis: Robina Institute of Criminal Law and Criminal Justice. https://sentencing.umn.edu/content/criminal-history-enhancement-sourcebook.

Griffin, Burt W., and Lewis R. Katz. 2002. "Sentencing Consistency: Basic Principles Instead of Numerical Grids." *Case Western Reserve Law Review* 53:1–75.

Griset, Pamela L. 1999. "Criminal Sentencing in Florida: Determinate Sentencing's Hollow Shell." *Crime and Delinquency* 45:316–33.

Hester, Rhys. 2015. "Prior Offense Weighting and Special Eligibility Rules." In *Criminal History Enhancements Sourcebook*, edited by Richard S. Frase, Julian V. Roberts, Rhys Hester, and Kelly Lyn Mitchell. Minneapolis: Robina Institute of Criminal Law and Criminal Justice.

Hester, Rhys, Richard S. Frase, Julia Laskorunsky, and Kelly Lyn Mitchell. Forthcoming. "Rethinking the Role of Criminal History in Sentencing." In *Handbook on Corrections and Sentencing: Sentencing Policies and Practices in the 21st Century*. New York: Routledge.

Hester, Rhys, Richard S. Frase, Julian V. Roberts, and Kelly Lyn Mitchell. 2018. "Prior Record Enhancements at Sentencing: Unsettled Justifications and Unsettling Consequences." In *Crime and Justice: A Review of Research*, vol. 47, edited by Michael Tonry. Chicago: University of Chicago Press.

Hindelang Criminal Justice Research Center. 2018. *Sourcebook of Criminal Justice Statistics*. Albany: University at Albany, State University of New York. https://www.albany.edu/sourcebook/tost_5.html#5_ab.

Hofer, Paul. 2019. "Federal Sentencing after *Booker*." In *American Sentencing*, edited by Michael Tonry. Vol. 48 of *Crime and Justice: A Review of Research*, edited by Michael Tonry. Chicago: University of Chicago Press.

Kansas Sentencing Commission. 2018. *FY 2017 Annual Report*. Topeka: Kansas Sentencing Commission. http://sentencing.ks.gov/document-center/annual-reports.

King, Ryan D., and Michael Light. 2019. "Have Racial and Ethnic Disparities in Sentencing Declined?" In *American Sentencing*, edited by Michael Tonry. Vol. 48 of *Crime and Justice: A Review of Research*, edited by Michael Tonry. Chicago: University of Chicago Press.

Maryland State Commission on Criminal Sentencing Policy. 2018. *Maryland Sentencing Guidelines Manual, Version 9.2*. College Park: University of Maryland. http://www.msccsp.org/Guidelines/Default.aspx.

Massachusetts Sentencing Commission. 2014. *Survey of Sentencing Practices, FY 2013*. Boston: Massachusetts Sentencing Commission. https://www.mass.gov/lists/surveys-of-massachusetts-sentencing-practices.

Mauer, Marc. 2007. "Racial Impact Statements as a Means of Reducing Unwarranted Sentencing Disparities." *Ohio State Journal of Criminal Law* 5:19–46.

Mauer, Marc, and David Cole. 2011. "Five Myths about Americans in Prison." *Washington Post*, June 17.

Miethe, Terrence, and Charles Moore. 1985. "Socio-economic Disparities under Determinate Sentencing Systems: A Comparison of Pre- and Post-guideline Practices in Minnesota." *Criminology* 23:337–63.

Mitchell, Kelly Lyn. 2015*a*. "Prior Juvenile Adjudications." In *Criminal History Enhancements Sourcebook*, edited by Richard S. Frase, Julian V. Roberts, Rhys Hester, and Kelly Lyn Mitchell. Minneapolis: Robina Institute of Criminal Law and Criminal Justice.

———. 2015*b*. "Prior Misdemeanor Convictions." In *Criminal History Enhancements Sourcebook*, edited by Richard S. Frase, Julian V. Roberts, Rhys Hester, and Kelly Lyn Mitchell. Minneapolis: Robina Institute of Criminal Law and Criminal Justice.

———. 2017. *Sentencing Commissions and Guidelines by the Numbers*. Minneapolis: Robina Institute of Criminal Law and Criminal Justice. https://sentencing.umn.edu/content/sentencing-commissions-and-guidelines-numbers.

Moore, Michael. 1997. *Placing Blame: A Theory of Criminal Law*. Oxford: Clarendon.

Morris, Norval, and Michael Tonry. 1990. *Between Prison and Probation: Intermediate Punishments in a Rational Sentencing System*. New York: Oxford University Press.

MSGC (Minnesota Sentencing Guidelines Commission). 1984. *The Impact of the Minnesota Sentencing Guidelines: Three Year Evaluation*. St. Paul: Minnesota Sentencing Guidelines Commission.

———. 2017. *2016 Sentencing Practices: Annual Summary Statistics for Felony Offenders*. St. Paul: Minnesota Sentencing Guidelines Commission.

———. 2018. *Minnesota Sentencing Guidelines and Commentary*. St. Paul: Minnesota Sentencing Guidelines Commission.

National Center for State Courts. 2008. *State Sentencing Guidelines: Profiles and Continuum*. Williamsburg, VA: National Center for State Courts. http://www.ncsc.org/Topics/Criminal/Sentencing/Resource-Guide.aspx.

Nellis, Ashley. 2016. *The Color of Justice: Racial and Ethnic Disparity in State Prisons*. Washington, DC: Sentencing Project.

Oldroyd, Richard J. 1994. "Utah's Conjoint Guidelines for Sentencing and Parole." *Overcrowded Times* 5(1):1,8–10.

Parent, Dale P. 1988. *Structuring Criminal Sentences: The Evolution of Minnesota's Sentencing Guidelines*. Stoneham, MA: Butterworth Legal.

Pennsylvania Commission on Sentencing. 2017. *Annual Report 2016*. Harrisburg: Pennsylvania Commission on Sentencing. http://pcs.la.psu.edu/publications-and-research/annual-reports.

———. 2018. *Proposed Sentence Risk Assessment Instrument, April 28, 2018*. Harrisburg: Pennsylvania Commission on Sentencing. http://pcs.la.psu.edu/news/guidelines/proposed-risk-assessment-instrument.

Pew Charitable Trusts. 2018. "National Prison Rate Continues to Decline Amid Sentencing, Re-entry Reforms." Philadelphia: Pew Charitable Trusts. http://www.pewtrusts.org/en/research-and-analysis/analysis/2018/01/16/national-prison-rate-continues-to-decline-amid-sentencing-re-entry-reforms.

Pizzi, William T. 1999. *Trials without Truth: Why Our System of Criminal Trials Has Become an Expensive Failure and What We Need to Do to Rebuild It*. New York: New York University Press.

Porter, Nicole D. 2014. "Racial Impact Statements." Washington, DC: Sentencing Project. https://www.sentencingproject.org/publications/racial-impact-statements/.

Reitz, Kevin R. 1997. "Sentencing Guidelines Systems and Sentence Appeals: A Comparison of Federal and State Experiences." *Northwestern University Law Review* 91:1441–1506.

———. 2011. "Reporter's Study: The Question of Parole Release Authority." In *Model Penal Code: Sentencing, Tentative Draft no. 2*. Philadelphia: American Law Institute.

———. 2018. "Measuring Change in Incarceration Scale." *Berkeley Journal of Criminal Law* 23.

Roberts, Julian V. 2015*a*. "Custody Status as a Criminal History Enhancement." In *Criminal History Enhancements Sourcebook*, edited by Richard S. Frase, Julian V. Roberts, Rhys Hester, and Kelly Lyn Mitchell. Minneapolis: Robina Institute of Criminal Law and Criminal Justice.

———. 2015*b*. "Justifying Criminal History Enhancements at Sentencing." In *Criminal History Enhancements Sourcebook*, edited by Richard S. Frase, Julian V. Roberts, Rhys Hester, and Kelly Lyn Mitchell. Minneapolis: Robina Institute of Criminal Law and Criminal Justice.

———. 2015*c*. "Severity Premium for Similar Prior Offending: Patterning Rules." In *Criminal History Enhancements Sourcebook*, edited by Richard S. Frase, Julian V. Roberts, Rhys Hester, and Kelly Lyn Mitchell. Minneapolis: Robina Institute of Criminal Law and Criminal Justice.

Roberts, Julian V., and Andrew von Hirsch, eds. 2010. *Previous Convictions at Sentencing: Theoretical and Applied Perspectives*. Oxford: Hart.

Robina Institute of Criminal Law and Criminal Justice. 2018. Sentencing Guidelines Resource Center. Minneapolis: University of Minnesota. https://sentencing.umn.edu/.

Ruth, Henry, and Kevin R. Reitz. 2003. *The Challenge of Crime: Rethinking Our Response*. Cambridge, MA: Harvard University Press.

Ryberg, Jesper, Julian V. Roberts, and Jan W. de Keijser, eds. 2018. *Sentencing Multiple Crimes*. New York: Oxford University Press.

Starr, Sonja B. 2015. "The New Profiling: Why Punishment Based on Poverty and Identity Is Unconstitutional and Wrong." *Federal Sentencing Reporter* 27:229–36.

Tonry, Michael. 1988. "Structuring Sentencing." In *Crime and Justice: A Review of Research*, vol. 10, edited by Michael Tonry and Norval Morris. Chicago: University of Chicago Press.

———. 1996. *Sentencing Matters*. New York: Oxford University Press.

———. 2010. "The Questionable Relevance of Previous Convictions to Punishments for Later Crimes." In *Previous Convictions at Sentencing: Theoretical and Applied Perspectives*, edited by Julian V. Roberts and Andrew von Hirsch. Oxford: Hart.

———. 2011. *Punishing Race: A Continuing American Dilemma*. New York: Oxford University Press.

———. 2019. "Predictions of Dangerousness in Sentencing: Déjà Vu All Over Again." In *American Sentencing*, edited by Michael Tonry. Vol. 48 of *Crime and Justice: A Review of Research*, edited by Michael Tonry. Chicago: University of Chicago Press.

Ulmer, Jeffery T. 2019. "Criminal Courts as Inhabited Institutions: Making Sense of Difference and Similarity in Sentencing." In *American Sentencing*, edited by Michael Tonry. Vol. 48 of *Crime and Justice: A Review of Research*, edited by Michael Tonry. Chicago: University of Chicago Press.

US Department of Justice. 1996. *National Assessment of Structured Sentencing*. Washington, DC: US Department of Justice.

———. 1998. *National Survey of State Sentencing Structures*. Washington, DC: US Department of Justice.

USSC (US Sentencing Commission). 1997. *National Sample Survey: Public Opinion on Sentencing Federal Crimes*. Washington, DC: US Sentencing Commission. https://www.ussc.gov/research/research-reports/survey-public-perceptions-and-federal-sentencing-guidelines.

———. 2003. *Survey of Article III Judges on the Federal Sentencing Guidelines*. Washington, DC: US Sentencing Commission. https://www.ussc.gov/research/topical-index-publications#surveys.

———. 2010. *Results of Survey of United States District Judges January 2010 through March 2010*. Washington, DC: US Sentencing Commission. https://www.ussc.gov/research/topical-index-publications#surveys.

———. 2015. *Results of Survey of United States District Judges: Modification and Revocation of Probation and Supervised Release*. Washington, DC: US Sentencing Commission. https://www.ussc.gov/research/research-reports/results-survey-united-states-district-judges-modification-and-revocation-probation-and-supervised.

———. 2016. *Federal Sentencing Guidelines Manual*. Washington, DC: US Sentencing Commission. https://www.ussc.gov/guidelines/2016-guidelines-manual.

———. 2018. *2017 Sourcebook of Federal Sentencing Statistics*. Washington, DC: US Sentencing Commission. https://www.ussc.gov/research/sourcebook-2017.

Utah Sentencing Commission. 2017. *2017 Adult Sentencing and Release Guidelines*. Salt Lake City: Utah Commission on Criminal and Juvenile Justice. https://justice.utah.gov/Sentencing.

Virginia Criminal Sentencing Commission. 2017. *2017 Annual Report*. Richmond: Virginia Criminal Sentencing Commission. http://www.vcsc.virginia.gov/reports.html.

———. 2018. "Nonviolent Risk Assessment, Larceny." Richmond: Virginia Criminal Sentencing Commission. http://www.vcsc.virginia.gov/worksheets.html.

Washington State Caseload Forecast Council. 2018. *Statistical Summary of Adult Felony Sentencing, Fiscal Year 2017*. Olympia: Washington State Caseload Forecast Council. http://www.cfc.wa.gov/default.htm.

Watts, Alexis L. 2016. "The Composition of Sentencing Commissions." Minneapolis: Robina Institute on Criminal Law and Criminal Justice. https://sentencing.umn.edu/content/composition-sentencing-commissions.

———. 2017. "Sentencing Guidelines and Correctional Resource Management." Minneapolis: Robina Institute on Criminal Law and Criminal Justice. https://sentencing.umn.edu/content/depth-sentencing-guidelines-and-correctional-resource-management.

———. 2018*a*. "Sentencing Guideline Grids." Minneapolis: Robina Institute on Criminal Law and Criminal Justice. https://sentencing.umn.edu/content/depth-sentencing-guideline-grids.

———. 2018*b*. "Sentencing Guidelines and Discretionary Parole Release." Minneapolis: Robina Institute on Criminal Law and Criminal Justice. https://sentencing.umn.edu/content/depth-sentencing-guidelines-and-discretionary-parole-release.

Zimring, Franklin E. 1976. "Making the Punishment Fit the Crime: A Consumer's Guide to Sentencing Reform." 1976 Hastings Center Report. https://chicagounbound.uchicago.edu/occasional_papers/16/.

———. 1992. "Are State Prisons *Undercrowded*?" *Federal Sentencing Reporter* 4:347–48.

———. 2005. "Penal Policy and Penal Legislation in Recent American Experience." *Stanford Law Review* 58:323–38.

———. 2010. "The Scale of Imprisonment in the United States: Twentieth Century Patterns and Twenty-First Century Prospects." *Journal of Criminal Law and Criminology* 100:1225–46.

Zimring, Franklin E., and Gordon Hawkins. 1991. *The Scale of Imprisonment*. Chicago: University of Chicago Press.

Paul J. Hofer

Federal Sentencing after *Booker*

ABSTRACT

The Supreme Court decision in *United States v. Booker* seemed to portend a new era for federal sentencing. By making federal guidelines advisory rather than "mandatory," and authorizing judges to critically review their development, *Booker* empowered judges to reject unsound guidelines. *Booker* has had, however, surprisingly little effect on sentence severity or imprisonment use. Sentencing below guideline ranges increased, but more from a general relaxation of guidelines' restrictions than from reasoned rejection of unsound guidelines. They continue to exert gravitational pull. Inter-judge disparity, modestly reduced by the earlier guidelines, increased after *Booker*. The commission claims that racial disparities increased, but the evidence is mixed and controversial. Bias in judges' decisions contributes less to racial disparity than do statutes and guidelines that disproportionately affect African Americans. *Booker* has the potential to reduce structural disparities caused by unsound guidelines. The federal system remains unbalanced, however, with control of sentencing concentrated largely in the hands of Congress and prosecutors rather than of the commission and judges. Only repeal of statutory mandatory minimums and many specific statutory directives to the commission will permit federal sentencing reform to work as intended.

Sentencing reform in the federal courts was sabotaged by Congress and compromised by the United States Sentencing Commission before the

Electronically published February 12, 2019
  Paul Jeffrey Hofer is policy analyst for the Sentencing Resource Counsel of the Federal Public and Community Defenders, and adjunct associate professor in the Department of Psychological and Brain Sciences, Johns Hopkins University. He thanks Vansh Bansal of William and Mary for help with data analyses and Amy Baron-Evans for tireless advocacy. Any errors are the author's. Opinions expressed do not necessarily reflect positions of the Federal Public and Community Defenders.

© 2019 by The University of Chicago. All rights reserved.
0192-3234/2019/0048-0004$10.00

guidelines took effect, and after 30 years no one has been able to fix it. The Sentencing Reform Act of 1984 (the SRA) was a bold plan nearly 10 years in the making. It created the commission as an independent expert agency in the judicial branch and charged it with developing detailed presumptive guidelines based on research and consultation with key stakeholders. The guidelines were to advance the purposes of sentencing and reduce unwarranted disparity. The commission was to "develop means of measuring the degree to which sentencing, penal, and correctional practices are effective." To prevent discretion and any resulting disparities from merely shifting from judges to prosecutors with the adoption of sentencing guidelines, the SRA tasked the commission with developing standards for plea agreements, and judges were tasked with enforcing them.

In the SRA itself, however, were signs that Congress would not avoid micromanaging the commission's work (Stith and Koh 1993). In addition to broad principles and lofty goals, the act contained specific directives that limited the commission's options, such as the so-called career offender provision (28 U.S.C. § 994(h); implemented at USSG § 4B1.1), which mandated lengthy prison terms for defendants with two prior drug or violent crimes.[1] Most important, in the Anti–Drug Abuse Acts of 1986 and 1988, Congress expanded the system of statutory mandatory minimum sentences, which form a parallel, and incompatible, system of coarse sentencing rules that override the guidelines whenever they conflict. By requiring sentences of at least 5 or 10 years for any offense involving certain quantities of a "mixture or substance containing a detectable amount" of a drug, the statutes constrained the commission, distorted the guidelines, complicated sentencing law, and shifted power away from the commission and judges and toward Congress and prosecutors.[2]

---

[1] In *United States v. LaBonte*, 520 U.S. 751 (1997), the Supreme Court made clear that the commission must comply with unambiguous statutory directives, even if in its judgment doing so creates unwarranted disparity. Judges are not legally bound by statutory directives to the commission. Many, however, in the wake of *Booker* continue to feel that congressional policies expressed in directives to the commission deserve deference.

[2] See 21 U.S.C. § 841, containing quantity thresholds created by the Anti–Drug Abuse Act of 1986, which were incorporated into the guidelines and expanded as the Drug Quantity Table at USSG § 2D1.1. While there is no question that statutory mandatory minimums bind judges, the extent to which they constrain the commission has been controversial. Commentators argued that the original commission could ignore the statutes and create the guidelines they deemed best, even if at sentencing the statutes would override any guideline recommendations that did not satisfy the minimum (Tonry 1996, p. 79). The original commission instead sought to incorporate the quantity thresholds, making

In *United States v. Booker*, 543 U.S. 220 (2005), the US Supreme Court made a fundamental change to the SRA to render the guidelines "effectively advisory" (p. 245). The decision excised provisions of the act that limited departures from the guideline range to extraordinary circumstances, and provisions that made the guidelines enforceable on appeal. This empowered judges to consider all relevant offense and offender characteristics that might make a sentence within the range greater than necessary to satisfy the purposes of sentencing, including factors that the commission had deemed "not ordinarily relevant."[3] Especially as clarified in the later decision of *Kimbrough v. United States*, 552 U.S. 85 (2007), judges were empowered to reject unsound guidelines, even in ordinary cases, if the guidelines recommendation fails to properly reflect the purposes of sentencing and other considerations listed at 18 U.S.C. § 3553(a). These include the traditional purposes of punishment—just deserts, protection of the public through deterrence and incapacitation of dangerous offenders, and rehabilitation and training of offenders. Sentences are to be "sufficient, but not greater than necessary" to achieve these purposes.

In the years since *Booker*, guideline application has become less rigid. Rates of sentences within the guideline range dropped by 10 percent immediately after the decision. They continued to decline steadily for

---

drug type and amount a major factor in assigning "offense levels," and pegging offense levels for first offenders to the thresholds and ratios in the statute. With mitigating adjustments, however, guideline ranges are sometimes below the statute, in which case the statutory minimum trumps the guideline recommendation. Several years after implementation of the guidelines, the commission departed from the statutory weighing method in cases involving LSD, due to extreme anomalies created by different carrier mediums by which the drug is distributed. See USSG App. C, Amend. 488 (Nov. 1, 1993). The Supreme Court in *Neal v. United States*, 516 U.S. 284 (1996) accepted the commission's approach for guideline calculation purposes, but not for application of mandatory minimum sentences. In recent years, the commission has felt legally constrained generally to conform the guidelines to the statutes.

[3] The "not ordinarily relevant" standard was developed by the commission to discourage departures from the guideline range for a variety of circumstances, such as employment record, family ties, or circumstances indicating a disadvantaged upbringing. The standard was loosened a few years after *Booker*, to enable judges to "depart" under provision of the guidelines in a wider variety of circumstances, rather than "vary" under their expanded powers granted by *Booker*. See USSC App. C. (amend. 739, eff. Nov 1, 2010). The typology of "departures" and "variances" to classify different types of sentences outside the guideline range was developed by the commission under the guidance of its chair at the time of the *Booker* decision, Judge Ricardo Hinojosa. The distinction has proven cumbersome to enforce and unhelpful for understanding judges' decisions. It was, however, the basis for the Supreme Court's allocation of the right to notice of a court's intention to sentence outside the guideline range, for reasons that make no sense from a procedural perspective (*Irizarry v. United States*, 128 S. Ct. 2198 (2008); Hofer 2009).

several years before reversing course and increasing slightly starting in 2015. Just fewer than half of defendants were sentenced within the guidelines range in fiscal year 2017. Judges regularly sentence below the guideline range for mitigating circumstances that were discouraged by the guidelines and appellate courts prior to *Booker*. Guidelines applying to several crimes, such as certain drug and child pornography offenses, are widely recognized to be excessive and are rejected by some judges in a large portion of cases.

But rendering the guidelines advisory could not address the biggest problems with federal sentencing. *Booker* did not amend the policy substance of the guidelines. The SRA's promise of guidelines that reflect best practices and empirical research remains unfulfilled. The commission's ability to amend the guidelines remains constrained both politically and legally. Even guidelines that lack any rationale or supporting evidence of effectiveness continue to exert a "gravitational pull," with substantial numbers of judges simply accepting that the guideline recommendation must have *some* sound basis.[4] Some appellate courts have actively discouraged sentencing judges from reviewing the soundness of guidelines through evidentiary hearings and expert testimony.

Sentencing judges for the most part have treated *Booker* as a general loosening of the constraints of the previous departure standard, rather than as a basis for reviewing the policies underlying the guidelines. They continue to search for unusual circumstances about the case that might justify departure rather than critically examine whether the guideline recommendation deserves deference in routine cases. The hope of reformers and academics for a critical jurisprudence, akin to the administrative law review given to rule-making by other agencies, has never emerged, despite unique circumstances of the sentencing guidelines that make it especially appropriate (Luby 1999; Miller and Wright 1999).

Most important, the parallel system of mandatory minimum sentence statutes remains in place, constraining both the commission and sentencing judges. These statutes, directly and indirectly, are the most important

---

[4] The most egregious examples were the guidelines applying to powder and crack cocaine until the revision of the 100:1 quantity ratio, as discussed below. Today, the career offender guideline (USSG § 4B1.1) requires prison terms at or near the statutory maximum for drug offenders with two prior convictions for drug or violent offenses, even though research has shown that the rule consistently overpredicts career offenders' risk of recidivism, makes the guidelines' criminal history category a worse risk prediction tool, and has severe adverse effects on African Americans (US Sentencing Commission 2004*a*, p. 134; 2004*b*, p. 9).

source of excessive severity and unwarranted disparity today. By giving prosecutors power to threaten and require severe punishments that are unreviewable by judges, these statutes enable prosecutors to pressure defendants to waive important procedural rights meant to bolster the system's truth-seeking functions. The statutory minimums constrain judges from imposing sentences best able to achieve the purposes of sentencing.

This essay begins with a review of *Booker* and subsequent decisions that raised hope that the SRA's vision of sentencing reform might be given new life. The second section presents data showing that, despite an immediate increase in imposition of sentences below the applicable guideline range, use of imprisonment did not decrease after *Booker*. Amendment of the drug guidelines and statutes governing crack cocaine sentencing reduced sentence severity more significantly than did the switch to advisory guidelines. Section III reviews reasons for this inertia, including the continuing gravitational pull of the guidelines and the failure of judges to develop a critical jurisprudence of the guidelines. The effects of the switch to advisory guidelines on various sources of unwarranted disparity are examined in Section IV. The final section discusses continuing problems caused by mandatory minimum penalty statutes, which both create unwarranted disparity and undermine the fairness of the federal sentencing process.

In sum, the switch to advisory guidelines had less effect on sentence severity and on judicial scrutiny of the guidelines' recommendations than the Supreme Court seemed to anticipate and reformers hoped. The commission and appellate courts have worked to discourage critical scrutiny and rejection of guidelines recommendations. Research suggests that inter-judge disparity has increased modestly following the decision. But despite suggestions from the commission that increased judicial discretion has increased racial disparity, the research is controversial and inconclusive. Moreover, judicial discretion is unlikely to be the greatest source of racial disparity in federal sentencing today. The *Booker* remedy of advisory guidelines has proven inadequate to address the most serious problems plaguing federal sentencing, in particular, congressional micromanagement of sentencing policy in the form of specific statutory directives and mandatory minimum penalties, many of which have unjustified adverse impacts. For the SRA's vision of sentencing reform to be realized, Congress and the commission will need to act. But current proposals for a return to more mandatory guidelines do not address the biggest problems with federal sentencing today.

I. What *Booker* Promised

The opinion in *Booker*, written by Justice Stephen Breyer, a principal author of the original federal guidelines when he was a member of the commission, suggested that the sentencing system envisioned in the SRA might have another chance. "The Sentencing Commission remains in place, writing Guidelines, collecting information about actual district court sentencing decisions, undertaking research, and revising the Guidelines accordingly" (p. 264). In this vision, the guidelines reflect the commission's expertise and its incorporation of empirical research and national experience. Judges review the guidelines recommendations but depart from them when appropriate to better advance the purposes of sentencing, explaining their reasons for doing so. The commission learns from this feedback and amends the guidelines as needed. Disparity created by prosecutors is controlled by guideline provisions—such as the standards for acceptance of plea agreements, and the relevant conduct rule (USSG § 1B1.3)[5]—while disparity created by judges is prevented by the guidelines themselves and by appellate review of unreasonable departures.

The problem is that this vision reflects more the dashed hopes of sentencing reformers than the realities of sentencing under the guidelines. The commission's own 15-year evaluation noted that "the goals of sentencing reform have been only partially achieved" (US Sentencing Commission 2004*a*, p. 144). Outside observers have been far less measured, declaring the federal system a "disaster" (Tonry 1996), a "dismal failure" (Cabranes 1992, p. 2), and "a cure worse than the disease" (Uelman 1992). Others were more moderate (GAO 1992), but very few found much to like (Cassell 2004). Some who initially defended the guidelines grew disillusioned (Bowman 1996, 2005). A widely held conclusion was: "Twenty-five years have produced a strong and informed consensus that the first

---

[5] This rule directs judges to consider facts beyond those entailed in the counts of conviction, permitting defendants to be held accountable for conduct that was never charged, or was covered in counts dropped as part of plea negotiations, or even conduct of which the defendant was acquitted. The intent of the rule was to prevent prosecutors' charging and plea bargaining decisions from limiting judicial options and creating disparity, but it also denies defendants the right to have certain facts proven to a jury beyond a reasonable doubt, even facts that are elements of potentially chargeable offenses. Justice Breyer has been a champion of the rule, which has been highly controversial (Breyer 1988; Reitz 1993).

bold and hopeful round of federal sentencing reform has largely failed" (Weisberg and Miller 2005, p. 35).

The reasons for this failure have been widely explored elsewhere and are greater and more numerous than the restrictions on departure that *Booker* addressed. Congress did not allow the commission to develop guidelines independently based on research and best practices. The commission did not articulate a substantive theory of the guidelines that explained how they advanced the purposes of sentencing, which could convince Congress and judges that the guidelines were worth defending and following. The Department of Justice came to appreciate mandatory minimums and congressional micromanagement of sentencing, which gave them powerful tools for threatening defendants and gaining their cooperation. Far from shielding sentencing from politics, the guidelines became the vehicle for political expression and professional advancement (Tonry 2006).

The tortured legal and political landscape of federal sentencing was reflected in the *Booker* decision itself. According to the five justices who joined the main opinion, the Sixth Amendment requires that juries, not judges, find facts that increase the maximum punishments to which defendants are exposed. The tops of the guidelines ranges were held to be such maximum punishments, because judges could not sentence higher without finding additional facts. Under this analysis, facts that the commission determines should increase a guideline range become in some respects like elements of an offense, requiring procedural rights such as inclusion in indictments and proof beyond a reasonable doubt.

But the procedural rights motivating the main opinion were effectively nullified by the parts of the opinion written by Justice Breyer, and joined by three other merit opinion dissenters plus Justice Ginsburg, which set out remedies to the constitutional problems. Justice Breyer reasoned that Congress would want to preserve the guideline system as much as possible to control disparity. For this to be possible with judicial fact-finding, this majority made the guidelines effectively advisory. While courts must still calculate and consider the guidelines range, judges can now impose any sentence within the statutory minimum and maximum for the counts of conviction, subject to appellate review under a "reasonableness" standard. The court invited Congress to adopt a different system if it wished.

In subsequent decisions, the court gave further content to *Booker*'s remedy. These made clear that the guidelines are the starting point, but sentencing judges should not presume they are reasonable and must address arguments that the guideline sentence does not comport with 18 U.S.C. § 3553(a). In *Rita v. United States*, 551 U.S. 338, 350 (2007), the court held that appellate courts may, but are not required to, apply a presumption of reasonableness to within guideline sentences. Most importantly, in *Rita*, Justice Breyer outlined a new type of challenge to the guidelines. As before *Booker*, judges may "depart" because the case "falls outside the 'heartland' to which the Commission intends individual Guidelines to apply" (*Rita*, at p. 351). But in addition, parties may "contest the Guidelines sentence generally under § 3553(a)," arguing that "the Guidelines sentence itself fails properly to reflect § 3553(a) considerations," that "the Guidelines reflect an unsound judgment," "that they do not generally treat certain offender characteristics in the proper way," or that "the case warrants a different sentence regardless" (p. 357).

In *Kimbrough v. United States*, 552 U.S. 85, 90–91 (2007), Justice Ginsburg, writing for the court, made clear that courts may reject guidelines recommendations based "solely on policy considerations, including disagreements with the Guidelines" (pp. 101–2). Moreover, it did not matter that the guideline in question—involving the 100:1 quantity ratio between powder and crack cocaine—originated in a policy determined by Congress. The court analyzed in detail whether the drug guideline was developed using the procedures set forth in the SRA and concluded that "the Commission did not use this empirical approach in developing the Guidelines sentences for drug-trafficking offenses. Instead, it employed the 1986 [Anti–Drug Abuse] Act's weight-driven scheme" (p. 96). She concluded that where a guideline "do[es] not exemplify the Commission's exercise of its characteristic institutional role," because the commission "did not take account of 'empirical data and national experience,'" it is not an abuse of discretion to conclude that the guideline "yields a sentence 'greater than necessary' to achieve § 3553(a)'s purposes, even in a mine-run case" (pp. 109–10).

With these and other decisions, the court appeared not just to "loosen" the standard for departure and increase judicial discretion. The court revived the vision of an evolving sentencing system that had never taken root prior to the decision and has failed to flower since. The commission would develop guidelines based on research. Courts would consider them, both in light of the facts of individual cases and in consideration of the applicable guidelines' method of development and supporting evidence.

II. Booker and Subsequent Cases' Effects on Sentencing

While *Booker* increased judicial discretion, it has done relatively little to address excessive severity and use of incarceration. Rates of sentencing below the guideline range increased immediately. But because the guidelines recommend sentences of incarceration for almost all defendants, rates of imprisonment were unaffected and continued their decades-long climb. Average sentence length fell by about 10 months but continued closely to track the guidelines recommendations.

A. Rates of Sentencing Below the Range

Booker had an immediate and undeniable effect on judges' willingness to sentence below the guideline range. Figure 1 shows the rates of below-range sentences in each quarter of fiscal years 2001 through 2017. Below-range sentences are divided between those that are sponsored by the government—as a reward for cooperation, or participation in an early disposition program, or otherwise part of plea negotiations—and other below-range sentences. A third line combines all below range. The data are taken from the commission's *Quarterly Sentencing Data Reports*, which are made available on the commission's website. The rate of sentences below the guideline range had begun to drop during the first term of George W. Bush, as the new administration began pushing a harder line in charging and plea negotiations. That administration's efforts to reverse what it incorrectly viewed as increasingly lenient sentencing by judges culminated in the Department of Justice working with Congress to enact the PROTECT Act of 2003, which eliminated departures below the guideline range for sex offenses involving children and directed the commission to discourage downward departures more generally[6] (Gregory and Kenner 2005; Schanzenbach 2005). The percentage of defendants sentenced below the guideline range fell through 2004.

---

[6] Prior to fiscal year 2001, the commission's data failed to properly differentiate between below-range sentences initiated by judges and those agreed to by the government. Much of the growth in below-range sentences prior to the PROTECT Act had been due to the informal growth of "fast track," or early disposition programs, which were developed in border districts to help manage the increased immigration caseload. These programs were formalized by the PROTECT Act, leading to the creation of the invited downward departure at USSG § 5K3.1 (US Sentencing Commission 2003). Like the distinction between departures and variances, the classification of sentences as government-sponsored or not depends on the reasons given by the court, which can often include a mix of reasons. In general, sentences involving at least one government-sponsored reason for departure are classified as government-sponsored departures.

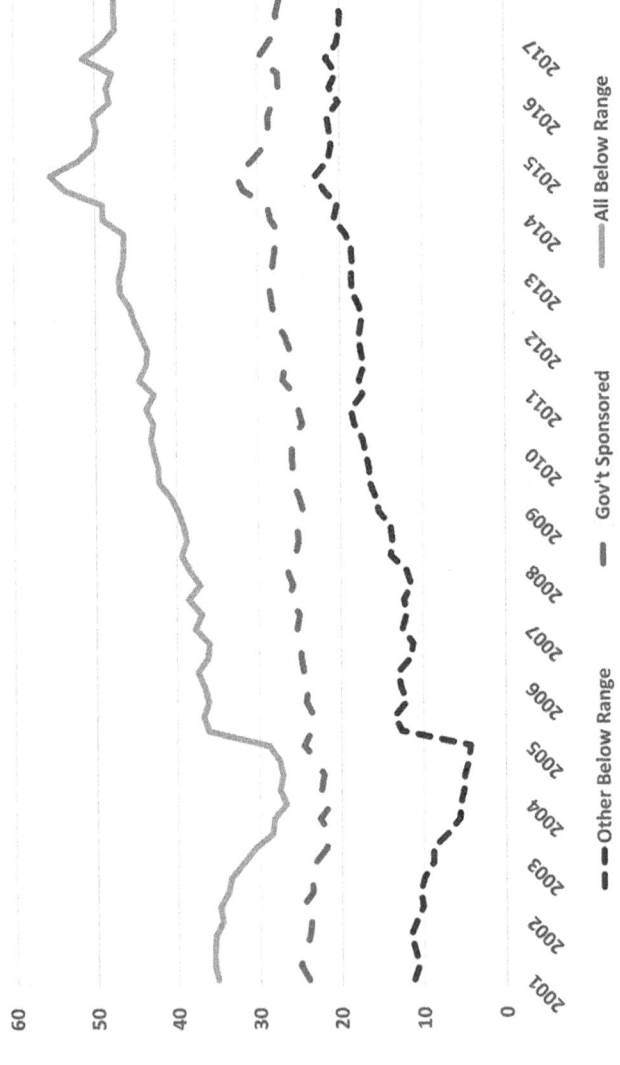

FIG. 1.—Percentage of defendants sentenced below the guideline range. Nationwide quarterly data, FY2001–FY2017. Source: USSC individual data files, FY2001–FY2017. Color version available as an online enhancement.

Immediately after *Booker*, however, the rate of sentences below the guideline range not sponsored by the government increased by just over 8 percent (Hofer 2007). After stalling and even falling slightly during the next several years of uncertainty, and appellate court efforts to restrain sentencing judges' discretion, by 2008 the rate began a slow and mostly steady rise. A temporary decrease in 2011 can be attributed largely to crack cocaine cases. Mandatory minimums and guideline ranges had been lowered by the commission and the Fair Sentencing Act of 2010, which replaced the infamous 100:1 ratio between powder and crack cocaine with an 18:1 ratio. Powder sentences remained the same, but the quantity thresholds for crack cocaine were increased, resulting in lower guideline sentences. These changes took effect in fiscal year 2011 and resulted in a larger portion of crack cases being sentenced within the guideline range.

Interestingly, the rate of sentences below the guideline range flattens and slightly reverses its upward trend again in fiscal year 2015. The reversal is again concentrated largely in drug trafficking cases, likely in response to amendment 782, which reduced base offense levels in the Drug Quantity Table for almost all drug offenses by two offense levels. In addition, the Department of Justice issued memoranda encouraging prosecutors to decline certain nonviolent, low-level drug cases, or to not charge quantities in the indictment that would bind judges to the statutory mandatory minimums.[7] This may well have reduced the number of mitigated cases for which judges had felt the guideline range was too high. It appears that changes to charging policy and amendments to the guidelines that make the guideline range appear more appropriate to sentencing judges can affect rates of sentencing within and below the range.

The most recent data as of this writing show that in the first half of fiscal year 2018, exactly half (50 percent) of sentences imposed under the guidelines were within the recommended guideline range (US Sentencing Commission 2018, table 8A). As has been true throughout the guidelines era, the government sponsors far more sentences below the range than are initiated by judges or imposed over government objections. The

---

[7] Memorandum from Eric Holder, US Attorney General, to US Attorneys and the Assistant Attorney General for the Criminal Division, Department Policy on Charging Mandatory Minimum Sentences and Recidivist Enhancements in Certain Drug Cases [August 12, 2013]; Memorandum from Eric Holder, US Attorney General, to Department of Justice Attorneys, Guidance Regarding § 851 Enhancements in Plea Negotiations [September 24, 2014].

commission, perhaps to suggest the continued relevance of its work, has taken to categorizing a larger group of 74.7 percent of cases as "sentences under the guidelines manual." This is achieved by including not only sentences within the guideline range, but also sentences outside the range for which the court cites at least one reason provided in the *Guidelines Manual*.

B. Types of Sentences Imposed

Despite the increase in the rate of sentences below the guideline range in the years following *Booker*, overall sentence severity was not dramatically affected by the switch to advisory guidelines. This is seen most dramatically in the continued increase in the already high portion of cases that receive sentences of imprisonment and continuing decreases in the portion that receive probation or some form of alternative punishment. Figure 2 displays data showing the percentages of offenders receiving imprisonment, probation, or alternative sanctions from fiscal years 1984 through 2017. In the first 4 years of guidelines implementation, the use of simple probation was cut in half. In 1987, 29 percent of offenders received sentences of probation, while in 1991 only 14 percent received simple probation.

Remarkably, the portion of offenders receiving probation has continued to fall after *Booker*. In 2017, only 6.9 percent received simple probation, while 2.1 percent received nonimprisonment alternatives, such as home confinement. While the SRA directed the commission to "minimize the likelihood that the Federal prison population will exceed the capacity of the Federal prisons" (28 U.S.C. § 994(g)), the Bureau of Prisons has exceeded its rated capacity throughout the guidelines era, including after *Booker*.

Booker did not amend the Guidelines Sentencing Table, which uses a zone system that makes probation or alternative confinement available as a within-guideline sentencing option only for relatively less serious offenses. The zones in which options are available have been only slightly expanded once since the guidelines were implemented. In 2018, the commission added commentary encouraging judges to consider a nonimprisonment sentence for nonviolent first offenders in zones A and B, at the lowest end of the offense seriousness scale. In 2017, just 20 percent of defendants fell in these zones, and 76 percent of these were detained prior to sentencing, which makes a sentence of probation or other alternatives

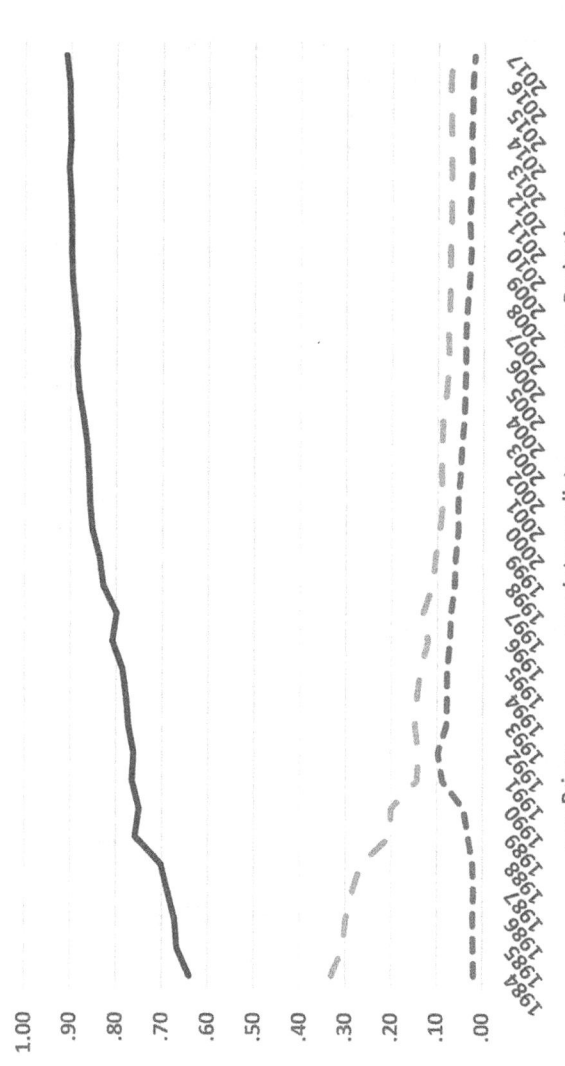

FIG. 2.—Percentage of defendants receiving various types of sentences. All defendants nationwide, FY1984–FY2017. Source: Federal Probation and Sentencing Supervision Information System Datafile, 1984–1990; USSC individual data files, FY1991–FY2017. Color version available as an online enhancement.

to incarceration unlikely. It seems unlikely that this change will have a substantial effect on rates of incarceration.

C. Average Sentence Lengths

The solid line in figure 3 shows the average sentence lengths in months for all cases in the fiscal years 2001 through 2017.[8] Strikingly, despite the large increase in the portion of below-range cases following *Booker*, average sentence lengths did not fall immediately after the decision. Average sentence lengths increased for 2 years due to increased prosecutions and higher guideline ranges for several types of crimes, particularly firearm and sex crimes. The subsequent decreases beginning in 2008 result to some extent from higher rates of below-range sentences, from amendments to the drug guidelines described above, and from lower guideline calculations in immigration cases.

Immigration offenses became the most common type of crime sentenced in federal court in 2010, nearly doubling from 17.5 percent of the caseload in 2001 to 34 percent in 2010. Immigration offenses therefore have an outsized effect on average sentences. Figure 4 shows the average sentences imposed on all offenses excluding immigration. Mean sentences for these offenses are both longer than with immigration included and show less of a decrease in the years following 2007. In 2017, the average sentence imposed in nonimmigration cases was 58.4 months, just a few months less than the peak of 61.3 months 10 years before.

III. Why Hasn't Booker Had a Greater Effect on Sentence Severity?

To people unfamiliar with how the guidelines were developed, half of federal sentences imposed below the guideline range may seem like a lot. But to people wanting punishments "not greater than necessary" to achieve the purposes of sentencing, it may seem like too few. Over three-quarters of defendants in federal court are sentenced under guidelines that were not developed independently by the commission but were instead shaped by statutory mandatory minimums or other congressional directives. Given

---

[8] These data were generated from the US Sentencing Commission individual data files for these fiscal years, using the same selection criteria as used in the commission's *Quarterly Reports*, fig. E. The average includes all cases, including those receiving zero months of imprisonment. Sentence lengths and guideline minimums are capped at 470 months, including sentences of life imprisonment.

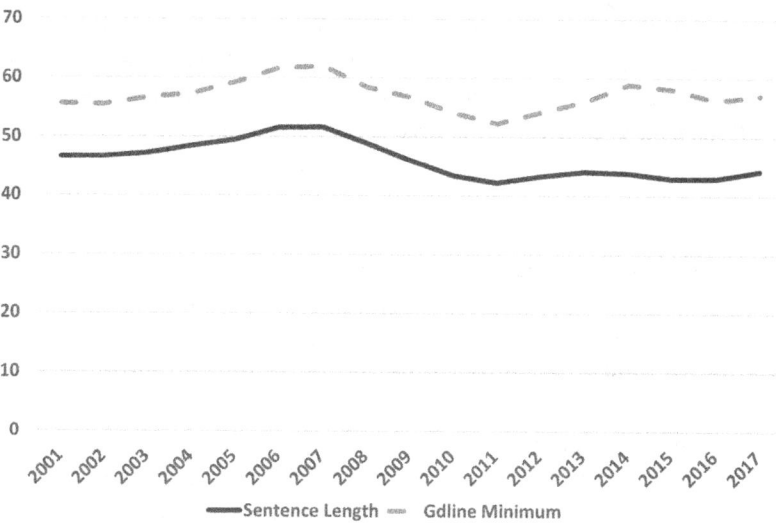

Fig. 3.—Mean sentence length and guideline minimum months. All defendants nationwide, FY2001–FY2017. Source: USSC individual data files, FY2001–FY2017. Color version available as an online enhancement.

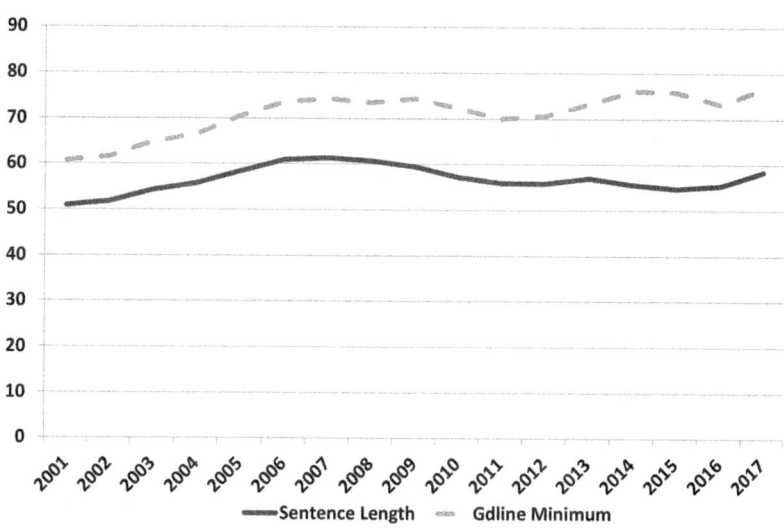

Fig. 4.—Mean sentence length and guideline minimum months. All defendants except immigration, FY2001–FY2017. Source: USSC individual data files, FY2001–FY2017. Color version available as an online enhancement.

that *Booker*, *Rita*, and *Kimbrough* invited judges to examine how the guidelines were developed, as well as research on their effectiveness and proportionality, the better question might be: Why do so many defendants continue to be sentenced within a range recommended by unsound guidelines?

A. The Guidelines Remain the Focus at Sentencing

The continuing influence of the guidelines and mandatory minimum sentence statutes on sentences is also reflected in figures 3 and 4. The dashed line above the sentence length line shows the average of the minimum of the guideline ranges applicable to these cases, including any statutory minimums that trump the otherwise applicable guideline ranges. Both prior to *Booker* and after until about 2013, trends in sentences imposed have closely paralleled trends in the guidelines' recommendations. The gap between the average guideline minimum and average sentence imposed grew slightly after *Booker*, as is especially visible in the nonimmigration cases in figure 4, as the rate of below-range sentences increased. But the slopes and plateaus in both lines follow the same trajectory over the years, including an upward trend in the 2 most recent years.

This illustrates that as a practical matter, the guidelines still exert a gravitational pull. Judges are directed by § 3553(a) to consider the "nature and circumstances of the offense and the history and characteristics of the defendant," all the traditional purposes of sentencing, and the guideline range. But the former are general and abstract, while the guideline range provides a concrete number. The guideline range acts as a psychological "anchor" against which even sentences outside the range are measured. As noted by one judicial observer: "Whether people like that number or not, even if they are angry about that number, does not matter; they will still be influenced by that number. That is the psychological fact. I think it is psychologically inevitable that the Guidelines will have a powerful influence on sentences, even if they are purely advisory" (Adelman et al. 2006, quoting Judge Gerald Lynch, pp. 17–18; Gertner 2006, 2007; Bennet 2014).

It is notable that the federal advisory guidelines have many of the attributes of what is considered a relatively mandatory system in the states (Reitz 2005). Judges are required to calculate the guideline range and to state reasons for departing from the range. Sentences are reviewable on appeal, and rates of compliance and departure are monitored by the commission, and even by some members of Congress. All of this makes the federal "advisory" system more like "mandatory" or "presumptive" systems in the states.

Another reason so many defendants continue to be sentenced based on unsound guidelines might be called fear of discretion. If the fairness and effectiveness of a guideline are doubted, judges may feel at a loss for objective standards and principles to help them determine the right sentence. The statutory purposes of sentencing are abstract and sometimes point in different directions. Because the commission has offered little explanation of *how* the specifics of many guidelines are intended to achieve the purposes of sentencing, judges are given little with which to evaluate whether a guideline is working in a particular case. Why undertake the hard work of scrutinizing the guidelines, explaining ones' reasoning, and risking appellate and congressional scrutiny, when the guidelines provide a safe harbor? Defense attorneys learned that arguing for mitigating circumstances was often easier and more likely to succeed than tackling the evidentiary bases of a guideline recommendation.

B. Courts Have Not Reached Consensus on Which Guidelines Are Unsound

A remarkable aspect of post-*Booker* sentencing is that rejection of a guideline's recommendation depends relatively little, at least in the aggregate, on a guideline's method of development or its supporting rationale and evidence. To be sure, a few judges have written extensive opinions criticizing particular guidelines. The guidelines for certain drug offenses have received critical scrutiny, especially regarding methamphetamine and its precursors (e.g., *United States v. Hayes*, 948 F. Supp. 2d 1009 [N.D. Iowa 2013]); MDMA [ecstasy], *United States v. Qayyem*, 2012 WL 92287 [S.D.N.Y. 2012] and Michelman and Rorty [2012]; synthetic marijuana, Gershel [2017]). So has the guideline for child pornography receipt and possession (*United States v. Grober*, 595 F. Supp. 2d 382 [D.N.J. 2008]). The so-called career offender guideline, which enhances sentences for drug and violent offenders with two prior convictions, has been repeatedly criticized (e.g., *United States v. Hodges*, 2009 WL 366231 E.D.N.Y. [2009]). But given that nearly a million defendants have been sentenced under the advisory system, the number of opinions rigorously evaluating the rationale and evidence for the guidelines' recommendations is small.

Apart from written opinions, another perspective into judges' views about different guidelines might be provided by comparing rates of sentencing within and outside particular guidelines' recommended ranges. It is easy to make too much of these comparisons, however. Rates of sentencing outside the range are affected by factors besides judges' satisfaction with the guideline. Some guidelines contain many more adjustments to the offense level than others, reducing the number of possible grounds for departure or variance. Some offenses are more narrowly defined and contain a narrower range of offense and offender characteristics. Rates of government-sponsored below-range sentences also vary, as do limitations to departure created by mandatory minimum sentence statutes.

Despite these complications, it is instructive to review rates of placement relative to the range to see if any patterns emerge. Table 1 shows these rates in fiscal years 2008 through 2017 for several of the most frequently applied guidelines. The public corruption and money laundering guidelines are among the least followed recommendations. Note, however, that in both cases high rates of government-sponsored below-range sentences may reflect prosecutors' interest in obtaining cooperation from

TABLE 1

Rates of Placement Relative to the Range: Selected Guidelines (FY2008–FY2017)

	Placement of Sentence Relative to the Guideline Range (%)			
	Within Range	Above Range	Gov.-Sponsored Below	Other Below
First-degree murder	48.9	1.0	38.3	11.8
Economic crimes	51.6	2.2	20.8	25.3
Robbery	49.8	6.0	22.5	21.7
Counterfeiting	62.8	2.5	13.4	21.3
Public corruption	27.2	1.2	41.2	30.4
Drug trafficking	41.0	1.0	37.7	20.2
Traffic listed chemicals	24.6	.4	39.3	35.7
Drugs protected locations	66.4	1.7	18.9	12.9
Travel for sex with minor	51.8	5.2	23.5	19.4
Child porn production	46.4	3.5	23.8	26.4
Child porn trafficking	34.3	1.9	17.7	46.1
Obstruction of justice	36.5	4.7	26.0	32.8
Firearm traffic or possess	59.4	3.4	14.9	22.4
Alien smuggling	46.3	2.2	41.3	1.1
Illegal entry into US	57.4	1.8	28.6	12.2
Money laundering	29.1	1.2	44.0	25.6
Structuring transactions	43.1	.9	28.4	27.6
Tax evasion	33.6	1.2	22.3	42.9

defendants in these cases more than judicial dissatisfaction with the guidelines. Surprisingly, the guideline with the highest rate of within-range sentencing is USSG § 2D1.2, involving drug offenses near protected locations.

Most noteworthy, however, is the absence of any obvious pattern in the types of guidelines whose recommendations are most commonly accepted or rejected by judges. Guidelines for offenses such as first-degree murder were developed by the commission relatively independently, in its characteristic institutional role, based on consultation with stakeholders, research into past sentencing practices, and other matters. Other guidelines, such as those concerning child pornography and sex offenses, or economic crimes like fraud, have been the subject of frequent congressional directives that override commission rule-making (Sentencing Resource Counsel 2016). With the exception of relatively low within-range rates for child pornography distribution and possession (trafficking), rates of compliance have little obvious connection to a guideline's pedigree, rationale, or supporting evidence.

A guideline heavily influenced by congressional micromanagement, both through statutory mandatory minimums and repeated congressional directives, is the main guideline for drug trafficking, USSG § 2D1.1. This, of course, is the very guideline criticized by the Supreme Court in *Kimbrough*. There is no better example of a guideline utterly lacking a consistent rationale or supporting evidence. The commission abandoned its research-based guideline development when Congress enacted mandatory minimums in the Anti–Drug Abuse Act of 1986 and simply incorporated and expanded the quantity thresholds and ratios in the statute (Skotkin 1990). And these were not based on research, or even normal legislative process (US Sentencing Commission 1995). There were no committee hearings or reports, and some amendments were added when the legislation reached the floor. Participants in this legislation described it as "like an auction house . . . this frenzied, panic atmosphere—I'll see your five years and raise your five years. It was the crassest political poker game" (Isikoff and Thompson [1990], quoting Eric Sterling at C1). The result was quantity thresholds that are far too low and have no relation to offense seriousness.[9] No other policy change had a greater effect on federal prison populations (Scalia 2002).

---

[9] Eric Sterling, "Testimony before the House Subcommittee on Crime, Terrorism, and Homeland Security, Committee on the Judiciary," in *Mandatory Minimum Sentencing Laws—the Issues* (Washington, DC: US Government Printing Office), 110th Cong., 1st Sess., June 26, 2007, at p. 166.

The 100:1 quantity ratio between powder and crack cocaine was heavily criticized for 24 years before Congress eventually revised it in 2010. But the penalties for many other drugs are similarly disproportionate and severe, compared both to pre-guideline sentencing practice and to sentences for other types of crime. The guidelines recommendations have little relation to the relative seriousness of different drug crimes, as measured by typical dosage weights, or to the public health harms caused by different drugs (Hofer 2015). Yet the rate of sentences within the drug trafficking guideline in the years since *Booker* is only modestly lower than the overall rate, and higher than several guidelines developed by the commission in its more characteristic institutional role.

Table 2 shows placement rates for various drugs in the 5 years since USSG § 2D1.1 was amended. Within-range rates are relatively low for MDMA, methamphetamine actual, and ICE (another name for relatively pure, smokable methamphetamine), all of which have been criticized by judges and other commentators for excessive severity. More perplexing is relatively high compliance with the guidelines for pseudoephedrine, a precursor to methamphetamine, for which the guidelines recommend extremely severe sentences—even higher than for the methamphetamine into which it could be made. Similarly, compliance with the revised crack cocaine guideline is as high as for powder, even though the revised guideline still treats crack far more harshly than similar quantities of the powder from which it is made. Sentences below the range

TABLE 2

Rates of Placement Relative to the USSG § 2D1.1 Range: Selected Primary Drugs (FY2013–FY2017)

	Placement of Sentence Relative to the Guideline Range (%)			
	Within Range	Above Range	Gov.-Sponsored Below	Other Below
Cocaine	38.1	1.2	33.1	22.6
Crack/base	38.7	1.7	32.7	26.3
Heroin	32.7	2.3	38.6	26.4
Marijuana	42.0	1.6	39.0	17.4
Meth	30.5	.6	47.7	21.1
ICE	28.3	.5	45.0	26.2
Ecstasy/MDMA	20.5	1.0	43.7	34.8
Meth actual	26.5	.4	50.2	22.9
Pseudoephedrine	38.4	.6	36.5	24.6

are more common for heroin than for crack, even though the guidelines recommend less severe sentences for heroin than for similar doses of crack, and opiates are the most dangerous major drugs for overdose risk (Hofer 2015).

In general, there does not appear to be a close connection between the rationale and evidence supporting a particular guideline's recommendations and judicial acceptance of those recommendations. Despite the invitation in *Rita* and *Kimbrough* for judges to review the guidelines in light of the purposes of sentencing, a critical jurisprudence has failed to develop. Perhaps this is unsurprising, because institutions that might have encouraged such a jurisprudence have largely done the opposite.

C. Appellate Courts and the Commission Have Not Encouraged Judicial Review of Guidelines

Prior to *Booker*, appellate courts surprised many with their willingness to enforce the guidelines with strict interpretation of the standards for departure. Since *Booker*, appellate courts have again seemed more concerned with maintaining the status quo than with improving the commission's rule-making and district courts' sentencing (Pratt 2016). Many appellate courts determined that sentences within the guidelines range would be considered presumptively reasonable, giving sentencing judges a safe harbor without fear of reversal (Hessick and Hessick 2008). The reasonableness standard for review of sentences outside the range bifurcated into procedural and substantive reasonableness (King 2006) and led largely to a retreat from meaningful substantive review of sentences both outside and inside the range. Guideposts in *Rita* and *Kimbrough* that might have developed into principles of review—such as distinctions between guidelines that were or were not developed by the commission in its "characteristic institutional role," or based on "empirical data and national experience"—were left dormant.

In the years since *Booker*, not a single appellate court has unambiguously held that sentences within a guideline are presumptively unreasonable, regardless of the evidence that a particular guideline was politically motivated and unsound. This includes several years during which neither the commission nor the Department of Justice defended the reasonableness of the 100:1 quantity ratio between crack and powder cocaine; indeed, both had determined that the ratio was unjust. Despite this lack of support, many judges continued to accept the crack guideline's unfair recommendations without fear of reversal. The Second Circuit, in *United States v. Dorvee*, 616 F.3d 174 (2010), came close to declaring the distribution of child pornography guideline unsound, writing that it is beset with "irrationality" that, "unless applied with great care, can lead to unreasonable sentences inconsistent with what § 3553 requires." But for the most part, rather than take up the Supreme Court's invitation to review and reject unsound guidelines, the appellate courts largely left sentencing judges to themselves.

Some appellate courts explicitly discouraged critical analyses of a guideline's pedigree and research basis. In the words of the Fifth Circuit:

> This Court has squarely held that district courts are not required to engage in "a piece-by-piece analysis of the empirical grounding behind each part of the sentencing guidelines" and ignore those parts that do not pass empirical muster. We fully agree with the Seventh Circuit that a rule to the contrary would render "sentencing hearings unmanageable, as the focus shifts from the defendant's conduct to the 'legislative' history of the guidelines." As we have said before, "empirically based or not, the Guidelines remain the Guidelines. It is for the Commission to alter or amend them." (*United States v. Malone*, 828 F.3d 331 [5th Cir. 2016], at p. 338 [internal citations omitted])

For these judges, *Booker*'s invitation to engage in a critical dialogue with the commission to help the guidelines evolve was simply declined.

The commission also squandered the opportunity created by *Booker* to encourage judges to seek fairer and effective sentences. Rather than embrace the decision and use it to harness expanded judicial discretion to the goals of the SRA, the commission resisted and minimized it. Rather than clarify the pedigree of different guidelines so that judges could evaluate how well they reflect research, consultation, and best practices, as opposed to congressional directives, the commission obscured such distinctions. The chair of the commission testified before Congress and claimed that all the guidelines had been developed with the procedures outlined in the SRA, completely ignoring that the commission's own policy development process for important guidelines like USSG § 2D1.1 had been abandoned when Congress intervened. He argued that all the sentencing procedures developed prior to *Booker*, such as probation officer calculation of the guideline range, should continue as before. And most tellingly, without mentioning the new type of challenge to sentences within the guideline range outlined in *Rita* and *Kimbrough*, he claimed that all the guidelines deserve "substantial weight," without regard to pedigree or supporting evidence.[10]

By removing the legal compulsion of mandatory guidelines, *Booker* seemed to require the commission to convince judges that the guidelines offered sound advice by providing more evidence and explanation of how the guidelines achieve the statutory purposes. But rather than embrace this requirement and use it as an argument to Congress that it must finally do the job it was given by the SRA, the commission acted less like an independent agency in the judicial branch and more like a junior partner to the political branches.

D. Understanding Congress's Role in Guideline Development

The SRA established broad principles to guide policy development but purportedly left to the commission the technocratic task of fashioning guidelines to advance those principles. Congress continued to intervene, however, even using the presumptive guidelines as a new tool for controlling sentencing directly. After *Booker*, two contradictory arguments developed about how judges should respond to guidelines whose recommendations were shaped by Congress instead of independent commission research. Some argued that a congressional pedigree should be seen as a red flag that a guideline might be a product of politics rather than the expertise envisioned in the SRA (Exum 2010; Hessick and Hessick 2010). How likely is it in a "tough on crime" era that Congress would arrive at sentences "sufficient, but not greater than necessary" to achieve the purposes of sentencing? How likely is it that congressmen and women, who never meet the defendants to whom their mandates apply, would recognize the range of characteristics and circumstances relevant to an appropriate sentence? By this reasoning, guidelines resulting from congressional micromanagement deserve less deference than guidelines that reflect the commission acting in its intended role as independent expert agency.

The other argument urged the opposite conclusion. The Supreme Court in *Harmelin v. Michigan*, 501 U.S. 957 (1991) held that legislatures

---

[10] Ricardo H. Hinojosa, "Prepared Statement of Ricardo Hinojosa Before the House Subcommittee on Crime, Terrorism, and Homeland Security, House Committee on the Judiciary, United States House of Representatives," in *The Implications of the Booker/ Fanfan Decisions for the Federal Sentencing Guidelines* (Washington, DC: US Government Printing Office), February 10, 2005, p. 3.

have nearly unconstrained constitutional authority to establish criminal penalties. So guidelines with a congressional pedigree are viewed by some as deserving more deference. Penalties under such guidelines reflect the will of the people as expressed through their elected representatives. Some judges may also be concerned that rejecting guidelines recommendations frequently and explicitly will attract unfavorable attention, both from the appellate courts and from Congress. Legislative efforts to obtain data on judicial "compliance" with the guidelines reinforced such concerns (Hewitt 2016).

Judges are indeed bound by legislative policies when expressed in unambiguous statutes such as mandatory minimum penalties. But there are important differences between statutes and the sentencing guidelines. Even prior to *Booker*, judges were permitted to depart from guideline recommendations—even when a guideline linguistically applied to a case—if there were circumstances not adequately taken into consideration by the commission. *Booker*, *Rita*, and *Kimbrough* further expanded this authority. Moreover, individualization is an important part of sentencing, as Justice Steven reminded in *Gall v. United States*, 552 U.S. 38 (2007).

In addition, the guidelines are part of a system that the SRA anticipated would entail certain methods of guideline development and implementation, and which should justify certain expectations in defendants. The guidelines should reflect the commission's expertise, not political posturing, and applying a guideline range to an individual defendant should reflect a judicial determination that the recommended sentence is "sufficient, but not greater than necessary" to achieve the purposes of sentencing. If judges merely assume that recommendations based largely on mandatory minimums or other statutory directives meet these criteria, they risk mechanically implementing congressional will rather than exercising individualized judgment. *Mistretta v. United States*, 488 U.S. 361, 407 (1989), upheld the constitutionality of the guidelines against a separation of powers challenge. But Justice Blackmun noted that the political branches should not be allowed to "cloak" their political decisions in the "neutral colors of judicial action." To prevent this seems to require that judges need to review the pedigrees of guidelines recommendations.

It is unfortunate that sentences outside the range the guidelines recommend, when motivated by critical review of a guideline rather than unusual circumstances present in a case, are often called "policy disagreements." This characterization evokes the philosophical differences among judges that led to much of the disparity the guidelines were designed to reduce. Several courts, including the Supreme Court, have even suggested in dicta that such "policy disagreements" might deserve greater scrutiny on appeal than more traditional departures based on mitigating circumstances. But guidelines can be rejected based on empirical evidence of the seriousness of a crime or the effectiveness of a guideline. These are findings that the guideline recommendation does not comply with the purposes of sentencing, not merely personal policy preferences. Critical examination of the guidelines by the courts might lead to a critical guideline jurisprudence and better reasoned sentences (Hofer 2006).

IV. Booker Increased Some Types of Disparity but Decreased Others

The legislative history of the SRA describes "shameful disparity" as a "major flaw in the criminal justice system" (S. Rep. No. 98-225, at p. 65 [1983]), and eliminating it was a primary goal of the SRA (Feinberg 1991). Given these concerns, the guidelines' success at reducing disparity, both before and after *Booker*, has naturally been the subject of much research and analysis. There was no consensus on whether the guidelines reduced disparity before *Booker*, however (US Sentencing Commission 2004), so it is unsurprising that the effect of the decision is also controversial (Hofer 2013). Some of the disagreements are methodological. Some are over definitions—what counts as unwarranted disparity and what types of disparity should sentencing guidelines try to control.

If we define disparity in terms of the purposes of sentencing, and examine all of its sources, there are reasons to believe total unwarranted disparity was greater after the SRA, the Anti–Drug Abuse Act, and promulgation of the distorted guidelines than it had been before. The pre-*Booker* guidelines modestly reduced inter-judge disparity but dramatically increased prosecutor-created and structural disparity that results from unsound sentencing rules. The shift of discretion to prosecutors resulted in charging and plea-bargaining decisions that could not be controlled by Department of Justice policies and that went unchecked by judicial review. Most important, unsound mandatory minimums and guidelines linked to them created profound adverse effects, especially on African American males. Commission research acknowledged that this structural disparity had a greater discriminatory effect on African American males than did the unstructured judicial discretion prior to the guidelines. In 2004 the commission reported: "Today's sentencing policies, crystalized into the sentencing guidelines and mandatory minimum statutes, have a greater adverse impact on Black offenders than did the factors taken into account by judges in the discretionary system in place immediately prior to guidelines implementation" (US Sentencing Commission 2004a, p. 135).

No statistical model invented so far is able to measure all sources of disparity in the system as a whole and definitively quantify whether *Booker* made things better or worse. Different types of research illuminate different pieces of the puzzle. Research suggests that some forms of disparity, particularly inter-judge disparity, have increased. Much has been made, especially by the commission and the Department of Justice, of a post-*Booker* increase in a particular type of "race effect" revealed by multivariate regression studies, which ignore disparity created by prosecutors and the adverse effects of the sentencing rules themselves. But *Booker* has also provided opportunities to reduce the types of unwarranted disparity ignored in multiple regression studies. The gap in average sentences between black and white defendants has shrunk in recent years, from a combination of commission actions, congressional reform of the crack statutes, and decisions of many judges to reject guideline recommendations based on unsound and discriminatory policies. More progress could be made if Congress and the courts applied disparate impact analysis to unsound sentencing rules with substantial adverse impact.

A. Judge-Created Disparity

A notable feature of research on federal sentencing disparity is that, until very recently, it has largely focused on a single type—racial disparity created by judicial decision-making. There are no good reasons to believe this is the only, or even the greatest, source of unfair racial disparity. But it has received the most attention for a variety of reasons, including the greater availability of data on judicial decisions and the long tradition of using multiple regression analyses to identify patterns of racial bias.

The type of disparity most clearly identified prior to enactment of the SRA, however, was disparity caused by philosophical differences among judges. This has been called inter-judge disparity and can be measured as the "primary judge effect"—the difference in average sentences among judges sentencing groups of similar cases (Hofer, Blackwell, and Ruback 1999). Because cases are randomly assigned to judges in most large federal courthouses, the primary judge effect can be assessed with a powerful natural experiment methodology. The best estimate is that the primary judge effect was reduced by an average of about 1 month under the pre-*Booker* guidelines system (Anderson, Kling, and Stith 1999). The commission viewed this reduction as "modest" but nonetheless "significant progress" (US Sentencing Commission 2004*a*, p. 99). Others, however, viewed this measure as missing the most important types of normative disparity, including structural disparity from unsound rules (Alschuler 2005).

The transition to advisory guidelines has resulted in an increase in the primary judge effect. An early examination of post-*Booker* sentencing by judges in one federal courthouse found such an increase (Scott 2010). A more recent nationwide study found that under the mandatory guidelines, the differences between harsher and more lenient judges sentencing similar caseloads varied on average, depending on the time period, by 2.5 to 2.8 months (Yang 2014). Following *Booker*, this increased to 4.8 months, and following *Kimbrough* and *Gall* it increased to 5.9 months. Differences among judges have been linked to some judicial characteristics, such as which president appointed them (Cohen and Yang 2018).

This confirms the finding of previous research that differences in sentencing philosophies can affect sentences, and presumptive or mandatory guidelines can constrain these differences to some extent. Disentangling the influences of judges and prosecutors is tricky, however, and "some of the inter-judge disparities may be attributable to prosecutors' uneven application of mandatory minimums" (Yang 2015). One author concluded that "the effect of the judge remains relatively modest" and noted that "inter-judge sentencing disparity is but one consideration among many in evaluating the federal sentencing system. It is entirely possible to conclude that *Booker*, *Kimbrough*, and *Gall* have improved federal sentencing, on balance, by allowing judges greater flexibility to reject unjust guidelines and impose just sentences" (Scott 2010, p. 41).

Although *Booker* increased inter-judge disparity, it also gave judges tools to combat structural disparity. Some of the inter-judge disparity today results from different judges deploying these tools in different ways. For example, imagine that prior to *Booker*, 10 judges in a district were constrained to sentence within the guideline range for so-called career offenders. After *Booker*, five of these judges review the evidence showing that the career offender guideline's recommendation to substantially increase sentences for defendants with prior drug offenses actually makes the criminal history category a worse predictor of recidivism—offenders assigned to the highest risk category by the career offender guideline have recidivism rates much lower than other offenders in that category. Moreover, the guideline has a significant adverse racial impact (US Sentencing Commission 2004a, pp. 133–34). If these five judges reject the guideline and sentence below the range, while the other five continue their prior practice, there would be an increase in inter-judge disparity. However, the structural disparity caused by the unsound guideline would be reduced by half. If a statistical model were able to measure all sources of disparity, the increase in inter-judge disparity would be accompanied by a decrease in the unfair adverse impact of the career offender rule.

The way to reduce both inter-judge and structural disparity would be for the guidelines to be revised to better reflect the research and the statutory purposes. It seems likely that many, if not most, of the judges who today feel bound to impose the guideline sentence for career offenders would be happy to impose sentences within an amended guideline range that better reflects these defendants' true recidivism risk and culpability. But that requires much more than a switch to advisory guidelines; it would take legislation repealing the specific directive in the SRA that required the commission to create the career offender guideline.

B. Racial Disparity in Judicial Decisions

The standard approach to studying racial disparity in judicial decisions (which is often mistakenly characterized as assessing racial disparity in sentencing more generally) is to use multiple regression to assess differences in average sentences among groups after controlling for "legally relevant differences" among members of each group. The logic is straightforward: first, obtain data on crimes, criminal histories, and other factors that might legitimately affect sentencing. In guidelines systems this has been done by using the "presumptive sentence"—the minimum sentence recommended by the guidelines themselves (Engen and Gainey 2000). Next, subtract differences in sentences that are correlated with these factors, then compare any remaining average differences among groups. It has long been known that legally relevant differences reduce the gap among groups. If a gap remains, however, researchers often attribute it to bias, unconscious stereotypes, or some other factor affecting judicial decisions.

Several problems have plagued such research. Multiple regression models are highly technical and rely on various assumptions that can go wrong and be misunderstood (Blank, Dabady, and Citro 2004). The data on legally relevant factors that might explain different treatment are incomplete. This is especially true for factors that might justify departure from the guidelines or that might influence the decision to imprison an offender or use an alternative sanction like home confinement. Whenever a factor is correlated with race and with sentences imposed—such as the type of gun used in the crime, or the defendant's role in supporting dependent minors—but is not included in the statistical controls, any effect of the factor will be mistakenly attributed to race.

In addition to problems with missing control variables, statistical models can be unstable and are frequently misspecified. In studies of federal sentencing, researchers have often failed to accurately model the ways that statutory mandatory minimums truncate or trump the guidelines range (Hofer 2016). Because this trumping and truncating are more common in cases of African American men, models that fail to capture it can attribute to judicial discretion race effects that are actually due to the mandatory statutes—a misattribution that can lead to wildly wrong policy implications. Results from multiple regression studies have also proven sensitive to variations in the populations analyzed and the definitions of outcomes (Ulmer, Light, and Kramer 2011; Ulmer and Light 2013).

Prior to the guidelines, a comprehensive review of research on racial disparity in judicial decisions in the federal courts found inconsistent results. Sentencing differences by race or ethnicity were uniformly small or insignificant and were affected by variations in the statistical models used (McDonald and Carlson 1993). The commission's examination of similar research on the guidelines during the pre-*Booker* era also found methodological differences and contradictory findings: "Different studies yield different answers as to whether discrimination influences sentences at all and, if so, how much" (US Sentencing Commission 2004*a*, p. 118). After conducting its own analysis and noting that results fluctuated from year to year, the commission concluded that "there is reason to doubt that these racial and ethnic effects reflect deep-seated prejudices or stereotypes among judges" (US Sentencing Commission 2004*a*, p. 125).

The proliferation of conflicting findings has continued in the post-*Booker* era. The commission has published four replications and variations of the multivariate regression analysis first introduced in the pre-*Booker Fifteen Year Review* (US Sentencing Commission 2004*a*, 2006, 2010, 2012, 2017). After controlling for the presumptive sentence and a few other legally relevant factors on which data are available, these results showed differences among sentences imposed on men and women, and also among racial and ethnic groups. The commission has especially highlighted differences between black and white men, which varied at the mean from an average of 5.5 months in the pre-*Booker* PROTECT Act era to 19.1 months in the most recent years (US Sentencing Commission 2017). Commission reports and recommendations have attributed the increase in racial disparity to increased judicial discretion resulting from *Booker* (Hofer 2013).

Outside researchers have replicated the commission's analysis and tried varying aspects of its methodology to see how the results were affected. Ulmer, Light, and Kramer (2011) tried excluding immigration offenses, which are handled differently in high-volume districts, and including a separate control variable for criminal history.[11] They also separated the sentencing decision into the initial decision to incarcerate, as opposed to using a sentencing option such as probation, and for offenders who are sent to prison, the length of imprisonment. They found that much of the disparity reported by the commission is explained by differences among groups in criminal history beyond its effect on the presumptive sentence, and arises mostly in the decision to incarcerate, not in lengths of imprisonment. In general, they found that racial disparity in the years after *Booker* was comparable to pre-2003 levels.

These conflicting findings led to a great deal of interest and were the subject of a special section in a leading criminology journal (Engen 2011). None of this controversy affected the commission, however, which continued to update its findings using largely the same regression model. The controversies demonstrated once again, however, that variations in the statistical model, or the population included in an analysis, can significantly affect results. Moreover, it became clear that different models answer different questions and that no model is perfect or capable of measuring all sources of disparity. The commission developed its regression model in 2004 to identify whether unwarranted racial, ethnic, or gender disparity could be detected in the decisions of judges, which is the traditional use of these models. But after *Booker*, attention naturally turned

---

[11] Adding criminal history category as a control in addition to the presumptive sentence assesses whether judges weigh criminal history differently from its effect on the guideline recommendation.

to a different, and much harder, question: whether *Booker* caused any changes in the amount of this disparity among demographic groups.

The commission did not confront the methodological challenges involved in inferring any causal effects of the decision on its measure of disparity (Starr and Rehavi 2013, p. 49). Rather than develop a unified model that assessed all time periods using the same control variables and weights, it simply applied its regression model to different time periods, before and after *Booker*, and compared the size of the race effect at these different periods. It did not attempt to disentangle other changes occurring over the same periods, including changes in caseload, prosecutorial priorities, and the interrelationships of the control variables in its model. Researchers outside the commission tackled the problem of inferring causation more directly, and this further highlighted limitations in the ability of statistical control and nonexperimental designs to assess causation.

For example, econometricians seeking to assess the causal effect of *Booker* differed sharply with the commission on several methodological issues (Fischman and Schanzenbach 2012; Starr 2013). One issue concerned whether the regression model should include control variables indicating whether an upward or downward departure was present in the case. When such controls are included, sentences in cases receiving departures are adjusted by the average reduction or increase for that type of departure. Sentencing differences among demographic groups are calculated after this adjustment, so any differences among groups in the rate of receiving such departures is controlled for (more defendants in groups with a higher rate of departure will receive the adjustment). Criminologists have generally included such controls, because the goal of criminological research has been to identify bias in the decisions of judges. If the presence of a departure represents real factual differences from cases that do not receive a departure, excluding this control risks attributing to demographics, and to judicial bias, differences that are better explained by factual differences.

Econometricians focusing on the causal effects of *Booker* see it differently. The most striking effect of *Booker* was to change the rate of below-range cases. These changes are endogenous—that is, causally related—to *Booker*. To the econometricians, controlling away the effects of departures is to control away the primary effect of *Booker*. If judges and prosecutors create demographic disparity by imposing and requesting sentences below the range more frequently for some groups than for others, including control variables for different types of departures conceals the effect. If departures reflect bias and not merely factual differences among cases, including the control variable conceals this bias.

There is no one correct resolution of this dilemma for all research purposes; either one includes the departure control variables and risks missing bias concealed as factual differences, or one excludes them and risks attributing as bias what are actually relevant factual differences among cases. The commission's resolution of it, however, is rather strange. In reports focused on the effects of *Booker*, the commission included the controls and thus controlled away the decision's primary effect. While they repeatedly warn that their multiple regression results should not be taken as evidence of judicial discrimination, the statistical model they used was designed for that purpose. The econometricians, however, focus on the effects of *Booker* and are less concerned with precisely controlling for every possible legally relevant difference among cases. They do not include controls for departures and rightly warn that their findings should not be taken to assess unconscious bias or discrimination on the part of judges.

This difference in statistical models yielded some surprising results. Fischman and Schanzenbach found racial disparity did not increase in the period immediately following *Booker*. It did increase in the period following *Rita*, *Kimbrough*, and *Gall*, but this appeared to result in part from more black offenders being sentenced at the statutory mandatory minimum. Judges were prevented by the statutory minimums from reducing sentences as often, and as far, for black defendants as for whites. They conclude "judicial discretion does not contribute to, and may in fact mitigate, racial disparities in Guidelines sentencing." And "policy makers interested in redressing racial disparity today should pay much closer attention to the effects of mandatory minimums and their effect on prosecutorial and judicial discretion" (Fischman and Schanzenbach 2012, p. 761).

Starr and Rehavi (2013) also rejected use of the presumptive sentence as a control for legally relevant factors and controls for departures. They argued that both the charges brought against defendants and the facts pressed at sentencing may reflect disparity in prosecutorial decisions and judicial fact-finding. To identify cases that were roughly similar prior to charging and plea bargaining decisions, they used data on the nature of crimes committed as noted in arrest records. They found racial disparity in the severity of charges faced by defendants arrested for seemingly similar conduct and in the likelihood of facing a charge that included a mandatory minimum penalty. This resulted in a 14 percent disparity between black and white defendants. But at least half, and possibly all, of the gap disappeared when differences between groups in mandatory minimum charges were taken into account. In an analysis focused on the causal effects of *Booker*, they found a temporary increase in the rate of charges carrying mandatory minimum penalties against black defendants, but "no evidence that *Booker* increased racial disparity in the exercise of judicial discretion; if anything it may have reduced it" (Starr and Rehavi 2013, p. 39).

Another methodological difference between the commission and outside researchers concerns the use of a unified model that includes all time periods at the same time. The commission's unconventional choice was to run separate regressions for several pre- and post-*Booker* time periods, which were defined by legal changes, such as enactment of the PROTECT Act or the *Booker* decision. This invites the interpretation that changes in the size of the demographic effects in each period reflect the different legal environments of each period. With separate regressions, however, the effects of the control variables are not held constant, because the weight of a factor can shift with changes in the caseload and the intercorrelations of control variables. With separate regressions it is impossible to know if changes in the size of the race effect reflect changes in the real world or changes in the weights of the control variables. The more conventional and safe approach is to use a unified model that treats time periods themselves as variables and examines the interaction effects of time periods with demographic factors.

For this essay, a research assistant and I replicated the commission's approach, using their variables and separate regressions for each time period.[12] The results were similar to the commission's. We then performed an analysis using the same variables in a unified model, with interaction terms for each time period and demographic combination. The commission found that the difference in average sentence lengths between black and white men was 5.5 months in the PROTECT Act period and 19.1 months in the most recent period. In the unified model, we found those differences were 11.9 and 14.1 months, respectively. Merely switching to a unified model dramatically reduced changes in the race gap between the two periods and reduced the gap in the most recent period by 5 months.

---

[12] Vansh Bansal assisted with these analyses.

When the unified model was further tweaked (in a variation following Ulmer, Light, and Kramer 2011) by including a criminal history control and excluding defendants who are noncitizens, the gap between black and white men in the most recent time period decreased to 3.7 months.[13] To reduce the influence of the in/out decision, the stage at which previous research showed much of the racial disparity arises, we performed this analysis excluding defendants in Zones A, B, and C of the Sentencing Table, where the guidelines invite judges to consider a nonimprisonment sentence. Under this unified model, among citizen defendants, with additional control for criminal history, the gap in imprisonment length between black and white males was eliminated entirely.

To summarize: research has consistently found that the race gap reported by the commission arises largely in the decision to imprison. There is concern that racial stereotypes about the dangerousness of black men may make judges less likely to favor nonincarceration sentences. In addition, for some judges, the in/out decision depends on considerations—such as a defendant's employment, or living situation, or responsibility for the care of dependent children—that may be correlated with race but for which we have no data. These omitted variables may explain some unknown part of the gap. Research has also consistently found that part of the race effect reflects differences among groups in criminal history that are not captured by the presumptive sentence. Under the guidelines that determine offenders' criminal history scores, the presumptive sentence does not distinguish persons with no prior contact with criminal justice from those with multiple arrests, or from those with convictions too petty or old to affect the criminal history score. Defendants' guidelines ranges, and thus presumptive sentences, are affected relatively little by criminal history compared to the seriousness of the current offense. The regression results show that judges give at least some aspects of offenders' criminal history greater weight than do the guidelines themselves.

Recent research using multiple regression analyses also confirms a lesson from previous eras: the model matters. Choices of what control variables to include, what populations to study, and what statistical model to employ all affect the results. No one approach is right for all questions.

---

[13] Like immigration offenders, noncitizens generally raise some unique considerations; for example, they may be subject to detainers, which limits use of alternatives to imprisonment.

No statistical controls can substitute for true experiments. No one measure captures all sources of disparity. Moreover, in retrospect, the focus of researchers on racial bias in judicial decision-making has been somewhat unfortunate, because it is increasingly apparent that judicial decisions are far from being the most serious source of unwarranted racial disparity in federal sentencing today. The effects of mandatory minimums and other unsound sentencing rules are far greater.

C. Adverse Impact of Unsound Rules

The most shocking fact of the guidelines era has been that, rather than reducing gross racial disparities, the implementation of the sentencing guidelines was accompanied by a dramatically widened gap between the average prison time served by African American defendants and other groups.[14] As shown in figure 5, average time served varied relatively little among racial and ethnic groups in the pre-guideline era. But once the presumptive guidelines and mandatory minimum statutes became effective, time served by African Americans soared above time served by others. In the years following the decisions in *Booker*, *Rita*, and *Kimbrough*, however, the gap between black and white offenders has narrowed considerably.

Simple averages like those in figure 5 obviously reflect a wide range of influences. Unlike multiple regression studies, there are no controls for differences in the types of crimes committed by different groups. In addition, the types of offenses prosecuted in federal court change over time. For example, the decreased average time served by Hispanic defendants certainly reflects the increased share of the caseload involving immigration offenses; they are predominantly committed by Hispanic defendants and receive relatively shorter sentences on average than many other crimes. Trends in simple averages can nonetheless reveal some things that are hidden in multiple regression analyses. The trends do not attempt to focus only on any bias in the decision of judges, but also to reflect changes in prosecutorial priorities and practices. Most important, these long-term trends reflect changes in sentencing policies.

---

[14] In addition to mandating the creation of sentencing guidelines, the SRA also abolished federal parole. Sentences imposed prior to the guidelines reflect prison time that most defendants never served. To understand changes in the severity of punishment and in prison populations, changes in estimated time served is a better measure (Hofer and Semisch 1999).

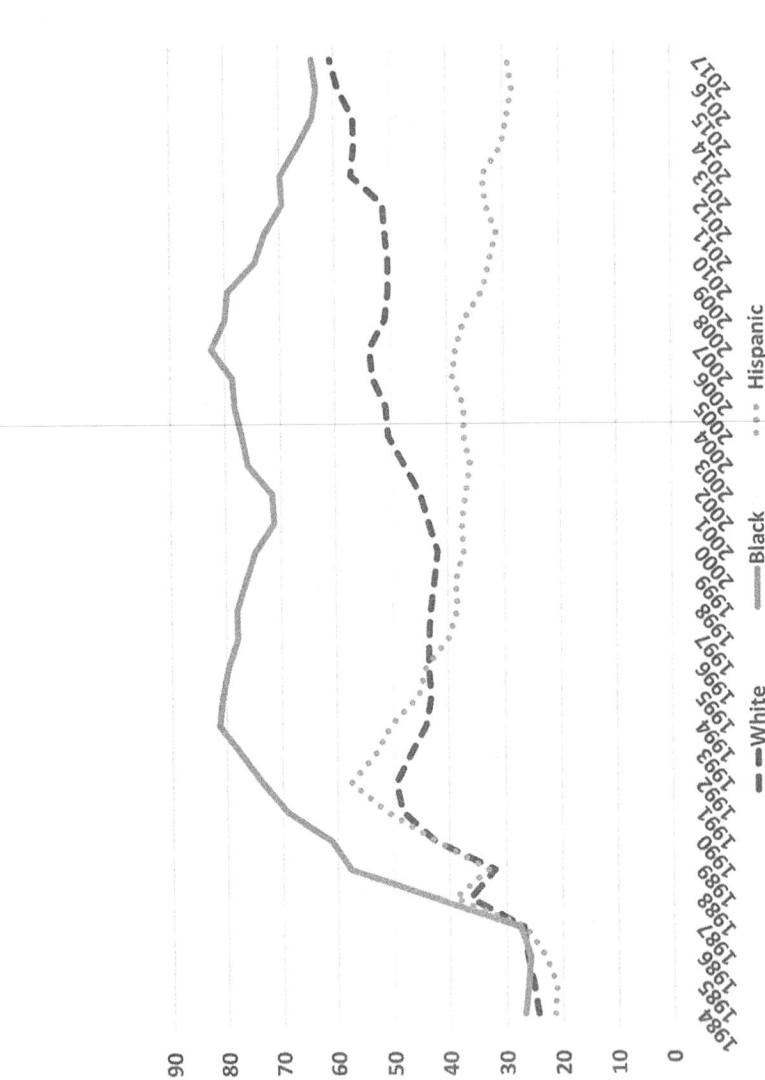

FIG. 5.—Average time served in months by black, white, and Hispanic offenders. All felonies, FY1984–FY2017. Source: Federal Probation and Sentencing Supervision Information System Datafile, 1994–1990; USSC individual data files, FY1991–FY2017. Color version available as an online enhancement.

In the multiple regression analyses performed by the commission and many others, changes in the laws governing sentencing are "legally relevant factors" that determine the presumptive sentence and are therefore controlled away before assessing any differences among groups. Any disparity caused by unsound rules is not measured; reductions or increases in disparity caused by changes to the law are not assessed. To interpret the changes illustrated by figure 5, we can be sure that judges did not suddenly start discriminating in 1989. The dramatic widening of the gap between African Americans and other groups at the time the guidelines and drug mandatory minimums were implemented *was due to the switch to guidelines and mandatory minimums and the policies they represented.*

Sentences got more severe at the time of guideline implementation, especially for the types of crimes disproportionately committed by and prosecuted against African Americans in the federal courts. In disparate impact analysis in employment law, a rule that disproportionately disqualifies members of a protected group must be shown to have a legitimate business purpose. One would hope that sentencing laws with severe adverse impacts could also be shown to have a legitimate sentencing purpose (Baumer 2013). Yet the commission reported as early as 1995 that the 100:1 ratio between powder and crack cocaine both had a severe adverse impact and was not justified by any purpose of sentencing (US Sentencing Commission 1995). Commission analyses later showed that this one rule was responsible for opening much of the racial gap (US Sentencing Commission 2004*a*, pp. 131–33) and that reducing the ratio would do much to narrow it. The trend lines reflect the series of changes to crack sentencing the commission started in 2008 and Congress continued in 2010. It also reflects the increased rates of below-guideline sentencing for crack and other offenses made possible by *Booker*.

Other unsound rules, such as the so-called career offender guideline, other drug recidivist provisions, and firearms statutes continue to contribute to racial disparity without advancing the purposes of sentencing. But Congress has not seen fit to change them. Within the limits of statutory mandatory minimum sentences, at least some judges have used their increased discretion following *Booker* to reject unsound guidelines and sentence below the guidelines recommendations. In this way, *Booker* has contributed and continues to contribute to a decrease in the most significant source of racial disparity. But addressing the remaining problems in federal sentencing will require action by Congress, the commission, and judges.

V. An Unbalanced System

Ensuring that a fearsome government power like criminal sentencing is exercised according to our constitutional ideals requires a system of checks and balances (Barkow 2005). The SRA envisioned such a system, with power to make sentencing rules and set individual sentences distributed among the commission, Congress, the Department of Justice, sentencing judges, courts of appeals, prosecutors, and defense counsel. Unfortunately, federal sentencing reform has demonstrated the dangers of imbalances of power among key players. As noted by Frank Bowman, a former prosecutor and early supporter of the guidelines: "The failures of the guidelines can be traced to the breakdown of the institutional balance the Sentencing Reform Act was supposed to create. Power has consolidated in the hands of prosecutors at the case level and an alliance of the Department of Justice with Congress at the policy level" (Bowman 2005, p. 1315; Miller 2004).

By the time the original commissioners began their work, the SRA's vision of policy making by a nonpartisan expert agency had faded in favor of "tough on crime" politics (Tonry 2015). The political branches began to undermine the commission's independence. Instead of insulating policy making and sentencing from political pressures, the guidelines and mandatory minimums became new legal tools for centralized, political control. The bluntest form of this control is the mandatory minimum statutes. These statutes override the policy development process envisioned in the SRA and wrest control of individual sentencing from both the commission and judges. Only slightly less blunt are specific statutory directives, which direct the commission, for example, to increase the guidelines offense level for certain crimes or add aggravating adjustments. The availability of these powers has also allowed Congress to control policy in more subtle ways, by threatening to enact new mandatory minimums if the commission does not itself increase punishment in response to various congressional concerns.

Restoring balance to federal sentencing will require Congress and the commission to return to the ideals of the SRA. This was made more possible by the switch to an advisory guidelines system, but it will require the guidelines to earn the respect of sentencing judges through the quality of the advice they offer rather than through legal compulsion. Unfortunately, the major proposals for changing the advisory system that have been touted by members of the commission have emphasized a return to legal compulsion rather than revision of unsound statutes and guidelines.

A. Post-Booker *Proposals for Reform*

Proposals for overhaul of federal sentencing in the wake of *Booker* have come from a range of stakeholders, including the American Bar Association (2005) and the Constitution Project (2006). Several chairs of the commission have offered detailed proposals for reinstating some form of presumptive system, often with simpler guidelines, broader sentencing ranges, and jury fact-finding for the most significant aggravating factors that increase the range (Sessions 2011; Pryor 2017). The main opinion in *Booker* seemed to provide an opportunity to address procedural concerns raised by the aspects of the federal guidelines, in particular the guidelines' infamous relevant conduct rule (Reitz 1993), which allows guideline ranges to be increased by some facts that have not been included in any indictment, or admitted by a defendant, or proven to a jury beyond a reasonable doubt. Indeed, guideline ranges can be increased even by facts underlying charges of which a defendant has been acquitted. Many of the proposed changes to the advisory system would provide for jury fact-finding for the most significant aggravating factors that would increase the presumptive sentencing range.

Despite these apparent procedural improvements, defense attorneys have not been supportive of these proposals (Baron-Evans and Stith 2012; Baron-Evans and Patton 2017), preferring the current system to what came before and to any likely presumptive system. This resistance is based in part on skepticism that a return to a presumptive system (defense attorneys prefer the term "mandatory") would bring the benefits that its proponents promise. Returning to a presumptive system risks again tying the hands of judges and transferring much of the power to determine the guideline range to prosecutors, who could effectively set sentences by the charges and facts included in plea agreements.

Moreover, any system that increases constraints on judges shifts sentencing power to the commission and to Congress, who can use the binding rules as instruments of centralized political control. Promises that excessive severity might be addressed by a return to presumptive guidelines have also been received skeptically. For example, commission chair Judge Pryor suggested that by returning to a presumptive system there would be "less need for statutory mandatory minimum penalties, except for the most egregious offenses" (Pryor 2017, p. 4). But of course, Congress enacted mandatory minimums during the previous presumptive era, and even under the relatively reform-minded Obama administration the Department of Justice reiterated its continuing support for mandatory minimums (Breuer 2010).

A primary argument made by proponents of a return to presumptive guidelines has been that the advisory system has increased sentencing disparity (Bowman 2012, 2014; Pryor 2017). Regarding inter-judge disparity, the research supports such concerns, as discussed above. But returning to compulsory guidelines is not the only or best remedy available for addressing variations in how different judges use their increased discretion. Better guidelines, more clearly explained, are likely to reduce the number of "policy disagreements" that currently divide judges and contribute to inter-judge disparity. Appellate review that encouraged critical examination of the pedigree and evidence supporting guideline recommendations might have developed into a reasoned guideline jurisprudence that could help control disparity. Absent that, commission research and consultation with key stakeholders could lead to changes to the guidelines that would win greater judicial acceptance and uniformity, as has already happened with the guidelines for crack and, to a lesser extent, other drugs.

The claim from critics of the advisory system that seems most likely to generate support for a change is that advisory guidelines and increased judicial discretion have increased racial disparity. But as reviewed above, the evidence for this claim is ambiguous at best and often misdiagnoses the sources of increased disparity and the mechanisms best able to ameliorate it. For example, the chair of the commission has attributed the increase in the race effect after *Booker* found in the commission's multiple regression studies to increased rates of below-range sentences based on individual characteristics, such as employment history, education and vocational skills, and family ties and responsibility (Pryor 2017, p. 98). The idea is that these characteristics are correlated with race, class, and gender, so that when judges use them to reduce sentences the benefits redound disproportionately to more privileged white male defendants, which creates an adverse impact against black males.

On closer scrutiny, however, this argument lacks both consistent empirical evidence and conceptual clarity. The data show that white defendants do benefit disproportionately from consideration of some of these factors, but the advantage is not overwhelming. And for some individual mitigating circumstances, such as education and vocational skills or disadvantaged upbringing, African Americans receive below-range sentences at higher rates than whites (Baron Evans and Patton 2017). Moreover, even if below-range sentences based on individual circumstances were consistently more common among white men, the commission's multiple regression model, by including a control variable for downward departures, *controls for any disproportionality among groups*. Differences among groups in the benefits of increased judicial discretion to consider mitigating factors simply cannot explain the commission's controversial finding of increased racial disparity after *Booker*.

Conceptually, consideration of mitigating factors correlated with race, class, or gender—such as child-care responsibilities or employment record—should not be considered to create an adverse impact leading to unwarranted disparity, so long as the factors are relevant to a legitimate sentencing consideration. It would be quite radical to consider *any* factor that affects different groups differently out of bounds and discriminatory, if the factor is relevant to a legitimate government interest. If taken seriously, Judge Pryor's argument seems to disfavor consideration of many factors currently taken into account by the guidelines, such as criminal history or use of a weapon, both of which disproportionately burden black male defendants. In sum, the argument that increased racial disparity is a reason for returning to a presumptive guideline system has been exaggerated and misconceived. The proposed solution of returning to a more mandatory system could actually be counterproductive for reducing racial disparity, as it would prevent judges from reducing the adverse impact of unsound rules.

Concerns about increased inter-judge disparity, while better supported by the empirical evidence, are better addressed by convincing judges that the guidelines are worth following. For guidelines based on research and consultation, this can be accomplished through more detailed explanations of how the commission intended the guideline to achieve the purposes of sentencing. For guidelines mandated by Congress whose recommendations are excessive or ineffective, this is not an option. Such guidelines should be amended. If they cannot be, reasoned rejection of the guidelines' recommendations by thoughtful judges should be welcomed, not resisted. Sentencing will not be improved by compelling all judges to comply with all the guidelines, even those that evidence shows are unfair and ineffective.

B. *Mandatory Minimums and Specific Directives Betray Sentencing Reform*

The move to advisory guidelines has highlighted conflicts between congressional micromanagement of sentencing rules and the evidence-based system envisioned by the SRA. When judges sentence within the guideline range, they rely "upon the Commission's own reasoning" to explain and justify the sentence, on the theory that the commission designed the guideline to achieve the same purposes of sentencing that judges are directed to consider, using the procedures for research and consultation outlined in the SRA (*Rita*, at p. 357). But when a guideline is based on a mandatory minimum or a congressional directive, the real explanation for the guideline's recommendation is that Congress set the policy. And in many cases, the reasons for Congress's policies are either unknown, or known to be flawed or brazenly political. Congressional micromanagement thus undermines the basis for accepting the guidelines' advice about what sentence is "sufficient, but not greater than necessary" to achieve sentencing purposes (18 U.S.C. §3553(a)).

Mandatory minimums and specific statutory directives also impede the commission's ability to receive and take account of feedback from judges, and to use empirical research to make its guidelines persuasive. As Justice Breyer has described, mandatory minimums thwart the evolution of the guidelines: "Statutory mandatory sentences prevent the Commission from carrying out its basic, congressionally mandated task: the development, in part through research, of a rational, coherent set of punishments. Mandatory minimums will sometimes make it impossible for the Commission to adjust sentences in light of factors that its research shows to be directly relevant. . . . They skew the entire set of criminal punishments, . . . and their existence then prevents the Commission from . . . writ[ing] a sentence that makes sense" (Breyer 1999, p. 184).

Mandatory minimums simply cannot be reconciled with sentencing guidelines, whether presumptive or advisory. The principle of just deserts, which underlies much of the guidelines' structure (Hofer and Allenbaugh 2003), requires that the severity of punishment be proportionate to seriousness of the crime (Frase 2005). For a guideline based on a mandatory minimum to comply with this principle, it must be sufficiently low for the least harmful offense that might arise under a statute, committed by the least culpable and least dangerous offender. But these are not the cases that Congress generally has in mind when it enacts a mandatory penalty. The penalties are attached to only one or two facts, such as drug type and quantity, while the details of the offenses are left to the imagination. The generic crime categories to which the penalties are attached—whether "child pornography" or "drug trafficking"—evoke stereotypes and misconceptions and extreme examples rather than the most mitigated cases. The result is that the penalties are applicable to many far less serious offenses than legislators had in mind when setting them.

Apart from overall severity, integrating mandatory minimums with guidelines is impossible due to the simplistic way the statutes characterize different crimes. By requiring a minimum punishment for any crime involving just one or two facts, the statutes give disproportionate weight to those facts while ignoring others that are equally or more important. In theory, guidelines can take account of many considerations and weigh each according to its importance compared to the others. And particularly when they are advisory, guidelines recognize that no set of rules can anticipate every relevant fact or how circumstances may combine to affect the appropriate sentence. Mandatory minimums, in contrast, assume that every single defendant whose crime involves those few facts deserves at least the minimum punishment. For all of these reasons, any hope like that of the Department of Justice that existing mandatory minimums might "work together" with a guidelines system is unfounded.[15]

C. Mandatory Minimums Result in Excessive and Disparate Sentences

The existing statutory minimums create sentencing floors that prevent the few mitigating adjustments in the guidelines from operating as the commission intended. They prevent judges from considering additional mitigating factors that might lower a sentence below the range. This problem of statutory override affects thousands of cases a year and is even worse under the advisory guidelines than it was in the pre-*Booker* era. In its 1991 report on mandatory minimum penalties, the commission found that the statutory minimum was greater than the bottom of the guideline range in 22.4 percent of cases with a conviction carrying a mandatory penalty, and that in 5.8 percent of cases, the mandatory minimum was greater than the top of the guideline range (US Sentencing Commission 1991, pp. 84–86). By 2017, the problem was far worse. In the 13,803 cases with a conviction under a statute carrying a mandatory minimum, the minimum was higher than the bottom of the guideline range in 41.7 percent of cases, and was higher than the top of the guideline range in 30.1 percent of cases.

---

[15] Sally Quillian Yates, "Testimony of U.S. Attorney for the District of Georgia, on Behalf of the U.S. Department of Justice, Hearing before the U.S. Sentencing Commission," in *Mandatory Minimum Sentencing Statutes*, May 27, 2010, pp. 5–6.

Many of these offenders qualified for a waiver of the minimum, due to the "safety valve" enacted in 1994 that waives the statutory minimum for certain first-time, nonviolent, low-level offenders, or because they assist in the prosecution of other persons. But 1,782 defendants, or 42.9 percent of those whose statutory minimum is greater than the maximum of the guideline range, did not receive such a waiver, meaning that judges could not sentence the defendant even within the range recommended by the guidelines. Mandatory minimums cause a large number of sentences to be outside the guideline range and thus excessive and disparate by even the commission's own definition. And of course, the guidelines themselves have been so distorted by the mandatory statutes that for whole classes of offenders, sentences within the guideline range are excessive and disproportionate to the seriousness of the crime or the dangerousness of the offender.

D. *Mandatory Minimums Are Corrosive to the Entire Criminal Justice Process*

In addition to their contribution to excessive severity and disparity, mandatory minimums are the biggest factor creating an unfair and unbalanced system (Hofer 2011). They vest prosecutors with enormous power to coerce defendants into forgoing important constitutional rights. These rights are not only crucial to ensure fair procedures but are also central to the truth-seeking function of the criminal justice system. Because judges are unable to check prosecutorial charging decisions, mandatory minimum penalty statutes are the most susceptible to abuse. Prosecutors file, or threaten to file, charges with harsh mandatory minimum sentences not because they result in appropriate sentences, but for the purpose of extracting guilty pleas, cooperation, appeal waivers, and various other concessions. Indeed, the Department of Justice has sought more and harsher mandatory sentencing laws, "not because the enhancements are inherently just or required for adequate deterrence, but precisely because higher sentences provide increased plea bargaining leverage" (Bowman 2007, p. 236).

Federal trial and acquittal rates are at historic lows because sentencing power in the hands of prosecutors makes it too costly to go to trial, even for those with an excellent defense (Wright 2005; Human Rights Watch 2013). When the difference between the sentence after trial and the sentence after plea is as high as it often is in the federal system, and prosecutors have a monopoly on granting any discount, the system produces less reliable results. Mandatory minimums also threaten the truth-seeking function of the criminal justice system by creating powerful incentives for informants and cooperators to provide exaggerated and false information—information that in most cases will never be tested because the risk of challenging it is too great.

E. The Guidelines Still Give Mostly Bad Advice

Ten years after *Booker*, the opportunity to use the increased judicial discretion it granted to critically evaluate the guidelines and help them evolve may be slipping away. But *Booker* alone was never enough. As long as the commission and the guidelines remain bound to statutory directives and mandatory minimums, the federal system can never function as intended. At this writing, limited reform of mandatory minimums is stalled before Congress, but even this proposed reform is relatively little, and far too late. What is needed is total repeal of mandatory minimum statutory penalties and specific statutory directives that have shackled the commission from the time of enactment of the SRA (Hofer 2008). Sentencing reform is still a good idea. Let's hope the federal system tries it sometime soon.

REFERENCES

Adelman, Lynn S., Nancy Gertner, Richard G. Kopf, Gerard E. Lynch, and Gregory A. Presnell. 2006. "Federal Sentencing under 'Advisory Guidelines': Observations by District Judges." *Fordham Law Review* 75:1–30.
Alschuler, Albert W. 2005. "Disparity: The Normative and Empirical Failure of the Federal Guidelines." *Stanford Law Review* 58:85–117.
American Bar Association, Criminal Justice Section. 2005. *Report on Booker and Recommendation*. Reprinted in *Federal Sentencing Reporter* 17:335–40.
Anderson, James M., Jeffrey R. Kling, and Kate Stith. 1999. "Measuring Interjudge Sentencing Disparity: Before and after the Federal Sentencing Guidelines." *Journal of Law and Economics* 42:271–308.
Barkow, Rachel. 2005. "Federalism and the Politics of Sentencing." *Columbia Law Review* 105:1276–1314.
Baron-Evans, Amy, and David Patton. 2017. "A Response to Judge Pryor's Proposal to 'Fix' the Guidelines: A Cure Worse Than the Disease." *Federal Sentencing Reporter* 29:104–25.

Baron-Evans, Amy, and Kate Stith. 2012. "Booker Rules." *University of Pennsylvania Law Review* 160:1631–1743.

Baumer, Eric P. 2013. "Reassessing and Redirecting Research on Race and Sentencing." *Justice Quarterly* 30:231–61.

Bennett, Mark W. 2014. "Confronting Cognitive 'Anchoring Effect' and 'Blind Spot' Biases in Federal Sentencing: A Modest Solution for Confronting a Fundamental Flaw." *Journal of Criminal Law and Criminology* 104:489–533.

Blank, Rebecca M., Marilyn Dabady, and Connie Citro. 2004. *Measuring Racial Discrimination: Panel on Methods for Assessing Discrimination*. Washington, DC: National Research Council, National Academy Press.

Bowman, Frank O. 1996. "The Quality of Mercy Must Be Restrained, and Other Lessons in Learning to Love the Federal Sentencing Guidelines." *Wisconsin Law Review* 1996:679–759.

———. 2005. "The Failure of the Federal Sentencing Guidelines: A Structural Analysis." *Columbia Law Review* 105:1315–50.

———. 2007. "American Buffalo: Vanishing Acquittals and the Gradual Extinction of the Federal Criminal Trial Lawyer." *University of Pennsylvania Law Review* 156:226–40.

———. 2012. "Nothing Is Not Enough: Fix the Absurd Post-*Booker* Federal Sentencing System." *Federal Sentencing Reporter* 24:356–68.

———. 2014. "Dead Law Walking: The Surprising Tenacity of the Federal Sentencing Guidelines." *Houston Law Review* 51:1227–70.

Breuer, Lanny A. 2010. "The Attorney General's Sentencing and Corrections Working Group: A Progress Report." *Federal Sentencing Reporter* 23:110–14.

Breyer, Stephen. 1988. "The Federal Sentencing Guidelines and the Key Compromises upon Which They Rest." *Hofstra Law Review* 17:1–50.

———. 1999. "Federal Sentencing Guidelines Revisited." *Federal Sentencing Reporter* 11:180–86.

Cabranes, José A. 1992. "Sentencing Guidelines: A Dismal Failure." *New York Law Journal* 11(February):2.

Cassell, Paul G. 2004. "Too Severe? A Defense of the Federal Sentencing Guidelines (and Critique of Federal Mandatory Minimums)." *Stanford Law Review* 56:1017–48.

Cohen, Alma, and Crystal S. Yang. 2018. "Judicial Politics and Sentencing Decisions." NBER Working Paper no. 24615. Cambridge, MA: National Bureau of Economic Research.

Constitution Project. 2006. *Recommendations for Federal Criminal Sentencing in a Post-*Booker *World*. Washington, DC: Constitution Project.

Engen, Rodney. 2011. "Racial Disparity in the Wake of *Booker/Fanfan*: Making Sense of 'Messy' Results and Other Challenges for Sentencing Research." *Criminology and Public Policy* 10:1139–49.

Engen, Rodney L., and R. R. Gainey. 2000. "Modeling the Effects of Legally Relevant and Extralegal Factors under Sentencing Guidelines: The Rules Have Changed." *Criminology* 38:1207–29.

Exum, Jelani Jefferson. 2010. "Making the Punishment Fit the (Computer) Crime: Rebooting Notions of Possession for the Federal Sentencing of Child Pornography Offenses." *Richmond Journal of Law and Technology* 16:3–44.

Feinberg, Kenneth R. 1991. "Commentary: The Federal Guidelines and the Underlying Purposes of Sentencing." *Federal Sentencing Reporter* 3:326–27.

Fischman, J. B., and M. M. Schanzenbach. 2012. "Racial Disparities under the Federal Sentencing Guidelines: The Role of Judicial Discretion and Mandatory Minimums." *Journal of Empirical Legal Studies* 9(4):729–64.

Frase, Richard S. 2005. "Excessive Prison Sentences, Punishment Goals, and the Eighth Amendment: Proportionality Relative to What?" *Minnesota Law Review* 89:571–651.

General Accounting Office. 1992. *Sentencing Guidelines: Central Questions Remain Unanswered*. Washington, DC: Government Printing Office.

Gershel, Brad. 2017. "Sentencing Synthetic Cannabinoid Offenders: 'No Cognizable Basis.'" *American Criminal Law Review* 45:50–57.

Gertner, Nancy. 2006. "What Yogi Berra Teaches about Post-*Booker* Sentencing." *Yale Law Journal* 115:Pocket Part 137.

———. 2007. "From Omnipotence to Impotence: American Judges and Sentencing." *Ohio State Journal of Criminal Law* 4:523–39.

Gregory, Becky, and Traci Kenner. 2005. "A New Era in Federal Sentencing." *Texas Bar Journal* 68:796–98.

Hessick, Carissa Byrne, and F. Andrew Hessick. 2008. "Appellate Review of Sentencing Decisions." *Alabama Law Review* 60:1–40.

———. 2010. "Five Years of Appellate Problems after *Booker*." *Federal Sentencing Reporter* 22:85–88.

Hewitt, Jillian. 2016. "Fifty Shades of Gray: Sentencing Trends in Major White-Collar Cases." *Yale Law Journal* 125:1018–71.

Hofer, Paul J. 2006. "Immediate and Long-Term Effects of *United States v. Booker*: More Discretion, More Disparity, or Better Reasoned Sentences?" *Arizona State Law Journal* 38:425–68.

———. 2007. "*United States v. Booker* as a Natural Experiment: Using Empirical Research to Inform the Federal Sentencing Policy Debate." *Criminology and Public Policy* 6:433–60.

———. 2008. "The Reset Solution." *Federal Sentencing Reporter* 20:349–51.

———. 2009. "How Well Do Sentencing Statistics Help in Understanding the Post-*Booker* Sentencing System." *Federal Sentencing Reporter* 22:89–95.

———. 2011. "Has *Booker* Restored Balance? A Look at Data on Plea Bargaining and Sentencing." *Federal Sentencing Reporter* 23:326–32.

———. 2013 "The Commission Defends an Ailing Hypothesis: Does Judicial Discretion Increase Demographic Disparity?" *Federal Sentencing Reporter* 25:311–22.

———. 2015. "Ranking Drug Harms for Sentencing Policy." http://dx.doi.org/10.2139/ssrn.2612654.

———. 2016. "Review of DOJ-Commissioned Report: Racial Disparity in Post-*Booker* Sentencing." *Federal Sentencing Reporter* 28:196–200.

Hofer, Paul J., and Mark Allenbaugh. 2003. "The Reason behind the Rules: Finding and Using the Philosophy of the Federal Sentencing Guidelines." *American Criminal Law Review* 40:19–85.

Hofer, Paul J., Kevin R. Blackwell, and R. Barry Ruback 1999. "The Effect of the Federal Sentencing Guidelines on Inter-judge Sentencing Disparity." *Journal of Criminal Law and Criminology* 90:239–306.

Hofer, Paul J., and Courtney Semisch. 1999. "Examining Changes in Federal Sentencing Severity: 1980–1998." *Federal Sentencing Reporter* 12:12–19.

Human Rights Watch. 2013. *An Offer You Can't Refuse: How US Federal Prosecutors Force Drug Defendants to Plead Guilty*. New York: Human Rights Watch.

Isikoff, Michael, and Tracy Thompson. 1990. "Getting Too Tough on Drugs: Draconian Sentences Hurt Small Offenders More Than Kingpins." *Washington Post*, November 4.

King, Nancy. 2006. "Reasonableness Review after *Booker*." *Houston Law Review* 43:325–40.

Luby, Joseph W. 1999. "Reining in the 'Junior Varsity Congress': A Call for Meaningful Judicial Review of the Federal Sentencing Guidelines." *Washington University Law Quarterly* 77:1199–1290.

McDonald, Douglas C., and Kenneth E. Carlson. 1993. *Sentencing in the Federal Courts: Does Race Matter? The Transition to Sentencing Guidelines, 1986–90*. Washington, DC: US Department of Justice, Office of Justice Programs, Bureau of Justice Statistics.

Michelman, Scott, and Jay Rorty. 2012. "Doing *Kimbrough* Justice: Implementing Policy Disagreements with the Federal Sentencing Guidelines." *Suffolk University Law Review* 45:1083–1127.

Miller, Marc L. 2004. "Domination and Dissatisfaction: Prosecutors as Sentencers." *Stanford Law Review* 56:1211–69.

Miller, Marc L., and Ronald F. Wright. 1999. "Your Cheatin' Heartland: The Long Search for Administrative Sentencing Justice." *Buffalo Criminal Law Review* 2:725–815.

Pratt, Robert W. 2016. "The Discretion to Sentence." *Federal Sentencing Reporter* 28:161–64.

Pryor, William H., Jr. 2017. "Returning to Marvin Frankel's First Principles in Federal Sentencing." *Federal Sentencing Reporter* 29:95–103.

Reitz, Kevin R. 1993. "Sentencing Facts: Travesties of Real-Offense Sentencing." *Stanford Law Review* 45:523–73.

———. 2005. "The Enforceability of Sentencing Guidelines." *Stanford Law Review* 58:155–73.

Scalia, John, Jr. 2002. "The Impact of Changes in Federal Law and Policy on the Sentencing of, and Time Served in Prison by, Drug Defendants Convicted in US Courts." *Federal Sentencing Reporter* 14:152–58.

Schanzenbach, Max. 2005. "Have Federal Judges Changed Their Sentencing Practices? The Shaky Empirical Foundations of the Feeney Amendment." *Journal of Empirical Legal Studies* 2:1–48.

Scott, Ryan W. 2010. "Inter-judge Sentencing Disparity after *Booker*: A First Look." *Stanford Law Review* 63:1–66.

Sentencing Resource Counsel. 2016. "Congressional Directives to the Sentencing Commission: 1988–2016." Unpublished manuscript. https://www.fd.org/sites/default/files/criminal_defense_topics/essential_topics/sentencing_resources/deconstructing_the_guidelines/congressional-directives-to-the-sentencing-commission.pdf.

Sessions, William K., III. 2011. "At the Crossroads of the Three Branches: The US Sentencing Commission's Attempts to Achieve Sentencing Reform in the Midst of Inter-branch Power Struggles." *Journal of Law and Politics* 26:305–57.

Skotkin, Ronnie. 1990. "The Development of the Federal Sentencing Guideline for Drug Trafficking Offenses." *Criminal Law Bulletin* 26:50–59.

Starr, Sonja B. 2013. "Did Booker Increase Sentencing Disparity? Why the Evidence Is Unpersuasive." *Federal Sentencing Reporter* 25(5):323–26.

Starr, Sonja B., and M. Màrit Rehavi. 2013. "Mandatory Sentencing and Racial Disparity: Assessing the Role of Prosecutors and the Effects of *Booker*." *Yale Law Journal* 123(1):2–80.

Stith, Kate, and Steve Y. Koh. 1993. "The Politics of Sentencing Reform: The Legislative History of the Federal Sentencing Guidelines." *Wake Forest Law Review* 28:223–90.

Tonry, Michael. 1996. *Sentencing Matters*. New York: Oxford University Press.

———. 2006. "Purposes and Functions of Sentencing." In *Crime and Justice: A Review of Research*, vol. 34, edited by Michael Tonry. Chicago: University of Chicago Press.

———. 2015. "Federal Sentencing Reform since 1984: The Awful as Enemy of the Good." In *Crime and Justice: A Review of Research*, vol. 44, edited by Michael Tonry. Chicago: University of Chicago Press.

Uelman, Gerald F. 1992. "Federal Sentencing Guidelines: A Cure Worse than the Disease." *American Criminal Law Review* 29:899–905.

Ulmer, Jeffery, and Michael Light 2013. "The USSC's 2012 *Booker* Report's Characterization of the Penn State Studies: Setting the Record Straight." *Federal Sentencing Reporter* 25:290–92.

Ulmer, Jeffery T., Michael T. Light, and John H. Kramer. 2011. "Racial Disparity in the Wake of the *Booker/Fanfan* Decision: An Alternative Analysis to the USSC's 2010 Report." *Criminology and Public Policy* 10:1077–1118.

US Sentencing Commission. 1991. *Mandatory Minimum Penalties in the Federal Criminal Justice System*. Washington, DC: US Sentencing Commission.

———. 1995. *Special Report to the Congress: Cocaine and Federal Sentencing Policy*. Washington, DC: US Sentencing Commission.

———. 2003. *Report to the Congress: Departures from the Federal Sentencing Guidelines*. Washington, DC: US Sentencing Commission.

———. 2004a. *Fifteen Years of Guidelines Sentencing: An Assessment of How Well the Federal Criminal Justice System Is Achieving the Goals of Sentencing Reform*. Washington, DC: US Sentencing Commission.

———. 2004b. *Measuring Recidivism: The Criminal History Computation of the Federal Sentencing Guidelines*. Washington, DC: US Sentencing Commission.

———. 2006. *Report on the Impact of U.S. v. Booker on Federal Sentencing*. Washington, DC: US Sentencing Commission.

———. 2010. *Demographic Differences in Federal Sentencing Practices: An Update of the* Booker *Report's Multivariate Analysis*. Washington, DC: US Sentencing Commission.

———. 2012. *Report on the Continuing Impact of* United States v. Booker *on Federal Sentencing*. Washington, DC: US Sentencing Commission.

———. 2017. *Demographic Differences in Sentencing: An Update to the 2012* Booker *Report*. Washington, DC: US Sentencing Commission.

———. 2018. *Quarterly Sentencing Updates*. http://www.ussc.gov/research-and-publications/federal-sentencing-statistics/quarterly-sentencing-updates.

Weisberg, Robert, and Marc L. Miller. 2005. "Sentencing Lessons." *Stanford Law Review* 58:1–36.

Wright, Ronald F. 2005. "Trial Distortion and the End of Innocence in Federal Criminal Justice." *University of Pennsylvania Law Review* 154:79–156.

Yang, Crystal S. 2014. "Have Inter-judge Sentencing Disparities Increased in an Advisory Guidelines Regime? Evidence from *Booker*." *New York University Law Review* 89:1268–1342.

———. 2015. "Free at Last? Judicial Discretion and Racial Disparities in Federal Sentencing." *Journal of Legal Studies* 44:75–111.

Julian V. Roberts

The Evolution of Sentencing Guidelines in Minnesota and England and Wales

ABSTRACT

Sentencing guidelines were an exclusively American enterprise until recently. Since 2004, however, other countries have joined in. Contrasting approaches are exemplified by systems developed by the Minnesota Sentencing Guidelines Commission and the Sentencing Council of England and Wales. Minnesota's guidelines are set out in grids that categorize cases by offense and criminal history. Each cell sets out ranges of sentences that are presumed to be appropriate. The English guidelines are step-by-step decision trees, one for each principal offense category. Each jurisdiction created an approach that fits its sentencing environment. The Minnesota grids are more restrictive and generate high levels of judicial conformity and consistency. The English guidelines allow greater discretion, possibly at the cost of consistency. However, the English approach provides ampler guidance on use of different dispositions, sentencing of multiple crimes, appropriate reductions to reflect guilty pleas, and other subjects. Neither the Minnesota Commission nor the English Council has been particularly self-critical. Minnesota's main grid has changed little since 1980. England's guidelines have evolved considerably, but the council has ignored calls to play a more active role in controlling the use of custody and hence the size of the prison population.

Until recently, the history of sentencing guidelines has been an exclusively American story. All that has now changed. Since 2004, several other countries have introduced guidelines for courts. In this essay, I explore con-

Electronically published February 12, 2019
  Julian Roberts is professor of criminology, Faculty of Law, University of Oxford, and member of the Sentencing Council of England and Wales, 2009–18. He is grateful to participants

© 2019 by The University of Chicago. All rights reserved.
0192-3234/2019/0048-0008$10.00

trasting approaches to guidance exemplified by the regimes in Minnesota and England and Wales. While guidelines (and sentencing grids) vary significantly across the United States, I use the Minnesota guidelines as an example of grid-based approaches to guidance. The English guidelines are an appropriate comparator since they have been evolving since 2004 and there is a limited, but growing, research record on which to draw. Modified versions of the English guidelines exist in South Korea, Uganda, Nigeria, Jamaica, and several Gulf states.

Courts in most common-law countries have long enjoyed wide discretion at sentencing, guided only by light-touch appellate review. All this changed in the 1970s with the introduction of presumptive sentencing guidelines. Guidelines were first implemented in the United States and proliferated across the country (for profiles of state guidelines, see Kauder and Ostrom [2008]; Mitchell [2017]). Guidelines drafted by a commission have since been adopted in 18 states, in the District of Columbia, and at the federal level (Frase 2019). Barkow and O'Neill describe the birth of the sentencing commission as "one of the most significant modern developments in criminal law" (2006, p. x). Minnesota established a commission in 1978, and in many respects its guidelines have proved the most influential. The best-known US guidelines system takes the form of a two-dimensional grid and is soon to mark its fortieth anniversary.[1] Sentencing grids share several common features. Most incorporate two primary dimensions: offense seriousness and criminal history, which is scored on the basis of the number and nature of prior convictions. Additionally, most contain dispositional and durational sentence recommendations, are sometimes presumptively binding on courts, and provide little additional guidance on sentencing factors or overarching considerations such as sentencing for multiple convictions and plea-based sentencing discounts (for discussion of the diversity of sentencing guidelines across the United States, see Frase [2005*a*, 2019] and Frase and Mitchell [2019]).

No other country has adopted a two-dimensional matrix structure for its guidelines.[2] However, elements of the US guidelines can be discerned in

---

in the May 2018 Minneapolis seminar for comments on the initial draft and for comments on subsequent drafts to Andrew Ashworth, Richard Frase, Arie Freiberg, David Faulkner, and Umar Azmeh.

[1] Some states such as Alabama and Virginia use worksheets that combine offense severity and criminal history rather than a grid; see Mitchell (2017) for a summary of cross-jurisdictional comparisons.

[2] The grid structure was studied and rejected by the Canadian Sentencing Commission (1986), the Western Australian government (1990), the New South Wales Law Commis-

the alternative schemes, many of which contain grid-like matrices. These contain "starting point" sentences—which courts use as a point of departure, moving up or down to reflect relevant sentencing factors—and sentence ranges for specific crimes, or categories of crime. The key difference between the US guidelines and those introduced elsewhere is that the latter are all offense specific. For example, the Korean guidelines, modeled on the English format, prescribe a standard sentencing range, applicable in most cases, and mitigated and aggravated ranges (Sentencing Commission of the Supreme Court of Korea 2014). Jurisdictions considering adopting guidelines for courts now have a range of models from which to choose. I attempt here to provide insight into the merits of the two principal methods of structuring discretion at sentencing.

Despite the common objectives of guidelines, scholars rarely make comparisons across systems. A number of authors have called for more comparative research to assess policies and structures across the United States (e.g., Stemen and Rengifo 2012; Reitz 2013; Subramanian and Shames 2013); but few such analyses have been conducted and fewer still compare the US guidelines to those in other countries. Reitz (2013) provides the only examination of the English guidelines within the context of the US experience. The limited comparisons typically relate one set of state guidelines to another or to the federal guidelines. I bridge the literatures on guidelines in the United States and elsewhere by comparing and contrasting the English and Minnesota experiences. My purposes are to highlight some important differences and draw lessons from experience with guidelines outside the United States. I pay particular attention to the structure of the two sets of guidelines. Although scholars have explored aspects of the state guidelines (e.g., Frase 2005*a*), few have asked questions about their fundamental structures.

Here is how the essay is organized. Section I explores the origins of the English guidelines. Section II describes the nature of the English Council. Section III explores the structure of the English guidelines, and Section IV summarizes the limited empirical research on use of the English guidelines. Section V contrasts the English and the Minnesota guidelines. I explore how the two sets of guidelines deal with some key issues, including the relationship between the guidelines and prison populations, the structure of the guidelines, the degree of discretion allowed courts, and the role of pre-

---

sion (1996), the Sentencing Commission Working Group in England and Wales (2008), and South Korea (2009).

vious convictions. Section VI draws preliminary conclusions and suggests some priorities for comparative research.

I. Origins of the Minnesota Commission and English Council

Several publications have discussed the origins of the US guidelines and, in particular, the Minnesota Commission (Parent 1988; Tonry 1993; Frase 2005*a*). This literature identifies the following triggers for the guidelines: rising state prison populations, a growing awareness of racial and other disparities in prison admissions and populations, a lack of offense-based proportionality (crimes involving property accounted for a high proportion of prison admissions), and a desire to make sentencing outcomes (and hence prison populations) more predictable. Many of these problems were attributed to, or were seen to be a consequence of, excessive indeterminacy in sentencing. This fueled a growth of interest in more determinate or structured sentencing. Addressing the "vexing issue" of disparate sentencing was particularly critical to the Minnesota decision to create a commission (Parent 1988, p. 1) and was a common objective of several early guidelines (Kilaru 2010). The pressing nature of these problems may explain why commissions settled on a guidelines format that would ensure consistent application and achieve rapid changes to sentencing practices. Cometh the hour, cometh the author: an important volume published in the 1970s had offered a solution to these problems.

Judge Frankel's *Criminal Sentences: Law Without Order* (1973) is generally accepted as the first proposal for sentencing commissions and guidelines (Weisberg 2012). In fact, prototypes had appeared much earlier, in Victorian England. An early sentencing monograph proposed a commission that would devise guidelines to "bring about an approach to uniformity" (Cox 1877, p. xix). A few years later, a prototype for a guidelines system appeared in an article entitled "Can Sentences Be Standardised?" The author advocated adoption of a sentencing table and guidelines system with sentences for common crimes, based on judicial practice, and containing "starting points from which the judge would make his reckoning" (Crackenthorpe 1900, p. 114). He also noted, "That there is at present no uniform scale of punishment—that equal justice is not meted out—is a notorious fact which requires no proof" (p. 104). Another Victorian had earlier observed that "the mode of fixing the lengths of sentences is from beginning to end little more than guessing" (Spencer 1860, p. 69).

These writings resulted in a key development, namely, the 1901 "Memorandum on Normal Punishments" prepared by Lord Alverstone for the judges of the King's Bench Division (Radzinowicz and Hood 1979; Wilkins 1987). This document established sentencing levels for various permutations of six offense categories (Radzinowicz and Hood 1986). However, these rudimentary "guidelines" were not updated or implemented, and there was little further public discussion of sentencing guidelines in England until the late 1980s, after the US experience became known. The evolution of the current guidelines has been documented in earlier publications (e.g., Ashworth 2008; Ashworth and Wasik 2010; Ashworth and Roberts 2013*a*; Wasik 2014). However, a brief summary may help contextualize the discussion that follows.

The Court of Appeal began to issue guideline judgments in the 1980s, although as with other common-law jurisdictions they were relatively rare, covering only a small percentage of offenses. Courts enjoyed wide discretion at sentencing, guided only by limited appellate review.[3] The standard of review was high: an appellate court interfered with a lower court sentence only when it was wrong in principle or resulted from an error in law.

Pressure began to build on the government to act on two growing problems: an increase in the size of the prison population and concern about the existence of sentencing disparities. The prison population grew rapidly in 1993–98, increasing by more than 24,000 prisoners (Ministry of Justice 2013, p. 6). Guidelines began to be seen as a plausible solution, and the US commissions served as a possible model. An academic conference involving scholars from the United States and the United Kingdom generated an important volume of essays addressing the guideline options (Wasik and Pease 1987). Over the next few years, specific proposals were advanced (see Ashworth and Roberts 2013*b*, p. 34), and a significant step was finally taken with the creation of the Sentencing Advisory Panel (SAP) in 1999. This body was conceived to provide advice to the Court of Appeal, which would draw upon the SAP's advice in crafting appellate judgments. The SAP had a broader membership than the Court of Appeal,

---

[3] An earlier set of guidelines covering most offenses had existed in the magistrates' courts for a longer period, although these were not legally binding. In contrast, magistrates' courts must now follow the guidelines issued by the Sentencing Council (see Ashworth 2003). The existence of these earlier guidelines may have facilitated acceptance by magistrates of the Sentencing Council's more binding guidelines.

including lay members.[4] It also had a research capacity and conducted empirical research that could then be considered by the Court of Appeal.[5] Within 5 years the SAP published draft guidelines for 12 offenses, and the Court of Appeal generally followed the panel's advice when crafting its judgments (Ashworth 2008).

Guidance arrangements for English courts appeared to have stabilized. However, in 2000 the government launched a sentencing review that ultimately recommended additional changes (Home Office Sentencing Review 2001). The review expressed concern about sentencing disparities and recommended a new statutory framework that, among other elements, would require guidelines based on graded seriousness levels, "entry point" or starting point sentences, and guidance on a range of other issues (chap. 8). In addition, the review proposed creation of a new authority to supplement the work of the SAP and the Court of Appeal (for more detailed discussion of the review's recommendations, see Tonry [2004, chap. 5]).

A second statutory body, the Sentencing Guidelines Council (SGC), was created in 2003. Unlike the SAP, it had a judicial majority, perhaps reflecting concern that any agency with powers to issue guidelines should be primarily judicial. The SAP and the SGC were designed to complement each other, with the SAP providing draft guidelines for the SGC, which issued guidelines for courts. The first such guidelines appeared in 2004.[6] The SGC had rejected the grid-based concept in favor of offense-based guidelines accompanied by guidelines applicable across all forms of offending, including one dealing with offense seriousness. The first offense-based guidelines contained multiple categories of seriousness, each with a range of sentences. For example, the guideline for assault provided four categories of harm, based on the level of injury to the victim. Courts would identify the level of harm reflected in the case. The guideline then provided a starting point sentence and a sentence range for each level of harm, and the guideline prescribed a stepped decision-making process for courts to follow (Sentencing Guidelines Council

---

[4] Initially the panel had 11 members, with four drawn from the judiciary.

[5] The SAP commissioned research on many sentencing issues, including public attitudes toward burglary and rape offenses, offense seriousness, and culpable driving offenses causing death (e.g., Roberts et al. 2008).

[6] These covered the determination of offense seriousness and the use of new sentences.

2008). In 2010 the SGC was replaced by a new council that began to issue its own guidelines with a new structure.

At this point there were effectively two sources of guidance for English courts: the SGC and the Court of Appeal. Growing concern over the prison population and inability to accurately predict future prison trends led the government to launch two additional inquiries. The first of these, by Lord Carter (in 2007), highlighted the rising prison population: by 2007 it was the highest on record (81,547). The report noted the alarming projections of the prison population, which predicted more than 100,000 prisoners within 7 years and criticized official projections of the size of the prison estate, which were very inaccurate (Carter 2007). The review identified the loose nature of the SGC guidelines (in contrast to Minnesota) as a reason why prison projections were far less accurate in England. Lord Carter clearly saw a need for a more structured sentencing framework implemented by a single guidelines authority (p. 3). At this point then, the move toward more binding guidelines was driven by a desire to better predict (and constrain) the prison population; concern over disparity receded in prominence.[7] It is ironic, if we fast-forward to the present, that there appears to have been no interest on the part of governments or the Sentencing Council to use the guidelines to curb the recent drift toward more and longer prison sentences. I return to this critical issue below.

Recommendations from Lord Carter's review led to the creation, in 2008, of the Sentencing Commission Working Group (Working Group) with a more specific mandate to review the guidelines, as well as the statutory bodies responsible for guidance. The Working Group visited several US state commissions and subsequently recommended significant changes to the English guidelines regime. Having studied the Minnesota grid-based guidelines, the Working Group concluded that the "inflexibility" of the US grid models "makes them unsuitable and unacceptable in England and Wales" (Sentencing Commission Working Group 2008, p. 31). The Working Group identified the weak compliance requirement in England as the principal reason why it was hard to predict sentencing patterns and hence prison populations (p. 7). At that time courts were required only to "have regard" to the guidelines, and the Working Group

---

[7] Research published at the time continued to document sentencing disparities. For example, one official report published at the same time as the Carter review found that both the custody rate and the average custodial sentence length varied significantly across the 42 criminal justice areas in England and Wales (Mason et al. 2007).

concluded that more rigorous wording would ensure greater compliance, leading to more predictable patterns of prison admissions and projections.[8]

The government acted on many of the Working Group's recommendations and legislated a new guidelines regime in the Coroners and Justice Act 2009. The wording of the compliance requirement was tightened by changing from "must *have regard to* any relevant guideline" to "must *follow* any relevant guideline" (Ashworth 2010; Roberts 2011). With respect to the guidelines authority, in 2010 both the SAP and the SGC were replaced by the Sentencing Council of England and Wales (English Council).

II. Structure of the Sentencing Council of England and Wales

The English judiciary has historically opposed the imposition of more structured sentencing. A good example may be found in the 1978 report of the Advisory Council on the Penal System. This council recommended a thorough overhaul of the maximum penalty structure in order to align the statutory maximums more closely to contemporary standards and levels of punishment. More specifically, the council recommended amending the historically high and unrealistic maximum penalties. The government declined to implement the recommendations largely because of judicial resistance. The judges took the view that the high maximums were necessary to address cases of exceptional seriousness. This suggests judicial concern to preserve significant discretion as reflected in the range of sentences available to courts. Why then did the English judiciary ultimately accept the creation of definitive sentencing guidelines? The explanation lies in the membership of the SGC and subsequently the English Council, the nature of their guidelines, the relaxed statutory compliance requirement, and the wide guideline sentence ranges. In a nutshell, the

---

[8] There are examples of one jurisdiction drawing on expertise from another. The Working Group appointed a leading US sentencing expert, Kevin Reitz, as academic advisor. Reitz provided an invaluable US perspective and was instrumental in several key recommendations, including the tightening of the compliance requirement and creation of a more comprehensive sentencing database that would permit adequate monitoring of the use of the guidelines. Similarly, the Home Office Review of 2001 and subsequent developments were influenced by the writings and input of Michael Tonry, who was a member of the review committee (see Tonry 2002, 2004).

guidelines proved acceptable to the judiciary once it became clear that they would be devised by a primarily judicial body, would be independent of government and the legislature, and would still permit courts a significant degree of discretion.

Knapp (1987) identified three models for a sentencing commission: "representative," "elite," and "judicial." In terms of this classification (and other characteristics), US sentencing commissions are "all over the map" (Dansky 2010, p. 159; for a concise summary of commission composition, see Mitchell [2017]). One common element is that judges are always in the minority.[9] The Minnesota Sentencing Guidelines Commission (MSGC) is composed of 11 individuals, including three judges. The other members include representatives of several criminal justice professions, and three places are reserved for members of the general public, at least one of whom must have been the victim of a felony crime. The MSGC conforms to the model described by Knapp as "representative" rather than "exclusively judicial" or "elite" (Knapp 1987, pp. 117–18).

The Sentencing Council of England and Wales does not fall neatly into one of Knapp's models.[10] The judiciary constitutes a majority of the English Council's 14 members, although representatives of key stakeholders are also included.[11] There are no members of the general public, and the perspective of victims is represented not by an individual crime victim (as is the case in several Australian sentencing councils) but by a professional working in a victim-related organization.[12] Some commentators have called for

---

[9] Judges are heavily outnumbered on some commissions. The least judicial is in North Carolina, where the Sentencing and Policy Advisory Commission has 30 members, of whom only three are sitting judges. The diverse membership includes a representative of the Retail Merchants' Association, a private citizen appointed by the governor, and six elected politicians. The Ohio Commission appears to be the largest, with 31 members, including 11 judges.

[10] It is unclear why the English guidelines authority (and those found in other countries such as Australia) uses the term "council" rather than "commission." Although the functions, powers, and activities vary, all these organizations provide advice to courts at sentencing. My personal view is that the US term was avoided in order to distance the English and Australian bodies from the grid-based guidelines that for years have been regarded negatively by judges in these other countries. Ironically, the original Victorian proposals for a guidelines authority used the term "commission" (e.g., Crackenthorpe 1900).

[11] Representatives of the police, probation, victims' groups, and an academic are included. Barkow (2012), an academic member of the federal US Sentencing Commission, argues that "guidelines are at their best and most effective when they are based on sound empirical data and professional expertise" (p. 1601). I agree, and the English Council conforms to this description.

[12] The Australian sentencing councils share a number of characteristics with the English Council and US commissions. For example, they all publish sentencing statistics of one kind

a broader and more diverse membership including ex-offenders,[13] but this has not happened (see Allen 2016; Bottoms 2018). Nor are any members drawn from the general public, although the SAP (replaced by the current English Council in 2011) included lay members (as do the Australian sentencing councils). Finally, the English Council is apolitical in the sense that it has no members representing political parties or with "political experience and connections" (Frase 1993, p. 369). The US commissions are clearly more political and populist than their counterparts in the United Kingdom. For example, it is unclear why there should be an equal number of members of the public and judges on a commission (as in Minnesota).

The English Council was created in close conjunction with the senior judiciary. The Lord Chief Justice serves as president, and membership overlaps with the Court of Appeal. The judiciary also appears to have influenced the nature of the enabling statute that created the council. This legislation specifies the kinds of guidelines the council should be developing and specifies the duties of a court, including the compliance requirement. This significant degree of judicial engagement was critical to ensuring acceptance by sentencers.[14] Some scholars question the judicial dominance of the council,[15] but the English guidelines would not have emerged if Parliament had created a council modeled on the MSGC. English judges would have rejected guidelines issued by a body without a judicial majority.

A judicial majority ensures greater independence. The Minnesota governor makes appointments to the MSGC, whereas, while an elected politician with responsibility for the court system (the secretary of state) appoints members to the English Council, decisions are made in conjunction with the Lord Chief Justice. To date, neither the government nor Parliament has intruded into the council's activities, and the council's ju-

---

or another. The principal difference is that unlike the US and English bodies, the Australian councils do not issue guidelines; their role is therefore primarily to inform the judiciary and the wider community about current issues and trends in sentencing (see, e.g., the website of the Sentencing Advisory Council, Victoria, https://www.sentencingcouncil.vic.gov.au/).

[13] Judge Frankel proposed that the commission include "present or former prisoners" (1973, p. 120).

[14] Some Australian councils (such as the Victorian Sentencing Council) have no judicial members, but these bodies do not issue guidelines.

[15] Tonry (2004) argued against a judicial majority for the English Council on the grounds that the presence of judicial members would inhibit development of guidelines by being excessively solicitous toward the views of sentencing judges (see also Berman 2017, pp. 103–4). Ashworth (2010) advocated for inclusion of lay members, and more recently, Allen (2016) urged the council to include more nonjudicial members.

dicial majority may explain this uncharacteristic reticence on the part of legislators. In contrast, the Minnesota commission has been under almost constant political pressure since its creation, resulting in an escalation in sentence severity over time. As early as 1991, Frase noted "the pressure for increased sentence severity and legislative control" (p. 732). In contrast, the English guidelines have not been amended in response to any external influences. The judicial dominance of the council may carry a cost, however. One consequence may be the more discretionary nature of the English guidelines.

A. Statutory Functions of the English Council

The enabling statute for the Minnesota commission and guidelines imposed few duties on the commission (Frase 1997, p. 389). In contrast, the enabling statute for the English Council—the Coroners and Justice Act 2009—goes much further than similar legislation in the United States or elsewhere in prescribing the nature of the guidelines and the role and responsibilities. In addition to specifying membership, it provides clear direction on the structure of the guidelines, the duties of the council, and the duties of the courts with respect to compliance with the guidelines. This tighter legislative mandate has consequences for the work of the English Council.

B. Descriptive or Prescriptive Guidelines?

An important consideration for any guidelines authority concerns its role in the sentencing environment. Should a sentencing commission prescribe sentencing practice or simply reflect existing trends in order to make them more consistent? Guidelines can be descriptive in nature, reproducing current judicial practice, or prescriptive, with a mandate to change current practice. The Minnesota guidelines are prescriptive (Frase 1993). In its first report to the legislature, the commission noted that in developing its guidelines, "we have been informed by, but not bound to, current practice" (MSGC 1980, p. 3).[16] Von Hirsch argued that "the enabling statute [of any commission] should make clear that the commission's role is a *policymaking* one" (1987, p. 62; emphasis in original). A related issue concerns

---

[16] One explanation for the English Council's reluctance to issue guidelines that depart more significantly from current practice may be apprehension that this will undermine judicial confidence in the guidelines, leading to less compliance (for discussion of this issue in the US context, see Kilaru [2010, p. 134]).

the relationship between the guidelines and prison capacity. Most US guidelines are sensitive to the prison population and have the potential to prevent serious overcrowding. The Minnesota commission interpreted its enabling legislation "to mean that the guidelines should produce prison populations which do not exceed the current capacity of state correctional institutions" (MSGC 1980, p. 2). Chapter 23 of the Minnesota Laws 1978 directs the commission to "take into substantial consideration current sentencing and release practices and correctional resources, including but not limited to the capacities of local and state correctional facilities." US academics appear to share the opinion firmly expressed by Frase that "an assumption of limited prison capacity is an essential component of guidelines development" (1991, p. 734).

Things are rather different in England. Unlike the Minnesota statute, the English legislation ascribes no power to the English Council to issue guidelines that take account of the size of the prison population. For this reason, the council issues guidelines based on judicial practice and designed to promote a more consistent approach to current practice; they *reflect* rather than *refract* judicial behavior. As the chair of the council noted in testimony before a parliamentary committee, "The first thing we look at when we are devising our guidelines is 'What is the current sentencing practice of the court?' By and large, that guides us as to the levels of sentencing and the sort of factors that are important in our guidelines."[17] This is the approach taken in other countries where judicially based guidelines have been introduced (see Dennison 2015, p. 9). Some UK scholars have criticized this approach, arguing that the English Council should address the high (relative to other western European nations) prison population in England and Wales by amending its guidelines (e.g., Allen 2016).

This is not the whole story, however, since the council has issued a few guidelines intended to change judicial practice. Four examples are illustrative. First, when devising its drug offenses guideline, the English Council concluded that sentences imposed on low-level drug couriers ("mules") were disproportionately high. To correct this, the council issued a guideline to reduce levels of sentencing for drug offenders with a lesser role (Sentencing Council of England and Wales 2012*a*). Subsequent research by the

---

[17] Testimony of the council's chair before the Justice Select Committee on July 11, 2018: http://data.parliament.uk/writtenevidence/committeeevidence.svc/evidencedocument/justice-committee/prison-population-2022/oral/86817.pdf.

council and independent researchers found that the guideline had successfully achieved shorter prison terms for this category of drug offender. A second example concerns the use of suspended sentences of imprisonment. For decades, courts in England and Wales used the suspended sentence order to replace community orders rather than the terms of immediate custody they were conceived to replace (Bottoms 1981; Roberts and Ashworth 2016). The tendency was particularly pronounced in the period 2005–14 when the volume of suspended sentences rose dramatically while the use of community penalties declined significantly (Irwin-Rogers and Roberts 2019, table 1). Having noted this misapplication of the suspended sentence, the council issued a guideline to ensure that suspended sentence orders were used only in cases in which custody would have been imposed (Sentencing Council of England and Wales 2016*a*).

A third example is a guideline for health and safety offenses that was designed to increase the magnitude of fines imposed and that has achieved the intended result. Finally, the sexual offenses guideline (2013) and the terrorism offenses guideline (2018*c*) also attempt to change current practice, albeit in the opposite direction (Sentencing Council of England and Wales 2018*b*).[18] The sentence for the most serious cases of rape increased under the council's guideline as did the sentence for certain terrorism offenses. These instances are corrections to departures from a proportionate sentencing regime (or the misapplication of a specific sanction) rather than significant changes in policy or an attempt to constrain the size of the prison estate.

The essential nature of the English guidelines remains conservatively descriptive, and the question is why? Even if the English Council wished to change sentencing trends, there are principled and practical impediments to reducing the size of the prison estate. The principled objection is that the council has no obvious legal authority to use its guidelines to reduce the volume or duration of custodial sentences. Although the council's drug offenses guideline had this effect for one group of offenders, this was an attempt to restore proportionality rather than to reduce the overall volume of drug offenders sent to prison. Nothing in the enabling statute directs the

---

[18] See testimony of the council's chair before the Parliamentary Select Committee on July 11, 2018, where he noted that with respect to some sexual offenses and to knife crimes, "We deliberately took the decision that that sort of offending required heavier sentencing" and acknowledged that this "will have had some effect on lifting sentences" (http://data.parliament.uk/writtenevidence/committeeevidence.svc/evidencedocument/justice-committee/prison-population-2022/oral/86817.pdf).

council's attention to the size of the prison population or the need to avoid prison overcrowding. The only statutory reference that might justify the council in issuing guidelines that would reduce the prison population concerns the effectiveness of sanctions. Section 120 11(e) of the Coroners and Justice Act 2009 states that in discharging its functions, the council must have regard to "the cost of different sentences and their relative effectiveness in preventing re-offending." The council could interpret this direction to conduct a review of current sanctions, and if it concluded that short prison terms were not cost-effective,[19] it might then reissue all its guidelines having adjusted them to promote suspended sentences and community orders at the expense of short prison terms. To date, the council has declined to take such a step; but were it to do so, it could affect the volume and duration of admissions to custody.

Practical problems arise from the use of separate guidelines issued sequentially over a lengthy period. The Minnesota commission can change the size of the prison population expeditiously by reducing the grid sentence ranges (assuming there is no legislative resistance to such changes). For example, it could reduce recommended sentence lengths by 10 percent across the entire grid. This would result in a reduction in sentence lengths and, ultimately, a smaller prison population without disturbing ordinal proportionality: all offenses would be affected to the same proportionate degree. Other US commissions such as the federal commission could also achieve expeditious reductions in the prison population. However, if the English Council wished to promote a greater use of noncustodial sentences for, say, assault offenders, this would require launching a professional and public consultation and then ultimately issuing an amended guideline. The typical duration for creation, consultation, and release of a guideline is approximately 12 months. Moreover, once sentences for assault changed, it would also be necessary to review all other guidelines for offenses against the person to ensure that proportionality across offenses was not undermined. This recalibration would then trigger additional rounds of consultation for each guideline, as required by the statute. This limitation is one of the drawbacks of an offense-specific approach.

---

[19] The UK Ministry of Justice has conducted extensive multivariate research to explore the relationship between different sanctions and recidivism rates. The research compared recidivism rates for short custodial sentences and suspended sentence orders and found that the 1-year reoffending rate was highest for those sentenced to short-term custody (see Mews et al. 2015).

Finally, it is not obvious that sentencing guidelines should shoulder the responsibility of constraining or reducing the prison population. There is at least an argument that they should be blind to prison capacity. If there has been a surge in serious crimes, resulting in an overcrowded prison estate, why should offenders sentenced in the aftermath receive milder punishments as a result of the state's failure to provide adequate prison capacity? Frase (1991) argued that a commission should respond to rising crime rates by recommending increases in prison capacity "or greater use of... intermediate sanctions" (p. 736). As a practical matter the legislature should be alerted to an impending problem of prison overcrowding, but the principle of adjusting sentence lengths or the dispositional line to respond to rising or falling crime rates is questionable. Moreover, should sentences rise back to precrisis levels of severity once the prison population falls back to earlier levels?

C. *Consistency of Outcome versus Consistency of Approach*

Judge Frankel's seminal volume inspired the creation of the MSGC (Parent 1988; Frase 2005*a*; Berman 2017). Disparity was the problem, and guidelines were the solution. In light of this, it is unsurprising that the Minnesota guidelines assumed the form of a simple grid that attempts to achieve predictable and consistent outcomes. More recently, however, scholars have called into question this emphasis on reducing disparities, linking such a goal to the high use of imprisonment. Adelman (2013) argues that "too much focusing on reducing inter-judge sentencing disparity is a major mistake" (p. 304). Barkow (2012, p. 1620) wrote that "the [guidelines] movement's reaction against the prior regime often placed too much emphasis on uniformity and not enough on individualization," while Stith (2000) and others have drawn similar conclusions about the federal guidelines. The grid-based approach has also been criticized by European scholars such as Wandall (2006), who argues that the Minnesota guidelines "bind sentencing structures closely to a concern for sentencing outcomes" (p. 26) and concluded that the Danish approach of discretionary sentencing without guidelines was "preferable" (p. 42).

The English Council on numerous occasions has stressed that its guidelines were not designed to promote greater consistency per se, but a more consistent approach to sentencing. The first chair of the council noted that its primary aim was to "promote a clear, fair, and consistent approach to sentencing" (Leveson 2013, p. 3). The distinction between promoting consistency and promoting a consistent approach is unclear, but it appears to distance the council from what it regards as an American approach to guidelines, namely, achievement of more consistent outcomes. The English Council has steered well clear of making any claims about reducing disparity, achieving greater consistency, or even a more consistent approach to sentencing (although there is evidence that sentencing is more consistent).[20] This constitutes another important difference between the English Council and the US commissions, each of which, as Tonry noted, "claim[s] that its guidelines have reduced sentencing disparities compared with sentencing patterns before guidelines took effect" (1993, p. 152).

D. Development of Guidelines: Concurrent or Consecutive?

Unlike the Minnesota commission, the English Council chose to develop and issue its guidelines *seriatim*; there was no "big bang" moment in the English guidelines experience when all offenses became subject to a guideline. The incremental approach confers benefits but also creates challenges. Guidelines are more expeditiously implemented if all offenses are assigned to a single grid or if all offense-specific guidelines are created at the same time. Constructing a separate guideline with different sentence recommendations, starting point sentences, and mitigating and aggravating factors takes much longer. The council might have taken several years to develop all its offense-specific guidelines in preparation for a mass release. Instead, it chose to identify key offenses and to issue guidelines one by one. The council began with high-volume offenses or crimes for which guidance appeared particularly necessary. The initial guidelines included assault, burglary, and drug offenses.[21] The first guideline (assault offenses) appeared in 2011 (Roberts and Rafferty 2011; Sentencing Council of England and Wales 2011). Most of the others have been offense-based guidelines, but the council has issued general guidelines applying to all cases. By 2020, a decade after its creation, the council will

---

[20] The more recently created Scottish Sentencing Council adopts the more direct approach found in the United States. Section 2a of the enabling statute states that the council "must, in carrying out its functions, seek to: (a) promote consistency in sentencing practice" (Criminal Justice and Licensing [Scotland] Act 2010).

[21] Other jurisdictions have taken the same incremental approach. The South African Law Commission proposed that guidelines would be developed one by one, over a 5-year period, although its recommendations were not implemented (see Law Reform Commission of South Africa 2000). The Ugandan guidelines, modeled on the English system, also adopted the gradual approach to guideline development (Kamuzze 2014).

have issued approximately 40 stand-alone guidelines covering all principal offense categories as well as several guidelines that apply across cases. In short, the English guidelines have taken much longer than those in Minnesota to cover all crimes.[22]

The second challenge arising from the offense-by-offense approach is that greater effort is required by the English Council to maintain ordinal proportionality across offenses. When developing the manslaughter guideline, for example, the council had to ensure that the sentence ranges and starting points were aligned with the guidance for the most serious assaults and other personal injury crimes.[23] It is easier to preserve ordinal proportionality when all offenses are assigned to a single grid. However, an advantage of the consecutive rather than concurrent approach is that the council can learn by trial and error, improving its guidelines over time, and this it has done. The first guideline (for assault offenses) attracted resistance from courts and critiques by practitioners;[24] accordingly, the council revised its format in later guidelines.

III. Structure of the English Guidelines

The principal structural difference between the two regimes is that Minnesota employs three grids to accommodate all offenses,[25] while the En-

---

[22] Other councils have taken even longer. The Scottish Sentencing Council was created in 2015 and is also issuing its guidelines sequentially. As of January 2019, it has yet to issue its first guideline.

[23] This task was further complicated by constant legislative interventions in sentencing and judicial interpretation of revised statutory sentences. For example, in 2003 Parliament introduced a comprehensive new regime of mandatory minimum periods of imprisonment for different categories of murder, all of which are subject to imprisonment for life. These new sentences had the effect, whether intended or not, of increasing sentences for other homicide offenses such as manslaughter, as well as the most serious assaults.

[24] The guideline contains categories of higher and lesser harm and culpability, but no "intermediate" or "medium" category. Some practitioners complained that this complicated the task of assigning cases to categories.

[25] An early published example of an offense-specific guideline can be found in the report of the Canadian Sentencing Commission (1987, app. A). The Canadian proposals were well received by US scholars such as Norval Morris and Andrew von Hirsch. However, once the Canadian Parliament declined to implement the recommendations, the commission's model sank without a trace. There has been little further discussion of guidelines in that country except for academic commentary. Several of the early American guidelines systems in the 1980s, e.g., in Delaware and Michigan, did adopt the offense-specific approach. Earlier, the US National Academy of Sciences report on sentencing reform described the offense-specific approach as the "telephone book" model in which sentencers look up the offense they are about to sentence (Blumstein et al. 1983).

glish guidelines provide separate (and individualized) guidelines for different categories of offending. The original Minnesota grid applied to all offenses; the MSGC has subsequently created separate grids for sex offenses and drug offenses (MSGC 2018), but all three grids share a common structure (App. A provides an extract from the main Minnesota grid).[26]

The Minnesota grid was effectively a transposition of the parole guidelines grid devised by Wilkins and his colleagues (Wilkins 1987; Tonry 1993; Frase 2005a).[27] The chief architect of the parole (and then sentencing) grid wrote, "By the end of the 1970s most paroling authorities had developed some form of guidelines.... The transition to sentencing guidelines was a natural development" (Wilkins 1987, p. 14). The Minnesota and other US commissions certainly thought it natural. But are the parole and sentencing functions really that interchangeable? The dimensions of seriousness and probability of recidivism (almost entirely determined by reference to prior record) are arguably more apposite to the decision to release than the more complex (and multidimensional) determination of sentence. Put simply, the parole decision is largely a function of the prisoner's risk of reoffending, and criminal history is more relevant to risk than retribution. In contrast to parole boards, sentencing courts balance potentially competing objectives of reducing risk and recognizing harm (retribution). The literature does not discuss why Minnesota adapted the parole grid model for the purposes of sentencing. The familiarity of the parole grid and the relative ease with which it could be transposed to sentencing probably explain the commission's decision. There has been no discussion since as to whether a two-dimensional structure remains the most appropriate one to follow and whether criminal history should still constitute one of the two dimensions. Perhaps there should have been.

A. The English Guidelines Format

The first English sentencing guideline appeared in 2004, approximately a quarter century after the inception of the Minnesota guidelines. Proposals

---

[26] The drug offender grid and the sex offender grid have fewer offense levels but the same number of criminal history categories and the same two-dimensional structure.

[27] Tonry (1993) notes that the early, voluntary guidelines emerged "expressly building on experience with parole guidelines" (p. 140). The voluntary guidelines then evolved into presumptively binding guidelines while retaining the two-dimensional structure. Tonry (2013) describes the creation of sentencing guidelines as the "logical next step" after parole guidelines, but this still does not justify the automatic read-across of the grid format.

had, however, emerged in England in the early 1980s. The current English format may be traced to several publications by Ashworth (1983, 1987). In these works, he outlined the principal elements of a sentencing guideline, namely, the grading of offenses, lists of factors that might aggravate or mitigate, and guidance on key issues such as criminal history and sentence recommendations.[28] He also proposed that sentencing levels be determined by examining current sentencing practice in conjunction with guidance provided by the Court of Appeal. This general approach was ultimately adopted by the Sentencing Guidelines Council and then its successor, the Sentencing Council of England and Wales. Despite some structural variation reflecting the nature of the offense, all the offense-specific guidelines contain a number of common elements. Broadly speaking, they require courts to follow a step-by-step methodology when determining sentence. A court in Minnesota will focus on the appropriate cell in the grid covering the offense being sentenced. The sentencing exercise is more protracted and complicated in England and Wales. Applying an offense-based guideline, a sentencer must follow up to nine steps, making decisions at each step of the process. This focuses the court's attention to a greater degree on the factors affecting the nature and severity of sentences.

B. *Example of an English Offense-Based Guideline: Street Robbery*

The Minnesota guidelines reflect a modified just deserts rationale, although the enabling statute articulates no single rationale (Knapp 1987). The English guidelines generally incorporate two primary dimensions, harm and culpability, the principal components of a proportionate sentence. The guidelines developed in other jurisdictions have also adopted the harm-culpability combination rather than the US crime–criminal history alternative.[29]

---

[28] For example, Ashworth noted that "there would be lists of aggravating and extenuating factors, which would help the sentencer to decide whether to go higher or lower than the [guidelines'] recommended penalty ... [and] a list of mitigating factors to be considered in conjunction with any representations on behalf of the offender" (1987, p. 101). This structure corresponds closely to the sentencing guidelines issued by the English Council. Ashworth's article highlights the importance of comparative research. Ashworth was well aware of developments in the United States, having, as editor of the *Criminal Law Review*, published several articles describing the US experience.

[29] These include South Korea (Park 2010) and China (Chen 2010; Roberts and Pei 2016). The New Zealand guidelines also follow this approach, although they have yet to be implemented (Young and King 2013).

The street robbery guideline lays down nine separate steps for courts to follow. Figure 1 presents an extract from the robbery guideline consisting of the categories at step 1 and the factors that determine which category is appropriate for the case being sentenced. (Appendix B shows the nine guideline steps for robbery.) In discussing the guidelines methodology, I assume that courts do work through all the steps. There seems no reason to question the professionalism of sentencers in this respect, but equally, there is no way of knowing whether they do. In this sense, the English guidelines are more opaque; a court could, presumably, ignore the step-by-step structure, decide the appropriate sentence, and then work backward to justify the decision. The use of the methodology must therefore be taken on trust.

STEP ONE
Determining the offence category

The court should determine the offence category with reference **only** to the factors listed in the tables below. In order to determine the category the court should assess **culpability** and **harm**.

The court should weigh all the factors set out below in determining the offender's culpability.

Where there are characteristics present which fall under different levels of culpability, the court should balance these characteristics to reach a fair assessment of the offender's culpability.

Culpability demonstrated by one or more of the following:

A – High culpability	• Use of a weapon to inflict violence • Production of a bladed article or firearm or imitation firearm to threaten violence • Use of very significant force in the commission of the offence • Offence motivated by, or demonstrating hostility based on any of the following characteristics or presumed characteristics of the victim: religion, race, disability, sexual orientation or transgender identity
B – Medium culpability	• Production of a weapon other than a bladed article or firearm or imitation firearm to threaten violence • Threat of violence by any weapon (but which is not produced) • Other cases where characteristics for categories A or C are not present
C – Lesser culpability	• Involved through coercion, intimidation or exploitation • Threat or use of minimal force • Mental disability or learning disability where linked to the commission of the offence

Harm
The court should consider the factors set out below to determine the level of harm that has been caused or was intended to be caused to the victim.

Category 1	• Serious physical and/or psychological harm caused to the victim • Serious detrimental effect on the business
Category 2	• Other cases where characteristics for categories 1 or 3 are not present
Category 3	• No/minimal physical or psychological harm caused to the victim • No/minimal detrimental effect on the business

(ROBBERY – STREET AND LESS SOPHISTICATED COMMERCIAL)

FIG. 1.—Extract from robbery guideline. Source: Sentencing Council of England and Wales (2016*b*).

The first step is the most important as it determines the limits of the sentence range that the court will work within as it proceeds through the remaining steps of the guideline. At step 1 the court assigns the case to one of three levels of harm and the defendant to one of three levels of culpability (high, medium, and lesser). Consistency at this crucial first step is promoted by requiring all courts to consider the same set of factors to determine which category of harm and culpability is appropriate. The list of factors at step 1 that determine the category sentence range is exclusive; courts may take other factors into account only later, at step 2. The exclusive nature of this list is one of the most restrictive elements of the English guidelines and aims to promote a more uniform approach across courts.

Once a court has determined which of the three categories of harm and culpability is appropriate (guided by the factors listed in the guideline and recommendations from the advocates), it proceeds to step 2, which contains a matrix with starting point sentences and sentence ranges for each category. For example, if the court decides that the offense involves intermediate harm (category 2), committed by an individual of the lowest culpability, the guideline provides a starting point sentence of 2 years' imprisonment and a range of 1–4 years. The court begins at the starting point sentence and then moves up and down within the category range considering a nonexhaustive list of mitigating and aggravating factors (along with any other factors proposed by advocates). This exercise results in a provisional sentence. Then the court works through additional steps, including awarding credit for any assistance to the police or prosecution (step 3) or for a guilty plea (step 4; see App. B). These two considerations are external to considerations of harm or culpability, and for this reason they are considered at a separate step. For example, assuming the provisional sentence after considering all relevant sentencing factors is 3 years' imprisonment, the court would reduce this by one-third if the defendant had entered a guilty plea at first court appearance. The one-third reduction arises from the recommendations contained in a separate guideline regulating plea-based discounts.

C. *"Generic" Guidelines Applicable to All Offenses*

Guidance from the Minnesota commission is contained within the guidelines manual and the three grids. No additional stand-alone guidance is issued, and this is typical of the US guidelines.[30] At best they offer

---

[30] The US Sentencing Commission has published several documents (referred to as "primers") to supplement the grid and the manual. For example, one deals with aggravating

broad policy statements. In addition to its offense-specific guidelines, the English Council has issued several "generic" guidelines that apply across cases. The most important of these, in terms of the number of cases affected, concerns plea-based sentence reductions.

Plea-based sentence reductions illustrate the benefits of guidelines that involve more than a grid and a guidelines manual. Judgments from the Court of Appeal have provided guidance regarding the appropriate levels of reduction and the factors affecting the magnitude of reductions, but a stand-alone guideline creates greater certainty and transparency. The statutory foundation for the practice in England and Wales is found in section 144(1) of the Criminal Justice Act 2003: "In determining what sentence to pass on an offender who has pleaded guilty to an offence in proceedings before that or another court, a court must take into account: (a) the stage in the proceedings for the offence at which the offender indicated his intention to plead guilty, and (b) the circumstances in which this indication was given." This provision offers no guidance on the magnitude of reductions appropriate to pleas entered at different stages of the criminal process or the circumstances that might justify greater or lesser reductions. For guidance on these (and other) issues, courts follow the guideline on sentence reductions.

The guideline states that defendants who enter a plea at first court appearance are entitled to a maximum sentence length reduction of one-third. The size of the reduction then diminishes the later the guilty plea is entered; defendants who change their plea to guilty on the day of trial should receive a reduction of only 10 percent (Sentencing Council of England and Wales 2017). The guideline thus creates a sliding scale of discounts to reflect the timing of the plea. Timing is critical to determining the level of reduction awarded, an arrangement consistent with other common-law jurisdictions (Roberts and Bradford 2015). Finally, plea may affect the nature as well as the quantum of punishment. Offenders convicted of a crime that justifies a term of custody may receive a noncustodial sentence in return for an early guilty plea (Sentencing Council of England and Wales 2017, p. 6).

---

and mitigating role adjustments, and others deal with the use of prior convictions. These documents are "provided by the Commission's Legal Staff ... to assist in understanding and applying the sentencing guidelines." They elaborate the guidelines and are not the equivalent of the English generic guidelines. See https://www.ussc.gov/sites/default/files/pdf/training/primers/2017_Primer_Role.pdf.

The English guidelines reflect a proportionate sentencing model. Plea discounts are unrelated to harm and culpability. Accordingly, if the discounts are very striking, proportionality is undermined. If offenders convicted of the same serious crime receive very different sentences because one pleaded guilty and the other was convicted after trial, proportionality and retributive parity will be affected. For this reason, some method of constraining the power of plea to reduce a sentence is necessary. In this respect, the guilty plea guideline is a useful element of the English regime in terms of reducing variability and protecting offense-based proportionality. Prior to the guideline, guilty plea reductions were less predictable, and courts periodically awarded reductions significantly above one-third in order to "crack" or resolve impending trials of great complexity or involving multiple defendants. Some defendants who ultimately pleaded guilty were denied any reduction on the basis that the crime was particularly heinous, a practice that still occurs in courts in Canada and other jurisdictions (Cole and Roberts 2018). These departures from a clearly established set of recommended reductions undermine fairness. They also impair the objectives of the reductions, namely, to elicit prompt pleas from defendants who elect to waive their right to trial. The existence of the definitive guideline prescribing specific reductions appropriate to the stage at which the plea was entered provides legal counsel and their clients a clear idea of what reduction to expect. The absence of a binding guideline regulating plea-based sentence discounts in Minnesota means that the likely benefit of entering a plea is unknown until the parties have secured a plea agreement.

D. Other Guidelines

The English Council has issued guidelines on a range of other issues. One guideline regulates the use of consecutive and concurrent sentences when an offender is convicted of multiple crimes. Such cases are not uncommon: the English Council estimated that approximately 40 percent of cases involved a defendant convicted of more than one offense. The sentencing exercise is much more complicated when the offender is convicted of multiple offenses, often varying in seriousness (see Ryberg, Roberts, and de Keijser 2017). Accordingly, guidance is useful. The English guideline provides guidance on the "totality" principle. This requires courts to consider the totality of the offender's crimes and, by using concurrent sentencing, to ensure that the total sentence is not disproportionate (Sentencing Council of England and Wales 2012c). The guideline explains the conditions under which a court would use concurrent as opposed to consecutive sentences in a way that preserves proportionality and prevents the total sentence from becoming excessive (as it would do if all sentences were simply added together).

To date, all guidelines, whether grids containing levels of seriousness (Minnesota) or offense-specific guidelines (England), focus on crimes. Yet courts can also benefit from guidance with respect to the application of different punishments. The English Council has issued a guideline that covers punishments rather than crimes. The dispositions guideline covers the three principal sanctions (immediate imprisonment, suspended sentences, and community orders). The guidance is relatively skeletal and has been criticized for this reason (Bottoms 2018). In addition, as Ashworth (2017) points out, the Court of Appeal paid little attention to the guideline when issuing judgments in multiple offense appeals. Nevertheless, there is merit in the principle of sentence-specific guidelines. Besides these topics, the council has issued guidelines on sentencing young persons, allocation to the superior court, breach of community sanctions, and determining crime seriousness. The council is in the process of issuing guidelines regarding the sentencing of offenders with mental health issues. A significant proportion of offenders appearing for sentence suffer from one or more mental health problems. A guideline that highlights these issues and proposes ways of considering them in the application of guidelines is surely a progressive useful reform.

As of January 2019, 32 guidelines have been issued (see Sentencing Council of England and Wales website).

IV. Evaluating the English Guidelines: Research Findings

Although they do not issue guidelines, the Australian sentencing councils have been subject to official evaluations, usually 5 years after their creation (e.g., New South Wales Department of Justice 2008). Surprisingly, the UK government has yet to conduct a comparable evaluation of the English Council,[31] although two independent evaluations have been published (Allen 2016; Bottoms 2018). In addition, the council's guidelines have attracted critical commentary from academics and practitioners (e.g., Lovegrove 2010; Cooper 2013; Dhami 2013; Padfield 2013; Secret Barrister

---

[31] The Justice Select Committee in Parliament reviews each English Council guideline and periodically invites the council's chair to appear to discuss the council's work, but the level of scrutiny is minimal. The committee usually suggests minor amendments to the

2017). Padfield (2013), for example, questioned whether the guidelines have generated fairer and more consistent outcomes, and a recurrent critique is that notwithstanding the 2009 amendments to the compliance requirement, the guidelines still permit too much judicial discretion at sentencing (e.g., Ashworth 2010; Young and King 2013). I do not attempt to summarize this literature here; the academic critiques focus on the failure of the council to address the comparatively high use of incarceration as a sanction. Some practitioners argue that the guidelines have undermined the individualized nature of sentencing (and possibly also the role of personal mitigation). The empirical literature on the guidelines is growing but remains sparse relative to the United States. A number of key questions have yet to be answered. Nevertheless, some preliminary conclusions may be drawn, particularly with respect to the use of the guidelines by the courts.

A. Offense-Specific Guidelines

Over the past 40 years the US guidelines and, in particular, the Minnesota guidelines have attracted much research and commentary. In light of their shorter life span, far less has been published on the English guidelines.[32] As with the Minnesota and other US commissions, the English Council publishes an annual report and monitors the impact of its guidelines. Since the total guideline range is so wide (running up to the statutory maximum in some cases), the percentage of sentences imposed within this range, and therefore compliant with the law, is relatively meaningless. In addition, prior to issuing a guideline the council always predicts the effect of the guideline on prison places (see, e.g., Sentencing Council 2018a). Again, the analysis is not very informative. Since the guidelines are designed to reflect judicial practice, the predicted effect of the guideline is almost always to be resource-neutral. In order to understand the effects of the guidelines, it is necessary to turn to the limited academic research. In keeping with the orientation of the guidelines, most of this research has explored the question of whether the guidelines are consistently applied rather than whether the outcomes are more consistent after introduction of the guidelines. Academic research suggests a positive effect on consistency across courts and the application of the offense-specific guidelines.

---

guidelines rather than examining the role and effectiveness of the council (e.g., House of Commons Justice Committee 2011).

[32] For essays examining the English guidelines, see Ashworth and Roberts (2013a) and Roberts (2015).

Pina-Sánchez evaluated the impact of the assault and burglary guidelines,[33] and he concluded that "consistency improved in all the offenses studied after the new guideline came into force" (2015, p. 87; see also Pina-Sánchez and Linacre 2013). Irwin-Rogers and Perry (2015) explored the application of guideline sentencing factors in cases of domestic burglary, and their analyses "provided a strong indication that the courts were sentencing in a manner that was consistent with the domestic burglary guideline and in particular the principle that the factors in step one of the guideline should have more of an influence on sentence severity than the factors in step two" (p. 210). As noted earlier, the drug offenses guideline was designed to change current sentencing practices, and research suggests it succeeded. Fleetwood, Radcliffe, and Stevens (2015) studied sentencing for low-level drug offenders and concluded that "the sentencing guideline appears to have achieved greater proportionality" (p. 435). That is, the disproportionately severe sentences imposed on low-level drug offenders had come down. These studies, while restricted in scope, suggest that the English guidelines have had a positive effect on promoting consistency and proportionality. More research is clearly needed, however.

Other guidelines designed to change judicial practice have also had an impact. The guideline for health and safety offenses was intended to increase the severity of sentencing for corporations and individuals (Sentencing Council of England and Wales 2014, p. 10). Webster (2017) reviewed sentences imposed within a year of the new guideline coming into force and found that the median corporate fine per breach had doubled, while the fines imposed on the most serious organizations increased very significantly. Custody was used more frequently for serious breaches by individuals, although the numbers of convictions were too small to draw general conclusions.

A critical question concerns the impact of the guidelines on the prison population. Frase (2019) has noted that states operating guidelines have generally experienced slower prison growth than states without guidelines. Analyses of sentencing trends over the period 2007–16 reveal that for certain offense categories, particularly crimes of violence and sexual aggression, the courts have been imposing more and longer prison sentences (Ministry of Justice 2016). Since this period included the introduction of the guidelines, the key question is whether they have contributed to this

---

[33] These guidelines were the first issued by the Sentencing Council of England and Wales (in 2011 and 2012; see Roberts and Rafferty [2011] for discussion) and have attracted the most research.

increase in sentencing severity. Research shows that the guidelines have neither constrained nor increased the size of the prison population. This is perhaps to be expected given that they were not designed to achieve reductions in the prison estate. But there are some exceptions. Prior to issuing a guideline, the English Council projects the likely impact on the need for prison places, and once the guideline has been operating for several years, the council revisits its projections. To date, these analyses have suggested a generally neutral impact. However, three early guidelines have had an unanticipated effect of increasing the proportion of admissions to custody (e.g., Sentencing Council of England and Wales 2015a; Carline et al. 2018). At the time of writing the council is currently considering how to address this unanticipated effect. Taken as a whole, however, there is no evidence that the guidelines have contributed to the rising prison population. Nor, however, have the guidelines reduced the volume of admissions, although as noted, a number of scholars have urged the council to pursue a reductionist strategy.

B. Critiques of Guidelines

Research has also addressed, again to a limited degree, some critiques of the guidelines. It has been suggested that the guidelines privilege consistency at the expense of individualization—a criticism that can also be leveled at the US grids. Browne (2017) argues that "the current system of English sentencing guidelines ... seeks consistency at the expense of individualised justice" (p. 150). Is there any evidence to support this critique? Roberts, Pina-Sánchez, and Marder (2018) employed two measures of individualization: the number of unique sentence lengths arising from the distribution of all custodial sentences imposed and the proportion of all cases falling into the most frequently imposed unique sentence lengths. A distribution of sentence lengths lacking individualization would require only a small number of specific sentence lengths to capture all cases. If the guidelines have constrained individualization, more cases will fall into a smaller number of unique sentences: The distribution of sentences will be captured by fewer sentences. Examining all sentences imposed after the introduction of the new guideline revealed that matters improved in terms of this measure of individualization in sentencing:[34] there were more, not fewer, specific sentence lengths being imposed.

---

[34] This finding is striking because it includes data from only the first year following introduction of the new guideline. It is reasonable to expect a new guideline to take at least a year

A related critique of the guidelines is that they inhibit individualization by undermining the consideration of aggravating and mitigating factors. Some advocates have argued that courts have paid less attention to speeches in mitigation, merely checking whether the guideline factors are present in the case. Researchers have tested the hypothesis that mitigation plays a diminished role under the English Council's new format guidelines by comparing the number of mitigating factors cited by courts before and after introduction of the guideline.[35] Findings revealed no decline in the number of sentencing factors cited by courts. In fact, the new format assault guideline had the opposite effect. Under the previous assault guideline an average of 3.65 sentencing factors were recorded across all cases. This average rose to 4.67 under the new assault guideline, a statistically significant increase. The number of mitigating factors rose, although the number of aggravating factors increased to a greater extent than the number of mitigating factors, reflecting possibly the greater number of aggravating factors contained in the guidelines.[36]

Assuming these findings replicate across other offenses, what might account for this increased degree of individualization following introduction of the guidelines? One explanation concerns the guideline structure that requires courts to consider individually a range of sentencing factors. A court sentencing without a guideline will have only submissions from the advocates to guide their application of principles and consideration of mitigating and aggravating factors. In contrast, the English guidelines require sentencers to proceed through a series of steps, and this may sensitize courts to important differences between cases, resulting in the use of a higher number of unique sentences. A second possibility is that courts take longer to sentence a case when applying a guideline with nine steps. This may provoke a deeper consideration of the case characteristics, generating greater discrimination between cases—and more unique sentence outcomes. It would be interesting to know whether requiring courts to spend

---

to "bed down" before achieving its anticipated effect on trial court sentencing practices, yet these data reveal statistically significant effects on individualization within 12 months.

[35] Cooper (2013) argued that "the council interprets personal mitigation very narrowly" (p. 160).

[36] This may be a weakness of guidelines that prescribe sentencing factors. There will always be more aggravating than mitigating factors, and by listing the factors the imbalance becomes clear. The result will likely be, as under the English guidelines, that aggravating factors exceed mitigating factors by a considerable margin. What is unclear is whether this conveys a message to courts about the relative weight of the two kinds of factors.

more time determining the sentence leads to a more reasoned or proportionate outcome. It seems likely that sentencing is more expeditious under the grid-based approach, and the question is whether this also has a cost.

C. Research on Public Attitudes to Sentencing

There is evidence, again limited, that the guidelines may have reduced public demands for harsher sentences or public criticism of current sentencing trends. Roberts et al. (2012) report findings from an experimental study involving a representative sample of the British public. All respondents were asked to evaluate specific sentences in a series of cases. One subsample was given information about the sentencing guidelines (the "informed" group), while the others rated the sentences without any information about the sentencing guidelines. Compared to respondents who had been given no prior information, people who had read about the guidelines were less punitive. For example, when asked to rate a typical sentence for domestic burglary, 57 percent of respondents without information about the guidelines rated the sentence as too lenient. Of the group that had been given information about the guidelines, only 37 percent perceived the sentence as being too lenient (Roberts et al. 2012, table 5). Moreover, people who had been informed about the guidelines expressed more confidence in the sentencing process (table 4). The difference in attitudes is consistent with responses to more general questions: 93 percent of the sample expressed the view that it was "a good idea" to have guidelines. Sixty percent chose "definitely a good idea" and 33 percent "probably a good idea" (p. 1083). To the extent that the public becomes aware of the council's guidelines, they may mitigate some criticism of the courts.

The limited research on the impact of the guidelines is encouraging but insufficient. It seems clear that the guidelines have resulted in greater transparency and are generally consistently applied by courts across the country. Many questions remain, however. I return to research priorities at the end of this essay.

V. Comparing Approaches to Guidance in Minnesota and England

The English guidelines require more from sentencers and provide more guidance on a wider range of issues. This can be demonstrated by considering a case of robbery in which an individual with no prior convictions has pleaded guilty to the offense. Under the Minnesota guidelines, this case falls into level 8 and criminal history category 0. Given this profile a court must impose a sentence of imprisonment between 41 and 57 months or find "substantial and compelling circumstances" to justify a departure. Judicial decision making therefore focuses on whether such circumstances exist and what sentence within the presumptive range is appropriate. Most of the time the sentence falls within the recommended range.

An English court would first apply the robbery guideline, proceeding through the nine steps enumerated above. Yet this guideline is not the only one that the court will have to consider. Since the guideline sentence ranges encompass both custodial and noncustodial dispositions, the court should consult the separate guideline on the use of the principal sanctions (Sentencing Council of England and Wales 2016*a*). If the defendant has pleaded guilty, the court will also apply the guideline regulating plea-based sentence reductions (Sentencing Council of England and Wales 2017). Finally, as noted earlier, additional guidelines address the factors affecting the determination of offense seriousness and the relationship among different offenses if this is a case involving more than one crime.[37]

The so-called custody threshold is an example of the deeper judicial processing required by the English guidelines. Under the Minnesota guidelines, armed with a copy of the grid, the defendant can know well in advance of sentencing whether the case falls in the custody zone of the grid. The approximate sentence that will likely be imposed can readily be ascertained by consulting the relevant grid. Offenders arrive at the sentencing hearing knowing that their fate has largely been determined by the decisions of the Minnesota commission. The dispositional departure statistics suggest that in most cases, this a priori classification will accurately predict whether he or she is incarcerated. In 2016, mitigated dispositional departures occurred in approximately one-third of cases (MSGC 2018, p. 27), and aggravated dispositional departures are extremely rare.[38]

---

[37] As with other commissions and councils, and particularly the sentencing councils in Australia (e.g., https://www.sentencingcouncil.vic.gov.au/), the English Council also publishes a range of statistical and analytic information relevant to sentencing in general and with respect to specific offenses (see https://www.sentencingcouncil.org.uk/). The Victoria Sentencing Council publishes "snapshots" of sentencing practices for specific offenses. These have proved useful to judges who cite them in their judgments. It is unclear how often the English material is accessed by sentencers or whether it affects judicial decision making.

[38] As the commission notes in its latest data release, defendants' requests for prison are included in aggravated dispositional departure rates; but without these, the rate would be 1 percent (MSGC 2018, p. 25).

Judicial reflection is required primarily to determine whether there are substantial and compelling circumstances to justify overturning the presumptive disposition.

A comparable individual appearing for sentencing in England will have less certainty about the outcome of the hearing because there is less clarity as to whether his or her case will fall into a specific level. The sentence ranges for many offenses encompass custodial as well as noncustodial options. For example, the category 3 sentence range for unlawful wounding (maximum penalty of 5 years) runs from a low-level community order to 51 weeks' custody.[39] A court must therefore decide whether the custodial threshold has been passed. In resolving this issue, the court will be assisted by submissions from the advocates. Whether the case should be assigned to category 2 or 3, for example, may well be the subject of argument in court among the advocates. In addition, even if the case does appear likely to fall into a guidelines range that includes only custody, consideration of his plea may result in the imposition of a suspended sentence, or even a high-level community order. Compared with offenders in Minnesota, advocates representing offenders sentenced under the English guidelines have more to play with in terms of mitigating the effects of prior offending.

The English guidelines are more demanding of judges yet less restrictive than their Minnesota equivalent. Does the English approach lead to a more reasoned sentencing decision? It is unclear what kind of critical test could be devised to determine whether one model is superior. Perhaps all we can conclude is that English sentencing involves a more in-depth judicial processing of all relevant variables.

A. Proportionality

Both sets of guidelines purport to reflect a retributive model of sentencing that privileges proportionality, yet they differ in their operationalization of this concept. Proportionality engages both harm and culpability, and the severity of assigned punishments should reflect some combination of these components. Fox (1994, p. 498) offered this concise definition: "The seriousness of a crime has two main elements—the degree of harm of the conduct and the extent of the offender's culpability." More recently, the leading proportionality scholar wrote that "the seriousness of crime has

---

[39] https://www.sentencingcouncil.org.uk/wp-content/uploads/Assault_definitive_guideline_-_Crown_Court.pdf, p. 8.

two elements: the conduct's degree of harmfulness and the extent of the actor's culpability" (von Hirsch 2017, p. 23).

Sentencing statutes echo and articulate these components. The key provision in England and Wales is in section 143(1) of the Criminal Justice Act 2003:[40] "In considering the seriousness of any offence, the court must consider the offender's culpability in committing the offence and any harm which the offence caused, was intended to cause or might foreseeably have caused." This provision is reaffirmed by the directions to the English Council in the Coroners and Justice Act 2009:

> When exercising functions under section 120, the Council is to have regard to the desirability of sentencing guidelines which relate to a particular offence being structured in the way described in subsections (2) to (9).
>
> (2) The guidelines should, if reasonably practicable given the nature of the offence, describe, by reference to one or more of the factors mentioned in subsection (3), different categories of case involving the commission of the offence which illustrate in general terms the varying degrees of seriousness with which the offence may be committed.
>
> (3) Those factors are—
>
> (a) the offender's culpability in committing the offence;
> (b) the harm caused, or intended to be caused or which might foreseeably have been caused, by the offence;
> (c) such other factors as the Council considers to be particularly relevant to the seriousness of the offence in question.

In Minnesota, proportionality is conceptualized differently, and this is clearly reflected in the axes of its grids. Frase (1993) observes that as defined by the Minnesota commission, "the goal of proportionality requires that sanction severity increase in direct proportion to increases in offense severity *and criminal history*" (p. 319; emphasis added). Frase also noted that the Minnesota Sentencing Commission assumed that seriousness and criminal history were "the only factors relevant to propor-

---

[40] Other jurisdictions take the same approach. Section 40b of the Sentencing Law of Israel notes, "The guiding principle in sentencing is proportionality between the seriousness of the offense and the degree of culpability and the type and severity of punishment" (Roberts and Gazal Ayal 2013), while sec. 718.1 of the Criminal Code of Canada articulates a similar relationship (Roberts and von Hirsch 1998).

tionality" (p. 295). The use of prior crimes as a primary dimension determining severity is inconsistent with most retributive definitions of proportionality.[41] The absence of a compelling retributive justification for considering prior convictions at sentencing raises questions about the proportionate nature of the Minnesota guidelines. If prior crimes are justified by risk rather than retribution, and if they carry great weight in the sentencing grid, this explains why the commission adopted the phrase "modified just deserts" to describe its guidelines. Research by the commission determined that crime seriousness and criminal history constituted the two principal predictors of sentence outcomes, and the grid reflects the primacy of these dimensions (MSGC 1979, p. 4).

As noted earlier, it is unclear from the scholarship on the origins of the Minnesota guidelines whether there was much discussion of alternative nongrid structures or different dimensions if a two-dimensional format was adopted. If a commission were to begin its work today, would it adopt a two-dimensional grid? Would it adopt the same two dimensions? It is worth recalling that Judge Frankel proposed assigning offenses to seriousness levels (he suggested five levels [1973, p. 114]), but nowhere did he propose that criminal history should constitute the second dimension of a grid. Frankel included prior record as simply one of several aggravating factors that would be contained within a sentencing code. It is hard to escape the conclusion that the criminal history dimension of the grid was adopted for three principal reasons: to promote consistency of application by means of a simple, "one felony, one point" scheme; to recognize the reality that after the crime, criminal history was the best predictor of sentence outcomes in the preguidelines period; and because criminal history had long been part of the parole guidelines matrix.

B. *Degree of Discretion: Statutory Compliance Requirement*

As noted, in Minnesota, courts have to find "substantial and compelling" reasons before departing from the guidelines. Courts are permitted greater discretion under the English guidelines. In England, the statutory compliance requirement is the following: Section 125 of the Coroners and Justice Act 2009 states that

---

[41] It may be more accurate to state that under the Minnesota guidelines a sentence is proportionate to the seriousness of the offense and the offender's risk of reoffending as reflected in his criminal history score. Almost all retributive scholars advocate limiting the role of previous convictions or eliminating them entirely from the sentencing equation (see Fletcher [1982] and, for conflicting perspectives, Roberts and von Hirsch [2010]).

(1) Every court—

(a) must, in sentencing an offender, follow any sentencing guidelines which are relevant to the offender's case, and
(b) must, in exercising any other function relating to the sentencing of offenders, follow any sentencing guidelines which are relevant to the exercise of that function, unless the court is satisfied that it would be contrary to the interests of justice to do so.

This wording suggests a relatively restrictive regime. However, a subsequent provision makes it clear that the constraint on courts is to impose a sentence within the total offense range rather than the category sentence range: "nothing in this section imposes on the court a separate duty ... to impose a sentence which is within the category range" (Coroners and Justice Act 2009, sec. 125(3)(b)).

For example, consider the offense of assault occasioning actual bodily harm. If a court decides at step 1 that the case falls into the intermediate category of seriousness, it begins to work within a category range running from a community order to 51 weeks' custody. However, for the purposes of complying with the statute, the court may impose any sentence within the total offense range, which is much wider (from a fine to 3 years' imprisonment; see Ashworth [2010] for commentary).[42] Finally, as in Minnesota, English courts may depart from the guideline range if it would be contrary to the interests of justice to remain within the range. The consequence is that courts have considerable discretion within the guideline ranges, as well as the ability to impose a sentence outside the guidelines range, if following the guideline would be contrary to the interests of justice.

To summarize, courts may exercise their discretion in three important ways under the English guidelines. First, although step 1 of the methodology requires a court to assign the case to a specific category of seriousness (and then sentence within that category's sentence range), the guideline notes that courts may "move outside the category range" if they believe it is justified by the presence of a significant number of aggravating or mitigating factors. Second, having settled on a provisional final sentence, a court is

---

[42] This definition of compliance was a late amendment to the draft bill. Previous versions had defined compliance more restrictively, in terms of the category range. Having selected category 2, a court would have had to remain within category 2's sentence range. The final wording of the legislation relaxed the compliance requirement to be the total offense range, which is of course much wider (see Roberts 2011).

not bound to remain within the category range of the offense but only the much wider total guideline range. Third, a court may always depart where it would be contrary to the interests of justice to follow the guideline recommendations. The flexibility of the English guidelines is captured in the description offered by the first chair of the council in testimony before a parliamentary committee: "The guideline creates an approach and within that approach *judicial discretion is entirely preserved*" (House of Commons Justice Committee 2011, p. 12; emphasis added). This surely overstates the case, but it seems reasonable to conclude that judges in England have greater freedom than their counterparts in Minnesota.

C. Compliance and Departure Rates

Departure rates are a key indicator of the health of any guidelines scheme. Monitoring judicial compliance is straightforward under the Minnesota guidelines. The commission publishes annual statistics of the volume and percentage of dispositional and durational departures from the grid sentence recommendations and ranges. In 2017, approximately one-quarter of cases were sentenced outside the guideline ranges (MSGC 2018, p. 22). This total includes dispositional as well as durational departures. The Minnesota departure rates have risen steadily over the lifetime of the guidelines, a trend noted by Frase (2005*a*). Although the trends are well documented, there is little commentary on the acceptable level of compliance. For example, is a departure rate of 30 percent high or low? The issue is worth more attention.

Determining compliance is more complicated in England and Wales. The "departure in the interests of justice" test is of little use as an indicator of judicial compliance, since courts are permitted to impose any sentence within the total offense range, which is very wide. The English Council publishes these statistics, and they reveal the expected: "departure" rates are typically very low, around 5 percent of all sentences imposed. In 2014, 97 percent of sentences for drugs, assault, and burglary offenses fell within the total guideline ranges (Sentencing Council of England and Wales 2015*b*, table 1). This is a consequence of the very broad sentence ranges found in the English guidelines. As is often the case, these statistics capture only part of the picture. Some of the guidelines—particularly those applicable across all cases—have not had the anticipated effects on courts. The guideline regulating sentencing in multiple offense cases is a good example. This guideline is seldom cited by courts (Bottoms 2018). Ashworth (2017) noted that although this guideline was introduced in 2012, 12 out of

14 appellate judgments dealing with the principle of totality failed to refer to it. If the Court of Appeal saw little need to consult or cite the guideline, it is unlikely to have had much impact on sentencers of first instance.

The issue of compliance is related to appellate review. In Minnesota, the clarity of definition makes it immediately apparent whether a sentence should be reviewed by the appellate courts. The absence of a clear trigger for appellate review means that in England an appeal must be brought by the defendant or the attorney general. This may suggest that trial court sentencing in England and Wales is less amenable to appellate scrutiny. It is a hard issue to resolve. The appellate jurisprudence in England reveals many examples of appellate intervention, and the Court of Appeal can evaluate the sentence against the relevant guideline. For example, it may note that the trial court placed the case in a higher category than could be justified by the factors determining the appropriate category at step 1.

More meaningful compliance data are available for the generic guideline regulating plea-based sentence reductions since this guideline prescribes specific levels of reduction against which judicial practice may be compared. In 2014, fully 89 percent of offenders entering a guilty plea at the first stage of proceedings (and thereby entitled to the full one-third reduction) were awarded exactly this level (Sentencing Council of England and Wales 2015b, fig. 6). More detailed data confirm the correspondence between guideline recommendations and judicial practice. Table 1 classifies cases into one of three categories, early, intermediate, and late guilty pleas (on or after the day of trial), and summarizes the levels of reduction awarded in each category.

The guideline recommendations were broadly being followed, with the greatest reductions awarded to offenders who entered a prompt plea ("early" pleas). Thus 80 percent of offenders in this category received ex-

TABLE 1

Empirical Sentence Reductions Awarded by Timing of Plea, England and Wales (%)

	Greater than ⅓	⅓	21%–32%	11%–20%	1%–10%	No Reduction Awarded
Early plea	9	80	9	2	<1	<.05
Intermediate plea	3	34	34	22	6	1
Late plea	1	11	9	24	49	6

Source.—Roberts and Bradford (2015).

actly the guideline recommendation; only 11 percent of offenders pleading guilty on or after trial onset (late plea cases) received this level of reduction. The reductions awarded to early plea cases cluster more tightly around the guideline's recommendation. Table 1 shows that almost all (98 percent) early plea cases fell within the guideline recommended column (one-third) or the columns immediately adjacent.[43] These data suggest that defendants in England and Wales—and indeed all parties with a stake or interest in sentencing—are better placed than their counterparts in most other jurisdictions where the likely sentence reduction resulting from a guilty plea is far less predictable. This may be one of the most important benefits of the council's guidelines.

D. Single versus Multiple Guideline Formats

In Minnesota, all offenses are subject to the same two-dimensional grid structure. Given the diversity of categories of offending, is this uniformity wise? The English guidelines vary to accommodate important differences in the offense. A good example of the advantages of adopting an offense-based approach to guidelines (rather than placing all offenses within the same two-dimensional grid) can be found in the English manslaughter guideline (Sentencing Council of England and Wales 2018*b*). For most offenses, the English guidelines employ two dimensions, harm and culpability. The two dimensions generally carry equal weight and create a two-dimensional matrix. Unlike most other offenses, and assuming a single victim, the harm of all manslaughter cases varies little, always entailing the loss of a human life. A manslaughter guideline that contained several different levels of harm would make little sense; what kinds of factors could justify classifying some cases as high harm and some as lesser harm? The culpability dimension is therefore paramount. For this reason, the council departed from its traditional harm-culpability formula in two important ways.

First, there are no levels of harm, only levels of culpability. For example, the lowest level of culpability is defined in the following way: "Death was caused in the course of an unlawful act which was in defence of self or other(s) (where not amounting to a defence) OR where there was no intention

---

[43] There is greater dispersal among the later plea cases, particularly the latest category. This more scattered distribution reflects the complexities of cases in which the guilty plea is classified as having been entered late. For example, if there has been undue delay in disclosure of the prosecution's case, the defendant may well be awarded the maximum reduction of one-third, even if the guilty plea was entered relatively late (see Sentencing Council of England and Wales 2017).

by the offender to cause any harm and no obvious risk of anything more than minor harm OR in which the offender played a minor role. The offender's responsibility was substantially reduced by mental disorder, learning disability or lack of maturity." Cases assigned to this category are subject to a starting point sentence of 2 years' imprisonment and a sentence range of from 2 to 4 years. The limited variation in harm—for instance, the degree of suffering inflicted on the victim prior to death—is captured by aggravating factors cited at step 2. For example, in the unlawful act manslaughter guideline, the aggravating factors include "death occurred in the context of an offence which was planned and premeditated" and "offence committed in the presence of children" (Sentencing Council of England and Wales 2018*b*, p. 6). As with other guidelines, these factors are used by the court to move the sentence up or down within the category sentence range. The second difference is that four culpability levels were employed instead of three. This decision reflected the council's recognition that the much wider range of culpable conduct encompassed by this offense required an additional level to provide more fine-grained guidance.

Drug offenses offer a second illustration of the benefits of varying the guideline structure to better reflect the nature of the offense. Most drug offenders are part of a collective enterprise, even if only loosely defined. Importers supply distributors who hire dealers. Harm is generally captured by the toxicity or danger associated with the illegal drugs. The culpability of the offender in such cases is primarily dependent on his or her role in the organization. One of the weaknesses of sentencing drug offenders has been that the harmfulness of the drug has predominated, creating disproportionate sentences for lower-level offenders such as drug mules. For this reason, the drug offenses guideline defines culpability largely in terms of role. Each offense has three levels of culpability defined as a "leading," "significant," or "lesser" role (Sentencing Council of England and Wales 2012*b*). The council conducted extensive road testing with its role-driven format, and this confirmed judicial support for this approach (Sentencing Council of England and Wales 2012*b*). Finally, by making role an explicit driver of the offender's level of culpability, the guideline makes it much clearer to the defendant how his category—and hence level of punishment—has been determined. Once this structure has been established at step 1, the guideline specifies a range of mitigating and aggravating factors that also bear on the offender's level of culpability; role is therefore the primary, but not the only, determinant of the offender's level of blameworthiness.

E. Mitigating and Aggravating Factors

Determining the relevance and weight of sentencing factors lies at the heart of the sentencing exercise. For this reason alone, courts would benefit from guidance on the matter. Concern over the use of extralegal factors at sentencing led the Minnesota commission to explicitly proscribe a list of such factors, accompanied by a list of factors that should or should not be used to justify a departure. These lists are useful for promoting a uniform approach to the decision to depart but offer no guidance for distinguishing cases remaining within the guideline ranges. The commission could have gone much further in its guidance, and the English Council does go further. Its guidelines provide more information and structure with respect to the key aggravating and mitigating factors at sentencing. First, each guideline contains its own bespoke list of relevant factors, although there is overlap across guidelines. Some guidelines contain up to 50 factors for courts to consider.

Second, although it is not explicitly stated, the guideline structure provides some structure to mitigating and aggravating factors. Determining the relative importance of different factors is challenging and is a source of variability at sentencing. The English guideline structure effectively creates two tiers of factors, those of primary relevance (located at step 1) and those of more limited relevance (assigned to step 2).[44] Sentencing factors relevant to the sentencing decision but unrelated to harm or culpability (state assistance, plea) are dealt with separately at steps 3 and 4. If all courts have the same basic set of factors to consider, this should promote more uniform outcomes. In addition, the English guidelines also give guidance regarding the cases in which certain factors may carry less or more weight. For example, in its rape guideline the council notes that "previous good character or exemplary conduct should not normally be given significant weight" (Sentencing Council of England and Wales 2013, p. 11). The council took the view that good conduct by the offender should carry less weight when the offense involves very significant harm.

---

[44] The guidelines note that the step 1 factors "comprise the principal factual elements of the offence" (see https://www.sentencingcouncil.org.uk/wp-content/uploads/Assault_definitive_guideline_-_Crown_Court.pdf, p. 4). The distinction between step 1 and step 2 is helpful because it guides sentencers as to the relative importance of sentencing factors, but it is not without problems. One obvious difficulty is that the council must be able to make valid assignment of factors that should be at step 1 rather than step 2. Readers reviewing the factor placements may perceive some anomalies: factors placed at step 1 when they might more reasonably be classified at step 2 (and vice versa).

F. Role of Prior Convictions

The role of previous convictions differs greatly under the two sets of guidelines. The Minnesota guidelines assign a central role to criminal history, which constitutes one of two primary dimensions. This arrangement arose at least in part from importing the structure of the parole guidelines.[45] Dale Parent, the first executive director of the Minnesota commission, writes that the commission "spent more hours defining the criminal history index than it devoted to any other aspect of guideline development" (1988, p. 65). With the benefit of hindsight, the fruits of the commission's labor seem meager.

Parent's account of the origins of the criminal history arm of the grid makes it clear that the commission adopted the approach to prior convictions advocated in *Doing Justice*, the seminal book by Andrew von Hirsch (1976) (von Hirsch also served as one of the commission's consultants; see Parent 1988, p. 38). That volume argued that prior convictions enhanced the offender's blameworthiness or culpability.[46] Again, Parent: "The commission's perspective meant that criminal history was to be used to increase sentence severity for offenders whose prior record indicated they were more blameworthy. *It was not used to predict which groups of offenders were more likely to commit new crimes in the future*" (1988, p. 66; emphasis added). The commission's publications also acknowledge this view. In its second progress report to the legislature, the commission noted that it had "decided against an index which would predict the probability of future criminality. Rather, the commission decided to construct an index measuring the extent and duration of prior criminality" (MSGC 1981, p. 1). In short, from the outset, criminal history enhancements in the Minnesota guidelines reflected retributive rather than preventive justifications. Whether that remains the case is open to question.

---

[45] Which raises the question of why prior convictions should play a primary role within even a parole grid. Why, for example should previous convictions acquired possibly many years earlier constitute one of the grid's two dimensions? Long-term prisoners applying for parole will have many years of custodial life containing more probative information about their risk of future offending. The literature on parole provides little justification for the primacy of criminal record in the guidelines. Blalock (1982, p. 93), e.g., merely notes that "offense severity and criminal history are the two basic considerations." It is unclear why this is the case.

[46] Von Hirsch subsequently abandoned this position in a later volume in which he endorsed a model unrelated to culpability (1985, chap. 7); however, the Minnesota commission stayed with his original formulation.

The role of prior crimes in the US guidelines has attracted considerable attention from scholars in recent years (e.g., Roberts 1994, 1997; von Hirsch 1994; Hamilton 2015; Hester et al. 2018; Frase and Roberts 2019), and there is a growing consensus that the US approach suffers from several problems. The principal deficiencies of the US approach (including Minnesota) are the reach of the guidelines and the magnitudes of enhancements. Most guidelines count all prior crimes, no matter how old. The commission provided four criteria guiding its criminal history index. One criterion was that it be "simple to use" (MSGC 1980, p. 7). Frase (1991) notes that "as the Minnesota commission recognized, simplicity of application is a separate and important goal" (p. 752). It is noteworthy that the criteria did not include predictive or retributive validity. Almost no validation work was conducted until the Robina Criminal History Project began work in 2013 (Frase et al. 2015; Hester et al. 2018).

In their desire to ensure that offenders receive consistent outcomes, the US guidelines operationalized prior conviction enhancements in a mechanistic fashion. Criminal history was unitized and converted to a score, which then triggers a harsher sentence. One consequence of regular, categorical increments in severity is that the regime poorly reflects the empirical pattern of reoffending rates—perhaps reflecting the emphasis on retribution in the early days of the commission. These issues are documented in greater detail in Hester et al. (2018) and Frase and Roberts (2019). However, one example is illustrative.

In Minnesota, a prior felony carries the same weight whether it was recorded 6 months previously or up to 15 years earlier. No discounting to reflect the declining retributive or predictive significance of a prior crime occurs. This practice is at odds with findings from recidivism research as well as surveys of the general public.[47] Thus an older prior is less predictive of reoffending than a recent conviction, and the public assigns less punishment to older priors, suggesting they recognize the relevance of the age of the conviction, whether from the perspective of risk or retribution (Mitchell 2015; Hester et al. 2017). Assigning the same weight to all prior felonies ensures consistency across cases, but only by abandoning the relationship between the level of enhancement and the variables of risk and retribution which justify the premium. This is the penal equiv-

---

[47] Public views are relevant because one of the justifications for prior record enhancements is that repeat offenders are more blameworthy, and public opinion can serve as a proxy for blameworthiness (see Roberts 2008).

alent of auto insurance that increases premiums in a linear fashion without regard to the nature of the driving violations or claims. The driver who rear-ended another car 14 years ago pays the same premium as the one who collided with his car last year. That cannot be right. This example illustrates the Minnesota commission's preference for consistency of application—and hence outcome—over a more complex approach that would more accurately calibrate the prior record enhancement to the individual offender's level of blameworthiness or risk.

As for the magnitude of the enhancements, the US guideline premiums escalate far more rapidly in severity than the corresponding risk or blameworthiness of the offender. Magnitude can be measured in various ways, but one common measure is a multiplier created by dividing the presumptive sentence for the highest criminal history score by the presumptive sentence for the lowest criminal history score on any given grid. Frase and Hester (2015, 2019) report that in Minnesota, averaged across all offense severity levels, the multiplier was 4.7.[48] Washington, Arkansas, and Kansas have even higher multipliers. Such high magnitudes threaten offense-based proportionality and have been criticized for many years. In 1994, von Hirsch wrote that the Minnesota guidelines "gave too much leverage to criminal record" (p. 45).

Forty years after the creation of the main Minnesota grid, the counting rules regarding prior crimes remain largely the same, despite the significant advances that have been made in our understanding of the relationship between prior and future offending. The most significant change to the criminal history score calculation involved expanding the look-back limit for felonies from 10 to 15 years. It seems unlikely that this reform can be justified in terms of increased crime prevention or enhanced blameworthiness, and of course counting the additional felonies carries significant costs in terms of prison beds and racial disproportionality.

The English guidelines are more nuanced and less punitive.[49] Prior convictions are considered at step 2 of the guidelines methodology. This

---

[48] It should be noted that although the Minnesota commission is criticized for allowing prior convictions so much influence (as evidenced in the high multiplier), criminal history played an even more powerful role in Minnesota sentencing prior to the guidelines. Parent (1988) notes that prior convictions were the "primary factor in deciding whether or not to incarcerate the offender" (p. 66).

[49] The Minnesota approach to the use of prior convictions has evolved somewhat since the first edition of the guidelines manual. Tonry (1993) described the revisions as making the use of prior convictions "subtler" (p. 185). Perhaps, but they are still more mechanistically applied

placement restricts their influence to determining the sentence within the category range rather than the selection of which category of seriousness is appropriate. Prior convictions therefore are a secondary factor under the English guidelines. No direct comparisons between Minnesota and England have been conducted, but a reasonable inference from research in the two jurisdictions is that prior convictions carry less weight in England. The long look-back period in Minnesota, which results in all prior felonies within a 15-year period being included in the criminal history score, is not matched in England.[50] There is no bright line rule in England and Wales regarding the relevance of older prior crimes; but unless the crime is particularly serious, previous convictions approaching a decade in age will have little (or no) aggravating effect on the sentence imposed for the current crime. The consequence is that English courts applying the guidelines assign less weight to prior crimes and disregard a number of earlier convictions as a result of their age or lack of relevance (Roberts and Pina-Sánchez 2014).

The English approach to criminal history enhancements has a cost. Under the Minnesota guidelines, an individual being sentenced knows in advance his or her own level of enhancement. The English guidelines are less prescriptive and do not supply an exact quantum of punishment, as in Minnesota. There are two consequences of this. First, a court will have to think through the issues of relevance and weight: are all the offender's priors relevant?[51] Are any sufficiently old to be disregarded entirely? How much weight should the relevant priors carry? The determination of relevance and the calibration of enhancement are thus more individualized

---

than in England and Wales (and other common-law jurisdictions). The more nuanced approach to prior crimes in England is not entirely due to the guidelines. The relevant statutory provision (sec. 143(2) of the Criminal Justice Act 2003) states, "In considering the seriousness of an offence ('the current offence') committed by an offender who has one or more previous convictions, the court must treat each previous conviction as an aggravating factor if (in the case of that conviction) the court considers that it can reasonably be so treated having regard, in particular, to—(a) the nature of the offence to which the conviction relates and its relevance to the current offence, and (b) the time that has elapsed since the conviction." This creates some judicial discretion to discount or disregard priors that are older or unrelated to the current crime. England is not unique in this approach; other common-law jurisdictions allow courts to disregard or discount older offenses.

[50] The look-back limit is an example of one way in which the Minnesota guidelines have become more punitive and less evidence-based; the original look-back limit for felonies was 10 years.

[51] In practice, English courts disregard a significant number of prior convictions on the grounds that they are too old or insufficiently related to the current offense (see data in Roberts and Pina-Sánchez [2014]).

and more closely reflect the degree of enhancement appropriate to the individual offender. The second effect is less desirable: The English system will result in less consistent prior record enhancements. The differences reflect the fundamental orientation of the two approaches to guidance. Minnesota privileges simplicity of application and consistency of outcomes;[52] the English guidelines favor a more individualized and therefore complex approach. Appropriate simplicity is a virtue,[53] but on balance my preference is for the latter approach rather than the formulaic grid-based guidelines. Appendix C provides a tabular comparison of key attributes of the two formats.

VI. Drawing Conclusions

The English sentencing guidelines constitute a revolution in English sentencing. Conceived as a dynamic system, this dynamism is reflected in the different forms of guidance issued to date. Creating a new guideline (or amending an existing guideline) does not require the formal approval of the legislature, only a public consultation. This freedom has two clear advantages. First, the English Council is less subject to political pressures to "get tough" with particular offenses or categories of offenders. Second, the council has the authority to issue (or amend) guidelines as it sees fit, without requiring the endorsement of the legislature or the government (although subject to a public and professional consultation exercise). These considerations may explain why the English guidelines have changed within a few years, with different formats emerging for different guidelines, whereas the architecture of the Minnesota main grid has remained relatively fixed over the 40 years since its creation.

Policy transfer in the area of sentencing usually arises in the context of specific high-profile initiatives such as "three-strikes" laws. Legislatures generally devise their own sentencing laws with little regard to developments in other jurisdictions, or cross-jurisdictional initiatives such as the American Law Institute's Model Penal Code: Sentencing project or

---

[52] Parent was very clear on this point: "The pivotal consideration for the commission was operational simplicity" (1988, p. 71).

[53] I am not so persuaded of the need for such simplicity. Simple schemes have disadvantages, and the US approach to criminal history enhancements would appear to be a good example of these limitations. Moreover, the additional complexity of the English approach does not appear to have created problems for sentencers in that jurisdiction.

the Council of Europe Sentencing recommendations. In 1992, the Council of Europe issued a document identifying key elements of a comprehensive approach to structuring judicial discretion at sentencing (Council of Europe 1993). The intention was that member states would adopt some or all of these recommendations. That uniformity never materialized; sentencing regimes across Europe still constitute a patchwork of different systems. The US guidelines broke new ground. The wide degree of variation across the United States in terms of the structure of the guidelines suggests that state commissions developed their guidelines independent of each other, without many comparative best-practice analyses. None of the US systems have been modified to reflect developments in foreign jurisdictions. Approached from the other direction, the English guidelines have evolved without drawing on the experience in the United States.[54] This is a regrettable state of affairs, as there are benefits associated with different approaches to structuring discretion at sentencing. Neither the Minnesota commission nor the English Council has been particularly self-critical over the years. In this final section, I make some suggestions for improvement in both sets of guidelines.

A. Lessons for the US Commissions

Comparative analyses are of particular benefit if they suggest best practices or ways in which one system may learn from another. In his essay exploring the English and US guidelines, Reitz (2013) offered a number of suggestions to improve the English regime.[55] Do the English guidelines contain any useful lessons for the US commissions? The commissions are unlikely to abandon formats developed decades ago, but the experience in other countries may provide some ideas for consideration. Four come to mind.

---

[54] It is perhaps natural that sentencing scholarship mirrors this insular approach. With the exception of volumes by Tonry and colleagues (e.g., Tonry and Frase 2001; Tonry 2016) and bilateral comparisons between the United States and other countries (e.g., Doob and Webster 2003; Frase 2005b; Roberts 2012), most scholars focus on a single jurisdiction. The few comparative articles (e.g., Frase 2001, 2014) do not examine guidelines structures.

[55] Reitz's proposals would have a salutary impact on the English guidelines. For example, he suggested placing a limit on the aggravating effect of prior convictions and advocated greater accountability by requiring courts to justify departures when they diverged from the middle category's starting point sentence (see Reitz 2013, pp. 196–200). Allen (2016) and Bottoms (2018), among others, have also advanced a number of reform proposals to improve the guidelines.

First, and consistent with much recent scholarship, commissions operating presumptive guidelines might wish to revisit the degree of judicial discretion allowed in the guidelines. Do they permit an adequate degree of discretion? Little commentary has focused on the appropriate rate of departures; are current rates too high or low? Do sentencers perceive that their ability to individualize to an appropriate degree is compromised by the "substantial and compelling reasons" requirement?

Second, it is unclear whether the prominent role and current structure of criminal history enhancements can be justified. At the very least, the levels of enhancement and the counting rules should be subject to greater empirical validation and scrutiny by commissions.[56] The academic literature makes a compelling case that offenders in states with a powerful criminal history enhancement receive severity premiums that cannot be justified on preventive or retributive grounds. The criminal history dimension of the grid has simply not been subject to sufficient scrutiny. It may be argued that the influence of prior crimes simply reflects acceptance in the United States that prior crimes should generate additional punishment. Period. That may be the case, but if commissions see their record-based enhancements as being primarily preventive, these arrangements deserve a second look. One obvious candidate for reform would be the severity increment between adjacent criminal history categories. The gap is the same across the grid. For example, level 9 offenses increase by a uniform 12 months from category to category.[57] It surely makes sense, on preventive or retributive grounds, to create a greater distinction between offenders with a zero score and all recidivists (Frase and Roberts 2019).

Third, US commissions might wish to consider whether the range of additional guidance available to sentencers in England and Wales carries benefits. Here a judicial "user survey" may identify issues for which US judges may wish to have additional guidance. The sentencing of multiple count cases is an obvious complexity in sentencing law. The English guideline on this issue is relatively skeletal, but judges may find additional information useful. Similarly, the Minnesota grids leave the courts with no guidance on complex issues such as the effect of mental health on

---

[56] Particularly those guidelines that involve the most powerful enhancements, thereby exacerbating racial disparities and correctional costs and undermining offense-based proportionality to the greatest degree (see Frase and Hester 2015).

[57] Interestingly, this was not always the case. In the first version of the grid, the severity increment varied depending on the categories (see MSGC 1981, p. 27).

the defendant's level of culpability or whether they may constitute a legitimate ground for departure. Leaving these kinds of issues to the appellate courts may be an abdication of responsibility on the part of the commission.

Fourth, the clarity of plea-based sentence reductions arising from a guideline may be attractive to Minnesota courts. Plea bargaining is more complex and more common in the United States; nevertheless, if the reductions were spelled out in guidance, the process would have greater transparency and predictability.

B. Lessons for the English and Other Offense-Based Guidelines

Racial disparities have been at the forefront of the guidelines movement in the United States. One of the principal early successes of the Minnesota guidelines was the reduction of racial disparities (Frase 2005a). Frase (2009) has documented the disproportionate effects of the prior conviction enhancements on racial minorities. Many commissions across the United States (including Minnesota) now routinely conduct racial impact analyses. The English Council has yet to engage with the issue of racial disparities. This is not due to an absence of evidence that visible minorities attract different sentences. The UK Ministry of Justice publishes annual statistics comparing sentencing patterns across different ethnic groups and routinely finds differentials for certain offense categories, although the statistics are uncorrected for confounding variables that might explain racial differences.[58] The true extent of racial disparities in England is therefore unclear, although earlier, academic research by Hood (1992) found modest racial differentials, suggesting that the problem is less serious in England.[59] Nevertheless, the council needs to ensure that its guidelines have not exacerbated any preexisting racial differences.[60] A recent report noted that within

---

[58] The most recent (2017) found that black and Asian offenders had a higher custody rate than whites. In addition, since 2012, the average sentence length has been consistently longer for all nonwhite ethnic groups. In 2016, of all offenders sentenced to immediate custody, black and Asian offenders received 24 and 25 months, respectively, compared with 18 months for white offenders (Ministry of Justice 2017, p. 53).

[59] The latest statistics released by the Minnesota commission as part of its demographic impact report reveal that although black Americans represent 4.3 percent of the state population, they account for 34.4 percent of the prison population. The statistics in England and Wales are less striking.

[60] For years scholars have urged more consideration of this issue. As far back as 2002, scholars such as Tonry had identified the development of the guidelines as a means of

drug offenses, the odds of receiving a prison sentence were 240 percent higher for offenders who self-identify as black, Asian, or minority ethnic compared with whites. The review then issued a challenge to courts, stating that "it is now incumbent on the judiciary to produce an evidence-based explanation for the finding" (Lammy 2017, p. 33). To date, the court system has failed to respond to this challenge, and the English Council could play an important role comparable to that of the US commissions.

A second lesson for the English Council concerns the use of imprisonment as a sanction. Earlier, I noted the impediments to the council's ability to regulate the size of the prison estate. The council could take some steps toward addressing the issue of a high use of incarceration in a way that is consistent with its statutory mandate. If there is no obvious authority to allow the guidelines to manage the prison capacity, the council could do more to reflect the costs (and cost-effectiveness) of different sanctions. A number of commentators have urged such a course of action (e.g., British Academy 2014, p. 106; Bottoms 2018, p. 19). This could be accomplished in a number of ways. For example, the English Council could publish research updates on the costs of imprisonment and other sanctions, as well as the latest reoffending statistics associated with these sentences and other sentencing trends. This may serve as a nudge to judges regarding the use of imprisonment as a sanction. If sentencers paid attention to such information, the council may play a role in reducing the use of the most expensive and least effective sanction, even without adjusting its guidelines. A similar initiative could see the council highlighting for the judiciary the findings of research on comparative reoffending rates. There is now a significant body of literature demonstrating that community orders and suspended sentence orders are associated with lower reoffending rates than imprisonment, having controlled for all relevant background variables. If an official body like the council were to bring this to the attention of the judiciary, perhaps in conjunction with the Judicial College, which offers judicial training, some judges may have second thoughts before imposing a short prison sentence.

Transparency may be a third area in which the non-US councils and commissions could learn from the US commissions. Meetings of the Minnesota commission are held in public, and time is reserved for members of

---

addressing racial disparities (Tonry 2002, p. 98). In the same volume, David Faulkner also highlighted the need to take greater account of race and ethnicity (Faulkner 2002, chap. 4).

the public to make a brief submission.[61] The transparency continues beyond the meeting; if individual commission members wish to discuss commission business outside of regular meetings, they must call a public meeting. In contrast, the sentencing councils in Europe, Asia, and Australia hold their meetings in private, and outsiders are not generally permitted to attend. The UK-based councils both publish minutes of meetings, but these are only skeletal in nature. It is hard to see the harm in opening meetings to a wider audience.

C. Research Priorities

Guideline structures are determined by the judicial culture in which they are set; they are not technological tools that can be easily implemented in any country, the way, say, in which room reservation software may be adjusted for the number of rooms and then deployed by diverse hotels around the world. Yet it would be useful to know more about the relative advantages of the various approaches to guidelines. Some years ago, Thibault and Walker (1975) set out to compare the adversarial and inquisitorial models of justice on a number of procedural justice indicators. They conducted laboratory-based simulation studies in several common-law and continental countries with a view to determining whether one system of criminal procedure was better for tasks such as generating facts or was more popular with litigants.

Comparable research could use judges from both jurisdictions (or from nonguidelines countries) to sentence offenders, having been randomly assigned to use either a sentencing grid (and manual) or the more complex offense-specific and generic package of guidelines used in England. Researchers could monitor the time taken to arrive at sentences, the degree of variability in outcomes, the number of mitigating and aggravating factors, as well as many other variables. Whatever the outcome of such experimental research, the Minnesota commission is no more likely to dismantle its grids than the English Council is to roll up all its offense-specific guidelines into a single matrix. Yet research of this kind would help us understand the ways in which these different formats function and would certainly be of interest to those contemplating adoption of a guidelines scheme. (Dhami, Belton, and Goodman-Delahunty [2015]

---

[61] Parent makes it clear that in the early days of the commission, meetings were even more open to participation; see the discussion in Parent (1988), in which he makes several comments to this effect: "members of the audience were permitted to enter the discussion at any point."

discuss research on different models of judicial decision making at sentencing.)

Another important and overlooked area is perceived legitimacy. There is a large and growing literature on perceptions of legitimacy at sentencing and the consequences of low levels of perceived legitimacy (e.g., Hough and Bradford 2010). We know very little about the reactions of defendants sentenced under these two different kinds of guidelines, and there are competing claims. A long-standing external critique of the sentencing grids is that they represent a mechanical and de-individualized means of determining sentence. If this is an accurate characterization, there may well be adverse consequences on litigants' perceptions of the legitimacy of the sentencing process. Adelman (2013) argues that there is no evidence that disparity causes resentment among prisoners or undermines perceptions of legitimacy. Again, comparative research would be useful. Are perceptions of legitimacy affected by the nature of the structures that determine sentencing outcomes? Do litigants and lawyers regard one approach to structuring discretion as more acceptable? Do offenders resent the use of a grid?

D. *Conclusions*

Ultimately, a legislature or guidelines commission needs to settle on a balance between binding guidelines that ensure formalistic consistency across cases and guidelines that are more flexible but fail to produce the same level of consistency of outcomes (Barkow 2012). The US guidelines emerged as a direct response to recognition that sentencing was unpredictable and inconsistent—the view best exemplified by Judge Frankel's volume. This desire to achieve more consistent outcomes has animated the grid-based guidelines ever since. In contrast, the English experience was somewhat different.

Although elements of the guidelines have changed periodically over the years, the essential architecture of the Minnesota grids remains the same.[62] The most significant development was the creation of additional grids for sex offenses and drug offenses. Amendments have been minor: offenses have been moved up or down the offense ladder and grid cell ranges and

---

[62] The transformation of the federal guidelines wrought by *Booker* changed the status of those guidelines, which became voluntary; but no substantial changes have been introduced to the federal grid, which retains its original structure of 43 offense levels and 256 cells. Similarly, although there have been changes to guidelines in several states over the years (Frase 2005*a*, pp. 1203–40; 2019), the basic structure of these guidelines has remained static.

the dispositional line have been adjusted periodically. To my knowledge, there has been no systematic review of the overall architecture of the grid or consideration of additional ways in which the commission might provide guidance for sentencers. Perhaps the time has come for further reflection. It would be unrealistic to expect a commission to review its guideline structure often, but there is surely scope for greater self-examination than has been the case to this point in Minnesota and other US states. After 40 years of use, the Minnesota commission is unlikely to abandon its grids. Yet there are important questions to be addressed with respect to a two-dimensional format. To what extent should it be described as a "sentencing machine" (Tonry 2015), albeit one less mechanized than the federal grid? Is the continued use of criminal history as a principal dimension justified? Beyond the architecture of the single grid, commissions should review some other policy issues such as whether multiple grids or nongrid structures would improve outcomes.

Where has this discussion led us? The key differences between the Minnesota and English approaches to guidance are the degree of individualization and the level of judicial discretion. Can we conclude that one approach is superior? Probably not. Ultimately, Frase (2005*b*) rightly observed that "there is no 'ideal' sentencing guidelines model; rather, each state must choose a combination of design features . . . appropriate to its local circumstances and political realities" (pp. 1231–32). Still, comparative research can help establish the strengths and weaknesses of the two competing approaches to guidelines. Having set themselves different objectives, the two sets of guidelines have achieved success in different ways. The Minnesota guidelines have been (relatively) successful in constraining prison populations, establishing more offense-based proportionality in prison admissions and populations, reducing racial disparities, and promoting more democratic accountability (see Tonry 1993; Frase 2019).

Finally, there is agreement that both schemes are preferable to the highly discretionary regimes they replaced. Frase (2019) states that "there is no better reform alternative" than a guidelines model, while Berman (2017, p. 109) concludes that "every serious modern study of US sentencing has reached the conclusion that a well-designed structure provides the best . . . to inform and shape individual sentencing outcomes and to promote transparency and the rule of law throughout a sentencing system" (see also Frase 2005*a*; Kilaru 2010). Most British scholars also appear to support the guidelines, although some express reservations about aspects of their structure and the loose nature of the compliance requirement (Ashworth 2010; Dhami 2013). Weisberg concludes that "consensus holds that the best possible sentencing scheme is a moderately flexible set of guidelines issued by a commission" (2007, p. 179). This consensus about the need for greater structure brings us full circle to Judge Frankel and, long before him, Lord Alverstone and the other jurists of Victorian England.

APPENDIX A
Extract from the Minnesota Sentencing (Main) Grid A

Presumptive sentence lengths are in months. Italicized numbers within the grid denote the discretionary range within which a court may sentence without the sentence being deemed a departure. Offenders with stayed felony sentences may be subject to local confinement.

SEVERITY LEVEL OF CONVICTION OFFENSE (Example offenses listed in italics)		CRIMINAL HISTORY SCORE						
		0	1	2	3	4	5	6 or more
Murder, 2nd Degree (intentional murder; drive-by-shootings)	11	306 261-367	326 278-391	346 295-415	366 312-439	386 329-463	406 346-480[2]	426 363-480[2]
Murder, 3rd Degree Murder, 2nd Degree (unintentional murder)	10	150 128-180	165 141-198	180 153-216	195 166-234	210 179-252	225 192-270	240 204-288
Assault, 1st Degree	9	86 74-103	98 84-117	110 94-132	122 104-146	134 114-160	146 125-175	158 135-189
Agg. Robbery, 1st Degree Burglary, 1st Degree (w/ Weapon or Assault)	8	48 41-57	58 50-69	68 58-81	78 67-93	88 75-105	98 84-117	108 92-129
Felony DWI Financial Exploitation of a Vulnerable Adult	7	36	42	48	54 46-64	60 51-72	66 57-79	72 62-84[2,3]
Assault, 2nd Degree Burglary, 1st Degree (Occupied Dwelling)	6	21	27	33	39 34-46	45 39-54	51 44-61	57 49-68
Residential Burglary Simple Robbery	5	18	23	28	33 29-39	38 33-45	43 37-51	48 41-57

☐ Presumptive commitment to state imprisonment. First-degree murder has a mandatory life sentence and is excluded from the Guidelines under Minn. Stat. § 609.185. See section 2.E, for policies regarding those sentences controlled by law.

☐ Presumptive stayed sentence; at the discretion of the court, up to one year of confinement and other non-jail sanctions can be imposed as conditions of probation. However, certain offenses in the shaded area of the Grid always carry a presumptive commitment to state prison. See sections 2.C and 2.E.

[2] Minn. Stat. § 244.09 requires that the Guidelines provide a range for sentences that are presumptive commitment to state imprisonment of 15% lower and 20% higher than the fixed duration displayed, provided that the minimum sentence is not less than one year and one day and the maximum sentence is not more than the statutory maximum. See section 2.C.1-2.

[3] The stat. max. for Financial Exploitation of Vulnerable Adult is 240 months; the standard range of 20% higher than the fixed duration applies at CHS 6 or more. (The range is 62-86.)

Fig. A1.—Extract from robbery guideline. Source: http://mn.gov/msgc-stat/documents/New Guidelines/2018/Guidelines.pdf.

APPENDIX B
Steps of the Street Robbery Guideline

STEP ONE
Determining the offence category

The court should determine the offence category with reference **only** to the factors listed in the tables below. In order to determine the category the court should assess **culpability** and **harm**.

The court should weigh all the factors set out below in determining the offender's culpability.

Where there are characteristics present which fall under different levels of culpability, the court should balance these characteristics to reach a fair assessment of the offender's culpability.

Culpability demonstrated by one or more of the following:

A – High culpability	• Use of a weapon to inflict violence • Production of a bladed article or firearm or imitation firearm to threaten violence • Use of very significant force in the commission of the offence • Offence motivated by, or demonstrating hostility based on any of the following characteristics or presumed characteristics of the victim: religion, race, disability, sexual orientation or transgender identity
B – Medium culpability	• Production of a weapon other than a bladed article or firearm or imitation firearm to threaten violence • Threat of violence by any weapon (but which is not produced) • Other cases where characteristics for categories A or C are not present
C – Lesser culpability	• Involved through coercion, intimidation or exploitation • Threat or use of minimal force • Mental disability or learning disability where linked to the commission of the offence

Harm
The court should consider the factors set out below to determine the level of harm that has been caused or was intended to be caused to the victim.

Category 1	• Serious physical and/or psychological harm caused to the victim • Serious detrimental effect on the business
Category 2	• Other cases where characteristics for categories 1 or 3 are not present
Category 3	• No/minimal physical or psychological harm caused to the victim • No/minimal detrimental effect on the business

(ROBBERY – STREET AND LESS SOPHISTICATED COMMERCIAL)

FIG. B1.—Step 1. Source: Sentencing Council of England and Wales (2016*b*).

STEP TWO
Starting point and category range

Having determined the category at step one, the court should use the corresponding starting point to reach a sentence within the category range below. The starting point applies to all offenders irrespective of plea or previous convictions. A case of particular gravity, reflected by multiple features of culpability or harm in step one, could merit upward adjustment from the starting point before further adjustment for aggravating or mitigating features, set out on the next page.

Consecutive sentences for multiple offences may be appropriate – please refer to the *Offences Taken into Consideration and Totality* guideline.

Harm	Culpability		
	A	B	C
Category 1	**Starting point** 8 years' custody	**Starting point** 5 years' custody	**Starting point** 4 years' custody
	Category range 7 – 12 years' custody	**Category range** 4 – 8 years' custody	**Category range** 3 – 6 years' custody
Category 2	**Starting point** 5 years' custody	**Starting point** 4 years' custody	**Starting point** 2 years' custody
	Category range 4 – 8 years' custody	**Category range** 3 – 6 years' custody	**Category range** 1 – 4 years' custody
Category 3	**Starting point** 4 years' custody	**Starting point** 2 years' custody	**Starting point** 1 year's custody
	Category range 3 – 6 years' custody	**Category range** 1 – 4 years' custody	**Category range** High level community order – 3 years' custody

The table on the next page contains a **non-exhaustive** list of additional factual elements providing the context of the offence and factors relating to the offender. Identify whether any combination of these, or other relevant factors, should result in an upward or downward adjustment from the sentence arrived at so far. In particular, relevant recent convictions are likely to result in an upward adjustment. In some cases, having considered these factors, it may be appropriate to move outside the identified category range.

FIG. B2.—Step 2. Source: Sentencing Council of England and Wales (2016*b*).

ROBBERY – STREET AND LESS SOPHISTICATED COMMERCIAL

Factors increasing seriousness

Statutory aggravating factors:

Previous convictions, having regard to a) the **nature** of the offence to which the conviction relates and its **relevance** to the current offence; and b) the **time** that has elapsed since the conviction

Offence committed whilst on bail

Other aggravating factors:

High value goods or sums targeted or obtained (whether economic, personal or sentimental)

Victim is targeted due to a vulnerability (or a perceived vulnerability)

Significant planning

Steps taken to prevent the victim reporting or obtaining assistance and/or from assisting or supporting the prosecution

Prolonged nature of event

Restraint, detention or additional degradation of the victim

A leading role where offending is part of a group activity

Involvement of others through coercion, intimidation or exploitation

Location of the offence (including cases where the location of the offence is the victim's residence)

Timing of the offence

Attempt to conceal identity (for example, wearing a balaclava or hood)

Commission of offence whilst under the influence of alcohol or drugs

Attempts to conceal/dispose of evidence

Established evidence of community/wider impact

Failure to comply with current court orders

Offence committed on licence

Offences taken into consideration

Failure to respond to warnings about behaviour

Factors reducing seriousness or reflecting personal mitigation

No previous convictions **or** no relevant/recent convictions

Remorse, particularly where evidenced by voluntary reparation to the victim

Good character and/or exemplary conduct

Serious medical condition requiring urgent, intensive or long-term treatment

Age and/or lack of maturity where it affects the responsibility of the offender

Mental disorder or learning disability (where not linked to the commission of the offence)

Little or no planning

Sole or primary carer for dependent relatives

Determination and/or demonstration of steps having been taken to address addiction or offending behaviour

FIG. B3.—Step 2 (*continued*). Source: Sentencing Council of England and Wales (2016*b*).

STEP THREE
Consider any factors which indicate a reduction for assistance to the prosecution
The court should take into account sections 73 and 74 of the Serious Organised Crime and Police Act 2005 (assistance by defendants: reduction or review of sentence) and any other rule of law by virtue of which an offender may receive a discounted sentence in consequence of assistance given (or offered) to the prosecutor or investigator.

STEP FOUR
Reduction for guilty pleas
The court should take account of any potential reduction for a guilty plea in accordance with section 144 of the Criminal Justice Act 2003 and the *Guilty Plea* guideline.

STEP FIVE
Dangerousness
The court should consider whether having regard to the criteria contained in Chapter 5 of Part 12 of the Criminal Justice Act 2003 it would be appropriate to impose a life sentence (section 224A or section 225) or an extended sentence (section 226A). When sentencing offenders to a life sentence under these provisions, the notional determinate sentence should be used as the basis for the setting of a minimum term.

STEP SIX
Totality principle
If sentencing an offender for more than one offence, or where the offender is already serving a sentence, consider whether the total sentence is just and proportionate to the overall offending behaviour in accordance with the *Offences Taken into Consideration and Totality* guideline.

STEP SEVEN
Compensation and ancillary orders
In all cases the court should consider whether to make compensation and/or other ancillary orders.

Where the offence involves a firearm, an imitation firearm or an offensive weapon the court may consider the criteria in section 19 of the Serious Crime Act 2007 for the imposition of a Serious Crime Prevention Order.

STEP EIGHT
Reasons
Section 174 of the Criminal Justice Act 2003 imposes a duty to give reasons for, and explain the effect of, the sentence.

STEP NINE
Consideration for time spent on bail
The court must consider whether to give credit for time spent on bail in accordance with section 240A of the Criminal Justice Act 2003.

FIG. B4.—Steps 3–9. Source: Sentencing Council of England and Wales (2016*b*).

APPENDIX C

TABLE C1
Key Characteristics of Sentencing Guidelines in Minnesota and England and Wales

	Minnesota (1980–2018)	England and Wales (2004–18)
Membership of commission or council	Judicial minority	Judicial majority
Guidelines subject to legislative approval	Yes	No
Degree of constraint imposed on courts	High: limited discretion permitted within the grid, and "substantial and compelling circumstances" required to justify a departure	Low: considerable discretion within guideline ranges; freedom to depart when contrary to the interests of justice guideline
Relationship to prison capacity	Policy and practice linked to prison capacity	No link to prison capacity
Nature of guidelines: descriptive or prescriptive	Prescriptive, and based on current sentencing practices	Primarily (but not exclusively) descriptive, based on current sentencing practices
Structure and evolution of guidelines	Grid based with two dimensions (offense seriousness and criminal history) containing dispositions and cell sentence ranges; format largely unchanged since 1980	Step-by-step approach beginning with categories of harm and culpability, each with sentence ranges and a starting point sentence; format has evolved significantly since 2012
Format	Same two-dimensional structure (offense seriousness and criminal history) applies to all three grids	Different formats to reflect variable nature of offenses, although they follow a common stepped approach

TABLE C1 (*Continued*)

	Minnesota (1980–2018)	England and Wales (2004–18)
Number of guidelines	Three grids in which all offenses are assigned to one of a small number of offense seriousness levels	Each principal offense carries its own specific guideline; approximately 25 in existence
Role of previous convictions	High impact; criminal history is a primary dimension; criminal history score affects both sentence type and sentence length	Low impact; no numerical guidance or quantification of prior crimes; prior convictions appear at step 2 of the guidelines methodology
Guidance on general sentencing issues	Limited guidance contained in guidelines manual	Guidance provided on a wide range of issues by "generic" guidelines, including sentencing multiple crimes, use of different sanctions, and plea-based sentencing discounts
Guidance on mitigating and aggravating factors	Lists of proscribed factors and factors that may justify departure; little additional guidance provided	Key factors relating to harm and culpability specified in each guideline and distinction made between primary and secondary factors
Appellate review and departure standard	Appellate review of "departures" and standard is "substantial and compelling circumstances"	Robust appellate review, and courts required to "follow any relevant guidelines unless it would be contrary to the interests of justice"

REFERENCES

Adelman, Lynn. 2013. "What the Sentencing Commission Ought to Be Doing: Reducing Mass Incarceration." *Michigan Journal of Race and Law* 18:295–316.
Advisory Council on the Penal System. 1978. *Sentences of Imprisonment: Report of the Advisory Council on the Penal System*. London: Her Majesty's Stationery Office.
Allen, Rob. 2016. "The Sentencing Council for England and Wales: Brake or Accelerator on the Use of Prison?" http://www.transformjustice.org.uk/wp-content/uploads/2016/12/TJ-DEC-9.12.16.pdf.
Ashworth, Andrew. 1983. *Sentencing and Penal Policy*. London: Weidenfeld & Nicholson.
———. 1987. "Devising Sentencing Guidance for England and Wales." In *Sentencing Reform: Guidance or Guidelines?* edited by Martin Wasik and Ken Pease. Manchester: Manchester University Press.
———. 2003. "Sentencing and Sensitivity: A Challenge for Criminological Research." In *The Criminological Foundations of Penal Policy: Essays in Honour of Roger Hood*, edited by Lucia Zedner and Andrew Ashworth. Oxford: Oxford University Press.
———. 2008. "English Sentencing Guidelines in Their Public and Political Context." In *Penal Populism, Sentencing Councils and Sentencing Policy*, edited by Arie Freiberg and Karen Gelb. Cullompton, UK: Willan/Federation.
———. 2010. "Coroners and Justice Act 2009: Sentencing Guidelines and the Sentencing Council." *Criminal Law Review* (5):389–401.
———. 2017. "The Evolution of English Sentencing Guidance in 2016." *Criminal Law Review* (7):507–20.
Ashworth, Andrew, and Julian V. Roberts. 2013*a*. "The Origins and Evolution of Sentencing Guidelines in England and Wales." In *Sentencing Guidelines: Exploring the English Model*, edited by Andrew Ashworth and Julian V. Roberts. Oxford: Oxford University Press.
———, eds. 2013*b*. *Sentencing Guidelines: Exploring the English Model*. Oxford: Oxford University Press.
Ashworth, Andrew, and Martin Wasik. 2010. "Ten Years of the Sentencing Advisory Panel." Annual report. http://www.sentencing.council.org.
Barkow, Rachel. 2012. "Sentencing Guidelines at the Crossroads of Politics and Expertise." *University of Pennsylvania Law Review* 160:1599–1630.
Barkow, Rachel, and Kathleen O'Neill. 2006. "Delegating Punitive Power: The Political Economy of Sentencing Commissions and Guideline Formation." *Texas Law Review* 84:1973–2022.
Berman, Douglas. 2017. "Sentencing Guidelines." In *Reforming Criminal Justice*, edited by Erik Luna, Barry C. Feld, and Michael Tonry. Phoenix: Sandra Day O'Connor College of Law, Arizona State University.
Blalock, Ira. 1982. "Parole Guidelines." In *Sentencing Reform: Experiments in Disparity*, edited by Martin Forst. London: Sage.

Blumstein, Alfred, Jacqueline Cohen, Susan E. Martin, and Michael Tonry, eds. 1983. *Research on Sentencing: The Search for Reform*. 2 vols. Washington, DC: National Academy Press.

Bottoms, Anthony. 1981. "The Suspended Sentence in England, 1967–1978." *British Journal of Criminology* 21:1–26.

———. 2018. *The Sentencing Council in 2017: A Report on Research to Advise on How the Sentencing Council Can Best Exercise Its Statutory Functions*. Cambridge: Institute of Criminology, University of Cambridge.

British Academy. 2014. *A Presumption Against Imprisonment*. London: British Academy.

Browne, Graham. 2017. *Criminal Sentencing as Practical Wisdom*. Oxford: Hart.

Canadian Sentencing Commission. 1987. *Sentencing Reform: A Canadian Approach*. Ottawa: Supply and Services Canada.

Carline, Anna, Emma Palmer, Mandy Burton, and Sally Kyd. 2018. *Assessing the Implementation of the Sentencing Council's Sexual Offences Definitive Guideline*. London: Sentencing Council of England and Wales.

Carter, Lord. 2007. *Securing the Future: Proposals for the Efficient and Sustainable Use of Custody in England and Wales*. London: Ministry of Justice.

Chen, Xiaoming. 2010. "The Chinese Sentencing Guidelines: A Preliminary Analysis." *Federal Sentencing Reporter* 22(4):213–16.

Cole, David, and Julian V. Roberts. 2018. "What's the Point of Pleading Guilty?" *Criminal Reports* 44:44–58.

Cooper, John. 2013. "Nothing Personal." In *Sentencing Guidelines: Exploring the English Model*, edited by Andrew Ashworth and Julian V. Roberts. Oxford: Oxford University Press.

Council of Europe. 1993. "Consistency in Sentencing: Recommendation to Member States and Explanatory Memorandum." *Criminal Law Forum* 4(2): 355–92.

Cox, Edward. 1877. *The Principles of Punishment, as Applied in the Administration of Criminal Law, by Judges and Magistrates*. London: Law Times Office.

Crackenthorpe, Montague. 1900. "Can Sentences Be Standardised?" *Nineteenth Century* (January):103–15.

Dansky, Kara. 2010. "A Blueprint for a California Sentencing Commission." *Federal Sentencing Reporter* 22:158–64.

Dennison, Brian. 2015. *Uganda's New Sentencing Guidelines*. Kampala: Uganda Christian University.

Dhami, Mandeep. 2013. "A 'Decision Science' Perspective on the Old and New Sentencing Guidelines in England and Wales." In *Sentencing Guidelines: Exploring the English Model*, edited by Andrew Ashworth and Julian V. Roberts. Oxford: Oxford University Press.

Dhami, Mandeep, Ian Belton, and Jane Goodman-Delahunty. 2015. "Quasirational Models of Sentencing." *Journal of Applied Research in Memory and Cognition* 4:239–47.

Doob, Anthony, and Cheryl Webster. 2003. "Looking at the Model Penal Code: Sentencing Provisions through Canadian Lenses." *Buffalo Criminal Law Review* 7:141–70.

Faulkner, David. 2002. "Taking Account of Race, Ethnicity and Religion." In *Reform and Punishment: The Future of Sentencing*, edited by Sue Rex and Michael Tonry. Cullompton, UK: Willan.

Fleetwood, Jennifer, Polly Radcliffe, and Alex Stevens. 2015. "Shorter Sentences for Drug Mules: The Early Impact of the Sentencing Guidelines in England and Wales." *Drugs Education, Prevention, and Policy* 22(5):428–36.

Fletcher, George. 1982. "Rethinking the Recidivist Premium." *Criminal Justice Ethics* 1:54–59.

Fox, Richard. 1994. "The Meaning of Proportionality in Sentencing." *Melbourne Law Review* 19:489–511.

Frankel, Marvin. 1973. *Criminal Sentences: Law Without Order*. New York: Hill & Wang.

Frase, Richard. 1991. "Sentencing Reform in Minnesota, Ten Years After: Reflections on Dale Parent's Structuring Criminal Sentences." *Minnesota Law Review* 75:727–54.

———. 1993. "The Role of the Legislature, the Sentencing Commission, and Other Officials under the Minnesota Sentencing Guidelines." *Wake Forest Law Review* 28:345–79.

———. 1997. "Sentencing Principles in Theory and Practice." In *Crime and Justice: A Review of Research*, vol. 22, edited by Michael Tonry. Chicago: University of Chicago Press.

———. 2001. "Comparative Perspectives on Sentencing Policy and Research." In *Sentencing and Sanctions in Western Nations*, edited by Michael Tonry and Richard Frase. Oxford: Oxford University Press.

———. 2005*a*. "Sentencing Guidelines in Minnesota, 1978–2003." In *Crime and Justice: A Review of Research*, vol. 32, edited by Michael Tonry. Chicago: University of Chicago Press.

———. 2005*b*. "State Sentencing Guidelines: Diversity, Consensus, and Unresolved Policy Issues." *Columbia Law Review* 105:1190–1232.

———. 2009. "What Explains Persistent Racial Disproportionality in Minnesota's Prison and Jail Population?" In *Crime and Justice: A Review of Research*, vol. 38, edited by Michael Tonry. Chicago: University of Chicago Press.

———. 2014. "Learning from European Punishment Practices—and from Similar American Practices, Now and in the Past." *Federal Sentencing Reporter* 27:19–25.

———. 2019. "Forty Years of American Sentencing Guidelines: What Have We Learned?" In *American Sentencing*, edited by Michael Tonry. Vol. 48 of *Crime and Justice: A Review of Research*, edited by Michael Tonry. Chicago: University of Chicago Press.

Frase, Richard, and Rhys Hester. 2015. "Magnitude of Criminal History Enhancements." In *Criminal History Enhancements Sourcebook*, edited by Richard Frase, Julian V. Roberts, Rhys Hester, and Kelly Mitchell. Minneapolis: Robina Institute in Criminal Law and Criminal Justice, University of Minnesota.

Frase, Richard, and Kelly Mitchell. 2019. "Sentencing Guidelines in the US." In *Handbook on Corrections and Sentencing*, edited by Cassia Spohn. New York: Routledge.

Frase, Richard, and Julian V. Roberts. 2019. *Paying for the Past: Prior Record Enhancements in the US Sentencing Guidelines*. New York: Oxford University Press.

Frase, Richard, Julian V. Roberts, Kelly Mitchell, and Rhys Hester. 2015. *Sourcebook of Criminal History Enhancements*. Minneapolis: Robina Institute in Criminal Law and Criminal Justice, University of Minnesota.

Hamilton, Melissa. 2015. "Back to the Future: The Influence of Criminal History on Risk Assessment." *Berkeley Journal of Criminal Law* 20:75–133.

Hester, Rhys, Richard Frase, Julian V. Roberts, and Kelly Mitchell. 2018. "Prior Record Enhancements at Sentencing: Unsettled Justifications and Unsettling Consequences." In *Crime and Justice: A Review of Research*, vol. 47, edited by Michael Tonry. Chicago: University of Chicago Press.

Hester, Rhys, Julian V. Roberts, Richard Frase, and Kelly Mitchell. 2017. "A Measure of Tolerance: Public Attitudes toward Sentencing Enhancements for Old and Juvenile Prior Records." *Corrections: Policy, Practice, and Research* 3(2):137–51.

Home Office Sentencing Review. 2001. *Making Punishments Work: Report of a Review of the Sentencing Framework for England and Wales*. London: Home Office.

Hood, Roger. 1992. *Race and Sentencing: A Study in the Crown Court; a Report for the Commission for Racial Equality*. Oxford: Oxford University Press.

Hough, Mike, Jonathan Jackson, Ben Bradford, Andy Myhill, and Paul Quinton. 2010. "Procedural Justice, Trust, and Institutional Legitimacy." *Policing* 4(3):204–10.

House of Commons Justice Committee. 2011. *Revised Sentencing Guideline: Assault*. London: House of Commons.

Irwin-Rogers, Keir, and Tom Perry. 2015. "Exploring the Impact of Sentencing Factors on Sentencing Domestic Burglary." In *Exploring Sentencing Practice in England and Wales*, edited by Julian V. Roberts. London: Palgrave Macmillan.

Irwin-Rogers, Keir, and Julian V. Roberts. 2019. "Swimming Against the Tide: The Suspended Sentence Order in England and Wales, 2000–2017." *Law and Contemporary Problems*, forthcoming.

Kamuzze, Juliet. 2014. "An Insight into Uganda's New Sentencing Guidelines: A Replica of Individualization?" *Federal Sentencing Reporter* 27(1):47–55.

Kauder, Neal, and Brian Ostrom. 2008. *State Sentencing Guidelines: Profile and Continuum*. Washington, DC: Pew Center on the States.

Kilaru, Rakesh. 2010. "Guidelines as Guidelines: Lessons from the History of Sentencing Reform." *Charlotte Law Review* 2:101–43.

Knapp, Kay. 1987. "Organization and Staffing." In *The Sentencing Commission and Its Guidelines*, edited by Andrew von Hirsch, Kay Knapp, and Michael Tonry. Boston: Northeastern University Press.

Lammy, David. 2017. *An Independent Review into the Treatment of, and Outcomes for, Black, Asian and Minority Ethnic Individuals in the Criminal Justice System*. London: Her Majesty's Stationery Office. https://assets.publishing.service.gov.uk/government/uploads/system/uploads/attachment_data/file/643001/lammy-review-final-report.pdf.

Law Reform Commission of South Africa. 2000. *Sentencing: A New Sentencing Framework*. Pretoria: Law Reform Commission of South Africa.

Leveson, Sir Brian. 2013. *The Parmoor Lecture: Achieving Consistency at Sentencing*. London: Judiciary of England and Wales.

Lovegrove, Austin. 2010. "The Sentencing Council, the Public's Sense of Justice, and Personal Mitigation." *Criminal Law Review* (12):906–23.

Mason, Thomas, Nisha de Silva, Nalini Sharma, David Brown, and Gemma Harper. 2007. *Local Variation in Sentencing in England and Wales*. London: Ministry of Justice.

Mews, Aidan, Joseph Hillier, Michael McHugh, and Cris Coxon. 2015. *The Impact of Short Custodial Sentences, Community Orders and Suspended Sentence Orders on Re-offending*. London: Ministry of Justice.

Ministry of Justice. 2013. *Story of the Prison Population: 1993–2012*. London: Ministry of Justice.

———. 2016. *Story of the Prison Population: 1993–2016*. London: Ministry of Justice.

———. 2017. *Statistics on Race and the Criminal Justice System 2016*. London: Her Majesty's Stationery Office. https://assets.publishing.service.gov.uk/government/uploads/system/uploads/attachment_data/file/669094/statistics_on_race_and_the_criminal_justice_system_2016_v2.pdf.

Mitchell, Kelly. 2015. "Decay and Gap Policies." In *Criminal History Enhancements Sourcebook*, edited by Richard Frase, Julian V. Roberts, Rhys Hester, and Kelly Mitchell. Minneapolis: Robina Institute in Criminal Law and Criminal Justice, University of Minnesota.

———. 2017. *Sentencing Commissions and Guidelines by the Numbers*. Minneapolis: Robina Institute in Criminal Law and Criminal Justice.

MSGC (Minnesota Sentencing Guidelines Commission). 1979. *Preliminary Analysis of Sentencing and Releasing Data*. St. Paul: Minnesota Sentencing Guidelines Commission.

———. 1980. *Report to the Legislature*. St. Paul: Minnesota Sentencing Guidelines Commission.

———. 1981. *Minnesota Sentencing Guidelines and Commentary*. St. Paul: Minnesota Sentencing Guidelines Commission.

———. 2018. *Minnesota Sentencing Guidelines and Commentary*. Minneapolis: Minnesota Sentencing Guidelines Commission.

New South Wales Department of Justice. 2008. *Evaluation of Sentencing Advisory Council*. Victoria, NSW: Department of Justice.

Padfield, Nicola. 2013. "Exploring the Success of Sentencing Guidelines." In *Sentencing Guidelines: Exploring the English Model*, edited by Andrew Ashworth and Julian V. Roberts. Oxford: Oxford University Press.

Parent, Dale. 1988. *Structuring Criminal Sentences: The Evolution of Minnesota's Sentencing Guidelines*. London: Butterworths.

Park, H. 2010. "The Basic Features of the First Korean Sentencing Guidelines." *Federal Sentencing Reporter* 22:262–71.

Pina-Sánchez, Jose. 2015. "Defining and Measuring Consistency in Sentencing." In *Exploring Sentencing Practice in England and Wales*, edited by Julian V. Roberts. London: Palgrave Macmillan.

Pina-Sánchez, Jose, and Robin Linacre. 2013. "Sentence Consistency in England and Wales." *British Journal of Criminology* 53(6):1118–35.

Radzinowicz, Leon, and Roger Hood. 1979. "Judicial Discretion and Sentencing Standards: Victorian Attempts to Solve a Perennial Problem." *University of Pennsylvania Law Review* 17(5):1288–1349.

———. 1986. *A History of English Criminal Law*. Vol. 5: *The Emergence of Penal Policy*. London: Stevens & Son.

Reitz, Kevin. 2013. "Comparing Sentencing Guidelines: Do US Systems Have Anything Worthwhile to Offer England and Wales?" In *Sentencing Guidelines: Exploring the English Model*, edited by Andrew Ashworth and Julian V. Roberts. Oxford: Oxford University Press.

Roberts, Julian V. 1994. "The Role of Criminal Record in the US Sentencing Guidelines." *Criminal Justice Ethics* 13:21–30.

———. 1997. "The Role of Criminal Record in the Sentencing Process." In *Crime and Justice: A Review of Research*, vol. 22, edited by Michael Tonry. Chicago: University of Chicago Press.

———. 2008. *Punishing Persistent Offenders: Community and Offender Perspectives on the Recidivist Sentencing Premium*. Oxford: Oxford University Press.

———. 2011. "Sentencing Guidelines and Judicial Discretion: Evolution of the Duty of Courts to Comply in England and Wales." *British Journal of Criminology* 51:997–1013.

———. 2012. "Structuring Sentencing in Canada and England and Wales: A Tale of Two Jurisdictions." *Criminal Law Forum* 23(4):319–45.

———, ed. 2015. *Exploring Sentencing Practice in England and Wales*. London: Palgrave Macmillan.

Roberts, Julian V., and Andrew Ashworth. 2016. "The Evolution of Sentencing Policy and Practice in England and Wales, 2003–2015." In *Sentencing Policies and Practices in Western Countries: Comparative and Cross-National Perspectives*, edited by Michael Tonry. Vol. 45 of *Crime and Justice: A Review of Research*, edited by Michael Tonry. Chicago: University of Chicago Press.

Roberts, Julian V., and Ben Bradford. 2015. "Sentence Reductions for a Guilty Plea: New Empirical Evidence from England and Wales." *Journal of Empirical Legal Studies* 12(2):187–210.

Roberts, Julian V., and Oren Gazal-Ayal. 2013. "Sentencing Reform in Israel: An Analysis of the Statutory Reforms of 2012." *Israel Law Review* 46:455–79.

Roberts, Julian V., Mike Hough, Jonathan Jackson, and Monica Gerber. 2012. "Public Attitudes toward the Lay Magistracy and the Sentencing Council Guidelines: The Effects of Information on Opinion." *British Journal of Criminology* 52(6):1072–91.

Roberts, Julian V., Mike Hough, Jessica Jacobson, Alan Bredee, and Nick Moon. 2008. "Public Attitudes to the Sentencing of Offenders Convicted of Offences Involving Death by Driving." *Criminal Law Review* (July):525–40.

Roberts, Julian V., and Wei Pei. 2016. "Structuring Judicial Discretion in China: Exploring the 2014 Sentencing Guidelines." *Criminal Law Forum* 27(1):3–33.

Roberts, Julian V., and Jose Pina-Sánchez. 2014. "Previous Convictions at Sentencing: Exploring Empirical Trends in the Crown Court." *Criminal Law Review* (8):575–88.
Roberts, Julian V., Jose Pina-Sánchez, and I. Marder. 2018. "Individualisation at Sentencing: The Effects of Sentencing Guidelines and 'Preferred' Numbers." *Criminal Law Review* (2):123–36.
Roberts, Julian V., and A. Rafferty. 2011. "Sentencing Guidelines in England and Wales: Exploring the New Format." *Criminal Law Review* (9):680–89.
Roberts, Julian V., and Andrew von Hirsch. 1998. "Conditional Sentencing and the Fundamental Principle of Proportionality in Sentencing." *Criminal Reports* 10:222–31.
———, eds. 2010. *Previous Convictions at Sentencing: Theoretical and Applied Perspectives*. Studies in Penal Theory and Ethics. Oxford: Hart.
Ryberg, Jesper, Julian V. Roberts, and Jan de Keijser, eds. 2017. *Sentencing Multiple Crimes*. Studies in Penal Theory and Philosophy. New York: Oxford University Press.
Secret Barrister 2017. *Stories of the Law and How It's Broken*. London: Macmillan.
Sentencing Commission of the Supreme Court of Korea. 2014. *Korean Sentencing Guidelines*. Seoul: Sentencing Commission of the Supreme Court of Korea.
Sentencing Commission Working Group. 2008. *Sentencing Guidelines in England and Wales: An Evolutionary Approach*. London: Sentencing Commission Working Group.
Sentencing Council of England and Wales. 2011. *Assault: Definitive Guideline*. London: Sentencing Council of England and Wales. http://sentencingcouncil.judiciary.gov.uk/.
———. 2012a. *Drug Offences: Definitive Guideline*. https://www.sentencingcouncil.org.uk/wp-content/uploads/Drug_Offences_Definitive_Guideline_final_web1.pdf.
———. 2012b. *Drug Offences Guideline Research Bulletin*. https://www.sentencingcouncil.org.uk/wp-content/uploads/Drug_offences_guideline_research_bulletin_web.pdf.
———. 2012c. *Offences Taken into Account and Totality: Definitive Guideline*. London: Sentencing Council of England and Wales. https://www.sentencingcouncil.org.uk/wp-content/uploads/Definitive_guideline_TICs__totality_Final_web.pdf.
———. 2013. *Sexual Offences: Definitive Guideline 2014*. London: Sentencing Council of England and Wales. https://www.sentencingcouncil.org.uk/publications/item/sexual-offences-definitive-guideline/.
———. 2014. *Health and Safety Offences, Corporate Manslaughter and Food Safety and Hygiene Offences Guidelines*. London: Sentencing Council of England and Wales. https://www.sentencingcouncil.org.uk/wp-content/uploads/Health_and_safety_corporate_manslaughter_food_safety_and_hygiene_offfences_consultation_guideline_web1.pdf.
———. 2015a. *Assessing the Impact and Implementation of the Sentencing Council's Assault Definitive Guideline*. London: Sentencing Council of England and Wales. http://www.sentencingcouncil.org.uk/wp-content/uploads/Assault-assessment-synthesis-report.pdf.

———. 2015b. *Crown Court Sentencing Survey, 2014: Annual Publication.* London: Sentencing Council of England and Wales. https://www.sentencingcouncil.org.uk/publications/item/crown-court-sentencing-survey-annual-publication-2014-full-report-2/.

———. 2016a. *Imposition of Community and Custody Penalties: Definitive Guideline.* London: Sentencing Council of England and Wales. https://www.sentencingcouncil.org.uk/wp-content/uploads/Definitive-Guideline-Imposition-of-CCS-final-web.pdf.

———. 2016b. *Robbery Offences: Definitive Guideline.* London: Sentencing Council of England and Wales. https://www.sentencingcouncil.org.uk/publications/item/robbery-definitive-guideline-2/.

———. 2017. *Reduction in Sentence for a Guilty Plea: Definitive Guideline.* London: Sentencing Council of England and Wales. https://www.sentencingcouncil.org.uk/publications/item/reduction-in-sentence-for-a-guilty-plea-definitive-guideline-2/.

———. 2018a. *Manslaughter Guideline: Final Resource Assessment.* London: Sentencing Council of England and Wales. https://www.sentencingcouncil.org.uk/publications/item/manslaughter-final-resource-assessment/.

———. 2018b. *Manslaughter Offenses: Definitive Guideline.* London: Sentencing Council of England and Wales. https://www.sentencingcouncil.org.uk/publications/item/manslaughter-definitive-guideline.

———. 2018c. *Terrorism Offenses: Definitive Guideline.* London: Sentencing Council of England and Wales. https://www.sentencingcouncil.org.uk/publications/item/terrorism-offences-definitive-guideline/.

Sentencing Guidelines Council. 2008. *Assault and Other Offences Against the Person: Definitive Guideline.* London: Sentencing Guidelines Council.

Spencer, H. 1860. "What Is to Be Done with Our Criminals?" *British Quarterly Review* (July):42–70.

Stemen, Don, and Andres Regifo. 2012. "Charting the Evolution of Structure and Determinacy in State Sentencing and Corrections Policies 1970–2010." *Justice Research and Policy* 14:1–30.

Stith, Kate. 2000. "Sentencing Guidelines: Lessons for the States." *Saint Louis Law Journal* 44:387–408.

Subramanian, Ram, and Alison Shames. 2013. *Sentencing and Prison Practices in Germany and the Netherlands.* Washington, DC: Vera Institute.

Thibaut, John, and Laurens Walker. 1975. *Procedural Justice: A Psychological Analysis.* Hillsdale, NJ: Erlbaum.

Tonry, Michael. 1993. "Sentencing Commissions and Their Guidelines." In *Crime and Justice: A Review of Research,* vol. 17, edited by Michael Tonry. Chicago: University of Chicago Press.

———. 2002. "Setting Sentencing Policy through Guidelines." In *Reform and Punishment: The Future of Sentencing,* edited by Sue Rex and Michael Tonry. Cullompton, UK: Willan.

———. 2004. *Punishment and Politics.* Cullompton, UK: Willan.

———, ed. 2013. *Crime and Justice in America, 1975–2025*. Vol. 42 of *Crime and Justice: A Review of Research*, edited by Michael Tonry. Chicago: University of Chicago Press.

———. 2015. "Federal Sentencing 'Reform' since 1984: The Awful as Enemy of the Good." In *Crime and Justice: A Review of Research*, vol. 44, edited by Michael Tonry. Chicago: University of Chicago Press.

———, ed. 2016. *Sentencing Policies and Practices in Western Countries: Comparative and Cross-National Perspectives*. Vol. 45 of *Crime and Justice: A Review of Research*, edited by Michael Tonry. Chicago: University of Chicago Press.

Tonry, Michael, and Richard Frase. 2001. *Sentencing and Sanctions in Western Nations*. Oxford: Oxford University Press.

von Hirsch, Andreas. 2017. *Deserved Criminal Sentences*. Oxford: Hart.

von Hirsch, Andrew. 1976. *Doing Justice*. New York: Hill & Wang.

———. 1985. *Past or Future Crimes*. New Brunswick, NJ: Rutgers University Press.

———. 1987. "The Sentencing Commission's Functions." In *The Sentencing Commission and Its Guidelines*, edited by Andrew von Hirsch, Kay Knapp, and Michael Tonry. Boston: Northeastern University Press.

———. 1994. "Sentencing Guidelines and Penal Aims in Minnesota." *Criminal Justice Ethics* 13:39–57.

Wandall, Rasmus. 2006. "Equality by Numbers or Words: A Comparative Study of Sentencing Structures in Minnesota and in Denmark." *Criminal Law Forum* 17:1–41.

Wasik, Martin. 2014. "Sentencing—the Last Ten Years." *Criminal Law Review* (7):477–91.

Wasik, Martin, and Ken Pease, eds. 1987. *Sentencing Reform: Guidance or Guidelines?* Manchester: Manchester University Press.

Webster, Mike. 2017. *The New Sentencing Guidelines One Year On: Their Impact on the Construction Industry*. http://mpwrandr.co.uk/the-new-sentencing-guidelines-one-year-on-their-impact-on-the-construction-industry/.

Weisberg, Robert. 2007. "How Sentencing Commissions Turned Out to Be a Good Idea." *Berkeley Journal of Criminal Law* 12:179–230.

———. 2012. "The Sentencing Commission Model, 1970s to Present." In *The Oxford Handbook of Sentencing and Corrections*, edited by Joan Petersilia and Kevin Reitz. New York: Oxford University Press.

Wilkins, Leslie. 1987. "Disparity in Dispositions: The Early Ideas and Applications of Guidelines." In *Sentencing Reform: Guidance or Guidelines?* edited by Martin Wasik and Ken Pease. Manchester: Manchester University Press.

Young, Warren, and Andrea King. 2013. "The Origins and Evolution of Sentencing Guidelines: A Comparison of England and Wales and New Zealand." In *Sentencing Guidelines: Exploring the English Model*, edited by Andrew Ashworth and Julian V. Roberts. Oxford: Oxford University Press.

Kevin R. Reitz and Cecelia M. Klingele

Model Penal Code: Sentencing—Workable Limits on Mass Punishment

ABSTRACT

The Model Penal Code: Sentencing (MPCS) rewrites the 1962 Model Penal Code's provisions on sentencing and corrections. Since the 1960s, use of all forms of punishment has exploded, including incarceration, community supervision, supervision revocation, economic sanctions, and collateral consequences of convictions. The MPCS provides an institutional framework for all major forms of punishment. It consists of a sentencing commission, sentencing guidelines, abolition of parole release discretion, appellate sentence review, and controls on correctional population size. It revamps sentencing procedures to inject greater fairness and transparency. It gives state legislators broad advice on how they can reform their systems as a whole, while improving decisions in each case. The MPCS recommends newly crafted limits on punishment through reasoned pursuit of utilitarian crime reduction goals, prohibition of disproportionate sentence severity, individualization of sentences that cuts through even mandatory minimum penalties, refinement of each type of punishment so it can achieve its core purposes, an attack on "criminogenic" sentences that do more harm than good, measures to prioritize and direct correctional resources to offenders who present the greatest risks and highest needs, and creation of institutional capacity to monitor, manage, and improve the entire system over time.

Electronically published February 13, 2019
   Kevin Reitz is James La Vea Annenberg Professor of Criminal Procedure at the University of Minnesota Law School. Cecelia Klingele is associate professor, University of Wisconsin Law School. They are reporter and associate reporter for the *Model Penal Code: Sentencing* and have worked the last 5 years with the Robina Institute of Criminal Law and Criminal Justice on projects designed to support MPCS drafting.

© 2019 by The University of Chicago. All rights reserved.
0192-3234/2019/0048-0007$10.00

The Model Penal Code is a venerable brand name in legal circles. The original code inspired legislation in 40 states and became a font of judicial precedent in every state and the federal courts (Lynch 1998, pp. 297–98; Dubber 2015, pp. 5–6). It was the most successful law reform project in the history of American criminal justice, worthy of comparison with the Uniform Commercial Code in commercial law or the American Law Institute's "Restatements" of contracts, torts, and other common-law subjects (Kadish 1988). The Model Penal Code has been a mainstay of law school curriculums for generations; it has been summarized and resummarized in hundreds of "hornbooks" for law students, and it continues to generate new scholarship to the present day.

The new *Model Penal Code: Sentencing* (MPCS) won final approval from the American Law Institute in 2017 after 15 years of study, debate, drafting, and redrafting (see American Law Institute 2017*a*, 2017*b*).[1] It is the first official amendment of any section of the original Model Penal Code and replaces about half of the old code—the half concerning sentencing and corrections.[2]

The MPCS is not legislation with force of law but recommended legislation addressed primarily to state legislatures in the United States. It is meant to collect best practices of the past and also to be "aspirational"— to propose reforms to push the law forward.

This essay does not attempt to summarize the entire MPCS project but focuses on several of its features, including foundational sections of the code that are key to understanding its more detailed pieces. Despite the many technical aspects of sentencing law addressed by the MPCS's 59 provisions, it approaches sentencing from a human, rather than a doctrinal,

---

[1] Citation of the new MPCS provisions can be tricky. The "Proposed Final Draft" (PFD) of the MPCS that was formally approved by the ALI membership (American Law Institute 2017*b*) is now being edited and updated, to be published in hardbound volumes in 2019. While there will be no changes in the substance of the PFD, most provisions have been renumbered to reflect their ultimate sequential order—and that final numbering does not match that in the PFD. (Over many years of drafting, the temporary section numberings were unsystematic.) Thus, in the short term, the PFD is the most complete source for the MPCS and its commentaries, but citations to the PFD will soon be past their expiration date. For the final numbering system, with back-and-forth cross-references to preapproval designations, see American Law Institute (2017*a*). Citations in this essay will follow the final MPCS nomenclature. When the PFD or other preapproval drafts are used as sources, page numbers will be cited rather than moribund section numbers.

[2] The "corrections" provisions were the least celebrated portions of the original Model Penal Code (Robinson and Dubber 2007, p. 326).

perspective. That is, it concerns itself with all the ways people convicted of crimes experience punishment. This perspective carries with it an extended time horizon. Under the MPCS, "sentencing" does not conclude with the judge's pronouncement of a sentence in court but continues forward through the lifespan of sentences as they are administered and experienced. The MPCS does not treat a sentence as having been fully determined until we can look back on it with hindsight. The full severity of a sentence, its shape and form, and the ways in which it pursues the policies of criminal law (or fails to pursue them) are continually unfolding until the sentence is over. Many official decisions taken during the life of a sentence are therefore treated by the MPCS as "sentencing decisions." Often, the process of defining a final sentence unfolds over a period of years. In some ways, the legal penalties imposed on people convicted of crimes in America are never ending.

This essay highlights a number of the MPCS's major proposals to introduce rational limits on sentences in individual cases as well as system-wide controls over aggregate sentencing severity. On matters of institutional structure, the MPCS recommends that every state should create a permanent sentencing commission with authority to develop "presumptive" sentencing guidelines—that is, guidelines with a degree of legal force but subject to judicial departures based on "substantial reasons." Trial court sentences are subject to appellate review under the MPCS. Unique to the MPCS, appellate courts are given authority to reverse any sentence—even if it is legislatively mandated—on the ground that it is disproportionately severe. The MPCS also includes a strong preference for a "determinate" sentencing system, in which parole boards have little or no authority to determine the actual time a person will serve in prison. Instead, under the MPCS, lengths of prison stay are primarily a function of the judicial sentence, with good-time allowances for prisoners who maintain a reasonably clean prison record and participate in in-prison programs. Among other advantages, the institutional structure endorsed in the MPCS has been associated with low prison-rate growth when compared with other types of American sentencing systems in the past several decades.

In addition, the MPCS addresses sentencing law and policy at the individual-case level and gives close attention to the distinctive principles at work for each sanction type. For example, it greatly restricts the utilitarian purposes that may be used to justify incarceration sentences. It would abolish all mandatory imprisonment laws but, because this is unlikely to happen all at once, it also proposes many mechanisms to dilute the application of mandatory penalties. In community supervision, the MPCS counsels in favor of smaller probation and parole populations, with more resources devoted to clients with the greatest needs. The MPCS advocates shorter supervision terms, the parsimonious use of conditions, and defined incentives that allow clients to earn early termination. It further takes the view that many people currently on probation do not need supervision at all, and many are hindered in their efforts to reenter their communities by probation restrictions. As a law-reform priority, diversion from probation is a significant goal under the MPCS, as well as diversion from prison. On the expanding panoply of financial sanctions imposed on criminal offenders (or, sometimes, suspected offenders) across America, the MPCS recommends drastic cutbacks. Perhaps most importantly, it provides that no economic sanction of any kind may be imposed if payment would prevent the defendant from providing for his or her own reasonable financial needs and those of his or her family. In the domain of collateral consequences of conviction—although these are usually classified as "civil" measures—the MPCS gives courts the power to exempt defendants from the mandatory effects of such sanctions. It also empowers courts to grant "certificates of rehabilitation" to ex-offenders after a period of years, which would clear away nearly all collateral sanctions. Further, the MPCS instructs sentencing commissions to draw collateral consequences within their jurisdiction of responsibilities, so that someone is required to collect and update information on the hundreds of collateral sanctions that exist in each state. The commission is also given responsibility for writing guidelines for the application of those sanctions and the use of judges' powers to soften their blows.

Here is how this essay is organized. Section I briefly describes the entire MPCS project. Section II addresses the historical context into which the code has landed. Section III focuses on the MPCS's provisions to combat racial and ethnic disparities in sentencing. Section IV discusses its overall policy framework for placing limits on mass punishment. The remaining sections discuss different modes of punishment the MPCS seeks to rationalize. Section V discusses prisons and jails; Section VI, probation; Section VII, "back-end" sentencing matters including postrelease supervision and provisions for the early release of prisoners serving extended prison terms (these are the MPCS's counterparts to the original Model Penal Code's provisions on parole supervision and release); Section VIII, economic sanctions; and Section IX, collateral consequences of conviction. We conclude with some consideration of the most important topic the MPCS failed to cover: conditions of confinement in American prisons and jails.

I. MPCS Overview

The new MPCS should not be seen as one project but as a collection of related projects spanning the sentencing landscape. Its major subject areas can be cataloged under the following headings—many of which, standing alone, could have justified multiyear law-reform initiatives in their own right:

- Purposes of Sentencing and the Sentencing System
- Institutional Framework of the Sentencing System
- Prisons and Jails
- Probation and Parole Supervision and Revocation
- Economic Penalties
- Collateral Consequences of Conviction
- Dispositions Short of Conviction
- Mechanisms to Address Racial and Other Disparities in Punishment
- Sentencing of Juvenile Offenders as Adults
- Mechanisms to Manage Correctional Resources
- Procedural Rules of Sentencing
- Mechanisms to Blunt Prosecutorial Control of Sentencing Outcomes
- Risk Assessment as a Sentencing Tool
- Victims' Rights at Sentencing
- Appellate Review of Sentences
- Sentence Modification and Prison-Release Mechanisms

Like the original Model Penal Code, the MPCS is rooted in 50-state legal research, wide consultation with practitioners, and study of the relevant legal and social science literatures. In some places, it is informed by comparative research.[3] Overall, it reflects investments of time and exper-

---

[3] In addition, the MPCS includes official comments and research notes for every provision. These add up to a treatise in American sentencing law and policy that will not be duplicated anytime soon.

tise that most legislatures or criminal justice agencies could not afford on their own.[4]

The MPCS's breadth of coverage is part of what makes it a valuable resource. Some of the 16 subjects listed above were receiving attention from policy makers and researchers before the MPCS project was launched, but just as many had been badly neglected. The study of all of them together, over a substantial period of years, was a unique strength of the American Law Institute process. This holistic scope permitted the MPCS to hammer out an approach to sentencing law that is internally consistent in its attempt to temper punishment with an appreciation of the cumulative weight of the many disparate sanctions—from fines to probation to collateral consequences—that criminal defendants experience as punishments for criminal conviction.

II. Context: Criminal Punishment in Twenty-First-Century America

The MPCS has arrived at a moment in American criminal justice history that is both tragic and, perhaps, a time of cautious optimism. Over several decades, from the early 1970s through the late 2000s, all American states expanded the per capita use and severity of every major form of criminal punishment—by stunning amounts.[5] We refer to this as America's "punishment buildup period." The across-the-board punitive eruption included imprisonment, jail confinement, probation supervision, victim restitution, fines, court and corrections fees (of many varieties), asset forfeitures, parole supervision, revocations from probation and parole supervision, and collateral consequences of conviction. All of these sanction types grew dramatically and over substantially overlapping periods.[6] Their social importance grew as well.

The basic facts of incarceration growth are well known. From 1970 to 2008, the 1-day counts of people in US prisons and jails multiplied from 357,292 to 2,325,633. Corrected for population growth, this was

---

[4] The MPCS also benefited from close alliance with the Robina Institute of Criminal Law and Criminal Justice. This added significantly to the project's resources over its last 5 years, especially in the areas of community corrections and economic sanctions.

[5] By "major forms of criminal punishment," we mean penalties imposed on large numbers of people.

[6] A similar pattern holds for the American death penalty, which saw a resurgence in the 1970s, 1980s, and 1990s, after nearly disappearing across the 1960s and early 1970s. Even at its recent peak, however, it affected a vanishingly small number of people compared with the many millions in prison and jail, or on probation and parole (Reitz 2018, p. 6).

a quintupling of the nation's incarceration rate (Cahalan 1986, tables 3–4, 4–1; Sabol, West, and Cooper 2009, table 5; Minton et al. 2015, table 2). No other country experienced a parallel incarceration explosion during the same period, and no country—including the United States—had ever seen such a historic phenomenon. By the 1990s, America had drawn neck and neck with Russia for the "leadership" position in the world's incarceration rates (The Sentencing Project 2001). The United States became the undisputed "winner" around the turn of the century and remains number one today.

We became an international leader in other ways, too. By the 1990s and 2000s, using available data, the United States had become an outlier among Western democracies in its uses of all mainstream forms of criminal punishment (Reitz 2018). To describe where the country ended up, we have no quarrel with the terms "mass imprisonment" or "mass incarceration," which have come into popular usage. Sadly, however, these terms underdescribe the current American predicament. We prefer to say that the nation has reached a condition of "mass punishment" that goes beyond incarceration and touches a far greater share of the US population than the 2 million in prison and jail.

For instance, across America there were 3.7 million adults under sentences of probation supervision on any given day in 2016 (Kaeble 2018, p. 1). In 1976, the average daily count of probationers was about 923,000 (Cahalan 1986, table 7–8A). Over the same 40-year period, the parole supervision population multiplied from 156,000 to 875,000. In other words, probationer counts quadrupled and parolees quintupled—during a time span in which the total US population grew by less than 50 percent. Trend lines this steep are worrisome in themselves, but it is equally illuminating to compare the United States with other countries in the wake of the community-supervision buildup. We do not know if America is the world leader in supervision rates (it could be), because we lack data for most countries. However, MPCS-allied research found that US probation supervision rates in 2014 were five to 10 times those of Western and Eastern European countries—roughly the same outsized ratio as comparative incarceration rates (Alper, Corda, and Reitz 2016; Rhine and Taxman 2018; van Zyl Smit and Corda 2018).[7]

---

[7] The research grew out of activities of the Robina Institute of Criminal Law and Criminal Justice, conceived to run in parallel with MPCS drafting. Reporters Reitz and Klingele were heavily involved in the planning and execution of Robina Institute projects from 2011–18, in symbiosis with their American Law Institute duties.

The same growth trends, and the same drive toward international preeminence, are apparent in America's use of economic sanctions and its ever-increasing slate of collateral consequences of conviction (Bannon, Nagrecha, and Diller 2010; Beckett and Harris 2011; American Law Institute 2017*b*, § 6.04 and comment *a*). Here are just a few of those developments. The victims' rights movement, first building momentum in the 1980s, brought about a revolution in victim restitution orders in criminal cases, which are now mandatory in many states regardless of the defendant's ability to pay. As local courts, governments, and criminal justice agencies have become poorer, they have increasingly looked to people accused of crime as new sources of revenue through the multiplication of fines, fees, costs, and other assessments—a trend that seems not to have abated. Police and county sheriffs' departments, allowed to retain assets seized from citizens via civil forfeiture laws (usually without criminal charges), have become ever more active in the forfeiture line of work. The "economic sanctions buildup" overlapped with a period of worsening wealth and income inequalities in the United States, which could only have amplified the felt intensity of these new punishment practices. We think it fair to include economic sanctions as a substantial component of the mass punishment buildup more generally. In much the same way, beginning in the 1980s, laws authorizing collateral consequences have been enacted at federal, state, and local levels, increasingly cutting off the ability of people who have served their criminal sentences to obtain employment, secure housing, obtain student loans, and vote (Pinard 2010; Meek 2014). Although data about the prevalence of collateral consequences in other nations are difficult to obtain, the available evidence suggests that, as in all other areas of sanctioning, the United States is an outlier, imposing more consequences, more automatically, on a larger segment of convicted individuals, for longer periods of time (Pinard 2010; Corda 2018; Demleitner 2018).

In addition to their sheer scale, criminal punishments in the United States are shot through with racial and ethnic disproportionalities. Generally speaking, across American prisons, jails, and parole and probation systems, the amplitudes of racial and ethnic disparities tend to increase in relation to the severity of the punishment type examined.[8] In other words, more severity often comes with greater disparity. Some mental adjust-

---

[8] Black-white disparities in imposition of the death penalty are similar to those in prison and jail populations. If we correct for representation in the general population, the black

ments need to be made when interpreting statewide or national statistics in this area. Within minority groups, the poor experience heightened risks of criminal punishment compared with the better off. Among the most disadvantaged Americans, especially African Americans, the felt intensity of criminal sentencing policy is far greater than is suggested by aggregated official statistics (Wilson 1987; Western 2006; Tonry 2011; Goffman 2015). And the official statistics are bleak enough.

The US Bureau of Justice Statistics reported that the nationwide African American imprisonment rate in 2016 was 5.2 times that for whites, the Latino rate was 2.6 times higher, and the Native American rate was twice as high (Beck and Blumstein 2018; Carson 2018, table 5, p. 7; table 6, p. 8). Disparities in jail confinement rates were also reported, albeit at lower levels than in the prisons (disparity ratios of 3.4, 1.1, and 1.2, respectively; Zeng 2018, table 1, p. 2). With more than 2 million people incarcerated overall, this adds up to a high level of "carceral intensity" experienced by discrete population groups as a constant feature of community life. The Pew Charitable Trusts reported that roughly "one in 9" (not a misprint) black men age 20–34 were in prison or jail on any given day in 2007 (Pew Center on the States 2008, p. 6). The ratio was even more shocking in the poorest black neighborhoods (Western 2006).

Racial and ethnic disparities also run through most of America's vast community supervision populations—totaling 4.5 million in 2016 on any given day. In that year, according to national statistics, the African American parole supervision rate was four times greater than for whites. The black-white ratio of probation supervision rates was more than 2:1. Hispanics and Native Americans were more than 10 percent overrepresented among parolee populations but were 9 percent underrepresented among probationers (Kaeble 2018, app. table 4, p. 17; app. table 8, p. 24).[9]

We have no official "counts" or "rates" to compare the intensity of application of economic sanctions and collateral consequences of conviction across demographic subgroups. We do have quite a bit of localized

---

rate of presence on death row in 2016 was 4.1 times the white rate. The Hispanic-white disparity ratio was 1.2:1, with no Native American statistics reported (Davis and Snell 2018, table 2, p. 4; estimates of Hispanic representation among blacks and whites based on Beck and Blumstein [2018, p. 862]).

[9] We do not know how to interpret these last underrepresentations on probation, except to say that prison disparities can be fueled in part by a tendency of particular groups to be refused probation more often than one would expect and receive prison sentences instead. This dynamic may also help explain the relatively "low" 2:1 black-white disparities among probationers, when disparities in incarceration and on parole are at least twice as large.

and anecdotal evidence, however. For example, the US Justice Department's investigation of the police department in Ferguson, Missouri, found that the collection of municipal fines and fees—largely used to support the local government—was concentrated in poor minority neighborhoods. The same thing has been happening in other parts of the country (US Department of Justice 2015; Lawyers' Committee for Civil Rights 2017). There have been many journalistic accounts of law enforcement agencies use of asset forfeiture laws around the country and many demonstrations at the local level that poor and black people suffer most (Lexington 2010; Stillman 2013; Balko 2017). In the domain of collateral consequences and their lifelong effects on the formerly convicted, we have strong circumstantial evidence of racial and ethnic disparities simply because the people who are arrested and convicted in the United States are disproportionately African American, Hispanic, and Native American. There is little question that the disabilities inflicted through collateral consequences have greater effects on poor people than on those better insulated by their money (Alexander 2010; Pinard 2010).

Today, the United States seems to be at a historical inflection point between the punishment buildup and whatever comes next. Thirty-five straight years of growth in national incarceration rates peaked in 2007–8, and since then there has been a slight decline. The nation's expanding community supervision rates also topped out in 2008 and dropped 18 percent by 2016 (Kaeble 2018, app. table 1, pp. 11–12). Although no longer included in the Model Penal Code, use of the death penalty has been dwindling in the twenty-first century, from a high of 98 executions in 1999 to 23 in 2017 (Death Penalty Information Center 2018, p. 1). Crime rates across the country have dropped a great deal since 1992—a massive change that followed a very long bad stretch. In the 30 years prior to the early nineties, the nation had lived through one decade of spiking crime rates followed by two decades of persistently high rates (Reitz 2018, pp. 22–28).[10]

All of these trends, with arrows pointing downward, may augur a weakening of the forces that drove the nation's buildup to mass punishment.[11]

---

[10] Ruth and Reitz (2003) called this the "crime spike" of 1962–72, followed by 20 years of a "high-crime plateau." Homicide rates doubled during the crime spike, and reported rates of robbery, rape, and aggravated assault skyrocketed even faster. From 1972–92, rates of serious violent crime oscillated over several-year periods, but the oscillation occurred around median levels established at the peak of the crime spike (pp. 98–102).

[11] It is harder to say whether there has been an overall softening in the uses of economic penalties and collateral consequences of conviction, partly because there is no reporting

There has been a great deal of talk, on both sides of the political aisle, about sentencing reform and broader criminal justice reform. So far, however, changes in law and practice have been modest. The good news is that there is a great deal of openness to reform in many state and local governments. There is widespread sentiment that the trajectory of criminal punishment over the past several decades was a serious mistake. Sentiment does not always translate into workable ideas for law reform, however, and can dissipate without much result.

If the present era holds genuine potential as a turning point, it would be a shame to squander the opportunity. Responsible officials need information about practical measures they can take to make their sentencing systems less gargantuan, more humane, less wasteful, more just, and more effective. Ideally, these should be lasting reforms, not crisis-driven Band-Aids. The MPCS is the product of years of effort to meet such practical needs. While it has no force of law, it does have the force that comes from speaking to subjects of dire necessity in need of invention.

III. Racial and Ethnic Disparities in Punishment

The primary MPCS approaches to disproportionalities in punishment are to ensure the issue never drops from sight, require sentencing commissions to search for causes of racial and ethnic disparities in the sentencing system on a continuing basis, charge the commissions to recommend ameliorative measures whenever disparities are found, and mandate that statistical demographic impact projections be prepared every time a change in sentencing law or guidelines is proposed—that is, a "demographic impact statement" to go alongside the familiar fiscal impact statement.

By itself, the demographic impact statement (or DIS) could fundamentally alter the evolution of American sentencing law. The goals of the DIS are to shine a spotlight on sensitive information when it matters the most, provoke debate before new laws are passed, and create a record for legislative accountability in the long run. These are not uninformed hopes.

---

system to keep track of the breadth of their use. Our guess is that economic and collateral sanctions remain on the increase in most states. New counterforces have appeared on the horizon, however, including upsurges in policy research, academic study, advocacy, public awareness, and law-reform initiatives. If we count expressions of concern as tea leaves of actual moderation in practice, then, again, there may be movement away from the punishment buildup.

Over the past several decades, sobering fiscal impact statements have caused many states to soften or abandon proposed sentencing legislation or guidelines. This has especially been true in the sentencing guidelines states that have developed the most sophisticated corrections modeling tools. Repeatedly, almost to the point of routine in some states, we have seen that credible forewarning of consequences can be a conversation changer.

One of the MPCS's cornerstone provisions, section 8.07, would require all state sentencing commissions to develop a "correctional forecasting model," building on the best practices already in use in a number of states. (In our experience, the states with the most advanced software do not consider it proprietary.) Taking a further step—and a big one—the MPCS advocates a broadening of the scope of the forecasting model to include anticipated changes in sentencing outcomes broken down by race, ethnicity, and gender (American Law Institute 2017a, § 8.07(1), (3)).

In 2007, Minnesota became the first state to experiment with the MPCS's proposal (Reitz 2009; London 2011). This was done as a matter of sentencing commission policy rather than statutory command (Minnesota Sentencing Guidelines Commission 2017).[12] Over the past decade, Iowa, Connecticut, Oregon, and New Jersey have enacted some form of "racial impact statement" legislation (Mauer 2009; The Sentencing Project 2018).[13] None of these states follows the MPCS recommendations exactly. Most DIS legislation was developed by states in partnership with The Sentencing Project, and the laws all bear scars of political compromise.[14] Still, the

---

[12] Although the MPCS as a whole did not receive final approval until 2017, the DIS proposal dates back to 2002 and won "tentative approval" as official ALI policy in 2007 (American Law Institute 2002, § 1.02(2)(e); 2007, § 6A.07(3)). The inspiration for the DIS was Michael Tonry's argument that Congress and other lawmakers should be held morally accountable for foreseeable racial disparities in punishment that result from their enactments (Tonry 1995, pp. vii–viii, 104–5).

[13] See Iowa Code § 2.56(1); Conn. Gen. Stat. § 2.24b; Ore. Rev. Stat. §§ 137.656, 137.683, and 137.685; and S. 677, 217th Leg. (N.J. 2018). The DIS goes by several different names. The Minnesota Sentencing Guidelines Commission used the term "racial impact statement" until 2017 and then switched to "demographic impact statement" (Minnesota Sentencing Guidelines Commission 2017). In recent New Jersey legislation, the DIS is named the "racial and ethnic community criminal justice and public safety impact statement" (S. 677, 217th Leg. [N.J. 2018]).

[14] For example, in Connecticut and Oregon, a DIS is not drawn up routinely when new laws affecting correctional populations are introduced. Instead, in Connecticut from 2008 through 2018, a DIS was prepared only when requested by a majority of the Joint Standing Committee of the General Assembly on Judiciary. In Oregon, a request must be lodged by at least two members of the Legislative Assembly from opposite parties (Ore. Rev. Stat. §

number of states that have taken an interest is encouraging. We can now count five states with active DIS statutes or policies of one form or another. In seven other states, DIS proposals have been put forward, so far without success (Erickson 2014).

To our knowledge, the uses and effects of the "demographic" or "racial" impact projections in the five adopting states have not yet been studied. The Minnesota sentencing commission, however, has generated more information on the use of the DIS than any other state. From this, we have evidence of the feasibility of preparing a DIS in addition to fiscal impact statements and solid examples of the kind of information a DIS can add to the lawmaking process.

In one early use of the tool, Minnesota's sentencing commission forecast the demographic effects of proposed legislation to raise the penalties for attempted robbery to the same level as for the completed crime (Minnesota Sentencing Guidelines Commission 2008). The DIS included projected effects on whites, blacks, Hispanics, Asians, and American Indians. To illustrate, we focus on the discussion of African Americans in comparison with whites.

The commission's impact report laid out some basic statistics of the current system before analyzing the proposed bill. In 2006, 4.3 percent of Minnesota's general population was black, yet blacks made up a much larger 32.1 percent of the state's prison population. In turn, whites were 86 percent of the general population and 61.6 percent of those in prison (Minnesota Sentencing Guidelines Commission 2008). While the commission's report did not calculate the "disparity ratio" between black and white prison rates, the math is easily done: the black prison rate at the time in Minnesota was more than 10 times the white rate.

The commission then estimated the effects of the new law, if passed. It found, based on felony conviction data for attempted robbery, that 61.1 percent of those expected to receive enhanced penalties under the new law would be black, and 25.9 percent would be white. In addition, the commission anticipated that the average increase in prison terms under the new law would be 10 months for blacks and 8 months for whites

---

137.683(2)(a)). In Connecticut, the absence of a routine-triggering mechanism has led to extremely limited use of the DIS tool. From 2008 through 2014, only one DIS was generated in the state, compared to 45 in Iowa over the same period (Erickson 2014, pp. 1447–48). Connecticut recently amended its law to require preparation of a DIS at the request of any member of the General Assembly, to take effect next year; see Conn. Gen. Stat. § 2.24b(a) (effective January 19, 2019).

(Minnesota Sentencing Guidelines Commission 2008, pp. 1–2).[15] Based on these projections, blacks in Minnesota would have been subject to the increased penalties for attempted robbery at 47 times the rate of whites, and the average increase in prison stay for blacks was expected to be 25 percent longer than for whites. In other words, the projected black/white disparities were jaw dropping.

The 2008 attempted robbery bill did not pass and was never reintroduced, but we cannot prove that the DIS was an important factor in its demise. No one has yet created a statistical measure, or oral history approach, to document the role actually played by a DIS in legislative debate or decision-making. Over 10 years of use, we have occasionally heard from Minnesota government insiders that a DIS has made a difference in stopping a particular bill. While such anecdotal opinions are encouraging, a serious study of DIS-caused effects should be high on the criminal justice research agenda.

With respect to the 2008 attempted robbery DIS, all we can say with confidence is that the information it contained was explosive. While that particular bill probably failed for other reasons,[16] it is useful to imagine how a similar DIS would play out in the debate of an otherwise popular bill. We firmly believe a DIS as extreme as the 2008 example would be a deal breaker, ethically and politically, for many legislators.

There are two more MPCS lines of attack on disproportionalities in punishment. The first is easy to overlook, but its importance should not be underestimated. Among the sentencing commission's data collection responsibilities, the MPCS adds a critical duty that no state currently imposes. Every commission must develop information systems to track the demographic characteristics of victims as well as offenders—a task that will require cooperation from other criminal justice agencies (American Law Institute 2017a, §§ 8.05(2)(c), 8.08(1), (2)). The importance of victim demographic information is potentially enormous. We know from studies of capital sentencing that the race of murder victims is a powerful predictor of which defendants receive the death penalty. In the most fa-

---

[15] The longer increase in time served for blacks was largely due to the fact that, in historical data, the average black person convicted of attempted robbery in Minnesota had a somewhat higher criminal history score than the average white person convicted of the same offense.

[16] At the time, we were told that all bills projected to increase prison costs were "dead on arrival" in the statehouse because of a statewide budget crisis. So, the DIS may have played no role at all or simply reinforced a preordained conclusion.

mous study, a murder case with a white victim was four times more likely to result in a death sentence than a case with a black victim. This victim-race-based effect was several times stronger than the disparity in outcome based on the race of the defendant (*McCleskey v. Kemp*, 481 U.S. 279 [1987]; Baldus, Woodworth, and Pulaski 1990).

If the race of murder victims had not been a focus of capital punishment research, the most shocking racial malfunctions in death penalty administration would not have been noticed. Yet, in the larger realm of subcapital sentencing, disparity research and statistical tracking focuses almost exclusively on offenders' personal characteristics, with no effort to collate victim demographics (Ruth and Reitz 2003). We predict that the collection of basic victim data could transform our understanding of racial and ethnic disparities in sentencing—possibly in unsettling ways. Stated more neutrally, no serious effort to combat disparities in criminal punishment in America can afford to ignore the currently unknown effects of victim characteristics on sentence severity. The MPCS would place the issue on every state's agenda, while today it is a question given no priority at all.

Finally, we believe the most consequential measures to ease the impact of US sentencing policies on minority communities will be overall reductions in the enormous scale and reach of any and all of the mainstream forms of punishment. Aggregate reductions could have very large indirect effects on the inequities of disparate punishment. For example, if the current ratio of black-white disparities in incarceration is 5:1, then a 25 percent reduction in aggregate prison and jail populations will benefit a much larger number of African Americans than whites, if all else is held equal. We will assume the 5:1 disparity ratio will remain unchanged and unimproved. On these assumptions, the "same" 25 percent overall incarceration drop would have five times more deincarcerative impact within black communities than among the white population.[17] The felt reduction of punitive intensity in the most disadvantaged black neighborhoods would be orders of magnitude greater.

---

[17] Using simplified numbers, suppose the black incarceration rate is 1,000 per 100,000 blacks in the general population, and the white incarceration rate is 200 per 100,000 whites. A 25 percent reduction in incarceration rates while holding the 5:1 disparity ratio constant would benefit 250 blacks per 100,000 but only 50 whites per 100,000. (The postreduction incarceration rates would be 750 per 100,000 for blacks and 150 per 100,000 for whites.)

On this reasoning, all of the MPCS limits on mass punishment, if effective, would carry benefits for every demographic group but could carry massive benefits for the minority subpopulations who were hit hardest and most disproportionately by the punishment buildup.

IV. General Sentencing Policy in the MPCS

To understand the MPCS's reexamination of mass punishment in America, we must begin with the first principles that drive everything else in the MPCS sentencing system. The opening section, the "purposes provision," lays out the affirmative objectives of sentencing and the sentencing system, and—just as importantly—places policy-driven limits on the pursuit of those goals (American Law Institute 2017a, § 1.02(2)). Indeed, line by line, the provision spends more ink on principles of restraint than on forward-driving objectives. In this respect, § 1.02(2) differs from most existing state legislation. Even more importantly, the statutory purposes of sentencing are enforceable throughout the MPCS system. In most states this is not so—a typical purposes provision is more decoration than law. To ensure its centrality in state sentencing laws, § 1.02(2) is expressly incorporated into dozens of later provisions and is made the backbone of many important decision points.

The MPCS describes its policy framework as "utilitarianism within limits of proportionality" (American Law Institute 2017b, p. 370). The general idea is that reasoned utilitarian sentencing is permissible and desirable, so long as the result is not a disproportionate punishment (see Morris 1974; Morris and Miller 1985; Frase 2013, pp. 82–84).[18] The most "Olympian" portions of § 1.02(2) lay out the core elements of the MPCS thought process:

Section 1.02(2). Purposes of Sentencing and the Sentencing System.
 The general purposes of the provisions on sentencing, applicable to all official actors in the sentencing system, are:

---

[18] Norval Morris famously named this theory "limiting retributivism"—a choice of wording the MPCS does not adopt. One reason for different terminology is that the idea of "retribution" has acquired negative connotations in the decades since Morris first wrote. Many people now associate retribution with unrestrained punitive impulses or see it as a dressing up of emotions of vengeance that should not be encouraged in law (Rubin 2001; Whitman 2003). To avoid such possible readings, the MPCS's use of "proportionality" emphasizes the inhibiting power of retributive thought.

(a) in decisions affecting the sentencing of individual offenders:

   (i) to render sentences in all cases within a range of severity proportionate to the gravity of offenses, the harms done to crime victims, and the blameworthiness of offenders;
   (ii) when reasonably feasible, to achieve offender rehabilitation, general deterrence, incapacitation of dangerous offenders, restitution to crime victims, preservation of families, and reintegration of offenders into the law-abiding community, provided these goals are pursued within the boundaries of proportionality in Subsection (a)(i);
   (iii) to render sentences no more severe than necessary to achieve the applicable purposes in Subsections (a)(i) and (a)(ii); and
   (iv) to avoid the use of sanctions that increase the likelihood offenders will engage in future criminal conduct.

The last two subdivisions above are entirely limiting in nature, and we do not discuss them further. They are both important—subsection (iv) is groundbreaking—but we trust the basic ideas are easy to grasp from their black-letter language. Subsections (a)(i) and (ii) are more complex. They articulate affirmative purposes to be pursued through criminal sanctions but are also self-regulating in two important ways. They create a "proportionality constraint" for all of criminal sentencing and an "assessment constraint" on the pursuit of utilitarian goals. These principles bear some explanation.

A. The Proportionality Constraint

Subsections (i) and (ii) in the excerpt above establish the MPCS's "proportionality constraint."[19] While proportionality in punishment is hardly an original concept, the MPCS attempts to implement it in new ways that will give it genuine meaning in American law. For one thing, the MPCS makes proportionality a meaningful and enforceable element of sentencing law, a benchmark "with teeth." It does so statutorily, with no reliance on constitutional law. The premise is that no legal principle of proportionality in punishment operated as an effective inhibitor of any part of

---

[19] Proportionality in § 1.02(2)(a)(i) also serves as an affirmative basis for punishment. The MPCS contemplates cases in which the consideration of proportionality is a sufficient condition for criminal punishment of some kind, including very serious cases in which anything short of an extended prison term would be disproportionately lenient (see American Law Institute 2017a, § 6.11(2)(b)).

the punishment buildup from the early 1970s through the late 2000s. The constitutional law of proportionality shrank to a weak and ineffectual stature during America's punishment buildup—just when, arguably, it was most needed (Ristroph 2006).

Over the past several decades, challenges to disproportionate sentences have mainly been rooted in the Eighth Amendment of the US Constitution. Most of them have been spectacularly unsuccessful. For instance, the Supreme Court in *Harmelin v. Michigan*, 501 U.S. 957 (1991); *Ewing v. California*, 538 U.S. 11 (2003); and *Lockyer v. Andrade*, 538 U.S. 63 (2003) upheld sentences of life without parole for a first-time drug offender caught with a large amount of cocaine and decades-long sentences for minor offenses under California's three-strikes law. To be found unconstitutionally "cruel and unusual" in cases like these, a sentence must be deemed "grossly disproportionate" in relation to an offender's crime, criminal record, and any danger the defendant might pose in the future. In applying this standard, courts have developed habits of extreme deference to legislative authorizations and sentencing court rulings. Putting aside juvenile and capital cases, gross disproportionality is a test that can almost never be met.

Despite the vacuum in constitutional jurisprudence, we know few people willing to complete the following sentence: "Disproportionately severe criminal punishments are justifiable, and should be recommended in model legislation, when. . . ." Or: "We are in favor of life sentences for people who don't deserve them when. . . ." If readers cannot comfortably fill in these blanks, or can think only of unreasonably extreme examples, then they are in substantial agreement with the MPCS that a proportionality constraint is needed whenever sentences are envisioned, threatened, imposed, or modified.

The harder questions come in the implementation of the idea. How is proportionality to be defined (if it's even possible to do so) and who gets to define it? Who gets to apply the principle in real cases? How do we avoid the trap of a toothless doctrine that is never used?

The first important step the MPCS takes is to reinvent proportionality as a statutory imperative. To make clear that a purely statutory power is envisioned, MPCS commentary uses the term "*subconstitutional* proportionality review" (American Law Institute 2017*b*, pp. 5, 9, 505–7, 523–24). The second step of the MPCS's strategy is to give its statutory proportionality review the range and horsepower to reduce any sentence otherwise authorized or required by state law—including the ability to override mandatory minimum prison terms (American Law Institute 2017a, §§ 10.01(2), (3)(b), 10.10(5)(b)).

Third, proportionality analysis under the MPCS must be applied to the entire package of legal sanctions that a criminal defendant will face as a result of conviction, including the nominally "civil" collateral consequences that are likely to be applied. Regardless of how collateral sanctions are formally classified, they add to defendants' subjective experiences of punishment and have ripple effects across all the utilitarian policies of criminal punishment. Therefore, the MPCS provides: "The court may not impose any combination of sanctions if their total severity would result in disproportionate punishment. In evaluating the total severity of punishment under this Subsection, the court should consider the effects of collateral consequences likely to be applied to the offender under state and federal law, to the extent these can reasonably be determined" (American Law Institute 2017a, § 6.02(4)).

Finally, the MPCS steers well clear of the permissive standards of review found in constitutional law and includes unusually strong wording intended to rule out the long-established norms of appellate court deference to sentencing judges' decisions: "The appellate courts may reverse, remand, or modify any sentence, including a sentence imposed under a mandatory-penalty provision, on the ground that it is disproportionately severe. The appellate court shall use its independent judgment when applying this provision" (American Law Institute 2017a, § 10.10 (5)(b)). To the legally trained ear, the "independent judgment" standard is a striking delegation of power to the appellate courts. Usually on subjective issues like this, standards for reversal are not triggered unless an appellate court finds an "abuse of discretion," "clear error," or an outcome no reasonable person can abide. The MPCS's innovation is warranted, however. Today, there is no final arbiter of sentencing proportionality in any American legal system. Only the distant goal line of "gross disproportionality" is ever—albeit rarely—policed.

The MPCS offers an institutional solution to this problem. Yes, proportionality is a principle that all actors in the MPCS system are called upon to honor, but it does not snap into an effective legal instrument until someone is given final, dispositive power. The buck must stop somewhere, or proportionality is adrift. As with much of the law, the identity of the decision-making authority is a question that can be answered, even if there is no prior consensus on correct answers. In the MPCS, the ultimate powers to define proportionality through precedent, and to reverse individual sentences that are disproportionately severe, are placed in the judiciary. It is a major advance in American law, we believe, to empower such a final "subconstitutional" decision maker.

B. The Assessment Constraint

The MPCS also introduces a new "assessment constraint" on the pursuit of utilitarian goals via criminal sentences. Utilitarian purposes may be pursued only "when reasonably feasible" (American Law Institute 2017a, § 1.02(2)(a)(ii)).[20] This standard is a creation of the MPCS, with no prior incarnation in American law. And yet, as explained in commentary, the assessment constraint codifies what ought to be an uncontroversial principle, in a relatively mild way:

> One test for the reasonable feasibility of a utilitarian penalty is whether there is a realistic basis to suppose that the specific utilitarian objective can be achieved through administration of a criminal sanction. Thus, for example, the intuition that a defendant will be dangerous in the future (formed, for example, by a judge or a parole board) would not be enough to support an extended prison term on incapacitative grounds. There must be some reasonable ground for the prediction of future criminal behavior. . . . The threshold of reasonable feasibility . . . does not require scientific proof that a given sanction imposed on a particular offender will yield a known result. It demands only that there be grounds that support a reasonable belief that the utilitarian benefit will be realized. (American Law Institute 2017b, pp. 9–10)

The assessment constraint is meant to bring the question of reasonable feasibility into the foreground, when in the past it has been overlooked to the point of obliviousness. Even a modest requirement of reasonable feasibility would be a seismic change in commonplace American sentencing practices. For example: the most difficult utilitarian strategy to defend, in light of current knowledge, is the pursuit of general deterrence through the use or threat of increasingly severe penalties. Serious criminologists have found little or no empirical evidence of the deterrence-through-severity hypothesis (in contrast with findings that increases in

---

[20] More prosaically, the idea of reasonable feasibility also rules out the consideration of purposes that are simply not apposite to a particular case, such as the goal of victim restitution when there is no victim.

the speed and likelihood of punishment can promote general deterrence; von Hirsch et al. 1999; Webster and Doob 2012; Nagin 2013; Travis, Western, and Redburn 2014, chap. 5). Similarly, some well-intended rehabilitative programs have been shown to increase, rather than decrease, participants' risk of reoffending (Martinson 1974; Cullen et al. 2005; Center for the Study and Prevention of Violence 2010). When persuasive evidence surfaces that a utilitarian intervention is not a plausible way to achieve its goals, the assessment constraint can be mobilized to discourage its continued use. As stated elsewhere in the purposes provision, one heartfelt goal of the MPCS is to weed out sentences that are themselves criminogenic (American Law Institute 2017*a*, § 1.02(2)(a)(iv)). Unfortunately, serious study of criminal sentences across the United States yields a surprising number of examples.

V. The MPCS on Prison and Jail Sentences

The problems of "mass incarceration" were high on the minds of everyone connected to the MPCS drafting process (although the term is not officially adopted in the MPCS or its comments). There was consensus from the beginning, never questioned over 15 years, that the MPCS should aim toward major changes in the scale and use of prison and jail sentences nationwide. This concern is embedded in nearly all of the MPCS, even in provisions with no express reference to incarceration policy.[21]

A. Institutional "System Design"

The entire institutional structure of the MPCS is designed to bring prison size, jail populations, and the use of all other correctional resources under the deliberate control and management of state policy makers. In broad brush, the MPCS system includes a permanent sentencing commission empowered to promulgate presumptive sentencing guidelines. Importantly, the commission must be required to create guidelines projected to yield sentenced populations that will fit the capacities of existing (or funded) correctional resources. An important component of such a

---

[21] Over the years of drafting, the ALI leadership and membership became convinced that all other forms of mainstream criminal punishments in the United States had exploded to crisis levels, along with prison and jail populations. This extended what otherwise might have been an 8- to 9-year project to a full 15 years.

system is a modicum of guidelines enforceability through appellate review of trial court sentences. Finally, several decades of experience suggest that it is difficult to control prison populations if parole boards are the central decision makers with power over time served. The MPCS, for this and other reasons, advocates that the prison-release discretion of state parole boards should be eliminated, so that lengths of prison stays are for the most part a product of judges' sentences and predictable goodtime discounts.

It is a fundamental goal of the MPCS system "to ensure that adequate resources are available for carrying out sentences imposed and that rational priorities are established for the use of those resources" (American Law Institute 2017*a*, § 1.02(2)(b)(iv)). The commentary calls this the capability of "correctional resource management" (CRM; American Law Institute 2017*b*, pp. 16, 32–33). CRM tools can inhibit or reverse prison growth, if those outcomes are desired in a particular state. They can also reprioritize the use of existing bed spaces (e.g., incarcerating serious violent offenders for longer terms and fewer drug offenders for shorter terms). Admittedly, CRM tools can also be used to push incarceration rates upward, if that is a state's policy goal (Zimring 1977; Tonry 1993). Indeed, the federal sentencing system was a splendid success at doing exactly this—for two solid decades. In the history of state sentencing systems, however, CRM has generally been used to slow or stop incarceration growth (Frase 2013). The main reasons for this, we think, are that prisons and jails are expensive, they are a significant chunk of all spending at state and local levels, and state governments must balance their budgets.

Importantly, CRM is not concerned only with the bottom line of total spending. It has been used in a number of states to "tilt" the use of existing prison spaces toward violent offenders (Wright 2002; Frase 2005). Incremental leniency can then be apportioned across nonviolent criminals, who are the much larger group among convicted felons. Line-by-line adjustments of this kind are possible with or without changes in prison size. In a deincarceration era, they are a way to make prison downsizing as policy responsive as possible.

CRM extends beyond incarceration to cover the resources required by community corrections and rehabilitative programming throughout the system. These are not separate issues. For example, a state may want to divert large numbers of drug offenders, currently receiving prison sentences, to treatment programs in their communities. In order to do so, the state must find ways to get trial judges to alter their sentencing patterns en masse, and the state must be in a position to project costs and fund the necessary community treatment slots in time for the inflow of new clients. Most states are extraordinarily poor at this kind of medium-term planning, but a few states (North Carolina is high on the list) have made strides toward purposeful resource allocation across different divisions of corrections (Wright 2002). In our view, successful deincarceration policy will often depend on a synchronized beefing up of community programming and services.

The major institutional building blocks of CRM in the MPCS are drawn from decades of experience in a handful of states, starting with Minnesota in 1980. The major elements of system design in the MPCS are in this sense "proven."[22] You need a sentencing commission with serious research capacity, good models for fiscal impact projections, and the ability to create sentencing guidelines that are, at least to a modest extent, legally enforceable. The commission must be ordered to tailor its guidelines to available resources or to whatever levels of funding the state desires to commit for the future. For the right degree of enforceability of guidelines, you need appellate review of sentencing decisions, with some deference to trial courts (but not too much), and full power to correct legal errors. With luck, this setup will generate a predictable bell curve of sentencing patterns centered on the "presumptive" sentences indicated by guidelines. If overall patterns are reasonably forecastable, so are future expenses. If the projected costs are too high, the commission can revise its guidelines accordingly (American Law Institute 2003).

For CRM to work, you also need some way to predict how long sentences will actually be, on average, after they are imposed. For this and other reasons, the MPCS recommends abolition of the prison release discretion of parole boards. In the traditional framework, parole boards can and do change prison policy with every governor, after every headline case of a released prisoner who does something horrible, with approaching elections, before and after lunch, or at the drop of some other hat (Travis 2002; Reitz 2012).

---

[22] Of course, "proven" successes of the past do not guarantee continued successes in the future. It is wrong to be entirely agnostic, however. We believe that the institutional model for the MPCS system—basically the Minnesota model—has worked well in a number of states because of sound design, down to the level of details, supported by reasons why it should work. Many hundreds of pages of commentary in the MPCS explain each "design decision" within the greater whole.

Contrary to conventional wisdom, parole boards in the 1980s, 1990s, and 2000s were not in the business of reducing sentences but were turning into "parole denial boards." Nationwide trends in parole release ran in the direction of greater severity and longer prison stays as boards became more vulnerable to political pressure and more risk averse. One trial judge in Pennsylvania complained to us that he once sentenced a defendant to 5–10 years in prison on the assumption that it would translate into 5 years of time actually served until release. In fact, by the time 5 years had gone by, the state parole board was keeping prisoners in for much longer than before, so that the defendant's actual prison term was likely to be much closer to 10 years. The parole board had effectively resentenced the defendant to more than the judge's intended punishment, out of sync with its own norms several years earlier. This pattern appears to have been a common one in paroling states. At the peak of the prison buildup, states with indeterminate sentencing systems had significantly more prison growth, and had reached much higher prison rates on average, than states that abolished their parole boards' release discretion. On average, states with determinate systems and sentencing guidelines experienced the least growth in prison rates during the buildup years (Stemen and Rengifo 2010; American Law Institute 2011, app. B).

On questions of system design and the benefits of CRM, the MPCS relies on decades of experience in states such as Minnesota, Washington, Kansas, North Carolina, and Virginia (Knapp 1986; Anderson 1993; Wright 1997; Hunt 1998; Boerner and Lieb 2001; Frase 2013). There is a track record standing behind all of the MPCS's recommendations, albeit in a small minority of states. To our knowledge, the American Law Institute did not produce any revolutionary ideas concerning institutional design.[23] Rather, the MPCS plagiarized from the more successful states and combined all of the best ideas the reporters could "borrow." In the model legislation business, this is considered an especially solid foundation (and not, we hope, intellectual thievery). The CRM

---

[23] The possible exception is the MPCS's provision on correctional overcrowding, which creates mostly administrative mechanisms to reduce prison, jail, probation, and postrelease supervision populations when they exceed operational capacities (American Law Institute 2017a, § 11.04). Emergency release statutes already exist in a dozen states for prison populations (a few for jails, too). These laws have not been used very often, however, and the MPCS tries to fashion a new approach that will be more effective. In addition, no state has ever created a safety valve for overcrowding in community supervision populations. This is probably the MPCS's major innovation in system design, but we have yet to see whether it will be attractive to state legislatures and successful when adopted.

tools created in Minnesota for controlling prison population growth have worked reasonably well in a number of states. This is an impressive achievement in criminal justice reform; most well-intentioned ideas fail miserably (Rothman 1980; Feeley 1983; Marvell 1995, p. 707). There may be other methods of bringing correctional populations under control, including ideas of our own, but the only proven and replicated approach is the presumptive-sentencing-guidelines-determinate-sentencing model pioneered in Minnesota.

B. Multiple Attacks on Mandatory Minimum Prison Sentences

A good sentencing guidelines system is one way to implement deliberate controls over prison and jail population sizes. The restraining power of guidelines can be thrown out the window, however, through operation of mandatory imprisonment laws that "trump" the guidelines. Mostly these are statutory, although a number have been brought in by voter initiative. In some states and the federal system, prison growth has been driven in large degree by mandatory minimum sentencing laws that, once enacted, take on a life of their own. Typically, sentencing commissions must work within a superstructure of sentencing statutes that they have no power to change. This is a recipe for uncontrollable incarceration rates.

The American Law Institute, like other law reform organizations, has long disapproved of all mandatory minimum imprisonment laws. The original Model Penal Code expressed its blanket condemnation by negative implication: Judges were always given the option to impose a probation sentence, or suspended prison term, no matter how serious the offense of conviction. "Mandatories," as they are sometimes called, were ruled out by omission (American Law Institute 2017*b*, p. 145).

The MPCS continues the original Model Penal Code's across-the-board policy with some added layers. First, the MPCS includes black-letter language that expressly supersedes all mandatory minimum penalties enacted in the past: "The court is not required to impose a minimum term of incarceration for any offense under this Code. This provision supersedes any contrary provision in the Code" (American Law Institute 2017*a*, § 6.11(8)).

Beyond this affirmative prohibition and repeal, however, the MPCS addresses the reality that all American states currently have a number of mandatory minimum penalties up and running in their criminal codes and are unlikely to repeal most of them for decades to come. This is so even though the American Law Institute, the American Bar Association, and others have laid down a firm line in the sand for decades. Realistically, therefore, Plan A (total abolition) should be accompanied by a Plan B. On the assumption that few states will rush to fall in line with § 6.11(8), the MPCS recommends a dozen additional, incremental measures that would mute the impact of mandatory minimums where they continue to exist (American Law Institute 2017a). These are, in order of appearance:

- § 6.04(3) (courts may order a deferred adjudication in a criminal case even when the offense charged is one that carries a mandatory prison penalty).
- § 6.14(6) (when sentencing defendants who were under age 18 at the time of their offenses, judges are not bound by otherwise-applicable mandatory sentences).
- § 6.16(5)(b) (sentencing judges may approve dispositions negotiated at victim-offender conferences even when they differ from an otherwise applicable mandatory prison sentence).
- § 9.03(6) (prohibits sentencing commission from formulating guidelines based on severity levels of mandatory-punishment statutes).
- § 9.08(3) (authorizes judges to deviate from a mandatory minimum sentence when an offender is identified through actuarial risk assessment to pose an unusually low risk of recidivism).
- § 10.01(3)(b) (grants sentencing judges an "extraordinary-departure power" to deviate from the terms of mandatory-penalty provisions).
- § 10.09(2) (on the government's motion, trial court may reduce sentence below the requirements of any mandatory prison penalty when defendant has provided substantial assistance in the investigation or prosecution of another person).
- § 10.10(5)(b) (creating a new statutory power in the appeals courts to reverse, remand, or modify any sentence, including sentences imposed in conformity with a mandatory prison penalty, on the ground that the sentence would be disproportionately severe; the standard of review is the appellate court's "independent judgment," with no deference to the legislature).
- § 11.01(3) (good-time credits are subtracted from the minimum term of a mandatory minimum prison sentence).

- § 11.02(5) (the MPCS's new sentence-modification power for extremely long sentences supersedes any mandatory minimum penalty originally imposed).
- § 11.03(8) ("compassionate release" for aged and infirm inmates, or based on other "extraordinary and compelling circumstances," supersedes mandatory minimum penalties).
- § 11.04(1.3) (granting emergency powers to corrections officials, sometimes requiring court approval, to release prisoners in conditions of prison overcrowding; these emergency powers supersede any mandatory minimum terms of incarceration imposed on otherwise eligible prisoners).

C. Other Strategies

We cannot summarize all of the hundreds of pages in the MPCS that speak to incarceration, but we discuss two highlights below.

1. *General Deterrence and the MPCS.* One of the MPCS's most important recommendations is that sentencing judges should not be allowed to consider general deterrence as a reason to sentence someone to incarceration or to extend the length of a confinement term longer than is justified on other grounds. Instead, the MPCS authorizes prison and jail sentences on only two grounds—incapacitation of dangerous offenders and seriousness of the offense (American Law Institute 2017*a*, § 6.11(2), (3); see also § 10.02(4)).

The omission of general deterrence as a justification for imprisonment prompted one of the most extended debates in the entire project.[24] One decisive argument for exclusion was that sentencing judges, in any particular case, lack reasonably trustworthy information that a harsher sentence will reduce crime in the outside world. A judge may have a strong personal belief that more punishment will yield better deterrence,

---

[24] The reporters' initial draft of § 6.11(2), omitting general deterrence, was supported overwhelmingly by the project's advisers (experts handpicked by the Institute; American Law Institute 2015*a*, numbered as § 6.06(2); ALI Model Penal Code Sentencing Advisers and MCG Participants 2016). In the ALI Council, however, the proposal met strong resistance. Many experienced judges (and others) argued that, especially in white-collar cases, it was important for judges to have discretion to tailor sentences to "send a message" to the community of potential offenders. They believed that, even if deterrence-through-severity was a failed policy in most contexts, it could be an effective disincentive in the risk-benefit calculations of white-collar offenders (American Law Institute 2015*b*).

but this is exactly the kind of unexamined utilitarian optimism the assessment constraint is designed to foreclose. Even if we believed deterrence-through-severity were a promising policy, judges would still have no information concerning the degree of extra severity needed in each case to bring about the desired effect. A belief that "more punishment is better deterrence" could support any increased use of incarceration. As Judge Patricia Wald phrased it, prison policy founded on general deterrence at sentencing "is a big weapon without a target mechanism" (Wald 2015).

The MPCS does not suggest that the theory of general deterrence can never play a role in a state's prison policy. Section 6.11(2) is addressed to sentencing courts and does not apply to policy making at the system-wide level. Thus, if general deterrence is to support some uses of incarceration, this should be expressed through statutorily authorized penalties and presumptive guidelines sentences. While we do not place stock in the deterrent effectiveness of heavy threats such as three-strikes laws or the felony murder rule, at least those measures convey the idea that all prospective criminals will suffer the threatened fate. It is even less plausible to seek general deterrence through sentence enhancements determined case-by-case according to the idiosyncrasies of each judge. Even at the broadest policy level, however, the MPCS would disapprove of deterrence-based punishment schemes without supporting information of (at least) reasonable feasibility. To date, that is lacking (Nagin 2013; Travis, Western, and Redburn 2014). Perhaps this will change for some types of crimes or offenders. For example, if there is someday reasonable support for the belief that white-collar offenders can be deterred by the threat of significant prison terms, a sentencing commission would be justified in writing guidelines based on that approach (but see Schell-Busey et al. 2016).

2. *"Evidence-Based" Risk Prediction and the MPCS.* The MPCS endorses incapacitation of dangerous offenders as a rationale for prison sentences, but only in limited and "domesticated" ways (American Law Institute 2017*b*, pp. 378–88). The code's premise is that American sentencing systems have been heavily responsive to judgments of recidivism risk for more than a century, but those judgments are usually of poor quality and, when they most count, are almost always administered through shabby, nontransparent processes. Risk-based sentencing is as American as apple pie, gone bad. In our experience, most current engines of American incarceration policy overpredict risk or are heavily biased by risk aversion. This can result in larger numbers of prison sentences, or ex-

tensions of time served, that are unnecessary by any reasonable measure (Piehl, Useem, and DiIulio 1999). Some observers have posited that incapacitation policy run wild was the largest single contributor to mass incarceration (Zimring and Hawkins 1995).

From the American Law Institute's viewpoint, crime prevention through incapacitation is a core value that no American jurisdiction would be willing to give up and is the only legitimate utilitarian purpose of incarceration that should be allowed to operate in case-by-case sentencing decisions (American Law Institute 2017*b*, pp. 151–53, 175–80).[25] The crucial task for the twenty-first century is to find appropriate principles of constraint. Limits on blunderbuss incapacitation theory are needed in any realistic program to reduce American incarceration rates.

We should mention the most obvious strategy of containment first: that risk-based sentencing is always subject to the MPCS's proportionality constraint, even in the face of a highly credible and highly worrisome risk score. As discussed earlier, the MPCS statutory version of proportionality is meant to be a lower ceiling than in pre-MPCS American law and is a tool courts are supposed to use without deference to other branches. If the MPCS succeeds in breathing life into "subconstitutional" proportionality review, risk-based sentencing is one of the most important contexts in which it will operate.

As a further deontological cut point, the MPCS rejects the use of incarceration for minor offenders, however prolific they may be. Incapacitation is not an eligible consideration in favor of a prison or jail sentence unless aimed at "dangerous" recidivism (American Law Institute 2017*a*, §§ 1.02(2)(a)(ii), 6.11(2)(a)). While the MPCS does not define dangerousness, it presumes that much generic recidivism risk will not count. The precise meaning of the term is left to the common law process in each state, one case at a time (Morris and Miller 1985).

The affirmative velocity of the MPCS's incapacitation policy is also inhibited by the assessment constraint. Prison policy based on the incapacitation of dangerous people is not "reasonably feasible" unless there is a reasonably accurate way to identify who the dangerous people are. The MPCS states that a court may not send someone to prison or jail

---

[25] The MPCS rejects rehabilitation by itself as a justificatory goal of incarceration, although it requires prisons and jails to provide reasonable opportunities to those incarcerated to participate in rehabilitative activities (American Law Institute 2017*a*, § 6.11(4)). And, as just explained, it disapproves the consideration of general deterrence by sentencing judges as a reason to incarcerate or to lengthen a term of stay.

unless it is "reasonable to believe" the defendant is a "dangerous offender," and that incarceration is "necessary" to prevent that risk of serious reoffending (American Law Institute 2017a, § 10.02(4)(a)). Most venues of American sentencing today would flunk this test. Moreover, under the MPCS, this is a standard the appellate courts must enforce on review.

If there were a genuine burden of proof placed on a finding of unacceptable recidivism risk in sentencing decisions, including prison release decisions, American incarceration rates would be lower than they are today. Even a forgiving burden of proof would topple most present-day practices. Nationwide, many risk decisions are supported only by "common sense" and hunches (Morris and Miller 1985). Actuarial tools, as they are used today, are not necessarily the cure. In general, the best available technologies for predicting serious criminal behavior are of middling-to-fair reliability, and most criminal justice decision makers are not using risk scales that are anywhere close to the state of the art. Some of the instruments are unforgivably bad, have never been validated in the state that is using them, or have been "modified" by nonexperts before being put in use (Reitz 2012; Desmarais, Johnson, and Singh 2016). In states that take the assessment constraint seriously, unasked questions about these common practices would be pushed to the foreground.

Overall, the MPCS would make judgments of recidivism risk a much more confined factor in American sentencing decisions than it is in most states today. It is especially concerned with risk-based decisions that ratchet up the harshness of prison sentences. In contrast, however, the MPCS encourages the use of risk assessment to identify and divert low-risk offenders who would otherwise be prison bound. Statistically speaking, it is much easier to find "true positives" for low risk of recidivism than for high risk. The number of people who will not commit serious crimes in their future lives is much larger than the number who will. Probabilistically, they provide a bigger target to shoot at (Gottfredson and Gottfredson 1985; Hayes and Geerken 1997). According to solid research findings, the use of risk assessment as a prison-diversion tool is more likely to prove "reasonably feasible" than an attempt to identify high-risk candidates for extralong prison terms. At least one state (Virginia) has shown that this can work (Kern and Farrar-Owens 2004; Kleiman, Ostrom, and Cheesman 2007; Reitz 2017).

The MPCS's most forceful move in addressing risk-based prison policy is to move it into the courtroom. In prison cases today, risk-based sentencing discretion is largely held by parole boards, in states where the boards are given a major share of discretion over lengths of prison terms. Among other problems, the procedural regularities that attend parole release decisions are intolerably poor. Prisoners have no right to a lawyer and are given no meaningful opportunity to challenge an adverse risk score. Indeed, they have no access to the worksheet, software, or instrument used by the board. In many states, prisoners have no right to see any section of their files. If someone has filled in a prisoner's criminal history score incorrectly, they have no recourse. If the person who prepared the report has no training or experience, this goes undiscovered. If the instrument itself is of abysmal quality, no one at the parole stage is in a position to speak up. If the instrument is discriminatory in its application, there is no one to detect the problem, let alone make a constitutional equal protection challenge (Reitz 2017).

The MPCS recommends the elimination of back-end release discretion in most cases and relocates the consideration of risk into the judicial sentencing stage (American Law Institute 2011, app. B; 2017*a*, § 6.11(9)). The primary reason for this preference is procedural fairness. There is a nonnegotiable Sixth Amendment right to counsel at judicial sentencing, which includes representation by an attorney at state expense if the defendant cannot afford to pay, and the right of adequate preparation before the sentencing hearing. Standard courtroom process permits factual and legal challenge to risk scores in individual cases and constitutional challenge of the instruments as a whole. Litigation may even provide expert defense witnesses at state expense, if needed to cross-examine the prosecution's allegations of risk. The elements of procedural fairness pile up further. As decision makers, judges are more insulated from political pressure than parole board members. Even elected judges cannot be fired by the governor at a moment's notice. There is a right to take a judicial appeal against sentence in every state, narrow in some jurisdictions and more fulsome in others, but in all instances more meaningful than prisoners' rights to appeal from a parole deferral. We cannot imagine, for instance, that any existing administrative appeals process in an American paroling system would seriously entertain a claim that a parole board's decisional instrument is constitutionally problematic. In every state, in contrast, it is ground for appeal that a judicial sentence was unconstitutionally imposed. Taken individually or as a whole, the standard procedural safeguards afforded to defendants at sentencing are nearly unimaginable at the parole release stage (see Rhine, Petersilia, and Reitz 2017).

The MPCS's policy of placing "risk discretion" in the courts is also supported by the current state of recidivism research, which teaches that sentencing judges are in as good a position as parole boards to evaluate recidivism risk, despite the fact that parole boards have the advantage of observing the offender over a passage of time. Contrary to conventional wisdom, studies show that a person's in-prison behavior does not tell you very much about how they will behave once they are released. One old but colorful quote by the late Hans Mattick, an influential corrections scholar in the 1960s and 1970s, was: "You cannot train an aviator in a submarine" (Morris 1974, p. 16). If we are trying to decide in a particular case whether a prisoner should be released after serving 2 years in prison, and we are committed to an evidence-based approach to risk of serious recidivism, the trial court already has the best information available to make a decision. There is no reason to wait 2 years for the parole board. Over years of prediction science, the addition of "dynamic" factors concerning an inmate's progress in prison has not been shown to add predictive value. Such factors exist in theory, of course, but have never been nailed down (Wong and Gordon 2006, p. 279; LeBel et al. 2008, p. 133; Skeem et al. 2017).[26] Indeed, the notion of parole boards' special competency to discern, person-by-person, which prisoners have been rehabilitated and which have not has never gotten a whiff of empirical support.

One benefit of the "domestication" of risk assessment, by moving it to the courtroom, may be to block the use of new machine-learning risk prediction tools until they are better understood. Right now, proponents of risk assessment through artificial intelligence concede that it is impossible for human beings to understand how artificial intelligence (AI) has reached a particular decision. We may be able to assess how often the algorithm is right and how often it is wrong, and some of the results look quite impressive, but present technology cannot tell us why it has sorted individuals into higher and lower risk categories. An AI does not "think" in a way that is recognizable to human beings (Berk 2012; Popp 2017). Even so, there is a good possibility that contemporary parole boards will

---

[26] As two leading researchers have put it, "empirical investigation of dynamic risk is virtually absent from the literature. . . . The field's next greatest challenge is to develop sound methods for assessing changeable aspects of violence risk. . . . To date, the scientific focus on dynamic risk and risk management has been more conceptual than empirical . . . it is unclear what the most promising dynamic risk factors are" (Douglas and Skeem 2005, pp. 347, 349, 352, 358).

soon begin to use such black-box prediction tools.[27] After all, their processes have always lacked transparency. The mysteries of machine learning do not look like much of a step down from a procedural fairness perspective. Indeed, if there is a strong empirical case that the AI predictions are more accurate than older generations of risk instruments, the culture of parole in America would suggest that only applause is in order.

We believe the use of machine-learning algorithms for "in-out" and length-of-incarceration decisions will receive a much more skeptical reception in the courts, by a mile, than in the low-visibility milieu of parole release. However much trepidation the reader may have today about actuarial risk assessment as a sentencing tool, and we agree trepidation is warranted, things could get much more frightening in the absence of greater transparency, adversarial testing, and decision makers with at least a fig leaf of political insulation.

VI. Probation

From its first use in the United States in the mid-nineteenth century, probation has been a popular disposition, serving the dual functions of surveilling probationers and offering them assistance in rehabilitation and reintegration (Klingele 2013). Even as imprisonment rates rose throughout the late twentieth century, probation's popularity did not diminish: probation rates continued to rise as well (Phelps 2013). Between 1970 and 2010, the number of individuals on probation more than quadrupled, growing from just over 800,000 to more than 4 million. Although the number of individuals on probation has fallen for 9 consecutive years, more than 3.6 million people remained on probation in the United States at the end of 2016 (Kaeble and Cowhig 2018).

Although probation has traditionally been framed as an alternative to incarceration—and therefore a counterpoint to the trend of growing incarceration rates—it is a sanction in its own right. Conditions of probation can impose significant restraints on individual liberty, and there are almost no legal constraints on the number and kind of conditions to which probationers can be subjected (Klingele 2013; Doherty 2016). In addition, and often as a result, many times probation sentences do not end successfully because a probationer has committed a new crime or has repeat-

---

[27] As of this writing, Pennsylvania was very close to doing so.

edly violated conditions of the terms of his or her release, which can range from participation in treatment programs to location monitoring to restrictions from associating with other convicted individuals. When probation fails, probationers often find themselves incarcerated, thereby increasing custodial populations.

One of the challenges to formulating model law on probation is the dearth of scholarly attention the subject has received in recent decades.[28] To help fill some of this gap, the MPCS reporters, through the Robina Institute of Criminal Law and Criminal Justice, helped lead a series of projects over 5 years that focused on better understanding of the use of probation, parole, and economic penalties across the country. Not only did these projects illuminate the day-to-day challenges faced by courts and correctional agencies in the area of probation supervision but they also revealed the wide disparities that exist between US and foreign rates of probation supervision. The discovery of "American exceptionalism in probation supervision" intensified the MPCS's efforts to create new provisions governing probation and probation revocation.

Recognizing that probation is the sentence imposed on more than half of all criminal defendants in the United States (Kaeble and Cowhig 2018), and that the revocation of probation is a significant contributor to prison population size, the MPCS addresses all of these issues. In doing so, the MPCS extends its preference for parsimony in punishment to community sentences.

It does so first by making clear that not all noncustodial sentences merit probation (American Law Institute 2017a, § 6.05(3)). In many jurisdictions, probation serves as a default sentence in cases where prison and jail are not imposed. As the comments to section 6.05 make clear, "the Institute disapproves of the use of probation when the sanction serves no definable purpose" (American Law Institute 2017a, p. 66). Probation should be imposed only in cases where it is needed to advance accountability or rehabilitation, or to plausibly reduce the risk of criminal reoffending.

---

[28] The MPCS project benefited from hands-on collaborations with state and local jurisdictions in more than a dozen states, which generated over 60 publications through the supportive research of the Robina Institute of Criminal Law and Criminal Justice at the University of Minnesota Law School. We believe that the MPCS provisions on community supervision and economic sanctions are stronger than they otherwise would have been, because they reflect the combined investments of the American Law Institute and the Robina Institute.

In cases where supervision is warranted, section 6.05 sets forth general principles governing probation and its attendant conditions. Recognizing that states vary tremendously in the authorized maximum length of supervision, the MPCS provides clear guidance to courts on appropriate sentence length. By prohibiting terms of supervision longer than 3 years for felony offenses and 1 year for misdemeanors, it attempts to focus limited probation resources and reduce the "contingent liability" created by the imposition of overly long probationary sentences that may begin to interfere with probationers' ability to reintegrate into the law-abiding community successfully.

Conditions of supervision receive significant attention in the MPCS. Courts retain broad discretion to impose probation conditions that promote accountability for criminal conduct, advance rehabilitation and reintegration, and reduce the risks of reoffense (American Law Institute 2017*a*, §§ 6.05(2), (8)). Nonetheless, the ability to impose conditions is not absolute. A key innovation is the requirement that courts apply the MPCS's core proportionality and do-no-harm principles to the cumulative weight of the conditions imposed in any given case by ensuring that no single condition or set of conditions "place[s] an unreasonable burden on [an] offender's ability to reintegrate into the law-abiding community" (American Law Institute 2017*a*, § 6.05(9)). In recognition of the need for parsimony, the MPCS permits courts to reduce conditions of supervision at any time during the probationary period but does not allow courts to increase the number or kind of conditions unless there has been a material change of circumstances that affects either the treatment needs or reoffending risk posed by a probationer.

Section 6.05(9) codifies a growing best practice in corrections: the use of incentives. Incentives have long been used by parents, educators, and businesses to improve performance. Not surprisingly, incentives can motivate positive behavior in probationers, too (Mowen et al. 2018). Section 6.05 encourages courts to offer incentives to probationers who meet treatment goals and demonstrate compliance with their supervision conditions. Such incentives might include reduction in economic sanctions, lightening of supervision conditions, or a reduction in the length of the sentence itself.

Even perfectly tailored conditions do not guarantee compliance with court orders. Often, probationers will fail to comply with some or all of the conditions to which they are subject. What to do when that happens is the subject of section 6.15, which jointly governs violations of probation and postrelease supervision. Under this section, community correctional agencies are appropriately treated as the frontline responders to rule violations. These agencies not only are positioned to detect violations but also to assess their relative seriousness. The MPCS encourages agencies to use a range of responses to rule violations, ranging from verbal reprimands through petitions for revocation.

Recognizing the seriousness of the liberty interests at stake when revocation is pursued, the MPCS ensures that probationers are guaranteed due process in accordance with both constitutional standards and basic principles of fair process. This includes a right to counsel at revocation hearings. When a court finds that a violation has occurred, it, too, has a range of responses at its disposal. The court may order revocation, but it may instead impose lesser sanctions, including formal reprimands, amended conditions of supervision, periods of home confinement, intermittent detention, or location monitoring. Whenever a sanction is formally imposed, whether by a probation agency or by the court, it must be "the least severe consequence needed to address the violation and the risks posed by the offender in the community, keeping in mind the purpose for which the sentence was originally imposed" (American Law Institute 2017a, § 6.15(4)).

Under the MPCS, accountability is not limited to probationers. Correctional agencies are required to fulfill their mission of providing appropriate supervision and services to those in their charge. Recognizing that the size of the community corrections population deserves as much attention as the size of the institutional correctional population, the MPCS requires the legislature to create a mechanism for reducing the size of any correctional population—including the number of people on probation—whenever the population exceeds the operational capacity of the relevant correctional agency. In the context of community corrections, this means that for more than 30 consecutive days the probation agency has reached "a threshold beyond which the supervising agency cannot supervise the offenders under its charge" in accordance with either professional standards or statewide standards (American Law Institute 2017a, § 11.04(1.2)(b)). Upon petition from the probation agency, a court that finds such conditions exist must "declare an overcrowding state of emergency," which authorizes the agency head to advance discharge for individuals approaching the end of their probationary terms, or those who have been in substantial compliance with their terms of supervision for 1 year or more. This provision extends to the community context the emergency release authority that exists in some states to manage prison overcrowding. In doing so, it recognizes that the restrictions on liberty probation imposes can only be justified so long as the sanction provides actual surveillance or support to those being supervised. When a probation agency loses its ability to do that due to extreme resource constraints, an adjustment in population size may be the only way to restore its ability to perform its legitimate functions.

VII. "Back-End" Sentencing Issues

A number of MPCS provisions look beyond fines, probation, jail, and prison sentences to what has often been referred to as the "back end" of the correctional system. Although the MPCS abolishes indeterminate sentencing—and with it, discretionary parole release—it recognizes the importance of and recreates two legitimate functions of parole. First is the supervision and assistance that accompanies a period of postimprisonment supervision. Second is the opportunity, in cases of lengthy sentences or those presenting unusual circumstances, to reexamine whether the full term of imprisonment imposed by the court is truly necessary to serve the purposes of punishment.

The first of these functions, surveillance and support, is recognized by section 6.13, which authorizes courts to impose a period of postrelease supervision following a term of custody to hold an offender accountable for his or her conduct, promote "rehabilitation and reintegration into law-abiding society," reduce the risks of reoffending, or address a need "for housing, employment, family support, medical care, and mental-health care during th[e] transition from prison to the community" (American Law Institute 2017a, § 6.13(2)). Conditions of postrelease supervision, like conditions of probation, may be broad ranging, but may not, either alone or in combination, "place an unreasonable burden on the offender's ability to reintegrate into the law-abiding community" (American Law Institute 2017a, § 6.13(9)). Although reasonable criticisms of the effectiveness of parole supervision have been offered (Scott Hayward 2011), the relatively higher risks and needs posed by those leaving custody justify postrelease supervision in at least a portion of cases. To minimize the risk that terms of postrelease supervision will interfere with achievement of the goals they are intended to promote, the MPCS specifies that terms of postrelease supervision are not required and when imposed may not last longer than 5 years for felony offenses or 1 year for a misdemeanor.

The decision to authorize postrelease supervision was uncontroversial among members of the Institute. Much more contentious was the decision to include provisions that authorize courts to revisit legally imposed sentences. Three provisions, of varying scope, invite judicial reexamination under a variety of conditions, including when a criminal statute has been repealed or invalidated (§ 10.09(3)(b)); when compelling circumstances, such as infirmity, arise (Principles of Legislation § 11.03); and when a person has served 15 or more years of any sentence of confinement (Principles of Legislation § 11.02).

New to the MPCS, but not to state practice, is section 10.09 that details technical circumstances in which sentences may be altered. Its primary provisions authorize courts to reduce sentences under circumstances in which most states allow adjustments to be made, including the correction of arithmetical, technical, or other clear errors, and to reward defendants who have offered substantial assistance in investigating or prosecuting crimes when the value of that assistance was not known or fully appreciated at the time of sentencing. While the MPCS goes further than most states in permitting these modifications to take place at any time before the termination of the sentence, it is the final subsection (3) that most significantly widens existing laws on sentence modification:

§ 10.09. Sentence Modification.

(3) Except as otherwise specified by the legislature, when doing so advances the purposes of sentencing set forth in § 1.02(2), the court may at any time prior to the termination of sentence, upon petition by either party or the department of corrections reduce the sentence of a defendant who is:

(a) serving a term of confinement, probation, or postrelease supervision based on a guideline sentencing range that has subsequently been lowered by the sentencing commission and made retroactive;
(b) serving a sentence for violation of a criminal statute that has subsequently been repealed by the legislature or interpreted by [the State Supreme Court or the United States Supreme Court] not to reach the conduct for which the defendant was convicted.

Subsection (3) gives courts discretion to reduce sentences when the maximum penalty or guidelines range for a crime has been reduced through a change the legislature has made retroactive, and in cases where the statute under which a defendant has been convicted has been repealed or otherwise invalidated. In both circumstances, the change in law calls into question whether, under prevailing moral norms, a defendant should be required to complete the full term of an earlier-imposed sentence. While requiring a person to serve such a sentence is legal, it may be neither necessary nor just. Section 10.09 gives the court discretion to apply the benefit of changing norms to these defendants. As the American prison population has grown, so, too, has the number of those who are elderly and infirm, as well as the number of prisoners who are parents of dependent children.

The second provision governing sentence reduction is section 11.03, which expands judicial power to alter sentences when a "prisoner's advanced age, physical or mental infirmity, exigent family circumstances, or other compelling reasons warran[t] modification of sentence" (§ 11.03 (1)), drawing on state statutes that authorize discretionary "compassionate release" to prisoners facing end-of-life issues and other significant hardships.

Section 11.03 provides several safeguards for the responsible exercise of judicial discretion in modifying sentences. Sentencing commissions are charged with developing guidelines for addressing petitions for sentence modification on the basis of compelling circumstances. In addition, courts are directed to develop procedures for the timely assignment of cases filed under this section, for screening and dismissing applications that plainly lack merit, and for scheduling hearings in cases where they are warranted. The broad power given to trial courts under this provision is checked by the core requirement that sentencing changes be made only when they are justified in light of the purposes of sentencing found in § 1.02(2). Consequently, while aging, infirmity, or other compelling reasons are a precondition to relief under section 11.03, they do not guarantee that a prisoner will receive a lesser sentence. Instead, those circumstances provide an opportunity for the court to reconsider whether the sentence originally imposed remains necessary to ensure the purposes for which it was imposed.

The most controversial new MPCS section pertaining to sentence adjustment is undoubtedly section 11.02, known colloquially as the "second-look" provision. It has no parallel in any state or federal code, and for that reason alone was opposed by some. This provision, styled as a "principle of legislation," directs the legislature to create a judicial panel or authorize a judicial decision maker to hear petitions for de novo resentencing brought by any prisoner who has served 15 years or more of a custodial sentence. Although no state has yet adopted this approach to reexamining long sentences, the provision has attracted notice from scholars and policy makers alike (Love and Klingele 2010; Ryan 2015; Charles Colson Task Force on Federal Corrections 2016).

In relevant part, the provision reads:

§ 11.02. Modification of Long-Term Prison Sentences; Principles for Legislation.[29]

(1) The legislature shall authorize a judicial panel or other judicial decisionmaker to hear and rule upon applications for modification of sentence from prisoners who have served 15 years of any sentence of imprisonment.

(2) After first eligibility, a prisoner's right to apply for sentence modification shall recur at intervals not to exceed 10 years. . . .

(4) Sentence modification under this provision should be viewed as analogous to a resentencing in light of present circumstances. The inquiry shall be whether the purposes of sentencing in § 1.02(2) would better be served by a modified sentence than the prisoner's completion of the original sentence. The judicial panel or other judicial decisionmaker may adopt procedures for the screening and dismissal of applications that are unmeritorious on their face under this standard.

(5) The judicial panel or other judicial decisionmaker shall be empowered to modify any aspect of the original sentence, so long as the portion of the modified sentence to be served is no more severe than the remainder of the original sentence. The sentence-modification authority under this provision shall not be limited by any mandatory-minimum term of imprisonment under state law. . . .

(9) The sentencing commission shall promulgate and periodically amend sentencing guidelines, consistent with Article 6B of the Code, to be used by the judicial panel or other judicial decisionmaker when considering applications under this provision.

(10) The legislature should instruct the sentencing commission to recommend procedures for the retroactive application of this

---

[29] This section was denominated § 305.6 during the preapproval drafting process.

provision to prisoners who were sentenced before its effective date, and should authorize retroactivity procedures in light of the commission's advice.

The MPCS, in most respects, embraces a determinate sentencing system. Not surprisingly, then, the introduction of wholesale resentencing for the longest (and, likely, most serious) cases initially struck many members of the Institute as inconsistent with the structure of the larger MPCS. But unlike indeterminate release mechanisms that vest release decisions in the hands of executive branch actors, section 11.02 returns to the judiciary the task of reconsidering the need for prolonged periods of detention. Judges, not parole officers, decide how much confinement is needed to serve the purposes of punishment, and they do so with the ability to reflect on ways in which advances in technology and shifts in punitive sensibilities may cast doubt on the wisdom of sentences imposed decades earlier.

There are several reasons for reconsidering lengthy sentences of the kind imposed in recent decades. Modern sentences are supersized, compared both to international punishment norms and to America's own traditional sentencing patterns and practices. Many of the long sentences being served by today's prisoners were imposed at a time when crime rates were high and the public demand for strict punishment was strong. As crimes rates have fallen steadily, and moral assessments of the needed severity of punishment have softened slightly, there is good reason to invite reexamination of the need for prolonged incarceration in individual cases. While decades-long detention may sometimes be necessary to punish extreme wrongdoing, the passage of time and changes in the ability of correctional agencies to deliver effective treatment and surveillance may reduce or eliminate the need for continued detention. As the MPCS explains, the second-look mechanism "reflects a profound sense of humility that ought to operate when punishments are imposed that will reach nearly a generation into the future, or longer still" (American Law Institute 2017*b*, p. 568).

There is no question that altering sentences many years after their imposition risks upsetting the expectations of crime victims and the broader community. To ensure that valid concerns are not ignored, the second-look mechanism requires courts to consider victim statements made at the time of sentencing, which may be supplemented with information about changed crime victim circumstances. Moreover, states are directed to develop procedures that guarantee fair process throughout second-look proceedings, and sentencing commissions are directed to create guidelines specific to second-look decisions. With these safeguards in place to guide the exercise of discretion, the American Law Institute agreed that the challenges created by America's unprecedented punishment buildup justify this new mechanism for ensuring that long sentences remain just and necessary to further the legitimate purposes of punishment.

VIII. Economic Sanctions

Although not widely appreciated, the nation's use of economic penalties surged in tandem with other punishments during the punitive buildup era. Across the criminal justice system, there has been steady growth in fine amounts, asset forfeitures, costs, fees, and assessments levied against offenders. At the same time, a wave of new statutes and state constitutional provisions has authorized or mandated victim restitution as part of a criminal sentence. Given the unpopularity of criminal offenders and the need for revenue to maintain growth in criminal justice institutions, the "piling on" of restitution, fines, fees, and forfeitures has found no natural stopping point. To make matters worse, the average person caught up in the criminal justice system has become less able to bear these penalties, as gaps between rich and poor have continued to grow.

The freedom with which economic sanctions are imposed in America does not proceed from a widespread belief that they are sufficient punishments for any but the least serious offenses. Economic sanctions in practice yield little retributive satisfaction. Instead, the general growth in economic penalties has been borne of need: sustained budgetary shortfalls have led governments and correctional vendors to turn to offenders as new sources of revenue for operating all facets of the criminal justice system, from courts to corrections.

Many of these new economic sanctioning policies raise questions about conflicts of interest in the administration of criminal law, felt most by agencies authorized to seize or collect assets from offenders and retain some or all for their own use. Asset forfeitures and a variety of costs, fees, and assessments, little used before the 1970s and 1980s, have in recent decades become major revenue sources for local and state criminal justice agencies. Fines, even at the level of traffic offenses, have become an important revenue source for local governments.

In some American jurisdictions, probationers and parolees are regularly charged with supervision and program fees, and the proceeds are used to help fund the probation and parole supervision agencies. Probation officers in some locales are perceived by their clients as bill collectors, with the imperative of collection displacing efforts to provide services and enforce nonfinancial conditions. It is common practice to extend probation terms for nonpayment of financial penalties, even if all other probation conditions have been met—it may be to an agency's advantage to keep "paying customers" on probation or parole even if early termination would otherwise be warranted. In addition, offenders are often barred from participating in needed treatment programs when they are unable to pay required program fees.

It is an understatement to say that research and policy debate have not kept stride with these larger trends, resulting in the adoption of laws and practices that are underexamined, unprincipled, and counterproductive to the goal of public safety (American Law Institute 2017b). The MPCS accordingly calls for an across-the-board rethinking of economic penalties—and significant reductions in their overall use.

Although the MPCS provides detailed guidance on the imposition and collection of restitution, fines, forfeitures, fees, costs, and other financial assessments, the single most important economic sanctions provision applies across the board. Section 6.06(6) states simply that "no economic sanction may be imposed unless the offender would retain sufficient means for reasonable living expenses and family obligations after compliance with the sanction" (American Law Institute 2017a). This language creates a new limiting principle of "reasonable financial subsistence" (RFS) to constrain governments' power to assess economic sanctions of all kinds, including victim restitution.[30] The RFS limit goes further than any existing constitutional or statutory command in American law.[31] If adopted, it would prohibit the use of financial penalties for a very large percentage of criminal defendants nationwide.

---

[30] The RFS provision supplements other limits on sentence severity in the MPCS, such as the statutory "subconstitutional" proportionality doctrine discussed earlier.

[31] Federal constitutional law, in theory, prohibits the use of incarceration for nonpayment when an offender lacks the "ability to pay" economic sanctions. This sets too low a floor for public-policy purposes. Also, enforcement of the rule is spotty.

In many ways, it seems obvious to require courts to consider a defendant's ability to meet his or her basic needs and those of his or her family before imposing a sentence that could intensify their poverty. Theoretically, it would not be an illegal abuse of discretion for sentencing judges to do so in many cases today. In fact, however, courts and other agencies do not calculate reasonable life expenses when considering whether defendants have the ability to pay economic sanctions—if they consider ability to pay at all. This results in many cases in which the total criminal justice debt levied on defendants is patently uncollectable. When this happens, the aggregate of economic penalties is a legal fiction and an exercise in futility, with little legitimacy from the defendant's point of view, and much demoralizing emotional force.

The primary rationale for the RFS constraint, however, is utilitarian. It is designed to prevent economic penalties from interfering with the overriding goal of returning offenders to productive, law-abiding lives. The best available evidence suggests that economic sanctions have negative effects on offender rehabilitation and reintegration when they disrupt the fundamentals of stable work, housing, and family life—or provide incentives to seek earnings in the illegal economy. Much like bankruptcy law, a primary goal of the sentencing system should be to reposition ex-offenders so they may become productive and successful participants in the law-abiding economy.[32] The RFS standard eliminates perverse incentives for offenders to offend, thereby undermining achievement of overriding goals of public safety, and instead promotes reintegration by ensuring offenders are not forced to choose between discharging their financial obligations to the criminal justice system and meeting their families' basic needs.

The MPCS also recommends mass abrogation of revenue-raising user fees and other surcharges (American Law Institute 2017*a*, § 6.10). Realistically, in the short or middle term, the best-case scenario is that a small number of jurisdictions will follow the MPCS's lead. It therefore offers a series of second-best recommendations addressed to states that do not implement a blanket prohibition on such revenue sources (American

---

[32] One of the most famous statements of the President's Crime Commission in 1967 was that "warring on poverty . . . is warring on crime." In the intervening 50 years, there has been much study and debate of the poverty-crime connection. Yet there are few who would say that the exacerbation of poverty is sensible crime-control policy.

Law Institute 2017a, alternative § 6.10). Every incremental step toward reducing criminal justice systems' reliance on costs, fees, and assessments makes their eventual abolition more practicable.

There are six second-order recommendations. First, the RFS standard would eliminate the imposition of many costs, fees, and surcharges in the first instance. Second, the MPCS provides that all costs and fees must be approved in advance by sentencing courts and may not be levied, increased, or supplemented with surcharges at a later time. In a related provision, sentencing courts are required to set a total dollar ceiling upon all financial sanctions that may be collected from an individual defendant. Third, no costs, fees, or assessments may be imposed in excess of actual marginal cost expenditures in the offender's case. Fourth, agencies or entities charged with collection of the fees are barred from retaining the monies collected, and collection surcharges or penalties may not be added. Fifth, the imposition of costs, fees, and assessments cannot violate statutory principles of sentence proportionality. Sixth, economic sanctions other than victim restitution may not be made formal "conditions" of probation or postrelease supervision—meaning that nonpayment cannot be a basis for sentence revocation.

While simple in theory, serious administrative obstacles impede states from adopting the MPCS economic sanctions provisions wholesale. Many courts, corrections agencies, police departments, and other government entities have become dependent on fines and "user fees" imposed on convicted individuals (Shaw 2015) and on remunerative asset forfeitures, which generally do not require a charge or conviction. Ending governmental agencies' dependence on funds received from offenders will require legislatures to step up financial support for core government institutions and functions.

IX. Collateral Consequences

Nearly 80 million Americans have criminal records (Murray 2018). As a result of these past contacts with the criminal justice system, individuals often face ongoing employment and licensing restrictions, disqualification from public benefits, registration requirements, and (for some) deportation. Since the 1980s, when "civil" collateral consequences of conviction were few, there has been an explosion in the collateral consequences authorized by state and federal law. The collateral consequence provisions of the MPCS attempt to ameliorate the punitive force of these laws that lie at the periphery of the sentencing process (or outside it entirely) but take effect only as the result of criminal conviction.

While collateral consequences are ostensibly "civil" by legal definition, they fall squarely within criminal sentencing policy. In some cases, the combined weight of collateral sanctions is far more punitive than the formal criminal sentence (Chin 2012). Their reach is broad and long: many persist for the remainder of the convicted person's life and can only be lifted by the increasingly elusive remedy of executive pardon (Love 2015). Article 7 treats collateral consequences policy as equal in importance to incarceration and community supervision policies, addressing collateral consequences in three ways. First, it requires public education about the civil restrictions that flow from criminal conviction. Second, it limits the degree to which legislatures may restrict the rights of convicted individuals to participate in the democratic process through voting and jury service. Finally, it creates mechanisms by which courts (or other designated government agencies) can provide individualized relief from mandatory collateral consequences.

Article 7 requires states to confront the number of collateral consequences that attach to any given offense. In most jurisdictions, they are scattered throughout statutes and regulations; policy makers cannot easily determine the cumulative effects of conviction for any given crime on convicted individuals. Section 7.02 requires the sentencing commission to "compile, maintain, and publish" a compendium that lists, for every crime contained in the state's criminal code, all penalties, disabilities, or disadvantages, however denominated, that are authorized or required by state or federal law as a direct result of an individual's conviction but are not part of the sentence ordered by the court. By doing so, the MPCS requires lawmakers, at a minimum, to confront the number and weight of the consequences that attach to each violation of the criminal code.

Section 7.04 is the centerpiece of article 7, setting forth the basic rules the court must follow with respect to notifying defendants about collateral consequences and granting relief from collateral consequences at sentencing, and for the duration of the sentence. This section provides the following guidance on when relief from collateral consequences should be granted:

§ 7.04(2). Notification of Collateral Consequences; Order of Relief.
At any time prior to the expiration of the sentence, a person may petition the court to grant an order of relief from an otherwise-

applicable mandatory collateral consequence imposed by the laws of this state that is related to employment, education, housing, public benefits, registration, occupational licensing, or the conduct of a business.

(a) The court may dismiss or grant the petition summarily, in whole or in part, or may choose to institute proceedings as needed to rule on the merits of the petition.
(b) When a petition is filed, notice of the petition and any related proceedings shall be given to the prosecuting attorney.
(c) The court may grant relief from a mandatory collateral consequence if, after considering the guidance provided by the sentencing commission under § 7.02(2), it finds that the individual has demonstrated by clear and convincing evidence that the consequence is not substantially related to the elements and facts of the offense and is likely to impose a substantial burden on the individual's ability to reintegrate into law-abiding society, and that public-safety considerations do not require mandatory imposition of the consequence.
(d) Relief should not be denied arbitrarily, or for any punitive purpose.

In addition to permitting courts to grant relief during the sentence pursuant to section 7.04, the MPCS provides relief mechanisms for otherwise mandatory collateral consequences under a variety of different circumstances. Courts may grant relief under section 7.05 to a person who has finished serving a criminal sentence, or who is serving a sentence in a different jurisdiction, if a mandatory collateral consequence will have an adverse effect on the person's ability to seek or maintain employment, conduct business, or secure housing or public benefits.

Other provisions of article 7 severely restrict the ability of jurisdictions to limit the right to vote and to serve on juries—rights that deeply affect convicted individuals' ability to reintegrate into the community. These two restrictions have well-documented disparate effects on minority communities (Cammett 2012; Roberts 2013). Section 7.03 strongly encourages jurisdictions to eliminate disenfranchisement as a consequence of conviction and prohibits barring individuals from voting except during the duration of a custodial sentence imposed for a felony offense. States are permitted to impose mandatory jury service exclusions only until the sentence imposed by the court, including any period of community supervision, has been served.

Finally, section 7.06 authorizes courts or other designated agencies to grant relief from most mandatory collateral consequences to individuals who are 4 or more years past the end of their most recent sentence and have no current charges pending against them. To maximize the availability of relief, the MPCS directs courts "not [to] require extraordinary achievement" and to show sensitivity "to any cultural, educational, or economic limitations affecting the petitioner" (American Law Institute 2017*a*, § 7.06(3)(b)).

Initially, the debate over whether to include article 7 in the MPCS rivaled the debate over the "second look" among project advisors and ALI members. The Institute engaged in deep discussion over the degree to which criminal courts should concern themselves with matters of civil law at all. There were also serious questions raised as to whether courts possess adequate expertise to determine when restrictions on housing, employment, licensing, and benefits can be lifted without imperiling public safety. Over time, however, as members became aware of the degree to which excessive collateral consequences continue to impede successful reintegration of former offenders, support grew for creating limited mechanisms for relief.

Article 7, accordingly, is careful to limit the court's role in deciding whether an individual offender should be prohibited from securing any particular benefit or opportunity. The court may decide only that, as a matter of law, the individual may not be categorically prevented from seeking the benefit or opportunity in question. Any order would not prevent authorized decision makers from later considering the conduct underlying a conviction when deciding whether to confer a discretionary benefit. The MPCS thus strikes a balance between the court's knowledge of the material facts of the particular case and the expertise of specialized agencies, such as licensing boards, to determine whether the facts of any individual's case justify denial of a particular benefit or opportunity.

X. Conclusion

In the end, the MPCS covers nearly all aspects of sentencing in America—if the field is defined to include those forms of punishment that are imposed on truly large numbers of people (measured in hundreds of thousands, or millions). The aggregate human consequences are immense. With groups this large, even incremental improvements can bring sizable benefits. The MPCS also defines "sentencing" as a subject best understood from the viewpoint of the human beings who must live through their sentences from beginning to end, from pronouncement in court to final discharge. Accordingly, it deals extensively with the ongoing—and sometimes never-ending—consequences that are experienced as punishments long after formal "sentencing" in the courtroom. In the eyes of the MPCS, a judicial sentence is merely a point along a line that stretches, unknowably, into the future. After the courts have done their part, many other officials will render later-in-time decisions with profound impact on offenders' experiences of their sentences. Scaled up from the individual to the societal level of policy concern, it is this experiential perspective that really matters. Cumulatively, it is all the actions taken during the life course of a sentence that determine whether the highest purposes of criminal punishment are served or frustrated.

The one major area of "sentencing-as-experienced" that the MPCS barely touches is the subject of conditions of confinement in America's prisons and jails. The topic was addressed in the original Model Penal Code, but not extensively. Fifty to 60 years later, the total US incarceration population is about seven times larger than at the close of the 1960s. Arguably, the subject of conditions of confinement has become seven times more important.

When the MPCS project was about 10 years into its 15-year course, however, the American Law Institute decided that a serious examination of prison and jail conditions would have to be done as a separate venture, if undertaken at all. For one thing, it would have added years to an already epic-length project. In addition, it was reasonable to ask whether the reporters, advisers, and other groups assembled for the MPCS had the necessary expertise to confront the various and difficult (some say intractable) problems strewn through the nation's prisons and jails. Going a step further, serious doubts were expressed about whether the ALI has the institutional competency to make a large contribution in this area, or whether such a project would end up as a well-meant waste of resources.

In our unofficial capacities as authors of this essay, not as ALI reporters, we hope the Institute will seriously consider, and ultimately launch, a new project on conditions of confinement in America. If we posit for a moment that America's prison and jail systems will remain large for decades to come, even if sentencing reforms begin to take hold, then the human stakes of "life inside" will remain enormous and, in some places, at crisis levels.

The experience of imprisonment and jail confinement across the United States is wildly different from place to place. We have no doubt there are "best practices" to be identified and "worst practices" to be ferreted out.

We fear the worst of these are not just slightly bad but merit extreme levels of concern. The law-abiding community tolerates the darkest of these realities largely because they are out of sight—which is perhaps the greatest attraction of incarceration as a criminal sanction. A project that shines a spotlight on conditions of confinement in America would make a contribution on that basis alone.

We also believe great progress is possible. On the side of optimism, there are many other countries that handle their (much smaller) prison populations in ways that are more humane and effective than average practice in America. A conditions-of-confinement project would not be an exercise in utopianism; it would fit the standard American Law Institute paradigm: build on precedent, while aspiring to do even better. A great deal of raw material for prison and jail reform exists, but it will take a well-resourced effort to marshal it and synthesize it into workable recommendations.

As to doubts about the ALI's competency, we wonder who else—that is, what other organizations of comparable stature—could possibly take this on. The American Law Institute is very good at recruiting the expertise it needs for its big projects. (Many of the group appointed to serve as MPCS advisers were not Institute members; many are nonlawyers.) Exploration of how the reporters and drafting groups might be constituted for a conditions of confinement project would be a worthwhile step, with some emphasis on cross-national expertise.

Ultimately, such a project would be a huge investment and could not be launched without considerable support from within the American Law Institute and its outside constituencies. We conclude this essay in the hope that such extensive support might materialize. Among other things, the project would complete a very large portion of the MPCS mission that the MPCS itself was unable to explore.

REFERENCES

Alexander, Michelle. 2010. *The New Jim Crow: Mass Incarceration in the Age of Colorblindness*. New York: New Press.

ALI Model Penal Code Sentencing Advisers and MCG Participants. 2016. "Memorandum to ALI Council Members re: MPC Sentencing Section 6.06 (2)." January 12.

Alper, Mariel E., Alessandro Corda, and Kevin R. Reitz. 2016. *American Exceptionalism in Probation Supervision*. Minneapolis: Robina Institute of Criminal Law and Criminal Justice.
American Law Institute. 2002. *Model Penal Code: Sentencing, Preliminary Draft No. 1*. Philadelphia: American Law Institute.
———. 2003. *Model Penal Code: Sentencing, Report*. Philadelphia: American Law Institute.
———. 2007. *Model Penal Code: Sentencing, Tentative Draft No. 1*. Philadelphia: American Law Institute.
———. 2011. *Model Penal Code: Sentencing, Tentative Draft No. 2*. Philadelphia: American Law Institute.
———. 2015a. *Model Penal Code: Sentencing, Council Draft No. 5*. Philadelphia: American Law Institute.
———. 2015b. "Transcript of October 2015 ALI Council Meeting Discussion of MPC Sentencing Section 6.06." Philadelphia: American Law Institute.
———. 2017a. *Model Penal Code: Sentencing, Official Statutory Text*. Philadelphia: American Law Institute.
———. 2017b. *Model Penal Code: Sentencing, Proposed Final Draft (Approved May 24, 2017)*. Philadelphia: American Law Institute.
Anderson, Ronald E. 1993. "Development of a Structured Sentencing Simulation." *Social Science Computer Review* 11:166–78.
Baldus, David C., George G. Woodworth, and Charles A. Pulaski Jr. 1990. *Equal Justice and the Death Penalty: A Legal and Empirical Analysis*. Boston: Northeastern University Press.
Balko, Radley. 2017. "Chicago Data Show Problems with Civil Asset Forfeiture." *Chicago Tribune*, June 14.
Bannon, Alicia, Mitali Nagrecha, and Rebekah Diller. 2010. *Criminal Justice Debt: A Barrier to Reentry*. New York: Brennan Center for Justice.
Beck, Allen J., and Alfred Blumstein. 2018. "Racial Disproportionality in US State Prisons: Accounting for the Effects of Racial and Ethnic Differences in Criminal Involvement, Arrests, Sentencing, and Time Served." *Journal of Quantitative Criminology* 34(3):853–88.
Beckett, Katherine, and Alexes Harris. 2011. "On Cash and Conviction: Monetary Sanctions as Misguided Policy." *Criminology and Public Policy* 10:509–37.
Berk, Richard. 2012. *Criminal Justice Forecasts of Risk: A Machine Learning Approach*. New York: Springer.
Boerner, David, and Roxanne Lieb. 2001. "Sentencing Reform in the Other Washington." In *Crime and Justice: A Review of Research*, vol. 28, edited by Michael Tonry. Chicago: University of Chicago Press.
Cahalan, Margaret Werner. 1986. *United States Historical Correctional Statistics, 1850–1984*. Washington, DC: Bureau of Justice Statistics.
Cammett, Ann. 2012. "Shadow Citizens: Felony Disenfranchisement and the Criminalization of Debt." *Penn State Law Review* 117:349–405.
Carson, E. Ann. 2018. *Prisoners in 2016*. Washington, DC: Bureau of Justice Statistics.

Center for the Study and Prevention of Violence. 2010. *CSPV Position Summary: D.A.R.E. Program.* Boulder, CO: Center for the Study and Prevention of Violence.

Charles Colson Task Force on Federal Corrections. 2016. *Transforming Prisons, Restoring Lives.* Washington, DC: Urban Institute.

Chin, Gabriel J. 2012. "The New Civil Death: Rethinking Punishment in the Era of Mass Conviction." *University of Pennsylvania Law Review* 160:1789–1833.

Corda, Alessandro. 2018. "The Collateral Consequence Conundrum: Comparative Genealogy, Current Trends, and Future Scenarios." In *After Imprisonment*, edited by Austin Sarat. Studies in Law, Politics, and Society. Bingley: Emerald.

Cullen, Francis T., Kristie R. Blevins, Jennifer S. Trager, and Paul Gendreau. 2005. "The Rise and Fall of Boot Camps: A Case Study in Common-Sense Corrections." *Journal of Offender Rehabilitation* 40:53–70.

Davis, Elizabeth, and Tracy L. Snell. 2018. *Capital Punishment, 2016.* Washington, DC: Bureau of Justice Statistics.

Death Penalty Information Center. 2018. *Facts about the Death Penalty.* Washington, DC: Death Penalty Information Center.

Demleitner, Nora V. 2018. "Collateral Sanctions and American Exceptionalism: A Comparative Perspective." In *American Exceptionalism in Crime and Punishment*, edited by Kevin R. Reitz. New York: Oxford University Press.

Desmarais, Sarah L., Kiersten L. Johnson, and Jay P. Singh. 2016. "Performance of Recidivism Risk Assessment Instruments in US Correctional Settings." *Psychological Services* 13:206–22.

Doherty, Fiona. 2016. "Obey All Laws and Be Good: Probation and the Meaning of Recidivism." *Georgetown Law Review* 104:291–354.

Douglas, Kevin S., and Jennifer L. Skeem. 2005. "Violence Risk Assessment: Getting Specific about Being Dynamic." *Psychology, Public Policy, and the Law* 11(3):347–83.

Dubber, Markus D. 2015. *An Introduction to the Model Penal Code.* 2nd ed. New York: Oxford University Press.

Erickson, Jessica. 2014. "Racial Impact Statements: Considering the Consequences of Racial Disproportionalities in the Criminal Justice System." *Washington Law Review* 89:1425–65.

Feeley, Malcom M. 1983. *Court Reform on Trial: Why Simple Solutions Fail.* New York: Basic.

Frase, Richard S. 2005. "Sentencing Guidelines in Minnesota, 1978–2003." In *Crime and Justice: A Review of Research*, vol. 32, edited by Michael Tonry. Chicago: University of Chicago Press.

———. 2013. *Just Sentencing: Principles and Procedures for a Workable System.* New York: Oxford University Press.

Goffman, Alice. 2015. *On the Run: Fugitive Life in an American City.* New York: Farrar, Straus & Giroux.

Gottfredson, Stephen D., and Michael Gottfredson. 1985. "Selective Incapacitation?" *Annals of the American Academy of Political and Social Science* 478:135–49.

Hayes, Hennessey D., and Michael R. Geerken. 1997. "The Idea of Selective Release." *Justice Quarterly* 14:353–70.

Hunt, Kim. 1998. "Sentencing Commissions as Centers for Policy Analysis and Research: Illustrations from the Budget Process." *Law and Policy* 20:466–89.

Kadish, Sanford H. 1988. "The Model Penal Code's Historical Antecedents." *Rutgers Law Journal* 19:521–38.

Kaeble, Danielle. 2018. *Probation and Parole in the United States, 2016*. Washington, DC: Bureau of Justice Statistics.

Kaeble, Danielle, and Mary Cowhig. 2018. *Correctional Populations in the United States, 2016*. Washington, DC: Bureau of Justice Statistics.

Kern, Richard P., and Meredith Farrar-Owens. 2004. "Sentencing Guidelines with Integrated Offender Risk Assessment." *Federal Sentencing Reporter* 16(3):165–69.

Kleiman, Matthew, Brian J. Ostrom, and Fred L. Cheesman II. 2007. "Using Risk Assessment to Inform Sentencing Decisions for Nonviolent Offenders in Virginia." *Crime and Delinquency* 53:106–32.

Klingele, Cecelia M. 2013. "Rethinking the Use of Community Supervision." *Journal of Criminal Law and Criminology* 103:1015–70.

Knapp, Kay A. 1986. "Proactive Policy Analysis of Minnesota's Prison Populations." *Criminal Justice Policy Review* 1:37–57.

Lawyers' Committee for Civil Rights. 2017. *Not Just a Ferguson Problem: How Traffic Courts Drive Inequality in California*. San Francisco: Lawyers' Committee for Civil Rights of the San Francisco Bay Area.

LeBel, Thomas P., Ros Burnett, Shadd Maruna, and Shawn Bushway. 2008. "The 'Chicken and Egg' of Subjective and Social Factors in Desistance from Crime." *European Journal of Criminology* 5:131–59.

Lexington. 2010. "A Truck in the Dock: How the Police Can Seize Your Stuff When You Have Not Been Proven Guilty of Anything." *Economist*, May 27. https://www.economist.com/united-states/2010/05/27/a-truck-in-the-dock.

London, Catherine. 2011. "Racial Impact Statements: A Proactive Approach to Addressing Racial Disparities in Prison Populations." *Law and Inequality* 29:211–48.

Love, Margaret Colgate. 2015. "Managing Collateral Consequences in the Sentencing Process: The Revised Sentencing Articles of the Model Penal Code." *Wisconsin Law Review* 2015:247–87.

Love, Margaret Colgate, and Cecelia Klingele. 2010. "First Thoughts about Second Look and Other Sentence Reduction Provisions of the Model Penal Code: Sentencing Revision." *University of Toledo Law Review* 42:859–80.

Lynch, Gerard E. 1998. "Towards a Model Penal Code, Second (Federal): The Challenge of the Special Part." *Buffalo Criminal Law Review* 2:297–349.

Martinson, Robert. 1974. "What Works: Questions and Answers about Prison Reform." *Public Interest* 35:22–54.

Marvell, Thomas B. 1995. "Sentencing Guidelines and Prison Population Growth." *Journal of Criminal Law and Criminology* 85(3):696–709.

Mauer, Marc. 2009. "Racial Impact Statements: Changing Policies to Address Disparities." *Criminal Justice* 23(4):17–20.
Meek, Amy P. 2014. "Street Vendors, Taxicabs, and Exclusion Zones: The Impact of Collateral Consequences of Criminal Convictions at the Local Level." *Ohio State Law Journal* 75:1–56.
Minnesota Sentencing Guidelines Commission. 2008. *Racial Impact for HF3175: Robbery—Increased Penalties*. Saint Paul: Minnesota Sentencing Guidelines Commission.
———. 2017. *Demographic Impact Statement Policy, Version 2.0*. Saint Paul: Minnesota Sentencing Guidelines Commission.
Minton, Todd D., Scott Ginder, Susan M. Brumbaugh, Hope Smiley-McDonald, and Harley Rohloff. 2015. *Census of Jails: Population Changes, 1999–2013*. Washington, DC: Bureau of Justice Statistics.
Morris, Norval. 1974. *The Future of Imprisonment*. Chicago: University of Chicago Press.
Morris, Norval, and Marc Miller. 1985. "Predictions of Dangerousness." In *Crime and Justice: An Annual Review of Research*, vol. 6, edited by Michael Tonry and Norval Morris. Chicago: University of Chicago Press.
Mowen, Thomas J., Eric Wodahl, John J. Brent, and Brett Garland. 2018. "The Role of Sanctions and Incentives in Promoting Successful Reentry: Evidence from the SVORI Data." *Criminal Justice and Behavior* 45:1288–1307.
Murray, Brian M. 2018. "Unstitching Scarlet Letters? Prosecutorial Discretion and Expungement." *Fordham Law Review* 86:2821–71.
Nagin, Daniel S. 2013. "Deterrence in the Twenty-First Century." In *Crime and Justice in America: 1975–2025*, edited by Michael Tonry. Vol. 42 of *Crime and Justice: A Review of Research*, edited by Michael Tonry. Chicago: University of Chicago Press.
Pew Center on the States. 2008. *One in 100: Behind Bars in America*. Washington, DC: Pew Charitable Trusts.
Phelps, Michelle S. 2013. "The Paradox of Probation: Community Supervision in the Age of Mass Incarceration." *Law and Policy* 35:51–80.
Piehl, Anne Morrison, Bert Useem, and John J. DiIulio Jr. 1999. *Right-Sizing Justice: A Cost-Benefit Analysis of Imprisonment in Three States*. New York: Manhattan Institute.
Pinard, Michael. 2010. "Collateral Consequences of Criminal Convictions: Confronting Issues of Race and Dignity." *New York University Law Review* 85:457–534.
Popp, Trey. 2017. "Black Box Justice." *Pennsylvania Gazette*, Aug. 28.
Reitz, Kevin R. 2009. "Demographic Impact Statements, O'Connor's Warning, and the Mysteries of Prison Release: Topics from a Sentencing Reform Agenda." *Florida Law Review* 61:683–707.
———. 2012. "The 'Traditional' Indeterminate Sentencing Model." In *The Oxford Handbook of Sentencing and Corrections*, edited by Joan Petersilia and Kevin R. Reitz. New York: Oxford University Press.
———. 2017. "'Risk Discretion' at Sentencing." *Federal Sentencing Reporter* 30(1):68–73.

———. 2018. "American Exceptionalism in Crime and Punishment: Broadly Defined." In *American Exceptionalism in Crime and Punishment*, edited by Kevin R. Reitz. New York: Oxford University Press.

Rhine, Edward E., Joan Petersilia, and Kevin R. Reitz. 2017. "The Future of Parole Release: A Ten-Point Plan." In *Reinventing American Criminal Justice*, edited by Michael Tonry. Vol. 46 of *Crime and Justice: A Review of Research*, edited by Michael Tonry. Chicago: University of Chicago Press.

Rhine, Edward E., and Faye S. Taxman. 2018. "American Exceptionalism in Community Supervision: A Comparative Analysis of Probation in the United States, Scotland, and Sweden." In *American Exceptionalism in Crime and Punishment*, edited by Kevin R. Reitz. New York: Oxford University Press.

Ristroph, Alice. 2006. "Desert, Democracy, and Reform." *Journal of Criminal Law and Criminology* 96:1293–1352.

Roberts, Anna. 2013. "Casual Ostracism: Jury Exclusion on the Basis of Criminal Convictions." *Minnesota Law Review* 98:592–647.

Robinson, Paul H., and Markus D. Dubber. 2007. "The American Model Penal Code: A Brief Overview." *New Criminal Law Review* 10(3):319–41.

Rothman, David J. 1980. *Conscience and Convenience: The Asylum and Its Alternatives in Progressive America*. Boston: Little, Brown.

Rubin, Edward L. 2001. "The Inevitability of Rehabilitation." *Law and Inequality* 19:343–77.

Ruth, Henry, and Kevin R. Reitz. 2003. *The Challenge of Crime: Rethinking Our Response*. Cambridge, MA: Harvard University Press.

Ryan, Meghan J. 2015. "Taking Another Look at Second-Look Sentencing." *Brooklyn Law Review* 81:149–78.

Sabol, William J., Heather C. West, and Matthew Cooper. 2009. *Prisoners in 2008*. Washington, DC: Bureau of Justice Statistics.

Schell-Busey, Natalie, Sally S. Simpson, Melissa Rorie, and Mariel Alper. 2016. "What Works? A Systematic Review of Corporate Crime Deterrence." *Criminology and Public Policy* 15:387–416.

Scott Hayward, Christine. 2011. "The Failure of Parole: Rethinking the Role of the State in Reentry." *New Mexico Law Review* 41:421–65.

The Sentencing Project. 2001. *US Continues to Be World Leader in Rate of Incarceration*. Washington, DC: The Sentencing Project.

———. 2018. "New Jersey Enacts Law to Examine Racial and Ethnic Impact of Sentencing Changes." Washington, DC: The Sentencing Project. https://www.sentencingproject.org/news/new-jersey-enacts-law-examine-racial-ethnic-impact-sentencing-changes/.

Shaw, Theodore M. 2015. *The Ferguson Report: Department of Justice Investigation of the Ferguson Police Department*. Washington, DC: Civil Rights Division.

Skeem, Jennifer L., Patrick J. Kennealy, Joseph R. Tatar II, Isaias R. Hernandez, and Felicia A. Keith. 2017. "How Well Do Juvenile Risk Assessments Measure Factors to Target in Treatment? Examining Construct Validity." *Psychological Assessment* 29:679–91.

Stemen, Don, and Andres F. Rengifo. 2010. "Policies and Imprisonment: The Impact of Structured Sentencing and Determinate Sentencing on State Incarceration Rates, 1978–2004." *Justice Quarterly* 28(1):174–201.
Stillman, Sarah. 2013. "Taken." *New Yorker*, August 12 and 19.
Tonry, Michael. 1993. "The Success of Judge Frankel's Sentencing Commission." *University of Colorado Law Review* 64:713.
———. 1995. *Malign Neglect: Race, Crime, and Punishment in America*. New York: Oxford University Press.
———. 2011. *Punishing Race: A Continuing American Dilemma*. New York: Oxford University Press.
Travis, Jeremy. 2002. *Thoughts on the Future of Parole*. Washington, DC: Urban Institute, Justice Policy Center.
Travis, Jeremy, Bruce Western, and Steve Redburn. 2014. *The Growth of Incarceration in the United States: Exploring the Causes and Consequences*. Washington, DC: National Academies Press.
US Department of Justice. 2015. *Investigation of the Ferguson Police Department*. Washington, DC: Civil Rights Division.
van Zyl Smit, Dirk, and Alessandro Corda. 2018. "American Exceptionalism in Parole Release and Supervision: A European Perspective." In *American Exceptionalism in Crime and Punishment*, edited by Kevin R. Reitz. New York: Oxford University Press.
von Hirsch, Andrew, Anthony E. Bottoms, Elizabeth Burney, and Per-Olaf Wikström. 1999. *Deterrence and Sentence Severity: An Analysis of Recent Research*. Cambridge: University of Cambridge, Institute of Criminology.
Wald, Patricia M. 2015. "General Deterrence Comments Sent to Stephanie Middleton (ALI Deputy Director)." November 16.
Webster, Cheryl Marie, and Anthony N. Doob. 2012. "Searching for Sasquatch: Deterrence of Crime through Sehtence Severity." In *The Oxford Handbook of Sentencing and Corrections*, edited by Joan Petersilia and Kevin R. Reitz. New York: Oxford University Press.
Western, Bruce. 2006. *Punishment and Inequality in America*. New York: Russell Sage.
Whitman, James Q. 2003. *Harsh Justice: Criminal Punishment and the Widening Divide between America and Europe*. New York: Oxford University Press.
Wilson, William Julius. 1987. *The Truly Disadvantaged: The Inner City, the Underclass, and Public Policy*. Chicago: University of Chicago Press.
Wong, Stephen C. P., and Audrey Gordon. 2006. "The Validity and Reliability of the Violence Risk Scale: A Treatment-Friendly Violence Risk Assessment Tool." *Psychology, Public Policy, and Law* 12:279–309.
Wright, Ronald F. 1997. *Managing Prison Growth in North Carolina through Structured Sentencing*. Washington, DC: National Institute of Justice.
———. 2002. "Counting the Cost of Sentencing in North Carolina, 1980–2000." In *Crime and Justice: A Review of Research*, vol. 29, edited by Michael Tonry. Chicago: University of Chicago Press.
Zeng, Zhen. 2018. *Jail Inmates in 2016*. Washington, DC: Bureau of Justice Statistics.

Zimring, Franklin E. 1977. "Making the Punishment Fit the Crime: A Consumers' Guide to Sentencing Reform." Occasional Paper no. 12. Chicago: University of Chicago Law School.
Zimring, Franklin E., and Gordon Hawkins. 1995. *Incapacitation: Penal Confinement and the Restraint of Crime.* New York: Oxford University Press.

Brian D. Johnson

Trials and Tribulations: The Trial Tax and the Process of Punishment

ABSTRACT

The jury trial has long been a keystone of the American criminal justice system. Few defendants exercise their right to trial, however, and those who do tend to receive significantly harsher punishments if convicted. This phenomenon, known as a trial tax or, conversely, as a guilty plea discount, is one of the most profound and consistent findings in the empirical sentencing literature. Estimates of its magnitude differ across studies and jurisdictions, but it typically involves a two- to six-times increase in the odds of imprisonment and a 15–60 percent increase in average sentence length. Recent changes to American sentencing policy may have exacerbated plea-trial disparities, raising a host of moral, legal, and procedural questions about fair and equal treatment of defendants who exercise their right to trial.

Juries are often portrayed as bulwarks of democracy, the backbone of the American criminal justice system. Criminal defendants are constitutionally guaranteed the right to a jury trial, yet research on sentencing consistently indicates that trial convictions result in harsher sentences (King et al. 2005). This phenomenon, alternatively labeled a trial tax for those convicted after a trial or a plea discount for those who plead guilty, presents a fundamental tension between defendants' constitutional rights and the organizational realities of courts. The trial penalty is consistently found

Electronically published February 13, 2019
Brian D. Johnson is a professor of criminology at the University of Maryland. He would like to acknowledge Raquel Hernandez for valuable research assistance in the drafting of this essay.

© 2019 by The University of Chicago. All rights reserved.
0192-3234/2019/0048-0005$10.00

across jurisdictions, offense types, and over time, and it is among the most robust findings in the empirical sentencing literature. In recent decades, guilty plea rates have grown dramatically, and plea-trial disparities have worsened.

In early colonial America, juries decided nearly all criminal cases (Hans, Vidmar, and Zeisel 1986). Today, the story is much different. The disappearance of the jury trial is one of the defining characteristics of the modern American justice system. Few defendants exercise their constitutional right to trial. Even for very serious crimes involving lengthy prison sentences, the vast majority of defendants plead guilty. Guilty pleas have become the sine qua non of criminal case processing. As Supreme Court Associate Justice Anthony Kennedy observed in *Lafler v. Cooper*, 132 S. Ct. 1376, 1388 (2012), "criminal justice today is for the most part a system of pleas, not a system of trials."

The rising prevalence of guilty pleas has diverse causes, but there is little doubt that changes in sentencing law are part of the explanation. Sentencing reform in the 1970s and 1980s focused on reducing judicial discretion but did little to constrain prosecutorial discretion. Mandatory minimum, truth in sentencing, three-strikes, and similar laws enhanced the power of the prosecutor to influence and determine punishments. Contemporary prosecutors carry many punishment hammers in their toolboxes that can be used to threaten long sentences and convince defendants to forgo trial (McCoy 2005; Wright 2005; Lynch 2016).

The eclipse of the jury trial is a product of the increased power of the prosecutor, along with growing risks of lengthy trial sentences and a lack of procedural or other controls on plea bargaining. Defendants convicted at trial consistently receive harsher punishments than defendants who plead guilty. Estimates of the trial tax vary but typically involve two- to sixfold increases in the odds of imprisonment with 15–60 percent longer sentence lengths. Trial defendants are also less likely to receive mitigated sentences, such as downward departures from applicable guidelines, and are more likely to receive sentence enhancements, including mandatory minimums. Plea-trial disparities have contributed to the booming guilty plea rate and can result in disproportionately severe punishments for trial defendants. Trial taxes are also associated with racial disparities. Racial differences in who goes to trial may reflect different plea offers, plea negotiation resources, or defendants' levels of trust in the justice system. Large trial penalties may also contribute to false guilty pleas; when plea-trial disparities are large enough, some innocents are likely to plead guilty.

Plea-trial disparities also raise numerous philosophical, moral, and legal questions about defendants' procedural rights and the ways the trial tax shapes court actors' and defendants' decisions.

Empirical research on the trial tax is extensive but beset by fundamental methodological challenges. Guilty plea and trial cases are difficult to compare because they often differ in important ways. Jury trials are more likely to involve serious violent crimes, repeat offenders, and minority defendants, and counterfactual outcomes are unobservable. Estimates of the trial tax depend on basic analytical choices, including the modeling of related punishment processes. Moreover, conviction charges are often altered during plea bargaining, and some defendants who go to trial are acquitted.

Despite these complications, there are persuasive reasons to believe the trial tax is real and substantial. Quantitative studies consistently unearth large plea-trial disparities, qualitative research confirms their existence, and attempts to address sample selection issues do not explain it. Most likely, common methodological problems result in systematic underestimation of the size of the trial tax.

Section I of this essay places plea-trial sentencing disparities in historical context. I discuss key changes in sentencing policy and various explanations for growth in guilty plea rates. I argue that modern sentencing reforms increased prosecutors' influence on sentencing and contributed directly to growing trial penalties and increased reliance on plea bargaining. In Section II, I survey empirical research on the magnitude of trial penalties and their effects on racial disparities and wrongful convictions. I also discuss key differences between viewing plea-trial differences as a trial tax and as a plea discount and conclude that conceiving of it as a trial tax is more consistent with philosophical notions of justice. In Section III, I discuss common limitations of empirical approaches used to estimate plea-trial disparities. Existing work likely produces underestimates because it fails to account for differences in who pleads guilty and who goes to trial. Finally, in Section IV, I consider moral and ethical issues raised by plea-trial disparities and discuss policy proposals that aim to reduce the trial tax, restore the balance of power between judges and prosecutors, and create a fairer, more just, and more equitable sentencing system.

I. Criminal Justice Reform and the Rise of Guilty Pleas

To appreciate the contemporary landscape of plea-trial disparity, it is useful to begin with the rise of modern sentencing reforms. In the 1970s, a sea change occurred. Against the historical backdrop of the Vietnam War and the civil rights movement, rising civil discord and waning public trust fueled deadly race riots in American cities (Kerner Commission 1968). Prison uprisings garnered national attention and drove concerns about inequalities in the justice system. Scholars criticized excessive judicial discretion (Frankel 1973) and the ineffectiveness of rehabilitation (Martinson 1974), which led to a new "just deserts" philosophy that prioritized deservedness, proportionality, and fairness in punishment (von Hirsch 1976). Both liberals and conservatives lobbied for change; liberals focused on justice, fairness, and equality and conservatives on rising crime and the need for tougher sentences. With bipartisan political support, sentencing reforms proliferated. Sentencing guidelines were promulgated in nearly half the states and the federal government, mandatory minimums flourished along with habitual offender and three-strikes laws, discretionary parole release was partly or fully abolished in many jurisdictions, and new truth-in-sentencing laws required many prisoners to serve at least 85 percent of their sentences (Tonry 1996).

Modern sentencing reforms altered the scale of American punishment (Travis, Western, and Redburn 2014). The United States today has the world's highest incarceration rate: it accounts for 5 percent of the world's population but 25 percent of its prisoners. People of color have been disproportionately affected, constituting more than 60 percent of US prisoners, and one in 10 young black men in America are incarcerated (Bureau of Justice Statistics 2016; The Sentencing Project 2017). Changes to sentencing law played a major role in the rise of mass incarceration (Blumstein and Beck 1999), shifted the balance of discretionary power between prosecutors and judges, and contributed to the modern decline of the jury trial.

A. The Rise of Guilty Pleas and the Decline of the Jury

The right to a jury trial is embedded in the American democratic ethos. Article III of the US Constitution declares, "The trial of all crimes... shall be by jury." In colonial America, jury trials were the norm, providing a means of maintaining democratic representation and ensuring public legitimacy. Although other Western democracies also guarantee a right to trial, estimates suggest that 80 percent of jury trials worldwide occur in the United States (Hans, Vidmar, and Stevenson 1986). By the late nineteenth century, guilty pleas emerged as a competing form of case disposition in major urban jurisdictions, and by the early twentieth century, they were commonplace.

Smith (2005) identifies several factors that contributed to the rise of guilty pleas, including escalating caseload pressures, longer and more complex trials, and increased professionalization of prosecution. Plea bargaining is often viewed as an expedient developed to manage extreme caseloads, but a number of scholars challenge this (Alschuler 1983; Meeker and Pontell 1985; Feeley [1979] 1992; McCoy 2005). Empirical evidence is inconsistent and has yet to resolve the controversy (Wooldredge 1989). In all likelihood, Mather (1973, p. 187) was correct when she asserted that "while caseload pressures are doubtlessly important, they may be overemphasized in the current literature." Far less empirical work examines other explanations. Langbein (1979) argues that early trials were summary affairs that provided little incentive for circumvention, and Feeley (1997) suggests that increased vigor and complexity in the trial process popularized guilty pleas. Related work emphasizes institutional changes in the roles of police and prosecutors. Advances in policing, for example, led to improvements in the quality of evidence (Friedman and Percival 1981). The shift in the mid-nineteenth century from central appointment to local election of prosecutors may have also created new incentives for high conviction rates (Ellis 2012).

Failed legal challenges throughout the twentieth century also played an important role.[1] The centrality of plea bargaining was strengthened in the 1970s when the US Supreme Court in *Santobello v. New York*, 404 U.S. 257, 260 (1971), concluded that plea bargaining was "an essential component of the administration of justice," which when properly administered "is to be encouraged." Subsequent decisions solidified the supremacy of plea bargaining. In *Bordenkircher v. Hayes*, 434 U.S. 357 (1978), the Court held that prosecutors may constitutionally enhance charges if a defendant refuses to agree to a plea bargain.[2] More recently, in *Missouri v. Frye*, 132 S. Ct. 1399, 1407 (2012), Justice Kennedy opined that "plea bargaining . . .

---

[1] Early court opinions highlighted legal concerns. In 1958, a federal court of appeals judge argued that "justice and liberty are not the subjects of bargaining and barter" (*Sheldon v. United States*, 242 F. 2d 101 [5th Cir.] [1958]). A few years later, another appeals court declared, "It is clear . . . that a plea of guilty induced by a promise of lenient treatment is an involuntary plea and hence void" (*Scott v. United States*, 349 F. 2d 641, 643 [6th Cir.] [1965]).

[2] In this case, a trial defendant received a mandatory life sentence under a newly filed habitual offender charge, which the Court ruled was "constitutionally legitimate" because "the simple reality" is that "the prosecutor's interest at the bargaining table is to persuade the defendant to forgo his right to plead not guilty" (*Bordenkircher v. Hayes*, 434 U.S. 357, 364–65 [1978]).

is not some adjunct to the criminal justice system; it *is* the criminal justice system." These rulings effectively immunized prosecutorial charging decisions from judicial review, even when harsher sentences are explicitly threatened.

On its face, plea bargaining benefits all actors in the system. For prosecutors it ensures convictions, streamlines case processing, and conserves limited resources. For defendants, pleading guilty can lessen punishment. For judges, it assists in clearing crowded dockets. Judges rarely use their limited powers to curb plea bargains, tending to "rubber-stamp" rather than vigorously scrutinize them (Alschuler 1976). Although denounced by critics as "coercive," "disastrous," and even "pathological" (Schulhofer 1992; Alschuler 2003; McCoy 2005), plea bargaining is firmly entrenched in the American justice system.

The prosecutor's ability to craft plea negotiations that determine punishments, however, has grown considerably in recent decades. Estimates are that 97 percent of convicted felony offenders in large urban courts plead guilty, up from 90 percent just two decades ago (Reaves 2013). Approximately every 2 seconds during regular business hours, someone somewhere in the United States pleads guilty, and some county prosecutors have never taken a case to trial (Colquitt 2001; Turner 2017; Stemen and Escobar, forthcoming). Trials in misdemeanor cases are even rarer (Kutateladze and Lawson 2018). As figure 1 demonstrates, the federal guilty plea rate increased steadily throughout the 1990s, with the percentage of cases settled by trial falling from 12.3 percent in 1990 to 2.7 percent in 2016. The increased power of the prosecutor to threaten defendants with protracted terms of incarceration if they exercise their trial right offers one compelling explanation for this trend.

B. The Growing Power of the Prosecutor

Prosecutors have always exercised broad discretion. However, by focusing narrowly on judges, sentencing reforms concentrated additional power in the hands of prosecutors (Miethe 1987). Unlike sentencing decisions, charge determinations are largely immune from procedural review, formal legal challenge, and public oversight (Bibas 2001).[3] Some commenta-

---

[3] Although public elections in theory provide a check on prosecutorial misconduct, district attorneys often run unopposed for reelection and are reelected at very high rates (Wright 2009). Some research has shown that elected officials become more severe as elections approach (Gordon and Huber 2007; McCannon 2013).

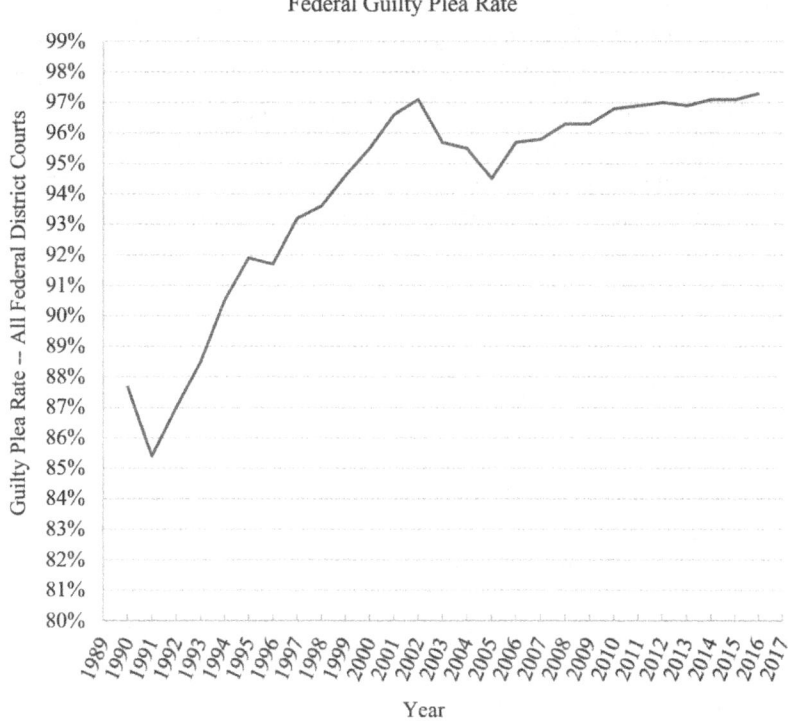

FIG. 1.—Federal guilty plea rates over time in US district courts. Source: USSC annual reports, 1990–95, and USSC Sourcebooks of Federal Sentencing Statistics, 1996–2016. Color version available as an online enhancement.

tors have likened the process to ordering from a menu of punishments (Stuntz 2004). Prosecutors have become the most powerful actors in the American justice system (Johnson, King, and Spohn 2016). Their discretionary powers have expanded so much that charging decisions are often de facto sentencing determinations (Bibas 2001).

Recent sentencing laws increased prosecutors' negotiating leverage. They can often threaten enormous sentences if defendants refuse to plead. This is especially true in federal courts, where US Attorneys can pressure reluctant defendants with an array of mandatory sentencing laws and enhancements. As the US Sentencing Commission (USSC 2004, p. 30) recognized, "Department policies allow prosecutors to invoke statutory minimum penalties and statutory enhancements as further incentives for guilty pleas." According to Lynch (2016, p. 80), once a defendant opts for trial, "all the options to worsen the client's situation [are] typically put into play." Mandatory minimums imbue prosecutors with immense plea-bargaining power and place considerable sentencing discretion in their hands (Nagel and Schulhofer 1992; Rehavi and Starr 2014).

Prosecutors can file superseding indictments if a defendant refuses to cooperate, and they control access to various types of mitigation, such as federal substantial assistance departures, which are available only at the prosecutor's request, and eligibility for "safety valve" provisions, which authorize sentences below statutory minimums (Stith and Cabranes 1998). As Federal Court of Appeals Judge Gerald Lynch (2003, pp. 1403–4) lamented, the prosecutor has largely replaced "the judge as arbiter of most legal issues and of the appropriate sentence to be imposed."

Although pleas bargaining dates back to the nineteenth century, it was less ubiquitous and less consequential before recent sentencing law changes. Prosecutors had less power, defendants were less at risk of excessive trial penalties, and parole release was available to mitigate punishments. Today, sentences imposed after trials often can be so severe that reasonable people, even if factually or legally innocent, may find it hard to refuse a proposed plea deal (McCoy 2005). "The distance between what is being offered and the potential sentencing exposure for those who go to trial" has become "so large that few defendants take the risk of turning down the offer" (Lynch 2016, p. 39). The empirical literature on the size and scope of the trial tax largely supports this observation.

II. The Size, Scope, and Impact of Trial Penalties

Defendants who plead guilty receive substantial sentence discounts. The evidence is overwhelming (Smith 1986; Johnson 2003; King et al. 2005; Ulmer and Bradley 2006; Ulmer, Eisenstein, and Johnson 2010; Bushway, Redlich, and Norris 2014; Johnson, King, and Spohn 2016). Diverse explanations have been offered, including offender remorse, concern for victims, and courtroom efficiency. One common argument is that guilty pleas are an expression of contrition that warrants sentencing leniency, in part because it is relevant to desert and culpability. Kramer and Ulmer (2009, p. 8), for instance, note that "a defendant's choice to plead guilty" has clear "ramifications for how court actors define his or her blameworthiness."

Although remorse is a legitimate sentencing consideration, there is little evidence that guilty pleas reliably indicate repentance. Defendants plead guilty for many reasons, including the expected punishment discount, making it difficult to isolate the effects of contrition from other considerations. At a minimum, high rates of guilty pleas (Ulmer, Eisenstein, and Johnson 2010) juxtaposed with high rates of recidivism (Bureau of Justice Statistics 2018) suggest that the plea itself is not a powerful marker of reformation.

A second rationale invokes victim hardship, arguing that guilty pleas enable victims to avoid the unpleasantness of testifying at trial. This argument is also unconvincing. If victim considerations were paramount, large plea-trial differentials would be expected only for crimes with victims, but this is not what research indicates. For example, Klein, Petersilia, and Turner (1990) found larger trial effects for burglary cases than for assaults or robberies in California courts. Moreover, large trial penalties exist for victimless crimes such as drug offenses in various states (King et al. 2005) and in federal courts (Lynch 2016).

A related claim is that plea-trial differences reflect "bad facts" that come out only at trial, when detailed offense behavior is dramatized to emphasize defendant culpability and dangerousness (Brereton and Casper 1982; Ulmer and Bradley 2006). This claim suffers from a similar shortcoming; it is difficult to imagine how "bad facts" explain the trial tax in garden variety property or drug cases. Moreover, bad facts are likely to encourage guilty pleas (Alschuler 1981), so cases with the "worst facts" may be less likely to go to trial.

By far the most common explanation for the trial tax is organizational efficiency: trial penalties incentivize guilty pleas to prevent high trial rates from immobilizing the justice system (Dixon 1995). A number of scholars have challenged this explanation, noting that the rise of plea bargaining was not associated with consistent increases in caseload pressure (Nardulli, Eisenstein, and Flemming 1988; Feeley 1992; McCoy 2005). Moreover, recent empirical work finds only modest associations between caseloads and trial rates (Ulmer and Bradley 2006; Ulmer, Eisenstein, and Johnson 2010). Overall, the weight of the evidence is tenuous and inconsistent (Wooldredge 1989).

Contrarily, some suggest that guilty pleas may produce more prosecutions, in the same "way that widening a highway can bring more traffic" (Sklansky 2018, p. 455). Whether or not this is the case, interviews with court actors repeatedly reveal a shared understanding that trial penalties are meant to encourage guilty pleas (e.g., Nardulli, Eisenstein, and Flemming 1988; Lynch 2016). As one trial judge in Chicago famously opined,

"He takes some of my time, I take some of his. That's the way it works" (Alschuler 1976, p. 1089).

A. The Plea Discount–Trial Tax Debate

There is disagreement over whether plea-trial disparities are plea discounts or trial penalties. Champions of discounts maintain that plea defendants receive rewards for admitting guilt and cooperating. Proponents of penalties argue that trial defendants are unfairly punished for exercising a constitutional right. This debate is more than semantic; it conveys implicit value judgments about appropriate punishments. The discount perspective assumes that appropriate sanctions are reflected in sentences after trial, whereas the penalty perspective treats sentences imposed after guilty pleas as the appropriate sanction.

The key question is whether differential treatment produces excessive sanctions for those convicted at trial. As Church (1979, p. 520) acknowledged in his spirited defense of plea bargaining, "trial sentences must be objectively *deserved*," which means the debate hinges on whether higher sentences following trial equate to warranted punishment or whether the trial tax itself exists primarily as a mechanism to encourage guilty pleas.

The idea of a plea discount made sense when trials were the norm, but that is no longer the case. Because the overwhelming majority of criminal defendants plead guilty, pleas have become the normative baseline. Bibas (2011, p. 1387) equates the guilty plea to buying a car in which "only an ignorant, ill-advised consumer would view the full price as the norm and anything less as a bargain." As Justice Anthony Kennedy observed in *Missouri v. Frye*, 132 S. Ct. 1399, 1407 (2012), trial defendants often receive "longer sentences than even Congress or the prosecutor might think appropriate, because the longer sentences exist on the books largely for bargaining purposes." This implies that the trial tax constitutes undue severity.

Court actors clearly rely on guilty pleas as benchmarks for appropriate punishment (Sudnow 1965), and plea-trial disparities are routinely justified by their plea-inducing powers (Alschuler 1968). Some suggest "that trials take place in the shadow of guilty pleas" rather than plea bargaining occurring in the shadow of judicial sentencing decisions (Wright and Miller 2003, p. 1415). The implication is that plea-trial disparities often result in excessive severity for trial defendants.

The choice of an appropriate baseline punishment is critical in estimating the magnitude of plea-trial disparities. Consider a case in which the expected sentence at trial is 10 years, and the expected sentence after a guilty plea is 5 years. Conceived of as a plea discount, the defendant receives a 50 percent reduction from the trial sentence; conceptualized as a trial penalty, he or she receives a 100 percent increase. Estimates of trial penalties will always be larger than equivalent plea discounts. One implication is that sentencing systems, as in England and Wales, that provide for explicit plea discounts underestimate potential trial penalties. The standard 33 percent sentence plea discount in the English system, conceptualized as a trial tax, becomes 50 percent.

B. The Magnitude of Contemporary Trial Penalties

Many studies provide point estimates for sentencing differences between plea and trial sentences, though few focus explicitly on explaining plea-trial disparities. Most include a measure of the mode of conviction while investigating other substantive issues. Much of this work examines the likelihood and length of incarceration; more recent work also considers additional sentencing decisions. Some studies focus on incarceration (e.g., Smith 1986), others separate jail and prison (e.g., Warren, Chiricos, and Bales 2012), and still others investigate only sentence lengths (Ulmer, Eisenstein, and Johnson 2010). Despite these and other differences, evidence demonstrating the trial tax is remarkably consistent.

Table 1 presents a selection of relevant work published in this century. It offers only a snapshot, not an exhaustive compilation, but it is useful for highlighting several findings. First, research on plea-trial differences is extensive. Most sentencing studies offer estimates of plea-trial disparity even when their focus lies elsewhere. Second, this work captures a wide array of jurisdictions that include many cities, different states, and the federal system. Some jurisdictions such as Pennsylvania and the federal courts are overrepresented because they have available, high-quality data. Third, the majority of studies focus on incarceration, sentence length, or, to a lesser extent, departures from sentencing guidelines. Only a few examine other outcomes such as charge reductions or use of community-based punishments. Finally, a stunning majority of studies report evidence of disadvantage for trial defendants. Figures 2 and 3 summarize typical effect sizes for trial conviction for the two most commonly examined outcomes: incarceration and sentence length. The evidence offers a clear and consistent pattern of harsher trial punishments.

It is important to acknowledge, however, that significant empirical issues complicate efforts to estimate plea-trial disparity. The standard

TABLE 1
Plea–Trial Differences in Criminal Punishment, Select Empirical Studies (2000–2018)

Authors	Year	Sample	Jurisdiction	Outcomes	Effect of Trial Conviction
Engen and Gainey	2000	$n = 36,949$ convicted offenders	Washington State	Sentence length	Average prison sentences are reduced between 6 and 13 months for defendants who plead guilty
Spohn and Holleran	2000	$n = 6,638$ convicted offenders	Chicago, Miami, Kansas	Imprisonment	Odds of a prison sentence are 2–7 times greater for trial defendants
Steffensmeier and Demuth	2000	$n = 89,637$ convicted offenders	Federal system	Imprisonment; sentence length	Trial conviction increases odds of imprisonment and results in 32–69 additional months of incarceration
Kautt	2002	$n = 21,474$ drug offenders	Federal system	Sentence length	Defendants convicted at trial receive sentences that are 39.5% longer on average
Johnson	2003	$n = 150,525$ convicted offenders	Pennsylvania	Guidelines departures	Jury trials reduce the odds of downward departure and increase odds of upward departures
Engen et al.	2003	$n = 51,844$ convicted offenders	Washington State	Departures; alternatives to incarceration	Guilty pleas are twice as likely to result in downward departures and more likely to involve alternatives
Ulmer and Johnson	2004	$n = 108,169$ convicted offenders	Pennsylvania	Incarceration; sentence length	Trial conviction increases odds of incarceration by 77%; average sentence lengths are 6 months longer

King et al.	2005	5 samples of convicted criminal cases from 5 states	5 states	Incarceration; sentence length	Plea-trial differences vary across offense types and jurisdictions but consistently suggest more severe penalties for trial defendants
McCoy	2005	$n = 2,772$ prison sentences	State Court Processing Statistics (SCPS)	Prison length	Defendants convicted by jury trial receive sentences that are 44.5 months longer on average
Wright	2005	$n = 704$ district-years	Federal	Guilty plea rates; acquittal rates	Guilty plea and acquittal rates are related to use of substantial assistance and acceptance of responsibility
Johnson	2006	$n = 148,590$ convicted offenders	Pennsylvania	Incarceration; sentence length	Odds of incarceration are 2 times greater for trial defendants and average sentence lengths are 60% longer
Ulmer and Bradley	2006	$n = 8,685$ serious violent offenders	Pennsylvania	Incarceration; sentence length	Odds of incarceration are 2.6 times greater for trial defendants and average sentences are 57% longer
Wooldredge	2007	$n = 2,954$ convicted felony defendants	24 Ohio counties	Incarceration; sentence length	Defendants who plea-bargain are about 1/3 as likely to be sentenced to prison and receive average prison lengths that are 16% shorter
Johnson et al.	2008	$n = 169,561$ convicted offenders	Federal system	Judicial departure; sub. asst. departure	The odds of judicial departure are .70 times lower for trial defendants and trial conviction all but precludes substantial assistance departures

TABLE 1 (*Continued*)

Authors	Year	Sample	Jurisdiction	Outcomes	Effect of Trial Conviction
Johnson and Betsinger	2009	$n = 188,937$ convicted offenders	Federal system	Incarceration; sentence length; departures	For trial defendants, odds of incarceration are twice as large, average sentence lengths are 19% longer, and guidelines departures are much less likely
Anderson and Spohn	2010	$n = 2,784$ imprisoned offenders	Minnesota, Nebraska, S. District of Iowa	Sentence length	Defendants who plead guilty receive sentences that are 4.1% or about 5 months shorter on average
Ulmer et al.	2010	$n = 115,440$ convicted offenders	Federal system	Sentence length	Average sentences are 37% longer for trial defendants
Abrams	2011	$n = 42,522$ criminal cases	Cook County, Illinois	Incarceration; sentence length	Plea defendants are twice as likely to be incarcerated and have sentences that are more than 1 year longer when trial acquittals are included in the sample
Bushway and Redlich	2012	$n = 1,808$ male burglary and robbery cases	5 cities	Incarceration	Predicted probability of prison at trial is 29.6% greater than in guilty plea cases
Johnson and DiPietro	2012	$n = 200,982$ convicted offenders	Pennsylvania	Probation; jail; prison; intermediate sanction;	Trial conviction reduces the odds of an intermediate sanction by 1/5 compared to prison and by 1/3 compared to jail.

Warren et al.	2012	n = 501,027 convicted offenders	Florida	Jail; prison; community supervision	Trial conviction increases odds of a jail sentence by 1.5 times and odds of a prison sentence by 6 times
Sutton	2013	n = 11,505 male defendants	State Court Processing Statistics (SCPS)	Pretrial detention; guilty pleas; sentence severity	Pleading guilty lowers the proportional odds of a more severe sentence by a factor of 2/3
Bushway et al.	2014	n = 1,664 judges, prosecutors and defense attnys.	All 50 states and Washington, DC	Plea sentence; conv. probability; exp. trial outcome	Plea deals are 60% shorter on average than expected sentences following trial conviction
Kim	2015	n = 207,352 federal offenders	Federal system	Sentence length (ln)	Sentence lengths are 64% longer for trial defendants after accounting for acceptance of responsibility
Kim et al.	2015	n = 2,686 federal offenders	Minnesota, Nebraska, S. District of Iowa	Sentence length (ln)	Sentence lengths decrease by 17% for defendants who plead guilty
Roberts and Bradford	2015	n = 43,108 Crown Court Sentencing Survey	England and Wales	Plea-based sentence reductions	The modal sentence reduction for pleading guilty is equal to a 1/3 discount on sentence length.
Hester and Sevigny	2016	n = 17,671 felony and serious misdemeanors	South Carolina	Incarceration; expected sentences	Odds of incarceration are 9 times greater for defendants convicted at trial
King and Johnson	2016	n = 866 black and white felony offenders	Minnesota	Sentence type; sentence length	Trial conviction increases the odds of an executed prison sentence by nearly 15 times but produces no difference in sentence lengths

TABLE 1 (*Continued*)

Authors	Year	Sample	Jurisdiction	Outcomes	Effect of Trial Conviction
Ulmer et al.	2016	$n = 192,446$ convicted offenders	Pennsylvania and federal system	Imprisonment; sentence length	Trial conviction quadruples the odds of prison and results in 27% longer sentences in PA; it doubles the odds of prison and results in 16% longer sentences in federal court
Zottoli et al.	2016	$n = 55$ adolescents and 42 adults	New York City	Qualitative data on plea discounts	Adults report average sentencing discounts of 80%, and adolescents 90%, relative to trial sentences
Johnson and King	2017	$n = 1,119$ convicted offenders	Minnesota	Sentence type	Trial conviction increases the odds of an executed prison sentence by 9.4 times relative to guilty pleas
USSC	2017	$n = 59,160$ convicted offenders	Federal system	Sentence length (ln)	Trial conviction increases average sentence lengths by 53%
Breen and Johnson	2018	$n = 2,473$ military courts-martials	US Air Force	Sentence severity; clemency	Defendants convicted by trial receive less sentence severity and are more likely to be granted clemency
Kutateladze	2018	$n = 170,572$ misdemeanor and felony cases	New York County	Charge decrease; charge increase	Cases disposed of via guilty pleas are more likely to result in cumulative decreases in charge severity
Metcalfe and Chiricos	2018	$n = 907$ (409 trials and 498 pleas)	Florida (1 county)	Type of conviction; plea value	Probability of receiving a charge reduction is significantly greater for defendants who plead guilty

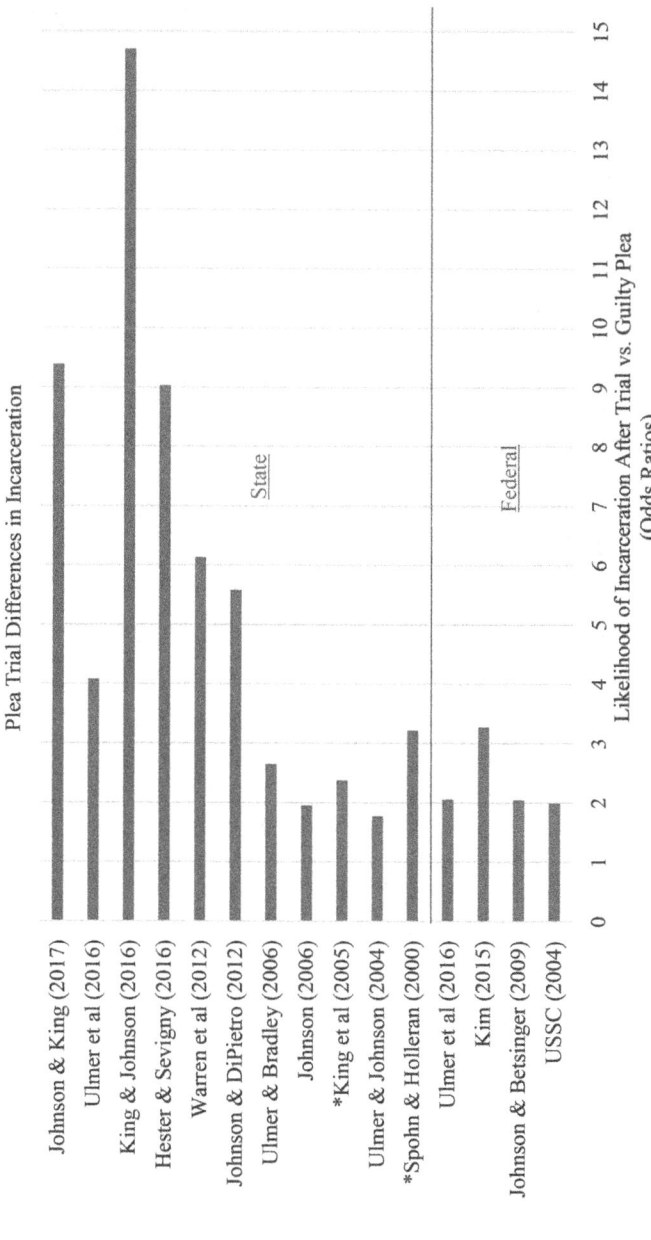

Fig. 2.—Plea-trial differences in incarceration across state and federal studies (2000–2017). Reported estimates are limited to jury trial/guilty plea comparisons. Average trial effects are shown for studies denoted by an * that report information for multiple subsamples. Color version available as an online enhancement.

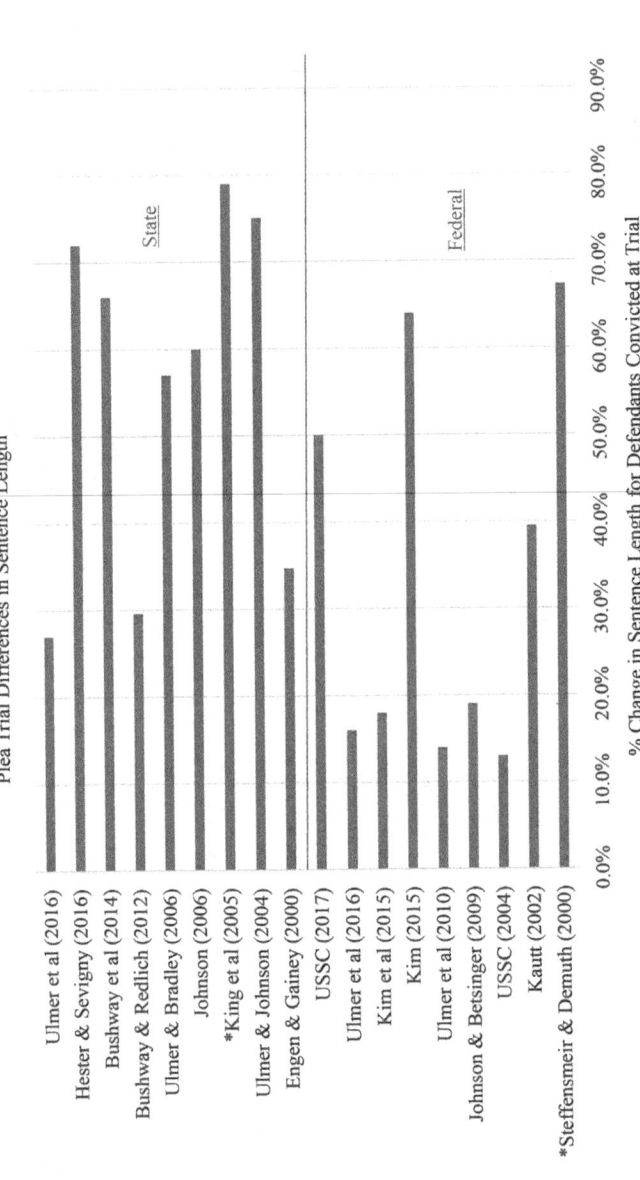

FIG. 3.—Plea-trial differences in sentence length across federal and state studies (2000–2017). Reported estimates are limited to jury trial/guilty plea comparisons. Average trial effects are shown for studies denoted by an * that report information for multiple subsamples. Color version available as an online enhancement.

approach compares defendants convicted by plea to defendants convicted by trial, after statistically controlling for other factors. This type of comparison is imperfect for several reasons: it does not account for selection processes that sort defendants into pleas and trials, it risks omitted variables related to mode of conviction and sentence severity, and it often fails to capture intermediate processes that condition trial effects in punishment. Despite these limitations, which I discuss in Section III, the consistency of results and the sheer magnitude of trial effects clearly support the existence of a substantial trial tax. Trial effects vary across offenses, jurisdictions, and individual studies, but they appear with remarkable consistency in both state and federal courts.

1. *The Trial Tax in State Courts.* Most empirical work has concentrated on a small number of states, usually early guidelines states in which sentencing data are readily accessible. The vast majority of studies investigate the likelihood and length of incarceration. Early work reported modest trial effects. For example, Miethe and Moore (1985) found that trial conviction in Minnesota increased the likelihood of incarceration by only 9 percent (cf. Moore and Miethe 1986; Frase 1993). Subsequent work, however, shows larger plea-trial disparities. Dixon (1995) found that trial conviction increased the odds of imprisonment by a factor of four and resulted in an extra year of incarceration. The most recent studies report even larger effects, from a nine- to 15-fold increase in the odds of imprisonment for trial defendants (King and Johnson 2016; Johnson and King 2017). Frase (2005a, pp. 178–79) has observed that "evaluations by outside researchers have revealed the continued existence of plea-trial disparities," which reflect "tacit or explicit sentence bargaining that causes reduced sentence severity for defendants who plead guilty."

In Pennsylvania, another early guidelines state, dozens of studies conclude that trial conviction increases the likelihood and length of incarceration. Steffensmeier, Ulmer, and Kramer (1998) estimated that the odds of incarceration were three times greater after jury trials than guilty pleas and that average sentences were more than a year longer. Ulmer and Johnson (2004) found odds of incarceration 77 percent greater for trial defendants and average incarceration terms that were 6 months longer. Ulmer and Bradley (2006) focused on serious violent offenders and reported similar-sized estimates, and Johnson (2006) found that trial cases were roughly twice as likely as guilty pleas to result in incarceration with terms of imprisonment that were 60 percent longer.

Studies from other states and local jurisdictions are less abundant but remarkably consistent. Early work in California reported that trial defendants were more likely to receive prison sentences, and for longer terms, in a number of different courts (Brereton and Casper 1982) and for various offense types (Klein, Petersilia, and Turner 1990). In Washington State, Engen and Gainey (2000) reported that average prison sentences were between 6 and 13 months less for defendants who pled guilty. In Maryland, Bushway and Piehl (2001) found that guilty pleas were among the strongest predictors of incarceration. Recent work from South Carolina, a state without sentencing guidelines, demonstrates that trial conviction is associated with a ninefold increase in the odds of incarceration (Hester and Sevigny 2016). Significantly, this large South Carolina trial penalty coexists with state trial rates of less than 1.5 percent. Research from Florida also reports large plea-trial differences; compared with sentences after guilty pleas, defendants convicted at trial are one and one-half times more likely to be sentenced to jail and over six times more likely to receive prison (Warren, Chiricos, and Bales 2012).

Even studies that compare diverse jurisdictions report consistent plea-trial disparities. Early work by LaFree (1985) examined robbery and burglary cases in six locales and discovered consistent evidence of trial disadvantages after controlling for strength of evidence, case severity, and various offender and offense characteristics. Recent multijurisdictional studies reach similar conclusions. Spohn and Holleran (2000) investigated sentencing disparities in three cities, Chicago, Miami, and Kansas City, and found large trial penalties in two of the three, with trial defendants between two and seven times more likely to be sentenced to prison. King et al. (2005), in a comparison of five guidelines states, found that the magnitude of trial effects varied across offense types and jurisdictions but concluded there was a consistent pattern of trial disadvantage with regard to both incarceration and sentence length.[4]

Recent work at the state level has investigated additional punishment outcomes, such as departures from sentencing guidelines (Johnson 2003),

---

[4] The five states were Kansas, Maryland, Minnesota, Pennsylvania, and Washington. Especially large trial penalties were found in Kansas for drug offenses involving depressants/stimulants, resulting in sentence lengths five times longer for trial defendants. In Maryland, trial conviction for cocaine distribution had the largest trial effects, increasing the odds of incarceration by 6.5 times. In Pennsylvania, assault offenses convicted by trial demonstrated the largest plea-trial disparities, increasing the odds of incarceration by 3.7 times. In Washington State, child molestation offenses received especially long sentences at trial, on average more than five times longer than following guilty pleas.

use of alternative sanctions (Engen et al. 2003), application of mandatory minimums (Ulmer, Kurlychek, and Kramer 2007), and charge reductions (Metcalfe and Chiricos 2018). Controlling for a wide range of relevant sentencing factors, defendants who go to trial are less likely to receive downward departures, which significantly mitigate punishment (Engen et al. 2003; Johnson 2003, 2005). Moreover, Engen et al. (2003) show that sentencing alternatives are more likely to be used following guilty pleas. Johnson and DiPietro (2012) report similar results for intermediate sanctions. Defendants convicted at trial are also more likely to receive mandatory minimums (Ulmer, Kurlychek, and Kramer 2007) and less likely to benefit from charge reductions (Metcalfe and Chiricos 2018). Collectively, this work suggests that traditional studies that focus only on incarceration and sentence length are likely to underestimate the cumulative trial tax.

2. *The Trial Tax in Federal Court.* Findings on federal plea-trial sentencing differentials are similar. Most studies indicate that tried cases are about twice as likely as guilty pleas to result in incarceration, with imprisonment terms between one-sixth and two-thirds longer (USSC 2004, 2010, 2017; Johnson and Betsinger 2009; Ulmer, Eisenstein, and Johnson 2010; Ulmer, Light, and Kramer 2011; Kim 2015; Kim, Spohn, and Hedberg 2015). Early research by the USSC (2004) reported a twofold increase in the odds of imprisonment for trial defendants. Recent work shows that average trial sentences are about 50 percent longer, even after controlling for a wide range of sentencing considerations (USSC 2017). A number of studies focus on drug offenders. Kautt (2002), for instance, found average plea-trial sentencing differentials of more than 2 years for federal drug traffickers, and Steffensmeier and Demuth (2000) reported trial penalties of 32 months for nondrug offenses and 69 months for drug offenses.

One complication with federal studies is that plea-trial differentials are closely related to intermediate case processing decisions, including acceptance of responsibility and downward departures. The federal system is unique in providing an explicit sentencing discount for "acceptance of responsibility." Defendants who plead guilty usually receive a two- or three-level reduction in their federal guidelines level, which equates to a sentence reduction of 25–35 percent (Schulhofer and Nagel 1989, 1997; O'Sullivan 1997).[5] Ironically, the federal sentencing commission made acceptance of

---

[5] The magnitude of the discount for acceptance of responsibility depends on the offense level of the current crime as well as the criminal history category of the defendant. For example, an offender charged with a level 26 offense who has no criminal history and receives

responsibility an independent reason to discount sentences because of concern that overt plea discounts would violate the constitutional right to trial. In practice, though, the reduction is nearly automatic in guilty pleas (Wilkins 1988; O'Hear 1997; Kim 2015).[6]

Federal plea-trial disparities are closely tied to other sentencing discounts, such as "substantial assistance departures" that are awarded for cooperation in the prosecution of another criminal case.[7] Research indicates that pleading guilty is effectively a requirement for receipt of the substantial assistance discount (Johnson and Betsinger 2009; Ulmer, Eisenstein, and Johnson 2010). The magnitude of federal plea-trial disparities depends on how researchers address these and other case processing factors (Kim 2015).

As in state courts, earlier studies of federal sentencing tend to find smaller trial effects than more recent work. Research conducted by the USSC suggests that plea-trial disparities have worsened in the wake of recent policy changes. After controlling for a wide range of sentencing variables, including guidelines departures and mandatory minimums, the commission reports that trial penalties increased from 24 percent in the post–PROTECT Act period (2003), to 36 percent in the post-*Booker* period (2005), to 51 percent in the post-*Gall* period (2007) (USSC 2010; Ulmer, Light, and Kramer 2011).[8] This final estimate is very similar to commis-

---

a three-level reduction for acceptance of responsibility would have his or her minimum recommended sentence under the guidelines reduced from 63 months to 46 months, or roughly 27 percent. At lower offense levels, acceptance of responsibility can be the difference between more than a year of prison and no incarceration at all.

[6] In its 15-year report on federal sentencing, the USSC (2004, p. 29) noted that the original commission established acceptance of responsibility so that "defendants retained sufficient incentive to plead guilty and the number of trials facing an already overburdened federal court system would not be increased"; it was intended "as a reward for offenders who plead guilty and also as a recognition of the reduced culpability of offenders who acknowledged guilt." Kim (2015) reports that 97 percent of defendants who plead guilty receive the discount.

[7] Upon motion of the government that a defendant has provided "substantial assistance" in the investigation or prosecution of another federal offense, the court may depart below the recommended range of the federal guidelines. The Assistant US Attorney must file a motion requesting this discount.

[8] The PROTECT Act was passed in 2003 and discouraged downward departures. It refers to the Prosecutorial Remedies and Other Tools to End the Exploitation of Children Today Act (Pub. L. No. 108-21, 117 Stat. 650 [2003]). *United States v. Booker*, 543 U.S. 220 (2005), made the federal sentencing guidelines advisory. *Gall v. United States*, 552 U.S. 38 (2007), held that courts of appeal must review all sentences using a deferential "abuse of discretion" standard.

sion analyses of the most recent data (USSC 2017). At least on the surface, then, the federal trial penalty is substantial and has increased inversely with declining trial rates. These results are consistent with the argument that the trial penalty drives the plea-bargaining machine (Brereton and Casper 1982).

US military courts provide a notable exception in the trial tax literature. Breen and Johnson (2018) show that trial conviction in the military justice system is significantly associated with sentence leniency and with increased odds of clemency, which they attribute to the military's distinctive organizational structure and culture. Jury trials are much more common in military courts, jury sentencing is often employed, and plea bargains provide only sentencing caps; bargaining chips and sentence discounts thus are less influential. This suggests that alternative approaches to structuring plea bargaining can have important consequences for plea-trial disparity.

Outside of this anomaly, though, research in state and federal courts finds consistent evidence of less favorable outcomes for trial defendants. This is consistent with early observations of the National Academy of Sciences panel on sentencing reform: "The strongest and most consistently found effect of case-processing variables is the role of guilty pleas in producing less severe sentences" (Blumstein et al. 1983, p. 18).

C. The Trial Tax and Social Inequality in Punishment

The pervasiveness of the trial tax has broader implications for social equality. Given the large effects trial conviction has on sentencing, it is important to consider who goes to trial and how this shapes patterns of disparity. Research indicates that certain types of defendants are more likely to exercise their right to trial. Defendants of color, in particular, are more likely than similarly situated white defendants to go to trial (LaFree 1980; Albonetti 1990; Frenzel and Ball 2008; Metcalfe and Chiricos 2018). According to Alschuler (1976, p. 1125), this is part of a broader phenomenon in which the guilty plea process is influenced by "penologically irrelevant considerations" including "defense attorney charm," "past favors," "friendship," and the "race, wealth or bail status of the defendant." Despite the storied legacy of empirical research on race and sentencing (Spohn 2000; Tonry 2011; Ulmer 2012), relatively little empirical work focuses on the intersections of race, guilty pleas, and trial penalties.

Albonetti (1990) showed that defendant race, along with certain case characteristics, predicted the likelihood of a guilty plea. African American defendants and those with serious criminal histories were more likely to go to trial, as were defendants whose cases involved weaker evidence and more serious charges. Other studies provide additional support for these findings (Frenzel and Ball 2008; Sutton 2013; Metcalfe and Chiricos 2018). Metcalfe and Chiricos, for instance, show that black defendants, and black men in particular, are less likely to plead guilty and receive less return on their guilty pleas.

Researchers have identified a number of reasons for this, including differential bargaining power (Savitsky 2012), quality of plea offers (Kutateladze et al. 2014), and perceived trust in the justice system (Hurwitz and Peffley 2005). Minority defendants often have less bargaining power because race and ethnicity are tied to broader patterns of social stratification, such as social and economic disadvantage (Sampson and Lauritsen 1997). At the same time, less favorable plea offers may induce more minority defendants to go to trial. This could result from several factors, including implicit racial biases on the part of prosecutors (Smith and Levinson 2012), racial differences in the timing of guilty pleas (Hood 1992), or differences in the quality or type of defense representation (Kutateladze and Andiloro 2014; Stemen and Escobar, forthcoming).

Differential trust in the criminal justice system may also be important. Plea bargains often involve a confusing and ambiguous process that requires defendants to trust in representatives of the state (Tata and Gormley 2016). Lower perceptions of the justice system's legitimacy likely translate into reluctance to cooperate with prosecutors. It is not surprising that defendants who perceive the justice system to be less equitable would be disinclined to enter into plea negotiations (Albonetti 1990). This logic aligns closely with broader perspectives on procedural justice that suggest that perceived legitimacy of the legal system is closely associated with compliance and cooperation with the law (Tyler 2006).

Finally, guilty plea outcomes may be affected by differential treatment at earlier stages of the justice system, such as biases in police interactions, enforcement patterns, and arrest behaviors (Kochel, Wilson, and Mastrofski 2011; Kurlychek and Johnson, forthcoming). Defendants who are mistreated at earlier stages are less likely to be cooperative at later stages, and they may be negatively affected by the accumulation of significant criminal histories. Minority status tends to be associated with less frequent and later guilty pleas, both of which likely contribute to racial disproportionality in punishment. If minority defendants are more likely to opt for trial and trial convictions result in harsher sentences, then disparities in guilty plea behaviors could contribute directly to racial inequalities in sentencing.

D. *The Trial Tax and False Guilty Pleas*

Large plea-trial sentencing differentials may coerce innocent defendants to plead guilty. Immense sentencing exposure at trial generates extreme pressure for defendants to consider the risk-reducing benefits of plea deals. Although it may seem counterintuitive that an innocent defendant would plead guilty, there are compelling reasons why it happens. Many defendants are passive participants in plea negotiations, are inexperienced in convoluted criminal procedures, and are challenged by a legal argot they do not fully understand. Often they have limited educational, social, and financial resources, and their decisions are shaped by the pressure, stress, and anxiety of facing criminal charges (Tata and Gormley 2016; Zottoli et al. 2016). In some cases, it may be rational to plead guilty because the costs of a trial clearly outweigh a lenient bargain.

Some scholars argue that false guilty pleas are particularly likely in low-level offenses and when trial penalties are especially large (Blume and Helm 2014). This is consistent with work by Feeley (1992, pp. 30–31), who argued that pleading guilty to low-level misdemeanors often makes sense because it avoids the "time, effort, money and opportunities lost as a direct result of being caught up in the system." For minor crimes, a small but certain punishment is often preferable, whereas for serious offenses, high ceilings for trial punishments provide strong inducements to plead guilty (Dervan and Edkins 2013; Bushway, Redlich, and Norris 2014).

Research demonstrates that innocent defendants do plead guilty when trial penalties are large enough (Alschuler 1968; Scott and Stuntz 1992; Garrett 2011; Bushway, Redlich, and Norris 2014; Redlich et al. 2014). False guilty pleas are most likely when plea-trial disparities are large, when incarceration or capital punishment is at stake, and when defendants are detained pretrial (Gross et al. 2005; Wright 2005; Blume and Helm 2014). Dervan and Edkins (2013, p. 17) argue that, although precise numbers are elusive, "it is clear that plea bargaining has an innocence problem." They found that more than half of innocents in vignette scenarios were willing to admit guilt falsely when plea discounts were large. Interviews with convicted defendants support these findings. Zottoli et al. (2016) asked offenders about their guilty plea decisions and found that roughly one in five adults and one in four juveniles reported that they pled guilty only because of the substantial discounts they were promised.

Additional evidence comes from exonerations (Blume and Helm 2014). The National Registry of Exonerations reports that about 18 percent of exonerated defendants pled guilty to crimes of which they were factually innocent. Other research shows that large plea discounts are the primary reason (Turner 2017), and it is likely that many more false guilty pleas escape detection.

This raises fundamental questions about whether trial penalties produce perverse incentives to plead guilty. As the "magnitude of the discount increases, so too, does the likelihood that innocent defendants will enter a guilty plea" (Roberts and Bradford 2015, p. 188). This implies that actual innocence will be most likely when trial penalties are most pronounced. If prosecutors scale plea discounts to the strength of the case, as evidence suggests (Bushway, Redlich, and Norris 2014), weaker cases will result in larger plea discounts, greater plea-trial differentials, and increased incentives for innocent defendants to waive their Sixth Amendment rights. This is consistent with theoretical arguments from the "shadow of the trial" perspective, which suggests that prosecutors are incentivized to offer larger discounts when conviction is less certain. If plea incentives are increased in cases with greater factual and legal doubt, it suggests that trial taxes contribute to false guilty pleas. Assessing the evidence, Zottoli et al. (2016, p. 257) conclude that "findings of deep discounts . . . bring into question the true voluntariness of plea decisions and speak to the need for a closer examination of the plea-bargaining process with respect to its potential to be coercive."

These concerns are especially strong for defendants held in pretrial detention, when a guilty plea can often resolve the charges and lead to immediate release. On any given day, two-thirds of American jail inmates are detained awaiting trial rather than because of a conviction (Bureau of Justice Statistics 2015). Monetary bail systems require financial resources for release and systematically disadvantage poor and indigent defendants (Demuth 2003; Schlesinger 2005; Wooldredge et al. 2015; Stevenson and Mayson 2017). Plea offers to "time served" in misdemeanor cases often mean defendants can go home, stacking significant personal, family, and economic pressures on the guilty plea decision (Heaton, Mayson, and Stevenson 2017). There is strong and consistent evidence that pretrial detention increases the likelihood of a guilty plea, the odds of trial conviction, and the severity of sentencing (Schlesinger 2005; Wooldredge et al. 2015; Stevenson and Mayson 2017). Financial release mechanisms thus enhance the significance of trial penalties, exacerbate pressure to plead guilty, and contribute to false guilty pleas among detained defendants (Bibas 2004). This highlights the potential for broader criminal justice reforms, such as restricting the use of monetary bail, to have salutary effects on other outcomes, including guilty plea decisions.

III. Conceptual and Empirical Issues in Estimating the Trial Tax

Defendants convicted at trial face a stark sentencing disadvantage, but its magnitude and meaning depend on how it is defined and operationalized. Estimates of the size of the trial tax vary along several dimensions. These include conceptual distinctions in questions asked, differences in analytic approaches, the data and jurisdiction under study, and whether and how estimates are adjusted for other factors, such as intermediate case processing decisions or the possibility of acquittal at trial.

First, disciplinary differences have led to a fundamental confusion between two related but distinct research questions. The first is "whether it is just to penalize defendants who assert their constitutional right to trial by jury and are convicted" (LaFree 1985, p. 292). This is consistent with analyses of conviction samples, the predominant approach, which report large and consistent trial penalties (Johnson 2003; King et al. 2005; Ulmer, Eisenstein, and Johnson 2010). The second is whether it "pays to plead guilty." This focuses on rationality in the decision-making processes of defendants and court actors. Studies asking this question often find that plea-trial disparities are small or nonexistent when acquitted defendants are included in analyses (Rhodes 1979; LaFree 1985; Smith 1986; Abrams 2011; Bushway and Redlich 2012; Bushway, Redlich, and Norris 2014). Early work by Smith (1986), for example, showed that defendants were almost 30 percent less likely to be incarcerated if they pled guilty, but that the majority of this effect was offset by the probability of acquittal at trial. Smith concluded that plea-trial disparity represents a rational balance between certain but discounted plea punishments and uncertain but severe trial sentences. LaFree (1985) and Bushway and Redlich (2012) also demonstrate how the possibility of acquittal counterbalances plea discounts.

Abrams's (2011) study of Cook County, Illinois, illustrates how these two questions can become muddled. After adjusting for the likelihood of acquittal at trial, he concludes that "a risk-neutral defendant seeking to minimize his or her expected sentence would do substantially better by rejecting a plea bargain," leading him to question the significance of the trial tax (p. 200). However, as Alschuler (2013) observes, acquittals do not change the pronounced sentencing disparities between those convicted by plea or trial.[9]

Much of the disagreement in the conceptual debate surrounding plea discounts and trial penalties reduces to a misunderstanding of these conceptual issues. When comparing outcomes of convicted offenders there is a pronounced and compelling trial tax in punishment. When considering whether it is "rational" to plead guilty, evidence often supports the hypothesis that plea discounts produce punishments roughly equivalent to trial sentences discounted by the probability of acquittal (Bushway, Redlich, and Norris 2014). Different empirical approaches are related to disciplinary norms: criminologists tend to focus on whether it is just to penalize individual trial defendants, whereas economists mostly focus on rationality in plea bargaining. Even an economist must admit, though, that it is little solace to trial defendants serving elongated prison terms to know that their added punishment is balanced out by the possibility of acquittals in other cases.

Second, the relative magnitude of plea-trial differences depends on how empirical analyses address other case processing factors. The decision to go to trial affects other factors related to punishment severity. Trial defendants are less likely to receive favorable charge reductions (Metcalfe and Chiricos 2018) or beneficial guidelines departures (Johnson 2005), and they are more likely to be affected by mandatory minimums and other sentence enhancements (Ulmer, Kurlychek, and Kramer 2007; Lynch 2016). In the federal system, they are effectively precluded from discounts such as "acceptance of responsibility" and "substantial assistance" (Johnson, Ulmer, and Kramer 2008; Ulmer, Eisenstein, and Johnson 2010; Kim 2015).

Studies that incorporate statistical controls for these types of intermediate outcomes almost certainly underestimate the full impact of trial conviction on punishment. For example, Ulmer, Eisenstein, and Johnson (2010) demonstrate that estimates of federal trial penalties shrink from a 37 percent difference in sentence length to a 14 percent difference when intermediate case processing factors are included. Kim (2015) argues that plea-related sentence discounts, such as acceptance of responsibility, are

---

[9] The Abrams (2011) study has been criticized on empirical grounds. Kim (2015) notes that estimates of conviction rates at trial mistakenly include all defendants whose cases ended without a conviction rather than only trial acquittals.

inseparably tied to the guilty plea process and therefore constitute an important element of the trial tax. He reports that trial sentences are 64 percent longer than guilty plea sentences when these additional influences are considered. Most studies of federal sentencing include controls for some but not all intermediate factors. For example, the USSC controls for guidelines departures in its statistical models but not acceptance of responsibility (USSC 2004, 2017).[10] At least some of the variation in plea-trial disparity, then, reflects analytical choices concerning indirect case processing factors.

Third, a persistent problem is that it is impossible to observe counterfactual punishments for alternative modes of conviction. As LaFree (1985, p. 291) explained, "Comparing sentence severity for guilty pleas and trials is difficult because they represent different processes to which defendants are non-randomly assigned." Any contrast of plea and trial defendants therefore risks comparing oranges to basketballs, so to speak. Trial and plea defendants often differ in key ways: trial defendants are more likely to be charged with more serious crimes, have longer criminal histories, and be male and minority (Albonetti 1990; Frenzel and Ball 2008; Abrams 2011; Metcalfe and Chiricos 2018). Quality empirical studies include a battery of covariates to account for these differences, but omitted variable bias remains a concern. Moreover, the punishment process itself differs in important ways depending on the mode of conviction. For example, prosecutors have far more control over the outcomes of negotiated guilty pleas, whereas judges tend to have greater influence in bench and jury trials (Johnson 2003).

A closely related issue is that sentences are based on offenses of conviction, whereas plea negotiations revolve around charges at arrest and arraignment. A dynamic process of charge alterations often takes place during the guilty plea process (Spohn, Beichner, and Davis-Frenzel 2001; Shermer and Johnson 2010; Kutateladze 2018). Because prosecutors often offer a reduction in the number, type, or severity of initial charges, the final conviction charge may differ considerably from the underlying offense behavior. Contemporary work in Wisconsin, for example, finds that

---

[10] The rationale for excluding measures such as acceptance of responsibility or obstruction of justice is that they are already incorporated into the presumptive guidelines recommendation, which is routinely included as a control variable; however, this approach precludes examination of the indirect influences these factors might have on plea-trial disparities in punishment (Ulmer, Eisenstein, and Johnson 2010).

one in three defendants plead to a lesser charge (Stemen and Escobar, forthcoming). Research in New York County shows that about 40 percent of felony arrests involve charge reductions between arrest and filing, and another 60 percent are reduced during plea bargaining; moreover, two-thirds of felony arrests in that jurisdiction end in misdemeanor convictions (Johnson and Larroulet, forthcoming). Because charge reductions are common, analyses that statistically "control" or match on the offense at conviction may end up comparing very different defendants. Newman (1956, p. 780) made this observation long ago pointing out that a "man's conviction record is assumed to be a quasi-automatic legal stamp which defines those activities which make him a criminal," yet "very few researchers would treat a person such as Al Capone as merely an income tax violator."

Comparisons of guilty pleas and trials are further complicated because defendants who go to trial may be acquitted while those who plead guilty forfeit this possibility. This is another bias that can skew comparisons of convicted defendants. Although the full scope of selection bias in trial tax research is difficult to quantify, it seems likely that it works to underestimate plea-trial disparity.

Because defendants who negotiate guilty pleas are often convicted of lesser crimes, they represent relatively more serious offenders, relative to their offenses at conviction. In theory, this should suppress estimates of the sentencing differential between plea and trial defendants.[11] This suggests that trial disparities would be even greater if we were able truly to compare oranges to oranges (or basketballs to basketballs), by restricting analyses of plea-trial differentials to offenders who *commit* the same offenses rather than compare offenders who are *convicted* of comparable crimes.

Little empirical research directly examines this issue, but several studies attempt to adjust for this form of sample selection bias. Abrams (2011) used an instrumental variable to address selection and found that it increased disparity estimates by 3–7 months. Other promising methods include counterfactual approaches, which generate estimates of expected plea or trial sentences for the same sets of defendants (Smith 1986; Bushway and Redlich 2012; Johnson and Larroulet, forthcoming) and exper-

---

[11] Consider a robbery defendant who pleads guilty and is convicted only of assault. When compared to a trial defendant who was originally charged and convicted for assault, the former is likely to be a relatively more serious offender.

imental case vignettes that allow for direct manipulation of the mode of conviction.[12]

Bushway and Redlich (2012) estimated plea discounts on the basis of what would have likely happened if plea defendants had gone to trial. They found that guilty plea sentences averaged 77 percent of expected trial sentences. Related work employing survey data from a large sample of prosecutors, judges, and defense attorneys found that court actors sentenced a hypothetical robbery case to 10 years following a trial conviction and to 6 years following a plea; this suggests a 40 percent plea discount or a 66 percent trial penalty (Bushway, Redlich, and Norris 2014). Overall, findings from alternative analytical approaches support the trial effect found in more traditional studies.

Future Directions for Research on the Trial Tax. Additional research should address a number of unresolved issues. Little work examines how other salient offense, offender, and case processing factors affect trial penalties. Some work suggests that larger trial penalties occur in serious cases facing the harshest punishments (Clark and Kurtz 1983; Ulmer and Bradley 2006; Ulmer, Eisenstein, and Johnson 2010). Wright and Engen (2006) argue that the magnitude of plea discounts depends fundamentally on the "depth and distance" of the legal code, which implies that trial penalties will vary with the seriousness of the offense. Few studies investigate this issue, but those that do find variation in trial penalties across offenses (Rhodes 1979; Clark and Kurtz 1983; Klein, Petersilia, and Turner 1990; King et al. 2005). Future work should try to establish how and why trial effects differ by crime type.

Other research points to the importance of timing (LaFree 1985; Tonry 2012; Kutateladze, Andiloro, and Johnson 2016). Plea discounts may be especially pronounced for defendants who plead earlier in the process. LaFree (1985) found no evidence of this, but Kutateladze, Andiloro, and Johnson (2016) reported that plea offers became less favorable over time in misdemeanor marijuana cases. That study was conducted in a jurisdiction with a "first-best" plea policy under which prosecutors provided the most favorable plea offer at arraignment, suggesting that the impor-

---

[12] The implicit assumption in this work is that the sentencing process does not differ for defendants who go to trial compared with those who plead guilty. Statistical coefficients are generated on the basis of one group (e.g., plea defendants) and then applied directly to the other group (e.g., trial defendants). Research has yet to test the validity of this underlying assumption.

tance of timing may differ across jurisdictions. In some countries, including England and Wales, parts of Australia, and New Zealand, plea discounts progressively decline with time in order to reward defendants who plead guilty sooner (Roberts and Bradford 2015; Brook et al. 2016).

The importance of the strength of evidence also warrants further study. Theoretically, cases with weaker evidence should result in more favorable plea offers, which should lead to larger plea-trial disparities. Early work consistently showed that the strength of the evidence influenced plea outcomes (LaFree 1985; Albonetti 1986, 1987; Spohn, Beichner, and Davis-Frenzel 2001). Recent scholarship reports less consistent results (Bushway and Redlich 2012; Kutateladze, Lawson, and Andiloro 2015).

Bushway and Redlich (2012) found that for defendants who pled guilty, evidentiary measures had small and inconsistent impacts on the expected probability of trial conviction. Kutateladze, Lawson, and Andiloro (2015) showed that charge bargains were less favorable when specific types of evidence were present, but that strength of the evidence mattered more for initial case acceptance than for plea bargaining. Bushway, Redlich, and Norris (2014) reported that weaker evidence was consistently associated with more favorable plea offers—a finding consistent with legal perspectives that emphasize the overarching importance of evidentiary problems, unsympathetic victims, and Fourth Amendment issues (Alschuler 1968, 1981; Spears and Spohn 1997; Bibas 2004; Sklansky 2018). Overall, relatively few studies examine quality measures of the strength of evidence.

Most scholars agree that quality of evidence is important, but it is unclear how it shapes plea-trial disparity. It may be, for instance, that defendants who go to trial in cases with strong evidence, or "dead bang" cases, are penalized more than defendants who go to trial when there are legal or evidentiary questions, but more research is needed on the topic.

Additional work should also investigate racial differences in guilty pleas, including why race matters and how guilty pleas shape broader patterns of inequality. One promising approach is to engage individual decision makers more directly. Early research tackled this challenge directly. Alschuler (1976) reports judicial anecdotes of the plea process, Newman (1966) and Casper (1972) offer analyses of defendant perspectives, and Alschuler (1968) and Mather (1973) provide insights from prosecutors and public defenders. This early work painted a detailed portrait of how principal actors understood and justified plea-trial sentencing differences, and it offered unique insights into defendant decision making. With few exceptions, though, this approach has seldom been applied in work on modern-day defendants or court actors.

Zottoli et al. (2016) is a noteworthy exception. The authors interviewed juvenile and adult offenders in New York City and illustrated the importance of the trial tax in defendants' decision making. On average, prosecutors offered trial sentences of 5 years to juveniles, though guilty pleas resulted in only 2 months of confinement. In adult cases, prosecutors threatened more than 12 years of prison at trial, but defendants received less than 3 years after pleading guilty. These numbers equate to roughly an 80 percent plea discount for adults and a 90 percent discount for juveniles, suggesting huge differences between threatened and actual sentences.

Unfortunately, this type of ethnographic approach has become an endangered species with the rise of the "big data" movement in sentencing research. Analyses of large-scale sentencing databases are invaluable but should be coupled with a return to more defendant-centric and qualitative approaches examining how and why defendants plead guilty, what they do and do not understand about the process, and how other external pressures shape their decision making (Lynch 2016; Zottoli et al. 2016).

Important differences may also characterize different types of pleas and trials. Although much of the rhetoric surrounding guilty pleas focuses on plea bargaining, defendants often plead guilty without a guarantee of formal concessions. These "nonnegotiated" pleas may occur when there is little doubt about factual guilt, or they may signify a form of "implicit plea bargaining" that involves assumptions of reduced punishment (Padgett 1985). Research findings show that the largest discounts occur in negotiated pleas, with smaller reductions in nonnegotiated cases (Johnson 2003).

The type of trial is also consequential. A number of studies find larger, more consistent trial penalties associated with jury than with bench trials (Kramer and Ulmer 2002; Johnson 2003; King et al. 2005). In his classic research on Philadelphia, Schulhofer (1984, p. 1063) showed that "expectations of leniency" led to frequent bench trials and that the "system of judicial assignments ... encourage[d] and reinforce[d] such expectations." Differential trial taxes for bench and jury trials are consistent with organizational efficiency arguments and with use in some jurisdictions of bench trials as an alternative mechanism for accepting "slow pleas" (Mather 1973; Eisenstein and Jacob 1977).

Finally, we know little about the broader sociopolitical contexts that shape plea-trial disparities. Only two studies explicitly focus on jurisdictional variation in trial effects, one in federal courts (Ulmer, Eisenstein, and Johnson 2010) and one in Pennsylvania (Ulmer and Bradley 2006). Both report significant jurisdictional variation in the effect of trial conviction, but neither explains much of this difference. Future work might benefit from expanding the range of predictors. For example, much discussion has focused on the importance of court cultures (Eisenstein and Jacob 1977), but few studies explicitly measure local norms (Ulmer and Johnson 2018). Moreover, contextual variation in trial penalties is complicated because "when differentials are most effective, they are least observable," so that "the strongest evidence for differentials" may be the absence of trial cases altogether (Brereton and Casper 1982, p. 50).

Interjurisdictional comparisons can be hazardous and require caution—differences in criminal procedures, criminal codes, sentencing structures, and local case processing norms all shape punishment in ways that are difficult to capture—but some work hints at contextual differences. Piehl and Bushway (2007), for example, investigated plea bargaining in two states, one with voluntary sentencing guidelines and one with stricter presumptive guidelines. They found larger plea discounts under presumptive guidelines, where judicial discretion was more constrained and trial sentences were more predictable. More work of this kind is needed, along with research that examines changes in trial penalties and trial rates over time. The presumption is that large trial penalties will lower the trial rate (Brereton and Casper 1982; McCoy 2005; Wright 2005), but little work examines these relationships over time or across courts.

Future work should also expand beyond its ethnocentric focus on US courts. As Turner (2017, p. 75) notes, plea bargaining has become "an increasingly popular feature of criminal justice reform" in countries "as diverse as France, Germany, India, Japan, Nigeria, Russia, and South Africa." However, the scope and salience of plea bargaining remain uniquely American. In most nations, the same arsenal of sentencing enhancements is not available, judges and prosecutors are career civil servants, prosecutorial powers to dismiss charges and recommend sentences are limited, and judicial determinations of facts are invariably required (Tonry 2012). Unlike other nations, the United States relies heavily on negotiated guilty pleas, meaning defendants explicitly bargain over the terms of their plea discount. This is distinct from nations that have institutionalized plea discounts in formal sentencing policies. In England and Wales, for example, defendants who plead guilty at the first opportunity receive a reduction of one-third of their custodial sentence and successively smaller discounts as the trial approaches (Roberts and Bradford 2015). In New South Wales, Australia, and in New Zealand, guilty pleas carry recommended sentence discounts of 10–25 percent (Brook et al. 2016). These process discounts are universally applied, with the discount scaled to the timing of the plea. This limits the magnitude of trial penalties but raises difficult questions about formally structured trial taxes and their effects on fairness and proportionality.

IV. Philosophical Debates and Policy Recommendations
Arguments about plea-trial disparities mirror ongoing debates over the merits and demerits of plea bargaining (Alschuler 1979, 1981; Bibas 2004; Stuntz 2004). Proponents maintain that plea bargaining streamlines case processing, saves time and resources, provides flexibility in punishment, ensures witness cooperation, and helps settle cases with difficult legal issues (Rosett and Cressey 1976; Church 1979; Easterbrook 1992; Wilkinson 2014). Critics counter that plea bargaining divests defendants of procedural safeguards; threatens transparency, accountability and proportionality in punishment; and amounts to a system of institutionalized coercion that forces defendants to accept pleas regardless of their guilt (Alschuler 1976, 1981; McCoy 2005; Wright 2005; Covey 2008; Stuntz 2011). Critics question how guilty pleas under the threat of extreme punishment at trial can be truly voluntary and argue that plea-trial sentencing differentials undermine the presumption of innocence (Tata and Gormley 2016). For the most part, these issues are normative and deontological in nature: they reflect value judgments at the nexus of core issues of justice, juxtaposed with the everyday organizational realities of the criminal courts.

A. Philosophical Debates on the Trial Tax

Frase (2005*b*) notes that widely accepted purposes of punishment include providing fair, just, and proportionate sentences; serving community protection and public safety; and striving to achieve uniformity and consistency, along with more traditional crime control goals such as deterrence, incapacitation, and rehabilitation. It is difficult to justify a significant trial tax on any of these bases. One of the most troubling features of the trial penalty is its potential to contribute to false guilty pleas (Blume and Helm 2014; Dervan 2015); but even when defendants are factually guilty, plea discounts can obscure transparency, reduce legitimacy, and thwart the goals of deterrence and proportionality in punishment.

Turner (2017, p. 75) notes that plea bargains contribute to "incomplete investigations, inadequate disclosure, limited adversarial testing," and "perfunctory judicial oversight." She worries that this reduces legitimacy in the justice system for defendants, victims, and the public alike—a concern consistent with survey research showing low levels of public support for plea bargaining (Herzog 2004). Smith (1986, p. 949) explains that plea-trial disparities can also "undermine the deterrent effectiveness of punishment" because they introduce uncertainty into the sentencing process. Roberts and Bradford (2015, p. 188) argue that large plea discounts often "have the effect of undermining ordinal proportionality in sentencing." Moreover, because the guilty plea decision is unrelated to retributive notions of desert and culpability, Alschuler (1981, p. 652) maintains that it "turns major treatment consequences upon a single tactical decision irrelevant to any proper objective of criminal proceedings."

All of this suggests that trial penalties are defensible only on utilitarian grounds related to organizational efficiency, because the raison d'etre of American plea bargaining is penologically limited to the principle of expediency (Langbein 1979).[13] As Alschuler (2013, p. 686) argued, if trial sentences are "imposed simply for the purpose of inducing guilty pleas," they may benefit defendants but only as "a gunman's demand for your money ... benefits you as well as the gunman." Plea discounts provide apparent rewards to defendants, but only in relation to the threat of more severe outcomes at trial. This poses the question whether expediency is a valid purpose of punishment or whether, as Darbyshire (2000, p. 901) argued, the trial tax represents a "stunning hypocrisy" for a legal system that "trumpets the right to trial."

Plea negotiations are an opaque form of administrative justice that requires defendants to sacrifice due process rights to gain putative sentencing leniency. The US Supreme Court in *North Carolina v. Alford*, 400 U.S.

---

[13] The American Bar Association standards for guilty pleas recognize that plea discounts may be appropriate in the "interest of the public in the effective administration of justice," but explicitly provide that "the fact that a defendant has entered a plea ... should not, by itself alone, be considered by the court as a mitigating factor in imposing sentence" and that "the court should not impose upon a defendant any sentence in excess of that which would be justified ... because the defendant has chosen to require the prosecution to prove guilt at trial" (American Bar Association 1999, 14-8(b)).

25 (1970), held that courts may accept guilty pleas from people who insist on their innocence if in the court's view there is strong evidence of guilt. Recent Supreme Court decisions require assistance of counsel in guilty plea cases and require defense counsel to inform defendants about plea offers and the rights they waive (*Padilla v. Kentucky*, 559 U.S. 356 [2010]; *Lafler v. Cooper*, 566 U.S. 156 [2012]; *Missouri v. Frye*, 566 U.S. 134 [2012]). However, those decisions do almost nothing to regulate prosecutorial power or protect the constitutional rights of defendants.

This is important because guilty plea discounts routinely require defendants to forfeit procedural rights in addition to the right to trial. Defendants are often required to waive their rights against self-incrimination, to confront witnesses or request a presentence report, to appeal the plea agreement or request postconviction review, and to challenge ineffective counsel (King and O'Neill 2005). In federal court, Hofer (2011) found that defendants often were required to waive their right to detention hearings, contest guidelines calculations, file motions to suppress evidence or request downward departures, and challenge errors in guidelines calculations. None of these limitations concern philosophical purposes of sentencing; they aim only to ensure administrative efficiency, insulate plea deals from judicial review, and prevent convictions from being overturned. Many defendants are unlikely to comprehend fully the rights they waive, suggesting that waivers contribute to uninformed pleas (Podgor 2011).

A final concern is that trial penalties may contribute to insufficient fact finding. The ability of public defenders to provide a high-quality defense is often limited by heavy caseloads, inadequate staffing and resources, and legal rules that restrict comprehensive defense investigations (Brown 2005). Encouragement of swift and certain guilty pleas may both enable and camouflage inadequate defense counsel. Prosecutors often expedite plea agreements in ways that make discovery of evidence difficult; criminal procedure rules require full disclosure before trial, but not before a guilty plea (Turner 2017). Federal Court of Appeals Judge Gerald Lynch (2003, p. 1404) observed that the ubiquity of plea discounts has enabled prosecutors to replace the judge and jury as the "central adjudicator of facts" in American courtrooms. In some jurisdictions, prosecutors use "exploding plea offers" that force defendants to except pleas quickly with limited opportunity to investigate the strength of the case against them (Zottoli et al. 2016). In theory, judges could assure fair, accurate, and informed plea outcomes, but in practice their role is limited (Alschuler 1976).

B. Reforms and Policy Recommendations

Critics have proposed numerous remedies. They include calls for total or partial bans on plea bargaining (Langbein 1978; Alschuler 1981; Schulhofer 1984; Gazal-Ayal 2005), fixed plea discounts (Covey 2008), and tighter prosecutorial regulation (Guidorizzi 1998). Not every criminal case can be decided at jury trial, but even in the absence of sentence discounts, the vast majority of defendants would likely plead guilty when there is clear and compelling evidence. Trials could be reserved for cases in which there are doubts about the defendant's guilt.[14] Several possible policy reforms offer promise.

First, the balance of power in plea negotiations should be restored. Prosecutorial domination of contemporary plea negotiations raises problems of injustice equivalent to earlier concerns about excessive judicial discretion (Frankel 1973). Increased transparency and accountability are needed in charging and plea negotiations, as is greater judicial oversight. One solution is to weaken prosecutors' ability to threaten severe punishments by repealing mandatory sentencing and similar laws that enable prosecutors to coerce guilty pleas. If the political will to do so existed, judges could be given other powers to review, revise, and reject proposed bargains (Tonry 2014).

A second partial solution is to require that guilty plea offers and subsequent alterations be reliably reported, accessible to the public, and subject to judicial review. Detailed reasons for charging decisions should be recorded and made reviewable by the trial judge, and ultimately by appellate judges (Miller and Wright 2008; Bibas 2009). This would make the plea-bargaining process more scrutable, fair, and transparent, and it would help prevent strategic overcharging.

Caldwell (2011, p. 65) points out that prosecutors have "a powerful incentive to begin the inevitable negotiating process from a position of strength, which often results in overcharging." Overcharging provides leverage to extract guilty pleas, allows for a broader range of negotiated concessions, and shapes implicit expectations of trial penalties (Alschuler 1968; Meares 1995). Although data on overcharging are elusive, the prac-

---

[14] It is important to acknowledge that the jury trial is no panacea for the ills of the criminal justice system. A separate corpus of work identifies many troubling issues with juries, from problems of eyewitness testimony to how juries are selected and how they make decisions (Hans, Vidmar, and Stevenson 1986; Vidmar and Hans 2007). These are distinct issues, however, and are unrelated to a defendant's constitutional right to a jury trial.

tice is believed to be commonplace. Improved record keeping is therefore a key requirement for advancing research and reform on prosecution (Johnson, King, and Spohn 2016). Better plea bargaining data could reveal aberrant charging practices and facilitate periodic audits to ensure fair and equal application of plea discounts. This would parallel the use of racial impact statements in some states (Mauer 2007).

A number of scholars have argued that it would be beneficial to have greater judicial oversight of negotiated guilty pleas (Turner 2006; O'Hear 2008). Although judges have authority to accept or decline plea agreements, in practice they seldom possess sufficient information to evaluate the merits of negotiated plea agreements. Sklansky (2018, p. 460) observes that a more thorough process is needed with expanded "judicial supervision over prosecutorial decisions regarding ... whether to file charges, what charges to file, what information to disclose to defense," and "what kinds of plea bargains to offer or to accept." That could rein in prosecutorial discretion and make prosecutors more accountable for their plea offers.

Creation of statutory caps on plea discounts to minimize the effects of trial penalties is a third reform possibility. This could further institutionalize discounts, but given their ubiquity, there is clear need to restrict their size. This might emulate the English model, which limits the size of discounts (Ashworth and Roberts 2013; Roberts and Bradford 2015). Covey (2008) proposes an alternative system of punishment ceilings in which trial sentences cannot exceed plea outcomes by more than a modest, fixed amount. This would ensure that trial sentences are not overly punitive rather than preventing leniency in plea offers.

These approaches would require additional limits on prosecutors' authority to shift defendants into new offense categories. American plea bargaining often involves charging manipulations that directly affect punishment, in contrast to other countries where prosecutors cannot dismiss or alter charges without judicial approval, and where judges are not bound by charging decisions (Tonry 2012). Companion reforms are therefore needed to limit the effects of charge bargaining on sentencing.

A final, more ambitious proposal is to develop binding guidelines for charging and plea bargaining, paralleling presumptive sentencing guidelines for judges. Many prosecutors' offices have internal charging policies, and some have independent "conviction integrity" units (Sklansky 2018). However, no US jurisdiction has developed comprehensive, legally binding, presumptive charging guidelines.[15] Such a system could provide standards governing what prosecutors can charge; how, when, and why charges can be amended; and what sentences are reasonably expected following plea bargaining (Pfaff 2017). This would shine a light into the shadowy realm of plea bargaining; rather than attempt to eliminate plea negotiations, it would structure them. It would also balance the playing field for prosecutors, defendants, and defense counsel by establishing clear benchmarks for plea deals that meet minimum standards of just punishment. Guidelines could increase transparency and accountability in charging decisions while structuring prosecutorial decision making, providing improved legal recourse to defendants, and limiting the coercive pressure of trial penalties.

C. Concluding Thoughts

It is difficult to justify a system of punishment that consistently metes out harsher punishments to defendants who exercise their constitutional right to trial. Yet the existence of plea-trial sentencing differentials is one of the most robust findings in empirical sentencing research: Across space, time, and offense, defendants convicted by judges or juries receive harsher sentences than if they had pled guilty. This represents a delicate balance between the organizational realities of everyday courts, striving to expedite cases and ensure the conviction of the guilty and acquittal of the innocent, and broader issues of procedural fairness and just and effective punishment.

Trial rates have fallen to unprecedented levels, largely because sentencing law changes have enhanced prosecutors' negotiating leverage by allowing them to threaten lengthy sentences if convicted at trial. The trial tax is large, contributes to broader patterns of social inequality, and increases pressure on innocent defendants to plead guilty.

Trial penalties have grown inversely with declining trial rates, threatening the eclipse of the American jury trial. This raises important questions about the voluntariness of guilty pleas, use of coercion in plea bargaining, and observance of principles of fairness, equality, and proportionality in punishment. The time has come to incorporate greater transparency and accountability in prosecution. The aims should be to structure charging

---

[15] Prosecutorial guidelines have been in use in other nations such as the Netherlands since the mid-1980s (Tak 2001; Tonry 2012).

practices, reduce excessive trial sentences, and create greater proportionality and equality in sentencing, regardless of whether a defendant pleads guilty or goes to trial. Criminal justice policy should never accept the false premise that "what is familiar" is "what is right" (Alschuler 2013, p. 707).

REFERENCES

Abrams, David S. 2011. "Is Pleading Really a Bargain?" *Journal of Empirical Legal Studies* 8(1):200–221.

Albonetti, Celesta A. 1986. "Criminality, Prosecutorial Screening, and Uncertainty: Toward a Theory of Discretionary Decision Making in Felony Case Processings." *Criminology* 24(4):623–44.

———. 1987. "Prosecutorial Discretion: The Effects of Uncertainty." *Law and Society Review* 21(2):291–314.

———. 1990. "Race and the Probability of Pleading Guilty." *Journal of Quantitative Criminology* 6(3):315–34.

Alschuler, Albert W. 1968. "The Prosecutor's Role in Plea Bargaining." *University of Chicago Law Review* 36(1):50–112.

———. 1976. "The Trial Judge's Role in Plea Bargaining, Part I." *Columbia Law Review* 76(7):1059–1154.

———. 1979. "Plea Bargaining and Its History." *Law and Society Review* 13(2):211–45.

———. 1981. "The Changing Plea Bargaining Debate." *California Law Review* 69:652–730.

———. 1983. "Implementing the Criminal Defendant's Right to Trial: Alternatives to the Plea Bargaining System." *University of Chicago Law Review* 50(3):931–1050.

———. 2003. "Straining at Gnats and Swallowing Camels: The Selective Morality of Professor Bibas." *Cornell Law Review* 88:1412–24.

———. 2013. "Lafler and Frye: Two Small Band-Aids for a Festering Wound." *Duquesne Law Review* 51:673–87.

American Bar Association. 1999. *ABA Standards for Criminal Justice Pleas of Guilty*. 3rd ed. Washington, DC: American Bar Association. https://www.americanbar.org/content/dam/aba/publications/criminal_justice_standards/pleas_guilty.pdf.

Anderson, Amy L., and Cassia Spohn. 2010. "Lawlessness in the Federal Sentencing Process: A Test for Uniformity and Consistency in Sentence Outcomes." *Justice Quarterly* 27(3):362–93.

Ashworth, Andrew, and Julian V. Roberts. 2013. "The Origins and Evolution of Sentencing Guidelines in England and Wales." In *Sentencing Guidelines: Exploring the English Model*, edited by Andrew Ashworth and Julian V. Roberts. Oxford: Oxford University Press.

Bibas, Stephanos. 2001. "Judicial Fact-Finding and Sentence Enhancements in a World of Guilty Pleas." *Yale Law Journal* 110(7):1097–1185.

———. 2004. "Plea Bargaining Outside the Shadow of Trial." *Harvard Law Review* 117(8):2463–2547.

———. 2009. "Prosecutorial Regulation versus Prosecutorial Accountability." *University of Pennsylvania Law Review* 157(4):959–1016.

———. 2011. "Regulating the Plea-Bargaining Market: From Caveat Emptor to Consumer Protection." *California Law Review* 99:1117–61.

Blume, John H., and Rebecca K. Helm. 2014. "The Unexonerated: Factually Innocent Defendants Who Plead Guilty." *Cornell Law Review* 100:157–92.

Blumstein, Alfred, and Allen J. Beck. 1999. "Population Growth in U.S. Prisons, 1980–1996." In *Prisons*, edited by Michael Tonry and Joan Petersilia. Vol. 26 of *Crime and Justice: A Review of Research*, edited by Michael Tonry. Chicago: University of Chicago Press.

Blumstein, Alfred, Jacqueline Cohen, Susan E. Martin, and Michael Tonry, eds. 1983. *Research on Sentencing: The Search for Reform*. Vol. 1. Washington, DC: National Academy Press.

Breen, Patricia D., and Brian D. Johnson. 2018. "Military Justice: Case Processing and Sentencing Decisions in America's 'Other' Criminal Courts." *Justice Quarterly* 35(4):639–69.

Brereton, David, and Jonathan Casper. 1982. "Does It Pay to Plead Guilty? Differential Sentencing and the Functioning of Criminal Courts." *Law and Society Review* 16:45–70.

Brook, Carol A., Bruno Fiannaca, David Harvey, and Paul Marcus. 2016. "A Comparative Look at Plea Bargaining in Australia, Canada, England, New Zealand, and the United States." *William and Mary Law Review* 57(4):1147–1224.

Brown, Darryl K. 2005. "The Decline of Defense Counsel and the Rise of Accuracy in Criminal Adjudication." *California Law Review* 93:1585–90.

Bureau of Justice Statistics. 2015. *Jail Inmates at Midyear 2014*. Washington, DC: US Government Printing Office.

———. 2016. *Prisoners in 2015*. NCJ 250229. Washington, DC: US Government Printing Office.

———. 2018. *2018 Update on Prisoner Recidivism: A 9-Year Follow-Up Period (2005–2014)*. Washington, DC: US Government Printing Office.

Bushway, Shawn D., and Anne Morrison Piehl. 2001. "Judging Judicial Discretion: Legal Factors and Racial Discrimination in Sentencing." *Law and Society Review* 35:733–64.

Bushway, Shawn D., and Allison D. Redlich. 2012. "Is Plea Bargaining in the 'Shadow of the Trial' a Mirage?" *Journal of Quantitative Criminology* 28(3):437–54.

Bushway, Shawn D., Allison D. Redlich, and Robert J. Norris. 2014. "An Explicit Test of Plea Bargaining in the 'Shadow of the Trial.'" *Criminology* 52(4):723–54.

Caldwell, Mitchell H. 2011. "Coercive Plea Bargaining: The Unrecognized Scourge of the Justice System." *Catholic University Law Review* 61:63–96.

Casper, Jonathan D. 1972. *American Criminal Justice: The Defendant's Perspective*. Englewood Cliffs, NJ: Prentice Hall.

Church, Thomas W. 1979. "In Defense of 'Bargain Justice.'" *Law and Society Review* 13(2): 509–25.

Clark, Steven, and Susan Kurtz. 1983. "The Importance of Interim Decisions to Felony Trial Court Dispositions." *Journal of Criminal Law and Criminology* 74:476–518.

Colquitt, Joseph A. 2001. "Ad Hoc Plea Bargaining." *Tulane Law Review* 75:695–776.

Covey, Russell D. 2008. "Fixed Justice: Reforming Plea Bargaining with Plea-Based Ceiling." *Tulane Law Review* 82:1237–90.

Darbyshire, Penny. 2000. "The Mischief of Plea Bargaining and Sentencing Rewards." *Criminal Law Review*, 895–910.

Demuth, Stephen. 2003. "Racial and Ethnic Differences in Pretrial Release Decisions and Outcomes: A Comparison of Hispanic, Black, and White Felony Arrestees." *Criminology* 41(3):873–908.

Dervan, Lucian E. 2015. "The Injustice of the Plea-Bargain System." *Wall Street Journal*, December 3. https://www.wsj.com/articles/the-injustice-of-the-plea-bargain-system-1449188034.

Dervan, Lucian E., and Vanessa A. Edkins. 2013. "The Innocent Defendant's Dilemma: An Innovative Empirical Study of Plea Bargaining's Innocence Problem." *Journal of Criminal Law and Criminology* 103(1):1–48.

Dixon, Jo. 1995. "The Organizational Context of Criminal Sentencing." *American Journal of Sociology* 100(5):1157–98.

Easterbrook, Frank H. 1992. "Plea Bargaining as Compromise." *Yale Law Journal* 101(8):1969–78.

Eisenstein, James, and Herbert Jacob. 1977. *Felony Justice: An Organizational Analysis of Criminal Courts*. Boston: Little, Brown.

Ellis, Michael J. 2012. "The Origins of the Elected Prosecutor." *Yale Law Journal* 121:1528–69.

Engen, Rodney L., and Randy R. Gainey. 2000. "Modeling the Effects of Legally Relevant and Extralegal Factors under Sentencing Guidelines: The Rules Have Changed." *Criminology* 38(4):1207–30.

Engen, Rodney L., Randy R. Gainey, Robert D. Crutchfield, and Joseph G. Weis. 2003. "Discretion and Disparity under Sentencing Guidelines: The Role of Departures and Structured Sentencing Alternatives." *Criminology* 41(1):99–130.

Feeley, Malcolm M. 1992. *The Process Is the Punishment: Handling Cases in a Lower Criminal Court*. New York: Russell Sage Foundation. (Originally published in 1979.)

———. 1997. "Legal Complexity and the Transformation of the Criminal Process: The Origins of Plea Bargaining." *Israel Law Review* 31:183–222.

Frankel, Marvin E. 1973. *Criminal Sentences: Law without Order*. New York: Hill & Wang.

Frase, Richard S. 1993. "Implementing Commission-Based Sentencing Guidelines: The Lessons of the First Ten Years in Minnesota." *Cornell Journal of Law and Public Policy* 2:279–337.

———. 2005*a*. "Punishment Purposes." *Stanford Law Review* 58(1):67–83.

———. 2005b. "Sentencing Guidelines in Minnesota, 1978–2003." In *Crime and Justice: A Review of Research*, vol. 32, edited by Michael Tonry. Chicago: University of Chicago Press.

Frenzel, Erika Davis, and Jeremy D. Ball. 2008. "Effects of Individual Characteristics on Plea Negotiations under Sentencing Guidelines." *Journal of Ethnicity in Criminal Justice* 5(4):59–82.

Friedman, Lawrence M., and Robert V. Percival. 1981. *The Roots of Justice: Crime and Punishment in Alameda County, California, 1870–1910*. Chapel Hill: University of North Carolina Press.

Garrett, Brandon L. 2011. *Convicting the Innocent*. Cambridge, MA: Harvard University Press.

Gazal-Ayal, Oren. 2005. "Partial Ban on Plea Bargains." *Cardozo Law Review* 27:2295–2349.

Gordon, Sanford C., and Gregory Huber. 2007. "The Effect of Electoral Competitiveness on Incumbent Behavior." *Quarterly Journal of Political Science* 2(2):107–38.

Gross, Samuel R., Kristen Jacoby, Daniel J. Matheson, and Nicholas Montgomery. 2005. "Exonerations in the United States 1989 through 2003." *Journal of Criminology and Criminal Law* 95:523–60.

Guidorizzi, Douglas D. 1998. "Should We Really 'Ban' Plea Bargaining? The Core Concerns of Plea Bargaining Critics." *Emory Law Journal* 47:753–82.

Hans, Valerie P., Neil Vidmar, and Hans Zeisel. 1986. *Judging the Jury*. New York: Plenum.

Heaton, Paul, Sandra Mayson, and Megan Stevenson. 2017. "The Downstream Consequences of Misdemeanor Pretrial Detention." *Stanford Law Review* 69:711–94.

Herzog, Sergio. 2004. "Plea Bargaining Practices: Less Covert, More Public Support?" *Crime and Delinquency* 50(4):590–614.

Hester, Rhys, and Eric L. Sevigny. 2016. "Court Communities in Local Context: A Multilevel Analysis of Felony Sentencing in South Carolina." *Journal of Crime and Justice* 39(1):55–74.

Hofer, Paul J. 2011. "Has *Booker* Restored Balance? A Look at Data on Plea Bargaining and Sentencing." *Federal Sentencing Reporter* 23(5):326–32.

Hood, Roger G. 1992. *Race and Sentencing*. Oxford: Clarendon.

Hurwitz, Jon, and Mark Peffley. 2005. "Explaining the Great Racial Divide: Perceptions of Fairness in the U.S. Criminal Justice System." *Journal of Politics* 67(3):762–83.

Johnson, Brian D. 2003. "Racial and Ethnic Disparities in Sentencing Departures across Modes of Conviction." *Criminology* 41(2):449–90.

———. 2005. "Contextual Disparities in Guidelines Departures: Courtroom Social Contexts, Guidelines Compliance, and Extralegal Disparities in Criminal Sentencing." *Criminology* 43(3):761–96.

———. 2006. "The Multilevel Context of Criminal Sentencing: Integrating Judge- and County-Level Influences." *Criminology* 44(2):259–98.

Johnson, Brian D., and Sara Betsinger. 2009. "Punishing the 'Model Minority': Asian-American Criminal Sentencing Outcomes in Federal District Courts." *Criminology* 47(4):1045–90.

Johnson, Brian D., and Stephanie M. DiPietro. 2012. "The Power of Diversion: Intermediate Sanctions and Sentencing Disparity under Presumptive Guidelines." *Criminology* 50(3):811–50.

Johnson, Brian D., and Ryan D. King. 2017. "Facial Profiling: Race, Physical Appearance, and Punishment." *Criminology* 55(3):520–47.

Johnson, Brian D., Ryan D. King, and Cassia Spohn. 2016. "Sociolegal Approaches to the Study of Guilty Pleas and Prosecution." *Annual Review of Law and Social Science* 12:479–95.

Johnson, Brian D., and Pilar Larroulet. Forthcoming. "The 'Distance Traveled': Investigating the Downstream Consequences of Charge Reductions for Disparities in Incarceration." *Justice Quarterly*.

Johnson, Brian D., Jeffery T. Ulmer, and John H. Kramer. 2008. "The Social Context of Guidelines Circumvention: The Case of Federal District Courts." *Criminology* 46(3):737–83.

Kautt, Paula M. 2002. "Location, Location, Location: Interdistrict and Intercircuit Variation in Sentencing Outcomes for Federal Drug-Trafficking Offenses." *Justice Quarterly* 19(4):633–71.

Kerner Commission. 1968. *Report of the National Advisory Commission on Civil Disorder*. Washington, DC: US Government Printing Office.

Kim, Andrew Chongseh. 2015. "Underestimating the Trial Penalty: An Empirical Analysis of the Federal Trial Penalty and Critique of the Abrams Study." *Mississippi Law Journal* 84(5):1195–1256.

Kim, Byungbae, Cassia Spohn, and E. C. Hedberg. 2015. "Federal Sentencing as a Complex Collaborative Process: Judges, Prosecutors, Judge-Prosecutor Dyads, and Disparity in Sentencing." *Criminology* 53(4):597–623.

King, Nancy J., and Michael O'Neill. 2005. "Appeal Waivers and the Future of Sentencing Policy." *Duke Law Journal* 55:209–12.

King, Nancy J., David A. Soule, Sara Steen, and Robert R. Weidner. 2005. "Panel One: Prosecutorial Discretion and Its Challenges." *Columbia Law Review* 105(4):959–1009.

King, Ryan D., and Brian D. Johnson. 2016. "A Punishing Look: Skin Tone and Afrocentric Features in the Halls of Justice." *American Journal of Sociology* 122(1):90–124.

Klein, Stephen, Joan Petersilia, and Susan Turner. 1990. "Race and Imprisonment Decisions in California." *Science* 247(4944):812–16.

Kochel, Tammy R., David B. Wilson, and Stephen D. Mastrofski. 2011. "Effect of Suspect Race on Officers' Arrest Decisions." *Criminology* 49(2):473–512.

Kramer, John H., and Jeffery T. Ulmer. 2002. "Downward Departures for Serious Violent Offenders: Local Court 'Corrections' to Pennsylvania's Sentencing Guidelines." *Criminology* 40(4):897–932.

———. 2009. *Sentencing Guidelines: Lessons from Pennsylvania*. Boulder, CO: Rienner.

Kurlychek, Megan C., and Brian D. Johnson. Forthcoming. "Cumulative Disadvantage in the American Criminal Justice System." *Annual Review of Criminology* 2.

Kutateladze, Besiki Luka. 2018. "Tracing Charge Trajectories: A Study of the Influence of Race in Charge Changes at Case Screening, Arraignment, and Disposition." *Criminology* 56(1):123–53.

Kutateladze, Besiki Luka, and Nancy R. Andiloro. 2014. *Prosecution and Racial Justice in New York County*. Award Technical Report no. 2011-DJ-BX-0038. Washington, DC: US Department of Justice, National Institute of Justice.

Kutateladze, Besiki Luka, Nancy R. Andiloro, and Brian D. Johnson. 2016. "Opening Pandora's Box: How Does Defendant Race Influence Plea Bargaining?" *Justice Quarterly* 33(3):398–426.

Kutateladze, Besiki L., Nancy R. Andiloro, Brian D. Johnson, and Cassia C. Spohn. 2014. "Cumulative Disadvantage: Examining Racial and Ethnic Disparity in Prosecution and Sentencing." *Criminology* 52(3):514–51.

Kutateladze, Besiki L., and Victoria Z. Lawson. 2018. "Is a Plea Really a Bargain? An Analysis of Plea and Trial Dispositions in New York City." *Crime and Delinquency* 64(7):856–87.

Kutateladze, Besiki L., Victoria Z. Lawson, and Nancy R. Andiloro. 2015. "Does Evidence Really Matter? An Exploratory Analysis of the Role of Evidence in Plea Bargaining in Felony Drug Cases." *Law and Human Behavior* 39(5):431–42.

LaFree, Gary D. 1980. "The Effect of Sexual Stratification by Race on Official Reactions to Rape." *American Sociological Review* 45(5):842–54.

———. 1985. "Adversarial and Nonadversarial Justice: A Comparison of Guilty Pleas and Trials." *Criminology* 23(2):289–312.

Langbein, John H. 1978. "Torture and Plea Bargaining." *University of Chicago Law Review* 46(1):3–22.

———. 1979. "Understanding the Short History of Plea Bargaining." *Law and Society Review* 13:261–72.

Lynch, Gerard E. 2003. "Screening versus Plea Bargaining: Exactly What Are We Trading Off?" *Stanford Law Review* 55(4):1399–1408.

Lynch, Mona. 2016. *Hard Bargains: The Coercive Power of Drug Laws in Federal Court*. New York: Russell Sage Foundation.

Martinson, Robert. 1974. "What Works? Questions and Answers about Prison Reform." *Public Interest* 35:22–54.

Mather, Lynn M. 1973. "Some Determinants of the Method of Case Disposition: Decision-Making by Public Defenders in Los Angeles." *Law and Society Review* 8(2):187–216.

Mauer, Marc. 2007. "Racial Impact Statements as a Means of Reducing Unwarranted Sentencing Disparities." *Ohio State Journal of Criminal Law* 5:19–46.

McCannon, Bryan C. 2013. "Prosecutor Elections, Mistakes, and Appeals." *Journal of Empirical Legal Studies* 10(4):696–714.

McCoy, Candace. 2005. "Plea Bargaining as Coercion: The Trial Penalty and Plea Bargaining Reform." *Criminal Law Quarterly* 50:67–107.

Meares, Tracey L. 1995. "Rewards for Good Behavior: Influencing Prosecutorial Discretion and Conduct with Financial Incentives." *Fordham Law Review* 64:851–919.

Meeker, James W., and Henry N. Pontell. 1985. "Court Caseloads, Plea Bargains, and Criminal Sanctions: The Effects of Section 17 PC in California." *Criminology* 23(1):119–43.

Metcalfe, Christi, and Ted Chiricos. 2018. "Race, Plea, and Charge Reduction: An Assessment of Racial Disparities in the Plea Process." *Justice Quarterly* 35 (2):223–53.

Miethe, Terance D. 1987. "Charging and Plea Bargaining Practices under Determinate Sentencing: An Investigation of the Hydraulic Displacement of Discretion." *Journal of Criminal Law and Criminology* 78(1):155–76.

Miethe, Terance D., and Charles A. Moore. 1985. "Socioeconomic Disparities under Determinate Sentencing Systems: A Comparison of Pre- and Postguideline Practices in Minnesota." *Criminology* 23:337–63.

Miller, Marc L., and Ronald F. Wright. 2008. "The Black Box." *Iowa Law Review* 94:125–96.

Moore, Charles A., and Terance D. Miethe. 1986. "Regulated and Unregulated Sentencing Decisions: An Analysis of First-Year Practices under Minnesota's Felony Sentencing Guidelines." *Law and Society Review* 20(2):253–78.

Nagel, Ilene H., and Stephen J. Schulhofer. 1992. "A Tale of Three Cities: An Empirical Study of Charging and Bargaining Practices under the Federal Sentencing Guidelines." *Southern California Law Review* 66:501–79.

Nardulli, Peter F., James Eisenstein, and Roy B. Flemming. 1988. *The Tenor of Justice: Criminal Courts and the Guilty Plea Process*. Urbana: University of Illinois Press.

Newman, Donald J. 1956. "Pleading Guilty for Considerations: A Study of Bargain Justice." *Journal of Criminal Law, Criminology, and Police Science* 46(6):780–90.

———. 1966. *Conviction: The Determination of Guilt or Innocence without Trial*. Boston: Little, Brown.

O'Hear, Michael M. 1997. "Remorse, Cooperation, and 'Acceptance of Responsibility': The Structure, Implementation, and Reform of Section 3E1.1 of the Federal Sentencing Guidelines." *Northwestern University Law Review* 91(4):1507–73.

———. 2008. "Plea Bargaining and Procedural Justice." *Georgia Law Review* 42:407–69.

O'Sullivan, Julie R. 1997. "In Defense of the US Sentencing Guidelines' Modified Real-Offense System." *Northwestern University Law Review* 91:1342–1433.

Padgett, John F. 1985. "The Emergent Organization of Plea Bargaining." *American Journal of Sociology* 90(4):753–800.

Pfaff, John. 2017. "Prosecutorial Guidelines." In *Academy for Justice: A Report on Scholarship and Criminal Justice Reform*, vol. 3, edited by Erik Luna. Phoenix: Arizona State University.

Piehl, Anne M., and Shawn D. Bushway. 2007. "Measuring and Explaining Charge Bargaining." *Journal of Quantitative Criminology* 23(2):105–25.
Podgor, Ellen S. 2011. "Pleading Blindly." *Mississippi Law Journal* 80(4):1633–47.
Reaves, Brian A. 2013. *Felony Defendants in Large Urban Counties, 2009—Statistical Tables*. Washington, DC: US Department of Justice.
Redlich, Allison D., James R. Acker, Robert J. Norris, and Catherine L. Bonventre, eds. 2014. *Wrongful Conviction: Stepping Back, Moving Forward*. Durham, NC: Carolina Academic Press.
Rehavi, Marit M., and Sonja B. Starr. 2014. "Racial Disparity in Federal Criminal Sentences." *Journal of Political Economy* 122(6):1320–54.
Rhodes, William M. 1979. "Plea Bargaining: Its Effect on Sentencing and Convictions in the District of Columbia." *Journal of Criminal Law and Criminology* 70(3):360–75.
Roberts, Julian V., and Ben Bradford. 2015. "Sentence Reductions for a Guilty Plea in England and Wales: Exploring New Empirical Trends." *Journal of Empirical Legal Studies* 12(2):187–210.
Rosett, Arthur I., and Donald R. Cressey. 1976. *Justice by Consent: Plea Bargains in the American Courthouse*. Philadelphia: Lippincott.
Sampson, Robert J., and Janet L. Lauritsen. 1997. "Racial and Ethnic Disparities in Crime and Criminal Justice in the United States." In *Ethnicity, Crime, and Immigration: Comparative and Cross-National Perspectives*, edited by Michael Tonry. Vol. 21 of *Crime and Justice: A Review of Research*, edited by Michael Tonry. Chicago: University of Chicago Press.
Savitsky, Douglas. 2012. "Is Plea Bargaining a Rational Choice? Plea Bargaining as an Engine of Racial Stratification and Overcrowding in the United States Prison System." *Rationality and Society* 24(2):131–67.
Schlesinger, Traci. 2005. "Racial and Ethnic Disparity in Pretrial Criminal Processing." *Justice Quarterly* 22(2):170–92.
Schulhofer, Stephen J. 1984. "Is Plea Bargaining Inevitable?" *Harvard Law Review* 97(5):1037–1107.
———. 1992. "Plea Bargaining as Disaster." *Yale Law Journal* 101(8):1979–2009.
Schulhofer, Stephen J., and Ilene H. Nagel. 1989. "Negotiated Pleas under the Federal Sentencing Guidelines: The First Fifteen Months." *American Criminal Law Review* 27:231–88.
———. 1997. "Plea Negotiations under the Federal Sentencing Guidelines: Guideline Circumvention and Its Dynamics in the Post-Mistretta Period." *Northwestern University Law Review* 91:1284–1316.
Scott, Robert E., and William J. Stuntz. 1992. "A Reply: Imperfect Bargains, Imperfect Trials, and Innocent Defendants." *Yale Law Journal* 101(8):2011–15.
The Sentencing Project. 2017. "Fact Sheet: Trends in US Corrections." Washington, DC: The Sentencing Project.
Shermer, Lauren O., and Brian D. Johnson. 2010. "Criminal Prosecutions: Examining Prosecutorial Discretion and Charge Reductions in US Federal District Courts." *Justice Quarterly* 27(3):394–430.
Sklansky, David A. 2018. "The Problems with Prosecutors." *Annual Review of Criminology* 1:451–69.

Smith, Bruce P. 2005. "Plea Bargaining and the Eclipse of the Jury." *Annual Review of Law and Social Science* 1:131–49.
Smith, Douglas A. 1986. "The Plea Bargaining Controversy." *Journal of Criminal Law and Criminology* 77(3):949–68.
Smith, Robert J., and Justin D. Levinson. 2012. "The Impact of Implicit Racial Bias on the Exercise of Prosecutorial Discretion." *Seattle University Law Review* 35:795–826.
Spears, Jeffery, and Cassia Spohn. 1997. "The Effect of Evidence Factors and Victim Characteristics on Prosecutors' Charging Decisions in Sexual Assault Cases." *Justice Quarterly* 14(3):501–24.
Spohn, Cassia. 2000. "Thirty Years of Sentencing Reform: The Quest for a Racially Neutral Sentencing Process." *Criminal Justice* 3:427–501.
Spohn, Cassia, Dawn Beichner, and Erika Davis-Frenzel. 2001. "Prosecutorial Justifications for Sexual Assault Case Rejection: Guarding the 'Gateway to Justice.'" *Social Problems* 48(2):206–35.
Spohn, Cassia, and David Holleran. 2000. "The Imprisonment Penalty Paid by Young, Unemployed Black and Hispanic Male Offenders." *Criminology* 38(1):281–306.
Steffensmeier, Darrell, and Stephen Demuth. 2000. "Ethnicity and Sentencing Outcomes in US Federal Courts: Who Is Punished More Harshly?" *American Sociological Review* 65(5):705–29.
Steffensmeier, Darrell, Jeffery Ulmer, and John Kramer. 1998. "The Interaction of Race, Gender, and Age in Criminal Sentencing: The Punishment Cost of Being Young, Black, and Male." *Criminology* 36(4):763–98.
Stemen, Don, and Gipsy Escobar. Forthcoming. "Whither the Prosecutor? Prosecutor and County Effects on Guilty Plea Outcomes in Wisconsin." *Justice Quarterly*.
Stevenson, Megan, and Sandra G. Mayson. 2017. "Pretrial Detention and Bail." In *Academy for Justice: Report on Scholarship and Criminal Justice Reform*, vol. 3, edited by Erik Luna. Phoenix: Arizona State University.
Stith, Kate, and Jose A. Cabranes. 1998. *Fear of Judging: Sentencing Guidelines in the Federal Courts*. Chicago: University of Chicago Press.
Stuntz, William J. 2004. "Plea Bargaining and Criminal Law's Disappearing Shadow." *Harvard Law Review* 117(8):2548–69.
———. 2011. *The Collapse of American Criminal Justice*. Cambridge, MA: Harvard University Press.
Sudnow, David. 1965. "Normal Crimes: Sociological Features of the Penal Code in a Public Defender Office." *Social Problems* 12(3):255–76.
Sutton, John R. 2013. "Structural Bias in the Sentencing of Felony Defendants." *Social Science Research* 42(5):1207–21.
Tak, Peter J. 2001. "Sentencing and Punishment in the Netherlands." In *Sentencing and Sanctions in Western Countries*, edited by Michael Tonry and Richard S. Frase. New York: Oxford University Press.
Tata, Cyrus, and Jay M. Gormley. 2016. "Sentencing and Plea Bargaining: Guilty Pleas versus Trial Verdicts." Oxford: Oxford Handbooks Online. DOI:10.1093/oxfordhb/9780199935383.013.40.

Tonry, Michael. 1996. *Sentencing Matters.* New York: Oxford University Press.
———. 2011. *Punishing Race.* New York: Oxford University Press.
———, ed. 2012. *Prosecutors and Politics: A Comparative Perspective.* Vol. 41 of *Crime and Justice: A Review of Research*, edited by Michael Tonry. Chicago: University of Chicago Press.
———. 2014. "Remodeling American Sentencing: A Ten-Step Blueprint for Moving Past Mass Incarceration." *Criminology and Public Policy* 13(4):503–33.
Travis, Jeremy, Bruce Western, and F. Stevens Redburn, eds. 2014. *The Growth of Incarceration in the United States: Exploring Causes and Consequences.* Washington, DC: National Academies Press.
Turner, Jenia I. 2006. "Judicial Participation in Plea Negotiations: A Comparative View." *American Journal of Comparative Law* 54(1):199–267.
———. 2017. "Plea Bargaining." In *Reforming Criminal Justice: A Report of the Academy for Justice on Bridging the Gap between Scholarship and Reform*, vol. 3, edited by Erik Luna. Phoenix: Arizona State University.
Tyler, Tom R. 2006. "Restorative Justice and Procedural Justice: Dealing with Rule Breaking." *Journal of Social Issues* 62(2):307–26.
Ulmer, Jeffery T. 2012. "Recent Developments and New Directions in Sentencing Research." *Justice Quarterly* 29(1):1–40.
Ulmer, Jeffery T., and Mindy S. Bradley. 2006. "Variation in Trial Penalties among Serious Violent Offenses." *Criminology* 44(3):631–70.
Ulmer, Jeffery T., James Eisenstein, and Brian D. Johnson. 2010. "Trial Penalties in Federal Sentencing: Extra-Guidelines Factors and District Variation." *Justice Quarterly* 27(4):560–92.
Ulmer, Jeffery T., and Brian Johnson. 2004. "Sentencing in Context: A Multilevel Analysis." *Criminology* 42(1):137–78.
———. 2018. "Organizational Conformity and Punishment: Federal Court Communities and Judge-Initiated Guidelines Departures." *Journal of Criminal Law and Criminology* 107(3):253–92.
Ulmer, Jeffery T., Megan C. Kurlychek, and John H. Kramer. 2007. "Prosecutorial Discretion and the Imposition of Mandatory Minimum Sentences." *Justice Quarterly* 44(4):427–58.
Ulmer, Jeffery T., Michael Light, and John H. Kramer. 2011. "Racial Disparity in the Wake of the *Booker/Fanfan* Decision: An Alternative Analysis to the USSC's 2010 Report." *Criminology and Public Policy* 10(4):1077–1118.
Ulmer, Jeffery T., Noah Painter-Davis, and Leigh Tinik. 2016. "Disproportional Imprisonment of Black and Hispanic Males: Sentencing Discretion, Processing Outcomes, and Policy Structures." *Justice Quarterly* 33(4):642–81.
USSC (US Sentencing Commission). 2004. "Fifteen Years of Guidelines Sentencing: An Assessment of How Well the Federal Criminal Justice System Is Achieving the Goals of Sentencing Reform." Washington, DC: US Sentencing Commission.
———. 2010. "Demographic Differences in Federal Sentencing Practices: An Update of the *Booker* Report's Multivariate Regression Analysis." Washington, DC: US Sentencing Commission.

———. 2017. "Demographic Differences in Sentencing: An Update to the 2012 *Booker* Report." Washington, DC: US Sentencing Commission.

Vidmar, Neil, and Valerie Hans. 2007. *American Juries: The Verdict*. New York: Prometheus.

von Hirsch, Andrew. 1976. *Doing Justice: The Choice of Punishments*. New York: Hill & Wang.

Warren, Patricia, Ted Chiricos, and William Bales. 2012. "The Imprisonment Penalty for Young Black and Hispanic Males: A Crime-Specific Analysis." *Journal of Research in Crime and Delinquency* 49(1):56–80.

Wilkins, William, Jr. 1988. "Plea Negotiations, Acceptance of Responsibility, Role of the Offender, and Departures: Policy Decisions in the Promulgation of Federal Sentencing Guidelines." *Wake Forest Law Review* 23(2):181–202.

Wilkinson, J. Harvie, III. 2014. "In Defense of American Criminal Justice." *Vanderbilt Law Review* 67(1099):1138–44.

Wooldredge, John D. 1989. "An Aggregate-Level Examination of the Caseload Pressure Hypothesis." *Journal of Quantitative Criminology* 5(3):259–83.

———. 2007. "Neighborhood Effects on Felony Sentencing." *Journal of Research in Crime and Delinquency* 44(2):238–63.

Wooldredge, John, James Frank, Natalie Goulette, and Lawrence Travis. 2015. "Is the Impact of Cumulative Disadvantage on Sentencing Greater for Black Defendants?" *Criminology and Public Policy* 14(2):187–223.

Wright, Ronald F. 2005. "Trial Distortion and the End of Innocence in Federal Criminal Justice." *University of Pennsylvania Law Review* 154(1):79–156.

———. 2009. "How Prosecutor Elections Fail Us." *Ohio State Journal of Criminal Law* 6:581–610.

Wright, Ronald F., and Rodney L. Engen. 2006. "The Charging and Sentencing Effects of Depth and Distance in a Criminal Code." *North Carolina Law Review* 84:1935–82.

Wright Ronald F., and Marc Miller. 2003. "Honesty and Opacity in Charge Bargains." *Stanford Law Review* 55:1409–15.

Zottoli, Tina M., Tarika Daftary-Kapur, Georgia M. Winters, and Conor Hogan. 2016. "Plea Discounts, Time Pressures, and False-Guilty Pleas in Youth and Adults Who Pleaded Guilty to Felonies in New York City." *Psychology, Public Policy, and Law* 22(3):250–59.

Ryan D. King and Michael T. Light

Have Racial and Ethnic Disparities in Sentencing Declined?

ABSTRACT

Blacks and Hispanics convicted of felonies are more likely than whites to receive prison sentences for their crimes, and they receive slightly longer sentences if imprisoned. Yet the majority of prior research compares sentencing decisions at a single point in time and does not give explicit attention to whether and how racial and ethnic disparities have changed. Decades of sentencing data from Minnesota, the federal courts, and a sample of large urban counties are used to assess the degree of change in racial and ethnic sentencing disparities since the 1980s. There has been some decline in the magnitude of racial and ethnic disparities, with changes in drug laws aligning with some of the reduction in disparity at the federal level. This trend, along with the pattern of findings from related studies, poses a challenge to prominent theoretical explanations of sentencing disparities, including racial threat theory and the focal concerns perspective. Each of four influential theoretical explanations of racial and ethnic disparities in sentencing includes significant empirical or logical shortcomings. Advancing theoretical understanding of racial and ethnic disparity will require new data that follow cases from the point of arrest through to final disposition and include information about citizenship and victims.

The past half century of American criminal justice is defined by two alarming trends. The first is the dramatic expansion of the size and scope

Electronically published February 13, 2019
Ryan D. King is professor of sociology at The Ohio State University. Michael T. Light is associate professor of sociology and Chicano/Latino studies at the University of Wisconsin–Madison.

© 2019 by The University of Chicago. All rights reserved.
0192-3234/2019/0048-0003$10.00

of the criminal justice system. By any metric, be it police force size, prison construction, or dollars spent on the administration of justice, the system has ballooned since the 1970s. This expansion is most evident when we look at the number of persons in prisons and jails per capita. During the first three-quarters of the twentieth century, the imprisonment rate was consistently around 100 prisoners per 100,000 population, or closer to 150 when including both prison and jail inmates. Then, beginning in 1974, the total US incarceration rate began a striking ascent, increasing fivefold to 767 per 100,000 by 2007. This rate makes the United States an extreme outlier on the world stage, so much that a separate axis is needed when the American rate is graphed alongside those of western European and North American countries.

Along with this sea change came a second and equally troubling characteristic: vast racial disparities. At the front end of the justice system, blacks are arrested at far higher rates than whites (Heath 2014), and racial disparities in arrests for drug crimes increased markedly during the war on drugs of the late twentieth century (Mitchell and Caudy 2015, p. 93). At the back end, the proportion of African Americans in prison easily surpasses their proportion in the general population. According to one recent estimate, the imprisonment rate for African Americans is over five times that of whites, and in some states (e.g., Oklahoma) an incredible one in 15 black males over the age of 18 are in state prisons (The Sentencing Project 2016).

Much legal and social science scholarship attempts to explain why racial disparities exist in just about every criminal justice statistic and to determine what causes them. Three contributing factors are investigated: racial differences in offending, enactment of ostensibly race-neutral laws that have disparate racial impacts (e.g., the infamous federal crack vs. cocaine disparity; Tonry and Melewski 2008, pp. 29–30), and unequal treatment by the justice system. In other words, how much of the disparity is due to discrimination by those who legislate, arrest, prosecute, and punish?

This question is central to the subset of criminal justice research that focuses on sentencing. No issue has received more attention in the scholarly literature on sentencing than whether nonwhite defendants are treated more harshly than similarly situated whites. The answer is consequential in several ways. Most fundamentally, the Fourteenth Amendment guarantees equal protection under the law, and this core principle of fairness is called into question if race infects the decision to punish.

Further, sending a convicted defendant to prison has ramifications well beyond the prison walls, as a bout of imprisonment adversely affects employment opportunities, wages, and long-term health (Pager 2003; Western 2006; Massoglia and Pridemore 2015). On that note, the sheer size of the imprisoned population and its racial disparities have motivated many scholars to claim that the criminal justice system is now a salient driver of racial stratification in the United States (Alexander 2012). As Wakefield and Uggen (2010, p. 401) state, "the prison has emerged as a powerful and often invisible institution that drives and shapes social inequality." Differential treatment in the criminal justice system can also foment cynicism toward our legal and political authorities, which in turn is associated with higher crime rates (Tyler 1990; LaFree 1998; Roth 2009; Kirk and Papachristos 2011). It is thus critical to understand whether race matters in sentencing decisions, and if so, why?

Given gross disparities in arrest and aggregate imprisonment rates, it may seem axiomatic that blacks, and perhaps members of other racial minorities, are more likely than whites to be sentenced to prison. If the question is posed simply as Are whites and nonwhites sent to prison at different rates? the answer is unequivocally yes. The odds of imprisonment given a conviction in the federal courts are over three times higher for black than for white males, and the difference for Hispanic compared with non-Hispanic white males is even greater (Ulmer, Painter-Davis, and Tinik 2016). Comparable raw disparities in the likelihood of imprisonment and in the duration of prison sentences are apparent in Minnesota (King and Johnson 2016; Frase 2019), Delaware (MacDonald and Donnelly 2017), and Pennsylvania (Ulmer, Painter-Davis, and Tinik 2016). It is not controversial to state that sizable racial disparities in sentencing exist, akin to what we see in arrest and imprisonment statistics. The more complicated question, and one that generates less consensus, is whether unwarranted racial disparities in sentencing exist. That is, do racial differences in punishments merely reflect racial differences in crime severity and the criminal records of defendants?

It seemed for a time that this may be the case. Reviews of noncapital sentencing studies as of the early 1970s concluded that the relationship between race and sentencing outcomes was effectively nonexistent once proper controls for offense severity and criminal history were considered (Hagan 1973, p. 378; Kleck 1981). As Kleck wrote of studies published as of 1979, "only eight [of 40 studies] consistently support the racial discrimination hypothesis, while 12 are mixed and 20 produce evidence consistently contrary to the hypothesis" (p. 789). Kleck added that it was a distinct possibility that nonwhites (blacks in particular) were treated more leniently.

Fast-forward 25 years, and authors tasked with reviewing the state of sentencing research reach a different conclusion. A meta-analysis of 71 studies through the year 2002 concluded that, even after controlling for the seriousness of the criminal offense and the criminal history of the offender, blacks are, on average, sentenced more harshly than whites (Mitchell 2005). In other words, racial differences in sentencing outcomes are not explained by characteristics of the crime or the defendant's criminal record. Sandwiched in between the early summary reviews and later meta-analyses are several additional canvasses of the sentencing literature that reach various conclusions. Some found little evidence of unwarranted racial disparity (Pratt 1998). Others conclude that race continues to infect sentencing decisions and that the "'discrimination thesis' cannot be laid to rest" (Spohn 2000, p. 428; Sweeney and Haney 1992; Baumer 2013).

Our objective here is not to conduct another meta-analysis or exhaustive summary of research on racial disparities in sentencing. Our reading of the literature leads us to the same summary statement that Baumer (2013, p. 12) offered: "The consistent finding from recent overviews on studies of race and sentencing in samples of convicted defendants is that there are often relatively small but statistically significant direct race differences in the probability of imprisonment to the disadvantage of blacks (compared to whites), and comparatively smaller and statistically nonsignificant direct race differences in prison sentence lengths between these groups."

Like Baumer, we note that racial disparity varies by jurisdiction, type of crime, and judge. Still, at this moment in history, the evidence suggests that racial disparities in sentencing exist and are not fully explained by the confluence of race with crime severity or the extensiveness of defendants' criminal records.

Rather than focus on the singular question of whether unwarranted disparities in sentencing exist in the aggregate, we give overdue attention to three larger themes. First, to what extent have sentencing disparities changed over time? Ironically, at the same time that studies in the 1970s found little evidence of unwarranted racial disparity in sentencing, sentencing reforms were being undertaken to eradicate racial disparities in sentencing by limiting discretion and increasing parity. Adding to the irony, studies of racial disparity after the implementation of sentencing guideline systems—for instance, in Pennsylvania, Minnesota, and the federal system—found evidence of racial disparities, although they appear to have diminished somewhat in Minnesota (Miethe and Moore 1985, p. 358). We cannot make perfect sense of this apparent disjuncture between research findings and policy shifts, but we can ask and try to answer a related question: have racial and ethnic disparities attenuated over time?

Second, it is time for a critical appraisal of theoretical explanations of race and sentencing. We identify four explanations that frequently motivate research on the topic, ranging from cognitive theories that emphasize implicit biases to macro-level theories that draw attention to county and state demographics. Not all theories square with the available evidence. For instance, the predictions of the oft-cited racial threat theory only sometimes pan out in empirical research. Other explanations, such as the focal concerns perspective on sentencing, arguably fit the data too well, raising questions about the theory's specificity and falsifiability. We weigh the merits of, and shortcomings with, theories of race and sentencing.

Third, we identify and expound on data problems that preclude a more complete assessment of the reasons for sentencing disparities. The off-the-shelf sentencing data used in most studies, including our own prior work, are inherently limited because of how they are collected. The data typically relate to convicted felony offenders who receive sentences, yet by that point in the process several earlier decisions have been made that almost certainly have consequences for sentencing outcomes. For instance, felony charges that result in misdemeanor convictions do not show up in felony sentencing files. Prosecutors' decisions to drop cases or to charge more severe crimes will affect which cases appear in the file and, if convicted, the ultimate sentence. Yet the exercise of prosecutorial discretion is not captured in most sentencing data. The few studies that follow cases from the point of arrest show that much of the racial disparity in sentencing reflects decisions made by prosecutors, particularly the decision whether to charge defendants under statutes that require mandatory minimum sentences (Rehavi and Starr 2014).

To accomplish these three objectives, we organize this essay into five sections. Section I provides an overview of recent scholarship on race and sentencing. Most research continues to find that blacks are more likely than whites to receive prison sentences, even when accounting for racial differences in criminal history and crime severity. A similar pattern exists for Hispanics relative to non-Hispanic whites, a difference that is even more pronounced for Hispanic noncitizens. In Section II, we turn to the question of whether racial and ethnic disparities in sentencing have changed during the past three decades. Our analysis of decades of data from the federal courts, Minnesota, and the State Court Processing Statistics Survey suggests some movement toward equality.

Section III appraises four frequently cited theories of racial disparity in sentencing: racial threat, focal concerns, implicit bias, and a loosely related set of ideas we combine under the heading "social distance." Our goal is to evaluate each theory's logic and fit with the pattern of findings from prior research. In our assessment, the racial threat explanation is not well supported, and the focal concerns perspective lacks specificity. Tests of the focal concerns perspective tend to highlight confirmatory evidence while minimizing findings that are inconsistent with predictions.

Section IV discusses the limitations of what Baumer (2013) calls the modal approach to sentencing, that is, the study of racial disparities based on samples of convicted felons provided by sentencing commissions. Gaining clearer understanding will require new data. The lack of data that follow cases from the point of arrest through to their final dispositions, and the near absence of victim information in noncapital sentencing research, impede the ability to explain why racial disparities exist.

Section V concludes with recommendations for future research. Two research issues warrant further attention. First, more work is needed on trends in disparities. We were surprised at how little has been written about changes over time. Our analysis in Section II provides a descriptive account but does not fully answer the question of why sentencing disparities appear to be declining. To this end, future work should take a hard look at policy changes that affect the presumptive sentence and use of criminal histories.

I. Summarizing the State of Research

In this section, we summarize the research on race, ethnicity, and sentencing in the United States. It suggests three patterns. First, after accounting for offense severity and criminal history, there is often a small but significant punishment gap between black and white defendants in the decision to imprison, to the detriment of blacks. This generally also holds true for Hispanics. We can draw no firm conclusions about the sentencing of Native Americans. Evidence from federal courts indicates that Asian defendants do not receive harsher sentences than whites and for some offense types may receive more lenient sentences. Second, sentencing disparities are often conditional on other offender attributes. Punishments are often most severe for young, minority men. Third, disparities vary across jurisdictions. However, no single county or court characteristic explains why some places have larger racial disparities than others.

A. Black-White Disparity

Blacks have long been the racial minority group most oppressed by the justice system (Tonry 1995; Cole 1999). Hundreds of studies from multiple jurisdictions have examined whether this is true for criminal sentencing. The key issue is unwarranted disparities, which refers to racial differences in sentencing outcomes that are not attributable to racial differences in crime severity, criminal history, or other legally relevant variables. We use this definition when referring to "disparity." There are three common findings.

First, blacks tend to receive harsher sentences than whites, even after taking crime severity and criminal history into account. The magnitude of this difference is usually small but nonetheless indicates a pattern of disparate outcomes. To illustrate this point, we present in table 1 two typical analyses of sentencing decisions for samples of blacks and whites for two jurisdictions, Minnesota and the federal system, for the years 2011–13. The outcome variable in each analysis is a dichotomous indicator of whether the convicted defendant received a prison sentence or an alternative, such as probation or a shorter jail sentence. The bivariate associations (models 1 and 3) are statistically and substantively significant, with the odds of receiving a prison sentence 72 percent higher for blacks relative to whites in Minnesota and 75 percent higher for blacks in the federal courts. These odds translate into an 11 percent difference in the percentage of each racial group imprisoned (e.g., 22 percent of whites in Minnesota, compared to 33 percent of blacks). In the second set of models (models 2 and 4), we introduce four variables that are taken into account in most analyses of sentencing: the offender's sex, age, criminal history, and given that each jurisdiction uses sentencing guidelines, the

TABLE 1
Logistic Regression Odds Ratios: Prison Sentences on Race and Control Variables, Minnesota and Federal Sentencing Data, 2011–13

	Minnesota		Federal	
	Model 1	Model 2	Model 3	Model 4
Black (vs. white)	1.720*	1.115*	1.752*	1.135*
Male		1.447*		2.466*
Age		.988*		.979*
Criminal history		1.406*		1.791*
Presumptive sentence		18.240*		16.630*
Observations	38,137	38,137	103,366	103,366

SOURCE.—MSGC monitoring data for 2011, 2012, and 2013 for models 1 and 2; USSC data for 2011, 2012, and 2013 for models 3 and 4.

NOTE.—Only blacks and whites are included in analyses. Other racial and ethnic groups are excluded.

* $p < .05$.

presumptive "in-out" recommendation prescribed by the guidelines.[1] The odds of receiving a prison sentence remain significantly higher for blacks relative to whites in each system. The magnitude of the disparity, however, is a fraction of the size: the odds are 11.5 percent higher in Minnesota and 13.5 percent higher in the federal system. In each case, this equates to about a 1 percent difference in the probability of an incarceration sentence for blacks relative to whites. These racial disparities are statistically significant, but the magnitudes are small.

The results shown in table 1 are symptomatic of a larger pattern in the study of race and sentencing. For instance, an analysis of federal sentencing shows that 64 percent of the black male (relative to white male) difference in imprisonment sentences is attributable to legally relevant factors (Ulmer, Painter-Davis, and Tinik 2016, p. 660). The same study finds that more than half of the black-white gap in the odds of imprisonment in Pennsylvania is explained by racial differences in the severity of the crime and criminal history of the offender. The probability of incar-

---

[1] In both the United States Sentencing Commission (USSC) and Minnesota data, criminal record is measured by the offenders' criminal history category—ranging from I (least serious) to VI (most serious)—based on the severity and number of their previous convictions. The presumptive "in-out" refers to whether the guidelines call for an imprisonment sentence relative to a stayed sentence. The latter often involves probation instead of imprisonment.

ceration in Delaware shows a similar pattern. MacDonald and Donnelly (2017) report a substantial (60 percent) baseline disparity in the probability of imprisonment for blacks relative to whites, yet the disparity shrinks to 11 percent after including measures of offense severity, criminal history, and other control variables. When we juxtapose our findings in table 1 with the findings from Delaware, Pennsylvania, the federal system, and a recent meta-analysis (Mitchell 2005), we think it uncontroversial to conclude that small but statistically significant racial disparities exist for the decision of whether to imprison a convicted defendant. These disparities are not fully explained by strictly legal characteristics of the case.

A second recurrent finding is that disparities between blacks and whites are more pronounced for the in-out decision than for decisions about sentence length (Mitchell 2005). Conditional on going to prison, whites and blacks tend to receive similar lengths of confinement for comparable crimes (Baumer 2013, p. 12).

Third, there is considerable heterogeneity in the relationship between race and sentencing. For example, research consistently finds that the association between race and sentencing outcomes is conditional on other offender attributes, such as gender and age. Steffensmeier, Ulmer, and Kramer (1998), for instance, show that the greatest observed disparities at sentencing were found for young black men (see also Doerner and Demuth 2010). In this same vein, the black-white punishment gap varies across communities and courtrooms (Britt 2000; Ulmer and Johnson 2004; King, Johnson, and McGeever 2010), although no clear set of characteristics explains this variation. For instance, Britt (2000) finds that racial disparities were more pronounced in some Pennsylvania counties than in others, but the differences were unrelated to county racial demographics or economic conditions, leaving him to conclude that links between social context and racial disparities are "unclear" (p. 729). Using data from the same state a few years later, Ulmer and Johnson (2004) reach a different conclusion: blacks and Hispanics received longer sentences in counties with larger black and Hispanic percentages, respectively. In a study of large urban courts, King, Johnson, and McGeever (2010) instead concluded that racial disparities were lower where the proportion of black attorneys in the county was higher. As these studies illustrate, there is not much consistency concerning why the white-black difference in sentencing is more pronounced in some places than in others.

B. Hispanics

As the United States grew more racially and ethnically diverse, sentencing studies expanded to assess whether black-white disparities were suggestive of a broader pattern of racial and ethnic inequities. Against the backdrop of higher immigration from Latin America since the 1980s, much of the contemporary work on sentencing disparities has focused on Hispanics. This emphasis is well placed. Between 1990 and 2010, the US Hispanic population more than doubled, from 21.8 million to 50.7 million, accounting for the majority of total population growth since 2000 (Passel, Cohn, and Lopez 2011). During this period, for the first time in US history, Hispanics surpassed African Americans as the largest demographic minority group in the United States.

Research findings for Hispanic relative to non-Hispanic white (Hispanic-white, hereafter) sentencing disparities are generally consistent with findings from black-white comparisons. Hispanic defendants receive more severe sentences, on average, than similarly situated white defendants (Ulmer 2012; Spohn 2015), and the disparity is most pronounced for young Hispanic men (Spohn and Holleran 2000). In a meta-analysis examining 34 published and unpublished studies, Mitchell and MacKenzie (2004) found that Latinos received significantly harsher penalties than whites, even when accounting for criminal history, offense severity, age, and other factors. This average effect, however, disguises heterogeneity in the Hispanic-white sentencing gap. As with the black-white findings, the largest disparities are observed for the incarceration decision. Hispanic defendants were significantly more likely than white defendants to be sent to prison, while Hispanic-white differences in sentence length were generally small and not statistically significant (Mitchell and MacKenzie 2004). Differences were also observed across offense types, with Hispanic ethnicity exerting the strongest influence in cases involving drugs. A summary review of 40 studies largely confirms this general set of findings (Spohn 2000).

In line with the recent, more nuanced approach in the contemporary race and sentencing literature, studies examine how other offender attributes, particularly gender and age, condition ethnic disparity. Once again, the results align with research on racial disparity by demonstrating interactions between ethnicity, gender, and age. Using data from the State Court Processing Statistics for 1990–96, Steffensmeier and Demuth (2006) demonstrate that Hispanic-white sentencing disparities (as well as black-white disparities) are highly dependent on gender; racial and ethnic sentencing disparities were largely confined to male offenders (see also Spohn 2013).

Following the lead of Steffensmeier, Ulmer, and Kramer (1998), Doerner and Demuth (2010) examined the joint effects of race/ethnicity, age, and gender using federal court data from 2001. Compared to young (ages 18–20) white males, they found that young Hispanic males are most likely to be incarcerated, while young black males received the longest prison sentences. For both sentencing decisions, none of the female groups (white or minority) received significantly harsher punishment than white males. On the contrary, many minority females received significantly lesser punishment compared to young white males (see Kramer and Ulmer [2009, chap. 5] for a similar analysis using data from the Pennsylvania Commission on Sentencing). Among females, Doerner and Demuth (2010) found few sentencing differences by race and ethnicity. Differences in the Hispanic-white punishment gap are also observed across contexts. Feldmeyer and Ulmer (2011) and Ulmer, Light, and Kramer (2011), for example, detect interdistrict variation in the effect of Hispanic ethnicity across US federal courts. Comparable findings were observed across county courts in Pennsylvania by Ulmer and Johnson (2004).

Some recent work suggests that Hispanics receive harsher sentences than similarly situated blacks. Steffensmeier and Demuth (2000) used data from US district courts for the years 1993–96 and found that Hispanic defendants received harsher punishment than both white and black defendants, particularly in drug cases. To explain their findings, they argued that "the specific social and historical context involving Hispanic Americans, particularly their recent high levels of immigration, exacerbates perceptions of their cultural dissimilarity and the 'threat' they pose," which in turn "contribute[s] to their harsher treatment in criminal courts" (p. 710). Steffensmeier and Demuth (2001) report a similar pattern in Pennsylvania. Brennan and Spohn (2008) report that Hispanic drug offenders in a large urban court in North Carolina were disadvantaged at sentencing relative to both white and black defendants.

On balance, however, the claim that ethnic disparity is now worse than racial disparity remains tentative. For instance, Spohn's (2000) review showed that while 43 percent of state-level studies reported significant black-white disparities, only 28 percent showed significant Hispanic-white disparities. In federal courts, 68 percent showed black disadvantage, compared to 48 percent showing significant Hispanic disadvantage.

In their meta-analysis, Mitchell and MacKenzie (2004) similarly report slightly greater black-white disparity than Hispanic-white disparity. Steffensmeier and Demuth's analysis of the State Court Processing Statistics provides little evidence that ethnic disparity has eclipsed racial disparity. For example, Demuth and Steffensmeier (2004) and Steffensmeier and Demuth (2006) report similar black-white and Hispanic-white differences in punishment, net of legally relevant controls. All in all, it appears that ethnic disparities are generally comparable to racial sentencing disparities.

C. Native Americans and Asians

Far less research exists on sentencing disparities for racial and ethnic groups other than blacks and Hispanics. A handful of studies examine whether the black-white disparities are comparable for Native Americans, albeit with mixed results (see Jeffries and Bond [2012] for a review). One set of findings suggests that Native Americans are treated differently than whites. For instance, Alvarez and Bachman (1996) use data from Arizona prisons to examine sentencing disparities for offenders convicted of homicide, sexual assault, robbery, assault, burglary, and larceny. Accounting for the prior felony record and demographic controls (e.g., age, gender), Native Americans received significantly longer prison terms than whites for robbery and burglary crimes but significantly shorter sentences in homicide cases. Native Americans have a higher probability of imprisonment than whites in Minnesota (Wilmot and Delone 2010). They receive longer sentences in federal courts, net of controls for criminal history and offense severity, particularly for violent offenses (Everett and Wojtkiewicz 2002). Franklin's (2013) analysis of 28 district courts with sizable Native American caseloads in 2006–8 suggests that Native American sentencing disparities are on par with or exceed those for black and Hispanic offenders.

However, other work shows no evidence of sentencing bias against Native Americans. Ulmer and Bradley (2018), for example, examined sentencing information for the same 28 federal district courts as Franklin (2013) for the years 2010–12. They found shorter prison sentences for Native Americans compared to whites, net of legal, demographic, and case processing controls. One plausible explanation for these discrepant findings relates to the distinct ways the analyses account for context. While Franklin (2013) includes district controls, Ulmer and Bradley (2018) investigate variation in the Native American disparity across districts and find that Native American leniency dissipates substantially with the size of the Native American population and in districts where federal courts have greater jurisdiction over criminal law enforcement in Indian country. Research from Washington State also found that Native Americans receive more lenient sentences (Rodriguez 2003) or no systematic differences in sentencing outcomes (Engen and Gainey 2000). Taken together, the small number of studies is, at best, suggestive that Native Americans may be disadvantaged at sentencing in comparison to similarly situated whites, although more work is needed before strong conclusions can be offered (see also Mitchell and MacKenzie 2004).

By comparison, the existing research on Asian American sentencing disparities generates more consensus. The most in-depth treatment of sentencing disparity among Asian offenders is provided by Johnson and Bestinger (2009). Using federal court data from the USSC from 1997 to 2000, they found evidence of sentencing leniency relative to black, Hispanic, and, to a lesser extent, white offenders. After accounting for a host of legally relevant controls, Asian defendants were more likely to be granted downward departures for "substantial assistance" to the government and significantly less likely to be incarcerated compared to white, black, and Hispanic offenders, although white defendants received significantly shorter prison sentences than Asians (see also Kutateladze et al. 2014). They argue that this difference in disparity among different racial and ethnic groups may stem from the relatively positive stereotypes of Asians as the "model minority" group. However, this sentencing advantage for Asians may not apply to noncitizen immigration offenders (Wu and Kim 2014).

II. Trends in Racial Disparity

The research just discussed is based on point-in-time estimates of racial and ethnic disparities. But have they changed over time? Are we trending toward more equity in this phase of the criminal justice process? Or have efforts to reduce bias, such as sentencing guidelines, failed to accomplish their objective? Worse still, might the sentencing reform movement have backfired and resulted in greater racial disparities?

We put these questions in context and then assess the degree of change on the basis of three unique data sets that collectively include over two million cases dating back to the 1980s or 1990s, depending on the data source. On balance, the observed trends provide reason for optimism, as the bulk of the evidence points to a downward trend in racial and ethnic sentencing disparities. A couple of indicators move in the opposite direction, but even these are balanced by countertrends. For example, the data show an increase in disparities for Hispanics relative to whites; yet further analysis shows that this is driven by noncitizens and that the sentencing disparity for US citizens of Hispanic origin has declined. The magnitude of the declines was substantial in some cases. The overall sentence length gap between whites and blacks in federal courts decreased by over 80 percent between 1996 and 2016, and by some measures the disparity decrease in Minnesota was nearly as strong. At the same time, few of the trend lines end at "zero disparity," suggesting that parity has not been reached.

A. Trends and Expectations

Racial disparity is a staple of sentencing research because it is a social problem that, as a society, we presumably want to eradicate. This is certainly the aim of widely read indictments of the justice system (Alexander 2012), documentaries along the same lines (*13th*), and organizations dedicated to sentencing reform (The Sentencing Project; e.g., Ghandnoosh 2015).[2] It thus seems prudent to assess whether the trend line for racial disparity in sentencing is up, down, flat, or sawtooth. More to the point, are we headed in the right direction? We are surprised at how little has been written on this question. It is hard to imagine a body of research on crime that did not give attention to crime trends or on imprisonment that did not focus on change over time.

Theory and prior research provide no clear guidance as to what we should expect, although four trends provide reason to believe that racial and ethnic disparities may have waned. First, racial disparities in many facets of social life have attenuated. The Pew Research Center reports that, since the 1960s, the white-black gaps have narrowed for measures of high school completion, college completion, poverty, and to a lesser extent family income (Parker, Horowitz, and Mahl 2016). Aggregate disparities on these outcomes certainly persist, but they are generally trending toward greater equality.

---

[2] The 2016 documentary film *13th*, directed by Ava DuVernay, places mass incarceration alongside other institutions that have historically suppressed the rights of African Americans.

Second, white Americans' support for discriminatory policies has waned. As Bobo et al. (2012, pp. 46–47) state in their work on trends in the General Social Survey since the 1970s, "A solid majority [of whites] turned against segregationist or Jim Crow principles in the domains of schools, housing, and racial intermarriage. By 1972, fewer than 15 percent of whites nationwide thought that black and white children should attend separate schools. That fell below 10 percent by the early 1980s. By 1985, so few people endorsed the segregationist response that the GSS dropped this item." Bobo et al. also show that a full 65 percent of whites opposed having a close relative marry a black spouse as late as 1990, yet this fell to below 30 percent by 2008. These trends in public opinion are congruent with other ways of measuring prejudice in American society. For instance, Google searches for racist jokes and antiblack hate crimes have declined since the early 2000s (Pinker 2018, pp. 218–20). To the extent that racial inequity in criminal justice reflects economic inequality and racist public sentiment, these trends may bode well for increasing fairness in criminal sentencing, particularly on the heels of a sentencing reform movement that made fair treatment a key objective (Spohn 2009).

Third, a recent report from the National Academy of Sciences shows that the imprisonment rate for blacks decreased from 6.5 times the white rate in 1980 to 4.6 times the white rate by 2010 (Travis, Western, and Redburn 2014, p. 58), and the pattern for Hispanics appears similar (pp. 62–63). The current racial disparity in imprisonment is large—excessively large in our opinion—especially when compared to black-white ratios and Hispanic-white ratios for measures of poverty or employment, but the trend line since 1980 appears to bend toward less disparity than in decades past.

Fourth, some prior work suggests that racial disparities in sentencing are indeed attenuating. In their review of Pennsylvania sentencing guidelines, Kramer and Ulmer (2009, pp. 111–12) compared sentencing disparities for the periods 1989–92 and 1997–2000 and found significantly less racial disparity in sentencing in the later period.[3] This was true for blacks and Hispanics relative to non-Hispanic whites.

---

[3] The authors find less disparity in the probability of receiving a prison sentence but no significant change in sentence length conditional on going to prison.

While these trends make us think that racial disparities should have declined, we also observe some countertrends. For instance, not all black-white economic disparities have narrowed. The wealth gap has widened since the early 1980s (Parker, Horowitz, and Mahl 2016, p. 24), and imprisonment disparities, which decreased when measured as the black-white ratio, increased between 1980 and 2010 when measured as the absolute difference between the black and white imprisonment rates (Travis, Western, and Redburn 2014, p. 58, table 2.2). In addition, early meta-reviews of the sentencing literature indicated little racial disparity in sentencing in the 1960s and 1970s (Kleck 1981), while more recent studies suggest significant racial disparities (Mitchell 2005). All of this raises a distinct possibility that racial disparities may be increasing.

Further, and with respect to federal cases, the federal sentencing guidelines have changed since their inception in ways that could influence racial sentencing disparities. For instance, following *Mistretta v. United States*, 488 U.S. 361 (1989), in which the Supreme Court upheld the constitutionality of the USSC and its guidelines, the percentage of cases sentenced within the recommended guideline range decreased from 77 percent in 1992 to only 49 percent in 2016. The number of judge-initiated departures also changed over this period. In 1992, only 6 percent of cases received judge-induced downward departures. In 2004, 12 percent of cases did. However, following *United States v. Booker*, 543 U.S. 220 (2005), which held the mandatory federal guidelines unconstitutional and declared them advisory, judge-initiated downward departures increased precipitously. They rose from 20 percent in the year immediately following *Booker* to 38 percent by 2016, in the wake of several other Supreme Court cases that granted more discretion to district court judges (*Rita v. United States*, 551 U.S. 338 [2007]; *Gall v. United States*, 552 U.S. 38 [2007]; *Kimbrough v. United States*, 552 U.S. 85 [2007]). To the extent that greater discretion corresponds to greater disparities, we might expect an increase in sentencing disparities in federal courts (Yang 2015; Hofer 2019).

We try to gain some clarity on this issue by analyzing three data sets: federal sentencing data from 1992 to 2016, Minnesota Sentencing Guidelines Commission data between 1981 and 2013, and State Court Processing Statistics Survey data collected between 1990 and 2009. Each data source has been used in prior research; additional details and notes about them can be found in the Appendix.

B. Federal Courts

The federal system through its visibility and prominence often exerts direct and indirect influence on the administration of justice at state and local levels. Thus, we begin by assessing whether racial disparities have changed over time in the federal courts. Two questions guide our inquiry: First, what are the raw disparities, without considering variations in presumptive sentences specified in the federal sentencing guidelines? Second, have disparities changed when we adjust our estimates to account for changes in the presumptive sentences?

Looking first at the raw disparities, the black line in figure 1 shows the difference in the proportion incarcerated among non-Hispanic black (hereafter black) offenders and non-Hispanic white (hereafter white) offenders. We refer to this as the black-white incarceration gap. The gray line shows the black-white gap in presumptive incarceration sentences, which is the proportion of black sentences for which the US guidelines recommended incarceration minus the proportion of white sentences for which the presumptive sentence was incarceration.[4] In the federal system, the presumptive sentence is determined by a combination of the prior record, the severity of the conviction offense, and other legally prescribed factors such as the application of federal mandatory minimum statutes. As shown in figure 1 (gray line), the presumptive gap suggests that black offenders were slightly more likely to have presumptive incarceration sentences during this period (mean = 3 percent over the study period). However, the actual black-white gap in prison sentences was considerably higher (mean = 9 percent). This incarceration gap has changed since the early 1990s. In 1992, blacks were 10 percent more likely than whites to receive an incarceration sentence in US district courts. This disparity increased during the next 4 years and peaked in 1996, when

---

[4] The main component of the Federal Sentencing Guidelines is the sentencing grid, on which the recommended sentence is determined by the combination of two numeric values: the offense level (range 1–43) and the criminal history category (range 1–6). To derive the offense level, a district judge uses the sentencing guidelines first to set the base offense level, which is determined by the crime of conviction. The guidelines then specify an extensive list of adjustments to this base offense level according to a variety of factors, such as harm to a vulnerable victim, the use of a gun, whether the offender played a major or minor role in the crime, and whether the offender accepted responsibility for his or her crime. The offender's criminal history category is then calculated on the basis of the number and severity of prior criminal convictions. The combination of offense severity and criminal history yields a sentencing range expressed in months. For the overwhelming majority of federal offenders over our study (88 percent), the guidelines recommended incarceration.

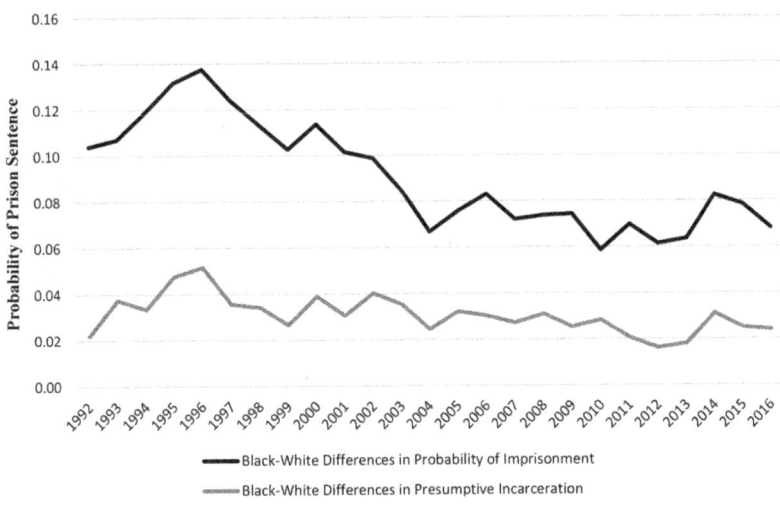

Fig. 1.—Black-white differrences in prison sentences, US district courts, 1992–2016. Sources: USSC (2016) and similar data files for felony and class A misdemeanor convictions in each year between 1992 and 2015.

blacks were nearly 14 percent more likely to receive a prison sentence. Then, between the mid-1990s and mid-2000s the black-white incarceration gap decreased considerably, from 14 percent to around 7 percent. A significant difference remains, yet the incarceration gap is smaller today than it was 20 years ago.

Figure 2 depicts the analogous trends for presumptive and actual sentence length differences. Two points are noteworthy. First, the trend toward parity is more vivid. On average, blacks received roughly 27 more months in prison than whites in 1992 (black line in fig. 2). By 1996, this had increased to 42 months. Since that time, the difference in black-white sentence lengths has decreased markedly, especially since 2009. In 2016, the black-white sentence length gap was 8 months; this is an 80 percent reduction from 20 years prior. Analyses of average sentence lengths for blacks and whites separately (not shown) indicate that this reduction is equally driven by lower average sentences for black offenders and higher average sentences for whites.

Second, there is significant consistency in the presumptive and actual black-white sentence lengths. This suggests that much of the disparity in black-white sentence lengths is driven by differences in their presumptive sentences. In other words, the observed disparities in sentence length

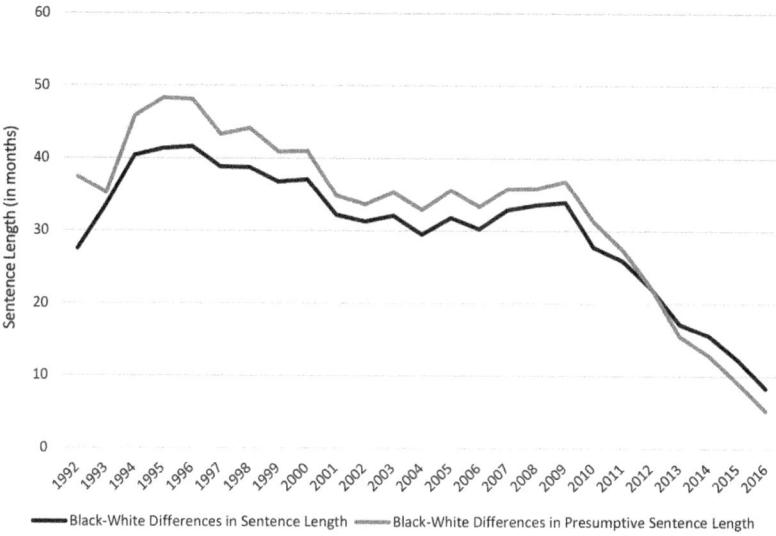

FIG. 2.—Black-white differences in sentence length, US district courts, 1992–2016. Sources: USSC (2016) and similar data files for felony and class A misdemeanor convictions in each year between 1992 and 2015.

are largely due to adherence to the sentencing guidelines. It also suggests that changes in presumptive sentences played a significant role in the dramatic decrease in average black-white sentence lengths observed over this period. It is important to note, however, that changes in presumptive sentences can be due to a variety of factors, including changes in criminal behavior, adjustments to the guidelines, or shifts in charging decisions (or a combination of each).

We next examine Hispanic-white differences in incarceration sentences in figure 3. In line with the racial differences observed above, we see a significant gap in the likelihood of incarceration for Hispanic offenders in each year (see the black line in fig. 3). For instance, the likelihood of a prison sentence in 1992 was 18 percent higher for Hispanics compared with whites. The magnitude of this disparity decreases during the 25-year observation period. In 2010, Hispanics were 12 percent more likely to receive incarceration, down from its peak of 20 percent in 1995. The trend line crept up in recent years, although disparities still remain lower than at any point in the 1990s. Interestingly, and in contrast to the case for blacks relative to whites, the presumptive sentence gap is consistently lower than the actual sentencing gap. Had the presumptive sentence de-

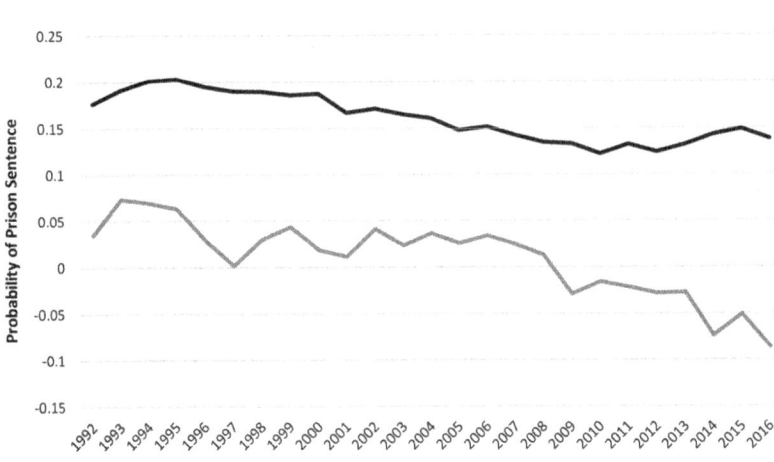

Fig. 3.—Hispanic-white differences in prison sentences, US district courts, 1992–2016. Sources: USSC (2016) and similar data files for felony and class A misdemeanor convictions in each year between 1992 and 2015.

termined the actual sentence, Hispanics should have been imprisoned less frequently than whites, which was clearly not the case. However, the trend in the presumptive sentence moves in the same direction, suggesting that the declining sentencing gap for Hispanics is partly driven by changes in the presumptive sentence.

We observe a similar pattern for sentence length in figure 4. As shown by the black line in figure 4, Hispanic offenders in 1992 received an average of 18 months' additional prison time than whites. By 2016, they received nearly 25 fewer months of prison than whites. This is due to increases in the average sentence for whites over this period, combined with substantial decreases in the average prison sentence for Hispanics. These trends appear to result from changes in Hispanic-white presumptive sentences (gray line in fig. 4).

It may initially appear surprising that sentences of Hispanic offenders are so far below those of whites. This apparent oddity results from the high number of federal immigration cases against non-US citizens. Enhanced border enforcement resulted in large numbers of noncitizens punished in US district courts, nearly all of whom are of Hispanic origin.[5]

---

[5] In 2016, 94 percent of non-US citizen offenders were Hispanic.

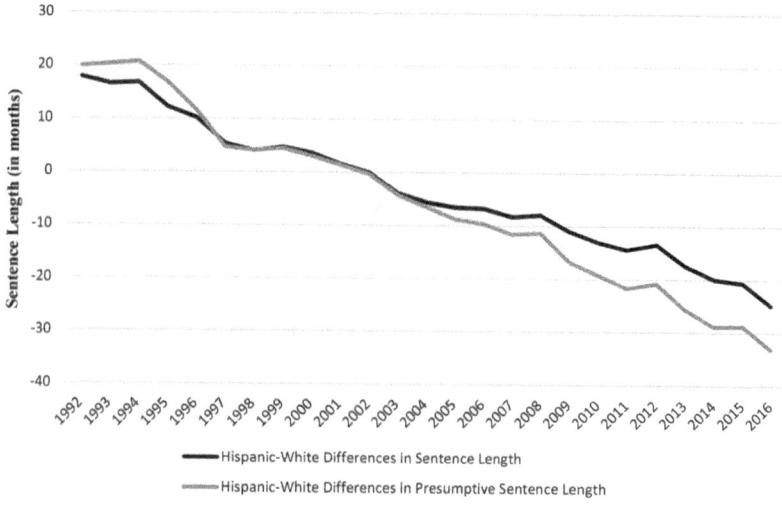

FIG. 4.—Hispanic-white differences in sentence lengths, US district courts, 1992–2016. Sources: USSC (2016) and similar data files for felony and class A misdemeanor convictions in each year between 1992 and 2015.

In 1992, roughly 8,000 non-US citizens were sentenced in federal court, representing 22 percent of the federal docket. By 2016, this had increased to over 28,000 cases, 42 percent of all cases. This is consequential when comparing sentencing outcomes for Hispanics and whites because nearly all non-US citizens receive prison sentences (97 percent in 2016), yet they are often short in duration.[6] In 2016, the average prison sentence for US citizens was 56 months; for non-US citizens it was 23 months.

As shown in figure 5, the trends in Hispanic-white sentencing look different when we look at US citizens. Most notably, the trend lines move closer to zero, indicating greater equity in sentencing. In 1994, the Hispanic-white sentencing gap for the decision to imprison was 15 percentage points. This dropped to 8 percent in 2016 (fig. 5, black line). In terms of average sentence lengths, there is little difference in months incarcerated between Hispanics and whites in 2016. This is a huge difference from the early 1990s: Hispanic US citizens received sentences that were 21 months longer on average (gray line and left axis in fig. 5).

---

[6] This likely reflects the relatively low base offense level assigned to immigration offenses. The average offense level for immigration offenses is only 8.6, substantially lower than for drug offenses (27.0), violent offenses (18.5), firearms offenses (19.1), and sex offenses (20.3).

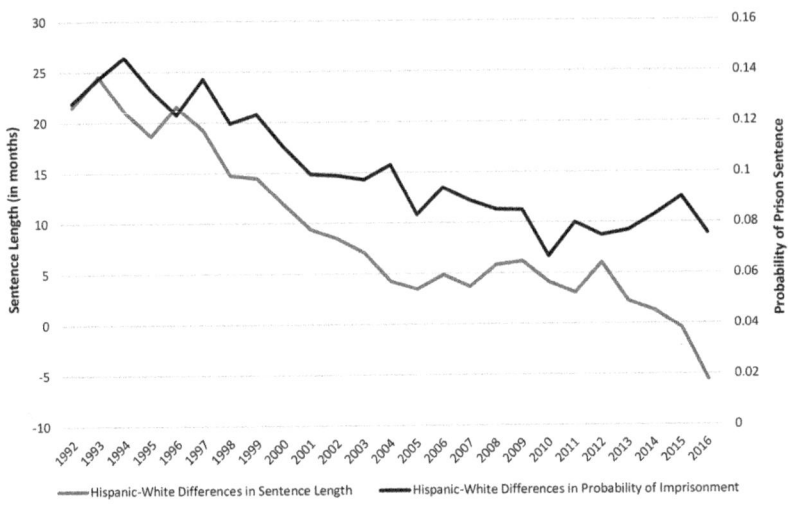

FIG. 5.—Hispanic-white differences in sentences for US citizens, US district courts, 1992–2016. Sources: USSC (2016) and similar data files for felony and class A misdemeanor convictions in each year between 1992 and 2015.

Overall, these descriptive findings suggest three patterns. First, in line with much of the previous sentencing research, we find greater racial and ethnic disparities in incarceration decisions than in sentence length decisions. The respective gray and black lines in figures 1 and 3 (imprisonment sentences) have daylight between them, indicating that the presumptive sentence is not determining the actual sentence. In contrast, the two lines are closely tethered in figures 2 and 4 (sentence length), which implies less disparity between guideline recommendations and actual sentences. Second, much of the racial/ethnic differences in sentence lengths is driven by differences in presumptive sentences. Third, we see some initial evidence of waning sentencing disparities between whites and the two largest groups of minority offenders.

Another way to look at sentencing trends is to focus on the adjusted disparity rather than the sentence gap. That is, do the declines in racial and ethnic disparity depicted in figures 1–5 persist after we account for the presumptive sentence? To "net out" the influence of the presumptive sentence, and thereby isolate the discretionary portion of the sentence, we examine the adjusted black-white sentence disparity. We calculate this value by dividing the average pronounced sentence (the actual sentence given by the judge) for blacks in a given year by the average presumptive sentence (the guideline recommendation) for blacks in that same year.[7] This gives us the average deviation from the guideline recommendations for blacks as a proportion of their prescribed sentence. We then do the same for whites and then subtract the white deviation from the black deviation. Stated more formally,

$$\text{Adjusted black} - \text{white sentence disparity} = (S_{bt}/P_{bt}) - (S_{wt}/P_{wt}), \quad (1)$$

where S indicates the average pronounced sentence and P is the average presumptive sentence in year t for blacks (b) and whites (w). This statistic can be interpreted as the proportional difference in imprisonment sentences for blacks relative to whites, net of the presumptive sentence, with positive values indicating more black-white disparity. More specifically, positive values indicate that black offenders receive less of a proportional discount from their presumptive sentence than whites. For example, 70 percent of white offenders received a prison sentence in 1992, but 86 percent of whites should have received imprisonment if judges simply followed the presumptive sentence specified in the guidelines. Whites thus received only 81 percent of the recommended prison sentences on average (70/86 = 0.81). That same year, 80 percent of sentenced blacks were imprisoned while the guidelines called for 89 percent to be imprisoned, and thus pronounced imprisonment sentences were 90 percent of the presumptive prisons sentences (0.80/0.89 = 0.9). Therefore, the adjusted black-white sentence disparity for that year is 9 percent (0.90 − 0.81 = 0.09).

How has the adjusted disparity changed over time? The gray line in figure 6 shows the adjusted black-white incarceration disparities. While disparities have declined, we have not reached parity. In each year the trend line is above zero, indicating that black defendants received harsher sentences than whites, even after taking into account differences in the presumptive sentences between groups. Consistent with the trends in the raw disparities, however, we find evidence of reductions in black-white imprisonment disparities. Given that racial disparities are most of-

---

[7] For the incarceration analysis, the average pronounced sentence is the proportion of black offenders who received a prison sentence. The average presumptive sentence is the proportion of black offenders who had a prison sentence recommendation from the guidelines.

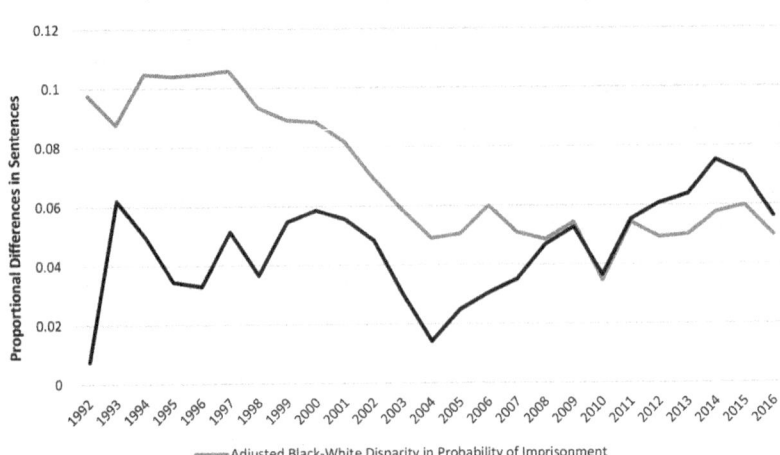

Fig. 6.—Adjusted black-white differences in sentencing, US district courts, 1992–2016. Sources: USSC (2016) and similar data files for felony and class A misdemeanor convictions in each year between 1992 and 2015.

ten found at the incarceration stage, this is promising news. Nevertheless, the reductions observed during the 1990s appear to have stalled in the 2000s, with minimal observed changes in adjusted black-white incarceration disparities.

The adjusted sentence length disparities are depicted by the black line in figure 6. For this analysis, we use the same equation as the adjusted imprisonment disparities, but the pronounced and adjusted sentences are calculated slightly differently. Here, the pronounced sentence is the average sentence length in months for a given group (e.g., white, black) in a given year. The presumptive sentence is the average minimum number of months of prison recommended by the guidelines (see the Appendix for further details) for a given group in a given year. For example, in 2016, the average black sentence was 63 months in prison, while the average black presumptive sentence was 79.4 months. For whites, the comparable figures were 54.6 months in prison relative to 74.1 recommended months. Applying equation (1) to these figures yields an adjusted black-white sentence length disparity of 0.06. That is, black offenders, on average, receive 6 percent longer sentences than whites in 2016, relative to their group-specific presumptive sentence lengths.

Turning to the overall trends in adjusted sentence lengths, we observe a pattern different from those shown for imprisonment disparities. The adjusted disparity is always above zero, suggesting that blacks receive proportionally longer sentences than whites, adjusting for their presumptive sentences. However, there is little evidence of either substantial decreases or increases over time. Indeed, with the exception of significant deviations in 1992 and 2004, there is only limited movement in the trend. For instance, the average adjusted black-white disparity between 1993 and 2003 was 0.047. Between 2005 and 2016, the average was 0.051. That said, there is evidence that this form of disparity has edged up slightly in the last 15 years.

We next turn to the adjusted disparities between white and Hispanic offenders (fig. 7). Beginning with sentence length differences (black line), our findings align with much of the extant research; in most years, Hispanics receive slightly longer sentences than whites, net of presumptive sentence (average over this period is 0.02). Yet the gap in sentence length between non-Hispanic whites and Hispanics is always 5 percent or less, and by 2016 there was practically no disparity between these groups in the federal system.

This is not the case, however, for imprisonment disparities (gray line). At first glance, the data appear to show worsening imprisonment disparities. That is, Hispanics were, proportionally, 17 percent more likely than whites to be incarcerated relative to their guideline sentence in 1992. By 2016, they were 26 percent more likely to be incarcerated, net of the presumptive sentence. Once again, however, citizenship status obfuscates this picture. When we omit non-US citizens from the analysis, as we do in figure 8, two different findings emerge. First, the adjusted Hispanic-white disparities in imprisonment decisions are far less pronounced (though still present). Second, the trend is in the direction of more equality, not less. In other words, adjusting for differences in the guideline recommendation, while disparities persist, there is less Hispanic-white disparity at the incarceration stage in 2016 than in the early 1990s, at least among US citizen offenders. It is also worth noting that there are virtually no Hispanic-white disparities in adjusted sentence lengths among US citizens; the average value across the study period is zero.

Our analysis of disparities between Hispanics and non-Hispanic whites underscores two additional points. First, citizenship status must be considered when making these comparisons (Light, Massoglia, and King 2014). As we demonstrated, what appeared to be increases in ethnic disparity in recent decades was actually an emerging disparity between citizens and noncitizens. This finding aligns with recent arguments that non-US citi-

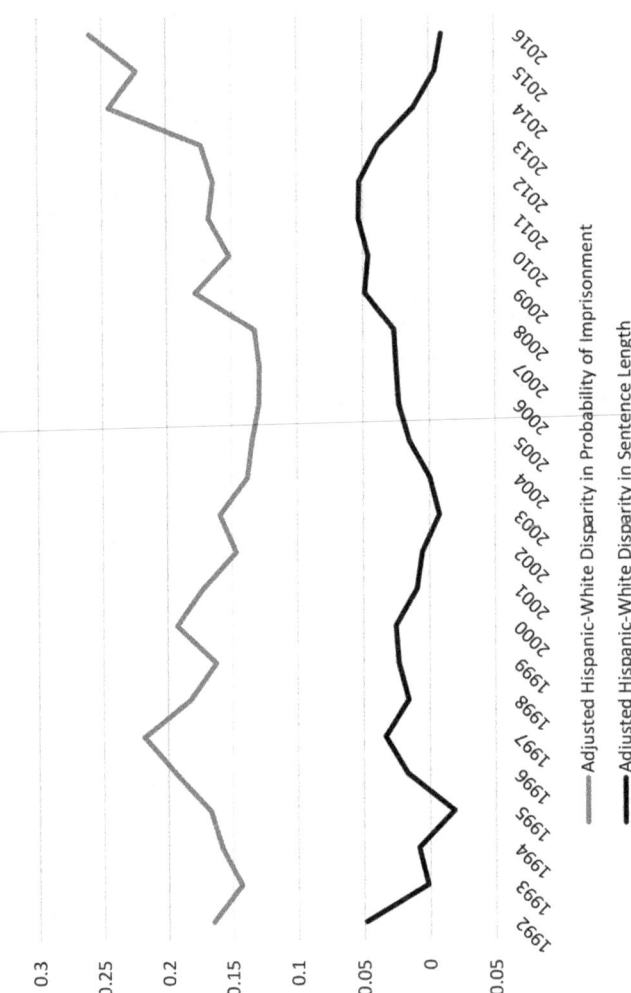

FIG. 7.—Adjusted Hispanic-white differences in sentencing, US district courts, 1992–2016. Sources: USSC (2016) and similar data files for felony and class A misdemeanor convictions in each year between 1992 and 2015.

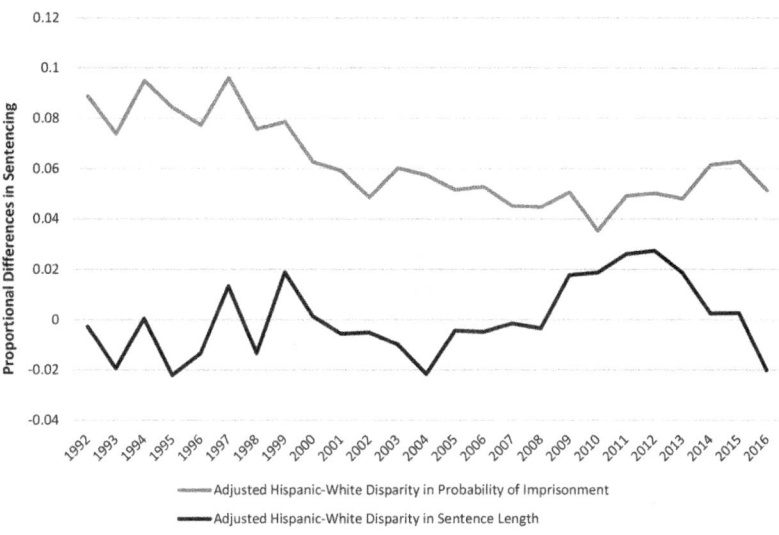

FIG. 8.—Adjusted Hispanic-white differences in sentences for US citizens, US district courts, 1992–2016. Sources: USSC (2016) and similar data files for felony and class A misdemeanor convictions in each year between 1992 and 2015.

zens, as opposed to racial or ethnic minorities, may be the new face of inequality in federal courts (Light 2014). Second, when accounting for citizenship status we find movement toward more equal sentencing outcomes for whites and Hispanics in federal courts. This trend is most obvious when looking at the adjusted disparity in Hispanic-white incarceration sentences, shown in figures 7 and 8. As seen in figure 7, which includes noncitizens, sentencing disparities clearly increased to the detriment of Hispanic offenders (compared to whites). However, when we focus only on US citizens in figure 8, the data show the opposite pattern: there is a clear trend toward less Hispanic-white disparity after taking presumptive sentence into account.

C. Minnesota Courts

We present a similar set of figures using data from the Minnesota Sentencing Guidelines Commission (MSGC), which maintains records for all felony sentences dating back to 1981 (our time series begins in 1982 because of missing data on sentence length in 1981). The trends for black-white sentencing disparities in Minnesota do not perfectly mirror those depicted above for the federal courts, but we again see some movement

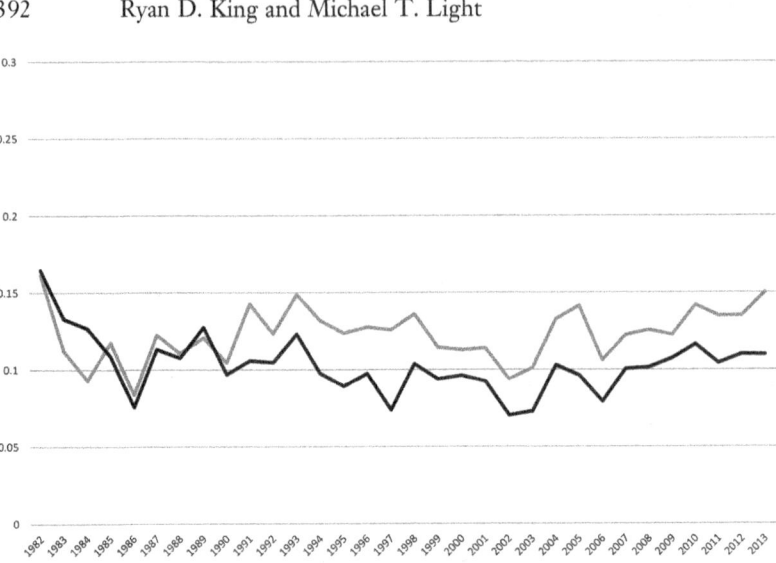

Fig. 9.—Black-white differences in prison sentences, Minnesota, 1982–2013. Sources: MSGC (2014) and similar data files for felony convictions in each year between 1982 and 2013.

toward less racial disparity, particularly when looking at black-white differences.

For instance, figure 9 shows the black-white gap in presumptive (gray line) and actual (black line) prison sentences by year.[8] Black convicted defendants received prison sentences a sizable 16 percent more often than whites in 1982, which is precisely what we would expect on the basis of the average presumptive sentence that year (gray line in fig. 9). The black-white gap in the presumptive sentence fluctuated during the next three decades, ultimately ending about where it began. However, the black-white gap in pronounced prison sentences followed a slightly different trajectory. The black line in figure 9 shows that the black-white gap in prison sentences dropped to a low of 7 percent in 2002 before reversing course and ending at 11 percent in 2013, which is 5 percent lower than the 1982 black-white difference.

---

[8] The presumptive (or recommended) sentence indicates whether the sentencing guidelines call for an imprisonment sentence relative to a stayed sentence (when analyzing the in-out decision) or the specific number of months identified in the guideline grid (when analyzing sentence length).

Have Racial and Ethnic Disparities in Sentencing Declined? 393

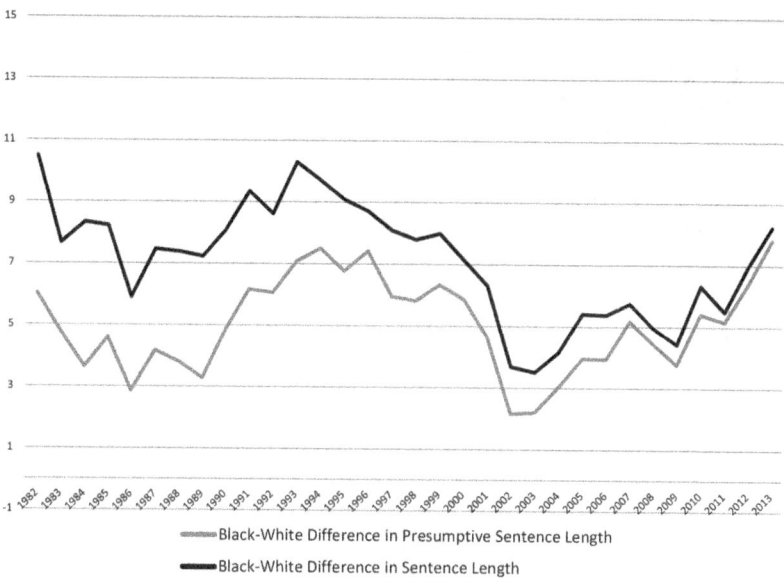

Fig. 10.—Black-white differences in sentence length, Minnesota, 1982–2013. Sources: MSGC (2014) and similar data files for felony convictions in each year between 1982 and 2013.

We see a similar pattern for sentence length during this period (fig. 10). The average presumptive sentence was 6 months longer for blacks relative to whites in 1982 (gray line), and the actual sentence disparity was even longer—10 months (black line). Both the presumptive and actual sentencing gaps ebbed and flowed over the next 30 years, but not in lockstep. That the two lines gradually converge over time is consequential for two reasons. First, it appears that Minnesota judges increasingly conformed to the presumptive sentence as time went on. Second, following the sentence length recommended by the guidelines meant that racial disparities in sentencing decreased from 10 months in 1982 to 8 months in 2013. Stated differently, the actual sentence length was more than 4 months higher than the presumptive in 1982 but nearly identical in 2013, which suggests a decrease in unwarranted racial disparity.

Another way to express this latter trend is to use the adjusted black-white sentence disparity, which we defined above when discussing the trends in the federal courts. As depicted in figure 11, the adjusted black-white disparity in the probability of receiving a prison sentence reached a high of 15 percent in 1984 (gray line in fig. 11). This indicates that black

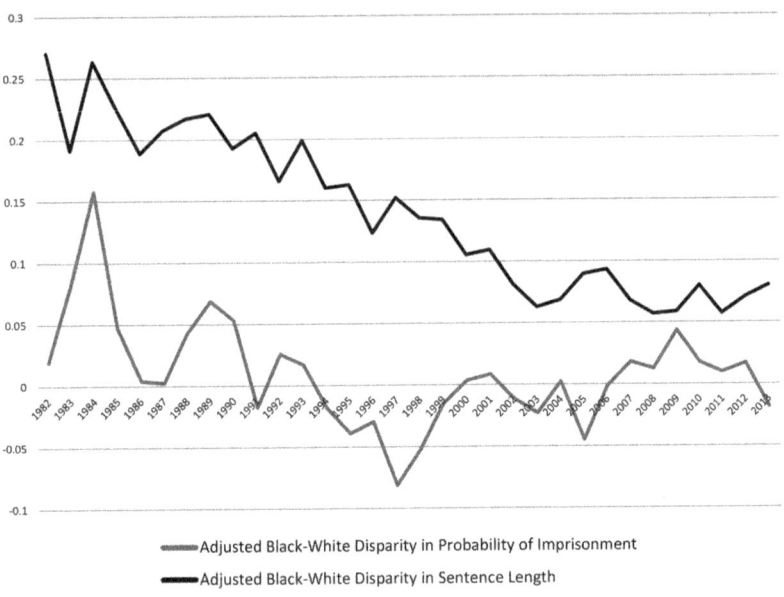

Fig. 11.—Adjusted black-white differences in sentencing, Minnesota, 1982–2013. Sources: MSGC (2014) and similar data files for felony convictions in each year between 1982 and 2013.

defendants were 15 percent more likely to receive a prison sentence than whites, relative to the race-specific presumptive sentences. The adjusted imprisonment disparity declined in sawtooth fashion during the next decade, reaching its low point in 1997 (−8 percent), indicating that blacks were less likely to be incarcerated than whites, relative to the presumptive sentence. The adjusted disparity then stayed close to zero for the remainder of the time series.

The adjusted black-white disparity for sentence length also declined over time (black line in fig. 11). For instance, the average black sentence was about 90 percent of the presumptive sentence in 1982, compared to 63 percent for the average white defendant (not shown in the figure), which yields a sizable adjusted sentencing disparity of 27 percent (black line in 1982). The adjusted disparity in sentence length was nearly cut in half, to 15 percent, by the mid-1990s, and then nearly cut in half again by 2013 (8 percent). Some racial disparity relative to the presumptive sentence clearly persists, but the adjusted racial disparity at the end of the time span is considerably lower than at the beginning.

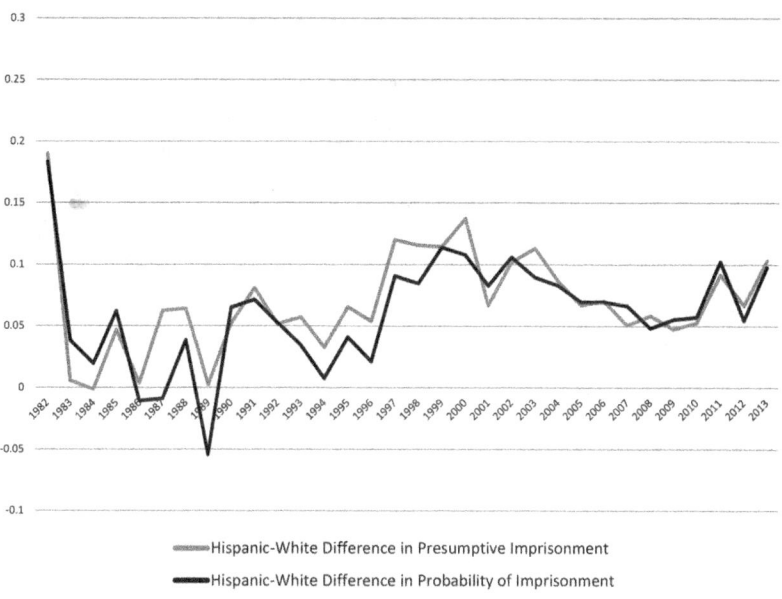

Fig. 12.—Hispanic-white differences in prison sentences, Minnesota, 1982–2013. Sources: MSGC (2014) and similar data files for felony convictions in each year between 1982 and 2013.

The trends in Hispanic-white sentencing disparities differ from the black-white differences. Figures 12 and 13 show the Hispanic-white gaps in presumptive and actual sentences, which reveal two points. First, the trends show more evidence of an increase than a decrease in disparities, especially for sentence length (fig. 13). Second, the Hispanic-white sentencing gaps are clearly driven by the presumptive sentences rather than judicial discretion. Whether looking at the imprisonment decision (fig. 12) or at sentence length (fig. 13), the Hispanic-white sentencing gap maps onto what we would expect on the basis of the presumptive recommendation in the state's sentencing guidelines. While it remains possible that the presumptive sentence is itself partially a product of judicial discretion (Fischman and Schanzenbach 2011), the analysis still underscores the importance of the sentencing guidelines in driving disparities. This is also apparent in figure 14, which shows the adjusted Hispanic-white disparities. The adjusted disparity for the imprisonment decision averages zero over the 32-year period, indicating that the presumptive sentence was driving the gap between Hispanics and whites. We observe greater dis-

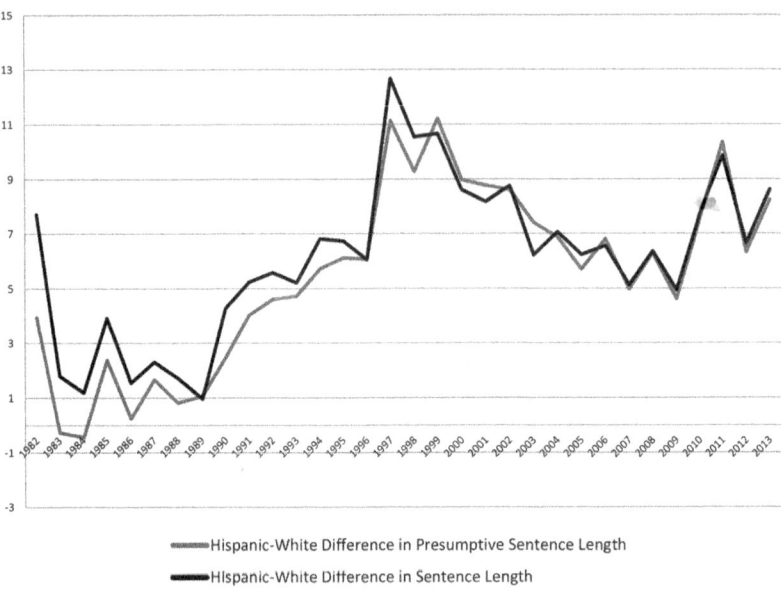

Fig. 13.—Hispanic-white differences in sentence lengths, Minnesota, 1982–2013. Sources: MSGC (2014) and similar data files for felony convictions in each year between 1982 and 2013.

parity in sentence length in the early years (black line), but the 1982 level is cut in half by the final observation year.

In sum, the Minnesota data indicate less black-white disparity over time, particularly when looking at the adjusted disparity (fig. 11). Raw differences between Hispanics and whites have increased slightly, although this is driven by the presumptive sentences.

D. State Court Processing Statistics

The last stage in our analysis examines data from the 1990–2009 waves of the State Court Processing Statistics Survey of Felony Defendants in Large Urban Counties (SCPS, hereafter). For our purposes, two important aspects of the SCPS are worth noting. First, the SCPS is widely used in research on race, ethnicity, and sentencing (Steffensmeier and Demuth 2006; King, Johnson, and McGeever 2010; Sutton 2013; Wang and Mears 2015). Second, and more importantly, unlike the federal and Minnesota data, the SCPS data come from multiple jurisdictions that span both guideline and nonguideline states. Of the 25 states represented in the 10 waves of data available, 11 of them do not have structured sentenc-

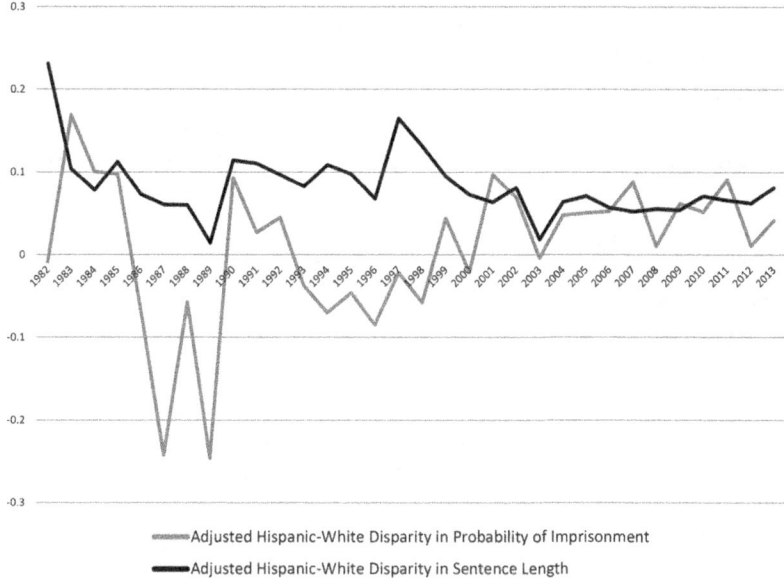

Fig. 14.—Adjusted Hispanic-white differences in sentencing, Minnesota, 1982–2013. Sources: MSGC (2014) and similar data files for felony convictions in each year between 1982 and 2013.

ing guidelines.[9] We can thus examine sentencing practices across a broad spectrum of geographical, political, and criminal justice contexts. Moreover, to the extent that the results in the SCPS are consistent with those found in Minnesota and the federal courts, we can have greater confidence that the findings are not idiosyncratic to only those jurisdictions. While the SCPS contains information on offenders who were not sentenced, we restrict our analysis to only those who were convicted of felonies to maintain consistency with the federal and Minnesota analyses reported above.

For parsimony, we begin with the analysis of adjusted racial and ethnic disparities. Because the SCPS includes both guideline and nonguideline jurisdictions, we cannot incorporate the presumptive sentence in the same way as our previous analyses. We thus use regression analysis to model the incarceration and sentence length decisions and examine the

[9] The data are available for the following years: 1990, 1992, 1994, 1996, 1998, 2000, 2002, 2004, 2006, and 2009. For details, see http://www.ncsc.org/~/media/microsites/files/csi/state_sentencing_guidelines.ashx.

trends in sentencing disparities. To reduce skewness, we log the sentence length variable in the regression models.[10] Following previous research, we account for several variables shown to affect sentencing decisions. The severity of the offense and extent of the defendant's criminal record are the two most salient determinants. We measure offense severity using 18 binary indicators representing the most serious conviction charge. Criminal history is captured by including the total number of prior convictions (top-coded at 10). Research suggests that offenders who go to trial and lose often pay a "trial penalty" at sentencing (Ulmer, Eisenstein, and Johnson 2010); we include a measure of whether the defendant was convicted at trial (1 = yes) as opposed to pleading guilty. In addition to race and ethnicity, we also account for the defendant's sex (male = 1) and age. As in our previous analyses, in all models we compare black and Hispanic offenders to whites (the reference group). To examine changes over time, we include a linear year term that captures each wave of data (1 = 1992, 2 = 1994, etc.). Our focal variables are interaction terms between race/ethnicity and time. Substantively, these interactions tell us how black and Hispanic offenders have fared over time relative to whites after adjusting for important case and offender characteristics. Finally, we include county fixed effects to remove all time-stable sentencing differences between counties.[11] By focusing on within-county change only, our models adjust for any legal, political, and jurisdictional differences in the SCPS that do not change over time.

We use logistic regression to model the incarceration decision and Tobit regression to model the length of incarceration. Tobit estimation accounts for selection into the incarcerated population by assuming that the outcome measure would be normally distributed if it were fully observed. It thus accounts for both the probability that the outcome exceeds zero (i.e., that the offender received a prison sentence) and the mean value of sentence length, adjusted by covariates.

Table 2 shows the results for the incarceration decision.[12] Model 1 assesses the trends in black and Hispanic incarceration disparities without controls; model 2 includes defendant and legally relevant case characteristics, and in model 3 we introduce county fixed effects. In line with

---

[10] We added a 1 prior to logging to retain those who received nonincarceration sentences in the analysis.

[11] There are a total of 71 counties represented.

[12] In line with previous research (King, Johnson, and McGeever 2010), incarceration sentences include both jail and prison sentences.

TABLE 2
Racial/Ethnic Disparities in Incarceration, SCPS, 1990–2009

	Model 1		Model 2		Model 3	
	b	SE	b	SE	b	SE
Focal measures:						
White (reference)	...	...	...	...	...	...
Black	.28***	.05	.16***	.05	.34***	.06
Hispanic	.98***	.06	.82***	.06	.54***	.07
Year	.01	.01	−.01**	.01	−.01	.01
Black × Year	.00	.01	.00	.01	.00	.01
Hispanic × Year	−.06***	.01	−.04***	.01	−.03***	.01
Controls:						
Male			.29***	.02	.42***	.03
Age			−.002*	.001	−.004***	.001
Trial			−.11**	.04	.16***	.05
Prior convictions			.18***	.00	.18***	.00
Offense effects?	No		Yes		Yes	
County effects?	No		No		Yes	
Constant	.61***	.04	3.22***	.42	2.02***	.44
Number of cases	66,181		66,181		66,181	

SOURCE.—State Court Processing Statistics (felony defendants in large urban counties in 1990, 1992, 1994, 1996, 1998, 2000, 2002, 2004, 2006, and 2009).

NOTE.—Models are estimated using logistic regression. Dependent variable is whether the offender received an incarceration sentence. Models include measures for 18 different offense types and county fixed effects.

* $p < .10$.
** $p < .05$.
*** $p < .01$ (two-tailed tests).

previous research, across each model we find that black and Hispanic offenders are more likely to be incarcerated, and these results hold even net of other case and defendant characteristics, including offense and criminal history controls. In reference to the trends in disparity, the interaction terms for black and Hispanic by sentencing year in model 3 suggest that there is virtually no observable trend in the black-white disparity, as indicated by the substantively small and nonsignificant interaction coefficient.[13] Hispanic-white disparity, on the other hand, attenuates over time, as indicated by the negative coefficient (−0.03 in model 3).

---

[13] We replicated this model using a quadratic function of year as well as interactions with race and sentencing year squared. The coefficients align with the descriptive findings, which show an initial decrease in black-white disparity followed by an increase in later years. None of these interactions, however, are significant at the $p < .05$ level. We thus give preference to the linear specification in the analysis.

TABLE 3
Racial/Ethnic Disparities in Sentence Length, SCPS, 1990–2009

	Model 1		Model 2		Model 3	
	b	SE	b	SE	b	SE
Focal measures:						
White (reference)	...	...	...	...	...	...
Black	.51***	.05	.28***	.04	.31***	.04
Hispanic	.85***	.05	.53***	.05	.36***	.05
Year	.02***	.01	.01	.01	.00	.01
Black × Year	−.02**	.01	−.01**	.01	−.01*	.01
Hispanic × Year	−.05***	.01	−.03***	.01	−.02**	.01
Controls:						
Male			.44***	.02	.49***	.02
Age			−.004***	.001	−.004***	.001
Trial			.54***	.03	.64***	.03
Prior convictions			.16***	.00	.16***	.00
Offense effects?	No		Yes		Yes	
County effects?	No		No		Yes	
Constant	.95***	.04	4.16***	.12	4.04***	.16
Number of cases	66,181		66,181		66,181	

Source.—State Court Processing Statistics (felony defendants in large urban counties in 1990, 1992, 1994, 1996, 1998, 2000, 2002, 2004, 2006, and 2009).

Note.—Models are estimated using Tobit regression. Dependent variable is the length of incarceration (including sentences of 0 months). Models include measures for 18 different offense types and county fixed effects.

* $p < .10$.
** $p < .05$.
*** $p < .01$ (two-tailed tests).

We next turn to sentence length (table 3). Given that our length specification includes nonincarceration sentences (i.e., those sentenced to 0 months of jail or prison time), these models arguably provide a better sense of the overall level of racial and ethnic sentencing disparity in the SCPS data. As with table 2, in table 3 we show three models. Beginning with model 1, two patterns stand out. First, consistent with previous research using the SCPS data, black and Hispanic offenders receive significantly longer sentences than whites. Second, the interaction terms suggest that the punishment gaps between whites, blacks, and Hispanics have significantly decreased since 1990. The next models examine whether this pattern holds after adjusting for covariates. While the empirical rigor increases across each subsequent model, the pattern of declining sentencing disparities persists. In our full specification (model 3), each of the focal interaction terms is negative and statistically significant.

To aid with interpretation, we graph the predicted trends in black and Hispanic sentences relative to whites in figure 15 (based on the results in table 3). Though a significant punishment gap remains between white and minority offenders, we find considerable convergence in the sentences meted out between these groups. As shown by the predicted values in figure 15, the black-white gap decreased by 36 percent between 1990 and 2009, and the Hispanic-white gap decreased by 42 percent.

III. Theoretical Explanations of Racial Disparity

In a 1984 article in the *American Sociological Review*, Ruth Peterson and John Hagan reflected on theoretical explanations of sentencing disparities and noted that "sentencing studies provide an example of an area of sociological research in which a static, simplistic understanding of race has impeded theoretical development" (Peterson and Hagan 1984, p. 56; see also Hagan and Bumiller 1983). Conflict theory, which was the predominant explanation at the time, predicted that the justice system was just another apparatus of the state that could preserve class structure by treating lower-class groups, including racial minorities, more harshly than whites and the wealthy. Yet the available evidence at the time of their writing did not necessarily align with this perspective (Kleck 1981). Peterson and Hagan suggested that theoretical explanations must explain why criminal sentencing does not always work to the detriment of nonwhites and that accounting for "anomalous findings" was the challenge of the day for sentencing research.

That challenge was met, and today we observe far more theoretical breadth in the sentencing literature. Yet it may again be time for some critical reflection on the current state of sentencing theory. Akin to Peterson and Hagan's critique of conflict theory in the 1980s, some current explanatory theories do not square with the evidence or are so vaguely formulated that testing them is difficult and confirmation bias is a serious risk. We assess four prominent explanatory perspectives: racial threat, focal concerns, implicit bias, and a set of related arguments that emphasize social distance and the demographics of courtroom actors. These are not the only theories of sentencing, but scholars frequently interpret racial

A. White-Black

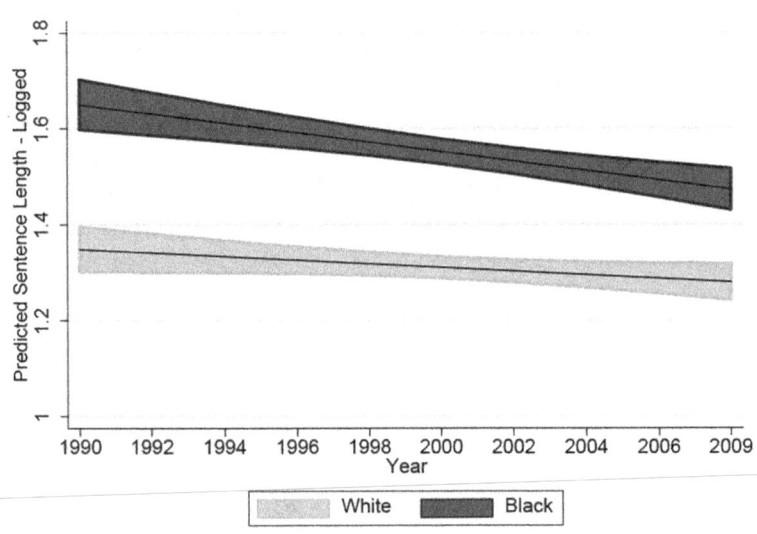

B. White-Hispanic

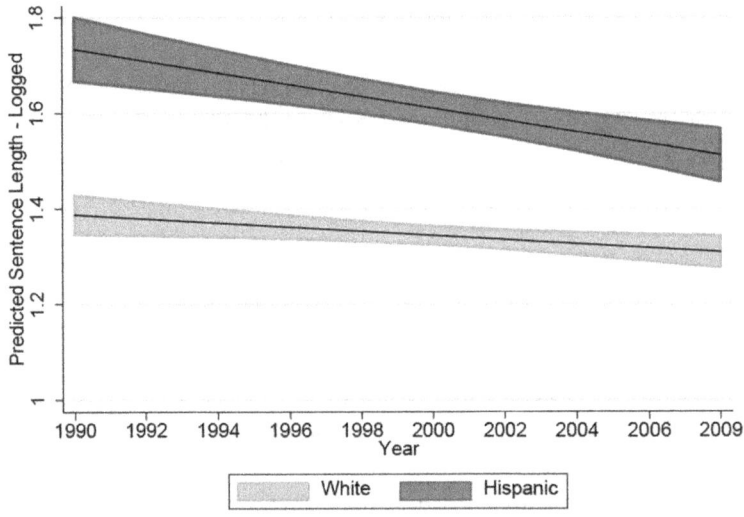

Fig. 15.—Predicted sentence lengths for white and black offenders, SCPS, 1990–2009. Note: Predicted sentence lengths are based on results in model 3 of table 3.

differences through these lenses. For each, we briefly summarize the key hypotheses pertinent to sentencing. We then draw attention to logical or empirical inconsistencies as relevant and relate the theory to the trends in racial/ethnic disparity observed in the previous section.

A. Racial Threat

In the inaugural article of the *Pacific Sociological Review*, the sociologist Herbert Blumer (1958) penned an essay that would serve as the foundation for decades of scholarship on racial prejudice. Neither "crime" nor "punishment" appears in the article, but Blumer's thesis found a home in the study of race and punishment by the century's end.

Blumer suggested that dominant groups in society—typically majority groups that have long held power—seek to maintain their advantaged position over "subordinate groups," which are typically racial minorities. The dominant group feels a sense of superiority and fears that the minority group will challenge its dominance or otherwise compete for economic and political control. As Blumer (p. 4) stated, prejudice includes "a feeling on the part of the dominant group of being entitled to either exclusive or prior rights in many important areas of life" (e.g., positions of authority in employment and government), and its members suspect that "the subordinate racial group is threatening, or will threaten, the position of the dominant group." As such, prejudice emerges as a response to perceived threats from minorities.

Blumer's work on prejudice is often cited in tandem with Hubert Blalock's (1967) seminal work, *Toward a Theory of Minority-Group Relations*. Like Blumer, Blalock saw much prejudice and discrimination as stemming from intergroup power contests (p. 109); a key driver of intergroup conflict was the relative size of the minority population. The specific functional form of the relationship between minority group size and discrimination depends on several factors, such as the nature of the discrimination (e.g., economic or political) and the economic conditions at the time (see Blalock 1967, chap. 5); but at the heart of his thesis is that discrimination and prejudice increase as the minority percentage gets larger. Blalock illustrates his point by showing that support for racist political candidates (e.g., the Dixiecrats in 1948) increased as the percent black increased in the area. Likewise, black voter registration in southern counties around 1950 decreased as the percent black increased, presumably as a result of voter suppression and discrimination (p. 163).

Blumer's and Blalock's ideas, referred to as "group threat theory," were supported by several studies of prejudice in the late twentieth and early twenty-first centuries (e.g., Giles and Buckner 1993; Quillian 1995; Taylor 1998). Given the substantial racial disparities in arrest and imprisonment rates in the United States, scholars queried whether the theory explains variation in punitive outcomes. Blalock devoted little attention to this subject in his original work but hinted at such a relationship (1967, pp. 167–68). He suggested that whites are more apt to express beliefs about the criminality of black men and demand greater control over deviants when the black population is proportionately larger. In line with his prediction, research finds that people perceive higher crimes rates where the size of the young black male population is larger, even after controlling for the crime rate (Quillian and Pager 2001). In a careful analysis of racial disparity in imprisonment rates in northern states between 1880 and 1950, Muller (2012) showed that disparities in imprisonment grew as more nonwhites (almost entirely blacks) migrated northward.

We have tested and found support for the group threat perspective in our own research but have become skeptical of the theory's relevance for explaining criminal punishment, including racial sentencing disparities. We do not reject the theory as applied to other social phenomena. For instance, recent work on voting laws finds a relationship between black voter turnout and restrictive voting laws, which is quite consistent with racial threat theory (Bentele and O'Brien 2013). Racial demographics also correlate with police decision making, as lethal use of force is more common in places with higher rates of black-on-white homicide (Legewie and Fagan 2016). However, we are less sanguine about the utility of racial threat for explaining sentencing disparities. Our criticisms relate to three aspects of the theory: its logic, the empirical measurement of key concepts, and its fit with available evidence.

The logic of the theory, meaning its assumptions about how key concepts fit together, is problematic when applied to the case of criminal sentencing. Blalock originally formulated the theory to explain variation in expressions of prejudice in a population. His logic was that large or growing minority populations represent a threat to existing power arrangements and thereby increase the level of prejudice expressed by majority group members. Yet we add layers of complexity when moving from attitudes in a population to decision making by professionals in formal roles. Most notably, it strains credulity to suggest that judges, in calculating fashion, are aware of demographic changes in the county and strategically use their power in the justice system to stymie the advancement of racial minorities in the political realm, or that judges deliberately give longer prison sentences in order to put blacks at a competitive disadvantage relative to whites. At a minimum, we would need some evidence beyond mere correlation between race and punishment to support such an inference. Further, even if we accept this logic, it seems improbable that such slight sentencing disparities (see table 1) are capable of accomplishing these sinister goals.

Accompanying this logical critique is a measurement problem. Blalock (1967) specified the functional form of the expected relationship between minority group size and prejudice. However, most of the empirical work on punishment has not followed his lead. Consider, for instance, the vast body of work testing for a relationship between racial demographics and a variety of criminal justice outcomes at case or aggregate levels of analysis. Collectively, this work measures the concept of racial threat by use of the percent black (King, Johnson, and McGeever 2010), the percent black squared (Stolzenberg, D'Alessio, and Eitle 2004), the natural log of the percent black (Campbell, Vogel, and Williams 2015), the year-to-year change in the percent black (Muller 2012), a dichotomous indicator of whether the percent black is above or below the median (Jacobs and Carmichael 2002), the percent black interacted with southern census region (King 2007), and the percent black interacted with the former Confederate states (Keen and Jacobs 2009). These measurement differences imply very different interpretations, such as whether racial demographics are consequential only in a region (e.g., the South) or whether there is an inflection point. Yet, despite important differences in interpretation, authors tend to view the correlations as consistent with group threat theory. To the extent that any correlation between the percent minority and punishment—regardless of functional form or contingency—supports group threat theory, it has lost precision and explanatory value to a point at which it hardly provides a clear framework for understanding variation in punishment.

Finally, and most importantly for our purposes, the theory does not square with the available evidence. Racial threat theory generates two hypotheses relevant to racial disparities in sentencing. First, at the heart of the theory are the notions that blacks are viewed as more aggressive and criminally inclined than whites (Blalock 1967, p. 167) and that such perceptions drive sentencing disparities. A second hypothesis relates to the racial demographics of the county in which sentencing decisions are made. Larger concentrations of racial minorities are expected to signal a greater threat; black-white sentencing disparities should be more pronounced in those jurisdictions.

Each of these hypotheses rests on a shaky empirical foundation. The first hypothesis is supported insofar as race is associated with perceived criminality (Quillian and Pager 2001). Sentencing decisions, however, are not necessarily associated with such perceptions. For instance, Johnson and King (2017) matched sentencing data on nearly 1,100 convicted felons with their booking photographs and then asked a team of research assistants with no knowledge of the suspects to give their initial impressions of whether the person in the photograph looked threatening. In line with threat theory and related research (Quillian and Pager 2001), black defendants were, on average, rated as more threatening in appearance than whites. However, perceived threatening appearance was uncorrelated with the severity of the sentences of the convicted felons and explained none of the black-white disparity. This is inconsistent with the racial threat thesis.

The second hypothesis, that racial demographics of counties are associated with sentencing disparities, fares no better. We can certainly identify studies showing the expected correlation of greater disparity where minority group size is relatively large (Bridges and Crutchfield 1988), but other studies found no association or even the opposite correlation. For instance, Ulmer and Johnson's (2004) analysis of sentencing in Pennsylvania found no correlation between racial disparity in prison sentences and percent black in the county, although the black-white disparity in sentence length increases with black population size. A related pair of studies on discretionary use of a habitual offender law in Florida, which effectively serves as a sentencing enhancement, found that racial disparities between black and white women in the use of habitual offender laws were more pronounced in places with large black populations (Crawford 2000). This offers "support for the straightforward black 'power threat hypothesis'" (p. 275).

Yet this finding is precisely the opposite of results from other samples of convicted women (Bridges and Beretta 1994) and is contrary to another study using essentially the same Florida data, but for a sample of male defendants (Crawford, Chiricos, and Kleck 1998). In the latter analysis, racial disparities among men were less pronounced where the percent black was higher. It seems unlikely that black women would pose a singular threat that would not materialize for black males. Thus the pattern of findings for habitual sentencing in Florida appears inconsistent with what we would expect given the assumptions of racial threat theory.

Further, several studies found that racial disparities in sentencing are uncorrelated with the percent black in the county or district (Britt 2000; King, Johnson, and McGeever 2010; Feldmeyer and Ulmer 2011). One study found that sentencing disparities between Hispanics and whites are smaller in federal judicial districts where the percent Hispanic is larger (Feldmeyer and Ulmer 2011). This is again contrary to the racial (or in this case ethnic) threat thesis.

Finally, the trends described in Section II are at odds with the racial threat thesis. The data by and large show a decline in racial disparities since the early 1980s in Minnesota and since the early 1990s in the federal system and in the SCPS data. During this same period, the black population in the United States increased by about 1 percent, from 11.7 percent in 1980 to 12.6 percent in 2010, and Minnesota experienced an even larger proportionate increase. From a racial threat perspective, these population changes should signal a greater threat and hence greater racial disparities in punishment. Our analysis of racial disparities suggests the opposite.

The findings regarding ethnic disparity are perhaps even more germane. Driven largely by immigration from Latin America, the United States experienced the largest influx of immigrants—in both absolute and relative numbers—in its history in recent decades. From a threat perspective, we would anticipate greater Hispanic-white disparity, yet our results from Minnesota, the federal courts, and the SCPS provide no evidence for this view, descriptive or otherwise. While it is plausible that the increases in citizenship disparity are consistent with the group threat perspective, the absence of similar patterns for Hispanics and blacks raises questions about the theory.

B. Cognitive Theories

The racial threat perspective assumes that the demographics of a city or county are correlated with explicit prejudice. Another perspective on racial disparities in sentencing draws attention to the related concept of implicit biases—stereotypical associations subtle enough that people often are unaware of them. Such biases are typically measured through responses to the Implicit Association Test (IAT). The "Race IAT" consists of a computer-based sorting task in which participants pair valuative words ("good" or "bad") and faces (white or black) (see Greenwald et al. [2009]

for a review). The IAT has been taken by millions of people and produced some distinctive patterns. Most notably, white Americans more quickly associate white faces with good words and black faces with bad words than vice versa. Black Americans, on the other hand, show significantly more variation on the IAT. While the average black American expresses a slight white preference, some report moderate to strong black preferences and others report strong white preferences (Nosek, Banaji, and Greenwald 2002).

Applying the IAT to 133 trial judges from different parts of the country, Rachlinksi et al. (2009) asked whether judges hold implicit racial biases and, if so, whether they predict decision making. They found that white judges, like the general population, exhibited a strong white preference as measured by the IAT and that black judges demonstrated no clear racial preferences. The authors then linked the IAT results with judges' decisions in hypothetical cases using criminal case vignettes, which revealed an association between implicit bias and judicial decision making. Judges with higher white preferences on the IAT and who were primed with black-associated words gave harsher sentences to hypothetical defendants described in a vignette. Those reporting a black preference on the IAT gave more lenient punishments when primed with black-associated words. However, when made aware of the need to be aware of racial bias, judges appeared to suppress their implicit biases and sentenced white and black offenders similarly. Levinson, Cai, and Young (2010) used a different version of the IAT that tested for associations between words like "black" and "guilty," with similar results.

Evaluating the role of implicit bias outside of the lab is a tall order, and hence the true impact of implicit bias is difficult to assess. However, we note that observational studies of sentencing are often congruent with experimental results, at least with respect to expected correlations. For instance, one method of priming implicit bias in lab experiments is to introduce variation in a defendant's skin tone, for instance, when participants view a video or pictures from a mock crime scene. Such experiments suggest that darker skin tones are associated with perceptions of guilt, which leads researchers to conclude that implicit racial biases underlie racial disparities in legal outcomes (Levinson and Young 2009).

To this end, sentencing research using court and prison data reveals a similar pattern of findings, albeit outside the context of experimental manipulation. For instance, dark skin hue is associated with longer prison sentences in a sample of Mississippi men (Gyimah-Brempong and Price

2006) and in a sample of North Carolina women (Viglione, Hannon, and DeFina 2011). Punishments are also more severe for defendants with Afrocentric features, which refers to "those physical features that are perceived as typical of African Americans (e.g., dark skin, wide nose, full lips)" (Blair, Judd, and Chapleau 2004, p. 674n1). King and Johnson (2016) examined skin tone and Afrocentricity for a sample of more than 800 black and white convicted defendants in Minnesota. They found that dark-skinned blacks were more likely to receive prison sentences in comparison with whites and also when compared to light- and medium-skinned blacks. Further, Afrocentric features mattered for understanding sentencing disparities, but only for whites.[14] That is, "whites with facial features that more closely resemble blacks are treated more harshly than other whites" (King and Johnson 2016, p. 111).

This conclusion is similar to Branigan et al.'s (2017) finding that skin tone is significantly associated with arrest for white respondents. It is unclear why intraracial variation matters for whites, although Branigan et al. speculate that law enforcers or judges notice phenotypic differences within groups more than across racial groups. For instance, same-race survey interviewers report more variation in skin color than do those interviewing persons of a different race (Hill 2002). As such, unconscious bias may surface against those with less conventional facial features.

These empirical findings are consistent with the notion of implicit bias, although we cannot say whether this is the specific mechanism producing racial disparities. It also bears mention that not all empirical results fit with the theory. For instance, implicit bias theory would presumably predict that white judges would sentence black defendants more harshly than white defendants, yet this is not necessarily the case (see subsection D below). Further, this type of cognitive theory must be reconciled with the substantial variation in sentencing disparities over time and across space. Implicit bias varies by state (Mooney 2014) and presumably over time, which provides an opportunity for researchers to examine whether times and places with higher levels of implicit bias show evidence of pronounced racial disparities in sentencing. This is an important and presumably em-

---

[14] The "Afrocentric features" variable was based on three coding items, each ranging from 1 through 7: (1) thin vs. full lips, (2) thin/narrow vs. full/broad nose, and (3) a global measure of whether the person had features that were more characteristic of Europeans or of Africans. Coding was based on booking photographs.

pirically testable question that bears on the relevance of implicit bias as a viable explanation of sentencing disparities.

In sum, implicit bias is a plausible reason for racial disparities in sentencing, although two issues must be reconciled. First, we would anticipate larger gaps between black and white judges when sentencing black defendants than appears to be the case. Second, the degree of racial disparity differs across jurisdictions and over time, and thus we would expect this variation to reflect spatial and temporal patterns of implicit bias. However, that pattern has not been demonstrated.

C. Focal Concerns

Cognitive perspectives on sentencing demonstrate that some judges have implicit biases, although this alone does not amount to a comprehensive theoretical model of sentencing. Consequently, scholars have sought to integrate findings from the study of prejudice with organizational theories of decision making. In Albonetti's (1991) uncertainty avoidance/causal attribution perspective, implicit biases factor into sentencing under conditions of "bounded rationality." That is, judges (and other courtroom actors) must often make consequential decisions under significant time and information constraints, which leaves them in want of more information. Judges, for example, have incomplete information about recidivism risks and the likelihood of rehabilitation for offenders. To reduce this uncertainty, they rely on "perceptual shorthands" (Hawkins 1981) that may be linked to negative stereotypical attributions regarding race, ethnicity, gender, or other social statuses. As Farrell and Holmes (1991, p. 536) describe, "Stereotypes about crime and social status are part of courts' normative organization and structure court actors' cognitive schemata, thus providing a basis for judgments regarding appropriate legal responses," which in turn "provide a shorthand basis for information-processing that facilitates routinized decision-making in an organizational context typically characterized by time and resource constraints."

Albonetti's insights motivated the most widely cited theoretical framework in the contemporary sentencing literature in sociology and criminology: the focal concerns perspective (Ulmer 2019). It posits that punishment decisions are determined by judges' subjective assessments of three focal concerns: defendant blameworthiness, protection of the community, and practical implications of decisions (Steffensmeier, Ulmer, and Kramer 1998). Within this framework, both legally relevant (e.g., criminal history) and extralegal factors (e.g., race) can condition the valuation of the focal concerns. Racial and ethnic disparities at sentencing thus might result from "court actors' beliefs that blacks and Hispanics are more dangerous, more likely to recidivate, and less likely to be deterred" (Steffensmeier and Demuth 2006, p. 246). More specifically, the combination of being young, black or Hispanic, and male is likely to signal dangerousness and higher risk of recidivism. Hence the theory predicts that these demographic characteristics should be associated with harsher sentencing relative to other demographic groups.

The three foci specified in the focal concerns model are most certainly relevant for sentencing decisions, yet the theory must grapple with two criticisms. First, it generates ambiguous predictions that make it difficult to prove or disprove. For example, Steffensmeier, Painter-Davis, and Ulmer (2017) use it to generate hypotheses about sentencing outcomes based on the intersectionality of race, gender, and age. They expect "large contrasts in sentence severity between some combinations of intersections of defendant statuses, for example, when comparing the sentences of young or older females with young minority male defendants" (p. 818). The hypothesis could be true, although the phrasing ("some combinations of intersections") makes it difficult to test. Some of this study's findings are consistent with focal concerns (e.g., the presence of racial disparities). Others are more ambiguous, such as the probability of incarceration being nearly identical for younger and older black males (p. 825).

Second, there appears to be confirmation bias that results in highlighting of empirical findings that are consistent with the theory and downplaying of those that are seemingly inconsistent. For example, Ulmer and Johnson (2004) derive nine hypotheses from the "practical constraints" aspect of the theory, each of which posits a direct or conditional association between sentencing and caseload pressures or jail capacity.[15] Three were supported in their analysis, five were not supported insofar as no statistical correlation emerged when one was predicted, and one hypothesis was not supported because the correlation was in the opposite direction of the hypothesized association (p. 167, table 6). The authors conclude that the findings "support the notion of the importance of focal concerns of sentencing" (p. 168), presumably because of the supported hypotheses. However, the absence of support for six of the hypotheses was not cited as contrary evidence.

---

[15] The authors develop six hypotheses, but three of them are separately tested for the in-out decision and the sentence length decision, thus totaling nine.

The trends in disparities discussed in Section II are not inconsistent with the theory. However, the vagueness of the focal concerns perspective, particularly as it relates to the contextual factors relevant to sentencing, makes it difficult to assess how the theory fits with the observed trends in racial disparity. Our reading of the literature is that stereotypes about racial and ethnic minorities are context specific (Steffensmeier and Demuth 2001, p. 145) and that "stereotypes and biases based on race/ ethnicity ... can influence the sentencing process *in social contexts where such stereotypes and biases are common*" (Ulmer 2018, p. 5; our emphasis).

The focal concerns perspective presumably predicts that racial disparities have waned because racial prejudice and stereotypes are less prevalent. This can be examined by aggregating attitudinal measures from survey data to the county level and assessing whether variation in racial sentencing disparities is associated with prejudicial attitudes, akin to what scholars have done in the study of policing (Stults and Baumer 2007). To our knowledge, no research has taken this approach to sentencing (save Baumer and Martin [2013] on homicide sentences).

In sum, focal concerns serve as a fine heuristic for thinking about what judges consider at sentencing, but the theory provides no clear guidance on when and where racial disparities should be most or least pronounced. It would benefit from clearer statements about what, precisely, is and is not consistent with the theory and whether it can be falsified. As currently articulated, the focal concerns perspective offers few testable propositions that would allow for invalidation, which limits its theoretical usefulness (on this point, see also Hartley, Maddan, and Spohn [2007]). In the case of racial disparities, the core question is this: what set of findings regarding racial disparities would be inconsistent with the focal concerns?

D. Social Distance and Demographic Change in the Legal Profession

The social distance perspective on sentencing disparity looks beyond the mere race of the defendant and draws greater attention to the racial dyad, namely, the defendant relative to the prosecutor or judge. In line with Black's (1976) theory of law, the key notion is that similarity between disputing parties breeds remedial and conciliatory punishments, while social distance (e.g., white judge and black defendant) produces comparatively punitive outcomes. Two hypotheses relevant to sentencing disparities follow from this logic.

The first is straightforward: disparities are more likely when the judge and the defendant are of different races. Black (1976, p. 77) alluded to this in *The Behavior of Law*, suggesting that, "In an American city, an Italian official is more likely to be lenient with an Italian, a Puerto Rican with a Puerto Rican, a Jew with a Jew. Scramble these, and law increases, whether by arrest, a judicial finding, or a parole decision." On this note, an early study of a single northeastern community found some evidence that black judges were more likely to send white defendants to prison while giving black defendants less severe sentences (Welch, Combs, and Gruhl 1988, p. 134). Johnson's (2006) study of Pennsylvania similarly found that nonwhite judges were more lenient with nonwhite offenders. A study of Chicago-area sentencing indicates that racial disparities in sentence length were smaller, by about 150 days, for black than for white judges (Abrams, Bertrand, and Mullainathan 2012).

However, at least as much evidence seems to contradict the social distance thesis. A study of Pennsylvania judges in the early 1990s found no evidence that black judges treated black defendants differently than white defendants (Steffensmeier and Britt 2001). The same was true for white judges; they treated black and white defendants approximately equally. A study of sentencing in Detroit found that judges, regardless of race, treated blacks more harshly than whites at sentencing but found no evidence that white judges treated black defendants more punitively (Spohn 1990). More recently, King and Johnson (2016, p. 112) found that sentencing differences based on skin color were not contingent on the judge's race.

A second related hypothesis is that racial disparities in sentencing attenuate with greater diversity in the courtroom work group, or even where there is diversity in the local legal profession. Judges and prosecutors are embedded in relationships with other attorneys, and the assumption is that racial dynamics of these work environments can indirectly influence sentencing decisions. There are at least two reasons why demographics of the courtroom workgroup, and not merely the race of the judge or prosecutor in a given case, could influence racial disparity. First, diversity could diminish apathy toward minority defendants and increase sensitivity to racial disparities, thereby serving as a counterweight to implicit racial bias (Ward, Farrell, and Rousseau 2009). In a court with little diversity, white judges may be freer to act on stereotypes and racial preferences. For instance, in their qualitative work on race and sentencing, Ulmer and Kramer (1996) interviewed judges in a county with no racial diversity on the bench or in the district attorney's office. One judge noted with respect to racial disparity in punishment, "You are reluctant to send white offenders to prisons that are largely black. It seems the prisons are becoming more and more black, and judges are leery because they have heard horror stories about things that have happened, violence and whatnot" (p. 400). The presence of nonwhite judges or prosecutors could disrupt these assumptions, force counter-stereotypical considerations, and "constrain automatic stereotypes and their impact on sentencing" (Ward, Farrell, and Rousseau 2009, p. 773).

Second, racial diversity among attorneys could increase the volume of discussion about race and punishment. This is difficult to observe and measure, although related work on legal education finds that discussions of race and law include more viewpoints when there is diversity in the classroom (Orfield and Whitla 1999). Research on gender composition in the workforce suggests that institutionalized discrimination against women is less tolerated where women are represented in management (Kulis 1997) and that the presence of women in management positions yields tangible benefits for female employees (e.g., Cohen and Huffman [2007] on wage inequality).

Each of these mechanisms suggests that diversity among attorneys could mitigate racial disparities in sentencing. In a test of this idea, Ward, Farrell, and Rousseau (2009) analyzed federal sentencing outcomes in 89 districts between 2000 and 2002 and supplemented the case-level data with demographic information about prosecutors and judges in each district. Three findings are noteworthy. First, diversity in the workforce varied substantially across districts. Some had no black judges or prosecutors, while in others blacks represented a quarter of the prosecutorial and a third of the judicial workforce (p. 783). Second, the probability of incarceration and average length of prison sentences decreased as the proportion of black prosecutors increased relative to the black population in the district. Third, white-black racial disparity in sentencing attenuated as the relative proportion of black judges—and especially of black prosecutors—increased. However, this interplay was not particularly large. As black representation in the prosecutor's office increased from zero to three times more diverse than the general population, the likelihood of imprisonment for a black defendant decreased by 3.4 percent (from 96.6 to 93.2; p. 790). Interestingly, the probability of a white defendant receiving a prison sentence increased by about 2 percent over the same range of prosecutorial diversity.

A separate analysis of state court data from 75 of the largest counties in the United States reached a similar conclusion, albeit with less precise measurement (King, Johnson, and McGeever 2010). The key variable was the racial composition of the local legal profession, which expands beyond prosecutors and judges. White-black racial differences in the probability of incarceration and average sentence length attenuated as the percentage of black attorneys in the county increased. A similar association emerged for Hispanic defendants: sentencing disparities between Hispanics and whites attenuated as the proportion of Hispanic attorneys in the local legal profession increased.

In sum, research on the race of judges relative to the race of defendants reveals no clear-cut association. However, the few studies of workforce racial diversity suggest that greater diversity in the bar is associated with less racial disparity in sentencing outcomes. This set of findings seems to fit with the trends in racial disparity described in Section II. The proportion of attorneys identifying as African American and Hispanic has slowly but steadily increased (Equal Employment Opportunity Commission 2003) as racial and ethnic disparities in sentencing decreased. This is a superficial correlation, and we make no causal claims. Changing demographics of the legal profession is nonetheless a plausible factor leading to less racial disparity, and one that ought to be the focus of future research.

IV. Sentencing Data and the Limits of the "Modal Approach"

Several data issues hamper our understanding of race and sentencing. The overwhelming majority of sentencing research, including our own, fits with what Baumer (2013, p. 4) calls the "modal approach." The typical study unfolds something like this. A researcher wants to investigate whether race, alone or in conjunction with other case characteristics, is associated with sentencing outcomes. She takes stock of the available data and finds that many state sentencing commissions (and the federal courts) make their data available for research purposes. The data file consists of most, if not all, felony convictions in the jurisdiction. With some simple recoding she creates two outcome variables: one indicating whether the convicted felon received a prison sentence and the other measuring the length of the sentence. The file also contains basic demographic information (age, sex, race) and some key control variables, including an indicator of the criminal history, the type of crime committed, the presumptive sentence recommended by the guidelines, and whether the conviction resulted from a plea or jury verdict. The researcher then assesses the partial coefficient for the race variable after controlling for the others, with the assumption that the net racial difference in sentencing reflects bias in the use of discretion.

We have learned much from the modal approach, but the statistical correlations they generate are tagged with many ifs and buts. For example, the data allow for a fair accounting of racial disparity if we assume there is no sample selection bias, yet this is not necessarily a tenable assumption. Further, we know from the research on capital sentencing that the race of the victim matters (Baldus, Woodworth, and Pulaski 1990), but rarely can we assess whether the victim's race influences noncapital sentencing. As a result, "the analysis of archival conviction data ... is not highly useful for shedding light about the sources or meaning of racial disparities in contemporary prison populations, nor is it (alone) well suited for detecting race differences in sentencing, identifying the presence (or absence) of racial discrimination in sentencing, or advancing knowledge about why race may (or may not) influence legal decision-makers" (Baumer 2013, p. 4).

To pinpoint sources of disparity and assess whether it results from discriminatory treatment, and for that matter by and against whom, requires a new type of data. It should allow for analysis of policy-making discretion as well as judicial discretion, allow researchers to follow cases from the point of arrest through to sentencing, include information on crime victims, and allow for simultaneous consideration of ethnicity and citizenship.[16] A data set with all of this information is unlikely to be attainable, but even incremental steps toward these ends would further our understanding of the causes of sentencing disparities. Scholars are making headway on some of these issues, sometimes with consequential results.

A. Beyond Judicial Discretion

The modal approach to sentencing generally uses the legally prescribed penalty (most often the presumptive sentence) to assess racial differences in the exercise of judicial discretion. Both statutory and sentencing guideline ranges can be quite broad.[17] This approach precludes an investigation of how much the laws and presumptive sentences themselves contribute to disparities. Mandatory minimum statutes and sentencing guidelines

---

[16] Information about both judges and prosecutors is highly important, although we do not discuss this issue here.

[17] In the federal sentencing guidelines, e.g., the presumptive minimum and maximum can vary by more than 6 years of incarceration at the higher end of the sentencing grid.

may encode racial biases, producing sentencing disparities in the absence of racially discriminatory decision making by judges. That is why Bushway and Forst (2013) argue that two types of discretion must be considered. The first, type A discretion, refers to individuals making decisions within a bounded set of rules and guidelines, such as prosecutors deciding whether and how to charge or judges deciding whether to sentence offenders at, above, or below guideline recommendations. The second, type B, refers to the discretion exercised by policy makers, such as legislators or guideline commissions, who establish the rules in the first place. The primary objective of sentencing research on racial disparities is to determine with as much precision as possible how type A and type B discretion contribute to inequalities.

The modal research design is ill-suited to accomplish this task. Prosecutors exercise considerable discretion when deciding whether and how to charge (type A discretion). Some scholars argue that prosecutorial discretion is fundamental for understanding the rise of imprisonment rates during the past four decades (Pfaff 2017). Other work shows that sentencing guidelines are structured in ways that systematically produce inequalities (type B discretion), for instance, by permitting judges to consider aggravating factors such as juvenile history that disproportionately affect blacks (Bushway and Piehl 2001) or by mandating more severe punishments for crimes with high racial imbalances in the arrest rate. The most obvious example is the 100∶1 difference for sentencing crack and powder cocaine offenses in the 1986 federal Anti–Drug Abuse Act. This law contributed heavily to racial disparity in federal imprisonment because blacks were far more likely than whites to be convicted of crack offenses (McDonald and Carlson 1994; Kennedy 1997).

The crack-powder disparity under federal law has long been criticized for its racially discriminatory impact (Provine 2011), including by the USSC. The commission reported in its 15-year assessment of the federal guidelines that "this one sentencing rule contributes more to differences in average sentences between African-American and White offenders than any possible effect of discrimination. Revising the crack cocaine thresholds would better reduce the gap than any other single policy change, and it would dramatically improve the fairness of the federal sentencing system" (USSC 2004, p. 132).

That statement emphasizes policy more than the exercise of judicial discretion as the key to understanding why more blacks than whites go to prison. Consider the data in figure 16. The figure shows the white-black

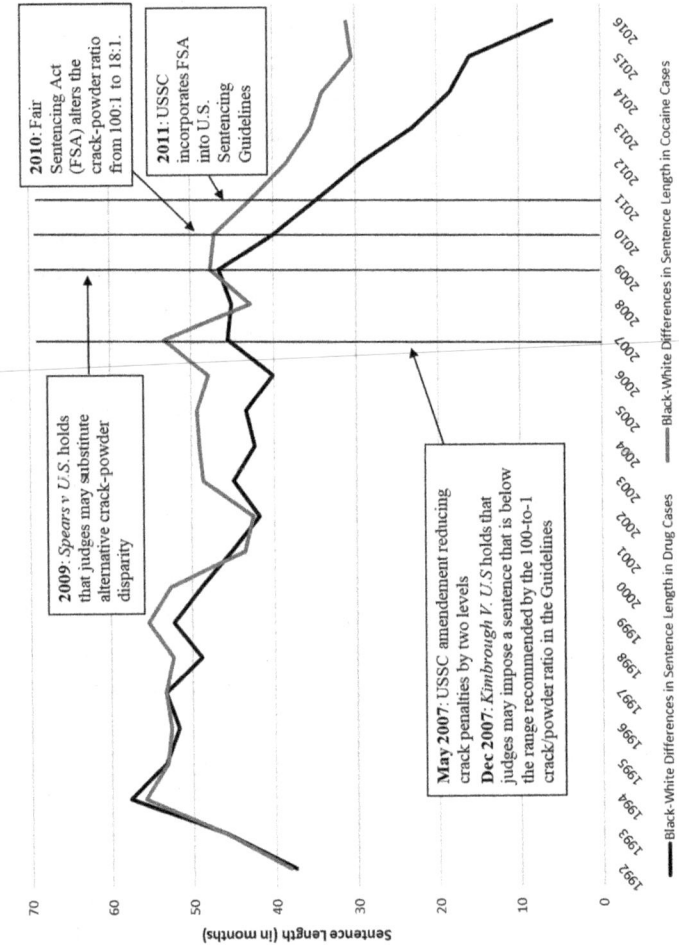

FIG. 16.—Black-white differences in sentencing for drug offenses, US district courts, 1992–2016. Sources: USSC (2016) and similar data files for felony and class A misdemeanor convictions in each year between 1992 and 2015.

gap in sentence length for all federal drug crimes (black line) and for cocaine convictions (powder as well as crack; gray line). Overall racial disparity has dropped dramatically since 2009–10. The 45-month difference in 2008 drops to less than 6 months by 2016. This is a stunning development considering that the average sentence length gap between 1992 and 2008 was an incredible 47 months. The timing of the overall reduction in disparity aligns with the decrease in white-black cocaine sentences. Most importantly, the declining disparities coincide with legal and policy changes aimed at reducing cocaine disparities in federal sentencing. For instance, in May 2007, the USSC voted to reduce the crack cocaine guideline penalties by two levels. In December 2007, the Supreme Court ruled in *Kimbrough* that judges could sentence crack offenders more leniently on the basis of disagreements with the crack-powder disparity in the federal sentencing guidelines. In 2009, the court held in *Spears v. United States*, 551 U.S. 261 (2009), that federal judges could substitute an alternative crack-powder ratio to avoid sentencing disparity under *Kimbrough*. In 2010, Congress passed the Fair Sentencing Act, which increased the amount of crack needed to trigger 5- and 10-year mandatory minimum sentences, altering the crack-powder ratio from 100:1 to 18:1. Finally, in 2011, the USSC permanently incorporated the provisions of the Fair Sentencing Act into the federal sentencing guidelines.

Those policy changes and court decisions almost certainly contributed to lower racial disparities in federal drug cases during the decade from 2006 to 2016 (Hofer 2019). We concur with Bushway and Forst (2013), Frase (2013), and others that more sentencing research needs to examine both the discretionary decisions made during criminal case processing (type A discretion) and legal and policy decisions that provide the framework (type B decisions) in which case processing operates. Given the amount of scholarly attention devoted to the crack-powder distinction, we are surprised how little research has looked at the efficacy of the Fair Sentencing Act in reducing racial disparities in federal sentencing. Beyond the federal courts, researchers should look outside guideline regimes because the consequences of strict sentencing policies for racial disparities require comparisons across guideline and nonguideline states. This will require suitable data from nonguideline jurisdictions. The focus on decision-making actors within the criminal justice system should be matched by research on actors such as lawmakers and sentencing commissions who shape the contours of the criminal justice process.

B. Beyond Conviction Data

All but a select few studies rely on conviction data, which is problematic for several reasons. Such data preclude analyses of discretionary decisions made prior to the point at which judges impose a sentence. Sentencing analyses often lack crucial information about the underlying criminal conduct that led to the conviction, such as the original arrest charge (Baumer 2013). As Rehavi and Starr (2014, p. 1321) observe, "Neither the crime of conviction nor the presumptive sentence is an exogenous measure of criminal conduct. Each is the product of highly discretionary and negotiated processes, including charging, plea bargaining, and sentencing fact-finding."

This endogeneity has consequences, especially since sentencing data often lack information on prosecutorial decisions regarding charge negotiation, plea bargaining, and sentencing recommendations. Each of these stages, in turn, can contribute to racial disparities. For instance, if whites are more likely than blacks to have their arrest charges downgraded from felony to misdemeanor, this group of whites would not appear in files of felony-sentenced offenders, such as the data we used from Minnesota. The result would be that studies may reveal weak or no racial differences in conviction data because the biased decisions occurred prior to conviction. As Daly and Tonry (1997, p. 230) note, if prosecutors screen out the less serious crimes perpetrated by whites but decide to prosecute crimes with similar evidence for black defendants, then by the sentencing stage the average white case would be more serious than the average black case. We might erroneously conclude that sentencing differences do not exist when they would be evident if the focus was on sanctions for the underlying crimes rather than for the underlying convictions. Or suppose that black offenders are more often charged with crimes that trigger mandatory minimums. If judges follow sentencing policy in color-blind fashion, no apparent bias will appear in an analysis based on conviction data, assuming we control for the legally prescribed sanction. However, that finding would be misleading if racial bias infected the initial charging decision. We have a problem of selection bias if race influences decisions made in the early stages of case processing.

Prior research shows that much racial disparity in federal sentencing is attributable to sentencing policies that affect blacks and Hispanics more than whites (Ulmer, Painter-Davis, and Tinik 2016). One of the few studies that include preconviction data reveals that prosecutorial discretion is key to understanding this differential exposure to harsh sentencing policies. Rehavi and Starr (2014) used linked data that connect federal sentencing information with arrest information for a sample of approximately 35,000 cases referred to federal prosecutors. They found that black men had 1.75 times the odds of white men of being charged with crimes that trigger a mandatory minimum. This decision is pivotal. According to Rehavi and Starr, mandatory minimum charging explains about half of the black-white racial disparity observed in federal sentencing between 2006 and 2008. Other research found that racial disparities exist in case processing prior to the point of conviction, including whether defendants receive a custodial plea offer (Kutateladze et al. 2014). Sutton (2013) found strong racial and ethnic differences early in the process, such as the decision to detain a defendant before trial, which in turn increase the odds of a prison sentence (see also Gottfredson and Jarjoura 1996; Demuth 2003).

This critique of sentencing data echoes others' laments for decades (Zatz 1987; Daly and Tonry 1997; Baumer 2013). But why does the problem persist, and what can be done? The challenge is both structural and technical. Because of the fragmented structure of the American criminal justice system, different agencies collect data using different identification methods, which results in a data linkage problem. Most arrest data are maintained by state agencies (e.g., Bureau of Criminal Investigation or similar title) and are tracked and linked via fingerprint information. Cases that move to the courts receive case identification numbers that cannot be easily matched to the fingerprint data. Furthermore, state agencies or sentencing commissions may request, but do not always receive, court disposition data. Following the "life course" of a criminal case can thus be a complicated task, even for the state agencies that manage the data. For instance, only about half of all arrests in Ohio's criminal history database include information on court dispositions (Bureau of Justice Statistics 2015).

Scholars and practitioners are making headway on the problem, sometimes with powerful results. The Federal Justice Statistics Program links convictions with arrests, which made possible an important finding about the role of mandatory minimums in producing racial disparities (Rehavi and Starr 2014). However, the federal system is distinctive in the types of cases it handles, and it handles only a small fraction of all cases. Further, the linkage method (based on name; see Kelly 2012) can be improved. We need similar efforts at the state level to open up a new generation of research on racial disparity. In the absence of this capacity to link arrest and conviction data, we are stalled.

C. Race of Victim

Decades of research show that the race of the victim is of greater consequence than the race of the offender in determining who is sentenced to death (US Government Accountability Office 1990). Baldus, Woodworth, and Pulaski (1990) famously found that the odds of a death sentence in Georgia for those who murdered white victims were over four times higher than if the victim was black. Their research was at the heart of *McCleskey v. Kemp*, 481 U.S. 279 (1987), a landmark decision on racial discrimination in capital punishment. Other research suggests that the chance of a death sentence is particularly high when the offender is black and the victim is white (Paternoster et al. 2004; Paternoster and Brame 2008).

The capital punishment studies, if generalizable, suggest that the victim's race should matter in noncapital cases as well. If jurors and judges place a greater value on white lives or impute greater dangerousness and moral culpability to black offenders with white victims, why should this be any different for crimes that do not trigger a possible death sentence? Research from the Netherlands (a non–death penalty country) finds that punishments are harsher for homicides involving Dutch victims than for homicides with non-Dutch victims (Johnson, Van Wingerden, and Nieuwbeerta 2010). In addition, American research on sexual assault similarly demonstrates that black men accused of assaulting white women are punished more severely than defendants in cases involving different victim-offender racial combinations (LaFree 1998). However, capital cases may be fundamentally different from others. They are much more likely than cases involving other crimes to involve trials and extensive sentencing hearings; more information about the victim may be available to judges and juries. As such, victim characteristics could be more influential in capital relative to noncapital cases.

Data to test the race-of-victim hypothesis in noncapital cases, unfortunately, are hard to come by. Three types of data sources may allow victim data to be linked with data used in traditional sentencing research. Government surveys, such as the Department of Justice's *Murder Cases in 33 Large Urban Counties in the United States* study (see Dawson and Boland 1993), might be used. This study used detailed victim data including race, age, and conviction history, although the data covered only homicide cases, which are a small proportion of interpersonal offenses (Baumer, Messner, and Felson 2000). Other analyses use data from state mortality files, which typically include information about characteristics of murder victims. Phillips (2009) used this kind of data to show that status characteristics of victims, such as education level and neighborhood income, are associated with capital sentencing. This source also, however, is limited to homicide cases.

A third possibility, which to our knowledge has not been tried, is to take advantage of the increasing amount of crime data available online. In one of our hometowns (Columbus, Ohio), the Division of Police maintains a web portal that includes information about crimes and victims. A few clicks allow one to select crimes against persons within a given time period and for each to learn the offense, location, case number, and race, age, and gender of the victim. If these data can be linked with data on case outcomes, researchers will be able to investigate whether victim characteristics are important predictors of sentence severity.

D. Citizenship

Sentencing research needs to broaden its focus beyond race and ethnicity to include citizenship, for two interrelated reasons. The first is demographic. There are more international migrants today than ever before: 258 million people live in a country other than their country of birth. This shows no signs of changing soon. Between 2000 and 2017, the number of international migrants increased by 49 percent (United Nations 2017). Migrants will inevitably, and increasingly, interact with the criminal justice institutions of their new countries. In addition, recent decades have witnessed dramatic and sustained expansions in use of the criminal law to control migration. The increasing criminalization of immigration—called "crimmigration" by some (Stumpf 2006) or the "criminology of mobility" by others (Aas and Bosworth 2013)—has affected legal systems in many Western countries. Nearly one in four prisoners in Europe are foreign nationals (Aebi, Tiago, and Burkhardt 2016).[18] In the United States, there were more criminal prosecutions for immigration offenses than for

---

[18] Foreign prisoners are usually defined as those without citizenship of the state in which they are incarcerated (van Kalmthout, Hofstee-van der Meulen, and Dünkel 2007). The overrepresentation of foreign nationals is only partly a reflection of differences between citizens and noncitizens in population structure and disadvantage. While the foreign-born are more likely to be young males with little education (i.e., the "crime-prone" population), in 2011 noncitizens made up less than 15 percent of working-age men (25–54) with only primary educations (or less) in the European Union.

all other federal crimes combined in 2016 (Transactional Records Access Clearinghouse 2016).

The second reason to give heightened attention to noncitizens is that their increased numbers in the criminal justice system obscure efforts to understand racial and ethnic sentencing disparities. Researchers have increasingly investigated the effects of Hispanic ethnicity at sentencing, but much of this work has overlooked citizenship. In an article arguing that Hispanics had replaced African Americans as the most harshly punished group, for example, Steffensmeier and Demuth (2000) removed noncitizens from their analysis of federal court data. This was not a minor adjustment; only 26 percent of Hispanics punished in federal court between 1992 and 2016 were US citizens. The overwhelming majority of Hispanic offenders punished in federal courts are noncitizens.

Recent work, including our analyses in Section II, suggests that accounting for citizenship fundamentally changes the picture of Hispanic-white sentencing disparities. Noncitizens receive substantially harsher penalties than US citizens, especially for incarceration decisions, and citizenship explains the majority of the punishment gap between Hispanic and white offenders (Light, Massoglia, and King 2014). Light (2014) demonstrated that the bulk of the increase in Hispanic disparity since 1992 is attributable to the treatment of noncitizens. Research from other Western societies also shows the increasing salience of citizenship in the legal system (Aliverti and Bosworth 2017). Citizenship may soon match or exceed race and ethnicity as a cause of disparate punishment.

Efforts to understand the effects of citizenship on punishment mostly involve the federal system, because of data constraints; few state court systems record citizenship status throughout case processing. None of the SCPS, Pennsylvania, Minnesota, or Washington State data sources record information about immigration status. This is not a minor omission: in 2012, state prisons held more than twice as many noncitizens as federal prisons (63,933 compared to 28,959; Carson and Golinelli 2013).

More recent estimates are difficult to make; data quality has gotten worse. California, for example, stopped reporting the number of noncitizens in custody to the Bureau of Justice Statistics in 2013. In 2016, California was joined by Nevada, New Hampshire, North Dakota, and Oregon in not reporting information on prisoners' citizenship. The bureau speculates that other states "likely provided undercounts" (Carson 2018, p. 13). As a result, we lack even basic descriptive information on the number of noncitizens entangled in state and local criminal justice systems.

Much more research is needed. Existing work provides imperfect guidance on whether and how immigration status affects local criminal justice practices (save Beckett and Evans [2015]).

Stark differences between citizens and noncitizens in federal courts may result from greater collaboration between federal criminal justice and immigration officials. To the extent that there is less collaboration between immigration and local officials, it may be that citizens and noncitizens of particular ethnic groups have comparable experiences in state courts (i.e., Latino noncitizens may be treated similarly to Latino citizens).

However, even at the local level, immigration status can affect criminal case outcomes because of the federal government's increasing reliance on arrests and convictions in immigration law enforcement. Eagly (2013, p. 1126), for example, demonstrates that immigration status checks have become a routine part of the booking process at local jails in several jurisdictions and that "immigration officials encourage criminal prosecutors to secure plea agreements that guarantee removal." Implications for case processing are unclear. The result could be longer spells of incarceration while local and federal officials work on both the criminal and immigration cases. Alternatively, individuals may be removed prior to completion of the criminal court process, leading to less incarceration.

The few studies of this issue indicate harsher treatment of noncitizens. Using prisoner data from California, Butcher and Piehl (2000) show that foreign-born prisoners designated to be released into the custody of the Immigration and Naturalization Service served substantially longer prison terms than either similarly situated native-born prisoners or foreign-born individuals without an "INS hold." More recently, Beckett and Evans (2015) offered similar findings using data from King County, Washington: noncitizens with a detainer from Immigration and Customs Enforcement served longer jail sentences than noncitizens without detainers. Each of these studies included race and ethnicity in its analyses. This shows that the negative consequences of immigration status are not simply reflections of racial or ethnic inequality in punishment.

Most "crimmigration" research focuses on the federal government, even though far more immigrants encounter local criminal justice officials. A substantial majority of incarcerated noncitizens are held in state, not federal, prisons. If the findings of our analyses of federal court sentencing are generalizable to state courts, accounting for citizenship status may change our understanding of racial and ethnic disparities at sentencing, particularly for Hispanics.

V. Conclusion

The findings reported and conclusions drawn in this essay have implications for future research and sentencing policy. We emphasize four.

First, our finding that racial and ethnic disparity is declining warrants further scrutiny and analysis. For instance, do the trends hold up in states other than those we looked at? And do they persist when different methodological choices are made? We can imagine different methods to calculate adjusted disparity, different ways to measure the presumptive sentence, and more sophisticated modeling of change over time that takes other case characteristics into account. Replications are needed before offering answers to a related important question: if disparities have attenuated, what explains the change?

Our descriptive analyses of federal and Minnesota data offer some clues, but much work lies ahead to pinpoint the reasons. Our analysis, like Frase's (2009) analysis of racial disparities in prison, indicates that racial differences in presumptive sentences cause much of the disparity. Figures 2, 4, 9, and 10 show that trends in pronounced sentences tether closely to trends in presumptive sentences. The adjusted disparity analyses suggest some additional reduction in racial and ethnic disparities, but in guideline systems the recommended sentence drives much of the change.

Second, our analyses do not estimate the precise contributions of the various factors that feed into presumptive sentences, such as sentencing policy, conviction offenses, and criminal histories. Future research could add specificity by decomposing the relative contributions of each, particularly as they contribute to changes in disparities over time.

Third, theories in use need elaboration and augmentation. Racial and ethnic disparities vary across jurisdictions and over time. A cogent explanation of racial disparity should incorporate these observations. We doubt that many of the most-often-cited theories accomplish this, although arguments stressing diversity of the workforce have promise for explaining disparities that are not attributable to racial differences in presumptive sentences, criminal histories, or crime severity (Ward, Farrell, and Rousseau 2009). Research on whether a diverse courtroom workgroup mitigates racial and ethnic sentencing disparities warrants high priority.

Finally, we believe that factors that contribute to determination of presumptive sentences in guidelines systems warrant further examination. Disparities in federal sentencing, figure 16 shows, appear to decline following changes in policies that have racially disparate impacts. Other factors such as criminal history (see Frase 2009, p. 265) that vary by race and

Have Racial and Ethnic Disparities in Sentencing Declined? 427

partly determine presumptive sentences should also be investigated. If we better understood which factors most contribute to racial differences in presumptive sentences, we could better understand the causes of inequities and whether apparent declines in racial disparity are likely to persist.

APPENDIX
Descriptions of Data Sets Used in Section II
Federal Sentencing Data
The federal court data come from the US Sentencing Commission's (USSC) Standardized Research Files. One of the chief missions of the USSC is to collect data on federal criminal cases sentenced under the Federal Sentencing Guidelines, and a primary aim of the guidelines is to ensure that sentencing is "entirely neutral as to race, sex, national origin, creed, and socioeconomic status of offenders" (28 U.S.C. § 994(d)). Our primary analysis uses data from 1992–2016.[19] The unit of analysis is the sentenced case and the universe is all offenders sentenced in US federal courts. The USSC file is a rich source of information on federal sentencing and provides detailed information on both the legal characteristics associated with a crime (e.g., guideline recommended sentence) and extralegal characteristics (e.g., race/ethnicity, citizenship) of defendants. We analyze a total of 1,605,564 cases. Throughout our analysis, we include all cases that had valid information for our three focal variables: race/ethnicity, final sentence, and presumptive sentence.

Race/ethnicity consists of white non-Hispanic, black non-Hispanic, and Hispanic individuals of any race. Combined, these groups make up 96 percent of the federal docket; "other" race individuals make up the remaining 4 percent. In the federal case files, we use the variable "newrace" ("race of defendant") for our race/ethnicity measures. Final sentence is created from two measures. The incarceration decision is a dichotomous outcome (1 = prison, 0 = no prison) created from the variable "sentimp" ("type of sentence"). Sentence length is measured in months from the variable "totprisn" ("total months of imprisonment ordered"). Following USSC protocol, we cap prison sentences at 470 months (including life sentences). The presumptive sentence comes from the USSC variable "glmin" ("adjusted guideline range minimum") and represents the minimum number of months of incarceration judges can sentence an offender within the specified guideline range. This measure accounts for the 43-point offense severity level, the 6-point criminal history scale, and sentencing adjustments (i.e., mandatory minimum penalties, obstruction of justice enhancements) that affect the final presumptive sentence. As for the final sentence, we cap the presumptive sentence at 470 months. In the incarceration analyses, we dichotomize this mea-

[19] In the late 1980s and early 1990s, the USSC largely relied on data from the Administrative Office of the US Courts offender database (Reedt and Widico-Stroop 2008). Our analysis is based on data files collected solely by the USSC.

sure: a value of 1 equals any amount of incarceration ordered, and 0 equals no incarceration presumed. In the sentence length analyses, the measure remains continuous (in months). For the analyses in which we examine the import of citizenship, we use the measure "citizen" ("nature of defendant's citizenship") to identify those offenders who are non-US citizens.

Minnesota Sentencing Data
Our analysis of the Minnesota data come from the state's Sentencing Guidelines Commission (MSGC). Minnesota was the first state in the country to implement sentencing guidelines in 1981, and since that year the commission has maintained data on all felony cases sentenced in Minnesota courts. We used the cumulative sentencing file as of 2013, which provided 355,554 cases for analysis. Four variables were particularly useful for figures 9–14 in the text. We used information on race of the defendant to measure disparities. White and black or African American are straightforward, although the Hispanic category is different from what we might find in the census. The MSGC data include Hispanic as a separate category of the race variable, not a separate ethnicity variable that can be cross-classified with race (e.g., white Hispanic, black Hispanic). The presumptive sentence measures were included in the MSGC data and required no calculation on our part. The imprisonment variable was coded 1 if the defendant received an executed prison sentence. Short jail sentences and stayed sentences were coded 0. Finally, we use the number of months sentenced as the outcome variable for sentence length. Note that a sentence length may be given even if a sentence is stayed.

REFERENCES

Aas, Katja Franko, and Mary Bosworth, eds. 2013. *The Borders of Punishment: Migration, Citizenship, and Social Exclusion.* New York: Oxford University Press.

Abrams, David S., Marianne Bertrand, and Sendhil Mullainathan. 2012. "Do Judges Vary in Their Treatment of Race?" *Journal of Legal Studies* 41(2):347–83.

Aebi, Marcelo F., Mélanie M. Tiago, and Christine Burkhardt. 2016. *SPACE I—Council of Europe Annual Penal Statistics: Prison Populations. Survey 2015.* Strasbourg: Council of Europe.

Albonetti, Celesta A. 1991. "An Integration of Theories to Explain Judicial Discretion." *Social Problems* 38(2):247–66.

Alexander, Michelle. 2012. *The New Jim Crow: Mass Incarceration in the Age of Colorblindness.* New York: New Press.

Aliverti, Ana, and Mary Bosworth. 2017. "Introduction to the Special Issue on Criminal Justice Adjudication in the Age of Migration." *New Criminal Law Review* 20(1):1–11.

Alvarez, Alexander, and Ronet D. Bachman. 1996. "American Indians and Sentencing Disparity: An Arizona Test." *Journal of Criminal Justice* 24(6):549–61.

Baldus, David C., George Woodworth, and Charles A. Pulaski. 1990. *Equal Justice and the Death Penalty: A Legal and Empirical Analysis*. Boston: Northeastern University Press.

Baumer, Eric P. 2013. "Reassessing and Redirecting Research on Race and Sentencing." *Justice Quarterly* 30(2):231–61.

Baumer, Eric P., and Kimberly H. Martin. 2013. "Social Organization, Collective Sentiment, and Legal Sanctions in Murder Cases." *American Journal of Sociology* 119(1):131–82.

Baumer, Eric P., Steven F. Messner, and Richard B. Felson. 2000. "The Role of Victim Characteristics in the Disposition of Murder Cases." *Justice Quarterly* 17(2):281–307.

Beckett, Katherine, and Heather Evans. 2015. "Crimmigration at the Local Level: Criminal Justice Processes in the Shadow of Deportation." *Law and Society Review* 49(1):241–77.

Bentele, Keith Gunnar, and Erin E. O'Brien. 2013. "Jim Crow 2.0? Why States Consider and Adopt Restrictive Voter Access Policies." *Perspectives on Politics* 11(4):1088–1116.

Black, Donald J. 1976. *The Behavior of Law*. New York: Academic Press.

Blair, Irene V., Charles M. Judd, and Kristine M. Chapleau. 2004. "The Influence of Afrocentric Facial Features in Criminal Sentencing." *Psychological Science* 15(10):674–79.

Blalock, Hubert M. 1967. *Toward a Theory of Minority-Group Relations*. New York: Capricorn.

Blumer, Herbert. 1958. "Race Prejudice as a Sense of Group Position." *Pacific Sociological Review* 1(1):3–7.

Bobo, Lawrence D., Camile Z. Charles, Maria Krysan, and Alicia D. Simmons. 2012. "The *Real* Record of Racial Attitudes." In *Social Trends in American Life: Findings from the General Social Survey since 1972*, edited by Peter V. Marsden. Princeton, NJ: Princeton University Press.

Branigan, Amelia R., Christopher Wildeman, Jeremy Freese, and Catarina I. Kiefe. 2017. "Complicating Colorism: Race, Skin Color, and the Likelihood of Arrest." *Socius* 3:1–17.

Brennan, Pauline K., and Cassia Spohn. 2008. "Race/Ethnicity and Sentencing Outcomes among Drug Offenders in North Carolina." *Journal of Contemporary Criminal Justice* 24(4):371–98.

Bridges, George S., and Gina Beretta. 1994. "Gender, Race, and Social Control: Toward an Understanding of Sex Disparities in Imprisonment." In *Inequality, Crime, and Social Control*, edited by George S. Bridges and Martha A. Myers. Boulder, CO: Westview.

Bridges, George S., and Robert D. Crutchfield. 1988. "Law, Social Standing, and Racial Disparities in Imprisonment." *Social Forces* 66(3):699–724.

Britt, Chester L. 2000. "Social Context and Racial Disparities in Punishment Decisions." *Justice Quarterly* 17(4):707–32.

Bureau of Justice Statistics. 2015. *A Survey of State Criminal History Information Systems, 2014: A Criminal Justice Information Policy Report*. Washington, DC: US Department of Justice, Office of Justice Programs.

Bushway, Shawn D., and Brian Forst. 2013. "Studying Discretion in the Processes That Generate Criminal Justice Sanctions." *Justice Quarterly* 30(2):199–222.

Bushway, Shawn D., and Anne Morrison Piehl. 2001. "Judging Judicial Discretion: Legal Factors and Racial Discrimination in Sentencing." *Law and Society Review* 35(4):733–64.

Butcher, Kristen F., and Anne Morrison Piehl. 2000. "The Role of Deportation in the Incarceration of Immigrants." In *Issues in the Economics of Immigration*, edited by George Borjas. Chicago: University of Chicago Press.

Campbell, Michael C., Matt Vogel, and Joshua Williams. 2015. "Historical Contingencies and the Evolving Importance of Race, Violent Crime, and Region in Explaining Mass Incarceration in the United States." *Criminology* 53(2):180–203.

Carson, Ann E. 2018. *Prisoners in 2016*. Washington, DC: US Department of Justice, Bureau of Justice Statistics, Office of Justice Programs.

Carson, Ann E., and Daniela Golinelli. 2013. *Prisoners in 2012*. Washington, DC: US Department of Justice, Bureau of Justice Statistics, Office of Justice Programs.

Cohen, Philip N., and Matt L. Huffman. 2007. "Working for the Woman? Female Managers and the Gender Wage Gap." *American Sociological Review* 72(5):681–704.

Cole, David. 1999. *No Equal Justice: Race and Class in the American Criminal Justice System*. New York: New Press.

Crawford, Charles. 2000. "Gender, Race, and Habitual Offender Sentencing in Florida." *Criminology* 38(1):263–80.

Crawford, Charles, Ted Chiricos, and Gary Kleck. 1998. "Race, Racial Threat, and Sentencing of Habitual Offenders." *Criminology* 36(3):481–512.

Daly, Kathleen, and Michael Tonry. 1997. "Race, Gender, and Sentencing." In *Crime and Justice: A Review of Research*, vol. 22, edited by Michael Tonry. Chicago: University of Chicago Press.

Dawson, John M., and Barbara Boland. 1993. *Murder in Large Urban Counties, 1988*. Special report. Washington, DC: US Department of Justice, Bureau of Justice Statistics, Office of Justice Programs.

Demuth, Stephen. 2003. "Racial and Ethnic Differences in Pretrial Release Decisions and Outcomes: A Comparison of Hispanic, Black, and White Felony Arrestees." *Criminology* 41(3):873–907.

Demuth, Stephen, and Darrell Steffensmeier. 2004. "Ethnicity Effects on Sentence Outcomes in Large Urban Courts: Comparisons among White, Black, and Hispanic Defendants." *Social Science Quarterly* 85(4):994–1011.

Doerner, Jill K., and Stephen Demuth. 2010. "The Independent and Joint Effects of Race/Ethnicity, Gender, and Age on Sentencing Outcomes in US Federal Courts." *Justice Quarterly* 27(1):1–27.

Eagly, Ingrid V. 2013. "Criminal Justice for Noncitizens: An Analysis of Variation in Local Enforcement." *New York University Law Review* 88:1126–1223.

Engen, Rodney L., and Randy R. Gainey. 2000. "Modeling the Effects of Legally Relevant and Extralegal Factors under Sentencing Guidelines: The Rules Have Changed." *Criminology* 38(4):1207–30.

Equal Employment Opportunity Commission. 2003. "Diversity in Law Firms." https://www.eeoc.gov/eeoc/statistics/reports/diversitylaw/lawfirms.pdf.
Everett, Ronald S., and Roger A. Wojtkiewicz. 2002. "Difference, Disparity, and Race/Ethnic Bias in Federal Sentencing." *Journal of Quantitative Criminology* 18(2):189–211.
Farrell, Ronald, and Malcolm Holmes. 1991. "The Social and Cognitive Structure of Legal Decision Making." *Sociological Quarterly* 32(4):529–42.
Feldmeyer, Ben, and Jeffery T. Ulmer. 2011. "Racial/Ethnic Threat and Federal Sentencing." *Journal of Research in Crime and Delinquency* 48(2):238–70.
Fischman, Joshua B., and Max M. Schanzenbach. 2011. "Do Standards of Review Matter? The Case of Federal Criminal Sentencing." *Journal of Legal Studies* 40(2):405–37.
Franklin, Travis W. 2013. "Sentencing Native Americans in US Federal Courts: An Examination of Disparity." *Justice Quarterly* 30(2):310–39.
Frase, Richard S. 2009. "What Explains Persistent Racial Disproportionality in Minnesota's Prison and Jail Population?" In *Crime and Justice: A Review of Research*, vol. 38, edited by Michael Tonry. Chicago: University of Chicago Press.
———. 2013. *Just Sentencing: Principles and Procedures for a Workable System*. New York: Oxford University Press.
———. 2019. "Forty Years of American Sentencing Guidelines: What Have We Learned?" In *American Sentencing*, edited by Michael Tonry. Vol. 48 of *Crime and Justice: A Review of Research*, edited by Michael Tonry. Chicago: University of Chicago Press.
Ghandnoosh, Nazgol. 2015. *Black Lives Matter: Eliminating Racial Disparity in the Criminal Justice System*. Washington, DC: Sentencing Project.
Giles, Michael W., and Melanie A. Buckner. 1993. "David Duke and Black Threat: An Old Hypothesis Revisited." *Journal of Politics* 55(3):702–13.
Gottfredson, Stephen D., and G. Roger Jarjoura. 1996. "Race, Gender, and Guidelines-Based Decision Making." *Journal of Research in Crime and Delinquency* 33(1):49–69.
Greenwald, Anthony G., T. Andrew Poehlman, Eric Luis Uhlmann, and Mahzarin R. Banaji. 2009. "Understanding and Using the Implicit Association Test: III. Meta-Analysis of Predictive Validity." *Journal of Personality and Social Psychology* 97(1):17–41.
Gyimah-Brempong, Kwabena, and Gregory N. Price. 2006. "Crime and Punishment: And Skin Hue Too?" *American Economic Review* 96(2):246–50.
Hagan, John. 1973. "Extra-Legal Attributes and Criminal Sentencing: An Assessment of a Sociological Viewpoint." *Law and Society Review* 8(3):357–84.
Hagan, John, and Kristen Bumiller. 1983. "Making Sense of Sentencing: Race and Sentencing Outcomes." In *Research on Sentencing: The Search for Reform*, edited by Alfred Blumstein, Jacqueline Cohen, Susan E. Martin, and Michael H. Tonry. Washington, DC: National Academies Press.
Hartley, Richard D., Sean Maddan, and Cassia C. Spohn. 2007. "Concerning Conceptualization and Operationalization: Sentencing Data and the Focal Concerns Perspective—a Research Note." *Southwest Journal of Criminal Justice* 4(1):58–78.

Hawkins, Darnell F. 1981. "Causal Attribution and Punishment for Crime." *Deviant Behavior* 2:207–30.

Heath, Brad. 2014. "Racial Gap in US Arrest Rates: 'Staggering Disparity.'" *USA Today*, November 18. https://www.usatoday.com/story/news/nation/2014/11/18/ferguson-black-arrest-rates/19043207/.

Hill, Mark E. 2002. "Race of the Interviewer and Perception of Skin Color: Evidence from the Multi-city Study of Urban Inequality." *American Sociological Review* 67(1):99–108.

Hofer, Paul J. 2019. "Federal Sentencing after *Booker*." In *American Sentencing*, edited by Michael Tonry. Vol. 48 of *Crime and Justice: A Review of Research*, edited by Michael Tonry. Chicago: University of Chicago Press.

Jacobs, David, and Jason T. Carmichael. 2002. "The Political Sociology of the Death Penalty: A Pooled Time-Series Analysis." *American Sociological Review* 67(1):109–31.

Jeffries, Samantha, and Christine E. W. Bond. 2012. "The Impact of Indigenous Status on Adult Sentencing: A Review of the Statistical Research Literature from the United States, Canada, and Australia." *Journal of Ethnicity in Criminal Justice* 10(3):223–43.

Johnson, Brian D. 2006. "The Multilevel Context of Criminal Sentencing: Integrating Judge- and County-Level Influences." *Criminology* 44(2):259–98.

Johnson, Brian D., and Sara Betsinger. 2009. "Punishing the 'Model Minority': Asian-American Criminal Sentencing Outcomes in Federal District Courts." *Criminology* 47(4):1045–90.

Johnson, Brian D., and Ryan D. King. 2017. "Facial Profiling: Race, Physical Appearance, and Punishment." *Criminology* 55(3):520–47.

Johnson, Brian D., Sigrid Van Wingerden, and Paul Nieuwbeerta. 2010. "Sentencing Homicide Offenders in the Netherlands: Offender, Victim, and Situational Influences in Criminal Punishment." *Criminology* 48(4):981–1018.

Keen, Bradley, and David Jacobs. 2009. "Racial Threat, Partisan Politics, and Racial Disparities in Prison Admissions: A Panel Analysis." *Criminology* 47(1):209–38.

Kelly, Jessica A. 2012. *Federal Justice Statistics Program Data Linking System*. Washington, DC: Urban Institute.

Kennedy, Randall. 1997. *Race, Crime, and the Law*: New York: Vintage.

King, Ryan D. 2007. "The Context of Minority Group Threat: Race, Institutions, and Complying with Hate Crime Law." *Law and Society Review* 41(1):189–224.

King, Ryan D., and Brian D. Johnson. 2016. "A Punishing Look: Skin Tone and Afrocentric Features in the Halls of Justice." *American Journal of Sociology* 122(1):90–124.

King, Ryan D., Kecia R. Johnson, and Kelly McGeever. 2010. "Demography of the Legal Profession and Racial Disparities in Sentencing." *Law and Society Review* 44(1):1–32.

Kirk, David S., and Andrew V. Papachristos. 2011. "Cultural Mechanisms and the Persistence of Neighborhood Violence." *American Journal of Sociology* 116(4):1190–1233.

Kleck, Gary. 1981. "Racial Discrimination in Criminal Sentencing: A Critical Evaluation of the Evidence with Additional Evidence on the Death Penalty." *American Sociological Review* 46(6):783–805.

Kramer, John H., and Jeffery T. Ulmer. 2009. *Sentencing Guidelines: Lessons from Pennsylvania*. Boulder, CO: Rienner.

Kulis, Stephen. 1997. "Gender Segregation among College and University Employees." *Sociology of Education* 70(April):151–73.

Kutateladze, Besiki L., Nancy R. Andiloro, Brian D. Johnson, and Cassia C. Spohn. 2014. "Cumulative Disadvantage: Examining Racial and Ethnic Disparity in Prosecution and Sentencing." *Criminology* 52(3):514–51.

LaFree, Gary. 1998. *Losing Legitimacy: Street Crime and the Decline of Social Institutions in America*. Boulder, CO: Westview.

Legewie, Joscha, and Jeffrey Fagan. 2016. "Group Threat, Police Officer Diversity, and the Deadly Use of Police Force." Columbia Public Law Research Paper no. 14-512. https://ssrn.com/abstract=2778692.

Levinson, Justin D., Huajian Cai, and Danielle Young. 2010. "Guilty by Implicit Racial Bias: The Guilty/Not Guilty Implicit Association Test." *Ohio State Journal of Criminal Law* 8:187–208.

Levinson, Justin D., and Danielle Young. 2009. "Different Shades of Bias: Skin Tone, Implicit Racial Bias, and Judgments of Ambiguous Evidence." *West Virginia Law Review* 112:307–50.

Light, Michael T. 2014. "The New Face of Legal Inequality: Noncitizens and the Long-Term Trends in Sentencing Disparities across US District Courts, 1992–2009." *Law and Society Review* 48(2):447–78.

Light, Michael T., Michael Massoglia, and Ryan D. King. 2014. "Citizenship and Punishment: The Salience of National Membership in US Criminal Courts." *American Sociological Review* 79(5):825–47.

MacDonald, John M., and Ellen A. Donnelly. 2017. "Evaluating the Role of Race in Sentencing: An Entropy Weighting Analysis." *Justice Quarterly*. DOI:10.1080/07418825.2017.1415368.

Massoglia, Michael, and William Alex Pridemore. 2015. "Incarceration and Health." *Annual Review of Sociology* 41:291–310.

McDonald, Douglas C., and Kenneth E. Carlson. 1994. *Sentencing in Federal Courts: Does Race Matter? The Transition to Sentencing Guidelines, 1986–1990*. Washington, DC: US Department of Justice, Bureau of Justice Statistics.

Miethe, Terance D., and Charles A. Moore. 1985. "Socioeconomic Disparities under Determinate Sentencing Systems: A Comparison of Preguideline and Postguideline Practices in Minnesota." *Criminology* 23(2):337–63.

Mitchell, Ojmarrh. 2005. "A Meta-Analysis of Race and Sentencing Research: Explaining the Inconsistencies." *Journal of Quantitative Criminology* 21(4):439–66.

Mitchell, Ojmarrh, and Michael S. Caudy. 2015. "Race Differences in Drug Offending and Drug Distribution Arrests." *Crime and Delinquency* 63(2):91–112.

Mitchell, Ojmarrh, and Doris L. MacKenzie. 2004. *The Relationship between Race, Ethnicity, and Sentencing Outcomes: A Meta-Analysis of Sentencing Research*. Final report to the National Institute of Justice. Washington, DC: US Department of Justice.

Mooney, Chris. 2014. "Across America, Whites Are Biased and They Don't Even Know It." *Washington Post*, December 8. https://www.washingtonpost.com/news/wonk/wp/2014/12/08/across-america-whites-are-biased-and-they-dont-even-know-it/?utm_term=.88000a67f27e.

MSGC (Minnesota Sentencing Guidelines Commission). 2014. *2013 Monitoring Data*. St. Paul: Minnesota Sentencing Guidelines Commission.

Muller, Christopher. 2012. "Northward Migration and the Rise of Racial Disparity in American Incarceration, 1880–1950." *American Journal of Sociology* 118(2):281–326.

Nosek, Brian A., Mahzarin R. Banaji, and Anthony G. Greenwald. 2002. "Harvesting Implicit Group Attitudes and Beliefs from a Demonstration Web Site." *Group Dynamics: Theory, Research, and Practice* 6(1):101–15.

Orfield, Gary, and Dean Whitla. 1999. "Diversity and Legal Education: Student Experiences in Leading Law Schools." Los Angeles: University of California, Civil Rights Project.

Pager, Devah. 2003. "The Mark of a Criminal Record." *American Journal of Sociology* 108(5):937–75.

Parker, Kim, Juliana Horowitz, and Brian Mahl. 2016. *On Views of Race and Inequality, Blacks and Whites Are Worlds Apart*. Washington, DC: Pew Research Center.

Passel, Jeffrey S., D'Vera Cohn, and Mark Hugo Lopez. 2011. *Census 2010: 50 Million Latinos: Hispanics Account for More than Half of Nation's Growth in Past Decade*. Washington, DC: Pew Research Center.

Paternoster, Raymond, and Robert Brame. 2008. "Reassessing Race Disparities in Maryland Capital Cases." *Criminology* 46(4):971–1008.

Paternoster, Raymond, Robert Brame, Sarah Bacon, and Andrew Ditchfield. 2004. "Justice by Geography and Race: The Administration of the Death Penalty in Maryland, 1978–1999." *University of Maryland Law Journal of Race, Religion, Gender and Class* 4(1):1–98.

Peterson, Ruth D., and John Hagan. 1984. "Changing Conceptions of Race: Toward an Account of Anomalous Findings of Sentencing Research." *American Sociological Review* 49(1):56–70.

Pfaff, John F. 2017. *Locked In: The True Causes of Mass Incarceration—and How to Achieve Real Reform*. New York: Basic Books.

Phillips, Scott. 2009. "Status Disparities in the Capital of Capital Punishment." *Law and Society Review* 43(4):807–38.

Pinker, Steven. 2018. *Enlightenment Now: The Case for Reason, Science, Humanism, and Progress*. New York: Penguin.

Pratt, Travis C. 1998. "Race and Sentencing: A Meta-Analysis of Conflicting Empirical Research Results." *Journal of Criminal Justice* 26(6):513–23.

Provine, Doris Marie. 2011. "Race and Inequality in the War on Drugs." *Annual Review of Law and Social Science* 7:41–60.

Quillian, Lincoln. 1995. "Prejudice as a Response to Perceived Group Threat: Population Composition and Anti-Immigrant and Racial Prejudice in Europe." *American Sociological Review* 60(4): 586–611.

Quillian, Lincoln, and Devah Pager. 2001. "Black Neighbors, Higher Crime? The Role of Racial Stereotypes in Evaluations of Neighborhood Crime." *American Journal of Sociology* 107(3):717–67.

Rachlinski, Jeffrey J., Sheri Johnson, Andrew J. Wistrich, and Chris Guthrie. 2009. "Does Unconscious Bias Affect Trial Judges?" *Notre Dame Law Review* 84(3):1195–1246.

Reedt, Louis, and Jessica Widico-Stroop. 2008. *Changing Face of Federal Criminal Sentencing*. Washington, DC: US Sentencing Commission.

Rehavi, M. Marit, and Sonja B. Starr. 2014. "Racial Disparity in Federal Criminal Sentences." *Journal of Political Economy* 122(6):1320–54.

Rodriguez, Nancy. 2003. "The Impact of 'Strikes' in Sentencing Decisions: Punishment for Only Some Habitual Offenders." *Criminal Justice Policy Review* 14(1):106–27.

Roth, Randolph. 2009. *American Homicide*. Cambridge, MA: Harvard University Press.

Spohn, Cassia. 1990. "The Sentencing Decisions of Black and White Judges: Expected and Unexpected Similarities." *Law and Society Review* 24(5):1197–1216.

———. 2000. "Thirty Years of Sentencing Reform: The Quest for a Racially Neutral Sentencing Process." In *Policies, Processes, and Decisions of the Criminal Justice System*, edited by Julie Horney. Washington, DC: National Institute of Justice.

———. 2009. *How Do Judges Decide? The Search for Fairness and Justice in Punishment*. 2nd ed. Thousand Oaks, CA: Sage.

———. 2013. "The Effects of the Offender's Race, Ethnicity, and Sex on Federal Sentencing Outcomes in the Guidelines Era." *Law and Contemporary Problems* 76:75–104.

———. 2015. "Race, Crime, and Punishment in the Twentieth and Twenty-First Centuries." In *Crime and Justice: A Review of Research*, vol. 44, edited by Michael Tonry. Chicago: University of Chicago Press.

Spohn, Cassia, and David Holleran. 2000. "The Imprisonment Penalty Paid by Young, Unemployed Black and Hispanic Male Offenders." *Criminology* 38(1):281–306.

Steffensmeier, Darrell, and Chester L. Britt. 2001. "Judges' Race and Judicial Decision Making: Do Black Judges Sentence Differently?" *Social Science Quarterly* 82(4):749–64.

Steffensmeier, Darrell, and Stephen Demuth. 2000. "Ethnicity and Sentencing Outcomes in US Federal Courts: Who Is Punished More Harshly?" *American Sociological Review* 65(5):705–29.

———. 2001. "Ethnicity and Judges' Sentencing Decisions: Hispanic-Black-White Comparisons." *Criminology* 39(1):145–78.

———. 2006. "Does Gender Modify the Effects of Race-Ethnicity on Criminal Sanctioning? Sentences for Male and Female White, Black, and Hispanic Defendants." *Journal of Quantitative Criminology* 22(3):241–61.

Steffensmeier, Darrell, Noah Painter-Davis, and Jeffery Ulmer. 2017. "Intersectionality of Race, Ethnicity, Gender, and Age on Criminal Punishment." *Sociological Perspectives* 60(4):810–33.

Steffensmeier, Darrell, Jeffery Ulmer, and John Kramer. 1998. "The Interaction of Race, Gender, and Age in Criminal Sentencing: The Punishment Cost of Being Young, Black, and Male." *Criminology* 36(4):763–98.

Stolzenberg, Lisa, Stewart J. D'Alessio, and David Eitle. 2004. "A Multilevel Test of Racial Threat Theory." *Criminology* 42(3):673–98.

Stults, Brian J., and Eric P. Baumer. 2007. "Racial Context and Police Force Size: Evaluating the Empirical Validity of the Minority Threat Perspective." *American Journal of Sociology* 113(2):507–46.

Stumpf, Juliet. 2006. "The Crimmigration Crisis: Immigrants, Crime, and Sovereign Power." *American University Law Review* 56(2): 367–420.

Sutton, John R. 2013. "Structural Bias in the Sentencing of Felony Defendants." *Social Science Research* 42(5):1207–21.

Sweeney, Laura T., and Craig Haney. 1992. "The Influence of Race on Sentencing: A Meta-Analytic Review of Experimental Studies." *Behavioral Sciences and the Law* 10(2):179–95.

Taylor, Marylee C. 1998. "How White Attitudes Vary with the Racial Composition of Local Populations: Numbers Count." *American Sociological Review* 63(4):512–35.

Tonry, Michael. 1995. *Malign Neglect: Race, Crime, and Punishment in America*. New York: Oxford University Press.

Tonry, Michael, and Matthew Melewski. 2008. "The Malign Effects of Drug and Crime Control Policies on Black Americans." In *Crime and Justice: A Review of Research*, vol. 37, edited by Michael Tonry. Chicago: University of Chicago Press.

Transactional Records Access Clearinghouse. 2016. *Immigration Now 52 Percent of All Federal Criminal Prosecutions*. Syracuse, NY: Syracuse University.

Travis, Jeremy, Bruce Western, and F. Stevens Redburn. 2014. *The Growth of Incarceration in the United States: Exploring Causes and Consequences*. Washington, DC: National Academies Press.

Tyler, Tom R. 1990. *Why People Obey the Law*. New Haven, CT: Yale University Press.

Ulmer, Jeffery T. 2012. "Recent Developments and New Directions in Sentencing Research." *Justice Quarterly* 29(1):1–40.

———. 2018. "Race, Ethnicity, and Sentencing." In *Oxford Research Encyclopedia of Criminology and Criminal Justice*. New York: Oxford University Press.

———. 2019. "Criminal Courts as Inhabited Institutions: Making Sense of Difference and Similarity in Sentencing." In *American Sentencing*, edited by Michael Tonry. Vol. 48 of *Crime and Justice: A Review of Research*, edited by Michael Tonry. Chicago: University of Chicago Press.

Ulmer, Jeffery T., and Mindy S. Bradley. 2018. "Punishment in Indian Country: Ironies of Federal Punishment of Native Americans." *Justice Quarterly* 35(5):751–81.

Ulmer, Jeffery T., James Eisenstein, and Brian D. Johnson. 2010. "Trial Penalties in Federal Sentencing: Extra-Guidelines Factors and District Variation." *Justice Quarterly* 27(4): 560–92.

Ulmer, Jeffery T., and Brian Johnson. 2004. "Sentencing in Context: A Multilevel Analysis." *Criminology* 42(1):137–78.

Ulmer, Jeffery T., and John H. Kramer. 1996. "Court Communities under Sentencing Guidelines: Dilemmas of Formal Rationality and Sentencing Disparity." *Criminology* 34(3):383–408.

Ulmer, Jeffery T., Michael T. Light, and John Kramer. 2011. "Does Increased Judicial Discretion Lead to Increased Disparity? The 'Liberation' of Judicial Sentencing Discretion in the Wake of the Booker/Fanfan Decision." *Justice Quarterly* 28(6):799–837.

Ulmer, Jeffery T., Noah Painter-Davis, and Leigh Tinik. 2016. "Disproportional Imprisonment of Black and Hispanic Males: Sentencing Discretion, Processing Outcomes, and Policy Structures." *Justice Quarterly* 33(4):642–81.

United Nations. 2017. *International Migration Report 2017: Highlights*. New York: United Nations, Population Division, Department of Economic and Social Affairs.

US General Accounting Office. 1990. *Death Penalty Sentencing: Research Indicates Pattern of Racial Disparities*. Report to Senate and House Committees on the Judiciary. Washington, DC: US General Accounting Office.

USSC (US Sentencing Commission). 2004. *Fifteen Years of Guidelines Sentencing: An Assessment of How Well the Federal Criminal Justice System Is Achieving the Goals of Sentencing Reform*. Washington, DC: US Sentencing Commission.

———. 2016. *Monitoring of Federal Criminal Sentences, Fiscal Year 2016*. Washington, DC: US Sentencing Commission.

van Kalmthout, A. M., F. B. A. M. Hofstee-van der Meulen, and F. Dunkel, eds. 2007. *Foreigners in European Prisons*. Oisterwijk, Netherlands: Wolf Legal.

Viglione, Jill, Lance Hannon, and Robert DeFina. 2011. "The Impact of Light Skin on Prison Time for Black Female Offenders." *Social Science Journal* 48(1):250–58.

Wakefield, Sara, and Christopher Uggen. 2010. "Incarceration and Stratification." *Annual Review of Sociology* 36:387–406.

Wang, Xia, and Daniel P. Mears. 2015. "Sentencing and State-Level Racial and Ethnic Contexts." *Law and Society Review* 49(4):883–915.

Ward, Geoff, Amy Farrell, and Danielle Rousseau. 2009. "Does Racial Balance in Workforce Representation Yield Equal Justice? Race Relations of Sentencing in Federal Court Organizations." *Law and Society Review* 43(4):757–806.

Welch, Susan, Michael Combs, and John Gruhl. 1988. "Do Black Judges Make a Difference?" *American Journal of Political Science* 32(1):126–36.

Western, Bruce. 2006. *Punishment and Inequality in America*. New York: Sage.

Wilmot, Keith A., and Miriam A. Delone. 2010. "Sentencing of Native Americans: A Multistage Analysis under the Minnesota Sentencing Guidelines." *Journal of Ethnicity in Criminal Justice* 8(3):151–80.

Wu, Jawjeong, and Dae-Young Kim. 2014. "The Model Minority Myth for Noncitizen Immigration Offenses and Sentencing Outcomes." *Race and Justice* 4(4):303–32.

Yang, Crystal S. 2015. "Free at Last? Judicial Discretion and Racial Disparities in Federal Sentencing." *Journal of Legal Studies* 44(1):75–111.

Zatz, Marjorie S. 1987. "The Changing Forms of Racial/Ethnic Biases in Sentencing." *Journal of Research in Crime and Delinquency* 24(1):69–92.

Michael Tonry

Predictions of Dangerousness in Sentencing: Déjà Vu All Over Again

ABSTRACT

Predictions of dangerousness are more often wrong than right, use information they shouldn't, and disproportionately damage minority offenders. Forty years ago, two-thirds of people predicted to be violent were not. For every two "true positives," there were four "false positives." Contemporary technology is little better: at best, three false positives for every two true positives. The best-informed specialists say that accuracy topped out a decade ago; further improvement is unlikely. All prediction instruments use ethically unjustifiable information. Most include variables such as youth and gender that are as unjust as race or eye color would be. No one can justly be blamed for being blue-eyed, young, male, or dark-skinned. All prediction instruments incorporate socioeconomic status variables that cause black, other minority, and disadvantaged offenders to be treated more harshly than white and privileged offenders. All use criminal history variables that are inflated for black and other minority offenders by deliberate and implicit bias, racially disparate practices, profiling, and drug law enforcement that targets minority individuals and neighborhoods.

Were the American philosopher Yogi Berra a social scientist, and alive, he would likely describe his reaction to recent debates about predictions of dangerousness in sentencing as déjà vu all over again. Except concerning technical statistical issues, all the major critiques offered in recent years

Electronically published February 11, 2019
  Michael Tonry is professor of law and public policy, University of Minnesota. He is grateful to Richard Frase, Jan de Keijser, Douglas Husak, John Monahan, and Kevin Reitz for insightful suggestions and to Richard Berk, David P. Farrington, John Monahan, and Alex Piquero for guiding him to pertinent specialist literatures.

© 2019 by The University of Chicago. All rights reserved.
0192-3234/2019/0048-0010$10.00

were offered in the 1970s and 1980s. Predictions of future violence by individuals are substantially more often wrong than right. Check. Minority offenders are more often incorrectly predicted to be violent than are white offenders. Check. Use of socioeconomic status variables in prediction instruments is per se unjust and disproportionately affects minority offenders. Check. Use of criminal history variables exaggerates differences between minority and white offenders and increases racial disparities. Check. It is unjust ever to punish someone more severely than he or she deserves because of a prediction of dangerousness (or for any other reason). Check. Increasing the severity of a sentence on the basis of risk prediction in effect punishes many offenders for crimes that would not have happened. Check.[1]

Those issues were on research and policy agendas four decades ago for several reasons.[2] Support for indeterminate sentencing and the rehabilitative aims said to underlie it had collapsed. Efforts were afoot to figure out what should come next. Retributivism was the leading candidate: punishment should be based mostly or entirely on offenders' blameworthiness, on what they "deserved." Among politicians—much less among scholars—an approach based on instrumental goals of deterrence and incapacitation was a leading candidate and had very different implications. Comparably blameworthy offenders could and should be treated differently if punishing one more severely than another would prevent crime more effectively.

Neither approach entirely won out. Retributivism was more influential in some times and places, consequentialism in others.[3] In practice, both approaches were influential and had to be reconciled. The normative literature on prediction of dangerousness considered how that might be done. Agreement quickly emerged among most legal scholars and philosophers, and many practitioners, that the offender's blameworthiness

---

[1] These issues were widely discussed (e.g., Morris 1974; Hoffman 1983, 1995; Monahan 1983; Morris and Miller 1985; von Hirsch 1985; Tonry 1987).

[2] Sources concerning intellectual and policy developments discussed in this introduction are well known. Tonry (2016, chap. 1) provides them.

[3] This is the term most often used in contemporary writing by philosophers and legal theorists to describe teleological punishment theories. Until a few decades ago, utilitarianism was in common use. Instrumentalism is a third, less commonly used alternative. The key point is that, whatever the term used, punishment is seen as a means, not an end, and must find justification in its beneficial effects. Deontological retributivism, by contrast, treats punishment as an end in itself. The only just punishment is a deserved punishment. Effects do not matter.

TABLE 1
US Parole Board, Salient Factors

	1973 Version	1976 Version	1991 Version
Convictions	Yes	Yes	Yes
Incarcerations	Yes	Yes	Yes
Age at first commitment	Yes	Yes	No
Age at current commitment	No	No	Yes
Recent commitment-free period	No	No	Yes
Not auto theft	Yes	Yes	No
Not check fraud	No	Yes	No
No parole revoke, offense on parole	Yes	Yes	Yes
Custody status			Yes
No drug dependence	Yes	Yes	Yes
Education	Yes	No	No
Employment	Yes	Yes	No
Family	Yes	No	No

SOURCE.—Hoffman (1976, 1983, 1995).

should set an absolute upper limit on punishment's severity; some argued that consequentialist considerations were irrelevant and others that they might be relevant but only if proportionate retributive upper limits were respected. Conservative social scientists and many policy makers were primarily interested in effective crime prevention.

Gradually, through the mid-1980s, something close to a consensus view emerged of how retributive and consequentialist views of the role of prediction could be reconciled. The evolution of the US Parole Commission's "Salient Factor Score," used in its release guidelines, is illustrative (see table 1).

1. *Only violence matters.* The initial scoring system included a record of auto theft convictions as an aggravating factor that, if present, would delay release. This made sense if the goal was to predict any future offense, including minor ones, since low-level property offenders often accumulate lengthy records. The commission decided that only risks of future violence could justify lengthier prison sentences. The auto theft factor was dropped. The addition and removal of a check fraud factor illustrate the same point.
2. *Racial disparities matter.* The initial system included "age at first commitment" as a factor because it is a predictor of later offending. The commission soon recognized, however, that ages at first com-

mitment were typically younger for blacks than for whites, partly because of racial differences in how police respond to young people's behavior. Use of age at first commitment as an aggravating factor meant that black offenders were held longer in prison than whites. The factor was dropped. The discussion below of social disadvantage factors illustrates the same point.

3. *Social disadvantage matters.* The initial system included education, employment, and family stability as factors because weak educational and employment records and unstable residential and family circumstances are predictors of later offending. The commission gradually recognized that use of these factors meant that more privileged people would be held in prison for shorter periods than disadvantaged people, who seldom in any meaningful sense choose to be poor, badly educated, or erratically employed or to live chaotic lives. Larger percentages of minority than white people live deeply disadvantaged lives; the socioeconomic factors increased racial disparities. They were all dropped.

The literature on ethical and legal issues in prediction dried up after the 1980s and has revived only in the 2010s. It dried up because the "tough on crime" movement matured in the mid-1980s. Mandatory minimum sentence, three-strikes, truth in sentencing, life without parole, and similar laws shifted the crime prevention focus from decisions by judges and parole boards in individual cases to extended confinement of whole categories of offenders defined only by the offenses of which they were convicted. Parole release was abandoned in a third of the states, made available only to people convicted of minor crimes in the 26 states that enacted truth in sentencing laws, fundamentally compromised by mandatory minimum, three-strikes, and life without parole laws, and where it remained available was granted much less often by politically risk-averse parole boards.

Explanations of why a literature on prediction of dangerousness has reemerged are more speculative. Correctional managers for three decades have been developing prediction instruments for use in classifying offenders for treatment and transferring offenders between programs. A private-sector industry has developed that long made its money by selling prediction instruments to correctional managers and, in recent years, has begun selling its products to courts for use in pretrial detention, sentencing, and probation revocation proceedings. Companies found new markets partly because of mass incarceration and efforts to diminish it. Starting with the reentry movement of the late 1990s, reformers emphasized the need to reduce recidivism rates, divert low-level and low-risk offenders from imprisonment, and reserve imprisonment for serious and violent offenders. Partly as a result, legislatures increasingly direct judges to take reoffending predictions into account in making sentencing decisions, sentencing commissions are building risk predictions into their guidelines, and courts are buying and using prediction instruments.

Predictions of dangerousness in our time present the same challenges and raise the same normative and policy issues as they did three decades ago. Eric Holder (2014) warned the US Sentencing Commission against using dangerousness predictions when he was attorney general and has repeatedly decried their use since.[4] Increased use of prediction instruments has attracted the attention of legal scholars and social scientists. The development of "big data" approaches to prediction has attracted the interest of statisticians who have extensively debated trade-offs between technical and ethical issues. Social scientists have been patiently working on development, refinement, and evaluation of correctional prediction instruments since the 1980s.

The normative and policy issues raised by use in sentencing of predictions of dangerousness are back on the table. The 1970s and 1980s debates about the same issues have largely been forgotten. In this essay I examine the fundamental issues. Following the lead of the US Parole Commission in the 1970s and 1980s, I focus on predictions of violent and otherwise serious crime. Reoffending is so common among chronic property, drug, prostitution, and public disorder offenders that use of predictive incapacitation strategies would generate palpably unjust punishments.[5] Blumstein,

---

[4] Holder's critique identifies many of the problems discussed in this essay: "By basing sentencing decisions on static factors and immutable characteristics—like the defendant's education level, socioeconomic background, or neighborhood—[risk assessments] may exacerbate unwarranted and unjust disparities that are already far too common in our criminal justice system and in our society. Criminal sentences must be based on the facts, the law, the actual crimes committed, the circumstances surrounding each individual case, and the defendant's history of criminal conduct. They should not be based on unchangeable factors that a person cannot control, or on the possibility of a future crime that has not taken place." He communicated his views to the US Sentencing Commission (letter, Jonathan J. Wroblewski, Director, Office of Policy and Legislation, US Department of Justice, to the Honorable Patti Saris, Chair, US Sentencing Commission, July 29, 2014).

[5] Andrew Ashworth and Martin Wasik (2017), both former chairs of England's Sentencing Advisory Panel, argue that chronic minor offenders should normally receive reduced sentences because their offending patterns signal the presence of fundamental social maladjustment, mental health problems, or serious personality disorders.

Farrington, and Moitra (1985) long ago showed that the probability of a subsequent arrest exceeds 90 percent for anyone who has been arrested eight or more times. Section I provides an overview of the current debates. To a large extent they consist of people talking past each other. Section II canvasses familiar objections to use of predictions of dangerousness in sentencing, including their inaccuracy; their reliance on ascribed characteristics such as age and gender;[6] their use of status characteristics such as education, marital status, and employment; and their reliance on criminal history indicators that are based in large part on discriminatory police practices. All of these characteristics of contemporary prediction methods systematically disadvantage poor and minority offenders relative to more privileged and white offenders.

Section III addresses justifications offered for predictive sentencing. One is that normative considerations related to punishment are too contested, unrealistic, or indeterminate to guide real-world decisions. Another is that racial, ethnic, age, and gender disparities caused by predictions are not troubling because they reflect real differences between groups. A third is that predictive sentencing raises issues indistinguishable from public health quarantines and use of actuarial predictions in medicine, public health, credit scoring, and insurance. A fourth is that predictive sentencing is an essential tool for minimization of crime.

In the final section, I show diverse ways competing claims and aspirations can be reconciled. The realpolitik claim is that predictions will be used one way or another, that crime is too emotional a topic for rational argument and analyses to be relevant, and, accordingly, that there is no point in explaining why predictive sentencing is unjust. I disagree with all those propositions. Better that officials treating other human beings unjustly be reminded again and again that that is what they are doing. Someday they may want and decide to do better.

That is not an unworldly aspiration. Conventional beliefs change. Some American southerners before the Civil War and during the Jim Crow period opposed racial discrimination on moral grounds. Theirs eventually became the prevailing view. Early feminists and sympathizers, notably in-

---

[6] Changes in gender self-identification are more common or more often declared in our time than in earlier times. They remain relatively rare, however. In the text, I use "gender" in its traditional bimodal sense. Inevitably, however, the issue will be raised in individual cases in which gender attributions matter whether individuals may or must be categorized according to birth-identified or self-identified gender (including none).

cluding Mary Wollstonecraft ([1792] 2009) and John Stuart Mill ([1869] 1997), argued, again against the odds, that subordination of women is wrong. That became the prevailing view. Consensual homosexual behavior remained a criminal offense in England until 1967 and in some American states until 2003. That is unimaginable now. Other countries' criminal law systems are committed to ideas of proportionality and equal treatment that leave little room for predictive sentencing (e.g., in Scandinavia; Lappi-Seppälä 2016). That may someday happen in the United States.

A critic might accuse me of being insensitive to the suffering of victims of crimes that would be avoided if their assailants had been incapacitated. I am not. Prevention of foreseeable harms, however, requires trade-offs between interests and costs. There is no cost-free way entirely to prevent many bad things—including crimes, automobile injuries and fatalities, occupational injuries, environmental degradation, and slips in bathtubs—from happening. No one is prepared to forbid use of automobiles, industrial production, or bathing. Instead we try to make activities as safe as they affordably can be while acknowledging their importance.

Crime is no different. There would be little violent crime in the community if all males between ages 16 and 30 were locked up; that is not going to happen. Human beings value their liberty and autonomy too much. Incapacitation resulting from predictions of dangerousness diminishes the liberty and autonomy of knowable individual people, disproportionately poor and disadvantaged ones, in exchange for predicted prevention of crimes to hypothetical future victims. Because the world changes, many predicted crimes may never have happened. Rates of violent crime, for example, declined by two-thirds in the past quarter century. Two-thirds of the crimes that were predicted as grounds for locking people up in 1995 did not happen, but those locked up lost much of their lives as free citizens. The trade-off is thus between punishing specific people much more than they deserve in order, on the basis of predictions that are much more often than not incorrect, to prevent an unknowable number of future crimes. That price, like the costs associated with banning private use of automobiles, is too high. Violent crimes are as much an inevitable fact of life as auto accidents. They are prices we pay for personal freedom.

I. The State of the Debates

People's views about use of predictions of dangerousness in sentencing sometimes appear to be irreconcilable, as two high-profile exchanges demonstrate. Hart, Michie, and Cooke (2007) evaluated use of several well-known instruments and concluded that the "group and individual risk estimates" they produce are too wide to be useful. The predictions are too often wrong, they said; using them does serious unjustifiable harm to individuals who would not have been violent. Statisticians Peter Imrey and Philip Dawid (2015) responded, insisting that the best-known instruments, their results, and their applications are based on sound statistical practice.

Imrey and Dawid did not understand, or pretended not to understand, the critics' objection. Individuals are not treated unjustly, they wrote: decisions are "individualized." A judge saying that would mean that he or she took into account all available information concerning a particular individual and thought carefully about what to do. What Imrey and Dawid meant was different: "individualized risk [is] derived from an external group and projected onto the subject" (2015, p. 39). That is, the riskiness attributed to an individual is not his or her own, but the average of a group in which he or she is included for purposes of statistical analyses. They distinguished this from "latent individual risk intrinsic to the subject herself." This, though obscurely phrased, is what most people mean when they say that a decision about a specific person is individualized.

The second exchange began when Angwin et al. (2016) analyzed Broward County, Florida, data on use of COMPAS, a proprietary prediction instrument licensed by a for-profit company.[7] Their title tells their conclusion: "There's Software Used across the Country to Predict Future Criminals. And It's Biased Against Blacks." Their three key findings: blacks had higher average risk scores than whites, relatively more blacks than whites were wrongly predicted to be violent (exposing relatively more

---

[7] Dressel and Farid (2018) report on a stunning analysis of 462 laypeople's predictions of dangerousness, using the Broward County, Florida, data set used by Flores, Bechtel, and Lowenkamp (2016), and find that laypeople's predictions of reoffending were as accurate as COMPAS's. Dressel and Farid presented short descriptions of the crimes with which 1,000 defendants were charged and (only) the defendant's sex, age, and previous criminal history. COMPAS, by contrast, uses 137 variables. In order to prevent participant exhaustion, defendants were divided into 20 sets of 50 cases. Each participant was asked for one defendant set to predict reoffending within 2 years of the defendant's most recent crime. In one round of questioning, participants were not given the defendant's race. In a second round, they were (for a different set of offenders than in the first round). The participants were recruited through Amazon's Mechanical Turk, an online crowd-sourcing marketplace in which people are paid to perform a wide variety of tasks. The participants' predictions in both rounds were as accurate as COMPAS's. Racial differences in false positive rates were lower than in Flores, Bechtel, and Lowenkamp's analysis.

black people to harsher treatment), and relatively fewer blacks than whites were wrongly predicted to be nonviolent (making fewer eligible for milder treatment). Those foreseeable racial disparities—crucially important to people they affect—are what the critics meant by "bias."

Flores, Bechtel, and Lowenkamp (2016) did not refute the racial disparity findings but insisted that the critics had not shown statistical bias. Blacks have higher crime rates than whites, they explained, and more often have socioeconomic and other characteristics correlated with offending: no bias, just sound statistical practice. They sidestepped the critics' objections.

Talented, passionate people were on both sides of those exchanges but could not find common ground. The prediction defenders viewed the issues as primarily technical: let the chips fall where they may. The critics viewed the issues as primarily substantive: knowingly treating blacks more harshly than whites is wrong.

Many fault lines permeate prediction debates. Some consider it irresponsible not to use state-of-the-art prediction methods. Others believe that punishments should be closely proportioned to offenders' blameworthiness and that it is unjust to punish some offenders more severely than others only because of predictions. Still others believe that reducing use of imprisonment depends on identifying offenders likeliest to reoffend, and locking them up, so that others need not be. Some people believe that racial, ethnic, and class disparities caused and exacerbated by prediction instruments are morally wrong and want them to end.

In writing the preceding paragraphs, I tried to avoid polemic. The facts, ma'am, just the facts, as Sergeant Joe Friday used to say. I did not mention assertions that political and ideological agendas and racial, ethnic, and class biases, conscious and implicit, underlay adoption in the United States of broad-based incapacitative crime control policies in the 1980s and 1990s, including increased use of prediction. Those allegations may be true, but here I set them aside. My interest is in the intellectual challenge posed by widely different, good-faith, views about prediction, and whether and how they can be reconciled.

The difficulty, as Isaiah Berlin (2002) long ago explained, is that the implications of equally valid first principles often conflict. Few would disagree that maintenance of public order and security is a Good Thing. Were that the only relevant consideration, it would be self-evident that efforts to diminish crime's effects on victims should be maximized.

Other no less important values, however, are at stake. If assuring that offenders be punished precisely as much as they deserve were all that mattered, predictions about future offending would be irrelevant. If only equal treatment mattered, people convicted of equally serious crimes should be punished equally severely; predictions would again be irrelevant. If avoidance of policies that cause or aggravate racial and ethnic disparities, or that rely on factors tinged with invidious bias, was overridingly important, all existing prediction systems would have to be abandoned.

The values underlying all of those things matter, and they conflict. People resolve the conflicts in different ways. Some allow one goal to trump others (e.g., reducing mass incarceration by using imprisonment only for "dangerous" people: Flores, Bechtel, and Lowenkamp 2016; reducing social and racial injustice: Harcourt 2008; preventing crime: Slobogin 2019). Imrey and Dawid (2015, p. 40), in an article sometimes described as the leading statistical work on actuarial risk assessment, observe, "If groups of individuals with high and low propensities for violence recidivism can be distinguished, and courts act upon such distinctions, recidivism will decline to the extent that groups most prone to violence are incapacitated.... And both society and offenders will be better served even if we cannot be sure ... from precisely which individual offenders this betterment derives." Offenders who are imprisoned, or held longer, because they were mistakenly predicted to be violent, however, are seldom likely to agree that they have been "better served."

Some writers acknowledge the problem but take no position. When writing about punishment theory generally, American philosopher Douglas Husak (2019*a*) observes, "Sentencing according to the principle of proportionality is crucial if the state is to treat offenders as they deserve." However, concerning risk prediction, he adopts a "pluralist" stance and writes, "Retributivists should preserve the role of desert while weakening its strength. . . . We can preserve proportionality but allow exceptions when we have a good rationale for them. . . . If we have good reason to inflict different amounts of punishment on two offenders who have committed equally serious crimes, we should not be worried that our decision does not preserve proportionality. Admittedly, the results produced [may be] messy; sentencing, like morality more generally, is not governed by an algorithm" (Husak 2019*b*).[8] English philosopher Matt Matravers (2019, p. 205) offers an account of punishment in which

---

[8] The newest and purportedly most accurate prediction devices employing big data and machine learning are algorithms (Berk et al. 2018; Berk 2019).

censure of blameworthy behavior and crime prevention are independent governing principles: "The results may well be counter-intuitive," he writes, to punish people convicted of less serious crimes more severely than people convicted of more serious ones, but "it is not inconsistent" so long as retributive and consequentialist goals are independent. The problem, which he does not explore, is in deciding what to do when the implications of the independent principles conflict.

Not everyone sidesteps. Psychologists John Monahan and Jennifer Skeem (2016) survey the literature, work through all the major problems, and propose ways to limit unwanted effects of prediction (notably by allowing them to be used to reduce but not to increase sentence severity).[9] Berk et al. (2018, p. 1) in one of a series of increasingly subtle analyses of trade-offs between ethical issues and predictive accuracy, observe, "Except in trivial cases, it is impossible to maximize accuracy and fairness at the same time, and impossible simultaneously to satisfy all kinds of fairness." However, they too throw up their hands: "In the end, it will fall to stakeholders—not criminologists, not statisticians, and not computer scientists—to determine the tradeoffs. . . . These are matters of values and law, and ultimately, the political process" (p. 33). Not terribly helpful or reassuring to anyone concerned about unjust treatment of individuals. The political process produced mass incarceration and three-strikes, life without parole, and similar laws.

II. The Indictment

Three sets of problems bedevil use of predictions in sentencing. The first is that they are seldom very accurate. When the aim is to predict serious sexual or other violence, more predictions are wrong ("false positives") than are right ("true positives"). If used to determine prison sentence lengths, many people who would not have committed serious violence will be held longer. The second set of problems concerns the variables used in nearly all prediction instruments: some over which individuals have no control, such as age and gender, are fundamentally unjust; some concern inherently personal matters such as marriage, work, and education; some relate to aspects of criminal records that are contaminated by

---

[9] This does not, however, reduce racial and class disparities. Minority and lower-social class offenders systematically score worse on risk prediction instruments and are thus less likely to benefit from mitigated sentences predicated on "good" risk scores.

conscious and implicit bias and discriminatory practices. The third set concerns racial and ethnic disparities; almost all variables used in prediction instruments correlate with race and ethnicity and inexorably make punishments of minority group members harsher than those of whites.

A. Accuracy

Violence is rare, even among known offenders. Predicting rare events accurately is inherently difficult. As a result, the technology of violence prediction is not very good. The predictions are more often inaccurate than accurate. I was astonished to learn, when reviewing the contemporary literature as background for writing this essay, that accuracy is little better now than it was four decades ago.

Norval Morris (1974), in an influential early synthesis, concluded that predictions of future violence were wrong two-thirds of the time. The most exhaustive contemporaneous analysis by John Monahan (1981) reached the same conclusion. Predictions that people will not be violent were overwhelmingly correct, but that is trivial: if only 10 percent are violent, a prediction that no one will commit a violent crime will be correct 90 percent of the time. Morris argued that then-current knowledge did not justify imposing longer prison terms on people predicted to be violent: "'Dangerousness' must be rejected for this purpose, since it presupposes a capacity to predict future criminal behavior quite beyond our present technical ability" (1974, p. 62). Locking up three people predicted to be violent when only one will be, he said, is deeply unjust. Two would be wrongfully deprived of extended periods of liberty.

Analyses of prediction studies conventionally distinguish, as Morris did, between true and false positives. True positives are predicted to reoffend, and do. False positives are predicted to reoffend, but do not. True and false negatives are defined similarly. In Morris's time, the state of the predictive art, as table 2 shows using Morris's example, was that two-thirds of individuals predicted to be violent were false positives.

The technology of violence prediction is vastly more sophisticated than it was four decades ago. The early studies were based on clinical predictions by doctors, mental health specialists, judges, and correctional personnel. The contemporary literature is actuarial and is based on mathematical models, sophisticated statistical analyses, machine learning, and "big data." One might expect that violence predictions today would be vastly more accurate than in the 1970s. They aren't.

TABLE 2
Violence Prediction, True and False Positives and Negatives: An Illustration

Crime Type	Prediction	Result—No Violence	Result—Violence
No violence	70	65 (true negatives)	5 (false negatives)
Violence	30	20 (false positives)	10 (true positives)
Total	100	85	15

Source.—Adapted from Morris (1974, table 1).

One leading meta-analysis of the accuracy of prediction instruments concludes that further improvements are unlikely: "After almost five decades of developing risk prediction tools, the evidence increasingly suggests that the ceiling of predictive efficacy may have been reached with the available technology" (Yang, Wong, and Coid 2010, p. 759). Consistently with this caution, two major meta-analyses conclude that the most commonly used violence prediction instruments are indistinguishable in their accuracy.[10]

The most influential meta-analysis, analyzing research on the nine most commonly used instruments, concluded that positive violence predictions are, on average, correct 42 percent of the time (Fazel et al. 2012; Fazel 2019). Morris, recall, was troubled that only one-third of positive predictions (two of six) were correct. Forty-two percent accuracy, put differently, means that two of five positive predictions are correct. As in Morris's time, substantially more than half of people predicted to be violent will not be.

Two of the leading meta-analyses conclude that positive predictions of future violence are too inaccurate to be used in sentencing:

> Because of their moderate level of predictive efficacy, they should not be used as the sole or primary means for clinical or criminal justice

---

[10] Yang, Wong, and Coid (2010, p. 759): "If prediction of violence is the only criterion for the selection of a risk assessment tool, then the tools included in the present study are essentially interchangeable." Campbell, French, and Gendreau (2009, p. 253): "This analysis found little difference among the predictive validities of actuarial and structured instruments for violent reoffending." Meta-analyses of research on instruments used to predict any, as opposed to only violent, reoffending reach the same conclusion: "Overall, no one instrument stood out as producing more accurate assessments than the others, with validity varying with the indicator reported" (Desmarais, Johnson, and Singh 2016, p. 213).

decision making that is contingent on a high level of predictive accuracy, such as preventive detention. (Yang, Wong, and Coid 2010, p. 761)

These tools are not sufficient on their own for the purposes of risk assessment.... The current level of evidence is not sufficiently strong for definitive decisions on sentencing, parole, and release or discharge to be made solely using these tools. (Fazel et al. 2012, pp. 5, 6)

Even outspoken defenders of risk prediction agree. Flores, Bechtel, and Lowenkamp (2016, p. 39), whom I discussed above concerning disagreements about racial bias, emphasized that "we want to make it clear that we are not supporting or endorsing the idea of using risk assessment at sentencing."

There is thus no credible scientific case to be made in favor of use in sentencing of predictions of future violence.

B. Unjust Variables

Except for race and, though they are seldom explicitly discussed, presumably also ethnicity, nationality, and religion, developers of prediction instruments include as variables any offense and offender characteristics on which they can obtain data. In other public policy settings, for example, education, public health, and medical research, equivalent strategies including use even of racial and other usually verboten data make sense. The aims are to improve public services generally, to understand and address problems affecting subpopulations, or to diagnose and treat individual health problems.

Violence prediction in courts is different.[11] The aim is usually to identify high-risk individuals for pretrial or postconviction preventive detention (though as Monahan [2017] argues, it could in theory be used to identify low-risk individuals for more humane treatment; I discuss this below). Public health and educational research and related policies seldom target individuals. Medical decision making does, but the aim is to

---

[11] Different considerations may be pertinent concerning some uses of prediction instruments in correctional settings. Some "culturally appropriate" treatment programs, e.g., target special needs of women or members of specific minority groups. Other treatment programs target "higher-risk" offenders on the efficiency rationale that low-risk offenders will usually not reoffend whether or not they participate. Prediction instruments are used to match offenders to treatment programs generally, to set or vary treatment or supervision intensity, and to measure changes relative to program goals. They are also used in institutional custody-level decisions, which may raise issues similar to those concerning sentencing.

attempt to prevent or minimize human suffering. Sentencing decisions are intended to cause human suffering. That is why Jeremy Bentham called all punishment, even when warranted, "evil."

Suspect variables fall into three categories. Race, gender, and age ought to be off-limits because they are basic human characteristics for which individuals bear no causal, personal, or moral responsibility. Increased punishments for any of these reasons are per se unjust. A host of socioeconomic characteristics including employment, education, marital status, living arrangements, and parental responsibilities are correlated with offending but are not the criminal law's business. These are matters of individual choice in a free society. Punishing people for making the "wrong" choices is also per se unjust. Socioeconomic and other personal characteristics including many related to criminal history are highly correlated with race and ethnicity; many are shaped by invidious discrimination. Their use causes and exacerbates adverse racial and ethnic disparities.

C. Immutable Characteristics

No one would think people should be punished more severely because of their eye or hair color or adult height, characteristics over which they have no control. Gender, race and ethnicity, and age raise the same issue. So, despite their greater mutability, would religion and nationality most of the time.

1. *Age.* Individuals have no more control of their age than of their eye color. Mentally responsible individuals do have control over their behavior. All else being equal, the age of an offender should not matter, except to mitigate the severity of punishments imposed on young and elderly offenders.[12] Young offenders in all Western countries, including the United States, have traditionally been punished less severely than adults and usually in specialized courts using specialized procedures and imposing less severe punishments.[13]

---

[12] Many European countries have created strong legal presumptions against imprisonment of the elderly (typically, 70 or older). That is why former Italian Prime Minister Silvio Berlusconi was sentenced to community service as a hospital orderly rather than to the multiyear prison sentence he would otherwise have received following conviction for public corruption offenses. As the Madoff Ponzi scheme and Bill Cosby cases and the reluctance of most American prisons to release terminally ill and elderly prisoners demonstrate, the United States, as in many penal policy matters, is an outlier.

[13] In western European countries, e.g., the age of criminal responsibility is typically 14 or 15 years (in Belgium 18 for most offenses). In most, waiver of young offenders to adult courts is not legally possible; nor is direct prosecution in adult courts. In German courts,

The reasons are self-evident. Most young offenders are less experienced and mature than most adults, are at a developmental stage during which risk taking, thrill seeking, and experimentation are common, and are more malleable. Research on "age/crime curves" and desistance has long shown that many adolescents commit crimes as teenagers, but most soon desist (Farrington [1986] and Laub and Sampson [2001] are the classic sources). Neurological and developmental research of the last two decades has documented details of adolescent brain development and behavioral controls that strengthen the rationale for more forgiving handling of young offenders (Monahan, Steinberg, and Piquero 2015). Even the conservative US Supreme Court is convinced. Banning mandatory life sentences without parole for juveniles, it emphasized that "children are constitutionally different from adults for purposes of sentencing" and that "mandatory penalties, by their nature, preclude a sentence from taking account of an offender's age and the wealth of characteristics and circumstances attendant to it" (*Miller v. Alabama*, 132 S. Ct. 2455, 2467 [2012]).

Nonetheless, youth is widely used as a variable in prediction instruments and as an aggravating factor in sentencing. I discuss Virginia's notorious sentencing guidelines, in use for more than 25 years, because they are premised on prediction-based incapacitation. They call for, all else being equal, harsher punishments for younger than for older offenders. This is wrong in principle and, in light of a growing body of research showing that imprisonment is criminogenic, perverse (e.g., Nagin, Cullen, and Lero Jonson 2009).

The Virginia guidelines set out criteria that identify nonviolent offenders for whom prison sentences are specified but whom judges are encouraged to divert to community-based punishments. In fraud guidelines, 22 "points" are given for being aged 20 or younger (Virginia Criminal Sentencing Commission 2014).[14] Being male adds 10 more points, for a total of 32. Only offenders who receive 31 or fewer points qualify for diversion; thus no matter how minor the offense or the criminal record, all males under 21 fail to satisfy the diversion criteria.

Virginia's remarkable treatment of young people becomes starker when compared with provisions for offenders 30 and over; they receive 7 "age

---

the vast majority of 18- and 19-year-olds convicted of serious crimes are sentenced as if they were juveniles (Tonry and Chambers 2012).

[14] The details are slightly different for larceny. Being male adds 9, not 10, points. The system is otherwise similar.

points." Five points are given for having one or two prior felony convictions and 4 points for having been incarcerated as an adult one to nine times. Put it together: A 30-year-old (7 points) male (10) with two prior felony convictions (5) and two prior adult incarcerations (4) totals 26 points and falls below the 31-point diversion threshold. An 18-year-old with no past criminal record does not.

There are three explanations for this strange policy. First, Virginia's guidelines were developed at the height of the "tough-on-crime" period under the administration of Republican Governor George Allen, who ran for office on a "parole abolition" platform (Tonry 2016). They were developed under the leadership of former US Attorney General William Barr, author while in office of the 1992 tract *The Case for More Incarceration* (1992). Second, selective incapacitation long before had been repudiated as a crime control strategy by the National Academy of Sciences (Blumstein et al. 1986), but Barr nonetheless made incapacitation the premise for the Virginia guidelines. Third, because of the age/crime curve, age is a powerful predictor of future offending (though most offenses involve property or drugs and most young offenders soon desist).

The more general question is whether youth should be included in any prediction instrument meant to be used, or that might be used, in deciding whom to imprison or for how long. The trade-off is between predictive accuracy and punishing people because they are young. If the trade-off concerned eye color, race, or religion, few people would consider it. Even if any of them predicted reoffending, basic requirements of justice forbid their use. Age is equally inappropriate.

2. *Gender.* Gender cuts in different directions in different contexts. Assiduous efforts are made in education, employment, and public health to prevent or minimize differential treatment of women. This is so even when actuarial rationales exist. Because they typically live longer than men, women traditionally paid lower life insurance premiums but also received lower monthly pension benefits. Those practices have been attacked as unjust, increasingly successfully, despite their actuarial justifications. So have higher automobile insurance premiums paid by men.

The early American sentencing commissions undertook research on past sentencing patterns and invariably found that women typically received less severe punishments than men. No commission, however, chose to promulgate separate, less severe guidelines for women or to make gender a mitigating factor. Gender-blind guidelines were expected to increase sentence severity for women, but everyone involved agreed that was required by respect for gender equality (e.g., Knapp 1984; Tonry 1996).

Gender blindness is a powerful idea. Treating people differently because they are male or female is wrong in the same way that treating people differently because they are of a particular race or religion is wrong. Gender blindness is sometimes set aside for sympathetic policy reasons. Examples targeting women include health care, maternity leaves, flexible work schedules, and help with child care. Even with such policies, movements are afoot as a matter of fairness to make comparable provision for men. What distinguishes these gender-conscious policies is that they aim to do something for women, not to them. They do not aim to treat men worse but to meet gender-specific needs of women.

That has not stopped developers of prediction instruments from incorporating maleness as a factor. Nor has it stopped policy makers from using maleness, all else being equal, to increase punishment severity. The 10 points given under the Virginia fraud guidelines for being male (compared with 1 point for being female) is an example. Theft and drug sale guidelines vary in detail, but all treat men and women differently.

The rationale is actuarial. Across crime, time, and country, men's offending rates are higher than women's. Locking up more otherwise comparable men than women will predictably prevent more future offenses. Just as with eye color, race, ethnicity, and age, however, that cannot justify punishing some equally culpable offenders more severely than others.

3. *Race and Ethnicity.* No American jurisdiction explicitly authorizes use of race or ethnicity (or religion or nationality) as criteria for making sentencing or parole release decisions. Doing so would violate long-settled constitutional equal protection doctrines (e.g., Starr 2014). Indirectly, however, race and ethnicity creep in when decisions are based in part on socioeconomic and criminal history variables that are correlated with them. On average, black and Hispanic Americans compared with whites have lower incomes, weaker employment records, less extensive educations, less residential stability, and more extensive criminal records. All are correlated with higher offending risks. This is one major reason why prediction instruments produce higher false positive rates for blacks than for whites and higher false negative rates for whites than for blacks.

A strong argument can be made, persuasive to many, that there is no moral difference between making invidious decisions on the basis of race and knowing that making decisions based on other considerations will affect members of different racial groups differently. If a law specifying

5-year prison sentences for black offenders and 2-year sentences for whites is wrong, why isn't it equally wrong to use prediction instruments that foreseeably produce the same result? This argument is why criminal law *mens rea* doctrine usually treats intention to cause a harm, knowledge that the harm will almost certainly result, and reckless disregard of a substantial and justifiable risk that it will occur as morally equivalent. Doing something knowing it will cause harm is little different from doing something intending to cause harm.

The legal and moral issues this argument raises are complex, but that does not weaken its force in relation to sentencing and punishment. There are other circumstances in which knowingly causing harm is justified. Criminal law defenses of self-defense, duress, and necessity provide examples. So does the Roman Catholic moral doctrine of double effect, which justifies harms that are side effects of actions taken to accomplish a good result (McIntyre 2014; an example: acting to save a pregnant woman's life though a fetus will likely die). Other times harms occur for which there is no remedy. The US Supreme Court famously decided that public authorities may not operate segregated schools on purpose (de jure discrimination) but segregated schools that are the outgrowth of residential patterns (de facto discrimination) are okay.

Criminal punishment is different from the harms involved in those other contexts. Sentences imposed by courts are state actions that are indisputably meant to cause pain to offenders. No decent person would say that black people convicted of a particular offense deserve to suffer greater pain than do white offenders convicted of the same offense. We know, judges know, designers of instruments know that use of predictions of dangerousness in sentencing causes black offenders to be punished more severely than white offenders convicted of the same offenses. We also know, though less confidently, that decision makers more often override risk predictions of black than white offenders and punish them even more severely than their individual risk classification would justify (Green and Chen 2019). Thus, a double whammy: black offenders are overpredicted to be violent and are then punished more severely than the prediction, even if correct, would call for.

Table 3, showing false positive and false negative rates calculated by Flores, Bechtel, and Lowenkamp (2016) in their reanalysis of COMPAS data, illustrates this. Half of whites predicted not to reoffend were rearrested, compared with only 28 percent of blacks predicted not to reoffend. The false negative rate for whites was nearly double that for blacks.

TABLE 3
Prediction Errors, Any Arrest within 2 Years, by Race: An Illustration

	False Positive Rates (%)	False Negative Rates (%)
Whites	22	50
Blacks	42	28

Source.—Flores, Bechtel, and Lowenkamp (2016, table 3).

Conversely, only 22 percent of whites who were predicted to reoffend did not, compared with 42 percent of blacks. The false positive rate for blacks was nearly twice that for whites. These are extraordinary differences. Blacks are much more likely than whites to be mislabeled as dangerous and, if this is reflected in sentencing, to be punished more severely than they otherwise would be. Conversely, whites are much more likely than blacks to be mislabeled as "not dangerous" and, if this is reflected in sentencing, to benefit from a mistaken prediction that they would not reoffend.

Harcourt (2008) showed that predictive sentencing has a ratchet effect that worsens racial and socioeconomic disparities. When risk predictions are used, minority and disadvantaged defendants are treated more severely, on average, than others the first time they are convicted. Each subsequent conviction has compounding effects and further increases increments of additional severity they suffer. Racial differences in criminal history are a primary cause of racial disparities in imprisonment (Hester et al. 2018).

Correlations between offending and race are not random. Both official police data and victim survey data show that black people commit some crimes at higher rates than whites. That is not surprising. In every country, members of some socially and economically disadvantaged groups commit crimes at higher rates than the majority population (Tonry 1997). In the United States, the social and economic disadvantages that disproportionately afflict black and Hispanic people, and are correlated with offending, are partly products of historical and ongoing discrimination and of diminished life chances at birth. Mentally responsible minority offenders, like other offenders, should be punished as they deserve for the offenses they commit; few people disagree.[15] It should be at least discomforting, however, that the use of prediction instruments in sentencing exacerbates the effects of disadvantage and causes many minority offenders to be punished more harshly than they deserve or would be if they were white.

---

[15] Minority and deeply disadvantaged offenders may, however, often deserve less severe punishments than do others (Tonry 2014).

D. Socioeconomic Characteristics

All of the early sentencing commissions rejected use of socioeconomic variables in their sentencing guidelines systems. The first principle set out in the "Statement of Purpose and Principles" of the Minnesota Sentencing Guidelines Commission (1980) provided, and still does, "Sentencing should be neutral with respect to the race, gender, social, or economic status of convicted offenders." Section 994(d) of the Sentencing Reform Act of 1984 directs the federal sentencing commission to "assure that the guidelines and policy statements are entirely neutral as to the race, sex, national origin, creed, and socioeconomic status of offenders." Section 994(e) elaborates: "The Commission shall assure that the guidelines and policy statements, in recommending a term of imprisonment or length of a term of imprisonment, reflect the general inappropriateness of considering the education, vocational skills, employment record, family ties and responsibilities, and community ties of the defendant."

The US Congress and Minnesota's sentencing commission rejected use of socioeconomic characteristics in sentencing because using them is unjust. It feels platitudinous to write this, but it is unchallengeably true: No one should be punished more severely than he would otherwise be because he is rich or poor, well or inadequately educated, married or single, working or unemployed. None of that has anything to do with an individual human being's blameworthiness. Even the Virginia Sentencing Commission, not renowned for its sensitivity to moral and ethical issues, removed the socioeconomic factors—employment and marital status—initially included in its diversion guidelines (Ostrom and Kauder 2012). The correlation of many socioeconomic characteristics with race makes their use doubly unjust.[16]

There is another fundamental reason why socioeconomic characteristics should not be cause for harsher punishment. Many result from legitimate lifestyle choices that are not the state's business. People living in free societies are entitled to decide whether to marry, to work a steady job, or to become well educated, even if being unmarried, lacking a stable work record, and being poorly educated are correlated with higher offending rates. Free citizens are entitled to decide to seek university degrees, join apprenticeship programs, or live lawfully hand to mouth, as street people and many artists, musicians, and writers do by some combination of choice and necessity.

---

[16] The US Parole Commission was concerned for decades that use of socioeconomic variables in its Salient Factor Score exacerbated racial injustices and, partly for that reason, removed them (Hoffman 1976, 1983, 1995).

Citizens are entitled to choose not to work at all and to live hand to mouth or on income from trust funds or indulgent parents.

Committing violent and property crimes, selling illicit drugs, and actively participating in criminal gangs also reflect personal choices, but they are choices of a different kind. So are choices by sentenced offenders to violate lawful conditions imposed on community punishments, such as compliance with curfews, desistance from crime, and not associating with former criminal associates. Those behaviors are unlawful; people who engage in them assume risks of arrest, prosecution, conviction, and punishment. They choose to live dangerous lives.

Prediction instruments and sentencing policies that take account of socioeconomic characteristics generally do so because research shows them to be correlated with offending. A cynic might say that anyone who chooses to live a vagabond life assumes the risk that he will be punished for it, so what's the problem? Many offenders, however, do not—in any fundamental sense—choose to be poorly housed, poorly employed or unemployed, poorly educated, or unmarried. Even if poor people's choices are more constrained than more privileged people's, they are lawful choices all the same. Punishing people because of their lawful lifestyle choices raises the same ethical issues for a disadvantaged inner-city resident as it would for a privileged trust fund beneficiary.

Anyone who believes in equal justice should oppose use in sentencing of race-skewing socioeconomic variables in sentencing generally, including in prediction instruments. That is why, more than 30 years ago, as table 1 shows, the US Parole Commission removed them from its prediction instrument even though that weakened the Salient Factor Score's accuracy (Hoffman 1983).

E. Criminal History

Criminal history raises more complex issues than is usually recognized, despite widely held intuitions that prior convictions justify harsher punishments for subsequent offenses (Roberts 2008; Roberts and von Hirsch 2010). Although it appears self-evident to Americans that people who have previously been convicted of crimes should be punished more severely for a new offense, all else being equal, it is not self-evident to people in other countries. In the Scandinavian countries, for example, the general assumption is that punishments should not be increased because of prior convictions (Asp 2010; Lappi-Seppälä 2011). The reasoning is that the offender has already been punished as much as he or she deserved for the former offense and should now be punished as much as is deserved for the new one. Prior convictions are often taken into account as aggravating factors in other common-law countries, but usually subject to sharp limits (Baker and Ashworth 2010; Freiberg 2014).

American policy makers and practitioners are unlikely soon to adopt or endorse the Scandinavian point of view and decide to take account of prior records not at all or only a little. Criminal history does, however, have dramatic aggravating effects in American sentencing. Under three-strikes, habitual offender, and career criminal laws, prior convictions make a huge difference. Under state sentencing guidelines systems, criminal history can result in sentences four to 15 times longer than are received by first offenders (Hester et al. 2018). Any searching inquiry into ethical issues in American sentencing would have to explore the rationales and justifications of those differences.

Criminal history variables are the primary drivers of risk predictions. It is difficult, however, to find a principled justification for increasing the severity of punishment because of an individual's criminal history. Even if one could be found, criminal history is entangled with racial bias and foreseeable disparate racial effects.

1. *Punishment Theories.* Retributivists believe that any punishment more severe than an offender deserves is per se unjust. Immanuel Kant, the archetypal retributivist, averred that punishment should be precisely calibrated to the seriousness of the offense: "But what kind and what amount of punishment is it that public justice makes its principle and measure? None other than the principle of equality (in the position of the needle on the scale of justice), to incline no more to one side than to the other. Accordingly, whatever undeserved evil you inflict on another among the people, that you [deserve]. . . . Only the law of retribution (*jus talionis*) . . . can specify definitely the quality and the quantity of punishment" ([1797] 2017, p. 115). This requires strict proportionality so that equally serious crimes are punished equally severely, and more and less serious crimes are punished appropriately differently. Almost all retributive philosophers and criminal law theorists who have considered the matter conclude that there is no convincing moral justification for treating people with prior convictions more severely than first-timers (e.g., Fletcher 1978; Lippke 2016).

Utilitarians and contemporary consequentialists should in principle permit harsher punishments for recidivists, but only if the reductions in suffering attributable to crimes thereby prevented are greater than the additional suffering imposed on offenders. Utilitarianism also has a strong proportionality principle, based on a deterrence logic: punishments should be scaled to offense seriousness to encourage offenders always to commit the less serious of alternative possible crimes. However, unlike retributive proportionality, utilitarian proportionality can be trumped by a frugality principle (Bentham's term; in our time, we say parsimony) that forbids unnecessary punishment. Bentham condemned and would forbid punishments that cause more suffering to offenders than their punishment prevents and punishments whose aims can more effectively be obtained by means of other preventive measures (Frase 2009*a*). For Bentham, the archetypal utilitarian, any punishments more severe than concerns for utilitarian proportionality otherwise permit are per se wrong: "All punishment is mischief: all punishment in itself is evil. . . . If it ought at all to be admitted, it ought *only* to be admitted in as far as it promises to exclude some greater evil" ([1789] 1970, p. 158; my emphasis).

The problem in our time for consequentialist supporters of predictive sentencing is that contemporary knowledge of deterrence, incapacitation (the rationale for prediction), and rehabilitation cannot "promise to exclude some greater evil." I have several times recently surveyed the relevant literature (Tonry 2016, 2018*a*), as have many others (e.g., Chalfin and McCrary 2017), including most notably the National Academy of Sciences Committee on the Causes and Consequences of High Rates of Incarceration (Travis, Western, and Redburn 2014, chap. 5). That august body concluded that deterrent and incapacitative effects of punishment are modest at best and that imprisonment is on balance criminogenic, making ex-prisoners more rather than less likely to reoffend. The evidence on rehabilitation is stronger. Well-designed, well-targeted, well-managed, and well-funded programs can reduce reoffending (MacKenzie 2006). Assignment to diagnostically appropriate treatment programs does not, however, require that individuals receive longer prison sentences.

2. *Racial Bias and Disparate Effects.* Even if punishment theories are set aside, difficult ethical issues relating to race and ethnicity remain. Blacks more often commit and are more often arrested for violent crimes than whites. In a system in which criminal history makes a big difference in sentencing, even that facially plausible explanation for differences in conviction rates means that criminal history factors disproportionately affect blacks. Use of criminal history factors systematically disadvantages members of minority groups. Frase (2009*b*), in the most comprehensive study ever published on racial disparities in a state sentencing system, found that two-thirds of racial disparities in Minnesota imprisonment result from use of criminal history factors in sentencing.

Aspects of criminal history that are commonly included as variables in prediction instruments—age at first arrest or commitment, custody status, and numbers of prior arrests, convictions, and punishments—result in substantial part from explicit and implicit racial bias and from conscious police targeting of poor and minority neighborhoods and individuals. Black and Hispanic people are arrested at younger ages and more often than white people for reasons that have as much to do with racially differentiated exercises of police discretion as with racial differences in offending behavior.[17]

Police sometimes arrest more young black people for invidious reasons but often would prefer to avoid arrests if they can. White and middle-class young people, however, can be returned to stable homes or referred to private treatment and mental health facilities more frequently than disadvantaged minority offenders. Schools refer more minority than white students to the police for conduct problems. Racial profiling by the police by definition mostly affects members of minority groups. Drug enforcement policies disproportionately target substances sold by minority drug dealers and the places where they sell them (Fellner 2013). All of these practices exaggerate the criminal records of members of minority groups compared with other people.

3. *Other Criminal History Issues.* Use of criminal history variables in sentencing, or in prediction instruments, raises other issues. When the sentencing provisions of the *Model Penal Code* were being developed in the 1950s, there was vigorous debate over whether criminal history should ever be taken into account. Paul Tappan (1947), chairman of the US Parole Board, and primary draftsman of the code's sentencing and corrections provisions, argued that with liberty at stake, only prior convictions should count. Arrests or prosecutions not resulting in a conviction should not. On the same logic, age at first arrest or commitment, custody status, prison commitments, all—along with arrests—commonly used as variables in prediction instruments, should not. Tappan's view is the contemporary norm in other Western countries: Only convictions count (Roberts and von Hirsch 2010). Here I only flag these issues. However, since predictions of dangerousness are often cited as reason to deprive "dangerous" offenders of more liberty than they otherwise would lose, they are as pertinent to the ethics of prediction as they are to sentencing.

---

[17] The classic Philadelphia birth cohort studies, e.g., found that 48.7 percent of non-white offenders in the 1945 cohort had their first police contact before age 14, compared with 30.8 percent for whites. The corresponding figures for the 1958 cohort were 41 and 27 percent (Tracey, Wolfgang, and Figlio 1990, chap. 10).

III. The Defenses

The indictment is pretty formidable. Predictions of future violence are more often wrong than right (Fazel et al. 2012): Of five positive predictions, three will be mistakes (false positives). The false positives are disproportionately black and other minority offenders (Angwin et al. 2016; Flores, Bechtel, and Lowenkamp 2016). Many prediction instruments incorporate variables such as youth and gender that are per se unjust. All prediction instruments incorporate socioeconomic status variables that produce systematically harsher dispositions of black, other minority, and disadvantaged offenders. All prediction instruments incorporate criminal history variables that are inflated for black and other minority offenders by racially biased and disparate practices, racial profiling, and street-level drug enforcement that targets minority individuals and neighborhoods.

The defenses are less weighty. One is that normative punishment theories provide no meaningful bar to reliance on predictions (Husak 2019*b*). A second is that prevention of predicted harms to victims is so overwhelmingly important that it trumps concerns about proportionality and equal treatment (Ryberg [2019], as devil's advocate). A third is that there is nothing special about subordinating individuals to collective or organizational interests on the basis of predictions. Happens all the time: actuarial statistics are used in credit scoring and setting insurance premiums; statistical analyses underlie public health policies and medical practices; quarantines confine individuals (Imrey and Dawid 2015; Douglas 2019). A fourth is that concerns about racial and other disparities in punishment are misplaced: people who score badly on predictive variables commit disproportionate numbers of crimes and should bear disproportionate preventive burdens (Slobogin 2019).

A. Punishment Theory

If everyone agreed that punishment policies and practices should be assessed only in relation to their crime-reductive effects, the elements of the indictment would be immaterial. As far as I can tell, no one believes that concerning themselves and people they care about.[18] The Christian

---

[18] As a matter of political self-interest, American politicians often support policies such as life without parole for minors, three-strikes sentences of 25 years to life for minor property offenders, and decades-long prison sentences for street-level drug sellers that cannot be justified by any principled theory of punishment. In the 1970s and 1980s, conservative politicians deplored US Supreme Court decisions that strengthened defendants' procedural protections. Throughout a long life of observing the criminal law, however, my experience has been that politicians and other powerful people charged with crimes believe

New Testament and Kant's categorical imperative agree that we should want and do for others what we want done for ourselves. Everyone believes that crime seriousness matters. Probably no one disagrees that lengthy imprisonment for routine traffic or parking offenses would be unjustly severe, even if an effective deterrent, and that probation for stranger rapes would be unduly lenient, even if harsher punishments had no preventive effects.

The likeliest theoretical justifications for predictive sentencing are utilitarian, trading justice to individual offenders for greater crime prevention. Bentham, however, did not believe that prevention of crime justifies injustice to individuals. He endorsed strong criminal law defenses—including insanity, intoxication, and ignorance of law—so that only blameworthy people are convicted. He argued that punishment is evil and—his frugality principle—should be imposed only when the offender's suffering would be outweighed by greater suffering averted for others. He insisted that punishments be proportioned to the seriousness of offenses—for deterrent, not retributive, reasons—and that sentencing decisions take sympathetic account of myriad personal characteristics of individual offenders (Bentham 1970, pp. 52, 158, 169). The only contemporary mainstream consequentialist theory, Braithwaite and Pettit's "Republican Theory of Criminal Justice" (1990, 2001), recognizes proportionate retributive upper limits on punishment. It otherwise rejects retributive values and calls in every case for the least punitive disposition on which the victim, the offender, and others close to them agree. Bentham's utilitarianism would not accommodate use of predictions of dangerousness in sentencing. The frugality principle forbids imposition in any individual case of punishments more severe than deterrent considerations justify. The false positive problem puts the kibosh on predictive sentencing; how for this defendant could a prediction that we know is probably wrong justify a harsher punishment?

Retributive theories vary. Kant's foundational account insists that offenders receive "definitely the quality and quantity of punishment" they deserve, no more, no less (2017, p. 115). That leaves no role for predictions, although it may permit them to be taken into account in

---

as to themselves, their families, and close colleagues that justice requires the full panoply of procedural protections, compassionate consideration of personal circumstances, and observance of general principles of justice in punishment including imposition of the least severe possible sentence.

choosing between punishments of equal severity (e.g., Ryberg 2019).[19] This was Andreas von Hirsch's view three decades ago (von Hirsch, Wasik, and Green 1989). In practice, however, it could apply to only a small minority of crimes. Few minor ones would warrant imprisonment in place of a community punishment, and there is no case to be made that a longer preventive prison term is punitively equivalent to a shorter one. For serious crimes, no sanction other than capital punishment has the same or greater incapacitative effect than imprisonment.

Kant and von Hirsch are "positive" retributivists who argue that offenders not only may but must be punished as much as they deserve. However, there are also "negative" retributivists who argue that blameworthiness sets only upper limits on severity; offenders may be punished as much as they deserve, but they need not be. This may be what Husak (2019*b*) had in mind when he wrote, "If we have good reason to inflict different amounts of punishment on two offenders who have committed equally serious crimes, we should not be worried that our decision does not preserve proportionality." The consensus view noted above among authors of leading meta-analyses that violence predictions should not be used in sentencing, however, casts serious doubt whether current knowledge provides "good reason" to allow pursuit of predictive goals to trump proportionality.

Husak's position rejects Kantian retributive and Benthamite utilitarian insistence on comparable treatment of people who committed comparable crimes.[20] It also abandons the almost ubiquitous belief among retributivists of all stripes that proportionality between offense seriousness and maximum punishment severity is a fundamental requirement of justice.

Although it can never be self-evident in a given case precisely what punishment is required, that problem was solved as a practical matter long ago. Wide agreement exists on the relative seriousness of different crimes. Uncontroversial scales of relative offense seriousness can be devised for particular places and times. So can parallel scales of punishment severity (Duus-Otterström 2019). The two can then be linked. Compa-

---

[19] Kant (2017, p. 115) wrote explicitly of substitution of punishments so they would be subjectively comparably burdensome. One example is that "someone of high standing given to violence could be condemned not only to apologize for striking an innocent citizen inferior to himself but also to undergo a solitary confinement involving hardship; in addition to the discomfort he undergoes, the offender's vanity would be painfully affected, so that through his shame like would be fittingly repaid with like" for an offense for which a "social inferior" would be called on only to apologize.

[20] But with major differences. Both want sanctions—for Kant, calculated on the gravity of wrongdoing, and for Bentham on deterrence calculations—to be adjusted to take account of differences (which Bentham called sensibilities) between offenders.

rably severe punishments can be specified for comparably serious crimes and proportionately different ones for diversely serious ones. There is no room for prediction; the overarching goals are to assure equal treatment by linking blameworthiness to punishment.

The alternative to Kant's view is negative retributivism. Monahan (2017), for example, has argued that predictions can be properly used as long as upper limits based on offense seriousness are respected and predictions are used to mitigate sentences for low-risk offenders but not to increase them for high-risk offenders. He refers to Virginia's approach that incorporates predictions into guidelines for diversion to alternative punishments of offenders otherwise bound for imprisonment.[21]

Morris's (1974) version of negative retributivism, "limiting retributivism," provided a more fully developed proposal. For every crime there is a maximum punishment that may justly be imposed. This varies with offense seriousness and thus provides proportionate limits. For some crimes—I used stranger rape earlier as an example—there may be minimums that must ordinarily be observed. The default is always the minimum; like Bentham, Morris urged recognition of a principle of parsimony that forbade imposition of unnecessary suffering. The minimum, however, can be exceeded for good reason.

From a predictive sentencing perspective, so far so good. Morris insisted that there be good evidence-based reasons to justify harsher-than-minimum punishment. Concerning predictions of dangerousness, he was emphatic: four false positives for every two true positives is not good enough. That would cause too much undeserved suffering. It is unlikely that improvements in accuracy over four decades—three false positives for every two true positives—would have changed his view. The general case to be made is weaker now than in 1974. Morris wrote before much evidence had accumulated on the racial disparities inexorably produced by predictive sentencing and without considering the implications of use of youth, gender, race-correlated socioeconomic status, and bias-contaminated criminal history variables. Morris's limiting retributivism does not provide the license prediction proponents might wish for.

Predictive sentencing is thus incompatible with mainstream retributive punishment theories. This is confirmed by the theoretical literature

---

[21] This does not really work at least in Virginia because the main guidelines are only advisory and judges may depart both downward and upward. Negative retributivist theories envision an unbreakable upper limit. The "normal" Virginia guideline recommendation is only that, not an upper limit. I discuss other problems below.

on the role of prior criminal history in sentencing new crimes. It is a cliché but true that past crimes are the best predictor of future crimes, which is why criminal history variables are the most predictively powerful (Hoffman 1983; Monahan 2017). Empirical evidence and common experience document that there is a "recidivist premium"; all else being equal, most judges impose harsher punishments on repeat offenders than on first offenders (Reitz 2010). There is solid evidence that most people think they should (e.g., Roberts 2008, 2011).

Nonetheless, nearly every retributivist philosopher who has considered the matter has concluded that it cannot be justified (e.g., among many more, Fletcher 1978; Ryberg 2001; Bagaric 2010; Lippke 2016): "did the crime, did the time"; "paid his or her debt to society." More punishment now for this crime for predictive reasons, because there was an earlier crime, is double counting, in effect attaching an increment of additional punishment to this crime to punish the earlier one more fully.

Several efforts have been made to argue that committing an earlier crime somehow increases an offender's culpability in relation to the new one. One argument is that recidivists deserve additional punishment because their behavior demonstrates defiance of the judge or the state or is evidence of bad character (e.g., Lee 2010). Those claims have no place in a free society: citizens are entitled to be defiant, eccentric, and difficult. "Bad character" is in the eyes of the beholder and in any case is nowhere a criminal offense. The other argument is that recidivists have a greater obligation than others to be law-abiding (Bennett 2010). The law, however, makes the same demands of all citizens. No one except possibly the arguments' proponents has been persuaded by either of these analyses.

If punishments may not justly be increased to take account of earlier convictions, it is difficult to imagine principled arguments for why punishments may be increased on the basis of predictions of future offending that are in turn substantially based on criminal history variables. Ryberg (2019) intensively mines retributive theories looking for an overlooked nugget that can justify predictive sentencing. No such luck. He concludes thusly: "Though there is some appeal in pursuing justice and in preventing future crimes, you cannot to a full extent get both."

B. *Public Safety*

Everyone is in favor of public safety, but that is not the only fundamental value involved. Sentencing also implicates fairness, proportionality, equal treatment, and parsimony (Tonry 2018*b*). Any rational person would want these additional values to be honored if he or she or a loved one was charged with a crime. It is difficult to develop a morally persuasive explanation for why we as individuals deserve those things but other people whom we do not know or care about do not. Unless someone can develop a fully elaborated consequentialist theory of punishment that does not incorporate those values and justifies predictive sentencing, a principled case for predictive sentencing cannot be made.

This does not mean that pursuit of crime prevention and public safety need be abandoned. Systems such as those in Scandinavian countries, Germany, and the Netherlands in which punishment is based primarily on blameworthiness and which allow only minor increases for criminal history do not have higher crime rates than the United States. Insofar as the operation of the criminal justice system deters wrongful behavior, systems of proportionate punishment will continue to do so. They will contribute to moral education by reinforcing basic social norms of right and wrong. Deserved terms of imprisonment will continue to incapacitate inmates from committing new offenses in the community. Other demonstratively effective strategies of community, developmental, and situational crime prevention, if pursued, will continue to do their work.

Expecting more than that from predictive sentencing is in any event unrealistic. The best available evidence cautions against believing that changes in sanctions policies have significant crime reduction effects (Travis, Western, and Redburn 2014, chap. 5; Tonry 2016).

C. Actuarial and Quarantine Analogies

Two arguments are made. The first is that, ho hum, there is nothing special about predictive sentencing: actuarial risk calculations affect private lives throughout modern society. There has been a "proliferation of statistical and other algorithmic prediction tools in banking, insurance, marketing, medicine, and other fields. . . . Prediction need not be highly accurate at the individual level for major collective benefit to accrue" (Imrey and Dawid 2015, pp. 25, 30).

So what's the problem? There are several. The most important is that the application of predictions in sentencing causes undeserved suffering to individuals whose punishments are increased, usually through lengthening of prison terms. Most other uses of actuarial prediction affect people's lives as private citizens. It may be disappointing to be denied a loan, insurance policy, or apartment lease, or be asked to pay higher rates, or not be offered a marketing opportunity. Those burdens, however, are not comparable to being imprisoned when otherwise a community punishment would be imposed or receiving a longer prison term. Actuarial predictions in medicine are used to benefit individuals by means of improved diagnostic capacities, not to cause suffering.

A criminal conviction is an authoritative declaration by the state that an individual engaged in morally blameworthy behavior. Punishment is meant to cause suffering—some philosophers approvingly refer to "hard treatment"—and is inherently stigmatizing in the eyes of the general public. Other uses of actuarial prediction are private and are neither intended to cause suffering nor handled in ways that expose individuals to public stigma. People who are denied loans or insurance policies may feel regretful, humiliated, even stigmatized, but only in private. No one else need know.

Arguments have been offered that predictive sentencing can be justified by analogy to public health quarantines. People carrying or exposed to contagious diseases are sometimes confined to eliminate or minimize the spread of contagion. However, except for rare circumstances such as the early periods of awareness of HIV when drug users and homosexuals were "blamed" for their afflictions, having a contagious disease (e.g., measles, typhoid, malaria, Ebola) is seldom personally stigmatizing. In rare circumstances when stigma attaches, decent people regard it as unjust and morally wrong. In any case, quarantines are not for lengthy fixed terms; they end when the risk passes or reaches acceptable levels. People subject to quarantines are not held in prisons and in a decent society receive sympathy and compassion. They are afforded the greatest material comfort that conditions allow, with as few limitations as possible on the freedoms enjoyed by other citizens. Preventive confinement based on risk predictions is not like that.

The arguments that preventive detention is morally equivalent to quarantine are unconvincing. Thomas Douglas (2019) tries mightily to demonstrate that quarantine is, or under some circumstances could be, indistinguishable. He assumes both sets of restrictions are morally undeserved (for offenders, because in excess of what could otherwise be justified). He sets aside the question of "soft moral difference," whether preventive detention is typically more morally suspect than quarantine, and considers only the narrower question of "hard moral difference," whether preventive detention is always in at least one respect more morally suspect.

Douglas concludes that preventive detention is not always worse in at least one respect. He may or may not be right, but in the real world, as he acknowledges, that is not important: "Whether preventive detention is *typically* more problematic than quarantine will depend heavily on the facts about how these two practices are typically imposed and what effects they normally have, on those subject to them, on those whom they are intended to protect, and on those required to fund them" (2019; emphasis in original).

Other arguments that quarantine offers a valid analogy to preventive detention are no more convincing. Gregg Caruso (2016) and Derk Pereboom (2014) argue that quarantine and preventive detention are indistinguishable to adherents of free will skepticism: "What we do, and the way we are, is ultimately the result of factors beyond our control and because of this we are never morally responsible for our actions in the basic desert sense—the sense that would make us truly deserving of blame or praise" (Caruso 2016, p. 26).

Caruso and Pereboom agree that neither "dangerous" offenders nor carriers of serious contagious diseases are morally responsible for the risks they pose and may be subjected to state controls to minimize risk. They posit reciprocal state obligations to offer minimal intrusions, humane conditions, and serious treatment efforts. Given their premise of free will skepticism, those are plausible and necessary ethical propositions.

Arguments about free will, hard determinism, and compatibilism are intellectually interesting and conceptually important. However, accepting the validity of Caruso's and Pereboom's analyses requires first accepting the validity of free will skepticism. That is unlikely on a widespread basis any time soon.

D. Group Differences in Offending

The argument is that the aim of prediction instruments is to predict crimes, that some instruments (e.g., COMPAS) predict future offending by black and white people with comparable accuracy, and accordingly that the instruments are not statistically biased (Flores, Bechtel, and Lowenkamp 2016). It may be regrettable, but if black, other minority, and disadvantaged offenders generally disproportionately have characteristics that predict future offending, so be it:

> COMPAS is based on an actuary designed to inform the probability of recidivism across its three stated risk categories. To expect the COMPAS to do otherwise would be analogous to expecting an insurance agent to make absolute determinations of who will be involved in an accident and who won't. Actuaries just don't work that way. This error discredits their [Angwin et al. 2016] main finding that Black defendants were more likely to be incorrectly identified as

recidivists (false positives) while white defendants were more likely to be misclassified as nonrecidivists (false negatives). (Flores, Bechtel, and Lowenkamp 2016, p. 45)

Two things about this quotation warrant mention. First, the quotation acknowledges no reason for concern about suspect variables: COMPAS uses every variable discussed in this essay except race.[22] Second, the claim that their analysis "discredits" Angwin et al.'s conclusions about racial distributions of false positives and false negatives is refuted by their own findings (see table 3 above presenting their findings on true and false positive rates for black and white offenders concerning general recidivism). What they presumably meant is that racial disparities do exist but are not important because they are simply by-products of an algorithm that is not statistically biased.

Flores, Bechtel, and Lowenkamp (2016) are interested only in predictive accuracy. This is made explicit when they offer two prediction models with very different false positive and negative rates but reject out of hand the model that makes fewer mistakes, as if any reasonable person would agree: "The [second model's effects]—a decrease in false positive rates and an increase in false negative rates—might be preferred by some, as it limits the number of individuals that are identified as 'high-risk.' For others with a low tolerance for recidivism and victimization, the [first model] would be preferred" (p. 42). Use of socioeconomic status and criminal history variables that differentially affect blacks and whites does not to them, as Lady Catherine de Bourgh would put it, signify. To people concerned about racial injustice, it does.

IV. The Summation

Predictive sentencing cannot thus be justified either empirically or morally. To many people, however, predictive sentencing, especially concerning violence, is intuitively plausible. It provides supporters opportunity to express sympathy toward hypothetical future victims and to express

---

[22] They note that when they added an interaction term between race and COMPAS into their analyses, it did not improve predictive accuracy (Flores, Bechtel, and Lowenkamp 2016, p. 43). This is irrelevant, as modelers have recognized for four decades (Fisher and Kadane 1983; Berk et al. 2018). Because race and other variables covary, most or all of any race effect is carried by the other variables. They most likely found no separate race effect because it was already present.

disdain for people believed likely to be violent. Probably in realpolitik terms, predictive sentencing will continue to command support from elected politicians and many criminal justice officials. What to do? A number of options are available.

A. Abandon Predictive Sentencing

This would be the correct approach. Prevention of crime is an important public policy goal, but so are justice, fairness, equal treatment, and parsimony. They importantly differ from crime prevention. Each derives from fundamental ideas about human dignity and limits state power over individual lives (Dan-Cohen 2002; Luban 2007; Waldron 2014). Predictive sentencing, by contrast, focuses only on hypothetical victims.

The way forward concerning punishment becomes clear when we recognize that punishment implicates multiple, competing values, including not only deserved punishment and crime prevention but also fairness and equal treatment. A comprehensive jurisprudence of just punishment would incorporate four propositions (Tonry 2018*b*):

- *Justice as Proportionality*: Offenders should never be punished more severely than can be justified by their blameworthiness in relation to the severity of punishments justly imposed on others for the same and different offenses (von Hirsch 1985).
- *Justice as Fairness*: Processes for responding to crimes should be publicly known, implemented in good faith, and applied evenhandedly (Rawls 1958).
- *Justice as Equal Treatment*: Defendants and offenders should be treated as equals; their interests should be accorded concern and respect when decisions affecting them are made (Dworkin 1977).
- *Justice as Parsimony*: Offenders should never be punished more severely than can be justified by appropriate, valid, normative purposes (Tonry 1994).

Preventive sentencing cannot be justified if those values are respected. The arguments concerning proportionality, equality, and parsimony are self-evident; predictive sentencing in its own terms violates them. It also violates the fairness requirement though possibly less self-evidently. Few prediction instruments have been validated using data for the populations affected and are thus arbitrary in their application to individuals. The bases for prediction instruments sold by private companies are not disclosed; this is deemed "proprietary information," akin to trade secrets. Thus judges and corrections officials who use them do not know on what basis they make decisions about individuals' liberty. Defendants, of course, cannot therefore challenge the basis of their sentences.

No country's legal system perfectly observes those values, but many in western and northern Europe try. In the United States, the case against predictive sentencing is likely to fall on deaf ears. Less bold options that would do less injustice are available.

B. Constrained Predictive Sentencing

Prevention concerns and prevailing emotionalism may make elimination of preventive sentencing unachievable. An unprincipled but more saleable option might be to establish limits on increments of additional punishment that can be imposed. Roberts and Frase (2019) propose maximum sentence increases of no more than 100 percent of the deserved sentence as a limit. I have proposed 50 percent (Tonry 2016).

A more discriminant proposal needs working out. Under Roberts and Frase's proposal, for example, predictions could justify a 2-month sentence if the starting point was 1 month, or a 40-year sentence if the starting point was 20 years, as in the United States it often could be. Under my 50 percent cap, a 20-year sentence could be increased to 30 years. All of these numbers are unjustly severe. A more constrained approach might allow increments ranging from the greater of 100 percent or 1 year for less serious offenses to the lesser of 100 percent or 3 years for more serious ones.

Those proposals, however, make pretty heroic assumptions about the willingness of American policy makers to constrain judges' authority and limit sentencing severity.

C. Predictive Mitigation

This is what Monahan (2017) proposes. It has the great defect that it will usually worsen racial and class disparities, all else being equal, because predictions of lower risk usually result from the absence of socioeconomic, criminal history, and other characteristics disproportionately associated with minority and disadvantaged offenders. The end result will be the diversion of more white and advantaged offenders. Norval Morris and I (1990) long ago argued that there may be something perverse about the argument that if some offenders will be treated unduly severely, concern for equal treatment requires that others also suffer unduly. Monahan's proposal might thus reduce severity for some offenders. Some people no doubt believe that is desirable, even if it exacerbates racial disparities (so Morris believed; I was doubtful). BUT—a big but—Monahan's proposal can work only if there are strong "normal" limits on sentencing severity, from which the mitigated sentence offers a reduction. Otherwise there will be nothing to stop judges and prosecutors from providing mitigated sentences to low-risk offenders and imposing aggravated sentences on high-risk offenders. This is what happens under Virginia's "advisory" guidelines.

D. Limiting Retributivism

A stronger version of Monahan's proposal is to allow mitigation for low-risk offenders but establish strong upper limits for all offenders based on offense seriousness. Only a handful of presumptive (Minnesota, Washington, Kansas) and mandatory (North Carolina) American guidelines systems establish meaningful upper limits. In such places, Morris's proposals could work. The presumptive normal sentence in every case would be set at the bottom of the guideline range. Low-risk offenders could receive sentences below the normal minimum, most offenders the normal minimum, and highest-risk offenders up to the maximum. This, however, could work only if guidelines systems were radically reformulated. Current approaches provide ranges for particular offenders that take account of both offense seriousness and criminal history. The limiting retributivism approach could work only if ranges were based solely on offense seriousness. Otherwise criminal history variables used in prediction instruments would be double counted.

E. Sanctions and Measures

Debates raged a century ago in the United States and Europe over the wisdom and justice of indeterminate sentencing (Pifferi 2012, 2016). Supporters argued that criminal behavior results primarily from environmental and psychological influences on individuals and that a rational sentencing system would reject retributive ideas and focus on rehabilitation and prompt release of the vast majority of corrigible offenders and the incapacitation of the rest. Opponents argued that moral blameworthiness should not be abandoned as an animating idea but should instead set limits on the state's punishment powers.

American jurisdictions—every one of them by the 1930s—adopted indeterminate sentencing. European countries including those in the United Kingdom rejected it as unjust. To deal, however, with the problem of seemingly incorrigible dangerous offenders, European countries created a distinction between sanctions, deserved punishments based on blameworthiness, and measures, crime prevention powers based on assessments of risk. In theory, measures are not punishments but extraordinary actions designed to deal with special problems. This is hypocritical, of course, since extended confinement will feel like additional punishment to any affected offender, but it has worked much as was intended (cf. de Keijser 2011). Measures targeting violence prevention are rarely used in any country (e.g., in Scandinavia, Lappi-Seppälä [2016]), but they are available for special cases. Anders Brejvik, the Norwegian mass murderer of 77 people in 2011, was sentenced to 21 years' imprisonment, the longest term possible, but was also made subject to a measure. If when his "sanction" expires he continues to be considered dangerous, the measure provides authority to continue to hold him.

The sanctions and measures distinction could in theory provide a mechanism for taming predictive sentencing in the United States. All offenders would receive proportionate sanctions based on the seriousness of their crimes and respecting concerns for fairness, equal treatment, and parsimony. A tiny number, a small fraction of 1 percent on the European pattern, might also be the objects of measures predicated on their dangerousness and permitting continued confinement after expiration of their prison sentences. Predictions could be used to identify cases in which a measure might be appropriate. For such a system to be a realistic option, however, there would need to be radical transformations in American popular, political, and legal cultures. That is unlikely in any foreseeable future.

REFERENCES

Angwin, Julia, Jeff Larson, Surya Mattu, and Lauren Kirchner. 2016. "Machine Bias: There's Software Used across the Country to Predict Future Criminals. And It's Biased Against Blacks." ProPublica, May 23. https://www.propublica.org/article/machine-bias-risk-assessments-in-criminal-sentencing.

Ashworth, Andrew, and Martin Wasik. 2017. "Sentencing the Multiple Offender: In Search of a 'Just and Proportionate' Total Sentence." In *More than One Crime:*

Sentencing the Multiple Offender, edited by Jesper Ryberg, Julian V. Roberts, and Jan de Keijser. New York: Oxford University Press.

Asp, Petter. 2010. "Previous Convictions and Proportionate Punishment under Swedish Law." In *Previous Convictions at Sentencing*, edited by Julian V. Roberts and Andrew von Hirsch. Oxford: Hart.

Bagaric, Mirko. 2010. "Double Punishment and Punishing Character: The Unfairness of Prior Convictions." *Criminal Justice Ethics* 19:10–28.

Baker, Estelle, and Andrew Ashworth. 2010. "Role of Previous Convictions in England and Wales." In *Previous Convictions at Sentencing*, edited by Julian V. Roberts and Andrew von Hirsch. Oxford: Hart.

Barr, William P. 1992. *The Case for More Incarceration*. Washington, DC: US Department of Justice, Office of Policy Development.

Bennett, Chris. 2010. "'More to Apologise For': Can We Find a Basis for the Recidivist Premium in a Communicative Theory of Punishment?" In *Previous Convictions at Sentencing: Theoretical and Applied Perspectives*, edited by Julian V. Roberts and Andrew von Hirsch. Oxford: Hart.

Bentham, Jeremy. 1970. *An Introduction to the Principles of Morals and Legislation*. Edited by J. H. Burns and H. L. A Hart. Oxford: Clarendon. (Originally published 1789.)

Berk, Richard. 2019. *Machine Learning Risk Assessments in Criminal Justice Settings*. New York: Springer.

Berk, Richard, Hoda Heidari, Shahin Jabbari, Michael Kearns, and Aaron Roth. 2018. "Fairness in Criminal Justice Risk Assessments: The State of the Art." *Sociological Methods and Research*. DOI:10.1177/0049124118782533.

Berlin, Isaiah. 2002. *Liberty*. Edited by Henry Hardy. New York: Oxford University Press.

Blumstein, Alfred, Jacqueline Cohen, Jeffrey A. Roth, and Christy A. Visher, eds. 1986. *Criminal Careers and "Career Criminals."* Washington, DC: National Academy Press.

Blumstein, Alfred, David P. Farrington, and Souymo Moitra. 1985. "Delinquency Careers: Innocents, Desisters, and Persisters." In *Crime and Justice: An Annual Review of Research*, vol. 6, edited by Michael Tonry and Norval Morris. Chicago: University of Chicago Press.

Braithwaite, John, and Philip Pettit. 1990. *Not Just Deserts: A Republican Theory of Criminal Justice*. New York: Oxford University Press.

———. 2001. "Republicanism and Restorative Justice: An Explanatory and Normative Connection." In *Restorative Justice: Philosophy to Practice*, edited by John Braithwaite and Heather Strang. Burlington, VT: Ashgate.

Campbell, Mary Ann, Sheila French, and Paul Gendreau. 2009. "The Prediction of Violence in Adult Offenders: A Meta-Analytic Comparison of Instruments." *Criminal Justice and Behavior* 36:567–90.

Caruso, Gregg D. 2016. "Free Will Skepticism and Criminal Behavior: A Public Health–Quarantine Model." *Southwest Philosophy Review* 32:25–48.

Chalfin, Aaron, and Justin McCrary. 2017. "Criminal Deterrence: A Review of the Literature." *Journal of Economic Literature* 55(1):5–48.

Dan-Cohen, Meir. 2002. *Harmful Thoughts: Essays on Law, Self, and Morality*. Princeton, NJ: Princeton University Press.
de Keijser, Jan W. 2011. "Never Mind the Pain, It's a Measure! Justifying Measures as Part of the Dutch Bifurcated System of Sanctions." In *Retributivism Has a Past: Has It a Future?* edited by Michael Tonry. New York: Oxford University Press.
Desmarais, Sarah L., Kiersten L. Johnson, and Jay P. Singh. 2016. "Performance of Risk Assessment Instruments in US Correctional Settings." *Psychological Services* 13:206–20.
Douglas, Thomas. 2019. "Is Preventive Detention Morally Worse than Quarantine?" In *Predictive Sentencing: Normative and Empirical Perspectives*, edited by Jan W. de Keijser, Julian V. Roberts, and Jesper Ryberg. Oxford: Hart.
Dressel, Julia, and Hany Farid. 2018. "The Accuracy, Fairness, and Limits of Predicting Recidivism." *Science Advances* 4(1):eaao5580.
Duus-Otterström, Göran. 2019. "Weighing Relative and Absolute Proportionality in Punishment." In *Proportionality in Punishment Philosophy and Policy*, edited by Michael Tonry. New York: Oxford University Press.
Dworkin, Richard. 1977. *Taking Rights Seriously*. Cambridge, MA: Harvard University Press.
Farrington, David P. 1986. "Age and Crime." In *Crime and Justice: An Annual Review of Research*, vol. 7, edited by Michael Tonry and Norval Morris. Chicago: University of Chicago Press.
Fazel, Seena. 2019. "The Scientific Validity of Current Approaches to Violence and Criminal Risk Assessment." In *Predictive Sentencing: Normative and Empirical Perspectives*, edited by Jan W. de Keijser, Julian V. Roberts, and Jesper Ryberg. Oxford: Hart.
Fazel, Seena, Jay P. Singh, Helen Doll, and Martin Grann. 2012. "Use of Risk Assessment Instruments to Predict Violence and Antisocial Behavior in 73 Samples Involving 24,827 People: Systematic Review and Meta-Analysis." *BMJ* 345:e4692.
Fellner, Jamie. 2013. "Race and Drugs." In *The Oxford Handbook of Ethnicity, Crime, and Immigration*, edited by Sandra Bucerius and Michael Tonry. New York: Oxford University Press.
Fisher, Franklin M., and Joseph B. Kadane. 1983. "Empirically Based Sentencing Guidelines and Ethical Considerations." In *Research on Sentencing: The Search for Reform*, edited by Alfred Blumstein. Washington, DC: National Academy Press.
Fletcher, George P. 1978. *Rethinking Criminal Law*. Boston: Little, Brown.
Flores, Anthony W., Kristen Bechtel, and Christopher T. Lowenkamp. 2016. "False Positives, False Negatives, and False Analyses: A Rejoinder to 'Machine Bias: There's Software Used across the Country to Predict Future Criminals. And It's Biased Against Blacks.'" *Federal Probation* 80:38–46.
Frase, Richard S. 2009*a*. "Limiting Excessive Prison Sentencing." *University of Pennsylvania Journal of Constitutional Law* 11(1):43–46.
———. 2009*b*. "What Explains Persistent Racial Disproportionality in Minnesota's Prison and Jail Population?" In *Crime and Justice: A Review of Re-*

search, vol. 38, edited by Michael Tonry. Chicago: University of Chicago Press.

Freiberg, Arie. 2014. *Fox and Freiberg's Sentencing: State and Federal Law in Victoria*. 3rd ed. Melbourne: Thomson Reuters.

Green, Ben, and Yiling Chen. 2019. "Disparate Interactions: An Algorithm-in-the-Loop Analysis of Fairness in Risk Assessments." Association for Computing Machinery (ACM) Conference on Fairness, Accountability, and Transparency (FAT* '19), Atlanta, January 29–31.

Harcourt, Bernard E. 2008. *Against Prediction*. Chicago: University of Chicago Press.

Hart, Stephen D., Christine Michie, and David J. Cooke. 2007. "Precision of Actuarial Risk Assessment Instruments: Evaluating the 'Margins of Error' of Group v. Individual Predictions of Violence." *British Journal of Psychiatry* 190:s60–s65.

Hester, Rhys, Richard S. Frase, Julian V. Roberts, and Kelly Lyn Mitchell. 2018. "Prior Record Enhancements at Sentencing: Unsettled Justifications and Unsettling Consequences." In *Crime and Justice: A Review of Research*, vol. 47, edited by Michael Tonry. Chicago: University of Chicago Press.

Hoffman, Peter B. 1976. "Salient Factor Score Validation: A 1972 Release Cohort." *Journal of Criminal Justice* 6:69–76.

———. 1983. "Screening for Risk: A Revised Salient Factor Score (SFS 81)." *Journal of Criminal Justice* 11:539–47.

———. 1995. "Twenty Years of Operational Use of a Risk Prediction Instrument: The United States Parole Commission's Salient Factor Score." *Journal of Criminal Justice* 22:477–94.

Holder, Eric. 2014. "Attorney General Eric Holder Speaks at the National Association of Criminal Defense Lawyers 57th Annual Meeting." Washington, DC: US Department of Justice. http://www.justice.gov/opa/speech/attorney-general-eric-holder-speaks-national-association-criminal-defense-lawyers-57th.

Husak, Douglas. 2019*a*. "The Metric of Punishment Severity: A Puzzle about the Principle of Proportionality." In *Proportionality in Punishment Philosophy and Policy*, edited by Michael Tonry. New York: Oxford University Press.

———. 2019*b*. "Why Legal Philosophers (Including Retributivists) Should Be Less Resistant to Risk-Based Sentencing." In *Predictive Sentencing: Normative and Empirical Perspectives*, edited by Jan W. de Keijser, Julian V. Roberts, and Jesper Ryberg. Oxford: Hart.

Imrey, Peter B., and A. Philip Dawid. 2015. "A Commentary on Statistical Assessment of Violence Recidivism Risk." *Statistics and Public Policy* 2:25–42.

Kant, Immanuel. 2017. *The Metaphysics of Morals*. Rev. ed. Translated by M. Gregor. (Originally published 1797.)

Knapp, Kay. 1984. *The Impact of the Minnesota Sentencing Guidelines: Three-Year Evaluation*. St. Paul: Minnesota Sentencing Guidelines Commission.

Lappi-Seppälä, Tapio. 2011. "Sentencing and Punishment in Finland: The Decline of the Repressive Ideal." In *Why Punish? How Much?* edited by Michael Tonry. New York: Oxford University Press.

———. 2016. "Nordic Sentencing." In *Sentencing Policies and Practices in Western Countries: Comparative and Cross-National Perspectives*, edited by Michael Tonry. Vol. 45 of *Crime and Justice: A Review of Research*, edited by Michael Tonry. Chicago: University of Chicago Press.

Laub, John H., and Richard J. Sampson. 2001. "Understanding Desistance from Crime." In *Crime and Justice: A Review of Research*, vol. 28, edited by Michael Tonry. Chicago: University of Chicago Press.

Lee, Youngjae. 2010. "Repeat Offenders and the Question of Desert." In *Previous Convictions at Sentencing: Theoretical and Applied Perspectives*, edited by Julian V. Roberts and Andrew von Hirsch. Oxford: Hart.

Lippke, Richard L. 2016. "The Ethics of Recidivist Premiums." In *The Routledge Handbook of Criminal Justice Ethics*, edited by Jonathan Jacobs and Jonathan Jackson. Abingdon, UK: Routledge.

Luban, David. 2007. *Legal Ethics and Human Dignity*. Cambridge: Cambridge University Press.

MacKenzie, Doris Layton. 2006. *What Works in Corrections: Reducing the Criminal Activities of Offenders and Delinquents*. Cambridge: Cambridge University Press.

Matravers, Matt. 2019. "Rootless Desert and Unanchored Censure." In *Penal Censure: Engagements Within and Beyond Desert Theory*, edited by Antje du Bois-Pedain and Anthony E. Bottoms. London: Hart/Bloomsbury.

McIntyre, Alison. 2014. "Doctrine of Double Effect." In *The Stanford Encyclopedia of Philosophy*, edited by Edward N. Zalta. Stanford, CA: Center for the Study of Language and Information, Stanford University. https://plato.stanford.edu/archives/win2014/entries/double-effect/.

Mill, John Stuart. 1997. *The Subjection of Women*. New York: Dover. (Originally published 1869.)

Minnesota Sentencing Guidelines Commission. 1980. *Report to the Legislature, 1 January 1980*. St. Paul: Minnesota Sentencing Guidelines Commission.

Monahan John. 1981. *The Clinical Prediction of Violent Behavior*. Washington, DC: National Institute of Mental Health.

———. 1983. "Ethical Issues in Prediction of Criminal Violence." In *Solutions to Ethical and Legal Problems in Social Research*, edited by Robert F. Boruch and Joe S. Cecil. New York: Academic Press.

———. 2017. "Risk Assessment in Sentencing." In *Reforming Criminal Justice: Punishment, Incarceration, and Release*, edited by Erik Luna. Phoenix: Arizona State University Press (for Academy for Justice).

Monahan, John, and Jennifer L. Skeem. 2016. "Risk Assessment in Criminal Sentencing." *Annual Review of Clinical Psychology* 12:489–513.

Monahan, Kathryn, Laurence Steinberg, and Alex R. Piquero. 2015. "Juvenile Justice Policy and Practice: A Developmental Perspective." In *Crime and Justice: A Review of Research*, vol. 44, edited by Michael Tonry. Chicago: University of Chicago Press.

Morris, Norval. 1974. *The Future of Imprisonment*. Chicago: University of Chicago Press.

Morris, Norval, and Marc Miller. 1985. "Predictions of Dangerousness." In *Crime and Justice: An Annual Review of Research*, vol. 6, edited by Michael Tonry and Norval Morris. Chicago: University of Chicago Press.

Morris, Norval, and Michael Tonry. 1990. *Between Prison and Probation*. New York: Oxford University Press.

Nagin, Daniel S., Frances T. Cullen, and Cheryl Lero Jonson. 2009. "Imprisonment and Reoffending." In *Crime and Justice: A Review of Research*, vol. 38, edited by Michael Tonry. Chicago: University of Chicago Press.

Ostrom, Brian J., and Neal B. Kauder. 2012. "The Evolution of Offender Risk Assessment in Virginia." *Federal Sentencing Reporter* 25:161–67.

Pereboom, Derk. 2014. *Free Will, Agency, and Meaning in Life*. Oxford: Oxford University Press.

Pifferi, Michele. 2012. "Individualization of Punishment and the Rule of Law: Reshaping Legality in the United States and Europe between the 19th and the 20th Century." *American Journal of Legal History* 52:325–76.

———. 2016. *Reinventing Punishment: A Comparative History of Criminology and Penology in the 19th and 20th Century*. Oxford: Oxford University Press.

Rawls, John. 1958. "Justice as Fairness." *Philosophical Review* 67:164–94.

Reitz, Kevin. 2010. "The Illusion of Proportionality: Desert and Repeat Offenders." In *Previous Convictions at Sentencing: Theoretical and Applied Perspectives*, edited by Julian V. Roberts and Andrew von Hirsch. Oxford: Hart.

Roberts, Julian V. 2008. *Punishing Persistent Offenders: Exploring Community and Offender Perspectives*. Oxford: Oxford University Press.

———. 2011. "The Future of State Punishment: The Role of Public Opinion in Sentencing." In *Retributivism Has a Past: Has It a Future?* edited by Michael Tonry. New York: Oxford University Press.

Roberts, Julian V., and Richard S. Frase. 2019. "The Problematic Role of Prior Record Enhancements in Predictive Sentencing." In *Predictive Sentencing: Normative and Empirical Perspectives*, edited by Jan W. de Keijser, Julian V. Roberts, and Jesper Ryberg. Oxford: Hart.

Roberts, Julian V., and Andrew von Hirsch. 2010. *Previous Convictions at Sentencing: Theoretical and Applied Perspectives*. Oxford: Hart.

Ryberg, Jesper. 2001. "Recidivism, Multiple Offending, and Legal Justice." *Danish Yearbook of Philosophy* 36:69–94.

———. 2019. "Risk and Retribution: On the Possibility of Reconciling Considerations of Dangerousness and Desert." In *Predictive Sentencing: Normative and Empirical Perspectives*, edited by Jan W. de Keijser, Julian V. Roberts, and Jesper Ryberg. Oxford: Hart.

Slobogin, Chris. 2019. "A Defense of Modern Risk-Based Sentencing." In *Predictive Sentencing: Normative and Empirical Perspectives*, edited by Jan W. de Keijser, Julian V. Roberts, and Jesper Ryberg. Oxford: Hart.

Starr, Sonja. 2014. "Evidence-Based Sentencing and the Scientific Rationalization of Discrimination." *Stanford Law Review* 66:803–72.

Tappan, Paul. 1947. "Who Is the Criminal?" *American Sociological Review* 12:96–102.

Tonry, Michael. 1987. "Prediction and Classification: Legal and Ethical Issues." In *Prediction and Classification: Criminal Justice Decision Making*, edited by Don M. Gottfredson and Michael Tonry. Vol. 9 of *Crime and Justice: A Review of Research*, edited by Michael Tonry and Norval Morris. Chicago: University of Chicago Press.

———. 1994. "Proportionality, Parsimony, and Interchangeability of Punishments." In *Penal Theory and Penal Practice*, edited by R. A. Duff, S. E. Marshall, R. E. Dobash, and R. P. Dobash. Manchester: Manchester University Press.

———. 1996. *Sentencing Matters*. New York: Oxford University Press.

———. 1997. "Ethnicity, Crime, and Immigration." In *Ethnicity, Crime, and Immigration: Comparative and Cross-National Perspectives*, edited by Michael Tonry. Vol. 21 of *Crime and Justice: A Review of Research*, edited by Michael Tonry. Chicago: University of Chicago Press.

———. 2014. "Can Deserts Be Just in an Unjust World?" In *Liberal Criminal Theory: Essays for Andreas von Hirsch*, edited by A. P. Simester, Ulfrid Neumann, and Antje du Bois-Pedain. Oxford: Hart.

———. 2016. *Sentencing Fragments*. New York: Oxford University Press.

———. 2018*a*. "An Honest Politician's Guide to Deterrence: Certainty, Severity, Celerity, and Parsimony." In *Deterrence, Choice, and Crime: Contemporary Perspectives*, edited by Daniel S. Nagin, Francis T. Cullen, and Cheryl Lero Jonson. New York: Routledge.

———. 2018*b*. "Punishment and Human Dignity: Sentencing Principles for Twenty-First-Century America." In *Crime and Justice: A Review of Research*, vol. 47, edited by Michael Tonry. Chicago: University of Chicago Press.

Tonry, Michael, and Colleen Chambers. 2012. "Juvenile Justice Cross-Nationally Considered." In *The Oxford Handbook of Juvenile Crime and Juvenile Justice*, edited by Barry C. Feld and Donna M. Bishop. New York: Oxford University Press.

Tracey, Paul E., Marvin E. Wolfgang, and Robert M. Figlio. 1990. *Delinquency Careers in Two Birth Cohorts*. New York: Plenum.

Travis, Jeremy, Bruce Western, and Steve Redburn, eds. 2014. *The Growth of Incarceration in the United States: Exploring Causes and Consequences*. Washington, DC: National Academies Press.

Virginia Criminal Sentencing Commission. 2014. *Manual*. 17th ed. Richmond: Virginia Criminal Sentencing Commission.

von Hirsch, Andrew. 1985. *Past or Future Crimes: Deservedness and Dangerousness in the Sentencing of Criminals*. New Brunswick, NJ: Rutgers University Press.

von Hirsch, Andrew, Martin Wasik, and Judith Greene. 1989. "Punishments in the Community and the Principles of Desert." *Rutgers Law Review* 20:595–618.

Waldron, Jeremy. 2014. "What Do the Philosophers Have Against Dignity?" Public Law and Legal Theory Research Series. Working Paper 14-59. New York: New York University Law School.

Wollstonecraft, Mary. 2009. *A Vindication of the Rights of Women*. Oxford: Oxford University Press. (Originally published 1792.)

Yang, Min, Stephen C. Wong, and Jeremy Coid. 2010. "The Efficacy of Violence Prediction: A Meta-Analytic Comparison of Nine Risk Assessment Tools." *Psychology Bulletin* 136:740–67.

Jeffery T. Ulmer

Criminal Courts as Inhabited Institutions: Making Sense of Difference and Similarity in Sentencing

ABSTRACT

An inhabited institutions perspective views institutions from the bottom up, as "inhabited" by individual and organizational actors who have agency, rather than as static, top-down structures. Criminal justice structures and policies, such as those that govern courts and their sentencing decisions, are dependent on court participants. From this perspective, several conclusions emerge. First, theory and methods in the study of courts and sentencing are out of balance: theories emphasize interpretation, culture, and processes, while empirical inquiries focus largely on statistical studies of aggregates and outcomes. Second, the inhabited institutions perspective blurs the lines between the discretions of specific participants such as prosecutors and judges. Rather than attempt to parse the discretion of individual actors, we should study the interactions that jointly produce discretionary decisions. Third, we should focus on specific organizational mechanisms that produce both uniformity and variation between courts. Finally, variation between courts in sentencing practices should be understood not as a nuisance in top-down imposition of sentencing policies, but as a valuable but underappreciated source of policy feedback and learning.

Intersections between organizational sociology and criminal court scholarship are seldom crossed. Organizational sociologists have paid little attention to criminal courts and punishment decisions, even though the

Electronically published February 7, 2019
Jeffery T. Ulmer is professor of sociology and criminology, Penn State University.

© 2019 by The University of Chicago. All rights reserved.
0192-3234/2019/0048-0002$10.00

court system is among the most consequential institutions in society. Scholars of courts and sentencing have made only sporadic use of concepts from organizational sociology. This is curious, given that decision-making dynamics, interorganizational relationships, and organizational and environment influences play out in criminal courts every day. Research on organizational processes within criminal courts can cross-pollinate both criminal justice studies and organizational sociology.

Individuals and organizations in courts continually navigate between formal rules and informal norms, expectations of diverse constituencies, law and practicality, and predictability and uncertainty. They have varying amounts of agency and power. Differences in criminal courts' conformity, uniformity, and variation in applying laws and policies offer an opportunity to test and apply general theories of complex organizations. These approaches focus on local organizational practices, actor agency, sense making, and variation in conformity to institutional rules. "Just as social psychologists call attention to 'individual differences'... students of organization have increasingly attended to differences among organizations in their response to the 'same' environment" (Scott 2008, p. 160).

I have several aims in writing this essay. The first is to present the "inhabited institutions" perspective and related concepts from organizational sociology. They provide rich and informative ways to understand and explain sentencing processes and outcomes. To lay a foundation for later detailed discussion I introduce a specialized vocabulary used in organizational sociology. The perspective views institutions as "inhabited" by individual and organizational actors who have agency, rather than as static, top-down structures. In this view, organizational participants constantly interpret and make sense of rules and structures. Organizational order and culture emerge from, and are changed by, participants' actions and interactions. From this perspective, implementation of criminal justice policies, including those that govern courts and sentencing decisions, are dependent on the people and organizations that inhabit them.

Second, I apply and connect the inhabited institutions approach to well-known theoretical frameworks in the study of criminal courts and sentencing, in order to illustrate that they exemplify broader themes in the sociology of organizations. I draw out close parallels between the court communities and focal concerns perspectives that animate much research on courts and sentencing and the more generic inhabited institutions approach. Third, I discuss selected areas of research that illustrate inhabited institutions themes and concepts, centering around conformity and variation in courts and their practices. These include death penalty sentencing, variation and similarity in court case processing practices, sentencing guidelines, and relationships between Native American tribal justice jurisdiction and federal courts. Finally, I suggest implications that flow from the melding of an inhabited institutions approach with theory and research on courts and sentencing.

Viewing courts and their workgroups as inhabited institutions enables scholars to use different theoretical lenses and look beyond examination of disparity in sentencing or case processing outcomes (though that is of continuing value). Melding of the inhabited institutions perspective and theoretical ideas in the study of courts and sentencing enables us to reframe old questions and ask better ones.

Several conclusions emerge. First, theory and methods are out of balance. Influential theories such as those that focus on court communities and focal concerns emphasize interpretation, culture, and processes, while methods and empirical inquiries increasingly rely on sophisticated statistical studies of aggregates and outcomes. We need more qualitative and multimethod research. Second, application of the inhabited institutions perspective to courts and sentencing blurs the lines between the discretions of specific participants, most notably prosecutors and judges. We would do well to study the interactions that jointly produce discretionary decisions. Third, we should orient research to studying organizational mechanisms that produce both uniformity and variation in application of laws and policies. Finally, variations between courts and their sentencing practices enable organizational learning. Variations in practices and outcomes are often viewed as a problem in top-down imposition of sentencing policy. Variations are better understood as valuable, and as yet underappreciated, sources of policy feedback and learning.

I. Inhabited Institutions

Neo-institutional theory in organizational sociology contains a rich set of generic concepts for describing and analyzing institutions and the organizations within them. Bourdieu (1977) coined the term "field" to refer to an arena in which individual or collective actors engage in "mutually organized striving" toward mutually recognized goals and develop distinctive conventions, rules, meanings, and practices (Martin 2003). Fields are sets of interacting groups, organizations, and agencies oriented around a common set of activities, and useful for analyzing a wide variety of organizational settings (Aldrich and Ruef 2006). Institutional fields are bounded by a shared normative system and cultural meanings (Scott 2008). Fligstein and McAdam (2011, p. 3) refer to institutional fields as "social order[s] where actors (who can be individual or collective) interact with knowledge of one another under a set of common understandings about the purposes of the field, the relationships in the field (including who has power and why), and the field's rules." Field boundaries are necessarily overlapping and are to some extent defined according to the research questions and focus of researchers (Aldrich and Ruef 2006). Here, I characterize court systems as institutional fields, in which laws, formal rules, and policies occasion opportunities for local court sense making, adaptation, and contention. However, fields can be conceptualized differently for different purposes: the criminal justice system itself could be considered a field, as could state court systems, policing, and different sectors of the correctional system.

A. Field Isomorphism

Organizations within a field display varying amounts of conformity to formal regulatory systems. This raises questions about the factors that explain the degree to which organizations in a field display similarity of form and activity, usually referred to as "isomorphism" (Morrill and McKee 1993). DiMaggio and Powell's (1983) typology, well-known throughout sociology, identifies three types of isomorphism in organizational fields: coercive, normative, and mimetic. Coercive isomorphism involves forced or coerced compliance by authorities. Normative isomorphism involves conformity motivated by institutionalized norms, behavioral expectations, and perceived legitimacy. Mimetic isomorphism involves conformity through the routine application of shared cultural and cognitive lenses. All three types of isomorphism are commonly seen in courts and the organizations interacting in them.

Scott (2008) describes three primary types of influence that produce conformity within a field: regulative (corresponding to coercive isomorphism), which entails coercive pressure toward conformity through formal consequences, costs, and benefits; normative (i.e., normative isomorphism), in which organizations conform through perceived fieldwide, typically informal, normative obligations, expectations, or shared morality; and cultural-cognitive (i.e., mimetic isomorphism), which involves conformity through shared meanings and common efforts at sense making (Weick 1995). The last involves the operation of constitutive rules that "take the general form: X counts as Y in context C" (Scott 2008, p. 64). Constitutive rules produce conformity by reducing uncertainty and devising categories and classifications that simplify complex decision-making processes. Examples of constitutive rules include perceptual shorthands, cognitive attributions, schema, and heuristics.

Laws, policies, and the courts that apply and make sense of them are an apt example of the potential importance of normative and cultural-cognitive influences, apart from any coercive pressures that might exist. Emphasizing the inherent uncertainty of decision-making and the frequent ambiguity of external constraints or expectations, Scott (2008, p. 54) observes, "law is better conceived of as an occasion for sense making and collective interpretation, relying more on cognitive and normative than coercive elements for its effects." In fact, "recent neo-institutional scholars argue that regulatory activities thought to embody coercive pressures often depend more on normative and cognitive elements" (Scott 2008, p. 136).

B. Organizational Variation

Neo-institutional scholars are fascinated by organizational differences and variation and have identified mechanisms through which the same institutional rules result in differences in organizational adherence (Aldrich and Ruef 2006; Scott 2008; Fligstein and McAdam 2011). Scott (2008) describes four: varying translations of institutional rules; varying attributes, relationships, or cultures that affect responses to institutional pressures; adaptations or innovations by users of rules; and strategic responses to environments by actors or organizations. The phenomena of variable organizational coupling between institutionalized rules and practices encompass all of these mechanisms.

1. *Organizational Coupling.* The term "coupling" is used in at least two different ways. The first refers to the degree of correspondence between formal institutional norms or rules and organizational practice. According to Meyer and Rowan (1977), organizations maintain the appearance of standardized, legitimated, formal structures, often through symbols and rituals that signal adherence to "macro myths." In criminal justice, for example, such macro myths might be equality and uniformity before the law, due process, and crime control through deterrence and

incapacitation. But exceptions to these rules will emerge in line within specific contexts that "highlight the inadequacies of the prescriptions of generalized myths" (Meyer and Rowan 1977, p. 356). Clashes among competing organizational goals and interests create "conflicts and inconsistencies in an institutionalized organization's efforts to conform to the ceremonial rules of production" (Meyers and Rowan 1977, p. 355). For example, court actors may believe both that justice requires comparable outcomes in comparable cases and that institutional resources must be preserved by encouraging or coercing most defendants to plead guilty. These goals can easily conflict in practice, as some of otherwise similar defendants receive rewards and others extra punishment depending on whether they plead guilty. In other words, macro myths and their categorical rules are often at odds with organizational realities, with competing interests, or with the contextual circumstances and constraints. The result is localized adaptation and selective circumvention of formalized rules and structures of control.

Loose coupling enables organizations to adhere to institutional macro myths and mandates while adapting practices to fit local contingencies and interests (Weick 1976). As Hallett (2010, p. 54) suggests, "macro myths provide legitimacy, but they often conflict with practical activity," which gives rise to local practices that are loosely within institutional norms and vary in substantively important ways across organizational contexts. One example of this sense of coupling is demonstrated by the "liberation hypothesis." It argues that informal discretion and potential for disparity are heightened in routine processing of less serious offenses concerning which legal norms and practice are only loosely coupled (Spohn and Cederbloom 1991). However, concerning serious, more highly visible crimes, court system practices become more tightly coupled to legal norms, decreasing informal use of discretion and limiting opportunities for disparity.

The second use of the terms *loose* or *tight* coupling refers to the connection between criminal justice organizations or stages: coupling between police and prosecutors, for example, or between courts and local political entities (Eisenstein, Flemming, and Nardulli 1988; Nardulli, Eisenstein, and Flemming 1988). John Hagan made both senses of organizational coupling central to his conceptualization of the criminal justice system. He argued that American criminal justice looks less like an integrated institutional system and more like a set of loosely coupled organizations that, under normal circumstances, "have a unique capacity to absorb changes in the surrounding political environment" (Hagan 1989, p. 119). For example, individual criminal justice organizations may become loosely coupled from one another and from centralized institutional rules, allowing the justice system to maintain the appearance of a legitimated formal structure while the activities of specific organizations within it have capacity to respond to their own organizational contexts, according to the interests of the actors and organizations involved. However, under certain circumstances, such as policy changes and differences in organizational environments, criminal justice organizations function with greater coordination and interdependence—tighter coupling. This variation in coupling has consequences for punishment and disparities within it (Hagan 1989).

2. *Inhabited Institutions and Processual Orders.* In light of this tendency toward localized adaptation and selective circumvention of formalized rules and structures, Weick (1995) argues that scholars should view institutions as inhabited by individual and organizational actors with agency, and argues that the actors' sense making drives organizational functioning (cf. Morrill and McKee 1993). Recent research in education policy has applied and extended this inhabited institutions perspective. Hallet's (2010) work on implementation of national education reforms showed how local teachers diversely interpreted and adapted to accountability structures imposed from above and meant to create uniformity, standardization, and clarity. Similarly, Everitt (2012, p. 204) argued that "the degree to which local practices and institutional mandates are coupled is contingent upon how actors negotiate that relationship through practical work activity with, and among, each other in specific social contexts." He elaborated: "If practice gets built from the ground up, so to speak, in a context where institutional rules come from the top down, as is the case with accountability mandates in education, then it is no surprise that varying degrees of coupling between individual activities and institutional rules persist.... Teachers both follow and deviate from external standards, but for different reasons depending on how they have made sense of experiences to that point in their careers" (Everitt 2012, p. 218). Hall (1997, p. 401), in discussing local implementation of national education policy, similarly observed that macro policies and rules, and the institutional authority they represent, limit some kinds of action and facilitate others. Thus, externally imposed structures, rules, and macro myths set boundaries and produce conformity through regulative, normative, and cultural-cognitive influences. At the same time, though, "later actors may reinforce,

clarify, subvert, or amend initial intentions and content" (Hall 1997, p. 401).

In this inhabited institutions view, the effects of institutional rules or policies on local practices are empirically indeterminate. Symbolic interactionist conceptions of policy likewise refer to policy formation and implementation as "the transformation of intentions" (Estes and Edmonds 1981; Hall and McGinty 1997). According to Hall (1997, p. 401), "policy actors, dependent upon those who follow them to complete their intentions, set the terms that both limit and facilitate later actions."

Anselm Strauss (1993) described the mechanism by which local organizational adaptations produce, maintain, and transform norms and practices as processual order. Processual order is the informal social order that continually emerges from strategic interactions between organizational participants. These interactions include negotiation, persuasion, manipulation, education, threat, and coercion. In other words, norms, decision rules, routines, and shared meanings emerge, endure, and change in organizations through interaction processes. Within this theoretical framework, all organizational culture is processual order. This is a dynamic, action-oriented view of organizational culture and order. They do not simply come about by fiat and remain static; they are constantly produced, reproduced, and changed through the actions of participants.

The importance and predominance of various forms of strategic interaction vary between organizations. Processual orders and their informal norms, conventions, and practices are "sedimented" outcomes (Berger and Luckmann 1967) of past strategic interaction processes. The role of negotiation in the development, maintenance, and change of informal organizational norms provides an important example. Informal norms and arrangements often emerge as negotiated solutions to problems not covered by existing rules, ambiguous or conflicting goals, or conflicts over resources. These solutions persist until challenging new situations render them inadequate. Then, new negotiation processes occur through which informal arrangements are adapted in an attempt to resolve the new problems. Local organizations thus produce informal cultures that have important consequences for how larger institutional rules are embedded in and transformed by local practice.

Of course, not all organizational actors have equal amounts of agency and power to shape processual orders and organizational practices. Some are in stronger or weaker positions to manipulate situations or constrain others' choices, to exercise or threaten coercion, to control resources that others depend on, or to set the terms of negotiation.

II. Courts Communities as Inhabited Institutions
Criminal justice is largely local in the United States and administered at state and county levels. Local variation in implementation of sentencing policies is a persistent theme in sociological research on state criminal courts (Myers and Talarico 1987; Nardulli, Eisenstein, and Flemming 1988; Flemming, Nardulli, and Eisenstein 1992; Dixon 1995; Ulmer 1997; Engen and Steen 2000). American criminal courts and their practices are well-described by the inhabited institutions perspective. That is, courts, their case processing and sentencing decisions, and their relationships to their larger institutional environments exemplify institutional fields, organizational isomorphism and variation, organizational coupling, and processual orders. The long-standing theme of conformity and variation between courts' sentencing practices relative to broader institutional policies or norms fits the focus of the inhabited institutions perspective. Widely used theoretical frameworks for understanding courts and sentencing are highly compatible with the inhabited institutions perspective, and explicitly incorporate concepts such as processual order and organizational coupling.

The court community model is one major lens through which to view such variation; it views courts as distinctive processual orders based on participants' shared workplace and on interdependent working relations between key sponsoring agencies such as the prosecutor's office, judges' bench, and defense bar (Eisenstein, Flemming, and Nardulli 1988; Flemming, Nardulli, and Eisenstein 1992). In turn, prosecutors' offices vary according to organizational type and prosecutorial style; the judges' bench varies in terms of ideology, consensus, and relations with prosecutors; and local defense bars vary in their adversarial vigor, resources, levels of experience, and relations with prosecutors and judges (Ulmer and Kramer 1998).

Individual representatives of these sponsoring agencies form courtroom workgroups that interact to process cases and make sentencing decisions (Eisenstein and Jacob 1977). They develop distinctive social orders that produce local organizational cultures, which in turn shape formal and informal case processing and sentencing norms. For example, court communities typically have locally distinctive, informal, and ever-evolving case processing and sentencing norms, or "going rates" as a key dimension of their processual order (Sudnow1965; Eisenstein, Flemming, and Nardulli 1988). Dixon (1995) demonstrates how workgroup case processing strategies differ across courts that vary in their social, political, and organizational contexts. These going rates often provide members of courtroom workgroups with cognitive and interactional "templates" for case processing strategies, typical plea bargaining terms, and sentences and are continually open to modification. Court communities' going rates or informal case processing norms thus represent a pragmatic processual order (Ulmer 2005).

Another key part of court communities' processual order is its "plea agenda." Nardulli, Eisenstein, and Flemming (1988) developed the concept to refer to sets of key "bargaining chips," concessions negotiated as a part of routine plea bargaining. The plea agenda represents "what is on the table" and the usual plea negotiation strategies in typical case processing. More broadly, plea agendas refer to issues, conventions, practices, tactics, and concessions around which the guilty plea process routinely centers. The plea agenda is a key ingredient of court community culture. Research has demonstrated variation in plea agendas among county courts in Pennsylvania (Ulmer and Kramer 1996, 1998; Ulmer 1997) and federal district courts (Ulmer 2005) and the importance of these variations for sentencing processes and outcomes.

Thus, court communities develop processual orders that produce distinctive local organizational cultures, and variations in informal norms and practices. Going rates and other informal case processing norms such as plea agendas represent the sedimented outcomes of past case processing or sentencing problem-solving through negotiation, unilateral manipulation, or adversarial conflict. These norms form an organizational "stock of knowledge" (Berger and Luckmann 1967) that can be drawn upon in similar situations. Such norms persist until perplexing new cases render them inadequate; new workgroups may adapt new informal arrangements to resolve the new problems.

However, court communities exist within a broader set of institutional fields. Courts' (and the organizations interacting within them) decision-making processes are constrained by overarching fieldwide rules, such as criminal laws, sentencing guidelines, mandatory minimum laws, administrative rules, legislative mandates, and policy and political influences. Criminal justice institutional fields therefore promote coercive, mimetic, or normative isomorphism in many ways and may exert strong pressures on courts to conform to law and policy. Particularly interesting (and understudied) are the mechanisms that produce cultural-cognitive influence, shaping "taken for granted reality" by establishing constitutive rules. Recall that cultural-cognitive influence entails the formulation and spread of shared cognitive meanings and common tools for sense making, and constitutive rules reduce uncertainty by devising categories and classifications that simplify complex decision-making processes. Examples include informal "rules of thumb," stereotypes, scripts, and cognitive schema.

At the same time, courts interpret formal institutional rules in locally distinctive ways that produce variation in organizational compliance (Kautt 2002; Ulmer 2005). This is what it means to speak of courts communities as inhabited institutions; courts are governed by institutional rules and laws but are inhabited by courtroom workgroup actors with agency and court community organizations with their own informal norms, culture, politics, and constraints. Sentencing guidelines, for example, and other externally imposed rules and policies may be field rules, but they may be interpreted and applied differently across contexts, illustrating a fundamental tension between formally rational reform efforts designed to promote uniformity in punishment, and substantively rational interests that emphasize flexibility, individualization, and localization of punishment (Ulmer and Kramer 1996).

Substantive rationality in legal decision-making refers to criteria guided by, or in service of, ideological factors and goals external to the law (Westby 1991). Substantive rationality in courtroom workgroup sentencing practices is thus a type of rationality that is oriented toward flexible and individualized decision-making in service of a potentially wide variety of extralegal goals (for helpful theoretical reviews, see Savelsberg [1992]; Marsh [2000]; Mears and Field [2000]). For example, substantive goals could focus on the welfare of the offender, the victim, or the community (Levin 1977). Other substantive goals could center on crime control or on organizational interests such as efficiency. The flexibility inherent in substantive rationality also permits the possibility of bias, discrimination, and unwarranted disparity.

Locally interpreted substantive rationality in court communities coexists in tension with formally rational criminal justice policies (Ulmer and Kramer 1998). Practical considerations that present exceptions to institutional field rules often result in circumvention of formally rational law and may inject value-based or ideological criteria into the process.

Savelsberg (1992, p. 1347) argues that "serious structural and cultural impediments in modern society" prevent formal adherence to neoclassical sentencing reforms like guidelines or mandatory minimums. Dixon (1995, p. 1158) notes: "the predominant rationality in the organization of sentencing varies across courts" in ways that produce consequential variations in punishment across social contexts.

Court communities and their workgroups, then, are an arena in which Scott's (2008) mechanisms of organizational variation play out: varying translations of institutional rules; varying attributes, relationships, or culture that affect responses to institutional pressures; adaptations or innovations by users of rules; and strategic responses to environments by actors or organizations. Criminal justice institutional fields contain rules and forces that foster isomorphism, but they are inhabited by court communities and their sense making, problem solving, negotiating, and by conflicting courtroom workgroups. Power imbalances exist between sponsoring agencies and courtroom workgroup members, and these imbalances shape the directions of variation from or conformity to institutional rules.

Conformity and deviation from sentencing guidelines provide an illustration. Guidelines are institutional rules, but over time exceptions emerge that "highlight the inadequacies of the prescriptions of generalized myths" (Meyer and Rowan 1977, p. 356). They take the form of cases or situations in which courtroom workgroup members feel the guidelines do not provide appropriate recommendations (Kaiser and Spohn 2014). Clashes among competing organizational goals create "conflicts and inconsistencies in an institutionalized organization's efforts to conform to the ceremonial rules of production" (Meyers and Rowan 1977, p. 355). The result is localized adaptations and selective circumventions. Local courts may become loosely coupled from one another and from centralized institutional rules, allowing the justice system to maintain the appearance of a legitimated formal structure while the activities of specific court communities respond to their distinctive organizational contexts. Informal norms such as going rates and plea agendas provide a template for workgroups' sense making (Weick 1995). Local norms, then, shape patterns of guidelines compliance and deviation in ways that are consistent with local court community culture and contexts but inconsistent with institutional rules.

Conceptualizing court conformity to institutional rules as various types of isomorphism does not imply that conformity is inherently "positive," desired, or beneficial to society. Likewise, organizational variation in practices between courts is not inherently "negative," problematic, or the source of injustice. Conformity and deviance are neither inherently positive nor negative, functional nor dysfunctional. Deviance, for example, is widely recognized as a potential engine of innovation and social change. Similarly, organizational conformity between courts does not necessarily entail justice, fairness, safety, or other socially desired outcomes, and between-court variation does not inherently signal unwarranted disparity, injustice, or socially undesired outcomes.

A. Focal Concerns: Courtroom Workgroup Sense Making

The focal concerns perspective directs attention to case-by-case interpretations of substantive rationality goals by individuals within the courtroom workgroup (Ulmer and Johnson 2004; Kramer and Ulmer 2009). It emphasizes particular kinds of substantively rational criteria that are embedded in the culture and organization of court communities. Building on earlier theoretical work (e.g., Albonetti 1991), it posits that three subjectively defined considerations—blameworthiness, protection of the community, and practical constraints—determine punishment decisions (Steffensmeier, Ulmer, and Kramer 1998). The focal concerns perspective "begins with the assumption that social control agents make sanctioning decisions in a context of managerial uncertainty based on a limited knowledge of the offenders under scrutiny and within a larger institutional environment that prioritizes both efficiency and legitimacy." It argues that the "focal concerns... are the vehicles by which social context intrudes on sanctioning decisions and by which substantive rationalities are brought to bear within formalistic social control regimes" (Lin, Grattet, and Petersilia 2010, pp. 762–63).

According to Albonetti (1991), sentencing suffers from operating in a context of bounded rationality (March and Simon 1958): court actors make important decisions under conditions of uncertainty, sometimes due to insufficient information, and sometimes due to other factors. Even when more information is available, the risk and seriousness of recidivism are never fully predictable for a particular defendant, a defendant's moral character is never fully knowable, and human decision-making processes have built-in limitations to the amount and complexity of information that can be considered. Judges and other court community actors make situational imputations about defendants' character and expected future behavior based on "perceptual shorthands" (Skolnick 1966), and assess the implications of these imputed characteristics in terms of their focal concerns. Court actors seem mostly to make character imputations based on legally relevant factors but may also consciously and unconsciously take account of stereotypes and schema based on defendants' characteristics such as race, ethnicity, gender, age, and social class.

Use of and reliance on these focal concerns characterizes courts generally, but the meaning, relative emphasis and priority, and situational interpretation of them are embedded in local legal and organizational cultures and surrounding sociopolitical contexts (Kramer and Ulmer 2009). Organizational norms concerning offender and offense characteristics that indicate heightened or lessened blameworthiness or dangerousness, and cases implicating salient practical constraints, can be seen as the kind of constitutive rules described by Scott (2008). Definitions of what kinds of offenses and offenders are especially blameworthy or dangerous, for example, are likely to vary with individual workgroup members' attitudes or ideologies, local sociopolitical and demographic contexts, and crime rates and patterns. The significance of practical constraints and consequences is likely to be shaped by factors such as local crime rates and patterns, court size, caseload characteristics, court resources, and local and state correctional resources (Ulmer and Johnson 2004). For example, the degree to which a court community's culture emphasizes efficiency as a goal will affect the salience of the need to move cases quickly by eliciting guilty pleas.

The interpretation of focal concerns and the navigation of formal rules like guidelines or mandatory minimums are forms of courtroom workgroup sense making, and manifestations of courts' nature as inhabited institutions. Just as the schools and teachers studied by Hall (1997), Hallet (2010), and Everitt (2012) diversely interpreted and adapted accountability structures imposed from above to create uniformity, standardization, and clarity, courtroom workgroups interpret and adapt laws, guidelines, policies, and institutional mandates. Varying degrees of coupling exist between court community activities and institutional rules, as workgroups apply and deviate from rules as they make sense in light of local contexts and interests.

III. Empirical Illustrations

Several areas of research illustrate how the notion of inhabited institutions aids understanding of court communities and their workgroups.

These include isomorphism and mechanisms of conformity between courts, but also variations in how court communities and workgroups navigate, negotiate, and make sense of sentencing guidelines, mandatory minimums, and other externally imposed policies. A full review of this literature is beyond my scope here. Instead, I examine selected subjects and studies.

A. The Influence of Individual Workgroup Members

Workgroup sense making and practices surrounding larger institutional rules loom large in criminal justice fields. Judges are the most visible workgroup members; much scholarly attention has been paid to judicial discretion. Johnson (2006), for example, examined the role of judges' personal characteristics on contextual and inter-judge variations in sentences in Pennsylvania. He found that between-judge variation accounted for a modest but meaningful proportion of overall sentencing variation. Black and Hispanic judges sentenced all offenders, and particularly minority offenders, more leniently than did white judges. Male judges sentenced female offenders more leniently. Wooldredge (2010) examined inter-judge variation in sentencing among 18 judges in Ohio and found wide variations in the effects of race, gender, or financial means. Half of the judges' sentences showed no significant influence by extralegal effects. However, five judges sentenced young black males less harshly than whites, and four sentenced them more harshly.

Anderson and Spohn (2010) examined sentencing decisions of judges in three federal district courts and found that variations between judges were largely accounted for by case and defendant characteristics. However, they concluded that judges considered legal and extralegal factors quite differently, varied greatly in the lengths of sentences they imposed as downward departures from guidelines as well as in their responses to prosecutors' motions for sentence reductions based on defendants having providing substantial assistance in prosecution of other cases. They also found that judges varied greatly in their responses to offenders' gender, employment status, and pretrial release status.

Johnson and DiPietro (2012) documented substantial differences among Pennsylvania counties in the use of intermediate punishments in place of imprisonment and in referrals to rehabilitative programs, in ways that seemed connected to local criminal justice resources and funding. Use of intermediate punishments also varied between individual judges within counties, but this was not explained by demographic differences between judges. This variation suggests differing judicial sense making about rehabilitative programs and also perhaps different focal concerns about community protection and practical constraints. Clair and Winter (2016) conducted interviews with 59 judges in a northeastern state that illustrated judges' perceptions of the influence of race on case processing. Some judges attributed racial disproportionality to differential treatment by themselves or others, while some attributed it to group differences in crime involvement resulting from different exposures to criminogenic conditions. Most judges (including most of those who explained disparities in terms of differential treatment) were reluctant to intervene to correct perceived disparities. A significant minority, however, actively used their sentencing decisions to address perceived biases. This research, then, suggests judges' individualized sense making and practices regarding racial disparity and its amelioration.

By contrast, Hester (2017) sheds light on novel sources of court isomorphism in South Carolina. His earlier quantitative research revealed less between-county variation in sentencing in South Carolina than is typical in findings concerning other states. Interviews with 13 trial judges pointed to the importance of a unique policy of judge rotation between counties. The rotation provided more interaction between judges and others across workgroups and court communities than is typical elsewhere and fostered "cross pollination" of informal norms. In terms of inhabited institutions, judicial rotation produced mimetic isomorphism through cultural-cognitive influence and shared perspectives on sense making, as well as normative influence through interaction and exchange. Judicial rotation led to "norm spreading" and "trading ideas" (Hester 2017, p. 227). However, differences among the rotating judges remained evident. Rotation "did not wash out all meaningful differences in the judges' approaches and sentencing philosophies," especially differing views and practices among judges and prosecutors in drug cases (p. 228). These between-judge differences enabled extensive "shopping" for lenient judges, even as judicial rotation blunted between-county differences in sentences.

Recent research shows how other workgroup members engage in localized sense making. Franklin (2010) found that prosecutorial charge dismissals reflected differences between counties in consideration of case-level and defendant factors (prior record, number and type of charges, gender, and age). He found that measures of racial composition and crime rates had little influence on prosecutorial charge reductions but that prosecutors in more conservative communities' were less likely to dismiss charges. Prosecutors in southern counties were less likely to dismiss charges against black defendants.

Hartley, Miller, and Spohn (2010) examined the effects of defense counsel on pretrial release, charge reductions, incarceration, and sentence length, using data from a random sample of Chicago offenders in 1993. They found no significant direct effects of attorney type, but that attorney type conditioned the effects of some case processing differences. Most notably, offenders represented by private attorneys incurred much more substantial trial penalties than did those represented by public defenders. Their explanation was that attorneys who are regular participants in the court community are more likely to secure more favorable outcomes for their clients. This, in turn, suggests that defense attorneys who are knowledgeable about court community norms and culture can obtain better outcomes for defendants.

A handful of studies have examined effects of courtroom workgroup familiarity and stability (Ulmer 1995; Hoskins-Haynes, Ruback, and Cusick 2010). Metcalfe (2016) examined the effect of courtroom workgroup familiarity and similarity on mode of conviction and time to disposition. She found that similarity and familiarity between the prosecutor and judge increased the likelihood of guilty pleas and reduced time to disposition. By contrast, defense attorney familiarity with other actors hindered plea bargaining.

Kim, Spohn, and Hedberg's (2015) study of federal courtroom workgroup pairings in three districts illustrates that sentencing is a complex collaborative process, influenced by the interactions between judges and prosecutors. Sentencing patterns varied substantially by judge, prosecutor, and judge-prosecutor dyad. Disparity between defendants was more attributable to the identity of the prosecutor than of the judge, and prosecutors moderated the sentencing influence of judges. Disparity patterns were distinctive in each of the three districts, with differing amounts of disparity attributable to the judge, the prosecutor, and the judge-prosecutor dyad. All of these studies and other similar research imply the importance of courtroom workgroup members' sense making and interactions.

B. Murder Sentencing

Emphasis on variation between local courts has been common in the general literature on courts and sentencing for decades but is underexamined in relation to murder case processing and death penalty decisions. The inhabited institutions perspective implies that administration of punishment of murder, including capital punishment, will not be fully understood until local decisional contexts are more fully mapped out. Garland (2010, p. 117) noted "the most important decisions about capital charging and sentencing remain matters for county-level decision makers." Paternoster (2012, p. 11) similarly observed: "What may be considerably more surprising, however, is that there is at least as much if not more variation in the inclination to impose the death penalty *within* death penalty states as there is *between* death penalty states."

Kramer, Ulmer, and Zajac (2017) examined disparities in administration of the death penalty in Pennsylvania. They collected basic statistical data on 4,274 homicide cases from 2000 to 2010. They then collected highly detailed data from courts and prosecutors' offices on a subset of 880 first-degree murder convictions in 18 counties that accounted for 87 percent of the state's murder convictions. Using propensity score methods to analyze first-degree murder convictions, they examined prosecutors' decisions to seek the death penalty, prosecutors' decisions to retract motions to seek the death penalty, and court decisions to sentence defendants to death or life without parole. The study focused primarily on racial and ethnic disparities, but other findings highlighted the importance of between-court variation in court community norms and practices. First, prosecutorial discretion loomed large in case processing and sentencing. Prosecutors filed motions seeking the death penalty in 36 percent of first-degree convictions but later retracted that filing in 46 percent of those cases. A predominant pattern emerged. Death penalty filings strongly predicted guilty pleas that, in turn, strongly predicted retraction of the death penalty motions. Second, there were very large differences between counties in the likelihood that prosecutors filed death penalty motions, that motions were retracted, and that courts imposed the death penalty. The county where a case was processed was the largest extralegal determinant of whether defendants faced or received the death penalty.

There were also notable differences related to defense counsel. Death penalty filings were less likely when public defenders represented defendants than when they had private or court-appointed attorneys. However, defendants represented by public defenders were more likely to receive the death penalty, and defendants represented by private attorneys were especially unlikely. These differences varied between counties. For example, public defenders in Philadelphia outperformed their peers elsewhere in avoiding the death penalty.

Baumer and Martin (2013) showed the importance of local variations and court contexts for noncapital murder in a study of effects of sociopolitical differences between counties on homicide conviction and sentencing. They analyzed nationwide murder data from Bureau of Justice Statistics files for 1988 that were merged with county contextual and General Social Survey data.[1] Multilevel analyses showed that murder convictions after jury trials (compared with acquittals) were more likely in more politically and religiously conservative counties. Defendants in more religiously conservative counties received longer sentences, leading to speculation that their courts gave greater emphasis than elsewhere to the focal concern of moral blameworthiness. County racial composition was also associated with increased conviction odds and sentence lengths. Baumer and Martin interpreted their findings as supporting the focal concerns perspective and showing that court and community differences shaped the outcomes of murder cases.

Murder is the most serious criminal offense. Its punishment is circumscribed by a complex scaffold of formal law. Yet studies such as these suggest that punishment of both capital and noncapital murder is shaped by focal concerns of sentencing filtered through the lenses of local decision makers and court communities. Sense making via focal concerns likely differs between courts according to court community culture, routine practices (processual order), local political conditions, and resource constraints. State laws concerning capital punishment and noncapital murder sentencing provide an institutional framework for handling murder cases, but that framework is inhabited by court communities in which workgroups make sense of cases and base decisions on local norms and practices.

C. Guideline Conformity and Deviation

1. *Sentencing Guidelines in State Courts.* Many studies have examined conformity with and departures from state sentencing guidelines, espe-

---

[1] The General Social Survey is an annual survey of a nationally representative sample of US individuals conducted by the National Opinion Research Center (http://gss.norc.org/about-the-gss). These survey data can be linked to aggregate data on respondents' geographic places of residence.

cially in connection with racial, ethnic, and gender disparity (see reviews by Spohn 2000; Ulmer 2012). Normative and cultural-cognitive influence likely looms large in producing between-court sentencing conformity in the many states with sentencing guidelines (state guidelines were never as presumptive or mandatory as the federal guidelines). Early research on Minnesota's sentencing guidelines showed that they reduced various forms of disparity, though some debate existed about how long those reductions lasted (Miethe and Moore 1985; Moore and Miethe 1986; Koons-Witt 2002; but see King and Light 2019). Research in Pennsylvania showed that, 10 years after their implementation, guidelines had become embedded in and relatively central to local courts' sentencing practices and workgroups' plea bargaining strategies (Ulmer 1997; Ulmer and Kramer 1998). The guidelines were useful tools for reducing uncertainty in case processing and served as legitimate normative benchmarks for typical cases. Later research also showed that the Pennsylvania guidelines produced substantial statewide changes in sentencing patterns in ways desired by the state sentencing commission (Kramer and Ulmer 2009). They seem to have fostered increased use of intermediate punishments in place of imprisonment in the late 1990s and early 2000s. Racial and ethnic disparities declined over time, with less disparity under the later, more detailed and structured versions of the guidelines than under earlier, less structured ones (Kramer and Ulmer 2009; King and Light 2019).

Engen and Steen (2000) demonstrated that drug sentencing in Washington was relatively tightly coupled to political factors and policy changes, but in ways driven by the interests of prosecutors. Changes in Washington's drug laws and sentencing guidelines produced statewide changes in drug conviction and sentencing patterns from 1986 to 1995. Drug convictions and sentence severity increased uniformly statewide. Local courts adapted in similar—though perhaps unintended—ways, with the result that prosecutors' ability to induce guilty pleas was substantially enhanced. Thus, Engen and Steen (2000) provide evidence of institutional isomorphism between courts that entailed both intended and unintended consequences.

Many other studies show evidence of court community variation in conformity to guidelines, and courtroom workgroup sense making around them. Johnson (2005), in particular, demonstrated important variation between court communities and between judges in Pennsylvania guideline departures. Kramer and Ulmer (2002, 2009) used the term "corrections to guidelines" to refer to local courts altering what they saw as inappropriate guideline sentences that did not match up with their own perceptions of offenders' blameworthiness, danger to the community, or practical constraints in individual cases. Johnson and Kurlychek (2012) compared courts in Pennsylvania and Maryland under presumptive and voluntary guidelines, respectively, in relation to guideline departures for juveniles. Downward departures were more likely for juveniles in Maryland, but in both states juveniles received greater upward departures (in sentence lengths) compared with adults. Qualitative analysis of departure reasons illustrated judicial sense making in juxtaposing the prescriptions of the guidelines and the meaning of youthful status. Judges in both states attributed less culpability to youth generally and wanted to give juvenile offenders second chances. For upward departures, however, judges did not acknowledge offenders' youthfulness, pointing instead to severe and atypical crime characteristics or severe victim injury.

2. *Sentencing Guidelines in Federal Courts.* The federal district courts best exemplify the dynamics of court communities as inhabited institutions. Federal courts are local organizational arenas in which punishment decisions are constrained by a set of overarching fieldwide rules—the sentencing guidelines—that feature a mixture of regulative, normative, and cultural force. The US Department of Justice, the US Sentencing Commission (USSC), and the Federal Judicial Center (FJC) are centralized organizations that potentially can produce normative, coercive, and mimetic isomorphism in federal district courts. For example, all US attorneys are appointed by the president and accountable to the US attorney general. The Department of Justice establishes policies and procedures for local US attorneys' offices and conducts various kinds of training for assistant US attorneys. The USSC promulgates the guidelines, monitors compliance, issues reports to Congress and the public, and conducts training seminars. The FJC conducts training in the use and interpretation of guidelines, and case law affecting them, for federal probation officers and new federal judges.

The federal guidelines were said by the commission to be "mandatory" until 2005 and were called the most rigid and complex sentencing rules ever enacted (Stith 2008) and "the most controversial and disliked sentencing reform initiative in US history" (Tonry 1996, p. 2). Some scholars argue that the guidelines produced great between-court conformity and uniformity, but at costs that many consider problematic: overly severe sentences, overly empowered prosecutors, overly restricted judicial discretion, and practical restrictions on the right to trial (Stith 2008; Scott 2011). However, in *United States v. Booker*, 543 U.S. 220 (2005), the US Supreme Court ruled that the guidelines would henceforth be advisory. Subsequent decisions, such as *Gall v. U.S.*, 128 S. Ct. 586 (2007), significantly expanded federal judges' sentencing discretion. Thus, the contemporary federal courts and their guidelines present an arena in which institutional rules seek to produce isomorphism with less regulative or coercive power than previously. Federal court communities are inhabited by actors and agencies that vary in their sensemaking practices and their perceptions of the normative legitimacy and practical usefulness of the rules (Ulmer and Johnson 2017). Tonry's (2012) demonstration of remarkable stability in sentencing patterns, including persistent between-district differences, before and after the *Booker* decision suggests the stability over time of local legal cultures and their processual orders.

Several studies have investigated between-court variation in federal guideline departures. Spohn and Fornango (2009) examined variation in federal prosecutors' likelihood of initiating substantial assistance departures in three districts. They found that about 24 percent of the variation between prosecutors was unaccounted for by case or defendant factors, and even less was unexplained in nondrug cases. Johnson, Ulmer, and Kramer (2008) examined interdistrict variations in application of substantial assistance and other downward departures for a variety of offense types in federal sentences from 1997 to 2000. Findings indicated considerable between-district variation in the probability of prosecutor-initiated substantial assistance departures. This was explained, in part, by organizational contexts such as caseload pressures (substantial assistance departures were more likely in districts with heavier caseloads) and by environmental considerations such as the racial composition of the district (substantial assistance departures increased with district black populations). Johnson, Ulmer, and Kramer (2008) summarized qualitative and survey evidence suggesting additional dimensions of variation between US attorneys' offices (see also Ulmer 2005).

In another important study, Kaiser and Spohn (2014; see also Hessick 2011) found that federal judges expressed policy disagreements with guideline recommendations for "nonproduction" child pornography sentences by departing downward at very high rates, while conforming more often to the guidelines for offenses involving production of child pornography. Similar patterns have been observed for drug offenses, with higher rates of downward departures for crack cocaine offenses than for cases involving other substances.

A recent study by Ulmer and Johnson (2017) supports the notion that federal courtroom workgroups interpret institutional rules in distinctive ways, with varying attitudes, relationships, and organizational cultures affecting localized conformity to and departure from institutional rules. This multimethod study drew on federal sentencing data, aggregated survey data from federal judges, and qualitative interviews. It found that federal sentencing practices were coupled to the guidelines to varying degrees, depending on the contours of local court communities, local court actors' interpretations and perceptions of the guidelines, and organizational constraints and uses. District-level conformity (and thus low judge-initiated departure rates) was fostered by judges' perceptions of the guidelines as normatively legitimate, by their perceptions of the coerciveness of their circuit court of appeal, and by the actions of district US attorney's offices. These perceptions exerted more influence on departure odds than did judicial punishment attitudes, concern with due process, or emphasis on organizational efficiency. Interview data showed that judges and assistant US attorneys in different court contexts varied in their perceptions of the guidelines and their normative power and legitimacy. They also differed about the relative discretionary power of sentencing judges, the restrictive influences of the circuit courts and US attorneys' offices, and the degree of reliance on guidelines as a tool for decision-making and uncertainty reduction. Ulmer and Johnson (2017) argue that their findings demonstrate that federal courts and the federal guidelines represent an inhabited institution in which local workgroup's sense making produces important variations in punishment outcomes for individual defendants.

Analyses of federal drug trafficking cases by Lynch and Omori (2014, p. 411) supported similar conclusions. They examined temporal and jurisdictional variations in federal sentencing tied to the *Booker* decision and concluded that "local legal practices not only diverge in important ways across place, but also become entrenched over time such that top-down legal reform is largely re-appropriated and absorbed into locally established practices." Federal court communities and their workgroups differed in their interpretive sense making around the guidelines, leading to varying processual orders and varying patterns of sentencing.

Yet, research shows that the guidelines continue to exert strong influence on federal sentencing. Judge-initiated departures have increased compared to pre-*Booker* years, but the majority of sentences conform to the guidelines well into the 2010s (Ulmer, Light, and Kramer 2011*a*, 2011*b*; US Sentencing Commission 2011, 2012; Kaiser and Spohn 2014). The post-*Booker* guidelines may illustrate Scott's (2008) contention that regulative, normative, and cultural-constitutive bases of conformity can intertwine in complex ways. For much of their history, the federal guidelines' influence likely derived from their regulative and coercive power (Stith 2008). But *Booker* made them advisory; their power to compel conformity and restrict departures was substantially weakened. They remain influential nonetheless.

This raises the possibility that institutional rules do not influence court actors merely (or even mostly) through constraints, but through normative cultural-cognitive influences. The guidelines seem to have become embedded in the fabric of federal court communities as sources of normative and mimetic isomorphism (Ulmer and Johnson 2017).

Scott (2008, p. 54) suggests that when legal constraint is reduced or ambiguous, the "law is better conceived of as an occasion for sense making and collective interpretation, relying more on cognitive and normative than coercive elements for its effects." This suggests that the extent to which advisory sentencing guidelines (not only the federal guidelines) increase uniformity in sentencing across courts likely depends on normative and cultural-cognitive influences. This could occur if guidelines become embedded as expected norms or as established constitutive rules, even if as in most state systems they were never mandatory, if they become taken-for-granted tools for reducing uncertainty and setting benchmark norms (Ulmer 1997; Kramer and Ulmer 2009; Anderson and Spohn 2010).

Guidelines could be seen as the embodiment of best practice, the product of a sentencing commission's careful research and prescriptions, and the source of macro myths of equality, crime control, and fairness (Meyer and Rowan 1977). To the extent that court actors conform to guidelines because they are viewed as legitimate and effective organizational policy, these influences are normative in nature. Concerning cultural-cognitive influence, guidelines may be viewed as a useful tool for reducing uncertainty in case outcomes and for streamlining complex decision-making processes, providing a benchmark for appropriate "going rates" for "normal crimes" (Sudnow 1965; Eisenstein and Jacob 1977). Once they become embedded in local sentencing practices as expected norms and constitutive rules (Ulmer and Kramer 1998), they are likely to continue to shape punishment even if their formal authority is substantially curtailed or was never strong to begin with.

Fieldwide isomorphism and conformity to institutional influences are not inherently desirable, uncontroversial, or fair—even if institutional influences are normative or cultural-cognitive rather than coercive. Recent and exemplary research by Lynch (2016) provides an example. She argues that the federal guidelines produced a systemwide "law enforcement machine" for federal drug crimes. They empowered prosecutors to threaten use of severe guideline and mandatory minimum sentences to exert unprecedented coercion on defendants to plead guilty, and to assist prosecutors and law enforcement by informing on others, wearing wires to record interactions, and testifying against others (Lynch 2016). Drug sentence lengths and federal imprisonment rates increased greatly and steadily under the federal guidelines, trials declined, and conviction rates dramatically increased (Lynch 2016). Lynch shows that the *Booker* decision and the era of advisory guidelines did not alter these patterns. Federal courts continued largely to conform to and rely on the guidelines, and prosecutors continued to use them to coerce guilty pleas (Lynch 2016).

D. *Federal Justice in Indian Country*

The federal courts' complex jurisdiction over crimes in Native American lands provides a final illustration of how inhabited institutions engage in consequential sense making and locally varying action strategies. The Major Crimes Act of 1885, amended in 2006, establishes federal criminal jurisdiction over crime in Indian country. It grants the federal government jurisdiction over 15 categories of crimes committed by Indians against either Indians or non-Indians, and by non-Indians against Indians. These include murder, manslaughter, kidnapping, various assaults, arson, burglary, robbery, felony child abuse and neglect, and drug trafficking.

Local federal officials have long been free to interpret and define justice jurisdiction and practice relative to Indian lands. The US Bureau of Indian Affairs (BIA) administers federal resources and services, including law enforcement (Droske 2008; Steinman 2012). BIA agents and agencies have long been semi-autonomous local policy makers (Steinman 2012). The experiences of tribes with formal federal policy were often widely divergent. "In practical terms, federal Indian policy regarding many dimensions was whatever field agents decided it was" (Steinman

2012, p. 1097). Thus, federal justice policy and jurisdiction exemplify dynamics of inhabited institutions. Furthermore, federal court communities and tribal courts and justice agencies display varying degrees of loose or tight coupling (Ulmer and Bradley 2018).

Tight federal-tribal justice coupling might sometimes take the form of "wardship," with federal authorities viewing Native American communities as wards subject to federal crime control efforts (Tredeau 2011; Franklin 2013). Tight federal-tribal coupling would foster greater federal justice involvement. Cases involving Native American defendants would make up a comparatively greater proportion of federal court caseloads, and US attorneys' offices would be proactive in prosecuting crime in Indian country, seeking to leverage greater federal capacity for incapacitation and deterrence than can state or tribal justice. By contrast, some federal districts might take a "hands off" approach, and tribal-federal justice might be relatively loosely coupled. This hands-off approach might take the form of federal underenforcement and neglect of crime, violence, and safety (Perry 2006), but also might foster the development and growth of sovereign tribal institutions.

A major arena of tightened federal-tribal justice coupling is the Tribal Law and Order Act (TLOA) of 2010, reauthorized in 2017. The TLOA appropriates funds to the BIA for public safety and justice programs, aims to increase federal-tribal justice coordination, and provides federally guided programs on illegal drug trafficking, alcohol and drug abuse prevention, and juvenile justice. The TLOA directs US attorneys' offices with jurisdiction over Indian lands to appoint an assistant US attorney as a tribal justice liaison and to use special assistant US attorneys to prosecute Indian country crime in consultation with tribal authorities. In addition, the TLOA contains a tribal sentencing enhancement program that enables the use of federal correctional resources for tribal sentencing of non–major crimes felonies.

Ulmer and Bradley (2018) provide empirical evidence of tribal-federal justice coupling for understanding how Native Americans are treated in federal courts. Their multilevel analysis compared sentencing of Native Americans compared with other types of defendants in 28 federal court districts with substantial tribal presence. Sentencing of Indian defendants varied considerably between courts in relation to measures of federal-tribal coupling. Measures of greater federal-tribal coupling were associated with markedly more punitive prison sentences.

One marker of varying federal-tribal coupling might be the use of "substantial assistance" departures and government-sponsored departures for Indian defendants. These types of guideline departures are well known as prosecutorial tools to leverage informant cooperation with federal law enforcement (Spohn and Fornango 2009). In districts with more integrated tribal-federal justice relations, more aggressive use of these prosecutor-controlled sentencing incentives might indicate more active and involved US attorneys' office investigative efforts. Supporting this notion, Ulmer and Bradley (2018) found that measures of tribal-federal coupling were associated with greater odds of Native American defendants receiving substantial assistance and government-sponsored downward guideline departures. Contemporary federal jurisdiction over crime in Native American lands illustrates how US attorneys' offices and federal courts make sense of, adapt, and manipulate relevant institutional rules and laws in locally distinctive ways.

IV. Implications

The inhabited institutions perspective integrates theory and research on courts at a more generic level of abstraction and provides useful conceptual tools for understanding similarities and differences between courts and their practices. Below, I sketch a number of implications.

A. Study What the Inhabitants Think and Do

One implication is that theories used in studying courts and sentencing are somewhat at odds with our data and methods. Theories emphasize court communities, workgroup interactions, sense making, focal concerns, attributions, and bounded rationality. Typical empirical efforts analyze sentencing and, less often, other case processing outcomes, sometimes with a focus on between-court variation and contextual influences on outcomes. Let me be clear: I do not denigrate or devalue such research, which will always be necessary. I do not want less of such research produced—quite the opposite. The issue is one of balance: our theories emphasize interpretation, culture, and processes, and our data and methods focus on sedimented outcomes. We need more qualitative and multimethod research that can flesh out the inhabited institutions we study—courts. We would do well to emulate the organizational sociology literature both methodologically and theoretically. Qualitative, survey, and multimethod research is quite common in organizational studies based on neo-institutional theory, along with sophisticated statistical analyses of organizational outcomes.

If we do not match a focus on modeling with a parallel focus on decisions and activities of courtroom workgroup participants, and how these are shaped by their surrounding court community contexts, our understanding of punishment will suffer (Ulmer 2012). There are, however, some recent exemplars of such multimethod and qualitative research. Research by Lynch (2016) and Hester (2017), discussed above, shows that integrating quantitative and qualitative data can yield unique insights into the complexities of between-court similarity and variation. An important study by Kohler-Hausmann (2013) also presents an exemplary treatment of formal and informal misdemeanor case processing norms and workgroup sense making in municipal courts of New York City.

B. Parsing Specific Actors' Discretion May Be an Illusion

A second is that: "courtroom decision-making, including sentencing, is shaped by workgroup dynamics" and that "sentences result not simply from the decisions of individual judges and prosecutors but also from interactions between judges and prosecutors" (Kim, Spohn, and Hedberg 2015, p. 617). In other words, we may not be able to isolate the discretion of this or that courtroom workgroup actor or sponsoring organization, because almost every case decision-making stage is interactive in some sense. Even seemingly unilateral decisions (like charging) are typically made in anticipation of the actions of others. However, a great many sentencing studies parse discretion over outcomes into this or that actor's domain (i.e., judges vs. prosecutors). For example, studies of guideline departures, especially in the federal courts, often try to isolate judicial or prosecutorial discretion by focusing on substantial assistance and other government-sponsored departures (representing prosecutorial discretion) compared with "judge-initiated" departures (e.g., Hartley, Miller, and Spohn 2007; Johnson, Ulmer, and Kramer 2008; Spohn and Fornango 2009; Anderson and Spohn 2010; Ulmer, Light, and Kramer 2011*a*). Studies of charging (e.g., Shermer and Johnson 2010; Bushway and Redlich 2012; Rehavi and Starr 2012; Bushway, Redlich, and Norris 2014), decisions to pursue mandatory minimums (Bjerk 2005; Ulmer, Light, and Kramer 2007; Starr and Rehavi 2013;), or the death penalty (Paternoster and Brame 2008; Kramer, Ulmer, and Zajac 2017) typically imply that these decisions are made unilaterally by prosecutors and elide interactive processes that may lie behind them. A great many theoretical and empirical treatments of sentencing in general depict sentencing as the province of the judge and the realm in which one can observe judicial discretion. More problematically, polemics criticizing judges and policies directed at constraining judicial sentencing assume that sentencing outcomes predominantly reflect judicial discretion (Tonry 1993; Stith 2008; Baron-Evans and Stith 2012). This is true only in a formal, legalistic sense but is dubious at best as a matter of real court community processes. It is sometimes useful to make such distinctions to gain analytical traction on particular research questions, but they caricature the interaction processes that produce these decisions.

In reality, most case outcomes result from interactions of courtroom workgroups, which are in turn embedded in and influenced by their larger court communities. The quest to isolate one particular set of actors' discretion over discrete case outcomes, while perhaps useful for specific analytic purposes, obscures the workgroup interaction at the heart of court communities as inhabited institutions.

C. Study Mechanisms That Produce Court Isomorphism and Variation

A third implication is that a major emphasis of the study of courts and sentencing should be on specific mechanisms that produce field isomorphism and conformity, as well as on those producing variation. This is not a new call, yet the contemporary literature continues to lack sustained attention to and understanding of how organizational mechanisms play out in court communities and their workgroups.

Research should focus on diverse mechanisms: mechanisms of regulative and legal constraint that produce coercive isomorphism among courts; mechanisms of how formal and informal norms emerge among courts communities and diffuse between courts throughout fields (see Hester 2017), thus producing normative isomorphism; and mechanisms of cultural-cognitive influence—how constitutive rules emerge and taken-for-granted practices become mechanisms producing mimetic isomorphism. Cultural-cognitive mechanisms may be most interesting and important of all, because constitutive rules and taken-for-granted practices are often used by courtroom workgroups as tools to reduce uncertainty and manage practical problems.

More research should investigate how the organizational variation-producing mechanisms identified by Scott (2008) play out. These include translations of externally imposed criminal justice institutional rules, policies, and laws; court community attributes, culture, and workgroup relationships that affect responses to constraints such as sentencing guidelines, mandatory minimums, and capital punishment laws; adaptations and innovations by courtroom workgroup actors and court communities in response to sponsoring agencies, surrounding field constraints, and externally imposed rules; and strategic responses to sociopolitical environments by workgroup actors or sponsoring agencies. Learning more about each of these four sets of variation-producing mechanisms will require in-depth examinations of court community processual orders and sense-making practices.

My discussion of sentencing guidelines conformity and deviation illustrates how a focus on organizational mechanisms of isomorphism and variation can lead to useful new research. There has been much discussion and emphasis on the degree of legal force of different kinds of sentencing guidelines, especially the federal guidelines. Some scholars and policy makers have framed the issue around "the assumption that, left to their own devices, judges will discriminate on the basis of race and gender" (Engen 2011, p. 1146). This assumption often underpins the argument that guidelines must tightly constrain discretion if there are to be meaningful reductions in unwarranted disparity (e.g., Paternoster 2011; Scott 2011). However, this framing of the debate centers on coercive isomorphism and ignores the potential influence of normative or mimetic isomorphism. Engen (2011, p. 1146) implies the importance of the normative and mimetic isomorphism-inducing power of sentencing guidelines: "Were the guidelines to be repealed entirely it is likely that the philosophy, values, and even the content of those guidelines would be carried forward as a part of local legal culture."

When guidelines' regulatory and coercive power is weakened (as with the federal guidelines post-*Booker*) or was never strong in the first place (as with some state sentencing guidelines), normative and cultural-cognitive influences are likely to be paramount in fostering conformity in practice. In such situations, guidelines' ability to structure sentencing may rest more on their perceived legitimacy as a norm-setting mechanism and their perceived practical usefulness at reducing uncertainty and establishing taken-for-granted reality than on coercive authority. Guidelines embedded in courtroom workgroup practice as constitutive rules and normative standards will continue to shape sentencing practices (producing conformity) even as they are subjected to local interpretation, organizational sense making, and adaptation. Additional research is therefore needed that examines the complex interplay between legal shifts in sentencing policy and patterns of conformity to and deviation from institutional rules (Engen 2009, 2018).

D. Policy Feedback and Institutional Learning

A final implication is that variation in court community practices and sentencing patterns is an important feedback signal for policy and field evolution. Sentencing and court policies can evolve through organizational learning (Daft 1989; Aldrich and Ruef 2006) with feedback from what court communities and their workgroups are actually doing. Organizational learning involves three steps: data gathering about organizational actions and environments, interpretation and debate surrounding the data, and debate and formulation of new organizational responses or actions (Daft 1989, p. 548). If such organizational learning occurred on a fieldwide level, involving field-level entities with authority to set formal institutional norms and rules, we could refer to this as institutional learning.

While I discussed conformity to sentencing guidelines as an example of isomorphism, departures from sentencing guidelines offer an often unrecognized source of feedback that could be useful for institutional learning. Institutional-level actors such as sentencing commissions and legislatures could look to variations in guideline departures as a source of data for organizational learning. Gottfredson, Wilkins, and Hoffman (1978) envisioned that kind of learning in early writings on guidelines. They wanted guidelines that would structure sentencing and parole discretion but monitor patterns of deviation from them as signals of the need for revisions.

Hessick (2011), Kaiser and Spohn (2014), and others (e.g., Stith 2008; Baron-Evans and Stith 2012) have argued that post-*Booker* federal guideline departures based on judicial policy disagreement are important policy signals to the USSC and to Congress. Patterns of departures can signal mismatches between policies and the situational realities faced in real court community contexts. Baron-Evans and Stith (2012, p. 1741) point out that federal guideline departures were "intended to allow individualized sentences and *constructive evolution* of the guidelines" (my emphasis). They characterize the post-*Booker/Gall* federal sentencing environment: "Indeed, for the first time, the frontline actors in sentencing—most importantly the Article III judges called upon to begin their sentencing deliberations by calculating the guideline range—are informing the Commission of the nature and extent of the problems with the guidelines" (p. 1741).

Guideline departures allow courtroom workgroups to communicate about mismatches between their own interpretations of focal concerns in a given case and the formal ratings of offender blameworthiness or dangerousness represented by guidelines (Kramer and Ulmer 2009). Aggregate patterns of departures, like those documented by Kaiser and Spohn (2014) concerning federal nonproduction child pornography guidelines, signal that the guidelines are off-target from the perspective of courtroom workgroups. Seen this way, departure sentences are not merely troublesome noncompliance. Instead, when they form patterned deviations from guideline prescriptions, they have corrective feedback value. Of course, as much research shows, guideline departures are often the site of unwarranted disparity. However, when we sharply restrict local courtroom workgroups' discretion, we lose a feedback mechanism, and local courts lose the ability to speak to policy.

Other areas of potential policy feedback and institutional learning include selective and locally varied prosecutorial application of mandatory minimums and selective seeking of the death penalty in capital murder. Bjerk (2005) found that prosecutors selectively used their discretion to circumvent three-strikes mandatories but were less likely to do so for male and Hispanic defendants. Similarly, Farrell (2003) found that blacks, males, and people convicted at trial were more likely to receive mandatory minimums for firearms offenses. Ulmer, Light, and Kramer (2007) found that prosecutors moved to apply drug and three-strikes mandatory minimums in only a minority of eligible cases and found considerable between-county variation in the application of mandatories. Prosecutors' decisions to seek or not seek mandatory minimums were intimately tied to plea bargaining and significantly affected by the type and characteristics of offenses and guideline sentence recommendations, prior record, gender, and Hispanic ethnicity. Local prosecutors sought the death penalty in a minority of eligible cases and varied widely in their decisions to file for the death penalty and retract those filings (Kramer, Ulmer, and Zajac 2017).

Findings from studies like these might signal that prosecutor-empowering sentencing policies like mandatory minimums and the death penalty do not fit the majority of cases that are exposed to them.

Unlike sentencing guideline departures, decisions to expose defendants to mandatory minimums and the death penalty rest with prosecutors and are relatively invisible and unaccountable. These and other prosecutorial decision processes therefore leave few organizational trails or data by which they can be monitored.

This points to a long-recognized imbalance of power and influence in courtroom workgroups. Moreover, from an inhabited institutions perspective, the opacity of prosecutorial decision-making short-circuits any policy feedback. If patterns and local variations in prosecutorial decisions and practices cannot be monitored, analyzed, and learned from, institutional learning and normative evolution cannot occur.

Fieldwide isomorphism is not inherently "good" or beneficial, and organizational variation is not inherently "bad." Fieldwide conformity among courts does not necessarily produce justice, fairness, or safety, and courts' deviation from institutional rules does not inherently signal unwarranted disparity or injustice. As the then US attorney general Eric Holder (2009, p. 1) noted, uniformity and the control of judicial discretion, per se, do not guarantee justice: "The desire to have an almost mechanical system of sentencing has led us away from individualized, fact-based determinations that I believe, within reason, should be our goal." Likewise, patterns of variation between courts have substantial and underrecognized value for criminal justice fieldwide institutional learning.

Examining variation between courts and attention to how their organizational contexts shape punishment is a mature scholarly enterprise; research has pointed to the importance of this variation for decades. The inhabited institutions perspective implies that the dynamics of similarity and difference that we observe among court communities are generic to institutional fields of all kinds. This implies that, as a generic principle, court communities will have distinctive processual orders that structure the sense making of their courtroom workgroups and implies that court communities will be variably coupled to institutional norms such as externally imposed laws and policies.

Criminal justice policies and institutional rules will always involve a "transformation of intentions," filtered through the processual orders of courts and their workgroups' sense making. Policy makers and scholars alike should recognize that formally rational policies and rules are dependent on those who inhabit them and that this cannot and should not be avoided.

REFERENCES

Albonetti, Celesta. 1991. "An Integration of Theories to Explain Judicial Discretion." *Social Problems* 38:247–66.

Aldrich, Howard, and Martin Ruef. 2006. *Organizations Evolving*. 2nd ed. Thousand Oaks, CA: Sage.

Anderson, Amy, and Cassia Spohn. 2010. "Lawlessness in the Federal Sentencing Process: A Test for Uniformity and Consistency in Sentencing Practices." *Justice Quarterly* 27(3):362–93.

Baron-Evans, Amy, and Kate Stith. 2012. "Booker Rules." *University of Pennsylvania Law Review* 160:1631–1743.

Baumer, Eric, and Kimberly Martin. 2013. "Social Organization, Collective Sentiment, and Legal Sanctions in Murder Cases." *American Journal of Sociology* 119(1):131–82.

Berger, Peter L., and Thomas Luckmann. 1967. *The Social Construction of Reality*. New York: Doubleday.

Bjerk, David. 2005. "Making the Crime Fit the Penalty: The Role of Prosecutorial Discretion under Mandatory Minimum Sentencing." *Journal of Law and Economics* 48:591–625.

Bourdieu, Pierre. 1977. *Outline of a Theory of Practice*. London: Cambridge University Press.

Bushway, Shawn, and Allison Redlich. 2012. "Is Plea Bargaining in the 'Shadow of the Trial' a Mirage?" *Journal of Quantitative Criminology* 28:437–54.

Bushway, Shawn, Allison Redlich, and Robert Norris. 2014. "An Explicit Test of Plea Bargaining in the 'Shadow of the Trial.'" *Criminology* 52(4):723–54.

Clair, Matthew, and Alix Winter. 2016. "How Judges Think about Racial Disparities: Situational Decision-Making in the Criminal Justice System." *Criminology* 54(2):332–59.

Daft, Richard L. 1989. *Organization Theory and Design*. New York: West.

DiMaggio, Paul J., and Walter W. Powell. 1983. "The Iron Cage Revisited: Institutional Isomorphism and Collective Rationality in Organizational Fields." *American Sociological Review* 48:147–60.

Dixon, Jo. 1995. "The Organizational Context of Criminal Sentencing." *American Journal of Sociology* 100(5):1157–98.

Droske, T. J. 2008. "Correcting Native American Sentencing Disparity Post-Booker." *Marquette Law Review* 91:723–813.

Eisenstein, James, Roy Flemming, and Peter Nardulli. 1988. *The Contours of Justice: Communities and Their Courts*. Boston: Little, Brown.

Eisenstein, James, and Herbert Jacob. 1977. *Felony Justice: An Organizational Analysis of Criminal Courts*. Boston: Little, Brown.

Engen, Rodney. 2009. "Assessing Determinate and Presumptive Sentencing: Making Research Relevant." *Criminology and Public Policy* 8:323–35.

———. 2011. "Racial Disparity in the Wake of *Booker/Fanfan*: Making Sense of 'Messy' Results and Other Challenges for Sentencing Research." *Criminology and Public Policy* 10(4):1139–49.

———. 2018. "What We Know, Do Not Know, and Need to Know about Sentencing and Mass Incarceration in the US and What 'Sentencing' Research Could Teach Us." In *Handbook on Punishment Decisions: Locations of Disparity*, edited by Jeffery Ulmer and M. Bradley. New York: Routledge.

Engen, Rodney L., and Sara Steen. 2000. "The Power to Punish: Discretion and Sentencing Reform in the War on Drugs." *American Journal of Sociology* 105(5):1357–95.

Estes, Carroll, and Beverly Edmonds. 1981. "Symbolic Interaction and Social Policy Analysis." *Symbolic Interaction* 4(1):75–86.

Everitt, Judson G. 2012. "Teacher Careers and Inhabited Institutions: Sense Making and Arsenals of Teaching Practice in Educational Institutions." *Symbolic Interaction* 35(2):203–20.

Farrell, Jill. 2003. "Mandatory Minimum Firearm Penalties: A Source of Sentencing Disparity." *Justice Research and Policy* 5(1):95–115.

Flemming, Roy B., Peter F. Nardulli, and James Eisenstein. 1992. *The Craft of Justice: Politics and Work in Criminal Court Communities*. Philadelphia: University of Pennsylvania Press.

Fligstein, Neil, and Douglas McAdam. 2011. "Toward a General Theory of Strategic Action Fields." *Sociological Theory* 29(1):1–26.

Franklin, Travis W. 2010. "Community Influence on Prosecutorial Dismissals: A Multilevel Analysis of Case- and County-Level Factors." *Journal of Criminal Justice* 38:693–701.

———. 2013. "Sentencing Native Americans in US Federal Courts: An Examination of Disparity." *Justice Quarterly* 30:310–39.

Garland, David. 2010. *Peculiar Institution: America's Death Penalty in an Age of Abolition*. Cambridge, MA: Harvard University Press.

Gottfredson, Don, Leslie Wilkins, and P. B. Hoffman. 1978. *Guidelines for Parole and Sentencing: A Policy Control Method*. Washington, DC: US Department of Justice.

Hagan, John. 1989. "Why Is There So Little Criminal Justice Theory? Neglected Macro- and Micro-Level Links between Organization and Power." *Journal of Research in Crime and Delinquency* 26:116–35.

Hall, Peter M. 1997. "Meta-Power, Social Organization, and the Shaping of Social Action." *Symbolic Interaction* 20(4):397–418.

Hall, Peter M., and Patrick J. W. McGinty. 1997. "Policy as the Transformation of Intentions: Producing Program from Statute." *Sociological Quarterly* 38(3):439–67.

Hallett, Tim. 2010. "The Myth Incarnate: Recoupling Processes, Turmoil, and Inhabited Institutions in an Urban Elementary School." *American Sociological Review* 75(1):52–74.

Hartley, Richard, Sean Maddan, and Cassia Spohn. 2007. "Prosecutorial Discretion: An Examination of Substantial Assistance Departures in Crack Cocaine Cases." *Justice Quarterly* 24:382–407.

Hartley, Richard, Holly Ventura Miller, and Cassia Spohn. 2010. "Do You Get What You Pay For? Type of Counsel and Its Effect on Criminal Court Outcomes." *Journal of Criminal Justice* 38:1063–70.

Hessick, Clarissa Byrne. 2011. "Disentangling Child Pornography from Child Sex Abuse." *Washington University Law Review* 88:853–902.

Hester, Rhys. 2017. "Judicial Rotation as Centripetal Force: Sentencing in the Court Communities of South Carolina." *Criminology* 55(1):205–35.

Holder, Eric. 2009. "Remarks for the Charles Hamilton Houston Institute for Race and Justice and Congressional Black Caucus Symposium 'Rethinking Federal Sentencing Policy 25th Anniversary of the Sentencing Reform Act.'" June 24, Washington DC. https://www.justice.gov/opa/speech/attorney-general-holder-s-remarksfor-charles-hamilton-houston-institute-race-and-justice.

Hoskins-Haynes, Stacy, R. Barry Ruback, and Gretchen Ruth Cusick. 2010. "Courtroom Workgroups and Sentencing: The Effects of Similarity, Proximity, and Stability." *Crime and Delinquency* 56(1):126–61.

Johnson, Brian D. 2005. "Contextual Disparities in Guidelines Departures." *Criminology* 43:761–97.

———. 2006. "The Multilevel Context of Criminal Sentencing: Integrating Judge and County Level Influences in the Study of Courtroom Decision-Making." *Criminology* 44:259–98.

Johnson, Brian D., and Stephanie M. DiPietro. 2012. "The Power of Diversion: Intermediate Sanctions and Sentencing Disparity under Presumptive Guidelines." *Criminology* 50(3):811–50.

Johnson, Brian D., and Megan Kurlychek. 2012. "Transferred Juveniles in the Era of Sentencing Guidelines: Examining Judicial Departures for Juvenile Offenders in Adult Criminal Court." *Criminology* 50(2):525–64.

Johnson, Brian D., Jeffery Ulmer, and John Kramer. 2008. "The Social Context of Guideline Circumvention: The Case of Federal District Courts." *Criminology* 46:711–83.

Kaiser, Kimberly A., and Cassia Spohn. 2014. "'Fundamentally Flawed?' Exploring the Use of Policy Disagreements in Judicial Downward Departures for Child Pornography Sentences." *Criminology and Public Policy* 13(2):241–70.

Kautt, Paula M. 2002. "Location, Location, Location: Interdistrict and Intercircuit Variation in Sentencing Outcomes for Federal Drug-Trafficking Offenses." *Justice Quarterly* 19:633–71.

Kim, Byungbae, Cassia Spohn, and E. C. Hedberg. 2015. "Federal Sentencing as a Complex Collaborative Process: Judges, Prosecutors, Judge-Prosecutor Dyads, and Disparity in Sentencing." *Criminology* 53(4):597–623.

King, Ryan D., and Michael T. Light. 2019. "Have Racial and Ethnic Disparities in Sentencing Declined? A Review of Theory and Evidence." In *American Sentencing*, edited by Michael Tonry. Vol. 48 of *Crime and Justice: A Review of Research*, edited by Michael Tonry. Chicago: University of Chicago Press.

Kohler-Hausmann, Issa. 2013. "Misdemeanor Justice: Control without Conviction." *American Journal of Sociology* 119(2):351–93.

Koons-Witt, Barbara. 2002. "The Effect of Gender on the Decision to Incarcerate before and after the Introduction of Sentencing Guidelines." *Criminology* 40(2):297–328.

Kramer, John H., and Jeffery T. Ulmer. 2002. "Downward Departures for Serious Violent Offenders: Local Court 'Corrections' to Pennsylvania's Sentencing Guidelines." *Criminology* 40:601–36.

———. 2009. *Sentencing Guidelines: Lessons from Pennsylvania*. Boulder, CO: Lynne Rienner.

Kramer, John H., Jeffery T. Ulmer, and Gary Zajac. 2017. *Capital Punishment Decisions in Pennsylvania, 2000–2010: Implications for Racial, Ethnic, and Other Disparate Impacts*. Harrisburg: Pennsylvania Interbranch Commission on Gender, Racial, and Ethnic Fairness. http://www.justicecenter.psu.edu/research/projects/files/the-administration-of-the-death-penalty-in-pennsylvania-pdf.

Levin, Martin. 1977. *Urban Politics and the Criminal Courts*. Chicago: University of Chicago Press.

Lin, Jeffrey, Ryken Grattet, and Joan Petersilia. 2010. "'Back End Sentencing' and Reimprisonment: Individual, Organizational, and Community Predictors of Parole Sanctioning Decisions." *Criminology* 48(3):759–96.

Lynch, Mona. 2016. *Hard Bargains: The Coercive Power of Drug Laws in Federal Court*. New York: Russell Sage Foundation.

Lynch, Mona, and Marisa Omori. 2014. "Legal Change and Sentencing Norms in the Wake of Booker: The Impact of Time and Place on Drug Trafficking Cases in Federal Court." *Law and Society Review* 48(2):411–45.

March, James, and Herbert Simon. 1958. *Organizations*. New York: Wiley.

Marsh, Robert M. 2000. "Weber's Misunderstanding of Chinese Law." *American Journal of Sociology* 106:281–302.

Martin, John Levi. 2003. "What Is Field Theory?" *American Journal of Sociology* 109(1):1–49.

Mears, Daniel P., and Samuel H. Field. 2000. "Theorizing Sanctioning in a Criminalized Juvenile Court." *Criminology* 38:983–1020.

Metcalfe, Christie. 2016. "The Role of Courtroom Workgroups in Felony Case Dispositions: An Analysis of Workgroup Familiarity and Similarity." *Law and Society Review* 50(3):637–73.

Meyer, John W., and Brian Rowan. 1977. "Institutionalized Organizations: Formal Structure as Myth and Ceremony." *American Journal of Sociology* 83:340–63.

Miethe, Terence, and Charles Moore. 1985. "Socioeconomic Disparities under Determinate Sentencing Systems: A Comparison of Preguideline and Postguideline Practices in Minnesota." *Criminology* 23:337–63.

Moore, Charles, and Terence Miethe. 1986. "Regulated and Nonregulated Sentencing Practices under Minnesota Felony Sentencing Guidelines." *Law and Society Review* 20:253–65.

Morrill, Calvin, and Cindy McKee. 1993. "Institutional Isomorphism and Informal Social Control: Evidence from a Community Mediation Center." *Social Problems* 40(4):445–63.

Myers, Martha, and Susette Talarico. 1987. *The Social Contexts of Criminal Sentencing*. New York: Springer-Verlag.

Nardulli, Peter F., James Eisenstein, and Roy B. Flemming. 1988. *The Tenor of Justice: Criminal Courts and the Guilty Plea Process*. Urbana: University of Illinois Press.

Paternoster, Raymond. 2011. "Racial Disparity under the Federal Guidelines Pre- and Post-Booker: Lessons Not Learned from Research on the Death Penalty." *Criminology and Public Policy* 10(4):1063–72.

———. 2012. "Capital Punishment." In *The Oxford Handbook of Crime and Criminal Justice*, edited by M. Tonry. New York: Oxford University Press.

Paternoster, Raymond, and Robert Brame. 2008. "Reassessing Race Disparities in Maryland Capital Cases." *Criminology* 46:971–1008.

Perry, Barbara. 2006. "'Nobody Trusts Them!' Under- and Over-policing Native American Communities." *Critical Criminology* 14:411–44.

Rehavi, M. Marit, and Sonja B. Starr. 2012. "Racial Disparity in Federal Criminal Charging and Its Sentencing Consequences." Working Paper no. 12-002. Ann Arbor: University of Michigan, Law School Program in Law and Economics. https://njoselson.github.io/pdfs/SSRN-id1985377.pdf.

Savelsberg, Joachim J. 1992. "Law That Does Not Fit Society: Sentencing Guidelines as a Neoclassical Reaction to the Dilemmas of Substantivized Law." *American Journal of Sociology* 97:1346–81.

Scott, Ryan W. 2011. "Race Disparity under Advisory Guidelines: Dueling Assessments and Potential Responses." *Criminology and Public Policy* 10(4):1129–38.

Scott, W. Richard. 2008. *Institutions and Organizations: Ideas and Interests*. Thousand Oaks, CA: Sage.

Shermer, Lauren O'Neill, and Brian Johnson. 2010. "Criminal Prosecutions: Examining Prosecutorial Discretion and Charge Reductions in US Federal District Courts." *Justice Quarterly* 27(3):394–430.

Skolnick, Jerome. 1966. *Justice Without Trial*. New York: Wiley.

Spohn, Cassia. 2000. "Thirty Years of Sentencing Reform: The Quest for a Racially Neutral Sentencing Process." In *Policies, Processes, and Decisions of the Criminal Justice System*, vol. 3, *Criminal Justice 2000*. Washington, DC: US Department of Justice.

Spohn, Cassia, and Jerry Cederbloom. 1991. "Race and Disparities in Sentencing: A Test of the Liberation Hypothesis." *Justice Quarterly* 8:305–27.

Spohn, Cassia, and Robert Fornango. 2009. "US Attorneys and Substantial Assistance Departures: Testing for Interprosecutor Disparity." *Criminology* 47(3):813–47.

Starr, Sonja B., and M. Marit Rehavi. 2013. "Mandatory Sentencing and Racial Disparity: Assessing the Role of Prosecutors and the Effects of Booker." *Yale Law Journal* 123(1):2–80.

Steffensmeier, Darrell, Jeffery Ulmer, and John Kramer. 1998. "The Interaction of Race, Gender, and Age in Criminal Sentencing: The Punishment Cost of Being Young, Black, and Male." *Criminology* 36:763–98.

Steinman, Erich. 2012. "Settler Colonial Power and the American Indian Sovereignty Movement: Forms of Domination, Strategies of Transformation." *American Journal of Sociology* 117:1073–130.

Stith, Kate. 2008. "The Arc of the Pendulum: Judges, Prosecutors, and the Exercise of Discretion." *Yale Law Journal* 117:1420–97.

Strauss, Anselm. 1993. *Continual Permutations of Action*. New York: Aldine de Gruyter.

Sudnow, David. 1965. "Normal Crimes: Sociological Features of the Penal Code." *Social Problems* 12(4):255–64.
Tonry, Michael. 1993. "Mandatory Penalties." In *Crime and Justice: A Review of Research*, vol. 16, edited by Michael Tonry. Chicago: University of Chicago Press.
———. 1996. *Sentencing Matters*. New York: Oxford University Press.
———. 2012. "The US Sentencing Commission's Best Response to *Booker* Is to Do Nothing." *Federal Sentencing Reporter* 24(5):387–93.
Tredeau, E. 2011. "Tribal Control in Federal Sentencing." *California Law Review* 99(5):1409–38.
Ulmer, Jeffery T. 1995. "The Organization and Consequences of Social Pasts in Criminal Courts." *Sociological Quarterly* 36(3):901–19.
———. 1997. *Social Worlds of Sentencing: Court Communities under Sentencing Guidelines*. Albany: SUNY Press.
———. 2005. "The Localized Uses of Federal Sentencing Guidelines in Four US District Courts: Evidence of Processual Order." *Symbolic Interaction* 28:255–79.
———. 2012. "Recent Developments and New Directions in Sentencing Research." *Justice Quarterly* 29(1):1–40.
Ulmer, Jeffery, and Mindy Bradley. 2018. "Punishment in Indian Country: Ironies of Federal Punishment of Native Americans." *Justice Quarterly* 35(5):751–81.
Ulmer, Jeffery T., and Brian D. Johnson. 2004. "Sentencing in Context: A Multilevel Analysis." *Criminology* 42:137–77.
———. 2017. "Organizational Conformity and Punishment: Federal Court Communities and Judge-Initiated Guideline Departures." *Journal of Criminal Law and Criminology* 107(2):253–92.
Ulmer, Jeffery T., and John H. Kramer. 1996. "Court Communities under Sentencing Guidelines: Dilemmas of Formal Rationality and Sentencing Disparity." *Criminology* 34:383–408.
———. 1998. "The Use and Transformation of Formal Decision-Making Criteria: Sentencing Guidelines, Organizational Contexts, and Case Processing Strategies." *Social Problems* 45(2):248–67.
Ulmer, Jeffery T., Megan Kurlychek, and John Kramer. 2007. "Prosecutorial Discretion and the Imposition of Mandatory Minimums." *Journal of Research in Crime and Delinquency* 44(4):427–58.
Ulmer, Jeffery T., Michael Light, and John Kramer. 2011*a*. "Does Increased Judicial Discretion Lead to Increased Disparity? The 'Liberation' of Judicial Sentencing Discretion in the Wake of the *Booker/Fanfan* Decision." *Justice Quarterly* 28(6):799–837.
———. 2011*b*. "Racial Disparity in the Wake of the *Booker/Fanfan* Decision: An Alternative Analysis to the USSC's 2010 Report." *Criminology and Public Policy* 10(4):1077–118.
US Sentencing Commission. 2011. *US Sentencing Commission's 2011 Annual Report*. Washington, DC: US Sentencing Commission.
———. 2012. *Report on the Continuing Impact of United States v. Booker on Federal Sentencing*. Washington, DC: US Sentencing Commission. http://www.ussc.gov

/news/congressional-testimony-and-reports/booker-reports/report-continuing-impact-united-states-v-booker-federal-sentencing.
Weick, Karl. 1976. "Educational Organizations as Loosely Coupled Systems." *Administrative Science Quarterly* 21:1–19.
———. 1995. *Sensemaking in Organizations*. Thousand Oaks, CA: Sage.
Westby, David L. 1991. *The Growth of Sociological Theory: Human Nature, Knowledge, and Social Change*. Englewood Cliffs, NJ: Prentice-Hall.
Wooldredge, John. 2010. "Judges' Unequal Contributions to Extralegal Disparities in Imprisonment." *Criminology* 48(2):539–67.

Index

A
Abrams, D. S., 339–340, 340n9, 342
Adelman, L., 201, 236
African Americans. *See* blacks
AI. *See* artificial intelligence
Alabama, 84, 89
Alaska, 83n3
Albonetti, C. A., 335–336, 410, 495
Alito, S., 63
Alschuler, A. W., 340, 344, 348
Alvarez, A., 376
Alverstone, R. W., 238
Amdahl, D., 26, 27
American Bar Association (ABA), 6, 9, 80, 85, 175
American Law Institute (ALI), 80, 85, 256, 279, 283. *See also* Model Penal Code: Sentencing
American Sociological Review, 401
Anderson, A., 497
Andiloro, N. R., 343
Anti–Drug Abuse Acts (1986, 1988), 138, 138n2, 144, 155, 161, 417. *See also* drug offenses
appellate courts and: overcrowding and (*see also* overcrowding)
Arizona, 71
Arkansas, 71, 99
Article III (US Constitution), 316, 514
artificial intelligence (AI), 286–287
Ashworth, A., 205n28, 443n5

Asian defendants, 371, 376–377
Australia, 344, 347

B
Bachman, R. D., 376
bail, 13, 54, 67, 70, 335, 338
Barker, V., 39
Barkow, R., 195n11, 201
Baron-Evans, A., 513
Baumer, E. P., 368, 370, 415, 501
Bechtel, W. K., 447, 452, 457, 472
Behavior of Law, The (Black), 412–413
Bentham, J., 453, 462, 465, 466n20
Berlin, I., 447
Berlusconi, S., 453n12
Bestinger, S., 377
BIA. *See* Bureau of Indian Affairs
Bjerk, D., 514
Black, D. J., 412–413
Blackmun, H., 160
blacks: Afrocentricity and, 409; below-range sentences, 176; black attorneys, 415; black-white differences (*see* racial disparity); DIS and (*see also* Minnesota); ethnic disparity and, 374 (*see also* ethnic disparity); guidelines and, 161, 165, 171 (*see also* guideline systems); Hispanics and, 3t, 11, 172f, 374–379, 398–399, 424 (*see also* Hispanics); imprisonment rates, 269n17, 366, 370 (*see also* racial

523

disparity); Jim Crow principles, 379; Minnesota and, 108, 267 (*see also* Minnesota); NAS report, 379; pleas and, 335–336, 346 (*see also* plea bargaining); prediction and, 15, 140, 282–287, 469–473; probation and, 10, 100, 118, 263, 287–291; *Thirteenth* (film), 378n2. *See also* racial disparity
Blakely v. Washington, 85
Blalock, I., 26
Blumer, H., 403–407
Bobo, L. D., 379
Booker decision, 97, 334, 505, 506; appellate courts and, 157; below-range sentences and, 150, 176; econometrics and, 167–168; federal sentencing and, 137–186 (*see also* federal courts); guidelines and, 104, 145, 236n62, 507 (*see also* guideline systems); inter-judge disparity, 163; judiciary and, 163 (*see also* judiciary); primary judge effect, 163; racial disparity and, 161–173 (*see also* racial disparity); reform and, 175; relevance standard, 139n3, 175; sentence severity, 150–161. *See also* ethnic disparity; racial disparity
Bordenkircher v. Hayes, 317
Bourdieu, P., 485
Bowman, F., 171n14
Bradford, B., 348
Bradley, M. S., 331, 376, 508, 509
Braithwaite, J., 465
Branigan, A. R., 409
Breen, P. D., 335
Breyer, S., 10n4, 142, 143, 144, 178
Britt, C. L., 373
Brown, J., 27, 45, 46, 50–51, 52, 65–67
Brown, P., 45
Brown v. Plata, 35, 37, 50, 63
Bureau of Indian Affairs (BIA), 507
Bureau of Justice Statistics, 263, 501
Bush, G. W., 145
Bushway, S. D., 332, 339, 343, 344, 346

C
Cai, H., 408
Caldwell, M. H., 350
California, 64; bail reform, 70; CCPOA, 46; Corrections Independent Review Panel, 64; cost internalization, 67; crime rates, 56; decarceration measures, 69–70, 72; determinate sentencing, 36, 42, 65; direct democracy, 36–37, 43–52, 60, 66, 67, 70–71, 72; enhancement and, 42, 43–44; incarceration rates, 36, 54–55, 58, 59; indeterminate sentencing, 36, 41; jails, 55, 56; law-and-order campaigns, 45; liberalism, 58; Little Hoover Commission, 45, 47; Marsy's Law, 44; mental health care, 59; negative externalities, 47; New York and, 39, 71; overcrowding and, 36, 54–55, 59, 64 (*see also* overcrowding); parole system, 47, 53; PLRA, 49; populism, 45; PRCS programs, 51; presumptive sentence approach, 128; Prison Law Office, 62; progressivism, 58; Proposition 8, 43; Proposition 13, 46, 47; Proposition 36, 37, 51, 66; Proposition 47, 37, 52, 56, 66, 72; Proposition 57, 37, 52, 60, 66, 67; Proposition 184, 43–44; realignment, 27, 37, 50–51, 55, 56, 59, 67; RICO law, 43; sentencing reforms, 35–77 (*see also specific topics*); STEP Act (1988), 43; Texas and, 57–58, 61; three-judge court, 37, 49, 50, 59, 63–66; three-strikes law, 37, 43–44, 51; Victims' Bill of Rights, 43, 44. *See also specific persons, groups, topics*
California Community Corrections Performance Incentives Act (2009), 49
California Correctional Peace Officers Association (CCPOA), 46, 47
Canada, 203n25
Caruso, G. D., 471
Casper, J. D., 344

Index   525

CCPOA. *See* California Correctional Peace Officers Association
charge-back, 118
child pornography, 140, 153, 155, 178, 504
China, 205n29
Chiricos, T., 336
Church, T. W., 322
citizenship, 423–425, 453–455. *See also* immigration offenses
Clair, M., 498
Coleman v. Brown, 48, 64
Coleman v. Wilson, 36, 48
colonial period (US), 314
community programs, 18–20, 95, 117
COMPAS data, 446, 457, 471
compassionate release, 281, 293
conflict theory, 401
Connecticut, 266
consecutive sentences, 88, 94, 101, 117–118, 202–203, 209, 240f
consequentialism, 115n41, 440, 449, 461, 462, 465, 469. *See also* retributivism
conservativism, vii, 2, 2n1, 17, 27, 45, 71, 199, 316, 464n18, 499, 501
Constitution Project, 175
control release, 120
Cooke, J., 446
Coroners and Justice Act (UK), 200
Corrections Independent Review Panel, 64
cost-benefit analysis, 3, 19–20, 38, 48, 53, 62, 67–69, 73, 114, 234, 300, 486. *See also specific types, topics*
coupling, institutional, 487–489
Covey, R. D., 351
Crackenthorpe, M., 190
criminal history, 91; career offenders and, 153–154, 173; enhancements and, 228, 229; guidelines and, 123, 126, 164, 173 (*see also* guideline systems); look-back limit, 229n56; prediction and, 282–287, 469–471; priors and, 153–154, 173, 232, 460–464; racial disparity and, 164–171, 458, 462–463 (*see also* racial disparity); recidivism and, 91, 93, 123, 164; retributivism and, 461; UK and, 226–230, 232
Criminal Sentences: Law Without Order (Frankel), 1, 190

D
Daly, K., 420
dangerousness, 439–452; ethnic groups and (*see* ethnic disparity); incapacitation policy, 283; racial disparity and, 15, 170 (*see also* racial disparity); recidivism and, 283; retributivism and, 440; socioeconomic variables, 14–15; violence prediction, 13–15, 286n6, 440, 441, 448–452, 451t, 464, 466
Darbyshire, P., 348
Davis, G., 45, 46, 47
Dawid, P., 446, 448
death penalty, 260n6, 262n8, 264, 268–269, 422, 485, 499–501, 510, 514
Delaware, 84, 89, 99
demographic groups. *See specific groups*
demographic impact statement (DIS), 265–270, 266n14
Demuth, S., 333, 375, 376
Department of Justice, 503
determinate sentencing, 1–2, 5, 36, 40–45, 65, 67, 190, 257, 278–279, 295. *See also* guideline systems
Deukmejian, G., 45
DiPietro, S. M., 333, 497
Discretionary Justice (Davis), 1
District of Columbia, 80, 99, 100, 104–105, 106n13, 188
Dixon, J., 331, 494
Doerner, J. K., 375
Doing Justice (von Hirsch), 226
Doob, Anthony, 5
Dorvee decision, 158
Douglas, T., 470
Dressel, J., 446n7

drug offenses, 199, 236, 332n4, 343, 375; 100-to-1 law, 12; Anti–Drug Abuse Act and, 417; England/Wales and, 224; enhancements, 43n10; guidelines and, 140–147, 504–505, 507; imprisonment rate, 366; mandatory minimums and, 24, 138n2, 147, 155, 173, 178; placement rates, 153, 156; quantity ratios, 155–157; racial disparity and, 366, 418f (*see also* racial disparity); Rockefeller laws, 43n10; school-zone laws, 125
DuVernay, A., 378n2

E
economic sanctions, 296–299
Eighth Amendment (US Constitution), 35, 36, 38, 48, 54, 60, 64
Eisenstein, J., 340, 492
elderly, 453–455
Engen, R. L., 333, 502
England. *See* United Kingdom
enhancements, 42–44, 226–230, 340, 346
ethnic disparity, 88, 172f, 233; *Booker* and, 165 (*see also Booker* decision); declines in, 365–437; gender and, 374; group threat theory, 404; Hispanics and (*see* Hispanics); immigration and, 150, 166, 170n13, 375, 377, 389–390, 423–425, 453–455; mandatory minimums and, 179–180 (*see also* mandatory minimums); prediction and, 456–458; racial disparity and, 165, 375 (*see also* racial disparity); SCPS and, 396–401; severity of punishment, 262–263, 265–270; supervision rates and, 263; trial penalty and, 398; white-Hispanic, 402f. *See also specific groups, topics*
Everitt, J. G., 489
evidence-based release, 20n9, 23, 49, 229n50, 234, 282, 286, 467

F
Fair Sentencing Act, 147, 419
Farid, F., 446n7

Farrell, A., 413
Farrell, J., 514
Farrell, R., 410
federal courts, 9–11, 137–186, 365; *Booker* and, 137–180 (*see also Booker* decision); citizenship and, 423–425; civil rights and, 64; disparities and, 165, 365, 370–393, 397, 419, 507–509 (*see also* ethnic disparity; racial disparity); District of Columbia and, 104; Federal Judicial Center, 503; guidelines and, 80, 104, 381n4, 419, 503, 510 (*see also* guidelines); incarceration rates, 367; inhabited institutions and, 503–507; judiciary and (*see* judiciary); modal approach and, 415; Model Penal Code and, 256; overcrowding and, 36, 108; plea agreements and, 319, 323; reform in, 137–138; SCPS data and, 396; sentencing ranges, 149f; Supreme Court (*see specific decisions*); trial effects, 331, 335, 346; trial tax in, 333–335; USSC data, 427–428; zone system, 148. *See also specific decisions, topics*
Feeley, M. M., 19, 317
Feldmeyer, B., 375
fines, 19, 101, 118, 199, 260, 262, 264, 291, 296–299
firearms, 24t, 42–43, 43n9, 165, 173, 381n4, 385, 514
first-offender waiver, 103
Fleetwood, J., 212
Flemming, R. B., 492
Fligstein, N., 486
Flores, A. W., 447, 452, 457, 472
Florida, 83n6, 84, 89
focal concerns: court communities and, 484–485, 495–498; disparities and, 365, 370, 411–412; guidelines and, 501, 514; problems of, 369, 370, 412; three foci, 410–411; topics of, 17, 17n7; variations in, 498, 501
Fornango, R., 504
Fourteenth Amendment (US Constitution), 366

Fourth Amendment (US Constitution), 344
Fox, R., 217
Frankel, M., 1, 4, 9, 80n1, 190, 201, 236, 238
Franklin, T. W., 376, 498
Frase, R. S., 4, 79–135, 201, 212, 237, 331, 347, 474
free lunch problem, 118

G
Gall v. United States, 160, 163, 168, 334, 504
gender: definition of, 444n6; departures and, 97; disparity and, 166, 373–375, 376, 410, 414, 497, 502, 512 (*see also* ethnic disparity; racial disparity); focal concern and, 496 (*see also* focal concerns); guidelines and, 176, 455, 459, 512–514 (*see also* guidelines); MPCS and, 266; nonrecord factors, 124; prediction and, 14, 439, 444, 449, 453, 455–456, 464. *See also specific topics*
General Social Survey, 379, 501, 501n1
Georgia, 62
Ginsburg, R. B., 143, 144
good-time reductions, 50, 53, 60, 62, 100, 120, 257, 280
Gottfredson, D. M., 1, 4n2, 20n9, 26, 513
GPS systems, 53
guideline systems, 85, 93, 114, 173, 381n4, 513; advisory/mandatory, 9; aggravating factors, 225; appellate courts and, 222–223; asymmetry and, 115n41; below-range sentencing, 145, 145n6, 150, 152, 154, 176; *Booker* and, 104, 504, 506, 507, 512 (*see also Booker* decision); characteristics of, 243–244; compliance rates, 104–105, 222; Congress and, 159–161; consecutive/concurrent approach, 203; control release and, 120; court actors and, 506; critiques of, 213; cultural-cognitive influences, 506; custody sentences, 122, 216–217; death penalty and, 515; decisions covered by, 88; departures, 96–98, 114, 121, 157–159, 214, 221–225, 232, 510, 513; drugs and, 141, 507 (*see also* drug offenses); enhancements and, 228; ethnic disparity and, 179–180 (*see also* ethnic disparity); evolution of, 187–253; federal courts and, 11, 236n62, 503, 510 (*see also* federal courts); field rules, 493; focal concerns and, 501, 514 (*see also* focal concerns); general effects, 23; grid-based approaches, 88–90, 122, 125, 187, 188; hybrid, 114–115; ideal, 127; impact/assessments, 116–117; individualization and, 214; inhabited institutions and, 485–491, 494; in-out recommendation, 372; isomorphism in, 512; jails and, 92, 95–96, 102, 110, 118; judiciary and, 83n5, 85, 86, 121, 141–145, 152, 155, 157, 160, 163–168, 176, 198, 211–212, 216, 235 (*see also* judiciary); just deserts and, 178; look-back limits, 92, 229n56; mandatory minimums and, 99, 102, 123, 174, 175, 178, 179, 515 (*see also* mandatory minimums); Minnesota and, 204, 238f, 243–244 (*see also* Minnesota); misdemeanors, 117; MPCS and, 101–102, 278, 280 (*see also* Model Penal Code: Sentencing); multiple formats, 223–224; multiple offenses, 94, 117–118, 221; non-prison sentences, 96, 118; nonrecord factors, 124; offense-by-offense approach, 203, 211–213; overcrowding and (*see* overcrowding); parole and, 100, 106, 107, 119–121, 171n14 (*see also* parole); patterning rules, 94; placement and, 154, 154t, 155; pleas and, 502 (*see also* plea bargaining); point-based systems, 92; policy issues, 117–125, 160; postprison supervision, 120; prescriptive/descriptive, 116; presumptive systems,

25, 175; pretrial detention, 122; primary judge effect, 163; prior convictions, 91, 92, 226–230 (*see also* criminal history); prison growth and, 87, 88, 105–112, 111t, 126, 201, 212 (*see also* overcrowding); probation and, 10, 100, 118–119, 287–291; proportionality and, 217–219; racial disparity and, 87, 103, 111, 112, 126, 171, 369, 512 (*see also* racial disparity); recidivism and, 123, 124, 126, 164, 173, 232; reforms of, 4, 102; research priorities, 235; risk assessment and, 123–124, 282–287, 469–471; rule/discretion in, 115–116; Sentencing Guidelines Resource Center, 85; Sentencing Table, 148; SEPS option, 95; state systems, 80, 80n2, 80n3, 82–83, 84t, 113–114, 146f, 147, 501–507 (*see also specific states*); steps in, 239–242; telephone book model, 203n25; transparency and, 234–235; types of, 82–112; UK and (*see* United Kingdom); unconvicted offenses, 90. *See also specific topics*

guns, 24t, 42–43, 43n9, 165, 173, 381n4, 385, 514

H

Hagan, J., 401, 488
Hallett, T., 488, 489
Harmelin v. Michigan, 159, 272
Hart, S. D., 446
Hartley, R., 499
health care, viii, 12, 19, 36, 46, 48, 59, 63, 68, 291, 444, 450, 452, 456, 464
Hedberg, E. C., 499
Henderson, T., 48, 63, 64
Hessick, C. B., 513
Hester, R., 498, 510
Hinojosa, R., 139n3
Hispanics, 463; age and, 15; blacks and, 3t, 11, 172f, 374–379, 398–399 (*see also* blacks); citizenship, 370, 389–390, 424; dangerousness and, 411; DIS and, 267; federal courts and, 427–428; Hispanic attorneys, 415, 497; Hispanic-white differences, 124, 262n8, 365, 367, 374–379, 383–386, 390f, 391, 391f, 395, 395f, 397f, 398–399, 402f, 456; mandatories and, 514; MSGC and, 428; probation and, 263; racial threat thesis, 407; sentence length, 171, 389, 390f, 391f, 396, 400, 400t, 415; socioeconomics and, 456, 458; urban courts and, 373

Hofer, P. J., 10, 137–186, 349
Hoffman, P. B., 513
Holder, E., 443, 515
Holleran, D., 332
Holmes, M., 410
Howard, J., 19
Humphrey decision, 70
Husak, D., 448, 466

I

immigration offenses, 150, 166, 170n13, 375, 377, 423–425, 453–455
Implicit Association Test (IAT), 407–408
Imrey, P., 446
indeterminate sentencing, vii, 1, 2, 4, 21, 27, 36, 40–42, 278, 291, 440, 475–476
inhabited institutions model, 483–518; agency and, 481; courts as, 491–496; federal courts and, 503–507; fields and, 485–491; processional orders and, 489
Irwin-Rogers, K., 212
isomorphisms, sociological, 486, 511–513

J

jails: bail, 70; class action and, 48; crowding in, 53, 62, 68 (*see also* overcrowding); guidelines and, 92, 96, 102, 110, 118, 126, 279 (*see also* guideline systems); immigration and, 425; MPCS and, 259, 260–263, 283, 291, 303; PLO and, 62; pretrial detention, 122, 338; prison/jail ratio, 54,

55, 57, 323, 366; racial disparity and, 263–265 (*see also* racial disparity); realignment and, 37, 50–56, 67; SEPS option, 95; sheriffs and, 53, 67–68; triple-nons, 51n18
Johnson, B. D., 54, 55, 313–363, 373, 377, 497, 502, 503, 505
judiciary: *Booker* and, 145, 166, 169, 181; disparity and, 162, 171, 404–408, 497 (*see* ethnic disparity; racial disparity); federal courts (*see* federal courts); focal concerns theory (*see* focal concerns); guidelines and, 83n5, 85, 86, 121, 141–145, 152, 155, 157, 160, 164–168, 176, 198, 211–212, 216, 235 (*see also* guideline systems); idiosyncrasies in, 17, 67; indeterminacy and, 115; judicial review, 8, 157, 160, 161, 318, 349, 350; Model Penal Code and, 256; MPCS and, 187, 190, 256, 285, 303 (*see also* Model Penal Code: Sentencing); pleas and, 344–351 (*see also* plea bargaining); primary judge effect, 162–163; reforms and, 4; rotation of, 497–498; SRA and, 138, 158; state courts (*see specific states, topics*); Supreme Court (*see* specific decisions); UK and, 192–198, 211–217, 221, 230–234. *See also specific topics*
jury trial, 313–316, 324f, 330f, 331, 335, 345, 350, 501. *See also specific topics*
just deserts, 86, 91, 115, 124, 139, 178, 205, 219, 316
Justice Reinvestment (JRI) program, 128, 128n48
juveniles, 2, 41n5, 52, 92, 98n28, 102, 123, 165, 259, 337, 345, 454, 464, 503

K
Kaiser, K. A., 504, 513, 514
Kansas, 90, 104, 107, 127, 278
Kant, I., 461, 465, 466, 466n19, 467

Karlton, L., 48, 64
Kautt, P. M., 333
Kennedy, A., 63, 64, 314, 317, 322
Kentucky, 71
Kim, A. C., 340
Kim, B., 499
Kimbrough v. United States, 139, 144, 155, 157, 158, 163, 168, 419
King, R. D., 365–437
Kleck, G., 367–368
Klein, S., 321
Klingele, C. M., 255–311
Knapp, K. A., 9, 26, 195
Koch brothers, 27
Kohler-Hausmann, I., 510
Kramer, J. H., 166, 170, 320, 331, 373, 375, 379, 500, 514
Kurlychek, M., 503
Kuteladze, B. L., 343

L
LaBonte decision, 138n1
Lafler v. Cooper, 314, 349
LaFree, G. D., 332, 339, 341, 343
Langbein, J. H., 317
Levinson, J. D., 408
liberalism, 58
liberation hypothesis, 488
Lieb, R., 26
Light, M. T., 166, 170, 365–437, 514
Lin, J., 68
Lockyer v. Andrade, 272
Louisiana, 62, 85
Lowenkamp, C. T., 447, 452, 457, 472
Lynch, G., 7, 152, 320, 349
Lynch, M., 45n13, 319–320, 507, 510

M
MacKenzie, D. L., 376
Madoff Ponzi scheme, 453n12
Major Crimes Act of 1885, 507
Maleng, N., 26, 27
Malone decision, 158
mandatory minimums, vii, 3t, 6, 7, 510; advisory sentencing and, 104, 123, 153; aims of, 23; ALI and, 279;

appeals courts and, 280; *Booker* and, 147, 150, 152, 163, 168–169, 173–181 (*see also Booker* decision); California and, 43, 47; Congress and, 141, 143, 155, 175; dangerousness and, 442 (*see also* dangerousness); departures and, 280; drugs and, 24, 138n2, 147, 155, 173, 178 (*see also* drug offenses); emergency powers, 281; ethnic disparity and, 179–180, 427 (*see also* ethnic disparity); federal courts and, 10, 137, 153, 165, 174, 334, 381, 419, 510 (*see also* federal courts); focal concerns and, 496–497; good-time credits, 280; guidelines and, 9, 23, 25, 26, 99, 102, 123, 152, 160, 161, 174, 175, 178, 179, 515 (*see also* guideline systems); guns and, 43 (*see also* guns); institutional context and, 492; judges and, 8, 157, 160, 163, 318, 349 (*see also* judiciary); local culture and, 16; minors and, 280; modal approach and, 416–417; MPCS and, 255–256, 266, 273, 277, 279–281 (*see also* Model Penal Code: Sentencing); parallel systems, 140; pleas and, 7, 180, 314, 333, 340, 514 (*see also* plea bargaining); problems of, 6–7, 16, 141, 171, 179–180, 369, 494; prosecutors and, 8, 23, 180, 507, 514, 515 (*see also* prosecutors); racial disparity and, 13, 16, 17, 169, 171, 179–180, 369, 420–421, 427 (*see also* racial disparity); reforms and, 24, 27, 71, 159, 177–179, 181, 279; safety valve provisions, 180, 320; SRA and, 138, 141, 160, 174; states and (*see* specific states); three strikes and (*see* three strikes). *See also specfic topics*

Marder, I., 213
Marsy's Law, 44
Martin, K., 501
Maryland, 62, 83n6, 99, 503
Massachusetts, 99
Mather, L. M., 317, 344
Matravers, M., 448

Mattick, H., 286
McAdam, D., 486
McGeever, K., 373
mental health, 19, 36–38, 59, 68, 71, 210, 232, 291, 443, 463
Metcalfe, C., 336
Meyer, J. W., 487
Michie, C., 446
Michigan, 83n6, 90
Miethe, T.D., 331
military courts, 328t, 335
Mill, J. S., 445
Miller, H. V., 499
Miller v. Alabama, 454
Minnesota, 98n27, 104, 107, 116, 127, 187–253, 502; CRM in, 277; DIS and, 266n13, 267–268; forecasting model and, 266; guidelines and, 238f, 243–244, 391–396, 428; just deserts and, 85; MSGC, 187, 195, 267–268, 391–396, 428, 459; prison growth and, 108; prison population and, 278, 279; racial disparity and, 365, 369, 371–373, 378; SCPS and, 397; UK and, 215–230, 243–244
Mississippi, 71
Missouri, 85
Missouri v. Frye, 317, 349
Mistretta v. United States, 9, 160, 380
Mitchell, L., 376
Model Penal Code: Sentencing (MPCS), 6, 9, 15, 27; appellate courts and, 22n10, 273, 280, 285; assessment constraint, 274–275; back-end sentencing, 285, 291–296; collateral consequences, 299–302; conditions of confinement, 303–304; control release and, 120; CRM and, 276–279; departure powers, 280; economic sanctions, 297; effects of, 256; emergency release, 278n23, 281; forecasting and, 266; gender and, 226 (*see also* gender); general deterrence and, 281–282; general policy, 80, 270–275; guidelines and, 101–102, 278–280 (*see also* guideline systems); inca-

pacitation policy, 283; incarceration and, 275–287; lengthy sentences and, 294–295; mandatory minimums, 255–256, 266, 273, 277, 279–281 (*see also* mandatory minimums); modification powers, 281; overcrowding and, 278n23 (*see also* overcrowding); parole and, 277, 278, 286; pleas, 22n10, 180, 514 (*see also* plea bargaining); postrelease supervision, 292; probation and, 287–291; proportionality in, 270–272, 273, 283; Proposed Final Draft, 256n1; recidivism and, 275, 282–287; rehabilitative programs, 275; retributivism and, 270n18; RFS limit, 297–298; risk prediction and, 282–287; second-look provision, 293–294; sentence modification, 292–296; spending and, 276; user fees and, 298–299; utilitarianism in, 270. *See also specific topics*

Model Sentencing and Corrections Act (1979), 9
Monahan, J., 13, 15, 449, 467, 474, 475
Moore, C. A., 331
Morris, N., 13, 14, 203n25, 270n18, 450, 451, 467, 474
murder, 41, 106, 154t, 155, 203n23, 268–269, 282, 422–423, 499–501, 514
Murder Cases in 33 Large Urban Counties (DoJ), 422–423
Myers, H., 26, 27

N
Nardelli, P. F., 492
National Academy of Sciences, 7, 335, 379, 462
National Advisory Commission on Criminal Justice Standard and Goals (1973), 9
National Commission on Reform of Federal Laws (1971), 8
National Registry of Exonerations, 338
Native Americans, 124, 263, 376–377, 485, 507–509

Neal v. United States, 139n2
Netherlands, 422
New Jersey, 56, 266
New York, 25, 39, 47, 56, 71, 110n10
New Zealand, 205n29, 344, 347
Newman, D. J., 342, 344
Ninth Circuit, 49
Norris, R. J., 344
North Carolina, 4, 5, 88, 90, 96, 97n 26, 100, 106, 127, 195, 277, 348, 375
North Carolina v. Alford, 348

O
Obama administration, 63, 175
O'Hear, M. M., 72
Ohio, 84, 89
Oklahoma, 71, 366
Oregon, 71, 96, 127, 266
overcrowding: California and, 44, 49, 56, 59, 64; control release, 120; emergency release, 281, 291; federal system and, 101; guidelines and, 87, 88, 102, 109–112, 116, 126, 198, 200; intermediate sanctions, 201; jails and, 41; measures of, 126; Minnesota and, 87; MPCS and, 120, 278n21; parole and, 20–23, 41, 109, 111, 111t; *Plata* and, 111; probation and, 290; second-look and, 102

P
Pacific Sociological Review, 403–407
Padilla v. Kentucky, 349
Painter-Davis, N., 411
Parent, D., 26, 226
parole, 3t, 107; abolition, 100, 107, 128; AI and, 286–287; appeals process and, 285; arguments against, 20–23; CRM and, 277; discretionary sentencing and, 128; effects of, 21; evidence-based, 286; federal, 171n14; functions of, 291; good conduct and, 100, 120; GPS and, 53; grid model, 204; guidelines and, 1, 100, 106, 119–121, 171n14; indeterminate sentencing and, 291; MPCS and, 277;

nonrevocable, 49; overcrowding and, 53, 106, 110–111, 111t; parole boards, 21, 277, 278, 286, 441t; Parole Commission, 443; postprison supervision, 120; prediction and, 286–287; recidivism and, 20n9; second-look and, 120; selection bias, 109; studies of, 20n9; supervision and, 291
Paternoster, R., 500
Patrick, D., 21
Pennsylvania, 90, 96, 104, 128, 323, 331, 497, 502, 503
Pereboom, D., 471
Perrit, P., 465
Perry, T., 212
Petersilia, J., 68, 321
Peterson, R., 401
Pew Center, 263, 378
Piehl, A. M., 346
Piehl, S. D., 332
Pina-Sánchez, J., 212, 213
Plata decisions, 36–37, 44, 48, 58–60, 63–64
plea bargaining, 6, 142, 142n5, 208, 233; balance of power, 350; bans on, 350; decision-making process, 339; effects of, 324t–328t, 329t–330t, 347; evidence and, 344; false guilty pleas, 337–339; guidelines and, 502; jurisdictional variation, 346; mandatory minimums and, 22n10, 180, 514; Model Penal Code, 22n10, 23; plea agenda, 492; prosecutors and, 349; racial disparity and, 344–346; trial tax and, 313–363; victim hardship, 321
populism, 35, 44, 45n13, 72
predictive sentencing, 15, 140, 282–287, 464, 469–471, 473
President's Commission on Law Enforcement and Administration of Justice (1967), 8
presumptive systems. *See* guideline systems
pretrial detention, 338
primary judge effect, 162–163
prior convictions. *See* criminal history

Prism Litigation Reform Act (PLRA), 36, 49, 59
Prison Law Office, 64
probation, 10, 100, 118–119, 263, 287–291
Process Is the Punishment, The (Feeley), 19
progressivism, 58
proportionality: *Booker* and (*see Booker* decision); community programs, 18–20, 18n8, 95, 117; constitutional, 102, 272, 297; criminal history, 123 (*see also* criminal history); defining, 272; drugs and, 212 (*see also* drug offenses); ethnic (*see* ethnic disparity); fines and, 299; guidelines and, 93, 152, 177, 190, 199, 217–219, 232n56, 237 (*see also* guideline systems); JRI and, 128n48; just deserts and, 299, 316, 448, 461–462, 466; justice as, 473; MPCS and, 271–273, 271n19, 283, 289; pleas and, 347, 348, 352 (*see also* plea bargaining); prediction and, 282–287, 464, 469–471, 473; prison population and, 200 (*see also* overcrowding); proportionality constraint, 271; racial (*see* racial disparity); UK and, 199, 203, 209, 445 (*see also* United Kingdom); utilitarianism and, 270. *See also specific topics*
Proposition 8, 43
Proposition 47, 72
prosecutors, 8, 16, 314, 318–320, 349, 481. *See also specific topics*
PROTECT Act (2003), 145, 145n6, 166, 169, 334
Pryor, W. H., 175, 177
public attitudes, 215
punishment, 3t; asymmetric theories, 114; community programs, 18–20, 18n8; death penalty, 260n6, 262n8, 264, 268–269, 422, 485, 499–501, 510, 514; determinate sentencing and, 1–2, 5, 36, 40–45, 65, 67, 190, 218, 257, 295; economic sanctions, 19, 101, 118, 199, 260–264, 291,

296–299; ethnic disparity (*see* ethnic disparity); four propositions, 473; guidelines for (*see* guideline systems); just deserts theory, 85, 86, 91, 115, 124, 139, 178, 205, 219, 316; MPCS and (*see* Model Penal Code: Sentencing); parsimony and, 473; proportionality (*see* proportionality); purposes of, 139; racial disparities (*see* racial disparity); theory of, 464–468, 473; Tonry on, 473; tough-on-crime laws, 8, 21, 23, 25, 27, 43–47, 159, 174, 316, 442, 455. *See also specific topics, types*
punishment theory, 464–468

Q
qualitative methods, 485. *See also specific topics*
quarantine, 470–471

R
Rachlinksi, J. J., 408
racial disparity, 3t, 10, 88, 124–125, 172f, 173, 233–234, 262–270, 502; attorneys and, 373, 413–414, 415; black-white differences, 269, 371–379, 381–386, 383f, 393f, 394, 394f, 399, 402f, 404–407, 418f, 456 (*see also* blacks; *specific crimes, topics*); Blumer/Blalock theory, 404; *Booker* and, 161–173, 165, 169 (*see also Booker* decision); cognitive theories, 369, 407–410; conflict theory and, 401; criminal history and, 164–171, 458, 462–463 (*see also* criminal history); dangerousness and, 15, 170 (*see also* dangerousness); death sentence (*see* death penalty); declines in, 365–437; definition of, 161; discrimination thesis, 368; dominant/subordinate groups, 403; drug offenses and, 366, 418f (*see also* drug offenses); economic disparities and, 380; education and, 378; ethnic disparity and, 165, 375 (*see also* ethnic disparity); federal courts and, 365, 371–391, 397, 419, 507–509 (*see also* federal courts); focal concerns, 370, 410–412; Fourteenth Amendment, 366; group threat theory, 404; guideline systems and, 87, 111, 112, 124, 126, 369, 377–401 (*see also* guideline systems); IAT, 407–408; impact statement, 266; implicit bias theory, 370, 409; judges and, 162–163, 171, 176, 498; length of sentence, 377–401, 379n3, 393–394, 393f; macro-level theories, 369; mandatory minimums and, 13, 171, 179–180, 369; Minnesota and, 369; modal approach and, 415–425; partial solutions, 13; perceived criminality, 406; phenotypic differences, 409; plea bargaining and, 344–345; poverty and, 378; prediction and, 370, 406, 469–471; priors and (*see* criminal history); probability of sentence, 379n3; rationalization of, 446; SCPS and, 396–401; size of, 367; social distance theory, 370, 412–415; stereotypes and, 11, 411–412; supervision rates and, 263; theoretical explanations, 401–405; trends in, 370, 377–401; trial tax and, 335, 398; victim and, 422–425. *See also specific topics*
Racketeer Influenced and Corrupt Organizations (RICO), 43
Radcliffe, P., 212
Reagan, R., 45
realignment, 38, 50–56, 68
recidivism: career offenders, 164; criminal history and, 93, 123 (*see also* criminal history); dangerousness and, 283 (*see also* dangerousness); guidelines and, 123, 124, 126, 164, 173, 232 (*see also* guideline systems); MPCS and, 282–287 (*see also* Model Penal Code: Sentencing); parole and, 20n9 (*see also* parole); prediction

and, 282–287, 469–471; realignment and, 38; UK and, 200, 200n19 (*see also* United Kingdom)
Redlich, A. D., 339, 343, 344
Rehavi, M. M., 168, 420–421
Reinhardt, S., 49
Reitz, K. R., 194n8, 231, 255–311
relevant conduct, 9–11, 142, 142n5, 175
Remington, F., 7
retributivism, 440, 448, 461, 465–466, 467
Rita v. United States, 144, 157, 158, 168
robbery, 205–206, 238f, 239–242
Roberts, J. V., 213, 348, 474
Robina Institute, 288
Ross, T., 26, 27
Rowan, R., 487
rural courts, 16, 17

S
Santobello v. New York, 317
Scalia, A., 63
Scandinavian countries, 460
Schlanger, M., 48
Schroeder, M., 49
Schulhofer, S. J., 345
Schwarzenegger, A., 47, 49, 64, 65
Scott, W. R., 486, 487, 494, 506
SCPS. *See* State Court Processing Statistics Survey of Felony Defendants in Large Urban Counties
second-look sentencing, 102
Sentencing Commission (US), 9–10, 137, 142, 150n8, 503
Sentencing Project, The, 266
Sentencing Reform Act of 1984 (SRA), 9, 87, 138, 144, 148, 159, 174, 459
sex offenses, 155, 199, 236
Sigler, M., 26
Sixth Amendment, 143, 285
Skeem, J., 449
Sklansky, D. A., 351
Smith, B. P., 317

Smith, D. A., 348
Smith, R. J., 339
socioeconomic characteristics, 456–460. *See also specific topics*
sociological theory, 483–518, 495
Soros, G., 27
South Africa, 202n21
South Carolina, 498
South Korea, 205n29
Spears v. United States, 419
Spector, D., 62
Spohn, C., 332, 497, 499, 504, 513, 514
SRA. *See* Sentencing Reform Act of 1984
Starr, S. B., 168, 420–421
state commissions, 6, 23, 24t, 25–27, 113–114. *See also specific states, topics*
State Court Processing Statistics Survey of Felony Defendants in Large Urban Counties (SCPS), 374, 376, 396
Steen, S., 502
Steffensmeier, D., 331, 333, 373, 375, 376, 411
Steven, S. J., 160
Stevens, A., 212
Stith, K., 201, 513
Strauss, A., 490
Street Terrorism Enforcement and Prevention (STEP) Act, 43
Struggle for Justice (American Friends Service Committee), 1
Stuntz, W., 7
substantive rationality, 493–494
Supreme Court (US). *See* federal courts; *specific decisions*
suspended sentence, 95
symbolic interactionism, 490

T
Tappan, P., 463
Tennessee, 71, 84
terrorism, 43, 155, 159, 199
Texas, 55, 57–58, 61–62, 71
Thibault-Walker studies, 235

Index

three strikes, 11, 24t, 37, 43, 51, 230, 272, 282, 314, 442, 449, 461, 464, 514
Tonry, M., 2–34, 18n8, 79, 83n5, 116n42, 192, 194n8, 196n15, 202, 204n27, 228n49, 231n54, 233n60, 237, 266n12, 420, 439–482
totality principle, 221–222
tough-on-crime laws, 8, 9, 21, 23, 25, 27, 41, 43–47, 159, 174, 316, 442, 455
Toward a Theory of Minority-Group Relations (Blalock), 403
trial tax, 313–363. *See also* plea bargaining
Tribal Law and Order Act (TLOA), 508
Turner, J. I., 346, 348
Turner, S., 321

U
Uganda, 202n21
Ulmer, J. T., 166, 170, 320, 331, 340, 373, 375, 376, 379, 411, 505, 508, 509, 514
United Kingdom, 191, 230, 344, 351; Advisory Council, 194; Australia and, 195n12; Carter review, 193; community penalties, 199; Coroners and Justice Act, 197, 200; Court of Appeal, 193; drug offenses and, 199, 224; enhancements and, 226–230; ethnic groups, 233; guidelines and, 187–253; harm-culpability model, 205–206; Knapp's models, 195; Minnesota and, 215–230, 243–244; plea bargaining, 208–209, 346–347, 351; prior convictions and, 226–230; prison population, 193; proportionate sentencing, 209; racial disparities, 233–234; recidivism, 200n19; Sentencing Advisory Panel, 191; Sentencing Council, 187, 192–198, 240f, 241f, 242f; sexual offenses, 199; Street Robbery and, 205–206; suspended sentences, 199; terrorism and, 199; US and, 231, 232–233. *See also specific topics*
United States v. Booker. *See Booker* decision
Utah, 89n12, 98n26, 99
utilitarianism, 461

V
variation, organizational, 494
victims, 43–44, 296, 297, 422–425
Virginia, 83n6, 89, 99, 105, 278, 459
voluntary, 5
von Hirsch, A., 197, 203n25, 466

W
Wald, P., 282
Wandall, R., 201
Washington State, 96, 103, 105, 121, 127, 278, 332, 377, 502
Wasik, M., 443n5
Webster, M., 212
Weick, K., 489
Weisberg, R., 27, 238
Wilkins, L. T., 1, 26, 513
Wilson, P., 45
Winter, A., 498
Wisconsin, 85, 341–342
Wollstonecraft, M., 445
women. *See* gender; *specific topics*

Y
Young, D., 408

Z
Zajac, G., 500
Zimring, F., 113
Zottoli, T. M., 337, 345